The Heaven Singing

MUSIC IN EARLY ENGLISH
RELIGIOUS DRAMA

Volume 1

The Heaven Singing

MUSIC IN EARLY ENGLISH
RELIGIOUS DRAMA

RICHARD RASTALL

Volume 1

D. S. BREWER

First published 1996
D. S. Brewer, Cambridge

ISBN 0 85991 428 3

D. S. Brewer is an imprint of Boydell & Brewer Ltd
PO Box 9, Woodbridge, Suffolk IP12 3DF, UK
and of Boydell & Brewer Inc.
PO Box 41026, Rochester, NY 14604–4126, USA

British Library Cataloguing-in-Publication Data
Rastall, Richard
    Heaven Singing:Music in Early English
    Religious Drama. – Vol.1
    I. Title
    781.71
    ISBN 0–85991–428–3

Library of Congress Cataloging-in-Publication Data
Rastall, Richard.
    The heaven singing : music in early English religious drama /
Richard Rastall.
        p.   cm.
    ISBN 0–85991–428–3 (hardback : alk. paper)
    1. Religious drama, English – Incidental music – History and
criticism. 2. Drama, Medieval – History and criticism. 3. Mysteries
and miracle plays, English – History and criticism. I. Title.
ML3275.R37   1996
781.5′ 52′09420902 – dc20   95–20687

The paper used in this publication meets the minimum requirements
of American National Standard for Information Sciences –
Permanence of Paper for Printed Library Materials, ANSI Z39.48–1984

Printed in Great Britain by
St Edmundsbury Press Ltd, Bury St Edmunds, Suffolk

CONTENTS

Preface and acknowledgements   ix
Bibliographical notes   xii
Abbreviations: play texts   xiii
Abbreviations: works frequently cited   xvi
List of Illustrations   xviii
List of tables   xix
List of musical examples   xx

1   **Introduction**   1
    1.1   Music in Middle English drama   1
    1.2   The repertory: historical and fictional drama   2
    1.3   The repertory: civic, community and institutional plays   10

2   **The Internal Literary Evidence**   16
    2.1   Introduction   16
    2.2   The manuscripts   17
    2.3   Dramatic directions   22
    2.4   Text references   31
    2.5   The proclamations and banns   50
    2.6   Lyrics and song-texts   57
    2.7   The use of Latin   78

3   **The Surviving Music**   85
    3.1   Introduction   85
    3.2   The Shrewsbury and Pepys fragments   88
    3.3   York   121
    3.4   Coventry   137
    3.5   Chester   152

4   **The Documentary Evidence**   160
    4.1   Introduction, and a note on money   160
    4.2   Guild accounts and related records   164
    4.3   Chelmsford: the summer of 1562   168

5   **Music as Representation**   175

    5.1   Introduction   175
    5.2   The music of Heaven   176
    5.3   The music of mortals   193
    5.4   The sounds of Hell   199
    5.5   Realism and representation   215
    5.6   Conclusion   219

6   **Music and Dramatic Structure**   221

    6.1   Introduction   221
    6.2   The dynamic functions of music   225
    6.3   The music of numbers: structure and proportion   233

7   **Music and Liturgy**   250

    7.1   The liturgical background   250
    7.2   The Presentation in the Temple   253
    7.3   The angelic announcement to the shepherds   256
    7.4   The Purification   258
    7.5   The Entry into Jerusalem   265
    7.6   The Last Supper: Maundy and Mass   272
          The Mandatum   272
          The Eucharist   276
    7.7   The Harrowing of Hell   278
    7.8   Miscellaneous sacraments and offices: 283
          Baptism   283
          Marriage   286
          Burial   289
          Sacrifice and blessing   293
    7.9   Questions of provenance   294

8   **The Performers**   300

    8.1   Professional and amateur   300
    8.2   The problem of female roles   308
    8.3   The Angels   328
    8.4   The Shepherds   344
    8.5   Instrumentalists   364
    8.6   The audience   368

Appendices: Editions and reconstructions

A	The Washington *Ave regina celorum . . . Mater*	380
B	The Chester *Gloria in excelsis*	384
C	*Wee happy heardsmen here*	386

| Bibliography | 392 |
| Index | 411 |

To the original

WEDNESDAY LUNCH-TIMERS

Lyne, Peter, Margaret and John, who helped to
prove that processional waggon staging works,

and especially Jane,

who had the idea and saw it through

PREFACE AND ACKNOWLEDGEMENTS

Medieval biblical plays were written to be performed, but even after almost a century of revivals it is not uncommon to find them considered as literature only, and questions concerning their performance regarded as trivial. Only such a limited approach could lead to the conclusion, recently expressed, by a literary scholar, that 'there are no fifteenth-century dramatic masterpieces.'

John Robinson's concern with medieval drama as a performing art stands at the beginning of his book and sets the agenda for the whole work.[1] Robinson was not alone on this issue, and over the last twenty-five years or more scholars and producers have sought to recreate the experience of medieval drama through scholarly debate and in productions reflecting the conditions and techniques of late medieval performance.[2] A primary concern has been the staging itself, but many other issues have been taken up: costuming, gesture, masks, pronunciation, lighting, the use of gunpowder, and many other matters of production have been studied through medieval literature, through documentary records, and through practical experiment in the plays themselves.[3] Scholarly work on the plays as drama rather than as literature – and this is not restricted to the biblical plays that were Robinson's main concern – goes back a very long way. Thomas Sharp, whose *Dissertation on the Pageants . . . at Coventry* was published in 1825, would no doubt have been delighted to think that the late medieval pageants might be played again in their original locations. Given the direction of his work towards staging matters, it is unfortunate that the blasphemy laws and other factors prevented such performances until recent times.[4]

In this quest for information on staging, and in the associated performances of

---

1 Robinson *Studies*, 1.
2 The practical reconstructions may be said to have started with Neville Denny's production of the Cornish Ordinalia at Piran Round in 1969, followed by Jane Oakshott's waggon staging of the York cycle at Leeds University in 1975. See Denny's essay in Denny 1973, 125–54, and Oakshott and Rastall 1982. These productions could hardly have taken place without considerable scholarly activity in the preceding years, and various earlier productions of medieval plays.
3 Some of the literature will be found in the Bibliography, below, especially in the collections of essays by Neuss, Mills, Riggio, Briscoe and Coldewey, Davidson and Seiler, and others. It is notable that *Medieval English Theatre*, a periodical dedicated to scholarship on performing matters, and *Records of Early English Drama*, a series presenting source-material for such scholarship, both started publishing in 1979 and were obviously part of the same movement that gave rise to the major cycle performances of 1969 onwards. The movement is not restricted to English drama: see Meredith and Tailby *Staging*, for instance.
4 Performance at original playing-places was a reason for Neville Denny's use of Piran Round for the Cornish cycle in 1969 and for Oakshott's attempts to perform the Towneley cycle in Wakefield (partly abandoned in 1977, when Roger Smith and Lesley Bloomfield mounted twelve pageants on waggons, and modified in 1980, when Oakshott presented the whole cycle less Towneley 12 on three fixed stages). Eight pageants from Oakshott's waggon-performance

medieval drama, music has suffered as much as other aspects of performance from a limiting view of the material as 'literature'. With music, however, there is additional reason to think the practicalities of staging to be 'trivial'. To a twentieth-century drama specialist, as to all of us, music traditionally plays a subsidiary, emotive, and ultimately dispensable role. 'Incidental music' is the phrase that comes to mind in dramatic contexts, but indeed to most of us music is incidental to our lives altogether. The dispensability of much of the music in late medieval drama is not in doubt, although it is significant in moulding the modern and erroneous feeling that the music is therefore *unimportant*. This feeling, unrecognised even in themselves by some who have done excellent work on staging medieval drama, is still one of the barriers against the proper understanding of the functions and effects of music in this context.

This book stems from my attempts to understand the place of music, of liturgy, and of other aural resources and effects in early English drama and to give that understanding comprehensible form in performances. The results do not always immediately feel right to us, for the reasons just given. Moreover, the evidence is incomplete to an extent that makes bootstrapping unavoidable, if only because there comes a point when we must trust our own, anachronistic, view of the situation for want of hard information from the historical period concerned. But if we are to test the playwrights on their own ground, to give them a fair hearing and to let the dramas speak for themselves, our first objective must be to examine the available evidence closely, to assess it carefully, and to draw what conclusions we can from it. I believe, with Robinson, that this dramatic repertory is as effective now as it was four or five centuries ago; that we are presently witnessing an explosion of knowledge and understanding that will soon completely change attitudes towards medieval drama; and that this will increase our understanding of the immense power of music in the plays.

This first volume is a general introduction to the subject. Although I have tried to make it self-explanatory, the reader will no doubt be aware that in the interests of brevity I have omitted some information and simplified discussions. Volume 2 is a detailed examination of the material on which this first volume is based, and will, I hope, make good such deficiences. There, a play-by-play discussion leads in each case to a cue list intended not only to make clear the situation but to offer producers any alternative solutions to the musical (and some other) problems confronting them. As my ultimate object is to facilitate the proper (by which I mean 'contemporary with the text') use of music in the plays, Volume 2 also includes a section on the practicalities of directing the music in a modern but historically-aware production. Only here does speculation – *informed* speculation, I hope – play a major role: elsewhere, I have been concerned only with what the evidence tells us about fifteenth- and sixteenth-century production.

of the complete Chester cycle were played at the High Cross in Chester, June 1983; a single waggon had been used for performance in York for many years before Meg Twycross and others played some York pageants on waggons in Stonegate and elsewhere in 1988 and again in 1992. Oakshott presented nine York plays on waggons in the streets of York as part of the York Early Music Festival on 10 July 1994.

*

In a work that has taken so long to write my debts are bound to be many, and I acknowledge them here with pleasure and immense gratitude. I have reused material originally published by the following: Early Drama, Art and Music; Leeds Studies in English; Medieval English Theatre; Basil Blackwell Publisher; Indiana University Press; and The University of North Carolina Press. For permission to do so I am very grateful to those publishers and their respective editors.

For permission to reproduce musical examples and illustrations my thanks are due to The British Library, the Master and Fellows of Magdalene College, Cambridge, the Dean and Chapter of Carlisle Cathedral, the Chairman and Governors of Shrewsbury School, the Board of Trustees of the National Gallery of Art, Washington DC, the Bodleian Library, Oxford, and the Department of Printing and Graphic Arts of the Houghton Library, Harvard University. I am grateful to the Librarian of Shrewsbury School, Mr J.B. Lawson, for the loan of a colour microfilm of Shrewsbury MS VI.

Many friends and colleagues have had a hand in this over the years, although after so long the precise nature of their kindnesses is in some cases rather hazy in my mind: perhaps by now they themselves have forgotten. I have received welcome help, information and advice of various kinds from Richard Beadle, Roger Bowers, Philip Butterworth, Nicole Chaplain-Pearman, John Coldewey, JoAnna Dutka, Peter Happé, Ruth Keane, Pamela King, David Klausner, David Lindley, Simon Lindley, J.E. Maddrell, David Mills, Gordon Oakshott, Andrew Taylor, Meg Twycross and Diana Wyatt: to all of them I am very grateful. If I have inadvertently omitted anyone from this list, I add my apologies to my sincere gratitude. To the Wednesday Lunchtimers I am grateful for many stimulating discussions, over sandwiches and at other times. I am especially indebted to Lynette Muir for her encouraging reminders of the wider European context of my subject, to Peter Meredith for his friendship and scholarship freely placed at my disposal on many occasions, and to David Bevington for his generous and encouraging advice.

Some of the work was written during my tenure of a William Evans Visiting Fellowship at the University of Otago, New Zealand, in 1988. I am grateful to that University for its hospitality; to Colin Gibson for his work in bringing me and my family to Dunedin and for many kindnesses; and especially to John Drummond for placing the resources and equipment of his Department at my disposal for seven months, in addition to his active friendship. I am grateful also to the University of Leeds for letting me take up the fellowship, and especially to Julian Rushton for his positive support of our venture, and of this book as a whole.

Most of all, I am grateful to Jane: for the first processional waggon cycle in modern times (the York cycle at Leeds, 1975) and for various productions before and since; for unceasing encouragement; and for raising three children while my thoughts were often in another century – in short, for making this book possible. Lastly, whatever Jane and I have done would have been more difficult or actually impossible without the love and support of our parents.

GRR
Leeds, March 1996

BIBLIOGRAPHICAL NOTES

(i) The abbreviations SD, MD and SH (sd, md, sh) are used for 'stage direction', 'marginal direction' and 'speech heading', respectively.

(ii) Internal references in the form '9.3' are to chapter and section as given in the Contents and in the running heads. References in the form 'York 2/13' or 'Mary Play 1224' are to collection/cycle, pageant and line or to play and line, as appropriate; '+sd', '+md' and '+lat' indicate the stage direction, marginal direction or Latin text following the line in question in the relevant edition; the form '1–' and '21+' refers to whatever precedes or follows the line concerned in the play under discussion. References in the form 'York 12₃' are to music cues (in this case, cue number 3 in York play 12), so numbered in the cue-lists of Volume 2: cues using a letter subscript, 'York 18ₐ', are putative cues for which the evidence is reasonable but speculative.

(iii) Plays are numbered according to the relevant modern edition or other authority: these are listed below, with their short references. Bibliographical references other than these abbreviations normally take the form of the author's name and a recognisable abbreviation: where the date is relevant or helpful I have used that in addition to, or instead of, the short title. Thus 'Stevens 1958' refers to John Stevens's article of that date in the *Proceedings of the Royal Musical Association*, while 'Cawley *Everyman*' refers to A.C. Cawley's 1956/1974 volume *Everyman and Medieval Miracle Plays*. Page references are always to the latest edition listed in the Bibliography. Some much-cited works have been given their own abbreviations, and these are included in the list on pp. xvi–xvii, below: for details, see the Bibliography.

(iv) Biblical quotations in Latin are from Gutenberg's 42-line Bible of c.1455, a facsimile of which has been published by Brussel and Brussel Inc. (New York, 1968) in three volumes. Translations of biblical texts are from the Authorized Version unless otherwise stated.

(v) Liturgical texts are quoted from the relevant service books, listed on pp. xvi–xvii and in the Bibliography.

(vi) In the discussions of music unspecified pitches are given capital letters: for instance, C is the note C but not in any particular octave (unless it is obvious from the musical context). Specific pitches are referred to by the Helmholtz system, in which c'-b' is the octave from middle C upwards.

ABBREVIATIONS: PLAY TEXTS

In this work, a name in roman type (e.g. Chester) refers to a cycle; names in italic (e.g. *Chester*) refer specifically to the edition listed here unless another is specified, or to an individual play (e.g. *Wisdom*). References to specific parts of a play text are given in **bold** type (e.g. **Towneley 13/50**, a reference to line 50 of Towneley play 13; **Castle 156**, a reference to line 156 of *The Castle of Perseverance*).

Adam	Lynette R. Muir, trans. 'Adam, a Twelfth-Century Play' in *Proceedings of the Leeds Philosophical and Literary Society, Literary and Historical Section* 13/5 (1970). 149–204.
Ashmole	'The Ashmole Fragment' in Norman Davis, ed. *Non-Cycle Plays and Fragments*. Early English Text Society s.s. 1. London: Oxford University Press, 1970. 120.
Brome	'The Brome Play' in Norman Davis, ed. *Non-Cycle Plays and Fragments*. Early English Text Society s.s. 1. London: Oxford University Press, 1970.
Burial	'Christ's Burial' in Donald C. Baker, John L. Murphy and Louis B. Hall, Jr., eds. *The Late Religious Plays of Bodleian MSS Digby 133 and E Museo 160*. Early English Text Society 283. London: Oxford University Press, 1982. 141–68.
Cambridge	'The Cambridge Prologue' in Norman Davis, ed. *Non-Cycle Plays and Fragments*. Early English Text Society s.s. 1. London: Oxford University Press, 1970. 114–15.
Castle	'The Castle of Perseverance' in Mark Eccles, ed. *The Macro Plays*. Early English Text Society 262. London: Oxford University Press, 1969. 1–111.
Chester	R.M. Lumiansky and David Mills, eds. *The Chester Mystery Cycle*. Early English Text Society s.s. 3, 9. London: Oxford University Press, 1974 and 1986: references are to volume I (Text) unless otherwise specified.
Coventry	Hardin Craig, ed. *Two Coventry Corpus Christi Plays*. Early English Text Society e.s. 87. London: Oxford University Press, 1902; 2nd edn, 1957.
Creacion	Paula Neuss, ed. *The Creacion of the World*. New York: Garland, 1983.
Delight	'The Reynes Extracts: A. A Speech of Delight' in Norman Davis, ed. *Non-Cycle Plays and Fragments*. Early English Text Society s.s. 1. London: Oxford University Press, 1970. 121–2.
Durham	'The Durham Prologue' in Norman Davis, ed. *Non-Cycle Plays and Fragments*. Early English Text Society s.s. 1. London: Oxford University Press, 1970. 118–19.
Dux Moraud	'Dux Moraud' in Norman Davis, ed. *Non-Cycle Plays and Fragments*. Early English Text Society s.s. 1. London: Oxford University Press, 1970. 106–13.
Everyman	'Everyman' in A.C. Cawley, ed. *Everyman and Medieval Miracle Plays*. London: Dent, 1956; rev. 2nd edn, 1974. 205–34.
Killing	'Candlemas Day and the Killing of the Children of Israel' in Donald C. Baker, John L. Murphy and Louis B. Hall, Jr., eds. *The Late Religious Plays of Bodleian MSS Digby 133 and E Museo 160*. Early English Text Society 283. London: Oxford University Press, 1982. 96–115. [This play is often called just 'The Killing of the Children'.]

Mankind   'Mankind' in Mark Eccles, ed. *The Macro Plays*. Early English Text
               Society 262. London: Oxford University Press, 1969. 153-84.

Mary   'Mary Magdalen' in Donald C. Baker, John L. Murphy and Louis B. Hall,
  Magdalen   Jr., eds. *The Late Religious Plays of Bodleian MSS Digby 133 and E Museo
               160*. Early English Text Society 283. London: Oxford University Press,
               1982. 24–95.

Mary Play   Peter Meredith, ed. *The Mary Play from the N.town Manuscript*. London:
               Longman, 1987.

Meriasek   Whitley Stokes, ed. and trans. *Beunans Meriasek: The Life of St Meriasek*.
               London: Trübner, 1872.

Newcastle   'The Newcastle Play' in Norman Davis, ed. *Non-Cycle Plays and Frag-
               ments*. Early English Text Society s.s. 1. London: Oxford University
               Press, 1970. 19–31.

Northampton   'The Northampton Play' in Norman Davis, ed. *Non-Cycle Plays and
               Fragments*. Early English Text Society s.s. 1. London: Oxford University
               Press, 1970. 32–42.

Norwich   'The Norwich Grocers' Play' in Norman Davis, ed. *Non-Cycle Plays and
               Fragments*. Early English Text Society s.s. 1. London: Oxford University
               Press, 1970. 8–18.

N-Town   Stephen Spector, ed. *The N-Town Play*. Early English Text Society s.s. 11,
               12. London: Oxford University Press, 1991.

Ordinalia   Edwin Norris, ed. *The Ancient Cornish Drama*. Oxford: Oxford Univer-
               sity Press, 1859. 2 vols. [The first and third days being called 'ordinale'
               in the manuscript, the Cornish cycle is often known as the Ordinalia.]

Passion Play   Peter Meredith, ed. *The Passion Play from the N.Town Manuscript*. London:
               Longman, 1990.

Pepys   The Pepys fragment in Cambridge, Magdalene College, MS Pepys 1236,
               ff. 127v–128r.

Pride of Life 'The Pride of Life' in Norman Davis, ed. *Non-Cycle Plays and Fragments*.
               Early English Text Society s.s. 1. London: Oxford University Press, 1970.
               90–105.

Resurrection   'Christ's Resurrection' in Donald C. Baker, John L. Murphy and Louis
               B. Hall, Jr., eds. *The Late Religious Plays of Bodleian MSS Digby 133 and E
               Museo 160*. Early English Text Society 283. London: Oxford University
               Press, 1982. 169–93.

Reynes   'The Reynes Extracts' in Norman Davis, ed. *Non-Cycle Plays and Frag-
               ments*. Early English Text Society s.s. 1. London: Oxford University
               Press, 1970. 121–23.

Rickinghall   'The Rickinghall (Bury St Edmunds) Fragment' in Norman Davis, ed.
               Non-Cycle Plays and Fragments. Early English Text Society s.s. 1. London:
               Oxford University Press, 1970. 116–17.

Sacrament   'The Play of the Sacrament' in Norman Davis, ed. *Non-Cycle Plays and
               Fragments*. Early English Text Society s.s. 1. London: Oxford University
               Press, 1970. 58–89. [This play is often known as the Croxton play.]

St Paul   'The Conversion of St Paul' in Donald C. Baker, John L. Murphy and
               Louis B. Hall, Jr., eds. *The Late Religious Plays of Bodleian MSS Digby 133
               and E Museo 160*. Early English Text Society 283. London: Oxford Uni-
               versity Press, 1982. 1–23.

Shrewsbury   'The Shrewsbury Fragments' in Norman Davis, ed. *Non-Cycle Plays and
               Fragments*. Early English Text Society s.s. 1. London: Oxford University
               Press, 1970. 1–7.

Towneley   George England and Alfred W. Pollard, eds. *The Towneley Plays*. Early

English Text Society e.s. 71. London: Oxford University Press, 1897; repr. Millwood, NY: Kraus, 1978.

Wisdom   'Wisdom' in Mark Eccles, ed. *The Macro Plays*. Early English Text Society 262. London: Oxford University Press, 1969. 113–52. [An incomplete version of the play is in the 'Digby' collection, pp. 116–40 in Baker, Murphy and Hall, eds. *The Late Religious Plays of Bodleian MSS Digby 133 and E Museo 160*. Early English Text Society 283. London: Oxford University Press, 1982.]

York   Richard Beadle, ed. *The York Plays*. London: Edward Arnold, 1982.

ABBREVIATIONS: WORKS FREQUENTLY CITED

Full references are given in the Bibliography

AM   *Antiphonale Monasticum.* Tournai: Desclée, 1934.

AR   *Antiphonale Romanum.* Paris: Descleé, 1924.

AS   *Antiphonale Sarisburiense,* ed. Walter H. Frere. London: Plainsong and Medi-aeval Music Society, 1901–15; repr. Farnborough: Gregg Press, 1966.

Aspects   Neuss, Paula, ed. *Aspects of Early English Drama.* Cambridge: D.S. Brewer, 1983.

BE   *Breviarium ad usum insignis ecclesie Eboracensis,* ed. Stephen W. Lawley. Durham: Surtees Society 71 and 75, 1879 and 1883.

BH   *The Hereford Breviary,* ed. Walter H. Frere and L.E.G. Brown. London: Henry Bradshaw Society, 1904–15. [See under 'Breviary' in the Bibliography.]

BS   *Breviarium ac usum insignis ecclesiae Sarum,* ed. Francis Procter and C. Wordsworth. Cambridge: 1879–86; repr. Farnborough: Gregg Press,1970.

Contexts Briscoe and Coldewey. *Contexts for Early English Drama.* 1989.

Essays   Lumiansky and Mills. *The Chester Mystery Cycle: Essays and Documents.* 1983.

GL   *The Golden Legend,* by Jacobus de Voragine, trans. Granger Ryan and Helmut Ripperger. 1941; repr. New York: Arno Press, 1969. [See also LA.]

GS   *Graduale Sarisburiense,* ed. Walter H. Frere. London: Plainsong and Mediaeval Music Society, 1891-4; repr. Farnborough: Gregg Press, 1966.

HS   *Hymnarium Sarisburiense.* London: James Darling, 1851.

IMEV   I   Carlton Brown and Rossell Hope Robbins, *The Index of Middle English Verse.* New York: Columbia University Press for the Index Society, 1943.
            II   Rossell Hope Robbins and John L. Cutler, *Supplement to the Index of Middle English Verse.* 1965.

LA   *Legenda Aurea,* by Jacobus de Voragine, ed. Th. Graesse. Vratistlavia [Breslau]: 3rd edn, Koebner, 1890. [See also GL.]

LH   *Liber Hymnarius.* Solesmes: Abbaye Saint-Pierre de Solesmes, 1983.

LMRP   Baker, Murphy and Hall. *The Late Medieval Religious Plays of Bodleian MSS Digby 133 and E Museo 160.* Early English Text Society 283. London: Oxford University Press, 1982.

LU   *The Liber Usualis, with Introduction and Rubrics in English,* edited by the Benedictines of Solesmes. Tournai: Desclée, 1938.

MDF   Leeds Texts and Monographs, Medieval Drama Facsimiles. Leeds: The University of Leeds School of English, 1973– . [See the Bibliography for a list of volumes.]

MisE   *Missale ad usum insignis ecclesie Eboracensis,* ed. William G. Henderson. Durham: Surtees Society 59 and 60, 1874.

MisS(D)   *Missale ad usum insignis et praeclarae ecclesiae Sarum,* ed. Dickinson, Francis H. Burntisland, 1861-83; repr. Farnborough: Gregg Press, 1969.

MisS(L)   *The Sarum Missal Edited from Three Early Manuscripts,* ed. J. Wickham Legg. Oxford, 1916; repr. 1969.

MPE   *Manuale et processionale ad usum insignis ecclesiae Eboracensis,* [ed. William G. Henderson]. Durham: Surtees Society 63, 1875.

MS   *Manuale ad usum percelebris ecclesiae Sarisburiensis*, ed. A. Jefferies Collins. London: Henry Bradshaw Society, 1960.
NCPF   Davis, Norman. *Non-Cycle Plays and Fragments*. Early English Text Society s.s. 1. London: Oxford University Press, 1970.
NG   *The New Grove Dictionary of Music and Musicians*, ed. Stanley Sadie. 20 vols. London: Macmillan, 1980.
OE   *Ordinale Exoniense*, ed. J.N. Dalton. 4 vols. London: Henry Bradshaw Society, 1909–40.
OED   *The Oxford English Dictionary*. Oxford: Clarendon Press, 1884-1987.
OS   *Ordinale Sarum sive Directorium Sacerdotum*, by Clement Maydeston, ed. William Cooke and Christopher Wordsworth. London: Henry Bradshaw Society 20 and 22, 1901–2.
PS(H)   *Processionale ad usum insignis ac praeclarae ecclesiae Sarum*, ed. William G. Henderson. Leeds: M'Corquodale and Co., 1882; repr. Farnborough: Gregg Press, 1969.
PS(P)   *Processionale ad Usum Sarum 1502*. Originally published by Richard Pynson. Facsimile repr.: The Use of Sarum 1. Kilkenny: Boethius Press, 1980.
WA   [Worcester Antiphoner] André Mocquereau, ed. *Antiphonaire Monastique . . . de Worcester*. Paléographie Musicale 12. Tournai: Desclée, 1922.

ILLUSTRATIONS

The plates follow p. 90

Plate 1   Shrewsbury School MS VI, f. 42v: by permission of the Chairman and Governors of Shrewsbury School.

Plates 2, 3   Magdalene College, Cambridge, Pepys MS 1236, ff. 127v–128r: by permission of the Master and Fellows, Magdalene College, Cambridge.

Plate 4   London, British Library, Add. MS 35290, f. 236r (Beadle 251r): by permission of The British Library.

Plate 5   London, British Library, Add. MS 35290, f. 241v (Beadle 256v): by permission of The British Library.

Plate 6   London, British Library, Add. MS 43645. Thomas Sharp, *A Dissertation on the Pageants or Dramatic Mysteries Anciently performed at Coventry* (1825), p. 116: by permission of The British Library.

Plate 7   London, British Library, MS Harley 2124, f. 42r: by permission of The British Library.

Plate 8   Master of the St Lucy Legend, *Mary, Queen of Heaven* (detail), c.1485–1500. Samuel H. Kress Collection: © 1996 Board of Trustees, National Gallery of Art, Washington.

Plate 9   *Compost et Kalendrier des Bergiers* (Paris: Guiot Marchant, 1541), frontispiece: Department of Printing and Graphic Arts, the Houghton Library, Harvard University.

Plate 10   Oxford, Bodleian Library, MS Douce 88, f. 73v (detail): by permission of The Bodleian Library, Oxford.

Frontispiece: Assumption of BVM (detail) by the Master of the St Lucy Legend c.1485–1500.

TABLES

1.	Evidence for music in the Chester cycle	3
2.	'Four-and-twenty to a long'	38
3.	Note-values in the Cambridge *Gloria*	40
4.	'Three breves to a long'	42
5.	Disposition of voice-parts in the source of Coventry 1	139
6.	Music in the drama at Chelmsford, summer 1562	170
7.	Angelic appearances in the York cycle	184
8.	Angelic appearances in the Chester cycle	186
9.	Music and the passage of time in Chester 3	227
10.	York 14, The Nativity	237
11.	York 11, Moses and Pharaoh	238
12.	York 35, The Crucifixion	239
13.	York 46, The Coronation of the Virgin	240
14.	York 9, The Flood	242
15.	York 12, The Annunciation and Visitation	244
16.	York 1, The Fall of the Angels	245
17.	York 45, The Assumption of the Virgin	248
18.	The Mandatum psalms and antiphons	275
19.	Timing of the Chester cycle	337
20.	The Coventry cycle and James Hewitt's doubling	343
21.	Shepherds' plays	348

MUSICAL EXAMPLES

1. Improvised textures on a chant   97

2. (a) Transeamus usque Bethelem   98
    (b) Salvatorem Christum   99

3. (a) Iam, iam ecce   102
    (b) O deus quis revolvet   104

4. Mane nobiscum   106

5. Reconstructed texture in 'Mane nobiscum'   107

6. Gloria tibi domine   108

7. Pepys 1236, ff. 127v–128r   111

8. (a) Antiphon 'Ierusalem respice'   114
    (b) 'Leva Ierusalem oculos' (antiphon and respond)   115
    (c) Antiphon 'Levate capita vestra'   117

9. 'Leva Ierusalem', second phrase   119

10. 'Leva Ierusalem', third phrase   119

11. 'Leva Ierusalem', third phrase   119

12. Starting and ending notes of the York music   127

13. 'Veni electa' B, ending   127

14. 'Veni electa' B, 'corrected' ending   128

15. Common cadence in A settings   128

16. Common phrase in 'Surge' settings   129

17. The phrases of 'Surge' A and B   129

18. Common material in 'Veni de Libano' A and B   130

19. Common material in the York music   131

20. Common material in the York music   132

21. Four-part chord in the York music   132

22. Equal-voice duet in 'Cantemus domino'   133

23. Equal-voice duet by Power   134

Musical Examples

24.	Vocal ranges of the York music	135
25.	Pitch centres of gravity of the York music	136
26.	The opening of 'As I out-rode'	141
27.	'As I out-rode', bars 3–5	142
28.	'As I out-rode', bars 5–7	142
29.	'As I out-rode', bars 7–9	143
30.	'As I out-rode', bar 9 to the end	144
31.	Phrases of the Coventry lullaby	145
32.	Error in phrase 6 of the Coventry lullaby	146
33.	Phrase 6 of the Coventry lullaby, corrected	146
34.	Coventry lullaby, verses 1 and 2 (voice I only)	147
35.	Coventry lullaby in Caldwell's rhythmic interpretation	149
36.	Coventry lullaby in ₵	150
37.	Voice ranges and pitch centres of gravity of the Coventry songs	151
38.	Chester Gloria	153
39.	Chant tunes for Gloria in excelsis deo	155
40.	Works using material like that of the Chester Gloria	156

1

INTRODUCTION

1.1 Music in Middle English drama

Faced with a Middle English play text and the task of providing music for a
production of it, we do not find it difficult to formulate the relevant questions.
Where in the play should there be music? What sort of music should it be? Who
performs it, and with what musical resources? Notated music is hardly ever present
in the text, and even when it is it does not solve the problems: for written music of
the period 1400–1600 or so is notoriously difficult to interpret when it comes to
making firm decisions about matters of performance-practice. That is probably why
the music itself has not been much discussed, and why studies of music in the plays
have generally taken the stage directions as their starting-point. The actual dialogue
in the plays, too, provides a good deal of information about music, and this has also
been something of a quarry for commentators.

   The incomplete nature of the evidence offered by written music, stage directions,
and text references is such that the available literary and notated information is
insufficient for the task. The scholar will therefore seek information in documentary
evidence such as the guild accounts that record financial transactions in respect of
the plays. This stratagem, started by Thomas Sharp in his *Dissertation on the Pageants
. . . at Coventry* (1825) and followed by Dutka, among others,[1] has greatly increased
our knowledge about the plays, in their musical aspects as in others. The enormous
strides taken in the study of this drama in the last two decades or so are in great
part due to the publication of relevant documentary evidence by the Records of
Early English Drama project,[2] although the publication of facsimiles and some
excellent editions has also had a considerable effect.

   But the records do not solve the problems, either. The information that they
contain was not put there for the benefit of twentieth-century commentators: we
are the inheritors of something that was not intended for our use, and it is hardly
surprising if the information is incomplete. Moreover, different types of evidence
often do not coincide chronologically, so that they refer to a particular drama at
different stages of its life. In this case different pieces of evidence do not necessarily

---

[1] Dutka *Use of Music* 1972.
[2] Influential pioneering projects on dramatic records were published by the Malone Society: see
especially those in the Society's *Collections* III (1954), VII (1965), VIII (for 1969, but published
1974) and IX (for 1971, but published 1977).

confirm one another. This chronological spread is exemplified by the evidence for the Chester cycle, shown in Table 1. Here the non-coincidence of different types of evidence is clearly a major problem: the documentary evidence coincides with neither play texts nor banns, and all of the main texts were copied long after the final performance in 1575. Moreover, the surviving documentary evidence and play texts contemporary with performances are clearly only a fraction of what once existed.

This would matter less if the plays had a static performance history, but of course they do not. Even in the civic cycles, where the performance traditions were particularly strong, the plays certainly evolved and were modified over the decades. Borrowing a play from elsewhere, revising or rewriting it, adding a scene, providing an alternative version of a scene or of only a few lines to take account of the presence of singers or the absence of a character – these are all situations to be seen in the surviving play texts, and all affect the use that can be made of whatever evidence remains.[3]

Such situations affect the use of music, too. After reviewing the evidence we can be sure that music had an important role in at least some of the plays. But what that role is in any particular play text is difficult to determine; what it *was* in any particular performance of the play, even more difficult. Chapters 3–8 attempt to throw some light on the problem, and in Volume 2 the plays are studied individually for that purpose.

1.2 The repertory: historical and fictional drama

At this stage I must define the limits and characteristics of the 'early English religious' repertory to be studied. The plays concerned are 'early' in the sense that they are pre-Shakespearean; but as I exclude the Tudor interlude from consideration, in effect the repertory is limited also to anonymous plays. Many of these are known from texts that are clearly much later than the plays themselves. As Table 1 shows, for instance, the Chester cycle survives in manuscripts dating from between 1591 and 1607: but the text transmitted certainly dates back to the middle of the sixteenth century and probably earlier. Apart from some earlier fragments, the plays considered here were first performed in the fourteenth and fifteenth centuries, with a performance history continuing into the sixteenth in many cases; the surviving texts were mostly copied in the fifteenth and sixteenth centuries; and the documentary evidence that we have is mainly for performances in the sixteenth century. In each case, therefore, their roots go back well beyond the middle of the sixteenth century, and most of them could be loosely regarded as 'late medieval' rather than 'renaissance' plays.

The Englishness of the repertory is shown principally in the fact that they are vernacular dramas written in late Middle English. In most cases the language is

---

3 On these issues see, for instance, Meredith 'Scribes, Texts and Performance' (1983).

TABLE 1 : EVIDENCE FOR MUSIC IN THE CHESTER CYCLE

Texts	Banns	Guild-Accounts	Notated Music
M ?C15 fragment: *Resurrection* P ?c. 1500: *Antichrist*			
	1539-40		
		1546 onwards: Blacksmiths *Purification* 1547 onwards: Shoemakers *Entry into Jerusalem, Simon the Leper* 1568 onwards: Painters *Shepherds* Coopers *Trial and Flagellation* (no music)	
		1575 : LAST PERFORMANCE	
Hm 1591: cyclic A 1592: "Group" MSS C 1599: Coopers: *Trial and Flagellation*			
R 1600: cyclic B 1604: "Group" MSS	1600		
H 1607: cyclic			Painters, MS H only: *Shepherds*

obviously older than Shakespeare's. The most important effect of the definition is the exclusion of plays not in the English language, such as the plays in Latin, both those which are substantially or wholly sung and the sixteenth-century humanist spoken dramas of the schools and universities. The Anglo-Norman plays, *Adam* and the *Seinte Resureccion*, are also excluded, although both are twelfth-century plays that might well have been written and performed in England. I have included the Cornish plays, however, which belong to the geographical area of England but are not in the English language. They (unlike the Anglo-Norman plays) belong to the same chronological period as the main group to be studied. Their language is Cornish: the Ordinalia use Latin for their directions and headings, but *The Creacion of the World* uses English as its second language and *Beunans Meriasek* (*The Life of Meriasek*) has additional directions in English although the principal ones are in Latin. All of the Cornish dramas use English loan words for musical matters, and it is well known that they also show important dramatic connections with the near-contemporary East Anglian drama. In general, therefore, it seems useful to include Cornish drama in this study, on the grounds that it is vernacular, geographically English, and chronologically close to the main repertory.

'Religious drama' is less restrictive than it may sound. The bulk of the dramatic texts surviving in Middle English (and all of those in Cornish) are firmly religious in character: they are usually categorised as biblical plays, saint plays or moralities, and there is also a single miracle play. The restriction to religious drama excludes the mumming plays and Robin Hood plays that the records show to have been performed, plays now usually referred to as 'folk drama'.

It is more difficult to exclude the various moral interludes dating from the late fifteenth century onwards, since many of these have clear religious implications, however Humanist or 'renaissance' their general outlook. The decision to discuss only three moralities here depends mainly on considerations of date, size and anonymity. Those that I include – *The Castle of Perseverance*, *Wisdom* and *Mankind* – are all from the fifteenth century, whereas most of the interludes are from the sixteenth. *The Castle*, at 3649 lines, is much the longest of them, and clearly distinct from the general run of interludes, which are typically 900–1500 lines long. *Wisdom* (1163 lines) and *Mankind* (914 lines) fall within the range of lengths for a Tudor interlude, and from this point of view match well with the slightly later fifteenth-century plays of the type – *Everyman*, *Nature* and *Fulgens and Lucres*. Of these, the last two are entitled 'Interlude', which *Wisdom* and *Mankind* are not, and are also ascribed to a specific author, Henry Medwall, whereas all the earlier plays are anonymous. Any attempt to distinguish the earlier moralities from the interludes on grounds of cast-size are dubious, although such a distinction would have been useful: it is possible that the earlier plays use larger casts, but by no means an established fact.

Another criterion used in the exclusion of Tudor interludes is that of civic production. In general I have not treated drama designed for private consumption indoors, and most of the plays discussed in this study were certainly performed out-of-doors and under civic or community control.[4] Attempts to distinguish between the earlier moralities and the Tudor interludes on these grounds is artificial at best, although it is pragmatically useful.

These various criteria – language, date, anonymity, civic outdoor production, and

---

4 This has been questioned in the case of *Wisdom*, which is thought by some to have been presented indoors, perhaps at St Edmund's Abbey in Bury: see Gibson, '*Wisdom*' in Riggio *Wisdom Symposium*, 39–66. I do not accept a St Edmund's provenance for *Wisdom*, but it is clearly more likely to be an indoor play than an outdoor one.

religious subject-matter – all cause anomalies when taken individually, and the decision to include or exclude a play has often been due to a fine balance of factors. The Cornish plays are included here, in the final analysis, because they have no other obvious place for discussion; *Mankind* and *Wisdom* because their medieval outlook aligns them with *The Castle of Perseverance* rather than with the more obviously 'renaissance' interludes from *Everyman* and *Nature* onwards. John Bale's biblical plays might have been included here, since it is arguable that he aimed to write a group of plays analogous to part of a medieval biblical cycle. They are excluded from this study ultimately because the biblical cycles, undoubtedly the inspiration behind Bale's biblical plays, were certainly not their model, and Bale's work – like other sixteenth-century biblical and saint plays of known authorship – cannot usefully be considered on the same terms as the anonymous late medieval biblical and saint plays.[5] And *Everyman*, the most anomalous of all, has the length and cast-size to be expected of an interlude, calls itself a 'treatise in the form of a moral play', dates from the earliest Tudor period in the last decade of the fifteenth century, is anonymous, but was printed and therefore may well have been intended for domestic performance by a professional company. These circumstances alone would be enough to suggest that it should properly be considered as a Tudor interlude: but its derivation from the Flemish moral play *Elckerlijc* casts other doubts on its postion in the repertory of English drama.

It is in the nature of drama, then, that definitions of genre cannot be applied rigorously in carving out a homogeneous repertory for study, and an element of pragmatism is needed. On the basis of the considerations just outlined, this book treats a total of three morality plays (*The Castle of Perseverance, Mankind,* and *Wisdom*), one miracle play (*The Play of the Sacrament*), three saint plays (*The Conversion of St Paul, Mary Magdalen,* and *The Life of Meriasek*), and a much larger number of biblical plays consisting of five cycles (the Cornish Ordinalia and the York, Towneley, N-Town and Chester cycles) and some sixteen single plays, some of which are the remains of cycles otherwise lost.

Historical drama

The terms 'biblical drama' and 'saint play' are however problematic. These and the term 'morality (play)' are modern, invented to make useful distinctions: but increased knowledge of material has changed our perception of the distinctions involved, and calls the distinctions themselves into question. Only 'miracle' is an older term, and that was originally used for saint plays and biblical plays, not just for plays on the miracles of long-dead saints.[6] 'Mystery', which is a post-medieval term taken from the French 'mystère', is likewise not specific enough to be useful.

Until recently 'biblical drama' was used to describe plays dramatising narrative

---

5 For a reference list of songs in the interludes see Happé 1991.
6 See p. 89, below, for instance.

episodes found in 'The Bible' – that is, those scriptures of the Judeo-Christian tradition accepted by the Church as divine revelation. This definition excludes plays based on apocryphal writings, legends, or medieval writings allegorising the eternal battle between Good and Evil over the soul of Man. The categories of 'morality' and 'miracle' plays are therefore theoretically quite separate.

The distinction between 'biblical' plays and 'saint' plays is more difficult to sustain. Our understanding of these categories has been distorted by the primacy given to the biblical cycles in medieval drama criticism. Throughout the nineteenth century and well into the second half of the twentieth the Creation-to-Doom cycle played processionally on waggons was felt to be the norm, with single biblical plays representing an anomalous sub-category. The lack of understanding about the purposes and occasions of dramatic performance in the fifteenth and sixteenth centuries resulted in commentators looking for evidence of a lost cycle to which any individual play could belong. It was always accepted, of course, that biblical plays included non-biblical material such as scenes featuring devils, and there has been some recognition that one could find in the cycles scenes that treated allegorical or hagiographic material in the manner of a morality or saint play. But it is only recently that the admission has been made that some so-called 'biblical' plays are nothing of the sort, and indeed would not be regarded as such if they did not appear in a 'biblical cycle'. Foremost among these are the Mary Play of the N-Town cycle, now recognised as an independent play split up and reworked as a substitute for various pageants in a civic waggon cycle,[7] and the physically separate Assumption play from the same cycle. These are clearly saint plays, the former largely independent of the canonic scriptures and the latter wholly so: yet their position in a 'biblical' cycle is traditionally such that scholars are not yet used to the idea that they are not 'biblical' plays. The category has been decided by the context of the manuscript source, then, not by the nature of the play itself. While this is clearly nonsense, at the same time the problem can be solved only by reference to the same context: devils' scenes in the 'biblical cycles' are not regarded as potential morality plays because there is no evidence that they were ever separate, while the N-Town Assumption *is* regarded as a saint play because of its demonstrable physical separateness from the cycle. This presents a serious dilemma. The *Assumption* play of the York cycle must be regarded as 'biblical' because of its position as part of a 'biblical cycle', yet if there were evidence of its former separateness from the rest of the cycle we should regard it as a saint play. The categories cannot be defined in this way.

The problem is compounded by the fact that the surviving saint plays in English all treat saints who appear in the New Testament. St Paul, Mary Magdalene and the Blessed Virgin can all be regarded as 'biblical' characters in the strictest sense and therefore suitable subjects for 'biblical' plays. This is very convenient in the case of the Blessed Virgin, who is an important figure throughout the Gospel narrative and whose life is a plausible compound of biblical fact, guesswork and outright legend.

[7] Separately edited by Peter Meredith (1987).

Mary Magdalene's life leans more heavily on guesswork, and most of all on legend: but the plays that include her, with a single exception, restrict themselves to biblical narrative and are normally classed as 'biblical' plays.[8] The exception is the independent play known as *Mary Magdalen* which, as a 'biographical' play specifically about that saint, demands much more material than the Gospels can provide. The case of St Paul raises the reverse question. Since *The Conversion of St Paul* treats a story that is wholly scriptural (it occurs in the Acts of the Apostles 9/1–26) the play could reasonably be regarded as 'biblical' drama. Again, it is seen as a saint play because it is free-standing: had it been incorporated into a biblical cycle it would have been treated as a biblical play even though unique in its subject-matter.[9]

The distinction between biblical drama and saint plays, then, is hardly a realistic one. On the one hand we have narrative plays based on biblical sources but including non-biblical material, while on the other there are plays on saints' lives, some of which incorporate biblical material or are even wholly based on it while others are largely or wholly based on legendary material. Apart from the quite unreal distinction of the play text and its context, the distinction between these two types of play depends on that between 'biblical' and legendary narrative.[10] This is however a distinction that most members of a contemporary audience did not recognise. In the first place, the medieval use of holy writings, including the liturgy itself, did not normally distinguish between authentic and fictional writing: and these terms would themselves have made no sense to the medieval man in the street. The lections at Matins made use equally of biblical material, legends of saints' lives, and patristic exegesis; and material such as the *Legenda Aurea* was designed to supplement the biblical material available for discussion in sermons. To the great majority of laypeople, then, and probably to most clergy, the story of a saint's life was as useful theologically and pastorally, and as authoritative, as much of the biblical narrative. Only the Gospels themselves had a special position in the medieval consciousness. Thus it is unlikely that medieval audiences thought of a 'biblical'

---

8 The classification is still a very broad one, of course. The Gospel narrative leaves in doubt such vital matters as Mary Magdalene's precise identity and whether she is the same as Mary the sister of Lazarus and Martha and/or the repentent sinner at the house of Simon the Leper. Any dramatist was bound to make decisions on these matters, and in such ways did the narrative of her life become strongly tinged with fiction.

9 This argument depends partly on our view of the concept of a 'cycle'. Here I need only say that I am content (unlike some scholars) to think of the York, Chester and Cornish compilations as 'cycles'; less happy about the Towneley plays, although I see no reasonable alternative; and least satisfied by the N-Town plays as a 'cycle'. It seems to me important to distinguish the unity of the *texts* from the unity of any *production*: the former is dubious in the case of Towneley and virtually a non-starter in N-Town, whereas any performance of a so-called cycle must have conformed to certain limits and therefore to a degree of unity imposed on it.

10 The one wholly non-biblical saint play treated here, *The Life of Meriasek*, has so many references to and parallels with the Gospel narrative that a medieval audience would hardly have looked on it as something different. The other non-biblical play in the historical genre, The Play of the Sacrament, has the Body of Christ as a principal protagonist; the first words of the play take us back to the biblical narrative: 'Now Cryst, þat ys our Creatour, from shame he cure vs'; and the banns carefully place and date the miracle at Rome in the year 1461, so that it can be seen as a continuation of biblical history (NCPF, 59, 60).

play on Abraham and Isaac as different in type from a 'saint' play on Mary Magdalene: the categories simply would not have made sense. In this case the categorisation of *The Conversion of St Paul* would not arise, either. Secondly, the arguments that eventually led to the distinction between a canon of scripture, the deutero-canonic writings, apocryphal writings (formerly canonic and then rejected) and non-authoritative writings were a difficult scholarly process that can have been of little interest to any but relatively few theologians.[11]

In this book, therefore, I follow Alan Knight in considering biblical plays and saint plays to belong to a category of 'historical' drama that includes them both.[12] This larger category also takes in a third sub-category, that of the 'miracle' play. Whereas a saint play is biographical, dealing with a living saint, a 'miracle' play concerns the miracles done by a saint who has died some time ago. Thus the miracle of the Jew's hand at the burial of the Blessed Virgin is biographical, whereas the Miracles of the Virgin, all of which took place long after the Virgin's death, count as 'miracles'. In the English dramatic repertory the only miracle play is the Croxton *Play of the Sacrament*. This seems atypical at first sight, since the main protagonist is the Blessed Sacrament itself: but the principle of the forceful action of a long-dead saint (in this case Christ himself) is intact.

According to Knight's categories, *The Play of the Sacrament* is nevertheless 'historical'. This term does not imply the historical truth of the subject matter of the plays but rather that contemporary audiences believed them to be historically true. More importantly, the historical plays deal with human beings in 'realistic' settings, and the battle is an outward one between two or more persons.[13] This is in contradistinction to the morality plays, in which spiritual truths are presented through allegorical characters, and the battle between Good and Evil is fought out in the protagonist's soul. This treatment is a recognisably fictional one: nobody in a medieval audience would have thought of the characters in a fifteenth-century morality play as historical, even if the plot included characters – such as God, his angels, and the Devil – who could equally have been included in historical drama.

What is the importance of this for music? The answer is two-fold. First, there has been a widespread belief that the use of music in the plays depended on the *genre* concerned, so that aspects of representation, 'realism', and so on had to be understood in relation to the type of drama under discussion. I hope to demonstrate in this volume that if this is true at all it is true only in a very different way from the understanding of the recent past. Second, music in the plays undoubtedly depended

---

11 There was a canonic collection of scriptures which was (and in the Roman Catholic Church still is) rather larger than that recognised in the Protestant churches. The Catholic Church, too, has never made as simple a distinction between canonic and apocryphal writings as the Protestant churches do. Historically, therefore, although 'the Bible' was a recognisable entity (seen in Gutenberg's print of c. 1455, for example) the concept of 'Holy Scripture' was a wider and much more widespread one than is now the case in Protestant countries.

12 Knight *Aspects of Genre* (1983), especially Chapter 2, pp. 17–40, 'History and Fiction'. Knight's terminology takes account of secular historical plays as well as of the religious dramas under examination here.

13 Knight *Aspects of Genre*, 104.

on the resources available for the production, and therefore on the social group involved, its relations with possible musical resources, and the methods of mounting the drama. In so far as these matters are related to the type of drama concerned, the *genre* is relevant to the issue of music in the plays.

Fictional drama

The moral drama is not easy to define, and I have given above my reasons for excluding early moral interludes such as *Everyman* and including *Wisdom* and *Mankind*, both of which are often regarded as interludes. I discuss here only three plays, therefore: in probable chronological order, *The Castle of Perseverance*, *Wisdom* and *Mankind*. They have in common a treatment of the spiritual journey of Mankind, dramatised as an individual but universal man, through life. The protagonists in the struggle between Good and Evil for the soul of Mankind are characters personifying the Vices, the Virtues, and so on. Thus the plays deal with the cosmic drama at the internal and spiritual level, as distinct from the external and social level treated in the historical plays.[14] Even in this some qualification is needed, however, for *The Castle of Perseverance* has a long final section devoted to The Parliament of Heaven, in which the Four Daughters of God debate whether Mankind shall be saved or not. Although this is found in only one of the English cycles (N-Town), and is there related to the question whether the Incarnation should take place, it fits perhaps more neatly into the historical view of Salvation than into the individual treatment. True, the Parliament section may well be a slightly later version of *The Castle*'s ending, but it is actually a very appropriate way to end that particular play.

The Castle is, indeed, the most extended of these three plays, although its 3649 lines, with a playing-time of around four hours, do not put it into the time-scale of the biblical cycles. Its cast of thirty-three nevertheless tends in the same direction, at least in comparison with the much smaller casts of the other plays: *Wisdom* has six speaking parts, though with many dancers, etc., and *Mankind* a cast of only seven.[15] *The Castle* is also the oldest of these plays, dating probably from the first quarter of the fifteenth century. Although some scholars consider it less than wholly successful,[16] it could hardly have been an isolated example, and we must assume that a number of large-scale dramas from that period are now lost. However this may be, the musical resources of the play do not seem to be in line with its size. For this, two factors may be responsible. First, the place-and-scaffold staging of *The Castle*, necessary for a cast and action on this scale and set down in the famous plan included in the manuscript, militates against music, which is difficult to make

---

[14] There is also a strong cosmological element in the biblical plays, of course: but one could perhaps make out a case for this as a transferred social element, Heaven being seen as its own type of society, recognisably related to human society.

[15] These look small against *Everyman*'s cast of seventeen speaking roles, and this is another way in which *Everyman* is anomalous, even if some doublings are possible.

[16] See Davenport *Fifteenth-Century English Drama*, 106–07.

effective in a setting so unhelpful acoustically. This effect is probably aggravated by playing in the round. Second, the dates of the play and the surviving manuscript are early enough to be in a period when either music was not much used or the indications for music had not yet reached the texts.

If *The Castle of Perseverance* is the most extensive of the moralities, *Wisdom* is the most political, concerning itself much more concentratedly on the best ways for the individual to achieve salvation. The possible contexts for this attitude have been discussed in the proceedings of the symposium on the play held at Trinity College, Hartford, in 1984.[17] Whatever the truth about the occasion of its original production, *Wisdom*'s genesis seems to lie in the internal questionings of a section of the Church itself. The use of dance is rare in Middle English drama, and in *Wisdom* it provides a uniquely masque-like quality otherwise virtually unknown in the latter half of the fifteenth century.

In comparison with *Wisdom*, and even to some extent with *The Castle, Mankind* seems a very popular play. This is not only because of its foolery, its use of 'popular'-style entertainment (such as the teaching of a song to the audience), and its colloquial and often indecent language: techniques such as the collection of money and the build-up to the entry of a 'star' character either deliberately parody popular drama or are actually a part of it. The play is probably not a popular production, however, and the musical resources used are appropriate.[18]

1.3 The repertory: civic, community and institutional plays

The plays under discussion here, then, hardly constitute a unified group of dramas. As will be apparent by now, the differences between the various plays in any sub-category are much more obvious than the similarities. It is true that the biblical cycles are all of much the same length, treat much the same material, and indeed in some cases are related textually. But their differences, too, are considerable, and in the relatively detailed context of the individual pageant are again more significant than the similarities. Even in the method of production no clear pattern can be seen: the York and Chester cycles were originally performed processionally on waggons as a series of separate plays; the Cornish Ordinalia clearly derive from a more continental view of cyclic drama,[19] and seem to be a single drama designed for performance in the round; Towneley, from Yorkshire but no longer thought to be from Wakefield, is a collection of plays, some of which were certainly waggon plays originally, apparently brought together as a drama to be played at a single location

---

[17] Riggio *The Wisdom Symposium* (1986).

[18] See Gibson *Theatre of Devotion*, 111. The music in these plays is discussed at the appropriate places in Volume 2.

[19] The language connects the Ordinalia with Breton and Welsh cultures, rather than with English, and the form of the drama, ending with the Ascension, relates it to the French biblical drama. In some of its details it shows parallels with the East Anglian plays.

by a single cast; and N-Town, of unknown provenance, is a collection of plays of disparate origins. It is this last cycle, especially, that underlines the dangers of making assumptions about the auspices under which any play was performed and the consequent role of music in that play.

Scholars tend to assume a civic context for the cycles, on the ground that only a town using its full authority and resources could undertake to mount such a huge dramatic event.[20] There is sense in this assumption, for the cost of mounting a cycle, as is shown by the financial accounts for those of known provenance, was enormous. Even so, the plays were individually the responsibility of the trade guilds that formed the background to civic organisation in the late Middle Ages. I need not repeat here the well-known facts of guild and civic production of the plays. It is important only to note the consequences for musical performance in the plays. Each guild, unless it had considerable musical resources of its own, would have to hire singers and instrumentalists from outside the guild, professional musicians over whom the guild would have only limited control. In the case of minstrelsy this made little difference: at no time did employers show any real interest in what particular tunes were played by a minstrel. In the case of singers, however, the effects are important.

For vocal music in the plays the guilds went, when we have any information on the matter, to the local cathedral or other large church for professional church singers, paying the church's own choir-trainer, or some other singing-man from that church, to rehearse the singing and to organise the details of the performance. While a particular liturgical piece may sometimes have been specified by the dramatist or producer, most of the dramatic directions that name Latin pieces seem to have been marginal directions originally, written probably as a record of what had been sung rather than as a directive (see 2.3). The guildsman actors, the organisers and the producer were non-musicians whose business was never liturgy or singing, and the plays were performed in a civic setting: so it is likely that when singers were procured from the local cathedral the guild was only too pleased to explain roughly what the play required in the way of music, and then to leave the singers to provide it in their own way. They, on their part, were outside their usual liturgical context and normally, no doubt, working with considerably fewer singers than the full complement. It is entirely possible that the producer did not always know, until the actors and singers first rehearsed together, what pieces had been chosen.[21] This rehearsal was probably late – the 'general rehearse' mentioned in guild accounts, which seems to have been the occasion on which the cast as a whole put the complete pageant together, rather than individual scenes being rehearsed with the limited cast concerned.[22] The relationship between guild-actors and the singers was therefore one in which each group dealt with its own concerns until the different groups fitted everything together at a late stage. Even when the singers took minor speaking

---

[20] See, for instance, Palmer 'Corpus Christi "Cycles" ', 220–21.
[21] See 8.3, below.
[22] See Wickham *Early English Stages* I, 299.

roles we can see that their roles were usually written in such a way that the singers did not need to rehearse with the guildsmen until a late stage. The twelve angels in **York 45** are a good example of this technique: their speeches form a self-contained section (**York 45/105–17**) which could be rehearsed separately and fitted into the rest of the play with a minimum of trouble.[23] This is however a quite different situation from that in which a singer, who by his training in voice-production and ceremonial movement was well qualified to perform in public, was used by the guild as a professional or otherwise imported actor for a major role. If Robert White did indeed play the singing role of Simeon in **Chester 11** in 1567 and 1568, for instance, he clearly had to rehearse with the Smiths as if he were a guildsman.[24]

The rather loose relationship between the trade-guild mounting a play and the professional church singers hired to provide vocal music for it probably obtained also for other plays mounted by the community as a whole. We know most about the circumstances in which trade guilds were responsible for dramatic performance under the control of the civic authority, but some plays were certainly not 'civic' in quite this sense. Peter Meredith has suggested that a proper context for the *Mary Play* could be found in the religious guilds and parish organisations of rural Norfolk in the fifteenth century, pointing to the probability of a St Anne's Guild existing at Acle that would have the precise interests needed by any group wishing to mount the play.[25] An alternative to civic production, then, is what might be termed 'community' drama[26] – drama mounted in a more rural context, by a religious guild or parish organisation. While this kind of production, too, would presumably require that singers be drafted in for the musical side, the relationship between production and singers might differ in two ways from that already discussed. First, the smaller the community concerned, the smaller are the available musical resources likely to be; but second, in such a situation the singers might well be a part of, or at least have close ties with, the group responsible. A religious guild mounting a play might have professional singers among its members, for instance, and a larger parish organisation similarly might be able to call on one or more singers. Basically, the larger the community concerned, the larger the available musical resources and the more professionally competent they are likely to be.

The situations in both civic and community drama are distinct from that obtaining in liturgical drama – that is, drama entirely sung, and in Latin. Although we are not concerned with Latin liturgical drama here, it will be useful to discuss this distinction, because it has a bearing on a section of the repertory. It is clear that some plays were mounted by more specifically institutional groups than religious guilds and parish organisations, exclusive communities of which individual religious houses and collegiate establishments were the main representatives and sung Latin drama the main repertory. In such a case those acting and singing were doing so in the circumstances, and with the techniques, of their normal everyday liturgical

[23] Further on this technique see below, pp. 328–9.
[24] See my argument for this in Lumiansky and Mills *Essays*, 134–5.
[25] Meredith *Mary Play*, 10–11.
[26] I am indebted to Lynette Muir for her recommendation of this term.

performance. They were using their specialist professional knowledge of liturgical singing, ceremonial and gesture; their costume was largely liturgical; they normally played the drama in the building in which they spent their professional lives; and even their audience was largely the usual congregation. Lastly, because liturgical drama was a special event, usually performed on a special occasion, the singers were likely to be there in full force.

I shall not discuss Latin liturgical drama further, but what has just been said is relevant also to vernacular drama performed in similar circumstances. It has been shown that the so-called 'Shrewsbury fragments', a fifteenth-century actor's part for three biblical plays in English, which includes part-music, belong to the corpus of processional music performed in liturgical ceremonies at Lichfield Cathedral.[27] The Shrewsbury music was sung, then, in circumstances not met with in the civic plays. It would therefore be very wrong to use it as evidence, for instance, that the shepherds at the Nativity might sing similar music in the civic cycles: this would be a serious methodological error that could lead to all sorts of wrong conclusions about the use of music in the civic plays.

This raises an important question: Do any other vernacular biblical plays have a similar provenance? A proportion of the repertory seems to have been designed for church performance, and may therefore have been under the aegis of church authority originally: but this does not mean that they were mounted by religious or secular houses. However, we might expect institutional drama to be more strongly influenced by liturgy than community drama, as the Shrewsbury plays are. Rosemary Woolf pointed out that the Bodley *Burial* and *Resurrection* plays demonstrate precisely this feature, and she suggested that they were intended for performance in a church:[28] it is thought that these plays probably originated at a Carthusian house in Yorkshire, perhaps Kingston on Hull.[29] It would be quite wrong to regard these two plays as 'liturgical' in the usual sense, and there is no evidence that they were even as closely related to the liturgy proper as were the Shrewsbury plays. On the other hand they were apparently intended to be performed on Good Friday and Easter Day, respectively – that is, at the proper liturgical time – and this may well be a normal feature of institutional drama in England. If this is correct, we should note that the singing of *Victimae paschali laudes* at the end of the play either had happened already on the day of a performance, or was going to happen.

It is also just possible that this performance of the Easter sequence was itself the liturgical performance, but this must be treated with great caution. In this case, the play would be acted after the Alleluia of the Mass: and because 'Alleluia' is not repeated on Easter Day the text immediately preceding the drama would be the Alleluia verse *Pascha nostrum*: 'Christ our Passover is sacrificed'. The play would then be the performance of both the sequence *Victimae paschali laudes* and the Gospel, and following the final speech of St John the Credo would begin the return to the

---

[27] Rankin 'Shrewsbury School Manuscript VI' (1976).
[28] Woolf *English Mystery Plays* (1972), 332, 335.
[29] LMRP, lxxxi–lxxxiii.

liturgical texts.[30] But this is supposition, and there is no real evidence that the Bodley plays were intended for liturgical performance, either as plays or in their original form as meditations: indeed, it is still supposition that the plays are institutional rather than merely intended for performance in a church. Propriety in liturgical time may have been the norm for liturgical plays, but it need not have been exclusively so: a play put on by a religious guild could well have been performed on the liturgically appropriate day also. The day in question, too, may not be more important to an institution than to a parish church community or a guild. *The Killing of the Children* was apparently intended for St Anne's Day, but this would not be a particularly appropriate time for an institution to perform a play unless it were one dedicated to that saint: the liturgically appropriate time would be the feast of the Holy Innocents (28 December) or the feast of the Purification (2 February). But the fact that the play treats both episodes, and that no one liturgical occasion would suit both, brings us back to the possibility of a religious guild: for St Anne's day *would* be a particularly appropriate occasion for a suitable play mounted by a guild dedicated to that saint. Similar considerations make it unlikely that the *Mary Play* was institutional. On the other hand, the amount of liturgical singing in the N-Town Assumption might well suggest performance by an institution in that play's earlier existence before incorporation into the N-Town cycle.

As always, the circumstances of performance, and therefore the type of drama under consideration, is important for music: it would be wrong to use the evidence of the antiphonal performance of *Victimae paschali laudes* in the Bodley *Resurrection* to draw any conclusion about its possible use and performance-mode in civic drama.[31] At the same time, evidence about music in the various types of play is too sparse for any real pattern of musical usage to be seen. To take an example, **N-Town 13** and **41** (the *Visitation* and *Assumption* plays) both clearly distinguish between the singing of angels and the speaking of mortals: this is not at all the stance taken by most civic plays, where the singing of mortals is not exceptional (see section 5.3). On the other hand, while the *Assumption* play clearly uses very full musical resources, this was probably not the case with the *Mary Play*, despite its strong liturgical background. Thus either the *Mary Play* was not mounted by a church but by a guild (perhaps without musical resources), or else it was mounted as a very special effort by a church in which musical performance played virtually no part. Much more information is needed before we can solve this kind of problem. It is relatively easy to discuss this matter in relation to the biblical plays because some of them can be related to the financial records of their production. When the saint plays and moralities are considered, the lack of financial records definitely associated with specific plays makes it impossible to draw firm conclusions, which is a great pity.[32] It follows from what was said above about the *Mary Play* and **N-Town 41** (the *Assumption*) that, if they are indeed community or institutional plays assumed into a civic cycle, the musical resources available for a production as part

---

[30] The Easter Day Gospel is from St Mark, but the play is evidently based on John 20.
[31] Stevens makes this mistake, 1958, 90.
[32] But see 4.3, concerning the plays at Chelmsford in 1562.

of the cycle may have been much less generous – or, perhaps, more generous – than those of the original saint plays. Whether these different levels of musical resourcing can now be discerned is another matter.

In this book, then, I shall not treat the biblical plays, saint plays and moralities as three homogeneous repertories. On the contrary, it is necessary to consider the various cycles and single plays separately, in order to take account of any circumstances known to belong to the play that would affect our assessment of its musical needs and the evidence for musical performance. Our next task must therefore be to look over the types of evidence available.

2

THE INTERNAL LITERARY EVIDENCE

2.1 Introduction

The incompleteness of the evidence has serious consequences for any study of the repertory. Most obviously, arguments *ab silentio* are unsatisfactory because a lack of evidence for music at any place in a play is not evidence for the absence of music there in performance. The question 'Where in this particular play should there be music?' is not necessarily easy to answer, therefore. Secondly, even when there is a full range of evidence – as there is for the Chester cycle, for example – whatever can be said about the provision of music at a particular point in a play often depends on the date concerned. That is, one set of evidence may be valid for, say, the late fifteenth century, while another set tells us only about the mid-sixteenth: and neither set can automatically be assumed for the other date.

The first consequence of these problems is that it is important to present any available positive evidence for the absence of music, since the demonstration that music was *not* used at a particular moment in a play is vital information. It tells us something positive about the play, and it also saves us from the mistake of trying to find a rationale for music (not to mention decisions about the repertory and its performance) in a place where this is unnecessary. Throughout this work I have therefore tried to offer evidence of a text being spoken rather than sung, or of an aural cue being for noise rather than for music, whenever possible.

Second, the temptation to use cross-comparison between plays is very strong. While cross-comparison may be helpful in making decisions for an actual production when the evidence is imperfect or absent, it should be a last resort: at a theoretical level it does not give us final solutions. Even within a sub-category (such as biblical plays for civic production) there is a wide variety of musical usage and of dramatists' and producers' attitudes towards music. In general, attempts to use cross-comparison to answer major questions about the use of music in particular plays are doomed to failure: we can draw conclusions on this basis only if we ignore the individuality of the separate plays – in other words, if we cease to recognise precisely those features that make the plays most interesting. The need, then, is to assess all available evidence for each play individually and only then to draw on indirect evidence (such as the content of related plays) or general evidence (such as our knowledge of the iconography of Heaven) to provide solutions.

There is always a danger, when this process is complete, that the provisional decisions thus made for the practical purpose of mounting a production may be seen as offering *final, theoretical* solutions. The use of cross-comparison is a matter of expediency and guesswork: its justification is that it enables informed productions of the plays to be performed, but no more. Our aim should always be to increase our knowledge to a point where we can know with reasonable certainty how a play was originally performed.[1]

This chapter and the next two are concerned with the direct evidence given by the play manuscripts and the documentary sources. Of the evidence provided by the sources, notated music is treated separately. This present chapter therefore covers only the internal literary evidence of the manuscripts, with discussions of 'stage directions', text references, the banns, the incidence of lyrics and song-texts, and the use of Latin.

Two types of evidence not treated in detail here are iconography and literature. Both are of course used in the book, but only for confirmation, not to give information absent from other types of evidence. It is not that they never provide the kind of information that we need, but that they must be regarded as secondary evidence. The relationship between iconography and drama is, despite the work of Clifford Davidson, Pamela Sheingorn and other scholars, neither close enough nor clear enough, in my view, for iconographical sources to be used with any certainty; and the same can be said of literary sources. When either type of source is cited in this book, therefore, it will be because it confirms what we know from other types of evidence; or an overwhelmingly high proportion of examples demonstrates the same thing; or assessment of the evidence suggests that a specific conclusion can reasonably be drawn.

The potential material for this chapter is much too extensive for the survey that I intend. The examples will not be comprehensive, therefore, but will attempt to offer a representative cross-section of the material as well as some of the most interesting items.[2]

2.2 The manuscripts

It is easy to assume, from a twentieth-century perspective, that surviving copies of any early vernacular drama were closely involved in performances of the play concerned, and that they therefore offer an authoritative record of the play text and its staging. In fact, the relationship between written text and the play as performed is a more complex one than that. If a play was performed over a period of many years, it may have changed, in which case the written text is a static reflection of perhaps several different stages in the play's development. A second reason concerns the nature of the performing body and the purpose of the manuscript in a

---

[1] This is so even when a director does not aim to reproduce the original methods and styles: no production can do a play justice unless the play itself (and that means its conditions and the relevant performance practices) is understood.

[2] This material is discussed fully in Volume 2.

largely illiterate age: we cannot always assume, for instance, that a performer learned his part from something like an individual copy of the relevant text.

Of the play manuscripts now surviving, only two seem likely to have been used by the performer. *Dux Moraud* need not concern us here, although it will be discussed in Volume 2.[3] The other, Shrewsbury School MS VI, has been shown by Susan Rankin to be a part book, one of three used for processional music at Lichfield Cathedral in the early fifteenth century.[4] In appearance it is such a book as might be described as a polyphonic processional. We must be careful about this, though. A normal processional, containing the texts and chants for liturgical processions, was certainly carried and sung from in procession: that much, at least, is clear from the size of most processionals – small for portability – and the fact that one of the largest of them has candle-wax all over the pages devoted to Candlemas.[5] Since the choir chants, as well as the priest's part, are included in a processional, it seems that not only the priest but also the choir singers carried such a book in procession. But even this is by no means certain: even if the choir knew the chants by heart the priest would still need a reference copy containing their music and texts as well as his own (a prompt copy, in dramatic terms) and it must be said that the wax-covered pages are in a finely-decorated manuscript that was certainly used by someone much more important than a choir singer.

In processions where plainsong was sung, then, it is far from certain that the singers carried service-books. The situation is no clearer when we consider the very unusual situation with polyphonic music in procession, although it is more likely that the polyphonists did read from a book. From the start, and until well into the fifteenth century, polyphony was a matter for soloists: the Shrewsbury processional, then, is not a choir singer's book in any case, but apparently that for a soloist. It is of course possible that the polyphonists learned the music from this or another copy, but still sang from memory in procession. This is perhaps not very likely, however, and I see no reason to doubt that the Shrewsbury manuscript was carried, with its companion volumes, by the polyphonists in procession in Lichfield Cathedral. Even so, we should note that the plays and their music were presumably *not* performed by actors who held books, and we should perhaps assume that the Shrewsbury manuscript was not carried during dramatic performances.

To sum up, there seems no reason to doubt that the Shrewsbury manuscript was used in procession, and we should therefore regard it as a performer's manuscript; but it probably was not used by a performer during dramatic performances.

The Shrewsbury manuscript is unusual among dramatic sources. The play was an institutional one with a large musical element, and as the institution concerned was

---

3 *Dux Moraud* is edited in Davis *Non-Cycle Plays and Fragments*, 106–13: for the type of manuscript, see especially p. cii.

4 The Shrewsbury fragment is edited in Davis *Non-Cycle Plays and Fragments*, 1–7: see Rankin 'Shrewsbury School Manuscript VI' (1976), *passim*, and section 3.2, below.

5 One of a pair of 14th-century Sarum processionals from Dublin, now MS Z4.2.20 in Archbishop Marsh's Library, Dublin: the other is Oxford, Bodleian Library, MS Rawlinson liturg. d.4. See Harrison *Music in Medieval Britain*, 98.

of a type that used liturgical books the plays were copied into those books as a matter of convenience.[6] The only other dramatic work that might have been contained in such a source is the Pepys fragment. Although the surviving fragment is part of a personal anthology, the type of music and the repertory of the Pepys manuscript as a whole suggests that this, too, might originally have been contained in a processional.[7] The provenance of the Pepys manuscript, which Roger Bowers considers to come from Christ Church Canterbury, supports this possibility, since Christ Church is an institution not unlike Lichfield Cathedral, albeit a monastic one. No other play sources, even among the possible institutional plays, have so important a musical element and the consequent affinity with a processional repertory, so it is not surprising that no other plays are found in service books.

Among other types of play, it is the northern civic play-cycles that present the clearest picture of source-types, although the picture is a complex one.[8] It seems that each of the trade guilds possessed an approved copy of its own play, called in the records the 'Original'. The Sykes Manuscript of the York Scriveners' play *The Incredulity of Thomas* is one of these.[9] So too are copies of two of the Chester plays and the surviving source of the Coventry Weavers' play and its associated fragments. The last of these must be part of the previous Original. The manuscript of the Shearmen and Tailors' play from which Sharp made his edition must also have been an Original.[10] When the time came to put the play into rehearsal, actors' parts, called 'parcels', were copied out from the Original and distributed among the actors so that they could learn their lines. These were obviously disposable manuscripts that would be subject to considerable damage; so although it is possible that such a manuscript will come to light – in a book binding, perhaps – it is not surprising that none is known at present. Our only information about 'parcels', in fact, comes from the guild records of payments for their copying.

Finally, a complete compilation of all the plays in the cycle was held by the civic authority. This was presumably a reference copy, and it could perhaps be used for the making of a new original should anything happen to the guild's own copy. We know, too, that this civic copy – called the Register, because it was the city's own official copy – could be used to monitor performances and to check the texts for purposes of censorship.[11]

This pattern is most clearly, though still incompletely, seen in the York cycle. The text that survives is the Register, copied for the city some time between 1463 and

---

[6] As John Caldwell has pointed out (Caldwell, 11), once tropers ceased to be used it was the processional that became most useful for housing dramatic works. This comment refers to sung Latin dramas, of course, not to vernacular spoken ones.

[7] On this source, see 3.2, below.

[8] For a brief account of the manuscripts of the civic cycles, see Meredith 'Scribes, texts and performance' in *Aspects*.

[9] See A.C. Cawley 'The Sykes Manuscript'. This play contains no music cues.

[10] Further on the Coventry manuscripts, see section 3.4.

[11] On the monitoring of performances, see Meredith 'John Clerke's Hand', *passim*; on censorship, see MDF 7, ix, and Stevens 'Missing Parts'.

1477:[12] it seems possible that this was the first complete (or intended to be complete) text compilation, and that the city authority demanded its copying in order to monitor the exact content of the plays. There is some evidence that the city sometimes asked a guild for its original so that the guild's text could be checked, and that either corruptions would then be removed from the original or (if the guild's changes were acceptable) the modifications would be incorporated into the Register. Most of the alterations in the Register, however, were apparently made while the Common Clerk of the city or his deputy was checking the performance against the Register at the first station.[13] Many of the additions concern music. The actual text performed, evidently, was subject to various kinds of alteration, including improvements incorporated into the guild's original as well as unwritten lapses and (perhaps) *ad hoc* amendments by the actors in performance.[14]

No other manuscript of a civic cycle tells the story of its compilation even as clearly as this. The manuscript of the Towneley cycle may be a civic register, although we do not know its provenance:[15] certainly some passages that were doctrinally dangerous in the mid-sixteenth century have been removed, which suggests the kind of centralised censorship that occurred at York.[16] In this manuscript, however, there is less of the kind of editorial activity seen in the York manuscript: some additions in red, probably by the main scribe, various minor additions and alterations by a sixteenth-century but slightly later hand, and the copying of one play out of sequence by a different and perhaps later hand than the main scribe.[17] If the Towneley manuscript was a civic register, as it seems, the administrative mechanism that kept and used it may have been a less formal one than at York.

The other surviving civic cycle, that of Chester, has no register extant. All the manuscripts of the cycle are late copies made out of antiquarian interest long after the plays had ceased to be performed. They therefore do not have the direct authority of sources used for a performance. They do tell us a great deal about the Chester cycle as it must have been in the mid-sixteenth century, however, because they seem to derive from a single copy, which Lumiansky and Mills call the Exemplar. Whether this Exemplar was the Chester Register or not is a moot point. Lumiansky and Mills regard it as itself derived from a Pre-exemplar which was compiled from the guilds' originals, or possibly itself compiled from originals. However this may be, the Exemplar includes such features as marginal notes, taken into the existing copies in various ways, and some extensive alternative passages

---

12 See section 3.3.

13 See Meredith 'Scribes, texts and performance', 16.

14 For the relationship between original and Register, see Meredith 'Scribes, texts and performance', 16–17, concerning the Sykes Manuscript.

15 On the manuscript's suitability as a register, see Epp 'Towneley Plays', 127–8. For a few years it was thought that the Towneley cycle was that of Wakefield, but this theory is now discredited: see Forrester 1974, Forrester and Cawley 1975, and Palmer 1987–8.

16 See Stevens 'Missing Parts' for a discussion of the lost material.

17 See MDF 2, ix–x.

that cannot be identified as obviously later and/or better readings.[18] As it is
impossible to discuss the music in the Chester cycle without referring to specific
manuscripts, I give here the abbreviations of the cyclic manuscripts as listed by
Lumiansky and Mills:[19]

Hm San Marino, Henry E. Huntington Library, MS 2. Copied in 1591 mainly by
   Edward Gregorie.

A   London, British Library, Add. MS 10305. Copied in 1592 by George Bellin,
   scribe of the Coopers' Guild, who worked also for the Ironmongers and for
   the Cappers and Pinners.

R   London, British Library, MS Harley 2103. Copied in 1600 by George Bellin
   (except for the proclamation).

B   Oxford, Bodleian Library, MS Bodley 175. Copied in 1604 by William Bedford (later Clerk to the Brewers' Guild).

H   London, British Library, MS Harley 2124. Copied in 1607 by James Miller
   and others.[20]

The first four of these are usually called 'the Group' because of the large measure
of textual agreement between them as opposed to the readings of manuscript H.

The remaining two cycle manuscripts present a different kind of problem. That
of the Cornish cycle, the Ordinalia, is apparently not a civic register: such evidence
as there is suggests that the play was mounted by the College of Glasney, so that
the Ordinalia should be regarded as institutional drama.[21] The N-Town cycle is
based on a civic pageant cycle, but with considerable additions and substitutions:
other dramas used in the compilation include a large play on the life of the Blessed
Virgin, a saint play on the Assumption, and a two-part Passion play. The scribe who
made the compilation attempted to graft these various elements together to make
a continuous drama to be performed on multiple fixed staging.[22] It is hard to believe
that he did it with no institution or specific projected performance in mind, but there
is no evidence of this. Indeed, the drama might have been compiled for a civic
authority mounting a continental-style civic project, but this seems unlikely. On the
whole, it seems more probable that the scribe was working for an institution or at
least a communal body such as a religious guild. Our lack of knowledge of the
provenance of such a manuscript makes it extremely difficult to assess the various
types of evidence, such as the stage directions.

[18] See *Essays*, Chapter 1, *passim*, and especially the summary, 85–6.
[19] See *Chester* I, ix and xii–xxvii.
[20] On the identity of James Miller, which Mills discovered after the publication of the edition,
   see Mills 'Will' and below, 3.5.
[21] See Longsworth 1967, 6; Bakere 1980, 31. The manuscript is now MS Bodley 791 at the Bodleian
   Library, Oxford.
[22] Opinions about the N-Town plays are still divided. Peter Meredith has developed a theory to
   explain the anomalous features of the collection, and has edited the *Mary Play* and the *Passion
   Play* separately. See Meredith 'N.Town Manuscript', *Mary Play* and *Passion Play*; also Spector
   N-Town, *passim*.

The histories of these various manuscripts, and the relationship of any surviving written text to performed text, demand a degree of interpretation, then, that is rarely attainable on the evidence available to us. Such matters as the validity of stage directions and alternative readings must however be assessed if we are to make any sense of the possible music cues in the dramas: and although this is largely an impossible process at present, research on the sources has allowed much headway to be made in the last few years. My next task is to study this evidence to see what we can learn from it about musical performance in the plays.

2.3 Dramatic directions

'Stage direction' suggests associations with the proscenium stage, or at least with the Shakespearian thrust stage, that are inappropriate for earlier religious drama. Some of the plays discussed in this book may well have been performed on a stage of some sort, and such platforms as pageant waggons could arguably be regarded as 'stages'. Even so, it will be better to avoid the more modern term. 'Performance direction' is more appropriate, but it begs the question of the intended recipient of the information transmitted. On the whole 'direction' by itself may be the best term: and I shall use 'dramatic direction' when necessary to avoid ambiguity.

I have however retained the abbreviations 'SD' and 'sd' for an original or principal direction in a play text, as these are well established. The distinction between that and a marginal notation of the same type is accomplished by the use of 'MD' and 'md' for the latter. By 'marginal' I mean literally marginal, written in the margin of the play text concerned, although (as will become apparent) this definition has to be somewhat modified.

The directions are one of three types of additions to the spoken text of a play. The boundaries between the various elements are not necessarily obvious, however. One type is those Latin texts supplied as authorities – footnotes, as it were – to the content of the play text. This subject is discussed in 2.7, below, because the boundaries between unspoken authority and spoken, sung or declaimed Latin text are difficult to locate. Another type, sometimes not easy to distinguish from a direction, is the speech heading (SH or sh). In its simplest form this is just the name or designation of the speaker of a section of text, such as 'Maria' or 'primus pastor'. Usually the speech heading is distinguished graphically from the spoken text by its size or style of writing, by underlining in red, by its position on the page (marginal or centralised, for example), or by some combination of these.

The speech heading moves more than half way to being a direction if the word 'says' or 'sings' is added: *Primus miles incipit* (**York 34/1–**) is a SH rather than a direction only because the text follows, set out in the usual place. The same is true even if an adjectival phrase is added, as in **Chester 12/240+**:

Jesus scribens in terra dicat:

where the direction element is very strong. But if the text incipit or the complete text itself is an extra-stanzaic element and follows on the same line, or in the same area of the page, as the verb, it has to be regarded as a direction: one example is a marginal annotation added by John Clerke as **York 29/23+md**:

Tunc dicunt Lorde

which has the same form as a direction to say or sing a text of which only the incipit is specified, as in **York 21/154+sd**:

Tunc cantabunt duo angeli Veni creator spiritus

Here, in contradistinction to the previous example, the text given is clearly not the entire text to be heard, but merely the incipit of a longer text already known to those concerned.

The boundary between direction and speech heading is hardly a realistic one, then, and I shall not attempt to distinguish between them. All such material will be discussed as directions. I shall however sometimes distinguish between the SD and SH *elements* in the material when a direction has a speech heading embedded in it:

Tunc cantabunt et postea dicat Tertius Pastor: (**Chester 7/447+sd**)

Such fine distinctions are not often needed for my present purpose, however.

From a musical point of view the directions can give some of the most important information available about the changing circumstances and approaches of the playwrights and directors. In many sources[23] at least two layers of directions can be seen. The situation is clearest in the case of the York register, where research has done much to expose the way in which the manuscript was used in the sixteenth century.[24] The 'original' directions are mainly in red ink and a more ornamental script than the main text, and were probably entered (by the two principal scribes) at the rubrication stage. Other directions written by the main scribe are in black and copied in the ordinary script, but the positioning of the directions at one side of the text-space ensures that they are not confused with the spoken text.[25] Whether these directions really are original or not it is impossible to decide, if by that we mean that they were composed by the dramatist rather than by a later reviser. They were however in the scripts from which the main scribe copied the York register, and were entered by him during the main copying process.

For whom were these directions written? Probably they were intended primarily for the directors of the plays concerned, but a lack of surviving actor's parts means that we cannot be sure to what extent, if any, they were designed for the individual

---

[23] I use 'source' in the musicological sense: a manuscript or print containing the work in question.

[24] See Meredith 'John Clerke's Hand'; also Beadle and Meredith 1983, xix–xxiii, and Beadle 1982, 16–19.

[25] See Beadle and Meredith 1983, xxx. At the International Medieval Congress in Leeds, on 6 July 1994, Frances Gussenhoven demonstrated that directions in the Towneley manuscript were written at the side of the text if they had to be put into effect during the speech: session 712, paper 2: 'Scribal Manuscript Practice and the Towneley Stage Directions'. This theory may well be applicable to other play manuscripts.

actor.[26] The provision of specified items of music is minimal, really, which would suggest that the music cues were written by the original playwright or perhaps by some reviser. Another indication of this is that the directions are in Latin. At the date of this manuscript's copying, c.1463–77, it would be natural for a dramatist or reviser – by definition an educated man and therefore almost certainly in at least minor orders – to write directions in Latin, whereas it would be very unlikely that a layman would write in anything other than English.

The directions written by the later scribes, and in particular by John Clerke, are of a quite different order.[27] These sixteenth-century annotations look to be of the same type as the original directions, but in fact have a different purpose. They were mainly entered by Miles Newton, the Common Clerk of York for twelve years or more before his death in 1550, and his assistant John Clerke, who succeeded him as Common Clerk in 1550 and held the post until 1567 or later. These are not prescriptive directions but descriptive memoranda: their purpose is to record what happened in a particular performance monitored by Newton or Clerke at the first station. They are mainly written at the side of the main text, in the margins of the manuscript, and are therefore best characterised as 'marginal' – literally so, as noted above. These marginal notes, by their nature, offer information that was not already available in the manuscript. While the majority are completely new entries, a few make additions or corrections to existing directions. Not surprisingly, Newton and Clerke generally wrote these annotations in an informal hand, without rubrication: but, being professional scriveners, they normally used Latin. Only one of these marginal directions, by Clerke, is in English.

These two layers of activity in the directions are easy enough to distinguish but not always so easy to interpret. The problems relating to music fall into two main areas: the historical period to which the additional information applied, and the precise history of the individual corrections.

The first of these problems may be illustrated by reference to the end of the York Annunciation and Visitation. At **York12/240+sd** (f. 47v) the main scribe's original direction reads simply 'Magnificat'. Since the Magnificat is Mary's text and she has just been speaking, we assume that this SD indicates that she speaks or sings it: but there is no indication of how it should be performed. Clerke's late addition *Tunc cantat* is placed above the original direction, in the margin next to **12/239**. While the spacing is perhaps less close than to justify putting both inscriptions together as a single SD *Tunc cantat Magnificat*, therefore, the effect is certainly to make it clear that Mary is to *sing* the Magnificat, not speak it. But then, what is the period of validity? Did Clerke merely note, some time around 1550, something that had always been the case since the 1470s, or did his addition mark the appearance of a change from speech to singing for this particular text? There is no general principle at stake here:

---

26 The manuscript of *Dux Moraud* gives no staging information. The other surviving actor's part, the Shrewsbury fragment, is a liturgical manuscript and therefore does not help in the present case. While the same question arises in the case of a liturgical rubric, we cannot assume that the answer is the same.

27 The material of this paragraph is taken from Meredith 'John Clerke's Hand'.

we can solve the problem only by deciding what the original SD meant to the dramatist and original scribe – whether the incipit 'Magnificat' automatically implied that the text should be sung – and, if singing was implied, why this was no longer the case around 1550. My own opinion in this case is that 'Magnificat' probably did imply singing c.1470, and that Clerke noted it c.1550 simply because the increased use of speech in church services made it advisable to do so: but this could be quite wrong.

The second problem is illustrated by a case in which a third layer of scribal activity can be discerned. At **York 42/176+sd** a late hand, apparently that of Miles Newton, has added a direction in the margin at the moment of Christ's Ascension (f. 239r):

Tunc cantat angelus Gloria in excelsys deo.

Granted that 'Gloria in excelsis deo' is sung by the angels at the Ascension in the Cornish Ordinalia, it nevertheless seems an odd text to sing here in view of its association with Christmas. Perhaps some director c.1550 thought this, too, and changed it, for John Clerke has crossed the incipit through and substituted 'Ascendo ad patrem meum'. On the face of it this is a more likely text for this moment in the play, although it ought properly to be sung by Christ himself.

The difficulties here need to be put in order. First, is it likely that there was always a music cue at the Ascension, despite the lack of an original direction there? The answer must surely be 'Yes': the Ascension is too important an event not to be marked by musical characterisation of the heavenly vision. The presence of a direction for the singing of 'Ascendo ad patrem meum' at this point in the Towneley Ascension play is circumstantial (but not strong) evidence for it: the two plays are closely related, and the Towneley version may well be the older.[28]

Second, is it likely in this case that the piece originally sung was 'Gloria in excelsis deo', as Newton's annotation states? Despite the support of the Cornish *Resurrectio Domini* (**Ordinalia 3/2528+sd**), I doubt it. The piece is used in the Cornish play only after the Fifth Angel has introduced it specifically, a usage that looks back to Isaiah's vision of Heaven (see 5.2, below): without such an introduction the Christmas associations of the piece would surely make it unsuitable for the York play. How the error could arise is another matter. Newton would hardly confuse the two pieces, and presumably he wrote the wrong well-known incipit in a moment of mental aberration while thinking of something else – no doubt the continuing performance of the play.

Third, it might be objected that, as 'Ascendo' ought to be sung by Christ, as it is in **Chester 20/104+sd+[a]**, Clerke's correction must itself be wrong. This will not stand up, however, since the text is sung by angels at **Towneley 29/253+sd**.

David Mills has undertaken a study of the Chester cycle's directions which is as

---

[28] The general view now seems to be that the York and Towneley cycles descend from a common ancestor, and that much of the Towneley pageants is based on an older version than the more extensively-revised York cycle.

thorough as Meredith's of the York ones.[29] This work has very important consequences for music in that cycle, just as it does for other matters of staging, since the
Chester cycle is particularly rich in directions. Two matters, in particular, set this
work aside from that on the York cycle. In the first place, the surviving copies of the
Chester cycle are late antiquarian copies, and Lumiansky and Mills have demonstrated the existence of alternative texts in the rather incoherent Exemplar from
which they all derive. The choices made go hand in hand with an element of editorial
activity on the part of the scribes, which included regularising such features as
marginal annotations. The result is that in the surviving copies some directions that
were obviously marginal in the Exemplar have been brought into the positions
occupied by 'original' directions. This process is detectable partly because the
various scribes used different positions on the page for 'original' directions and have
carried the process through inconsistently. Thus the Chester manuscripts show how
marginal annotations are 'legitimised' and brought into the main body of a text by
editorial intervention, but also allow us to identify those directions that were
marginal in the Exemplar.[30]

Second, it is clear that the marginal annotations were made under rather different
circumstances from those in the York register. Whereas the latter were official
comments made by a professional scribe on behalf of the civic authority, and are
therefore normally in Latin, most of those in the Chester Exemplar were apparently
written by producers making notes for performances, and are in English. Thus there
is generally a difference of language between SD and MD in the Chester cycle,
although the equation is not entirely simple.[31]

The full list of differences between SD and MD in the Chester cycle is given by
Lumiansky and Mills as follows:

(1) Language. Original SDs are normally in Latin, production-notes in English;
(2) Function. MDs often give supplementary information, rather than information that could not be deduced from elsewhere; or they may refer to choices
among alternatives in the text; and they may be addressed to the individual
actor;
(3) Terseness. The MDs tend to brevity. This may be partly because of the
shortage of space in a margin, but their origins are such that full grammatical
construction was unnecessary.

These two studies suggest that the history of accretion and editing of directions in
any text may be a long and complex one; that it is desirable to unravel it so that the
precise authority and function of any direction can be assessed; and that it may often
be difficult or impossible to carry out this process of assessment. If we consider the
directions in the N-Town cycle, it is clear that many directions, having both Latin
and English elements, have probably come into existence by a process of addition,

---

[29] Mills 1981.
[30] Lumiansky and Mills deal fully with SDs and MDs in *Essays*, 28–32, and are careful to note (p.
29) the paradox that 'it is not a necessary feature of a MD that it should appear in the margin
of an extant manuscript'.
[31] See *Essays*, 29–30.

one or more secondary layers having been added to an original direction. But it is equally clear that the distinction of earlier and later layers is difficult, and that no element can be identified as having been an MD at any time. Consider a situation, for example, in which the York register had been copied by an antiquarian in the late sixteenth century and the register itself thrown away or lost. The direction *Tunc cantat Magnificat* at **York 12/240+sd**, discussed earlier, would be seen as an original SD for singing, there being no reason to think that any of it was a late addition to an existing text.

With this in mind it will be instructive to examine some of those directions that cause particular problems, not in order to solve the problem (which in most cases is impossible) but to avoid misinterpretations that might wrongly be thought good evidence. The first is a direction from the Coventry Weavers' play when, having travelled to Jerusalem, Joseph, Mary and the twelve-year-old Jesus enter the Temple (**Coventry 2/805+sd**):

> *There the all goo vp to the awter and Jesus before. The syng an antem.*

On the face of it, Mary and Joseph process to the altar, preceded by Jesus, and either during or immediately after this procession the three of them sing an anthem (or perhaps antiphon). Discussions of the logistics of this, and of the repertory to be performed, might well obscure the fact that the direction itself is not as coherent as it seems. If it is recognised that the two parts of the direction are not of equal status and were not conceived together, then it is easier to see that 'There the all goo vp to the awter and Jesus before' is a prescription for the movement of the Holy Family, probably an original prescription by the dramatist, while 'The syng an antem' is a more general, impersonal statement, meaning 'An anthem is sung'.[32] And since an anthem would normally be sung in the Temple by a choir or smaller body of professional singers it is hardly necessary to specify who 'they' might be. It is unfortunate for us, certainly, that an original direction and a marginal production note added to it both have the pronoun 'they' for a subject although they refer to different people. A sixteenth-century producer would never suppose that Mary, Joseph and Jesus would walk into the Temple and start singing a liturgical item: and for us there is a clue in what Joseph says immediately afterwards:

> [JOSEPH] All thyng ys done ase yt schuld be
> And serves song full sollamle   (**Coventry 2/808–9**)

Everything has been done properly, then, and the service 'sung full solemnly', which means with all due ceremony. In fact, the Weavers' accounts for 1560 show that James Hewitt played the regals with the singers, which suggests precisely this.[33]

Not all additions of a late layer to an existing direction form such a poor match.

---

[32] On the timing of these two events, see p. 224, below.

[33] The relevant Weavers' accounts are in *REED.Coventry*, 124, for the older version of the play, and *ibid.*, 156–208 *passim* for the play as we have it: later payments showing Hewitt and the singers together are in *ibid.*, up to 292, *passim*. Further on Hewitt and his singing colleagues, see section 8.3, below.

A much more serious problem is encountered in the final direction of the York cycle, **York 47/380+sd**, simply because the match is apparently so good:

> *Et sic facit finem cum melodia angelorum transiens a loco ad locum.*

Lucy Toulmin Smith's edition follows the manuscript reading faithfully in offering no punctuation, and her division into two lines (at *melodia / angelorum*) suggests no significant analysis of the grammatical construction. Later editors and translators have tended to place a comma after 'finem', which suggests that 'cum ... locum' is a discrete unit subordinate to the first four words. A second comma after 'angelorum' would have avoided this rather important result, which produces an error that looks both persuasive and interesting for its staging implications:[34]

> *Et sic facit finem, cum melodia angelorum transiens a loco ad locum.*
>
> And thus he makes an end, with the melody of angels crossing from place to place.

This punctuation is not entirely unambiguous, but it clearly makes 'crossing' agree with either 'melody' or 'angels'. With this wording, a translation without the comma has much the same effect:[35]

> And so he makes an end with a melody of angels passing from place to place.

The ambiguity is still there: and although 'crossing' / 'passing' might be held to agree with 'melody', at least one scholar has decided that it was the angels who did the crossing.[36]

I shall discuss possible reasons for this understanding in a moment. For the present it is important to note that any translation making 'crossing' agree with either 'melody' or 'angels' by implication labels 'transiens' as an error. I see no reason to assume that the latinity of the SD is incorrect, however, and prefer to treat 'transiens' as agreeing with the subject of the sentence, which by implication is Deus (i.e. Christ), who has the last speech of the play.[37] This being so, the problem lies not in the grammatical construction (which is not particularly complex) but in the word-order of the direction: *Et sic facit finem transiens a loco ad locum cum melodia angelorum* would be clearer, if less pleasing at 'locum cum'. Peter Happé, alone of editors and translators as far as I know, translates the syntax correctly and changes the word-order to make sense of the whole:[38]

> And thus crossing from the place to the place, he makes an end with the melody of angels.

---

34 Cawley *Everyman*, 203; Beadle 1982, 415; Beadle and King 1984, 279. Beadle and King omit 'the'.

35 Purvis 1957, 382.

36 See Davidson in Davidson and O'Connor *York Art*, 185: '[York 45] ends with heavenly music as the angels cross the pageant stage back and forth'.

37 The grammatical status of 'transiens' was pointed out to me by J.E. Maddrell.

38 Happé *English Mystery Plays*, 645 (edition) and 694 (translation).

the procedure by blessing all of the saved souls around the waggon before the tableau can end and the waggon move off the station.

It may be thought that few directions will cause as much trouble as that at the end of the York cycle, and indeed most do not. On the other hand, the two examined here – admittedly representative of many that must be assessed carefully before a producer can use the information that they transmit – were chosen because reasonable solutions are possible. Many directions present insoluble problems, unfortunately, and for a variety of reasons. Some use scribal suspensions that cannot be expanded with certainty, like the *Tunc cant'* of **York 37/35+md**, which leaves us in doubt as to the number – and therefore the identity – of the singer(s); some give information in so cryptic a fashion that it is impossible to be sure of the meaning, like the marginal annotations (for they are hardly real directions) *Staffe, Sword, Cast up*, and so on of **Chester 8**;[44] and occasionally the cryptic utterance certainly relies on a main clause that is no longer present in the text, or perhaps never was, like the *Cantando* of **York 46/80+md** (what would the main direction have been?).[45]

These examples are far from exhausting the range and nature of the directions that cause interpretational problems. They will however be enough to show that, informative as the directions are in many plays, they do not solve our problems in providing music in performance. Much of the reason for this is that they are in the nature of *aide-mémoires* rather than fully prescriptive instructions. They seem to assume that certain items of information are known to the reader – producer or actor – and therefore need not be transmitted: but the direction then does not give all the information that a modern observer requires. The missing information may be part of a continuing tradition of performance in a particular place or by a particular group ('we know what happens here: we played this pageant last time'), or it may be part of a wider tradition, such as that of liturgical ceremony. It is not always clear which it is, of course, and therein lies the major problem: for a direction relying on such a tradition cannot be interpreted without recourse to it, yet by its nature such a tradition is difficult, or even impossible, to track down. In the fields of literary tradition, musical performance and liturgy, among others, there is a substantial body of knowledge, however, and there is a reasonable chance of making good the omissions in the information transmitted by the directions. We turn now to the next of these types of evidence.

2.4 Text references

Internal references to music in the plays take various forms. The largest group consists of those that refer to, describe or comment on actual performances. This is an indication of the importance of music in the play concerned, for comment on a

---

[44] See Peter Meredith's discussion in *Aspects*, 25–6, for an imaginative and convincing explanation of these.
[45] Compare the same construction in the Peniarth version of the Chester Antichrist (*Chester* I, 495): *Tunc resurgendo dicat Primus Mortuus*. Here the main clause is present.

performance is relevant to the play text only to the extent that the performance itself is relevant to the drama. To a large extent, then, these references must be designed to emphasise the effect of the performance on the audience. It may also serve to define the nature of one or more characters more closely, by characterising them as godly or evil (see Chapter 5, below).

Such references have the effect of binding this particular form of representation very firmly into the fabric of the drama. A dramatist or reviser who felt strongly about the use of music as an aid to representation could use this to make known his wishes for music in the drama and to ensure that the provision of music in the play would not be reduced by successive producers. A text reference can give information that then need not appear in a direction, a technique used to the full in the York Crucifixion play. The advantage for the dramatist was probably that a text reference cannot be ignored by a producer, whereas a stage direction certainly can.

It is a commonplace of drama production that the text must be read very carefully for information on staging matters, of which music may well be one of the most important. References to music can also provide information about a different part of the play, or even about a different play altogether. On this point I wish to examine two instances. The first concerns the music in the Coventry Shearmen and Tailors' pageant. I shall discuss this further in section 2.6, but here I wish to demonstrate that information on the music can be gained by reading the text in various places. The immediate information tells us about a total of six music cues, as follows:

Coventry

1_1 **263+sd**   *There the angelis syng Glorea in exselsis Deo*
This SD tells us of the pronunciation of 'excelsis' but gives no other information about the performance or the extent of the text sung. Only in the next few lines, 264–77, do we discover that the angels were in a high place, that their music was pleasant to hear (a group of terms requiring considerable interpretation), and that the text sung included 'et in terra pax hominibus'. This is as expected. Joseph's comments at 1/278–81 about a 'noise' (i.e. musicians) of 'grett solemnete' certainly refer to this, although cue 1_2 occurs meanwhile.

1_2 **277+sd**   *There the scheppardis syngis Ase I owt Rodde . . .*
No other information is given. The notated music that Sharp found at the end of the play text (for which see 2.6 and 3.4, below) has no demonstrable connection with this SD other than the title of the song.

1_3 **281+sd**   *There the angellis syng Gloria in exsellsis ageyne*
No other information is given.

1_4 **331+sd**   *There the scheppardis syngith ageyne and goth forthe of the place . . .*
No other information. Craig wrongly identified this as the notated song 'Downe from Heaven': see p. 67.

1_5 **539+**   The SD here is for Herod's exit: but the previous three lines state his

intention of having minstrelsy ('Trompettis, viallis, and othur armone', line 538) and this would probably be the best place at which
to start this music. It is however problematic.

1₆   829+sd   *Here the wemen cum in wythe there chyldur syngyng them ...*
No other information. For the surviving song, see 2.6 and 3.4, below:
but note that there is nothing to connect this song with the original
intention of the dramatist, who may have had a quite different song
in mind.

This is a fairly normal range of cues in which the information is sparse. In this play
there is more evidence, however, because the two prophets who separate the two
main sections of the biblical narrative rehearse the outlines of the Incarnation story,
including the episode of the shepherds and its sequel, with some attention to the
details of musical performance.

The First Prophet tells the Second of two performances by the shepherds, and
this provides new information. He makes the point (**1/445**) that the shepherds told
people what they had seen at the stable in Bethlehem, not secretly but out loud
(**1/446–8**),

[I. PROFETA]	For the song ase lowde	
	Ase eyver the cowde	
	Presyng the kyng of Isarell.	**(Coventry 1/449–51)**

This, then, was what the shepherds sang as they left the stable, i.e. the song heard
immediately before the Prophets appear, at **331+sd** (cue **1₄**). Here, if we needed it,
is the demonstration that **1₄** is not the song 'Downe from Heaven'. On being pressed
for more information the First Prophet states that when the shepherds left the stable

I. PROFETA	Forthe the went and glad the were	
	Going the did syng	
	With myrthe and solas the made good chere	
	For joie of that new tything.	**(Coventry 1/467–9)**[46]

The First Prophet then continues with a part of the story that does not occur in the
play text:

[I. PROFETA]	And aftur asse I hard the[m] tell	
	He reywardid them full well	
	He graunt them hevyn ther-in to dwelle	
	In ar the gon with joie and myrthe	
	And there songe hit ys Neowell.	**(Coventry 1/470–4)**

This is the end of the shepherds' story, then. They have been allowed into Heaven,
and their song there is 'Nowell'. At first sight this may seem to have no immediate
relevance, except that it confirms our understanding of the relationship between

---

[46] The numbering of Craig's edition goes wrong by one line at this point.

music and the doing of God's will.[47] But it is possible that the play would have illustrated this part of the story as well. The Heaven has twice offered a musical set piece in the first half of the play, and after the Prophets' scene an angel twice delivers messages – at **1/725–32** to the Kings and at **1/818–22** to Mary and Joseph. Although it is hardly mentioned in the text, therefore, Heaven is an important and spectacular location in this play: so this narrative surely means that the shepherds ascend to Heaven at some stage after their exit at **1/331+sd** and sing in the Heaven with the angelic choir. The simplest solution would, in fact, be for them to go there, still singing to cover the entry of the Prophets. In this case the song of praise to the King of Israel is also a *Nowell* song, but the two ideas are quite compatible.

This is now speculation, but the audience might well be surprised to hear of the shepherds' entry into Heaven without it being both visible and audible. The corollary to this, if true, is that the play demonstrates an integration of text and performance going well beyond the immediate information given at any particular point in the text.

A second occasion of distant reference to music occurs in the York Entry into Jerusalem. **York 25/287+md** is a late direction, *Tunc cantant*, which refers to the children of the citizens singing during the procession of Christ to the city gate:

I BURGENSIS Go we þan with processioun
　　　　　　 To mete þat comely as vs awe
　　　　　　 With braunches floures and vnysoune
　　　　　　 With myghtful songes her on a rawe
　　　　　　 Our childer schall
　　　　　　 Go synge before þat men may knawe.　　　　　　**(York 25/260–5)**

The 1415 *Ordo paginarum* entry for the play is more specific:[48]

　　　　　　 ... viij pueri cum ramis palmarum cantantes Benedictus &c, ...

The *Ordo* may not refer to the play as we have it, but the specified eight children do match the eight citizens in the play text.

This procession with its music is commented on by the Blind Man, for whom the Poor Man gives a brief description (**25/288–313**), but the sung text is not specified. For that information we have to go five plays later, to the pageant of Christ's first appearance before Pilate. Here the beadle tells Pilate about Christ's entry, stating that he rode on an ass (**30/339**) and that the people sang 'Osanna [to] þe sone of Dauid' (**30/343**). Play 30 is attributed to the playwright known as the York Realist, but play 25 is not thought to be one of his: so play 25 either is the play that the York Realist already knew when he embarked on the composition of play 30 or it has at least many of the same features, and certainly the same text for the music at **25/287+md** (cue 25₁). In fact, I think that we can be fairly certain of this last, since the *Ordo paginarum* shows that cue 25₁ had the text *Benedictus, etc.* This is presumably *Benedictus qui venit in nomine domini*, and although it apparently contradicts the

---

[47] See 5.2 and 5.3, below.
[48] *REED.York* I, 20; MDF 7, A/Y Memorandum Book, f. 253v.

evidence of the beadle in play 30, this need not be so. The beadle's *Osanna* [to] *þe sone of Dauid*, presumably an item to the Latin text *Hosanna filio david*, is not incompatible with the *Ordo* text, since the Palm Sunday antiphon *Hosanna filio david* includes both:[49]

> Osanna filio dauid
> benedictus qui uenit in nomine domini rex israel
> osanna in excelsis.

Although the exact relationship between the 1415 Ordo, the Entry play that the York Realist knew and the pageant that he wrote with references to the Entry's music is unclear, it seems obvious that when the York Register was copied, c.1463–77, the beadle's comments in play 30 were accurate with regard to the existing play 25. At least, it seems unlikely that an audience would be satisfied with non-congruence between the information given in play 30 and the performance already heard in play 25. However the situation arose, therefore, this is a genuine case of information shared between plays some way apart in a cycle, a situation that in practice must have obtained for a century or so, until the York cycle performances were discontinued.

The second type of text reference consists of those giving technical or theoretical information. These vary between the simplest and briefest form of description to an extended conversation. The subject-matter falls into three broad areas: the sound of singing, the technical means used in performance, and the technicalities of music itself and its notation.

The first of these, which is the most common, is seen in the bishop's prescription for music in the procession of the Holy Sacrament in the Croxton play:

[EPISCOPUS]   Thys holy song, *O sacrum Conuiuium,*
              Lett vs syng all with grett swetnesse.   (**Sacrament, 840–1**)

The naming of the Corpus Christi antiphon *O Sacrum Convivium* might well have occurred in a direction but would be a bonus to us even so.[50] More importantly for our present purpose, the bishop makes a comment on the style of performance, saying that the piece should be sung 'with great sweetness'. This is now a general and non-technical term, but in the fifteenth century it was more precise, and the remark therefore tells us something about what was expected in a good performance.

Audrey Ekdahl Davidson has pointed out that for Isidore of Seville, writing c.600,

---

[49] AS, 206. There are other Palm Sunday pieces that have the relevant words, but none fits the description as well as this antiphon.
[50] In the Sarum Rite this was the Magnificat antiphon at Second Vespers. The text is in BS, mlxxiv f., but it is not in AS; the text and music can be found in LU, 959. However, the version intended in the play is presumably the rather simpler setting used at the end of the procession before Mass in PS(P), 119v.

the perfect voice was high, sweet and clear:[51] These three adjectives were almost universal in medieval descriptions of fine singing,[52] and 'sweet' is especially common in the plays. Davidson explains that the term may have been applied to different sounds at different times, the techniques of singing – and therefore the aesthetic – changing slightly from time to time. There seems to have been a change to a more relaxed style of singing in the sixteenth century, so that 'sweet' singing may not have meant precisely the same in the late sixteenth century as it did in the late fifteenth. Of the many quotations supplied by Carter for 'sweet', 'sweetly' and 'sweetnesse', several support his definition of 'sweetnesse' as 'Any pleasing combination of musical qualities; melody, harmony'.[53] But 'harmony' in the late Middle Ages implied the proper relationship between notes spaced out in time, as well as between those sounded simultaneously,[54] so that the implication of 'sweet' is both wider and more specifically technical than it would now be. Thus a description of a performance, either vocal or instrumental, as 'sweet' may mean not merely that the performer has a pleasant-sounding voice or instrument, but that all aspects of the performance are of high quality, satisfactory musically and intellectually.

The word 'clear' also, used as either an adjective or an adverb, implied more than merely a healthy openness of the throat without excessive vibrato. Carter's quotations show that for singing the word suggests both a distinct and therefore a carrying sound and a certain accuracy of performance. The very first line of the Coventry shepherds' discussion of the angelic Gloria, then,

III PASTOR   Harke! the syng abowe in the clowdis clere!   (**Coventry 1/264**)

shows that this is a fine performance even before we hear their various comments on the angels' 'armony' and 'the swettnes of ther songe' (**Coventry 1/267, 269**).

More specific comment on performance often uses the technical terms 'crack', 'knack' and 'hack', and these too help an understanding of the kind of performance at issue.

Crack 'Crak' normally means 'to tell out loud' or to pronounce something briskly or with *éclat*: that meaning survives in the phrase 'to crack a joke'. In a musical context in the plays 'crack' implies uninhibited performance.[55]

Knack 'Knak' means 'to break', and more specifically to striking with hard, sharp blows; but its musical use is for singing or playing in a lively and ornate manner, with trills and runs.[56] Technically, then, 'knak' refers to the breaking of a large note into many small ones, the technique of ornamentation known as 'divisions'. While

51 Davidson 'Performance Practice', 3, citing Isidore of Seville, *Etymologiarum*, ed. W.M. Lindsay (Oxford, Clarendon Press, 1911), book III.
52 See the correspondence from Joseph Dyer in *Early Music* 4 (1976), 489–90.
53 Carter *Dictionary*, 483–4.
54 Carter *Dictionary*, 14ff. (under 'Armonie').
55 Carter *Dictionary*, 102–3; OED, sub 'crack' v, I.6. See below, also, pp. 205–07, concerning cracking a fart. 'Crack of thunder' must be another survival of this usage, and, less obviously, 'crack of dawn'.
56 Carter *Dictionary*, 226–7; OED sub 'Knack' v.4.

'crak' could presumably be used for an incompetent performance, therefore, 'knak' probably could not, implying a high-quality and usually professional performance.

Hack 'Hak' is entirely to do with breaking and splitting,[57] but (rather surprisingly, since it appears in the Towneley cycle) Carter does not include it in his *Dictionary*. The non-musical meaning may be the principal one, therefore, any musical meanings being subsidiary and directly derived by analogy. This suggests a use for derogatory comments rather than for fine performances, but the Towneley references are one of each. The first equates Gill's groaning with the pangs of childbirth and Mak's out-of-tune singing:

> TERCIUS PASTOR   will ye here how thay hak? / oure syre lyst croyne.
> PRIMUS PASTOR   hard I never none crak / so clere out of toyne.
>
> **(Towneley 13/476–7)**

Here 'hak' has something of the modern implication of incompetence and the undirected expenditure of energy,[58] while 'crak' is clearly a neutral term indicating only loud noise. However, this play later uses 'hak' (and 'crak', too) in describing the music of the angelic Gloria:

> SECUNDUS PASTOR Say, what was his song? / hard ye not how he crakyd it?
>   Thre brefes to a long. /
> TERCIUS PASTOR   yee, mary, he hakt it.
>   was no crochett wrong / nor no thyng that lakt it.
>
> **(Towneley 13/656–8)**

Again, 'crakyd it' is a fairly general term for an uninhibited performance, but 'hakt it' must bear a more specific meaning close to that of 'knak'. The melodic line is clearly a florid one, then, demanding a fine performance by a professional singer. We shall return to this passage in a moment, and also in section 8.4. The most technical aspects of the shepherds' conversation must however be dealt with here.

In the first shepherds' play it is clear that the angel sang very well. The First Shepherd remarks that '[The song] was wonder curiose / with small noytys emang' (**Towneley 12/306**): the idea of small notes is brought up again by the First Shepherd, who says that the angel had 'throng on a heppe' many notes (**12/416–17**). It is however the Second Shepherd who gives the technical information necessary to make the meaning clear:

> [SECUNDUS PASTOR]   ... / it was a mery song;
>   I dar say that he broght / foure & twenty to a long.
>
> **(Towneley 12/413–14)**

Twenty-four notes to a long must give five notational levels: long, breve, semibreve, minim and semiminim. Each of the first three levels could in theory divide into either two or three of the next level down:[59] but 24 factorises as 3 x 2 x 2 x 2, so only

---

[57] OED, *sub* 'hack' v.6.

[58] Compare my comments on hellish noise, pp. 207–08.

[59] The division of minim into semiminims was binary in 15th-century English music.

TABLE 2 : "FOUR-AND-TWENTY TO A LONG"

(a)

(the beat)

(b)

(the beat)

(c)

one triple-measurement relationship is possible. The twenty-four semiminims could theoretically be distributed in any of the three ways shown in Table 2, therefore.

The first of these, with a semibreve beat dividing twice, has notes for both a whole bar and a pair of bars together; it would be transcribed into modern notation in 3/4 time, with quavers and semiquavers below the crotchet beat. This is the metre used in five of the six Gloria settings in MS Pepys 1236 (see section 3.2, below).[60] The second example, also with a semibreve beat, would be transcribed in 6/8 time with the quavers divided into semiquavers. The two-voiced *Gloria* setting in Cambridge University Library Add. MS 5943 has exactly the metrical structure of this organisation, with all note-values used. Table 3 shows sections of this piece, with the semibreve beat transcribed as a (dotted) crotchet.[61] This second metre would have been old-fashioned at the time the Towneley manuscript was copied, although this particular piece is florid enough to match the shepherds' rather excited description of the angelic music. The metre of the Pepys settings looks less exciting, but a good performance of those settings would in fact be a very memorable event, and of course the date is much closer to the Towneley cycle as we have it.[62]

The more famous Second Shepherds' Play offers a parallel discussion about the angelic Gloria, with much the same kind of technical information being given by the Second and Third Shepherds:

SECUNDUS PASTOR Say, what was his song? / hard ye not how he crakyd it?
                    Thre brefes to a long. /
TERTIUS PASTOR   yee, mary, he hakt it.
                    was no crochett wrong / nor no thyng that lakt it.
                                              (**Towneley 13/656–8**)

The angelic song was evidently florid and impressive, for the angel 'crakyd it' (**13/656**), 'hakt it' (**657**), and sang all the short notes in the right places (**658**).[63]

'Three breves to a long' is the listener's description of music in *modus perfectus*, the threefold division of the long into breves. In the fifteenth century (and for that matter in most of the fourteenth) this would be a background metre, working at the

---

[60] See Charles *The Music of Pepys MS 1236*. Of the three settings à 2, nos. 47 and 71 are in triple time and are chant-based in the upper voice, while no. 82, in duple time, is probably not chant-based; the two settings à 3 (nos. 7 and 36) are both in triple time and are chant-based in the top voice; no. 76, à 4, is in triple time and is probably not chant-based.

[61] Cambridge, University Library Add. MS 5943, ff. 166v–167r: see facsimiles in *A Fifteenth-Century Song Book* (Leeds: Boethius Press, 1973) and *Two Fifteenth-Century Song Books* (Aberystwyth: Boethius Press, 1990), both with introductions by Richard Rastall; and the edition in Rastall *Four Songs in Latin*, 4–5.

[62] The Towneley manuscript seems to date from around 1500; the Cambridge *Gloria* was copied c.1400; and the Pepys manuscript was compiled c.1460–75. See the introductions to MDF 2 and Rastall *Two Fifteenth-Century Song Books*, and below, 3.2.

[63] A 'crochett' is a semiminim, a short-duration note with a hook at the end of the stem: the French still use the word *croche* for the quaver (eighth-note). On the reason why our modern crotchet is flag-less, and how it and the modern quaver derive their shapes from different forms of the semiminim, see Rastall *Notation*, 94–5.

TABLE 3 : NOTE-VALUES IN THE CAMBRIDGE *GLORIA*

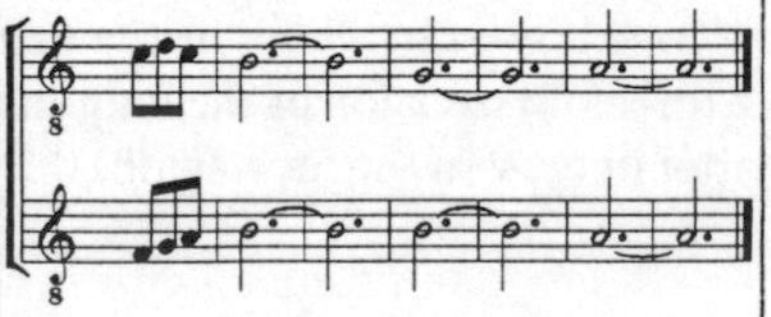

(Text omitted)

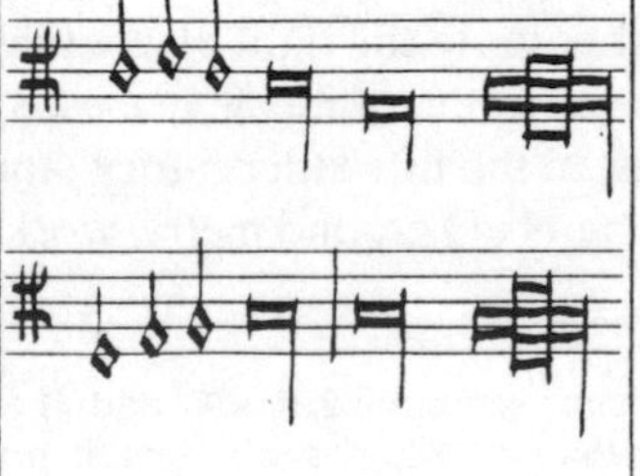

level above that of the beat, which would be the semibreve. *Modus perfectus* could easily be audible: but in the later fourteenth and fifteenth centuries it was normally used only for rather complex music in which *Tempus* and *Prolatio* (the breve/semibreve and semibreve/minim relationships, respectively) were also perfect, i.e. threefold. It is possible that the music was notated in an old-fashioned way, with the breve as the beat: but then if the Third Shepherd is correct in his mention of 'crochetts' these short notes would be a full three levels below the beat. This would make some very florid music indeed, with very fast notes against a very slow beat. Of course, the Second and Third Shepherds may be showing off, not having the expertise to make an accurate technical description of the music: in other words, this passage may be a joke of the playwright's.

On the other hand the playwright was likely to be as musical as any of his audience, and more musical than most, so he may have intended the technical details to be correct. The shepherds' descriptions are consistent, in that the 'hacking' of notes would result in small note-values such as semiminims ('crochetts'); the metre of *modus perfectus* would also result in a florid melodic line if small values were used, and this is something that the angelic song clearly is. In the absence of an obvious Gloria setting for this play it may be safest to assume that the shepherds' use of technical terms is accurate. If so, the metre of the music is as in Table 4. This metre would now be transcribed in 9/8 time (i.e. three beats in a bar, each divided by three), but the listener would also hear a grouping of bars into threes. It will be seen that it gives six semiminims to the beat, or 54 to the long.

At this stage I must make a brief digression. In her influential article on the music in this play, Nan Cooke Carpenter offered a metre for this music based on only 24 notes to the long:[64] this is the third metre shown in Table 2, above. As can be seen, the long divides into three breves, but then the breve and lower values are all subject to the binary division. This metre would be transcribed in 4/4 time (with a larger-scale grouping each bar-and-a-half), or perhaps in 3/2 but with the crotchet as the beat. Possibly this metre was used, but with a semibreve beat it seems rather unlikely: with the old-fashioned breve beat it would certainly give a very florid melodic line. I do not know of an example of this metre (although it may exist), but in fact it need not be considered. Carpenter conflated information from two different plays, taking 'foure and twenty to a long' from **Towneley 12/414** and 'thre brefes to a long' from **13/657**. This is an inadmissible procedure even when, as here, the plays belong to a cycle, are by the same playwright and are closely related textually. I must reiterate that if we take the two shepherds' plays separately, and treat the material that they offer as an entity in each case, we can make sense of the technical information given: but if we try to supplement the information given in either play by transferring material from the other, we shall come to the wrong conclusions. The general form of this statement is also true: the procedure is inadmissible, whatever the two plays concerned.

In a comment about Mak's singing quoted above (p. 37), the First Shepherd

---

[64] Carpenter *Secunda Pastorum*, 215–17.

TABLE 4 : "THREE BREVES TO A LONG"

	𝄽 (long)	
𝅝 (breve)	𝅝 (breve)	𝅝 (breve)
◊ ◊ ◊	◊ ◊ ◊	◊ ◊ ◊
♪♪♪ ♪♪♪ ♪♪♪	♪♪♪ ♪♪♪ ♪♪♪	♪♪♪ ♪♪♪ ♪♪♪
(semiminims, grouped)	(semiminims, grouped)	(semiminims, grouped)

remarks that he has never heard anyone 'crak / so clere out of toyne' (**Towneley 13/477**). 'Crack' has its usual meaning (see above), and 'clear' has the general meaning 'obviously' rather than a specifically musical meaning. 'Out of tune' can be taken to have its modern meaning of singing just off the note, and the First Shepherd of the Prima Pastorum apparently means that the angel's intonation was good when he remarks that the angel's small notes, which have excited so much admiration, were

> [PRIMUS PASTOR] ... gentyll and small,
> And well tonyd with all.   (**Towneley 12/418–19**)

Carter cites these quotations in his articles on 'Tone' (sb) and 'Tonen' (vb), respectively. His articles divide into six sections between them, which is a measure of the complexity of the terminology.[65] The comment about Mak's singing is listed in the section dealing with the 'key, or tonality, of a musical composition'. This is not the meaning that we now have for 'out of tune', and it did not in any case quite coincide with modern ideas of tonality, but it is certainly a usage that must be considered. The major pitch problem before 1600 or so was the difficulty of knowing where the semitones came in the scale. Three notational aids were devised to help with this problem: clefs (still in use), solmisation syllables (still in use as a separate notational system, 'Tonic sol-fa'), and coloured stave-lines (discontinued in the eleventh

---

[65] See Carter *Dictionary*, 503–06; these quotations are cited on pp. 505 and 506, respectively. Carter takes 'tone' and 'tune' together, except that 'tune' as a melody is treated separately.

century).[66] Singing 'out of tune', then, could mean failing to sing the semitones in the right place.

It is perhaps more likely, however, that Mak's singing was out-of-tune in the modern sense. He is singing by ear, so that the question of correspondence between a notated tune and the tune as sung hardly arises, although his pitching of individual notes is almost certainly very inaccurate. With the angel, on the other hand, the technical question may well be relevant. The *Gloria in excelsis deo* would normally be sung from a service book with the musical notation given, so that the accurate rendition of the tune's intervals is relevant to the performance. It is notoriously difficult, in fast and intricate music, both to sing the semitones properly and to sing all the notes in tune. In view of our knowledge that the angel must have been played by a professional singer, it seems probable that both of these meanings were intended by the playwright (the Wakefield Master).

A similar question arises in *Mary Magdalen* when the Priest and his boy sing their service:

PRYSBY[TYR]	Now, boy, I pray þe, lett vs have a song.	
	Ower servyse be note, lett vs syng, I say.	
	Cowff vp þi brest, stond natt to long,	
	Begynne þe offyse of þis day.	1225
BOY	I home and I hast, I do þat I may	
	Wyth mery tvne þe trebyll to syng.	
	Syng both	
PRYSBY[TYR]	Hold vp. Þe dyvll mote þe afray,	
	For all owt of rule þou dost me bryng.	

(Mary Magdalen 1222–9)

This is an incompetent performance, with the Priest's injunction to the boy to clear his throat being answered by an equally amateurish assurance that the boy is preparing himself to sing (lines **1224, 1226**). The Priest apparently sings the plainsong tune, to which the boy sings a 'treble' – that is, a secondary line at a higher pitch. Whether this is a true counterpoint or simply the same tune at a different pitch level, there is no means of telling. The performance is so poor that the Priest protests, apparently in the middle of the piece: 'Stop! You are making me go wrong!' (lines **1228–9**). Since the Priest has the easier task in singing the plainsong tune, this says little for his own musical ability. 'All owt of rule' implies that there is a body of theoretical knowledge in use, and that the boy is causing the Priest to make mistakes within that area.[67] If they are singing mensural music it may be rhythmic errors that are occurring, but this seems unlikely: plainsong was not usually measured. The probability is, therefore, that the boy is causing pitch problems, perhaps by misplacing the semitone intervals in his part and so singing in the wrong mode. Specifically, then, the Priest loses his place in the hexachord system. The boy may cause this in any case, but it will be most obvious if the boy sings precisely the same music at a

---

66 See Rastall *Notation*, 30–2 and 128–31.
67 See Carter *Dictionary*, 417–18 ('Rule').

different pitch – that is, in strict organum. This will result in instability of the interval between the two parts, which should be a fixed perfect interval (a fourth, fifth or octave): then the Priest may begin singing at the wrong pitch (singing in the wrong key would be the modern equivalent), and he will also sing wrong notes (B-flat instead of B-natural, etc.). For most people, out-of-tune singing and out-of-time singing both follow on from such problems.

In addition to references about actual performances of music, the dramatists made metaphorical references. These fall into three main groups: the use of 'sing' as a substitute for 'speak'; the use of 'dance' as a substitute for 'go'; and the general use of musical terms in non-musical contexts. The incidence of metaphorical references in any play is probably some measure of a dramatist's attitude towards music and may also be related to the amount of actual music in a play. In the first case, of course, the contention is impossible to prove. Metaphorical references tend to bunch together in certain plays or groups of plays, and reading them sometimes gives a strong sense of the dramatist's attitude, often in clear contrast to plays in which there are no such references. This is particularly the case in the York cycle, but it is also true elsewhere. As for the relationship between metaphorical usage and the provision of actual music, the statistical indications are far from conclusive, although some plays that use music most are also those with most metaphorical references. There are also instances of a metaphorical reference being made into an actual reference by the later provision of music, which may indicate that the relationship between them is not a simple one. It is however impossible to demonstrate such examples conclusively.

One of the most common types of musical metaphor is the use of 'sing' for some other verb. The following selection is far from comprehensive, but it will show a range of uses:

I REX	For solas ser now may we synge	**(York 16/357)**
III MILES	3a, he may synge or he slepe of sorowe and angir	**(York 33/422)**
[CAIAPHAS]	of care may thou syng	**(Towneley 21/129)**
[FROWARD]	I may syng ylla-hayl	**(Towneley 21/375)**
[IHESUS]	Of sorrow may every synfull syng.	**(Towneley 30/393)**

In these examples there is a high proportion of instances in which grief or pain is involved, and this is probably representative of this type in general. Although there are instances of joy involving metaphorical references to singing, a large number of such references do of course attract an actual performance.

A particularly interesting extension of this idea is found in **Towneley 30/537–8**, where the metaphor is made specific and technical:

SECUNDUS DEMON   The meyn shall ye nebyll
           And I shall syng the trebill.

The demonic provision of an unwanted counterpoint to the 'singing' of a damned soul is unusual, and even here would probably not have been presented without the discussion in **13/186–9** that prepares the way for it:

PRIMUS PASTOR	lett me syng the tenory.
SECUNDUS PASTOR	And I the tryble so hye.
TERCIUS PASTOR	Then the meyne fallys to me.

The three shepherds actually do sing in three parts, of course, so that the later reference can make use of the audience's memory of their song. Moreover, **Towneley 30/537–8** is from one of the stanzas towards the end of the play generally regarded as being an addition by the Wakefield Master, the dramatist of play 13:[68] the same playwright, then, is responsible for these two uses of musical part-names.

A usage related to that of 'sing' for 'speak' is that of 'pipe' with a similar meaning. The word is twice used in the Towneley cycle for scornful speech about the character who has just spoken. In the first, Caim refers slightingly to God; in the second, the First Shepherd insults Mak:

[CAIM]	we! who was that that piped so small?	**(Towneley 2/298)**
PRIMUS PASTOR	Who is that pypys so poore?	**(Towneley 13/195)**

Again, the Wakefield Master is responsible for both plays.

This kind of metaphor can exist in different forms. A not uncommon one is the use of singing as a noun rather than a verb:

MARIA	Alas may ever be my sang /	**(Towneley 23/406)**
MARIA	Sore syghyng is my sang /	**(Towneley 23/429)**

These are not part of the Wakefield Master's work, although he wrote a single stanza earlier in this play.

'Alas' is one of those words of grief that attracts the metaphor, then, and there is an example in the York cycle and in the parallel position in the Towneley cycle:

[DEUS]	His sange ful sone sall be allas.	**(York 11/128)**
[DEUS]	ful soyn hys song shall be alas	**(Towneley 8/141)**

Another word that often attracts the singing metaphor is 'Welaway':

[DIABOLUS]	of oure myrthis now xal 3e se and evyr synge welawey.	**(N-Town 19/244–5)**
[OMNES ANIME]	now may oure songe be wele-Away	**(N-Town 41/29)**

In the first of these we should note the perversion of heavenly mirth: it results not

---

[68] Cawley *Wakefield Pageants*, xviii.

in the joyful singing of the mirthful person but in someone else metaphorically singing sadly.

Most uses of 'welaway' are non-musical, at least in the sense that the word 'sing' is not present. The question is, then, whether the non-musical uses of 'welaway' occur because of a musical connection or not. In the York cycle there are four 'welaway' occurrences – two by Lucifer and two by Adam – which are all non-musical; those in the N-Town cycle are one from Eve, two from Cain, two from Joseph in his trouble about Mary, one from the midwife Salomee when her hand is withered for her disbelief, and one from Martha at the death of Lazarus. Although these are mainly characters for whom actual singing would be a godly act, this does not in itself answer the question. The proportion of singing to non-singing citations in the Oxford English Dictionary is similar to that in the cycles, which suggests that, whatever the precise situation, the plays did not take a radically different stance from other writings in this matter. It is probably impossible to draw firm conclusions about this, but we should bear in mind that the use of 'welaway' may have suggested singing by association even when 'sing' is not the verb involved.

It is not always easy to distinguish metaphorical references from real ones. Den's comment on Mary's pregnancy in the N-Town pageant of The Purgation of Mary and Joseph clearly makes sense if taken metaphorically but could well have been intended at face value, since one would expect a mother to sing a lullaby to her baby:

[DEN] Ffayr chylde lullay sone must she syng.   (**N-Town 14/164**)

On the other hand an apparently metaphorical reference turns out to be an actual performance, as the SD following it shows:

[EVA] therfor owr handes we may wryng with most dullfull song.
And so thei xall syng, walkyng together about the place, . . .   (**Norwich A/88, +sd**)

(The text of their song follows, **A/89–90**) There is no evidence here that a metaphorical reference has been turned into a reference to actual performance by the addition of a (marginal) direction, and indeed A/88 is most unlikely as a metaphorical reference. There are certainly places where that process can be demonstrated, however, such as **York 9/259–60, 266+md**:

[NOE] mare joie in herte never are I hadde,
       We mone be saued, now may we synge.
            . . .
Tunc cantent Noe et filii sui &c.

Here line **260** is a perfectly acceptable metaphorical reference, but the late marginal direction six lines later turns it into a reference to an actual performance.

Another metaphorical usage is of the verb 'dance'. Two examples from the York cycle can exemplify the type:

CAYME   Ya, daunce in þe devil way, dresse þe downe.   (**York 7/52**)

REX (PHARAOH)   Nay, nay, þat daunce is done.   **(York 11/225)**

For the first of these Beadle glosses the verb 'dance' as 'go, proceed': but he also gives the whole phrase as an intensification of 'in the deuel way' (glossed as 'in the devil's name'), with the meaning of 'hence, away, in the devil's name'.[69] However, he also glosses 'in waye' as 'along the way',[70] so that the whole phrase could mean 'go, along the devil's way', which is close to the more recent 'go to the devil'. This metaphor seems to refer not to the orderliness of dancing, but rather to the wasted expenditure of energy characteristic of the devil's service.[71] The characters who use it are all the devil's agents: others in the York cycle are Herod's messenger (**19/96**), Caiaphas (**29/395**), and Herod himself (**31/423**). In the second quotation Beadle's gloss on 'dance' is 'business, affair':[72] thus the phrase means 'that business is finished with' or, more specifically in this context, 'the situation is altered'.

Two examples from the Towneley cycle show a more inventive application of the dancing metaphor, but without altering the conclusions already drawn:

[PRIMUS TORTOR]   .../ we must hop and dawns
                         As cokys in a croft.   **(Towneley 21/354–5)**

TERCIUS TORTOR   I shall lede the a dawnse / Unto sir pilate hall.
                                                          (Towneley 22/80)

The third and last type of reference concerns musical terms used with everyday non-musical meanings. The commonest in the plays is the phrase 'loud and still': in a musical sense 'loud' is a technical term referring to instruments such as trumpets, drums and shawms, while 'still' is the parallel adjective for stringed instruments and the soft winds such as recorders. The terms are applied also to the resulting music.[73] In the plays 'loud and still' can have a variety of meanings, such as 'great and small', 'important and unimportant' (of people) and, generally, 'in all/various situations'. This phrase is not confined to any particular plays or group of plays, but it will be convenient to examine those in the York cycle.

NOE A, lorde, I lowe þe lowde and still   **(York 8/41)**

[NOE] I lowe þe lare both lowde and stille   **(York 8/145)**

[I ANGELUS] And thanke hym hartely, both lowde and still.   **(York 21/58)**

[JOHANNES (BAPTISTA)] Thy subgett lord, both lowde and still   **(York 21/139)**

[JOHANNES (the Evangelist)] We love God lowde and still   **(York 23/47)**

[I APOSTOLUS]   A, lorde, we loue þe inwardly
                    And all þi lore, both lowde and still   **(York 24/75–6)**

---

[69] Beadle 1982, 487.
[70] Beadle 1982, 529.
[71] See below, pp. 207–08.
[72] Beadle 1982, 487.
[73] See Bowles *Haut and Bas*.

[I APOSTOLUS]   I loue þe, lord God allmyghty;
        Late and herely, lowde and still,
        To do thy bidding bayne am I.   **(York 47/204–6)**

Just as the metaphor of the dance is used by the devil's agents, so the 'loud and still' metaphor, however divorced from its musical context in this usage, was the property of those who do God's will. Moreover, they use it in speaking of matters pertaining to the Kingdom: of their love for God (Noah and John the Evangelist), of thanksgiving (the angel), of love for his Law (First Apostle at **24/76**, here associated with love for God), and of their intention to do his Will (John the Baptist, First Apostle at **47/205**, again associated with love for God). There are relatively few 'lowde and still' references in the Towneley cycle but, as at York, the speakers are those doing God's will: two occurrences are in speeches by John the Baptist **(Towneley 19/8, 101)**, and one is spoken by the First Doctor in stating the first Commandment **(Towneley 18/122)**. In each case the phrase is connected with speeches in which God's will is done.

A more problematic metaphor is the use of 'gam', which normally means 'game': Beadle glosses it with the meaning of joy, pleasure or sport.[74] Thus Simeon's comment

[SYMEON]   Nowe certys then shulde my gamme begynne
        And I myght se hyme, of hyme to tell   **(York 17/103–4)**

means that the coming of Christ will turn his sadness to joy. Later in this play the Priest puts 'gam' and 'glee' together in a way that is frequently met also in the Towneley cycle and elsewhere:

[PRESBITER] Thowe art our beylde, babb, our gamme and our glee
        (York 17/318)

Beadle gives no gloss for this occurrence, although his glossing of 'glee' as pleasure or joy both suggests a similar meaning for 'gam' and introduces a tautology. While 'glee' does have a later musical meaning, 'game and glee' as a phrase does not imply music,[75] and there is no real reason to look for a musical origin in **17/318** or in most other uses of the phrase (such as in **Towneley 1/84** and **3/529**). In the case of **York 17/103**, however, 'gamme' may bear its musical meaning of the scale, sung up and down as a vocal exercise with the syllables of the hexachords.[76] In 1567 or so, when the play was entered into the York register,[77] this would be more likely than a century earlier, and would fit with Simeon's presumed knowledge of the practice of liturgical music. In this case line **103** would mean 'Then should I accomplish the actions for which I was ordained'. There is no firm evidence that this was intended, however, and the simpler interpretation, 'then should my joy begin', fits the context perfectly well.

[74] Beadle 1982, 496. See also Coldewey 'Plays and "Play"'.
[75] Carter *Dictionary*, 169–70.
[76] Carter *Dictionary*, 160–1; Rastall *Notation*, 128–34.
[77] Beadle 1982, 434.

This discussion illustrates the major problem in dealing with metaphorical references to music and musical matters: it is often difficult to be certain of the dramatist's precise intention. I shall not make claims for the musical thinking of any dramatist, therefore, beyond what the evidence clearly shows: but on the other hand it is always worth exploring possibilities in the hope that those usages currently found to be rather obscure may one day become better understood. As I hope to have shown, this problem is not necessarily a simple one. A reviser or producer may have a different understanding of a term or its usage from the dramatist, and that understanding may also change with time.

Finally in this section I wish to consider an undoubted musical simile of obscure meaning:

SECUNDUS MILES   Ffor swerdys sharpe
                 as An harpe
                 quenys xul karpe
                 and of sorwe synge.   (N-Town 19/65–8)

Although the concentration of musical metaphor here is greater than usual, the pageants of the N-Town protocycle do use musical metaphor much more than the Mary Play and other substituted sections of the cycle as we have it. But what exactly does this first metaphor mean? In what sense is a harp 'sharp'?

Spector's commentary and glossary give no extra meaning for either 'sharp' or 'harp' in this quotation.[78] Carter lists two relevant meanings for 'scharpe': 'shrill, high-pitched', and 'capable of emitting a shrill musical sound'.[79] The first of these relates to pitch, while the second ('shrill' as opposed to 'soft') is a quality of sound: in neither case is any particular volume implied. Thus while a sharp sound is often assumed to be a loud sound this is not necessarily so. Similarly, 'soft' does not mean 'quiet', although a 'soft' sound is more often than not a quiet one.[80] 'Sharp' and 'soft', then, imply an approach, resulting in sounds of a particular quality: in modern terms, the harmonics of the former will be richer and more dissonant. Of Carter's various quotations, three using 'sharp' as an adjective relate to the harp, as do two in which 'sharp' is an adverb. In all cases the sound is received with approval.

The sound at issue, then, is pleasant, but it is distinguished by its ability to carry, its penetration. Carter cites a quotation from Lydgate that refers to the strings themselves as sharp, but this is presumably a transferred epithet: two other Lydgate quotations show that it is the touch of the fingers that produces the sharp or soft sound. Technically, there are three ways to produce a sound rich in dissonant harmonics: one can pull the string further, which also results in a *louder* sound; one can pluck the string at a particular position (such as one-seventh or one-eleventh of the way along, as these odd-numbered harmonics are the dissonant ones); or one

---

[78] Spector *N-Town* II, 478, 593 and 632.
[79] Carter *Dictionary*, 424; as an adverb, *ibid.*, 425.
[80] 'Soft' was not used for low volume in music until the second half of the seventeenth century: in the first half of that century the English direction for a quiet passage was 'away'.

can use a more angular agent, such as finger-nails or plectrum, for plucking instead of the rounded finger-ends.

The stated parallel between a sword and the sound of a harp in **N-Town 19/65–6** suggests that it is the penetrating power of the instrument that makes the metaphor a usable one; and that its carrying sound-quality was regarded as one of the harp's virtues. This may point towards a metal-strung clarsach rather than a gut-strung harp as the instrument best known to an East Anglian audience.

2.5 The proclamations and banns

The terms 'proclamation' and 'banns' have been used indiscriminately in the past, but there is now a move towards distinguishing them. Recent writers have used 'proclamation' as the civic authority's public demand that a play or cycle be mounted, or brought forth in an orderly fashion, and 'banns' as the advertisement by the company concerned of the time and place of a forthcoming performance. Proclamations are rare; a few sets of banns survive, and it is likely that the Towneley cycle did originally include banns at the beginning of the manuscript.[81] The majority of play texts survive without banns, however, and it is impossible to know whether banns were a usual method of advertising performances of plays. Nor is there any evidence that other types of advertisement were used as an alternative to the banns.

The surviving banns fall into two geographical groups. The first consists of three sets found at the beginning of play texts from East Anglia. *The Castle of Perseverance*, the oldest of the morality plays, survives in a manuscript apparently dating from around 1440. The play is of 3649 lines, with a playing time of about four hours, while the banns – the first 156 lines of the text – probably take about 10 minutes to perform. In these banns two banner-bearers (*vexillatores*) rehearse the story of the play in order to encourage their audience to attend the drama at a later time. The banns are being proclaimed in an open space such as a market-place, and in a town, for Primus Vexillator addresses

> . . . all þe goode comowns of þis towne þat beforn us stonde
> In þis place.   (Castle 8–9)

The name of the town concerned is not stated, the manuscript having a blank space for it:

---

81 See Stevens 'Missing Parts', 256–7. Stevens argues convincingly that the whole of the missing Quire [a] was taken up with the banns: but he goes on to say that, since existing Towneley gatherings are of eight leaves containing 800–900 lines, and since the manuscript does not contain blank leaves between plays, 'the missing Towneley banns must have been considerably longer than the N-Town 528-line banns of the plays, the longest set of banns surviving from the English mystery cycles.' This may be turning the argument on its head: it is likely that the banns would be contained in their own gathering, and therefore that, whatever the usual size of gathering in the text as a whole, Quire [a] was the size demanded by the material contained in it – perhaps smaller than later gatherings.

SECUNDUS VEXILLATOR   Os oure lyuys we loue 3ou, þus takande oure leue.
        3e manly men of . . ., þer Crist saue 3ou all!   (Castle 144–5)

The banns are being cried in the town where the performance is to take place, apparently, on 'the green' in seven days' time. Another blank was left probably for the time of starting to be specified:

[PRIMUS VEXILLATOR]   þese parcellys in propyrtes we purpose us to playe
                Þis day seuenenyt before 3ou in syth
                At . . . on þe grene in ryal aray.   (Castle 132–4)

There is no way of telling what would be a reasonable starting-time, but the organisers wanted the audience to be there in good time:

[PRIMUS VEXILLATOR]   And loke þat 3e be þere betyme, luffely and lyth,
                For we schul be onward be vnderne of þe day.
                                              (Castle 137–8)

What does 'be onward' mean here? Is it that the play must have started, or be well under way 'be underne of the day', whatever that means? Davis's glossary suggests '?afternoon' for the latter, which would imply that the play must start in the late morning at the latest. On the other hand, 'we schuld be onward' may mean 'we [the players] must be moving on to the next place'. This would imply that the company travelled in the afternoon in order to play elsewhere the following morning, in which case the play must have started at 8 a.m. even if there were no breaks in the performance, and considerably earlier if the performance were not continuous. An early-morning start was usual for the cycle plays, as we shall see: so although there is no evidence for plays such as *The Castle* the possibility is there.

Secundus Vexillator ends with some conventional commendations to the audience, and then commands one or more minstrels to

                Trumpe up and lete vs pace.   (Castle 156)

There is loud music, then, as the banns-criers depart. Although there is no evidence of it, we can probably assume that the minstrels played before the banner-bearers began, as well, to draw a crowd and to warn them to listen to what followed.

The Croxton *Play of the Sacrament* has banns showing some of the same features. This miracle play may date originally from the 1460s or 1470s. The language is East Anglian, so the Croxton mentioned in line **74** of the banns is probably a Norfolk one: that on the Bury St Edmunds side of Thetford is the most likely, since in the play the Doctor is said to live 'besyde Babwell Myll' (line **621**), and Babwell is on the Thetford road from Bury St Edmunds, about 12 miles from that Croxton.[82] The banns take up the first 80 lines of the play text, which runs to 1007 lines altogether: so for a play about an hour long there are banns lasting something over five minutes. Here, too, two banner-bearers give a prècis of the plot, which they present as being the true story of events that occurred in 1461. Secundus Vexillator ends by

---

[82] See Davis's introduction to the play, NCPF, lxxxiv–lxxxv.

explaining that this drama will be played 'at Croxston on Monday', and that any of their present audience will be 'Hertely welcum' at the performance (**Sacrament 74–6**); he adds some conventional wishes for the well-being of the hearers' souls, and finally calls for music:

SECUNDUS [VEXILLATOR]   Now, mynstrell, blow vp with a mery stevyn.

(**Sacrament 80**)

It is possible that Primus Vexillator is the minstrel, but this is far from certain; nor is it clear that a single minstrel is involved, rather than a group, for 'mynstrell' certainly could be plural. What is not in doubt is that here, as in the banns-crying of *The Castle*, the banner-bearers departed from their pitch to the sound of minstrelsy; and here too we can reasonably assume that they also arrived with minstrelsy, the sound of loud music bringing the crowd to hear what they had to say.

The purpose of these banns is evidently to bring in an audience to Croxton, where the play is to be performed, from the surrounding area, and it was presumably made at a number of different places. 'At Croxton' (line **74**) suggests that this area could not be a very large one, since there are other Croxtons in Norfolk, Cambridgeshire and Lincolnshire; and 'on Monday' (line **74**) shows that the banns preceded the performance by less than a week. In the past something has been made of the possibility of this play being a touring performance. Norman Davis remarked that the naming of Croxton 'need not define the provenance of the play closely, for the very nature of the proclamation implies a travelling company'.[83] It is certainly possible that the Croxton performance was only one of several in different places, but the banns provide no evidence for that. What we have, on the face of it, is an advertisement made around a rural area for a single performance in a single location.

The question is an important one for music, for a touring play is likely to use fewer resources than a play mounted by the citizens of the town where it is to be performed. *Prima facie* the Croxton play, an hour long with a small cast, is much more likely to be a touring play than the huge *Castle of Perseverance*, which is a major undertaking however it is performed. In fact, *The Castle* demands loud minstrelsy in performance, as well as singing, while the Croxton play needs only two sung items. It is true that the minstrels are likely to be those that have already accompanied the banns, but there is a great difference between organising and financing loud minstrelsy in a major dramatic production and using them simply for fanfares before and after the banns.

The next set of banns, also from East Anglia, is that for the N-Town plays, which survives at the start of the play text. It is delivered by three banner-bearers, and at 528 lines – half-an-hour or more, probably – it is a large enough piece of text for the use of a third *vexillator* to be sensible. This is not for the N-Town plays as known to us, but for the proto-cycle of pageants on which the collection was built. The content

---

[83] Davis NCPF, lxxxiv.

of forty pageants is described.[84] The purpose of this is certainly to draw a crowd to the performance, and the banns tend to concentrate on those features of the plays that a potential audience will find most exciting. The music mentioned is therefore confined to the set pieces on spectacular occasions: the singing of the angels at the Creation in Pageant 1 and at the Nativity in Pageant 15 (stated to be 16, but the numbering is confused at this stage). Strangely, the Last Trumpet is not mentioned for Pageant 40.[85]

Finally, Tercius Vexillator announces that the play will be given the following Sunday, beginning 'at vj of the belle' in 'N-town' (**N-Town 525–7**). There is no indication that the banner-bearers are accompanied by trumpeters.

It will be useful at this stage to make a brief digression to examine the prologues and epilogues to certain plays. A.C. Cawley pointed out that the introduction to *Everyman* is closely related to banns in describing the content of the play before the performance, the difference being that banns relate to a performance due to happen some time in the future, whereas an introduction is part of a performance that is just starting.[86] Poeta's introduction to *The Killing of the Children* ends with an exhortation to the minstrels to play, and the direction following shows that 'the virgins' (of the Temple) then danced:

> And ye menstrallis, doth youre diligens!
> And ye virgynes, shewe summe sport and plesure,
>   These people to solas, and to do God reuerens!
> As ye be appoynted, doth your besy cure! (**Killing 53–6**)

The introduction by Poeta to *The Conversion of St Paul* ends with a late additional direction 'Daunce', so for that play too at least one performance in the middle of the sixteenth century included such an entertainment to separate the prologue from the body of the play (**Saint Paul 13+md**).

In a similar way, there are epilogues which end with music just as the East Anglian banns do. *The Killing of the Children* ends with the Prophetess Anna telling the virgins of the Temple to show 'summe plesure', after which a dance takes place (**Killing 549–50+sd**, and cf. **Killing 54**, above): and then Poeta delivers an *envoi* at the end of which there is another dance by the virgins, accompanied by minstrels:

> Wherfore now, ye virgynes, er we go hens,
> With alle your cumpany, you goodly avaunce!

---

[84] This is not necessarily a processional cycle on the northern model, although the proto-cycle is a complete Creation-to-Doom cosmic drama. Kathleen Ashley has noted that the community concerned seems to be a smaller one than the northern towns with cycles, and perhaps a rural community, while Peter Meredith believes that it could be for a fixed stage (both at the N-Town Symposium in Toronto: 5 May, 3 May 1987, respectively).

[85] Spector's edition (in which the Judgement is play 42) sensibly does not try to match up the pageant-numbers of the banns (which are for the proto-cycle) with those of the existing collection.

[86] In *Revels History* I, 40, n. 3.

> Also, ye menstralles, doth your diligens;
> Afore oure departyng, geve vs a daunce!   (**Killing 563–6**)

This kind of ending is seen also in various of the Cornish plays, where one of the dramatic characters normally steps out of role to deliver the epilogue. In *The Life of Meriasek* the Count of Vannes tells the pipers to play for what seems to be intended as a general dance:[87]

Dywhy banneth meryasek	To you the blessing of Meriasek
ha maria cambron wek	And of sweet Mary of Camborne,
banneth an abesteleth	The blessing of the Apostles!
evugh oll gans an guary	Drink ye all with the play
ny a vynagis pesy	We will beseech you
kyns moys an plaeth	Before going from the place.
Pyboryon wethugh in scon	Pipers, blow at once.
ny a vyn ketep map bron	We will, every son of the breast,
moys the donsya	Go to dance.
eugh bo tregugh	Go ye or stay,
wolcum vethugh	Welcome ye shall be
kyn fewy sythen omma.	Though ye be a week here.

(Meriasek 4557–68)

This is presumably a loud band of shawms; the first and third days of the Ordinalia end with musicians playing, King Solomon announcing the music at the end of the *Origo Mundi* and the Emperor telling the musicians to 'strike up a brisk tune' for (again, perhaps general) dancing at the end of the *Resurrexio Domini* (**Ordinalia 1/2845–6, 3/2645–6**);[88] and a similar ending to *The Creacion of the World* has Noah encouraging what seems to be a traditional ending:

Mynstrells, grewgh theny peba,	Pipe up for us, minstrels,
May hallan warbarthe downssya,	That we may dance together,
Del ew an vaner han geys.	As is the manner and the custom.

(Creacion 2547–9)

If this was indeed traditional (in East Anglia as well as in Cornwall), it is perhaps comprehensible as an extension of the method of ending plays with liturgical music in praise of God. Indeed, the lack of music at the end of the second day of the Ordinalia, *Passio Domini*, underlines the suitability of music and dancing elsewhere and suggests that we can regard the endings of the various plays as showing a spectrum of possibilities – silence, a said 'Amen', a sung liturgical piece, or loud minstrelsy and dancing – that were utilised as appropriate by the dramatists.

---

[87] As is often the case, Markham Harris changed the line-order for a more flowing speech:
'The blessing of Meriasek, of beloved Mary of Camborne, and of the Apostles go with you. Before you leave, we urge you to take something to drink for the benefit of the play. Now, pipers, blow, and let everybody join the dancing. Go home if you must, but if you can stay on, you'll be welcome though you were with us for a week!'
[88] This translation is from Harris *The Cornish Ordinalia*, 247.

Returning to the banns and proclamations, the second geographical group is that of the northern cities with their centrally-organised productions mounted by the trade-guilds. The earliest of these belongs to York, and is one of four entries dating from 1415 in the A/Y Memorandum Book of that city.[89] All four are official civic documents concerned with the ordering of events on Corpus Christi day, with the maintenance of law and order during the plays, and with making sure that the guilds concerned produce the proper plays in good order. Two of these entries – the torch list and the additions to it – we can ignore for present purposes. The proclamation was to be made on the eve of Corpus Christi – that is, the day before the performance.[90] It is concerned with a ban on the carrying of arms so that the peace shall be kept and the plays allowed to process unhindered; the guilds are warned to play only at the designated playing-places, to supply the torches necessary, and to bring out their pageants in good order with the players properly costumed and able to speak their lines; and notice that the players should be ready to start the performance at 4.30 a.m., the second and subsequent pageants following after the first in order.[91] The proclamation ends with a list of the guilds and the episodes that they play.

This material was registered by Roger Burton, who became the Common Clerk of the city of York in 1415. In front of it is a fuller list of guilds and the material that they played, registered by Burton as the *Ordo paginarum ludi Corporis Christi*. This list of the contents of each play gives rather fuller descriptions, although still not as full as we should like. The entries for the Nativity and the Shepherds, for instance, mention the angel speaking to the shepherds but do not indicate that there is any music. However, the play of the Entry into Jerusalem is said to include 'viij pueri cum ramis palmarum cantantes Benedictus & c.'; there is singing mentioned at the Coronation of the Virgin (although the entry is badly damaged and much of it is now illegible); and the Last Judgement play is stated to include 'iiij^{or} angeli cum tubis'.[92]

Clearly the needs of a large northern city that mounted a cycle regularly were quite different from those of a smaller, perhaps rural, community putting on a play only occasionally. In the former case it was hardly necessary to advertise in the countryside around in order to attract an audience, while there was a very great need to maintain law and order and to ensure that the performance ran smoothly. By the late fifteenth century it was perhaps necessary also to show that the material to be played was theologically acceptable. Even as early as the proclamation of the N-Town cycle there was apparently a need to state the authority of the material presented:

---

[89] These are edited in *REED.York*, 16–26, and can be seen in facsimile at the end of MDF 7.

[90] This is clearly a proclamation (not banns) as defined earlier in this section.

[91] This passage is a little confused, and has caused problems. It cannot mean that everyone must be ready at 4.30 a.m. even though some will not start playing until several hours later: it must mean that the first pageant starts at 4.30 and the others follow it in due course, in proper order and at the right time.

[92] The *Ordo paginarum* is clearly for the plays as they were before the revisions of the mid-15th century. In the existing Judgement play there are only two angel trumpeters.

> Of Holy Wrytte þis game xal bene,
> And of no fablys be no way.   (N-Town 520–1)

From the 1530s onwards this evidently became a very important issue, as we can see in the two sets of banns from Chester, read on St George's Day before a summer performance.[93] The Early Banns were probably composed in their present form by 1540. Lumiansky and Mills suggested that they were originally written at the time when the plays were moved from Corpus Christi to Whitsunday, which had happened by 1521. They postulated later emendations to account for the change from performance on a single day to the three-day presentation (by 1531) and some erasures following the suppression of the feast of Corpus Christi in 1548.[94] Clopper has expressed similar views, suggesting initial composition in the period 1505–21 and the final (but uncut) version in the mayoral year 1539–40.[95]

Lumiansky and Mills considered that the fundamental purpose of the Early Banns was 'to create high expectations for the coming performance' by enumerating 'selling points' to the potential audience.[96] Certainly the visually-effective parts of the plays tend to be mentioned, and one would think that music, being often associated with spectacular effects in the plays, would be mentioned as well. But this is not the case, which may indicate that music played a smaller part in the cycle before 1540 than it did in the second half of the century. However, the usual *caveat* obtains for the Early Banns: omissions cannot safely be regarded as positive evidence. In fact, the Early Banns are antedated by the charter of the Painters, Glaziers, Embroiderers and Stationers, which dates from 1534–5 and which mentions their play of 'þe shepperds with þe Angells hyme'.[97]

The Late Banns were apparently written as a Protestant replacement for the Early Banns, but Lumiansky and Mills did not hazard a guess at the date of composition.[98] They noted, though, that there was increasing Protestant opposition to the plays from about 1560 onwards, and that the tone of the Late Banns is defensive. Clopper considered the Late Banns to be part of the attempt to persuade the City Council to allow a performance in 1572,[99] while Ruth Keane has put forward the view that they were a statement by the City Council itself of its attitude towards the plays.[100] Whatever the truth of this, the Late Banns are surprisingly silent about music, considering the number of music cues that we know of in the cycle.[101] They do however mention music in the entries for plays **7** (The Shepherds), **11** (The

---

93   The sources are fully discussed and an edition of the texts presented by Lumiansky and Mills in *Essays*, 272–310; the banns have also been edited by Clopper in *REED.Chester*, 31–9 and 240–7.

94   *Essays*, 166–7 and 190.

95   In 'History and Development' (1978).

96   *Essays*, 179.

97   Edited by Clopper in *REED.Chester*, 29–30, and by Lumiansky and Mills in *Essays*, 218.

98   *Essays*, 190.

99   See 'History and Development'.

100   Keane *Kingship*, 8–13, and especially 12.

101   I have listed the cues in *Essays*, 139–42: a fuller listing will appear in Volume 2 of the present work.

Purification) and **24** (The Last Judgement). These three items are discussed else-where,[102] and only a summary is needed here. The Late Banns item for the Painters' and Glaziers' play requires them, among other things, to see that *Gloria in Excelsis* is sung merrily. The incipit, given as 'Gloria in Excelsus', is written in red ink in manuscript R, and the item was clearly regarded as important. The Late Banns, lines 101–2, do in fact identify this liturgical piece as the basis of the whole play. The Blacksmiths, who played the Purification, are required in the Banns to supply three minstrels – pipe, tabret and flute. It is not clear what these would be used for, since they would be inappropriate for the only musical item in the text, Simeon's singing of *Nunc dimittis*. Perhaps they accompanied the waggon and entertained the crowd at the different stations before and after the play.[103] Finally, the Late Banns mention that 'Come hither, come hither, Venite benedicitie' is to be sung in the Last Judgement. There is neither direction nor reference for this performance, but Christ does paraphrase the liturgical text *Venite benedicti*, beginning 'Come hither', at **Chester 24/453–6**, so presumably a tradition grew up of Christ singing the liturgical piece before speaking the English version.[104]

The banns do tend to emphasise the differences between the various types of drama, and to raise important questions about the methods of performance. The information that they give about music is generally a little disappointing: but they suggest a rather wider view than the usual one of the musical (or otherwise) endings to the plays, and indicate also that in southern areas there may have been a tradition of general dancing after a performance.

2.6 Lyrics and song-texts

Reading through many of the plays gives a strong impression of varied literary resources being used, even when a play maintains a uniform stanza-pattern. Of course, the poetic form is broken up by such elements as sung liturgical pieces: but beyond that, a feeling of purely *poetic* variety remains. Some passages are reminiscent of other types of writing and seem to be discrete examples of particular literary styles embedded in the plays. The question is bound to arise, therefore, whether any pre-existent material was used in the plays and, if so, how it is treated. In this section I shall discuss only non-liturgical verse texts.[105]

At first sight the incorporation of pre-existent lyrics into the dramatic texts seems improbable. The dramatic directions do not usually provide copies of liturgical texts that already existed in easily-obtainable books. The case of musical settings is similar. As Chapter 3 will show, complete musical settings are apparently those that do not exist elsewhere: pre-existent pieces were not copied into the play books

---

[102] *Essays*, 130–2.

[103] This matter is discussed in *Essays*, 130–1 and 134–7.

[104] See *Essays*, 131–2.

[105] Liturgical texts are discussed in 2.7 and Chapter 7.

because that would be unnecessary. The 'hilare carmen' of **Chester 7/447+sd** is perhaps an example. An MD in manuscript Hm gives the title 'troly loly loly loo', the spelling of this title being rather garbled in ARB. This title may be relevant to only a single performance, however, and from the performance point of view we need not be too concerned about the song's identity. According to John Stevens 'Trolly lolly lo' was 'a common refrain' in the sixteenth century, but he cites only one other song.[106] There are examples in a song book from Henry VIII's court, however. 'Hey troly loly loly: My love is lusty, plesant and demure' is a three-part round that would demand professional singers with equal voices: it is an unlikely candidate for Chester 7, which requires Garcius to teach it to 'all men', making a relatively simple unison song most likely. The text is not unacceptable for that use, however.[107] 'Hey troly loly lo, Mayde whether go you?' is a milkmaid-seduction text unsuitable for use in Chester 7.[108] No doubt there are other contenders, and perhaps in any case the one concerned has not survived. Robert Laneham, writing in 1575, rehearses a list of eight or nine 'ballets & songs all aunncient' sung by Captain Cox, in which it is not clear whether 'So wo iz me begon, troly lo' is one song or two.[109] A song by William Cornish dating from c. 1515 seems the only one to fit the title as the Chester manuscripts perhaps intended it:[110]

> Trolly lolly loly lo,
> Syng troly loly lo!
> My love is to the grenewode gone,
> Now aftyr wyll I go;
> Syng trolly loly lo loly lo!

This three-voiced song is unique to BL Add. MS 31922: the top line alone would make a perfectly adequate unison song. Stevens believed the piece to be 'probably complete, even though short',[111] but this seems to me unlikely: there were surely other verses that were not copied into the surviving source. Whether second and subsequent verses were as innocent as this first one, I doubt. That may be irrelevant, however, if Garcius was indeed teaching the song to the audience, for he would be free to make use of any version, including parodies and completely new verses.

It is possible that the copyists of the Chester manuscripts did not have this text in front of them, or they would surely have come closer to a correct version: as it is, the variants *troly loly loly loo / troly loly troly loe / troly loly lo / troly holy holy loo*[112] suggest that the refrain was not well known in the late sixteenth century, at least to the Chester scribes. On the other hand it must have been well known earlier in the

---

106 This is in *Complaint of Scotland*, 1549: Early English Text Society 83 (1872), no. 64.

107 Stevens *Henry VIII*, no. 75; *Music and Poetry*, 413–14.

108 Stevens *Music and Poetry*, 424; musical setting in Stevens *Henry VIII*, no. 109. The words could have been altered for dramatic use, of course.

109 *REED.Coventry*, 274.

110 The text is in Stevens *Music and Poetry*, 243 and 401, and Cornish's setting in Stevens *Henry VIII*, no. 39.

111 Stevens *Music and Poetry*, 401.

112 In Hm, A, R and B, respectively. See above, p. 21, for the Chester manuscripts.

century when the direction was written into the play, or a fuller description of the song would presumably have been given.[113]

It is also worth noting that in considering musical settings we find ourselves in a tradition that thrived on the transportation of pre-existing material. The poetry books of the second half of the century regularly make use of the formula 'To the tune of . . .' when identifying a musical setting for a new verse.[114] Here again, it was not considered necessary to re-present material that was well known: the singer would be able to fit the new words to the existing tune.

It seems unlikely, then, that pre-existent lyrics would be copied into the plays: indeed, it seems likely that any lyrics were copied precisely because they were *not* pre-existent. Nevertheless, we cannot discount the possibility of such lyrics turning up in other sources; and we may, too, be able to identify existing lyrics as models on which play-lyrics were based.

Of the various lyrics or possible lyrics in the plays, the most immediately important are obviously those that have actually been set to music. Here we must include not only those texts for which the musical settings survive but also those stated to be songs but surviving only in poetic form. The latter *may* never have been set to music, of course, although this would have been an improbable accident of history. I shall discuss the texts concerned in chronological order.

The earliest is the indecent song taught to the audience by the worldlings in *Mankind*: there is no musical notation.[115] The text reads as follows:

[NOUGHT]   Yt ys wretyn wyth a coll, yt ys wretyn wyth a cole,
NEW GYSE, NOWADAYS   Yt ys wretyn wyth a colle, yt ys wretyn wyth a colle,
NOUGHT   He þat schytyth wyth hys hoyll, he þat schytyth wyth hys hoyll,
NEW GYSE, NOWADAYS   He þat schytyth wyth hys hoyll, he þat schytyth
                        wyth hys hoyll,
NOUGHT   But he wyppe hys ars clen, but he wype hys ars clen,
NEW GYSE, NOWADAYS   But he wype hys ars clen, but he wype hys ars clen,
NOUGHT   On hys breche yt xall be sen, on hys breche yt xall be sen.
NEW GYSE, NOWADAYS   On hys breche yt xall be sen, on hys breche yt xall
                        be sen.
Cantant OMNES   Hoylyke, holyke, holyke! holyke, holyke, holyke!

(Mankind 335–43)

As can be seen, each of the first four text lines is presented twice by Nought and the whole repeated by New Gyse and Nowadays, apparently leading the audience. Thus each text unit is sung four times in a row. If the audience repeat is ignored, the

---

[113] It is impossible to know when this was: but since the text incipit was apparently in the Exemplar, it was presumably in the first half of the sixteenth century (see *Essays*, 48).

[114] For example, of the 32 items in *A Handfull of Pleasant Delites* (1584), 26 name a tune and another can be sung 'To anie pleasant tune': see *Handfull* (facsimile), Rollins 1924/1965, and Ward, 'Music for *A Handefull of pleasant delites*'.

[115] I follow Chaplan, 148, n. 5, in using Kathleen Ashley's term 'worldlings' for these characters, who are neither devils nor vices. Further on the representational function of this song, see pp. 199–200, below.

song still has repeated lines, which seem to give it the form of a children's song. It clearly is *not* a children's song, however, though it could no doubt be a parody of one. Is there any chance at all that it was pre-existent?

If such scatalogical songs had any common currency, they apparently failed to enter the written tradition and remained in the oral one. Some parts of *Gammer Gurton's Needle* are reminiscent of the *Mankind* song, but there is no direct connection and the chronological gap must be eighty years or so. If they belong to a continuing tradition, it was still an oral one. This text, though, does sound like one written for the purpose, specially for *Mankind*: its apparently innocent first line followed by concentrated indecency neatly divided up between the next three lines surely indicates that it was written with this specific purpose in mind. It is hard to imagine the continuation of a pre-existent song that started this way, or indeed how it began if this is not the start.

On the other hand, the speech heading 'Cantant OMNES' for the refrain line, rather than Nought for the first half-line and New Gyse and Nowadays for the repeat, might at first sight suggest the reverse. If the audience, as well as the worldlings, are to sing from the beginning of the line, clearly they were expected to know the refrain line even if the worldlings are teaching them the rest. Second thoughts suggest, however, that since only the worldlings are specified in previous speech headings for the song, OMNES refers only to them: and in this case it merely requires all three worldlings to deliver this refrain line at its first presentation. The audience – if they are still singing by then, which is surely doubtful – can still sing the repeat ('holyke, holyke, holyke!'), as before. On balance, then, I see no reason to think that this is either a pre-existent song or a (recognisable) parody of one. No doubt a *tune* well known to the audience was chosen for it, but that is a different question.

The fifteenth-century *Ordinalia* from Cornwall provide two possible lyrics. The first, from the *Origo Mundi*, is apparently derived from Psalm 150, perhaps with over-tones of Daniel 3/5 ('at what time ye hear the sound of the cornet, flute, harp, sackbut, psaltery, dulcimer, and all kinds of musick, ye fall down and worship the golden image . . .'):

whethoug menstrels ha tabours	Blow minstrels and tabours;
trey-hans harpes he trompours	Three hundred harps and trumpets;
cythol crowd fylh he savtry	Dulcimer, fiddle, viol, and psaltery;
psalmus gyttrens he nakrys	Shawms, lutes, and kettle drums;
organs in weth cymbalys	Organs, also cymbals,
recordys ha symphony.	Recorders, and symphony.

(Ordinalia 1/1995–2000)

King David is speaking. The list of instruments is reminiscent of banquet scenes in medieval romances, but there are such lists in the Psalms of David (Psalm 80 (AV 81) for instance). Every instrument-name here is a loan-word from English: literally they are tabors, (three hundred) harps, trumpeters, citole, crowd, viol (?fiddle), psaltery, shawm, gittern, nakers, organs (presumably in the specific sense, not meaning 'instruments of music'), chime-bells, recorders and symphony. Psalm 150 mentions the instruments in the following order:

v.3: laudate eum in sono tubae;   [trumpet
         . . . in psalterio et cithara.   [psaltery and harp
4:      . . . in tympano et choro   [tabor and symphony
         . . . in chordis et organo.   [strings and organ
5:      . . . in cymbalis benesonantibus;   [chime-bells
         . . . in cymbalis jubilationis.

The order of instruments in the *Origo Mundi* is certainly not that of the psalm, and seems to have been decided mainly by the need to keep to the aabccb rhyme-scheme. It is no doubt for similar reasons concerning the versification that the 'chordis' of the psalm has been expanded into a list. One result of this is the appearance of several instruments not specified in the psalm – citole, crowd, viol/fiddle, shawm, gittern, nakers and recorders.

Robert Manning's translation (1303), with a much simpler tail-rhyme versification, keeps the instruments in something close to the order of the psalm, with the trumpet and psaltery after the harp, tabor and symphony:

> Yn harpe, yn tabour, and symphan gle,
> W[u]rschepe god yn trumpes and sautre.
> Yn cordes, and organes, and bellys ryngyng,
> Yn alle þese, w[u]rschepe 3e heuene kyng.
>   (Mannyng *Handlyng Synne*, 4773–6)

The Cornish passage has 'organs' in the plural, as Manning does but the Psalter does not,[116] and it also spells out a number of stringed instruments, not specified by the Psalter and Manning. It is tempting even so to suspect that the *Ordinalia*'s 'recordys' is a mistake for 'cordys', but there are considerable difficulties with the apparent meanings of these instrument names, and 'recordys' may well reflect the English translation 'pipe', as in the 1549 prayerbook:[117]

> Prayse him in the sounde of the trumpet:
> prayse hym vpon the lute and harpe.
> Prayse hym in the cymbales and daunse:
> praise him vpon the stringes and pipe.
> Prayse him vpon the wel tuned cymbales:
> praise hym vpon the loud cymbales.

No doubt other commentaries and translations have similar variants, although the three hundred harps (which would be impossible to stage) seem to be a unique reading. Otherwise, the dramatist apparently intended a recognisable allusion to Psalm 150 without directly quoting any one source.

In *Resurrectio Domini* the three Maries three times say or sing a couplet that seems to be the refrain of a recognisable song:

---

[116] 'Organs' is what we should now call 'an organ', but it can also mean 'instruments of music'. The first meaning is apparently intended here.

[117] Staley 1903, 261; Harrison 1910, 207–8.

61

ellas mornyngh y syngh mornyngh y cal
our lorde ys deyd that bogthe ovs al.

(Ordinalia 3/733–4, 753–4, 779–80)

The fact that this is in English, not Cornish, suggests that it might be part of a pre-existent lyric, and its use as a refrain – albeit a sung refrain to spoken dialogue, it seems – strengthens the supposition. I have not been able to find this text, however.[118]

The next texts to be considered are found in the two surviving plays from the Coventry cycle. Both of these plays are revisions by Robert Croo of earlier texts; both plays included songs in English; and in both cases the songs are collected at the end of the manuscript, with the name of Thomas Mawdycke attached.[119]

The Weavers' play of the Purification and Doctors in the Temple survives in what is apparently the guild's own prompt copy. The document still belongs to the guild – now the Broadweavers and Clothiers – but is held in the Coventry City Record Office for safe keeping.[120] A colophon on the penultimate page states that the text is a revision made by Robert Croo and completed on 2 March 1534.[121] Two leaves of an earlier text, apparently that from which Croo worked, survived with Croo's revision.[122] On the last page, following Croo's colophon, are the texts of two songs. These song texts are written in two different hands which King says are 'roughly contemporaneous with the [play] text'. The name 'Thomas Mawdycke' appears at the top of the page in yet another hand, which King characterises as 'seventeenth-century'.[123] It has always been assumed that these song texts belong to the play, although in fact there is no real evidence that they do.

The first song text is in two stanzas and has the name 'Rychard' at the end. King reviews the evidence concerning men called Richard, but comes to no conclusion

---

118 If this is a refrain, rather than a carol burden, it would probably never be indexed. The new resource of texts on CD-ROM will eventually overcome this problem, presumably.

119 Further on this matter, see 3.4, below.

120 King ['Introduction'], [21]. Dr King's work on this manuscript is the first substantial study since Craig's edition. I am grateful to her and to Peter Meredith for allowing me to see a typescript of the introduction to the forthcoming facsimile.

121 Croo completed his revision of the Shearmen and Tailors' play on 14 March that year. Ingram gave the year as 1535, since the Coventry civic and guild records use old-style dates with the year starting on 25 March. In this he is followed by Lancashire: see *REED.Coventry*, liii, and Lancashire, 115. However, the play manuscripts are not records of that sort, so that old-style dates cannot be assumed. In addition, 14 March 1535 was Passion Sunday, and even if Croo were working on that day, one might expect him to have mentioned it. In 1534, 2 March was a Monday and 14 March a Saturday. Croo names the mayor and the masters of the two guilds at the date he gives, but the relevant Coventry records are lost and the problem cannot be solved by ascertaining their dates of office.

122 See Craig *Two Coventry Plays*, xxxv–xxxviii. On Robert Croo, see *REED.Coventry*, *passim*, and Wickham *Early English Stages* I, 299.

123 King ['Introduction'], [12]. These hands are however impossible to date with any certainty within a period of some decades. It is notable that Mawdycke did not write any explanation of the songs for the Weavers' play, as he did for those of the Shearmen and Tailors' play: this suggests to me principally that he did not have the musical settings in front of him when he appended his name to the manuscript of the Weavers' play.

as to his identity, nor as to whether he was the copyist, composer, poet, or more than one of those.[124] The song was evidently written specifically for the dramatic situation concerned, Simeon's rejoicing at the angel's message that he will see the Messiah. At the narrative level, then, this text fits into the play after line 636, where Craig suggests it.[125] It is not quite as simple as this, however, since the dialogue requires Simeon's assistants to ring the bells at this stage, and to sing only on Christ's arrival:[126] but the direction 'Cantant' there is marginal and later than Croo's text, so it apparently indicates a necessary directorial amendment to the play at the time that the songs were added to it.

The song text itself, 'Rejoyce, rejoyce, all that here be', has no known concordance. Greene lists only one Candlemas carol, which is not as specific to the occasion as this song, and none beginning 'Rejoyce'.[127] The nearest reminiscence I can find is in the 'Carol for Christmas Day' that starts 'From Virgin's womb this day', written by Francis Kindlemarsh c.1570 and set by Byrd in his *Songs of Sundrie Natures* (1589):[128] here the two-line refrain is

> Rejoice, rejoice, with heart and voice,
> In Christ his birth this day rejoice.

This reproduces the metre, but not the rhyme-scheme, of the four-line Coventry stanza. I give here the first stanza of the two:

> Rejoyce, rejoyce, all that here be,
> The Angell these tythyng hath browght,
> That Simion, before he dye,
> Shalle se the Lorde which all hathe wrowght.   (Craig *Coventry*, 70)

The date may or may not be about right: all we can say about the Coventry song text is that it postdates Croo's revision in 1534 and was probably copied into the manuscript no later than the last performance, which was that of 1579.

The second song in this play also seems to be without concordances. The first stanza seems quite unsuitable for the Weavers' play:

> Beholde, now hit ys come to pase,
> That manye yeres before was tolde,
> How that Christ, owre ryght Messyas,
> By Jwdas scholde be bowght and solde!   (Craig *Coventry*, 70)

The remaining two stanzas seem equally irrelevant to the play, for they deal with

124 *Ibid.*, [12]–[13]. In a private communication Dr King has noted that the hand is close to that of Richard Pixley, who wrote his name elsewhere in the margins; and that the positioning of the name on the page does not suggest 'Richard' 's role as copyist, composer or poet. The lack of a surname probably argues against these roles, also.
125 Craig *Coventry*, 45.
126 See p. 264, below.
127 Greene *Early English Carols*, 84–5 and *passim*.
128 Edited by Edmund H. Fellowes as *The English Madrigal School* 15 (London: Stainer & Bell, 1920), no. 35.

the Crucifixion in relation to the process of Salvation.[129] This matter is however discussed in Simeon's rehearsal of messianic prophecy in **Coventry 2/233–46**,[130] and there are resonances in the language that suggest a connection: compare, for instance, the b-rhyme and fourth line of the following,

> SIMEON   O feythefull frynde and louer dere!
>   To you this texte ofte haue I tolde,
>   That the lyght of Leyve amonge vs here
>   In Isaraell schuld be boght and sold.   **(Coventry 2/233–6)**

with those of the stanza quoted above; and part of Simeon's prayer,

> [SIMEON]   Reycomforde [me] when hit ys thy plesure.   **(Coventry 2/282)**

with the last two lines of the song:

>   Reycownfort vs bothe gret and small,
>   that yn thy trewth we lyve and dye!   (Craig *Coventry*, 71)

It is also possible that the song belongs somewhere between the Crucifixion and the Resurrection, in a play now lost. As we have seen, such resonances and connections of language and material between plays are known elsewhere. In this case, indeed, there is an external connection in James Hewitt, whose name (as 'Iamis hewyt') appears below the song, as if he were the poet, composer or scribe. Hewitt was well known in Coventry, and not least for his involvement with the plays: Ingram offers a brief biographical note,[131] but Hewitt deserves a thorough biography. For the present, however, it will be enough to say that he was a city wait and organist, and to state the part he played in the pageants of various guilds.[132]

Hewitt played his own regals (reed organ) in the Weavers' pageant in various years starting in 1554 (his earliest appearance in any records) and ending in 1573 (although later payments to an un-named musician may be to Hewitt). He also played the regals for the Drapers between 1563 and 1568.[133] The Smiths hired the city waits for their play in 1549, and perhaps also in 1555 and 1561, so Hewitt may have been involved there, too. The records raise the possibility, in fact, that Hewitt performed for all three guilds in 1561 and perhaps in other years: but, as the discussion in 8.3 below suggests, the logistics of the performance almost certainly did not allow this. Hewitt may have been paid by the Smiths for work on their part

---

[129] Craig *Coventry*, 71.
[130] I am grateful to Dr King for reminding me of this.
[131] *REED.Coventry*, 573, quoted in King, [13]; see also *REED.Coventry*, 566, where Ingram discusses the songs.
[132] The information in the next paragraph is taken from *REED.Coventry*, *passim*.
[133] Hewitt apparently performed for both companies in all the years when he is named in the Drapers' accounts – i.e. 1563 and 1565–8 inclusive. As I demonstrate below, pp. 341–3, it was almost certainly possible for him to do this.

of *The Destruction of Jerusalem* in 1584.[134] He was probably retired or dead by 1590, by which time the trumpeter Goldston had become leader of the waits.[135]

It is interesting to note that in 1573 and 1577 the other three waits – Richard Sadler, Thomas Nicholas and Richard Stiff – are recorded as singing men in Holy Trinity Church,[136] so that at that time the four waits could have formed a singing group led by the chief wait, Hewitt, supporting the voices on the regals. Richard Sadler and Richard Stiff are two of the candidates offered by Ingram (albeit without much conviction) as the copyist of 'Rejoyce, rejoyce'. The suggestion is given some credence by the appearance of another wait, Thomas Nicholas, as the copyist of songs for the Cappers. In all there are five payments for the production of songs or written music in the plays (page-numbers in parentheses refer to *REED.Coventry*):

  (1)   1563, Cappers: 'to the syngers & makynge the songe ij s iiij d' (223)
  (2)   1566, Cappers: 'for prikynge the songes xvj d' (236)
  (3)   1566, Drapers: 'to Thomas nycles for settyng a songe xij d' (237)
  (4)   1568, Cappers: 'for prikynge the songes, xij d' (245)
  (5)   1569, Cappers: 'Thomas Nyclys for prikinge þe songes xij d' (249)

To 'prick' a song is to copy it, so there is no doubt about the activity in question in (2), (4) and (5): evidently the songs for the Cappers' play had to be recopied frequently, presumably for rehearsal purposes. The Cappers' accounts seem to make a distinction between 'make' and 'prick', however, which suggests that in 1563 the songs were being composed. That is certainly the meaning of 'setting', so that we can be sure that Thomas Nicholas was the composer of a song for the Drapers in 1566. The only other person named as pricking songs in the Coventry records at this time was Thomas Wotton, who copied 'songs' for Holy Trinity Church in 1559–60.[137]

These items, then, tell us that at least one of the Coventry waits in the 1560s could compose a song for the plays. As noted above, the 'Rychard' of *Rejoice, rejoice* is most likely to be Richard Pixley and – whoever it was – not the poet or composer. We need not consider Stiff or Sadler in these roles, therefore, although it is possible that they were capable of such work. On the other hand, James Hewitt's name does seem to be an attribution, and it will not be unreasonable to think of him as a possible poet or composer of the song 'Beholde, now hit ys come to pase'. The Cappers probably played the Harrowing of Hell, the Resurrection, and the post-Resurrection appearances;[138] where this song would certainly be suitable. 'Beholde, now hit ys come to pase' may belong to the Cappers' play, then, and there is consequently a possibility that this is the song composed in 1563.

---

[134] The payment to 'Hewette for fetchynge of the hoggesheaddes' is surely not to the musician; and I am almost as doubtful about that to 'Hewet for hys paynes', although this follows shortly after a payment to drummers and before those to the actors. Both are in *REED.Coventry*, 308.

[135] *REED.Coventry*, 588.

[136] *REED.Coventry*, 491.

[137] *REED.Coventry*, 494. 'Song' at this time could mean any piece of music, not necessarily vocal or texted, and not always secular.

[138] Craig *Two Coventry Plays*, xv–xvi; Craig *English Religious Drama*, 287–91; Lancashire, 115–16.

The two songs in the Shearmen and Tailors' play of the Nativity and Slaughter of the Innocents had survived with their musical settings intact when the play was edited by Thomas Sharp. The manuscript from which Sharp worked, like that of the Weavers' play, was evidently the guild's own prompt copy. Croo's colophon says that he finished revising the play on 14 March 1534, only twelve days after he completed his work on the Weavers' play. The manuscript was destroyed in a fire at the Birmingham Free Library in 1879, however, and Sharp's edition in his *Dissertation on the Pageants . . . at Coventry* (1825) is now the only source of the play.[139] It is a quasi-facsimile which purports to show the orthography and layout of the original. King has compared Sharp's Abbotsford Club edition of the Weavers' play with the manuscript, and regards Sharp's work as an accurate edition in which signs of 'creative editing' are absent: and she therefore concludes that we can 'take an optimistic view of his [edition of the Shearmen and Tailors' play] as being a reasonably accurate copy of that now missing manuscript'.[140] There are no song texts in the body of the play, although SDs show that the shepherds sing twice and the mothers of the Innocents once: but at the end of the play text three songs are copied, first the words alone and then the musical settings in the same order.[141] In both places the songs are headed 'Song I.', 'Song II.' and 'Song III.', respectively.

There are two general headings above the song texts. The first reads:[142] 'Theise Songes / belonge to / The Taylors & Shearemens Pagant. / The first and the last the shepheardes singe / and the second or middlemost the women singe.' Below this is the second heading: 'Thomas Mawdycke / die decimo tertio Maij anno dñi millessimo quingentesimo nonagesimo primo.', followed by a note of the mayor and 'consuls' of that year. This second heading was evidently written by or for Mawdycke on 13 May 1591, then, as an explanation for what follows: but what of the first? Could it have been written by Sharp as an editorial explanation of his material, or was it also written by Mawdycke, or by someone else? The orthography of that first heading rules out Sharp, and indeed anyone later than c.1650, but it is still possible that someone other than Mawdycke collected the songs together, perhaps even some decades later.

It is however most likely that Mawdycke himself was responsible for the first heading. As already mentioned, his name appears also at the head of the song texts at the end of the Weavers' play, so that he had apparently undertaken the task of collecting material for music in at least two of the Coventry plays.[143] A probable reason for this is suggested by the facts surrounding the cycle at Coventry in the

---

139 There was in fact an earlier edition by Sharp, in 1817, from which the better-known publication of 1825 differs very little. The 1825 edition was published in facsimile in 1973.

140 King ['Introduction'], [22]. Sharp's edition of the Weavers' play is *Presentation* (1836).

141 Sharp *Dissertation*, 113–118. Further on the musical settings and the underlaid text, see 3.4, below.

142 This heading and the next (beginning 'Thomas Mawdycke') are centred on the page and use a variety of fonts and type sizes. I have not attempted to reproduce the typographical details, which (as distinct from the orthography) I think irrelevant for our present purpose.

143 However, the writer of the note does not say that the song texts at the end of the Weavers' play actually belong to it: see also n. 123, above.

late sixteenth century.[144] The performance of the cycle in 1579 was, as it turned out, the last one. Although civic drama continued in Coventry, the next production – that of 1584 – was the less costly *Destruction of Jerusalem*, and even that was not performed annually. There was a question of a performance of some kind in 1591, however, for on 19 May that year the Council acceded to a request by the citizens for a drama to be played, and allowed *The Destruction of Jerusalem*, *The Conquest of the Danes* or *The History of King Edward IV* '& non other playes' to be presented.[145] This decree came only six days after Mawdycke had written his heading on the music for the Shearmen and Tailors' play, and the closeness of the dates surely cannot be coincidental.[146] Probably at least some people hoped for a return to the city's traditional cycle drama, and this, after a gap of twelve years, would certainly entail a review of texts, properties, and so on, and the kind of collection of relevant material such as Mawdycke's activities represent. Mawdycke's first heading, then, is an explanation of the use to which the songs were put in the play, presumably for the benefit of a possible director. Since that performance did not take place, and the cycle was never played again, we are probably very lucky indeed that the music survived with the play text.

The next problem with these songs concerns their order. 'Song I.' is, as John Stevens pointed out,[147] only the first verse of the song, for 'Song III.' is set to the same music and constitutes a second verse. 'Song II.' is the lullaby sung by the mothers of the Innocents, the famous 'Coventry carol'. The present order of the songs is incorrect, then, for the shepherds do not reappear after the scene of the Massacre of the Innocents, so that Songs I and III must both be sung before Song II. In fact, however, Songs I and III are not sung (as all previous commentators have suggested)[148] on separate occasions. The Prophets whose discussion separates the two main parts of the play say clearly that the shepherds left the stable praising God (**Coventry 1/449–51** and **466–9**), a description that will not fit Song III, 'Down from Heaven'. It seems, then, that at **Coventry 1/277+sd** ('There the scheppardis syngis ASE I OWT RODDE . . .') the shepherds sing both verses of 'As I out-rode' (that is, Song I and Song III),[149] some other song, not identified, being performed at **1/331+sd** ('There the scheppardis syngith ageyne . . .').

Who put the songs in this order, and who numbered them? The order was made,

---

144 For this period in the city's dramatic history, see *REED.Coventry*, xix.

145 *REED.Coventry* xix, 332. The words '& non other playes' seem designed to prevent the cycle or any other politically-unacceptable drama from being played.

146 Mawdycke's activity could of course have been simply that of an antiquarian, and indeed his care to date his presentation of the material suggests this: but the evidence of civic consideration of the drama at this time makes it probable that his purpose was a more immediate one.

147 Stevens 1958, 91.

148 Craig *Coventry*, 12, followed by Stevens 1958, 91, and Dutka 1980, 7. Further on this matter, see my comments in *Contexts*, 203. My suggested identification of Mawdycke with the copyist of the songs, however, I now withdraw, for reasons given here.

149 The director has some flexibility here, presumably: the shepherds do not necessarily *need* to sing both verses, but the production may demand the time required for this. All things being equal, there is no reason for the shepherds not to sing both verses.

or at least authenticated, by the writer of the first heading, and this was probably Mawdycke, as we have seen. The numbering could have been added by any interested party, including Mawdycke or Sharp. Whoever numbered the songs did so according to the order given in the first heading, so the songs were in the wrong order as early as 1591. It seems to me unlikely that Mawdycke was responsible, however: if the songs were written on three separate sheets of paper which were simply shuffled into the wrong order, it seems strange that Mawdycke read the play carefully enough to see who sang which song but not carefully enough to see that the shepherds cannot have sung after the Massacre scene. The most likely solution is that someone prior to Mawdycke had numbered the songs, incorrectly, at the top of each, and Mawdycke did not correct this numbering but merely gave the necessary information about the performers. Of course, Mawdycke's acceptance of the incorrect numbering would be virtually inevitable if the songs were not only numbered but also physically fixed in the present order – perhaps stitched or glued together (although not, apparently, bound in with the play) – when they came into his hands. This is a question that presumably will never be answered.

We must nevertheless speculate on the reason for this ordering. It may be an accident of the scribe's layout that the two stanzas of 'As I out rode' were on separate pieces of paper or parchment, but I think not. The copy of 'Doune from heaven' demands a knowledge of 'As I out rode', because the treble part is incomplete: it breaks off in the middle of the refrain, so that the singer must either know the refrain already or have the copy of 'As I out rode' alongside that of 'Doune from heaven'. (This matters only in rehearsal, of course: in performance the song must have been memorized anyway, presumably.) But the decorative final note and 'finis' of the tenor part of 'As I out rode' need to be explained. Perhaps the copyist had forgotten that there was a second stanza to come: certainly the lack of these features in the treble and bass parts is evidence that 'As I out rode' was not the only stanza in existence at the time. On the other hand a copyist is likely to copy what is there rather than to add what is not, which suggests that the decorative ending and the 'finis' were there already. If they were at the end of the treble and bass parts as well, the copyist remembered not to include them, knowing that there was a second stanza, but forgot this when he copied the tenor part. The two stanzas were probably separate, then, at that time. It seems to me possible, therefore, that the song originally consisted of the first stanza only; that the second stanza was added at some stage, perhaps to reduce the considerable discrepancy between a very short shepherds' song and the much longer lullaby, on a separate piece of paper or parchment; and that this format confused the scribe of the copy used by Sharp. The copy known to Sharp may have been the original copy of the second stanza, of course; and the addition of the second stanza may be related to the move from the old version of the play to Croo's revision, although it need not have been.

The question of numbering depends on another factor: Who copied the separate texts? Sharp himself might have provided them as an edited text to which he could refer in his notes,[150] but he clearly did not: first, he does not tell us of his addition

---

[150] *Dissertation*, 123f.

2.6 *Lyrics and Song-texts*

although he tells us, for instance, of his addition of accents to assist pronunciation;[151] second, the orthography of the text does not follow the underlaid text of any particular voice throughout, but nevertheless keeps within the bounds of orthographic variants there; and third, the song texts at the end of the Weavers' play are in sixteenth-century hands. These latter appear on the last page (f. 17v) of the Weavers' manuscript and are therefore not physically separate from the text of the play.[152] Either Mawdycke or (more probably) someone earlier copied the separate song texts in the Shearmen and Tailors' play.

The date of composition of these songs cannot be determined with any accuracy (see 3.4, below). Their style is compatible with a date contemporary with Croo's revision in 1534, but would equally have been possible in 1591. On balance, however, the vocabulary and orthography suggest to me a date in the earlier part of this period. In the shepherds' song the word 'enderes' would surely be out of date by the middle of the sixteenth century, as would the spellings 'ioli' and 'mereli'; similarly, the use of the thorn suggests a date in the first half of the century (the Y is used in the music's underlaid text, but this is presumably because the italic typeface used there did not include a thorn among the punches), as does the abbreviation 'shepp^{ds}' in the underlaid text. The lullaby is if anything a little more old-fashioned in these respects: the use of 'yongling', the spelling of 'tyne', 'chargid' and 'thi', and the abbreviation 'þ^w' for 'thow', with its thorn, all suggest a date perhaps even earlier than that of the shepherds' song. On the whole, these texts could easily be older than Croo's revision, in which case the direction for 'Ase I owt Rodde' at **1/277+sd** may well be for the text (and perhaps the music) as we have it.

As to the texts themselves, although there are no known concordances there are certainly a number of relatives. Compare the opening line of the shepherds' song, for instance,

> As I out rode this enderes night

with some of the opening lines listed by Greene:[153]

> Als I me lay this endryes nyth (no. 149b)
>
> Als I me rode this endre dai (no. 450)
>
> As I me went this enderday (no. 149c).

None of these is otherwise close to the Coventry song. (No. 149 is however a lullaby). Similarly, there are many songs of the 15th and 16th centuries that use the refrain 'Tyrly tyrlo', which Greene says is an onomatopoeic phrase for the sound of a pipe.[154] Closest to the Coventry shepherds' song, which Greene lists as no. 79B, is a fifteenth-century carol that uses the *Tyrly tyrlow* phrase in the burden and is also

---

[151] *Dissertation*, 83.

[152] King ['Introduction'], [3]. The *recto* of this last leaf bears the end of the play text, including Croo's colophon.

[153] *Early English Carols*, index on p. 508.

[154] *Early English Carols*, 360 (notes to no. 79): Greene presumably means a bagpipe.

69

close to other Coventry lines. The similarities are all in the burden and first two stanzas (of seven):

> Tyrle, tyrlo,
> So merylye the shepperdes began to blowe.

1   Abowt the fyld thei pyped full right
Even abowt the middes off the nyght;
Adown frome heven thei saw cum a lyght.
   Tyrle, tirlo.

2   Off angels ther came a company
With mery songes and melody
   . . .

When this is compared to the complete Coventry song it becomes clear that the poet of the latter probably knew this song – of which, incidentally, Greene lists a sixteenth-century version.[155]

> As I out rode this enderes night
> Of thre ioli sheppardes I saw a sight
> And all a bowte there fold a star shone bright.
>   They sange terli terlow
>   So mereli the sheppards ther pipes can blow.
>
> Doune from heaven, from heaven so hie,
> Of angeles ther came a great companie
> With mirthe and ioy and great solemnitye.
>   The sange terly terlow . . .
>   (Craig *Coventry*, 31–2; Sharp *Dissertation*, 113–15 and 118)

As Dutka points out, the third line of the Balliol College version of the first stanza is even closer to the Coventry song: 'Adown frome heven that ys so hygh'.[156]

Comparison with the complete text of 79A also suggests that the Coventry text is incomplete.[157] We are not told what the angels sang, although it is clearly the *Gloria in excelsis deo*, as we discover in 79A and many other shepherds' songs. This fact is obscured by the refrain, however, for in the second stanza we hear 'The sange terly terlow' as referring to the angels (and therefore erroneously as completing the sense of the stanza), although it actually refers to the shepherds. Thus it seems to me possible that the Coventry shepherds' song was pre-existent or, more likely, that the song originally consisted of more than the two stanzas that have survived. Another shepherds' song – one that can be identified as non-dramatic – similarly has an

---

155 *Early English Carols*, no. 79A.b. Both versions are now in Oxford: the 15th-century one, no. 79A.a, is from the Bodleian Library, MS Eng. poet. e. 1, f. 60r, while the 16th-century one is from Balliol College MS 354, f. 222r. In view of this carol, could the 'can' of the Coventry refrain be a mishearing for the '[be]gan' of the carol's burden?

156 Greene *Early English Carols*, 41–2; Dutka 1980, 76.

157 Not, however, in the way that Greene's '[burden lacking]' suggests: *As I out rode* is not a carol but a strophic part-song with refrain. (The common but inaccurate designation of these songs as 'carols' is in relation to their appropriateness to the Christmas season, not to a technical description of them as having a formally-separate burden.)

opening pair of stanzas that could be appropriated for use in a shepherds' play. This song, *Wee happy heardsmen here*, has been suggested as a dramatic song, and is discussed in Appendix C.

The lullaby 'Lully lulla thow littell tine child' is also unique but with some close relatives. Greene lists twelve lullaby carols of which 'lullay' is the first word of the burden and/or the first stanza,[158] including (burden/first line)

> Lullay lullay litel childe/Lullay lullay litel child (no. 155a)
>
> Lullay lullay my lityl chyld/How suld I now . . . (no. 147)
>
> Lullay lullay thow lytil child/Thys other nyghth (no. 151C)
>
> Lullay lullay thow lytil child/Lullay lullay litel child (no. 155b)

Greene has more than eighteen pages of lullaby carols (nos. 142–55),[159] although they do not all start with the word 'lullay'. Reading through them establishes a strong feeling of a tradition resulting in inter-related texts – in fact, overlapping traditions, as the first stanza-line of no. 151C suggests (see also the comment on no. 149b, p. 69 above). Of these songs, however, only the Coventry one (Greene's no. 112) is a lullaby sung by anyone other than the Virgin Mary or to anyone other than the Christ-child.[160] Of the lullabies listed in the *Index of Middle English Verse* only one is not a lullaby of the BVM, and even so it is closely related to some in Greene's list.[161] Greene's collection of carols of the Innocents (nos. 108–12) reveals no relatives of the Coventry lullaby, and the IMEV shows nothing related, either. These lists are far from comprehensive, it is true, but the lack of related material suggests even so that the Coventry lullaby stems from a general tradition only, and that it is unusual in not being a song of the Blessed Virgin to the Christ-child.[162] Here, even more than in the case of the shepherds' song, it seems likely that the text was written specially for the play.

The remaining song-texts are without musical settings. We shall consider next the drinking song in **Chester 3**. Lumiansky and Mills dated the Exemplar from the first half of the sixteenth century, but there is of course no way of telling how old is the play that has come down to us.[163] The song consists of three stanzas:

> 29   The fludd comes fleetinge in full faste
>   One everye syde that spredeth full farre.

---

[158] *Early English Carols*, index on p. 511.

[159] When referring to Greene's listing it is necessary to note that not all of the texts presented are technically carols, although most are.

[160] This song is sung by the mothers of the Innocents to their children. Although one can imagine the song starting as a lullaby of the Virgin to the Child, the line 'O sisters too' suggests otherwise.

[161] IMEV, no. 2025: see *ibid.*, pp. 318–19.

[162] There was a tradition relating Rachel, the mothers of the Innocents, and the Blessed Virgin, however.

[163] *Essays*, 48.

> For fere of drowninge I am agaste.
> Good gossippe, lett us drawe nere.
>
> 30 And lett us drinke or wee departe
> For oftetymes wee have done soe.
> For at one draught thou drinke a quarte
> And soe wyll I doe or I goe.
>
> 31 Here is a pottell full of malnesaye good and stronge
> Yt will rejoyse both harte and tonge.
> Though Noe thinke us never so longe
> Yett wee wyll drinke atyte.   **(Chester 3/225–36)**

The passage is variously headed 'The Good Gossips' (HmRB), 'The Good Gossip' (H), and 'The Good Gossipes Songe' (A): the heading is a SH in HmARH, but it is marginal in B. The absence of the word 'song' in HmRBH does not positively preclude singing, but we should be clear that A is the only version to mention a song.

Despite the SH in manuscript A, some commentators have treated only stanza 31 as the song, preferring to see the two previous stanzas as introductory speech.[164] One reason for this may be that manuscript H omits stanza 31 entirely, and that because of the undue importance accorded to this by Deimling and Matthews's use of H as their base text, this omission was seen as the difference between the singing SH of A and the non-singing SH of H. Perhaps, like Dutka, they followed F.M. Salter in regarding stanzas 29 and 30 as a late revision, only stanza 31 being part of the original song.[165] Certainly stanzas 29 and 30 have a different rhyme-scheme, while stanza 31 reverts to the form of the 'Chester' stanza, but even so this seems too speculative: to treat the passage thus is to claim that we can distinguish speech (stanzas 29 and 30) from song (stanza 31), and there is no firm evidence to support such a claim. If it is possible to see the whole passage as a song as it is transmitted in manuscript A, then we should need very good evidence that stanzas 29 and 30 ought to be spoken before we can regard that SH as untrustworthy.

The different versions transmitted by the various Chester manuscripts may result from an Exemplar reading that reflects directorial choices made in the past. The passage can be spoken rather than sung, and stanza 31 may be omitted. In fact, the SHs seem to offer three possibilities for performance: spoken, by more than one gossip (HmRB); sung (A); and spoken, by a single gossip (H). The text shows however that a single gossip is addressing Mrs Noah in stanzas 29 and 30, while stanza 31 could be spoken/sung by a single gossip (acting as spokeswoman for the group) or by two or more. The singular reading 'Gossip' in manuscript H, then, is sensible for stanzas 29 and 30, and this manuscript omits stanza 31. Although the SH of HmRB suggests that two or more gossips are speaking or singing, that of manuscript A is ambiguous, and could therefore be singular – the song of a good gossip. One way in which the different readings could have arisen, then, is as follows:

---

[164] Deimling and Matthews I, 57n; Kolve, 262; Carpenter 1968, 16.
[165] Dutka 1980, 78–9; Salter 'Banns', 452.

(1)   Manuscript A's heading, with a singular interpretation, is the original one: 'The good gossip's song';

(2)   The editorial omission of 'songe', intended only to reduce singing to speech, accidentally gave rise to the plural reading of HmRB: 'the good gossip[']s [. . .]' thus became a true speech heading, 'the good gossips';

(3)   Manuscript H gives the correct reduction: 'the good gossip'.

If the SHs can indeed be explained in this way, then stanzas 29–30 are a solo song, with the other gossip(s), and perhaps Mrs Noah, joining in stanza 31. This would account for both the change to the plural pronoun in the text of stanza 31 and for the omission of that stanza from manuscript H, which prefers not to present the 'chorus' to a spoken text.

The three stanzas are firmly specific to the play. There is a request to Mrs Noah ('good gossippe') to let her friends 'drawe nere' – that is, enter the Ark – and Noah himself is named. Moreover, the dramatic situation is a dynamic one such as even narrative songs cannot easily encompass: between stanzas 29 and 30 the gossips change from terror of the flood to an easy-going suggestion of a drinking-party that will delay evasive action, while stanza 31 shows that this is a deliberate ploy.[166] These considerations in themselves show that the text was not pre-existent but was written specially for the play. There is in addition an external reason for thinking that this text is late – probably later than the rest of the play – and therefore not pre-existent. I have suggested elsewhere that **Chester 3/260+sd** in manuscript H, which prescribes the singing of the psalm 'Save mee, O God', shows that Noah and his household sing a metrical version of Psalm 68 (AV 69), and that this would be the version by John Hopkins, first published in Sternhold and Hopkins's psalter of 1561.[167] That being so, then stanza 29 would awaken some powerful allusions to the well-known psalm text about to be sung, for it expresses an anxiety that parallels the spiritual anguish of the psalm, while there are distinct verbal references:

> Saue me O God, and that with speede,
>   the waters flow full fast:
> So nye my soule do they proceede,
>   that I am sore agast.
>
> (Sternhold and Hopkins *Psalter*, edn of 1579)

These references in **Chester 3/225–36** to the psalm to follow may have been subconscious on the dramatist's part, but they could hardly be coincidental. The obvious inference to draw is that the song text was written after 1561, with the metrical psalm in mind, and perhaps by the same man who chose the psalm for **Chester 3/260+sd**. This is not the only solution (the dramatist may have known an earlier version of the psalm, or Hopkins may have drawn on common imagery and vocabulary), but it must certainly be borne in mind. It should be said that stanza 29 is not a parody, and the song cannot be sung to the tune of the metrical psalm.

---

[166] Further on the deceit of the gossips, see below, pp. 201–02.
[167] *Essays*, 157–60.

The Norwich Grocers' play of the Expulsion from Eden provides two lyrics that could be pre-existent. Both were originally set to music, and the stage directions give some information on the settings: but the music is not extant in either case. The earlier text, which Norman Davis calls Text A and which was in use in 1533,[168] requires Adam and Eve to 'syng walkyng to gether abowt the place wryngyng ther handes' after their expulsion from the Garden (**Norwich A/88+sd**). The text of the song is given as the next two lines:

> Wythe dolorous sorowe we maye wayle & wepe
> both nyght & day in sory sythys full depe.   (**Norwich A/89–90**)

According to the direction that follows, these two lines are 'set to musick twice over / and again for a Chorus of 4 parts' (**A/90+sd**). This is at best ambiguous, but I think that it is intended that lines **89–90** shall be sung three times in all, the last occasion being choral.

According to **A/80+sd2** lines **81–88** – which form two stanzas, one each for Adam and Eve – are spoken: '. . . they schall speke this foloyng'. The opening of this passage, however,

ADAM   O with dolorows sorowe we maye wayle & weepe,

suggests that these two stanzas might once have been part of the song. This would certainly require some editorial activity in the text, including the changing of **A/80+sd2** to read 'speke'. It is possible, though, that the whole of **A/81–90** was originally set to music; that for practical or other reasons the amount of singing was cut down; and that the sung part – now only two lines – was then so short that the setting was sung three times in all to make an adequate ending to the play. This is however entirely conjectural: and while it offers an alternative and more music-filled ending for a modern production, it is perfectly possible that lines **89–90** were intended simply to provide a verbal link with the preceding speeches.

This is not quite the end of the matter, however. The Grocers' records for the performance of 1533 show that Sir Stephen Prowet was paid 12d 'for makyng of a newe ballet', while John Bakyn was paid for playing an organ that had been borrowed for the occasion.[169] No singers were paid for this performance, so the heavenly 'Musick' demanded by **A/80+sd1** after the Expulsion must have been instrumental music – that is, the organ-playing of John Bakyn.[170] Prowet's 'ballet', then, has to be this vocal item at **A/88+sd** with **89–90** as the text. This is certainly a short text for a ballet, however, and especially one for which a respected composer

168 NCPF, xxiv.
169 *REED.Norwich*, 339–40. 'Ballet' must here have its early 16th-century meaning of a metrical song, not its later implication of an Italian dance-song with fa-la-la refrains.
170 For heavenly music at the restoration of Divine Order, see p. 183, below, and Stevens 1958, 83. 'Musick' would in any case normally mean *instrumental* music.

was commissioned at a fee of 12d.[171] This is perhaps circumstantial evidence for the surviving song text being a shortened version of what was originally set.

A second song text is in the later version of the play (Text B), which is a reworking dated 1565. There appear to be no concordances for this text, although it contains verbal similarities with the refrain of Francis Kindlemarsh's 'Carol for Christmas Day', mentioned earlier:[172]

> With hart & voyce, let us reioyce, & prayse the Lord alwaye, for/
> this our Joyfull daye, to se <of> this our god his maiestie. who he/
> hath given himselffe. over us, to raygne, & to gouerne us./
> Lett all our harte reioyce together and let us all lifte/
> up our voyce on of us with another.   (**Norwich B/154–61**)

The punctuation and line-ends shown here are according to the oldest extant source, a transcript made by the Norfolk antiquarian John Kirkpatrick (1687–1728) of material originally owned by the Grocers:[173] the word 'of' (in < >) is interlined above, with a caret. At the end is a footnote to 'god his maiestie', which Kirkpatrick has underlined: he says that the original had 'maiestratʃ' at first, and then ?'mai-ralty', and eventually as he gives it.

Kirkpatrick presented the text in continuous prose, probably because the original material did so: but it is obviously in verse, and Davis orders it as a poem.[174] In doing so, however, he notes that the last three lines 'can hardly be restored to regularity'. There is certainly some corruption in the last three lines (and perhaps in the last five), although here, as in lines three and four, there is apparently a neat play of an end-rhyme with an internal rhyme (alwaye / daye, reioyce / voyce). Davis almost gives up on the last three lines, and the result is not satisfactory:

> With hart & voyce
> Let us reioyce
>   And prayse the Lord alwaye
>   For this our joyfull daye,
> To se of this our God his maiestie,
> Who hath given himselffe over us to raygne and to governe us.
> Lett all our harte[s] reioyce together,
> And lett us all lifte up our voyce, on of us with another.

Davis notes two emendations by Manly, but adopts only one, the change to 'hartes'

---

171 Bowers 1980, 318, identifies Prowet as the Dom Stephen Prowett known as the composer of two five-part Latin antiphons surviving in part-books of c.1530, and whose will, proved in 1560, shows that he possessed 'a payer of Clavycords'. Dutka notes (1972, 22) that John Bakyn was an executor of Prowett's will.
172 See p. 63, above.
173 The Grocers' Book, containing the original texts and records, had disappeared by 1856, and nineteenth-century editions used an eighteenth-century transcript as a source. Norman Davis's EETS edition (1970) relied on Robert Fitch's publication of 1856 as the oldest source, but only two years later Kirkpatrick's transcript came to light. For the details of this story, see Davis 1970, xxii–xxvi; Dunn 1972; and Dutka 1984, 1–2. Dutka 1984 prints a facsimile of the Kirkpatrick transcript, which is now in the Norfolk Record Office, Norwich.
174 NCPF (1970), 18.

in the seventh line. Manly presumably made this change on the assumption that the final letter was really an -is sign (ꝑ), used for -es endings in English.[175] But the -e is in fact perfectly clear in Kirkpatrick's manuscript, and Davis would no doubt have reversed that emendation if he had known it. In any case the singular 'harte' is in accord with the 'voyce' of the last line.

Despite Davis's disclaimer about the last three lines, it is surely possible to get a little closer to a putative original. Much depends on the relative importance of various possible internal rhymes and on the possible stress-patterns, so it is rather a matter of taste. I offer here an alternative layout, with punctuation as in Kirkpatrick's transcript:

> With hart & voyce
> let us reioyce,
> & prayse the Lord alwaye,
> for this our Joyfull daye, to se
> of this our god his maiestie.
> who he hath given himselffe over us,
> to raygne, & to gouerne us.
> Lett all our harte reioyce together
> and let us all lifte up our voyce
> on of us with another.

In the sixth line 'given' should be a single syllable ('giv'n'), and in the seventh 'raygne' must take the time of two syllables.

This poem has not been traced. It has the feel of a psalm-paraphrase, and indeed presents the main ideas and some of the vocabulary of Psalm 144 (AV 145), verses 1–7: but these are not unusual in the context of the Psalms.

We learn from the stage direction for this song that it was 'Old Musick Triplex Tenor Medius Bass' (**Norwich B/153+sd**). Davis notes that this direction was 'evidently added by Fitch', but we now know that it appears in Kirkpatrick's transcript and therefore may be original. At first sight this appears to describe music already existing, so that we can posit a copy of the music kept with the Grocers' Book and presumably lost with it. There is however another possibility: namely, that the Grocers never possessed a copy of the music – indeed, perhaps it had not been composed – and that the note is wholly prescriptive of music still to be provided. Our interpretation of it may depend partly on our understanding of the word 'old' – whether it means that the music existed and was in an identifiably 'ancient' style, or that it had been composed a long time ago, or simply that it was in an old manuscript. It is possible, I think, that the musical setting never existed. However, JoAnna Dutka has weighed the evidence carefully and believes that this SD originated with Kirkpatrick, apparently a non-musician whose interest in the verbal text did not extend to the notated music that he saw.[176]

---

[175] See Hector *Handwriting*, 33 and 39; and Petti *English Literary Hands*, 23.
[176] In a private communication.

Of the lyrics or possible lyrics examined here, most seem to have been written specially for the play concerned and are unlikely to have survived in a concordance. On the other hand some apparent lyrics in the plays certainly demonstrate stylistic relationships with non-dramatic literature – in itself far from surprising – and a very few give some cause for hope that a diligent search will have some chance of success in tracking down a pre-existent version. The subject is in any case worth pursuing further, if only to give a better understanding of the various literary types and styles found in the plays. For example, various salutations in which the first word of successive lines is 'Hail' may well belong to a non-dramatic genre, if the descent is not in the other direction. Such passages as Mary's greeting to her Child in **York 14/57–63**, Joseph's in **York 14/106–12**, the Magi's in **York 16/309–44**, the Shepherds' in **Towneley 12/458–84** and **13/710 36**, or the angel's welcome to Mary at her Assumption in **N-Town 40/91–4**, all echo such passages as the opening of Richard Rolle's *A Salutation to Jesus*, 'Heyle Jhesu my creatowre', and the various 'Hail' lyrics listed by Greene.[177] Of course, many such lyrics are based on or derived their impetus from Latin hymns and other liturgical texts beginning 'Ave': so, for example, the third verse of James Ryman's carol *Ave regina celorum* would not be out of place in an Assumption play:[178]

> Haile, flos campi of swete odoure;
> Haile, modur of oure Sauyoure;
> Haile, virginall floure of grete honoure,
>   Velud rosa vel lilium.

It is easy, but not yet very fruitful, to point out such possible connections. At present it is my purpose only to suggest that in trying to decide on the possibility of pre-existent lyrics in the plays, we come up against a much larger literary context, which it is to be hoped will be explored in the future.[179]

Finally, a similar question should be asked about the English paraphrases of Latin texts. Here, too, is a gold-mine – or is it a minefield? – of literary allusion and stylistic interrelation that needs to be examined. One can imagine that a dramatist needing to write a passage of translation of a psalm, say, in English verse might well see advantages in 'lifting' a pre-existent one. The advantages would be for his audience,

---

[177] Rolle *English Writings*, 48; Greene *Carols*, 509. Robinson *Studies*, 71–2, used the word 'lyric' in discussing the first two of those I cite here.

[178] Greene *Carols*, no. 202. This carol quotes the *Ave regina . . . mater regis* text, used in paintings of the Assumption: see Kenney *Walter Frye and the Contenance Anglois*, 69–73, and Rastall 'Repertory', *passim*. For the relations generally between Latin liturgy and English or macaronic lyrics, see Wehrle *Macaronic Hymn Tradition*.
   In relation to discussions of the *Ave regina . . . mater regis* text by Kenney and myself it is interesting that Wynkyn de Worde's York Manual of 1509, which suggests the reciting of five 'Aves' in honour of the Five Joys of Mary, uses this *Ave regina* text for the purpose: see T.F. Simmons, ed., *The Lay Folk's Mass Book* (EETS, 1875), 79.

[179] See Robinson *Studies*, 40, for instance. Robinson's discussion should remind us that a lyric is not necessarily for *singing*. *Ibid.*, 71–3, relates the 'Hail' lyrics of **York 14** to changes of speech register used in manipulating the structural dynamics of the play.

too, and not just for himself: for the recognition of a paraphrase known in a non-dramatic context would make the lessons of the drama more real, and would perhaps also relate the liturgical and homiletic texts more closely to the biblical narrative. Did it ever happen? One would expect that someone would have recognised it by now if that were the case. The inference is, then, that dramatists preferred – or simply found it just as exciting or just as easy – to write new paraphrases as they were needed: and, of course, the metre and rhyme-scheme of the play would not always be compatible with those of a pre-existent poetic text. It is not likely that we shall ever find a pre-existent lyric in a dramatic context, but it is not impossible.

2.7 The use of Latin

The most common use of Latin in the plays, apart from the directions written in Latin, is as the *incipits* of Latin liturgical pieces in the SDs. But the plays also introduce Latin texts and fragments, to a varying extent, in the body of the text. Sometimes it is not clear whether the Latin phrase is intended as a spoken text, as part of a SD, or with some other purpose. There is a spectrum of types of appearance, not all of which are intended to provoke sung performances of Latin liturgical texts. It is therefore important to examine the use of Latin with a view to deciding which was the playwright's intention in each case.

There is no general discussion of the use of Latin in the repertory, but some editors have seriously addressed the matter in relation to individual plays. The subject has been fully treated by Lumiansky and Mills in regard to the evocation of authority in the Chester cycle.[180] According to them, biblical or other authority is evoked in that cycle in order to defend material that is potentially or actually under attack. Lumiansky and Mills considered that many of the Latin quotations in the text started life as MDs, later incorporated into the Exemplar, the copy of the cycle from which the surviving copies were made.[181] By implication, such MDs are likely to date from the middle of the sixteenth century. Lumiansky and Mills list 57 biblical quotations in Latin,[182] with others not readily identifiable as biblical.[183]

The examples discussed fall into three broad categories: the singing of (normally) liturgical items; the use of Latin as an integral part of the stanza-form; and the citing of authority.

First, it is sometimes clear from the dialogue or a SD that a Latin quotation is to be sung. As Lumiansky and Mills point out, in such cases the text is 'liturgical in connotation rather than biblical'.[184] A brief digression is needed to explore the

---

180 *Essays*, 99–110.
181 *Essays*, 101.
182 They also list a further seven in manuscript H's version of Play 5, only one of which corresponds to a quotation given by the Group manuscripts of that play.
183 *Essays*, 100–01. They here use 'biblical' in its widest sense, since they go on to say that the text might be liturgical. 'Scriptural' might have been a better adjective.
184 *Essays*, 102.

implications of this remark.[185] The great majority of liturgical texts are, of course, biblical, a wide range of books being used although the Psalms are the most common source. Non-biblical material in the liturgy consists largely of accretions such as hymns and sequences, which are usually in verse form: these frequently take their ideas directly from biblical sources, however, and may do so in biblical language.[186] Further non-biblical material, usually in prose, appears as the homilies and other readings (from saints' lives, for instance) that form the lessons of the offices: these are in addition to the biblical readings found in both the offices and the Mass. The offices for saints canonized in the Middle Ages were written specially, and are therefore mainly or entirely non-biblical in origin.

Even when a liturgical text was taken directly from the Scriptures, however, it did not usually correspond precisely with the text found in that book known as 'the Bible'. While the Bible itself was usually read in the version by St Jerome known as the Vulgate, liturgical texts mainly derived from older translations, in particular from the *Vetus Latina*. The subject of biblical translations is a complex one that need not be pursued further here, though I shall follow its consequences a little further in Chapter 7. For the moment it is enough to state that, in any scriptural quotation of more than a few words, we may expect that the slight variations between the different Latin versions will show the quotation to be from the Bible itself – that is, the Vulgate – or from the liturgy. To take a well known example, most people educated in medieval subjects, if asked for the opening words of the angelic annunciation to the shepherds, will offer 'Gloria in excelsis deo'. This is in fact the liturgical version, the Vulgate wording being 'Gloria in altissimis deo'.

This brings me to the last stage of my digression. 'The Bible' was not widely read in the Middle Ages: those who could read, understand and discuss it were the few whose task it was to present the doctrine of the Church to the many who could neither read it nor understand it. Liturgy, on the other hand, was the unceasing round of praise in which everyone, to a greater or lesser extent, participated. The distinction made by Lumiansky and Mills between 'liturgical' and 'biblical' connotations is a radical one, then. It is also a vital one for performance of the plays.

Lumiansky and Mills list sixteen occasions in the Chester cycle in which Latin texts are indicated to be sung, and other cycles and plays are comparable in this respect. Examples have been given in sections 2.3 and 2.4, above, and need not be multiplied here. We must however note that the intentions of the original dramatist and those of a reviser or scribe/editor may not be the same, and indeed that a scribe/editor may misinterpret the intentions of the playwright, just as a director may misinterpret the intentions of both. The problem, then, is twofold: first, to disentangle the intentions of those concerned, and to date those intentions; second, to work out precisely what those intentions were.

Rather easier to discuss in terms of performance are those quotations that form

---

[185] For further discussion of this matter, see Chapter 7 below, and especially section 7.1.

[186] See pp. 181–2 below, for instance, for the relations between Isaiah's vision and the prose hymn *Te deum*.

an integral part of the stanzaic text itself. Lumiansky and Mills cite four examples of this, together with eight examples in which a speaker indicates an intention to quote a Latin text. When the text is part of the stanza-form it is clear that the Latin will be spoken, not sung. If the speaker states an intention to quote a text (i.e. the play script does not quote the text at the place where it should be performed), that is an indication that the text will be heard but not that it will be spoken rather than sung. On the other hand, unless it is a liturgical text and there is clear evidence (in SD or text) that it is sung, the assumption must be that it is to be spoken. Can we imagine the Latin being sung, for instance, in such a case as Peter's citation of a text in persuading his fellows to choose a replacement for Judas?

> [PETRUS]   Therfore, as the psalter mynd mase,
>   fullfylled nowe must bee:
>   'Fiat habitatio eius deserta et non [sit] qui habitet in eo. Episcopatum
>   eius accipiat alter.'   (Chester 21/31–2+lat)

Peter continues speaking after this. Clearly the Latin must be heard: it is part of Peter's justification to the Apostles and of the dramatist's justification to us, his audience. But could it be sung rather than spoken? Clearly it could, and if it is a liturgical text – that is, a text that normally *would* be sung – then singing would have some validity as a performance mode for the quotation. It may be worth experimenting with the singing of such quotations in the plays, therefore. On the other hand, there is no reason why it *should* be sung, and singing might even be disruptive of the message being transmitted. In this particular case, as it happens, singing is probably not an option: Lumiansky and Mills identify the quotation as Acts 1/20, which is based on Psalm 68/26 (AV 69/25) and 108/8 (AV 109/8),[187] and this is not, as far as I know, a liturgical text.[188] Some examples of this type cited by Lumiansky and Mills occur in the speeches of characters such as the demons and Antichrist. There, for reasons that will be explained in Chapter 5, singing would seem very unlikely, even if the text in question were a liturgical one.

Lumiansky and Mills are concerned particularly to deal with the texts that seem to be cited as a sort of reference, giving the scriptural authority for the ideas expressed. Although they note that oral performance cannot be demonstrated in every case, they also point out that in some cases where oral performance can be shown the actual biblical reference is given as part of the quotation – for example, in **Chester 23/119–20+lat**:

> [ANTECHRISTE]   I shall rehearse here readelye
>   that clarkes shall understand:

---

187 *Chester* II, 308.

188 By this I mean two things. First, it is not as far as I know a text that actually appears in the liturgy: if it were, the chances are that it would be a spoken/recited text, and a strictly musical performance would not be likely anyway; second, and more particularly, it seems not to be a solo or choral item such as an antiphon, responsory, etc., that would if possible be sung to its own chant tune. These two types of item may be thought of as readings/recitations and 'set piece' musical items, respectively.

'Expecta me in die resurrectionis meae in futurum quia judicium ut congregem
gentes et colligam regna.' Sophoni 3.

The edition's quotation marks are not there, of course, in the original, where there
is nothing to show that the reference has a status different from that of the quotation
itself. Should we, then, assume that the whole is spoken, reference and all? There is
perhaps no reason why it should not be: if the purpose is authentication (which it
is), then the authentication should be presented to everyone, orally, rather than just
to the reader, visually. Although this seems alien to our modern concept of drama,
there is nothing inherently undramatic about it.[189] This does however confirm a
feeling that liturgical singing is not normally appropriate as part of a discourse.
Even if the quotation were a liturgical one, the presence of an orally-presented
reference would seem to preclude singing.

Chester is something of a special case in this regard, for no other cycle or play is
so rich in referenced quotations. It is not unique, however, and so it will be useful
to form a general view of Latin quotations included for reference or authority-giving
purposes: even if the text is a liturgical one, and even if the character presenting the
text is an appropriate one, an oral presentation is likely to be spoken rather than
sung. We should however note that, just as Lumiansky and Mills admit the occasional possibility of a choice as to whether the text is to be declaimed or not, so we
must accept that there may be alternative ways of presenting a text orally – that a
particular director just might wish to have a text sung even if all the indications are
that traditionally it would be spoken.

On reading through a play text it soon becomes apparent that in many cases a
Latin quotation is followed or (more rarely) preceded by a translation, paraphrase
or exegesis of the passage in question. It is indeed one of our problems that this
sometimes makes the oral presentation of the Latin text unnecessary, which is a
reason for thinking that directors may have been able to exercise choice in such
matters. This problem can be solved only through textual criticism, and we need
editors to treat the Latin quotations of other cycles and plays with the thoroughness
of Lumiansky and Mills's treatment of those in the Chester cycle. At the same time,
it will help to have a broader understanding of this problem in European drama
generally, since the use of Latin quotations is common in other vernacular repertories.[190]

The Latin+English (or English+Latin) situation is so common in the repertory
that occasionally one can guess that it is in operation when the pattern is in fact
incomplete. As I have noted elsewhere, the late banns for the Chester cycle mention

---

[189] I can say this from experience, having played Ezechiel in **Chester 22** during Oakshott's 1983
production of the cycle. There was no feeling of incongruity in the prophets of Antichrist
giving the reference after each quotation.

[190] See, for example, the Sterzingen Passion of 1496, in which German texts are first sung and
then spoken and sung Latin is followed by a paraphrase: Walter Lipphardt and Hans-Gert
Roloff, eds., *Die geistlichen Spiele des Sterzinger Spielarchivs* (Bern: Peter Lang, 1988) II, especially 294–329.

the singing of *Venite benedicti* during **Chester 24**, the Judgement.[191] Although there is no indication of this in the play text, the text of the antiphon *Venite benedicti* is paraphrased by Christ in lines **453–6**: hence the banns must refer to the singing of that text, by Christ, after **24/452**. However, the late banns date from later than the Exemplar, so that it is possible that performances did not include the singing of *Venite benedicti* until very late in the cycle's performance history: that is something that we shall probably never know.

The English translations or paraphrases may also tell us the extent of a Latin text. In the case just mentioned, the lack of Alleluias in **Chester 24/253–6** suggests that the liturgical text is the antiphon *Venite benedicti*, which has no Alleluias, rather than the Introit *Venite benedicti*, which has them. The English can sometimes provide evidence also of the number of verses of a multi-stanza work that should be performed: for example, the apostles' paraphrase of *Veni creator spiritus* in **Chester 21/121–148**, which is laid out in seven stanzas, shows that the apostles must have sung the complete hymn at **21/120+sd**. At least, it seems reasonable to suppose that, in general, the translation or paraphrase will deal with neither more text nor less than the Latin did, or at least that that was the dramatist's intention.[192] While a musical director might choose the 'wrong' version of a text, therefore, or a later director might add a MD giving a Latin text that does not quite match the playwright's English text, we can surely consider it probable that the dramatist started with a clear idea of the Latin text and its meaning. In the present case, therefore, there is at least some evidence that Simeon's singing of *Nunc dimittis* at **Chester 11/166+** utilises a version that includes the whole text of the canticle but has no doxology – in other words, the Tract, not some other setting of verses from *Nunc dimittis*.[193]

This kind of evidence is far from firm, and it should be used cautiously and preferably only to confirm other evidence. To take a more problematic example, **Towneley 29/253+sd** requires the singing of *Ascendo ad patrem meum*, while the angel's speech immediately following, **254–69**, paraphrases the text of *Viri Galilei*. This might suggest considerable editorial activity at some time: not only is the angel's speech a paraphrase of the wrong text, but **29/253+sd** requires *Ascendo ad patrem meum* to be sung by angels, whereas it is of course a text belonging to Christ himself. We might reasonably postulate an original text in which Christ sang *Ascendo ad patrem meum*, followed by a spoken English paraphrase, with the angels

---

191 See Mills *Staging Chester*, 79–80, and Lumiansky and Mills *Essays*, 131–2 and 153–4. For the relevant lines of the late banns see *Essays*, 293, and *REED.Chester*, 246.

192 But see 7.2, below, for a case where this principle may be modified.

193 The normal way of singing the Psalms was to chant the psalms of the day to one or more psalm tones, which are short tunes designed for the purpose. On these occasions each psalm was concluded with the lesser doxology, *Gloria patri* ('Glory be to the Father, and to the Son . . .'). However, psalm-texts form the bulk of liturgical set-piece items, such as antiphons and responsories, though only one or two verses are normally used for these. The Tract, which is sung (when it is sung at all) before the Gospel at Mass, is a complete psalm or canticle sung from beginning to end but without the doxology. (The longest psalms, notably Psalm 119, are split up in performance.)

then singing *Viri Galilei* and one of them speaking the paraphrase of that text. Two major pieces of editorial revision are then necessary: first, the paraphrase of *Ascendo ad patrem meum* has been deleted; second, the two – now adjacent – SDs have been amalgamated so that Christ ascends while the angels sing *Ascendo ad patrem meum*. But this is sheer speculation, and depends entirely on a rigid system by which a Latin text and its English paraphrase (in whichever order they come) are always inseparably bound together.[194]

The best we can say, perhaps, is that in a case where we know there was singing and the next speech offers a translation or paraphrase of a liturgical text – by definition a suitable text, unless the dramatist or editor has made an error – the paraphrase offers a sensible and probably correct solution to the problem of choosing the item to be sung.

It must also be said that, without a SD or other firm piece of evidence for singing, it would be wrong to assume that singing takes place merely because a liturgical text is paraphrased. Just as the paraphrase of *Venite benedicti* would have been without its Latin original unless the late banns had mentioned it, so there are other portions of the play texts that in fact paraphrase liturgical items in the absence of the Latin texts. Clear examples are the paraphrase of *Nunc dimittis* in **York 17/415–24** (which leaves no space for the singing of the Latin text because of its positioning across two stanzas, and is therefore not a parallel to other Purification plays); and the allusion to *Sacerdotes domini* at the beginning of the N-Town Conception of Mary play (**N-Town 8/1–2**, which is **Mary Play 26–7**). Another example is the opening of Chester 6, where lines 1–4 are based on the liturgical *Ave Maria* texts rather than on the Gospel version.[195] The existence of the *Venite benedicti* evidence in the banns, as I have suggested, is not evidence that any other such paraphrase must once have been associated with the appropriate Latin text.

The use of the Latin+English pattern is in any case a well-known device that, in its usual manifestations, has nothing to do with music and does not always have to do with liturgy either. It is a common device for popular exegesis, and therefore may be taken to have a more general application, and perhaps more general modes of application, than a dramatic context alone might suggest. The pattern is seen, for example, in the Lay Folk's Mass Book and in the English Psalter of Richard Rolle, as well as in more specific instructional books such as that of Peter Idley.[196] In all these, the layout is as for a glossed Bible or other text, with the text itself (sometimes in larger script) followed by a considerably longer explanatory gloss or exposition taking the text as its starting point. Indeed, if one reads such exigetical Middle English texts one finds that passages such as the exposition of the Creed in **Chester 21/311–58**, where the apostles in turn recite a verse and then speak an explanatory

---

[194] It is hardly evidence against a speculation of this sort, but it must also be said that it is very hard to reconstruct SDs that might credibly have been amalgamated to make the SD that we have – '& *sic ascendit, cantantibus angelis* Ascendo ad patrem meum'.

[195] See Keane 'Kingship', 78. In Luke 1/28 Gabriel does not address Mary by name.

[196] See T.F. Simmons, ed., *The Lay Folk's Mass Book* (EETS, 1879), *passim*; Rolle *Psalter*, *passim*; Idley, *passim*.

stanza in English, are exactly in line with the wider tradition. A.C. Cawley introduced his 1974 paper 'Medieval Drama and Didacticism' by proposing a hypothesis 'that the vernacular plays, containing as they do both biblical episodes and doctrinal matter, have a didactic aim and may therefore be seen as a part of the Church's total efforts to bring religious instruction to lay people'.[197] Cawley further suggested that the matters with which the plays concerned themselves were the Creed, the decalogue, the seven sacraments, the seven corporal works of mercy, the seven principal virtues, and the seven deadly sins: his paper clearly demonstrated the relationship between the popular instructional works and the vernacular drama.

Before leaving the subject of Latin for the time being, I wish to note briefly two uses of Latin that derive neither from the Bible nor from liturgy. As has been noted often enough before, one of the Towneley shepherds quotes the Virgilian 'prophecy' of Christ's birth in a rare example of a quotation of a classical author (**Towneley 12/386–8**). Finally, we may note that evil characters use Latin a surprising amount, sometimes quoting or misquoting scripture, sometimes creating a parody of liturgy, sometimes translating indecent texts or making complete nonsense (though often with indecent allusions). This use of Latin, which should be regarded as an important form of perversion that is part of the characterisation of evil, takes many forms. The subject is further discussed in section 5.4, below.

[197] In [Rastall] *Drama*, 3; and 'Middle English Metrical Versions of the Decalogue', 132.

3

THE SURVIVING MUSIC

3.1 Introduction

It would be natural to assume that notated music written into a play text is the most important evidence for our study, and we certainly cannot work on a musical repertory unless we have some record of it that is translatable into musical terms. For music of the late Middle Ages and Renaissance such a record is normally a matter of musical notation. It is disappointing, then, to find that there is hardly any notated music in the manuscripts of early English plays. Why is this? What music should be used for music cues where none is notated? And what relationship does the notated music bear to the unnotated music on one hand and the non-dramatic musical repertory on the other?

This chapter seeks to answer the last of these questions: but the first two also demand some sort of discussion before we can proceed, for they lead towards the major stumbling-block to any understanding of the place of music in the plays concerned. In the context of the study as a whole the notated music is not the ultimate goal of work on 'music in early English religious drama' but almost a side-issue. Notated music is rare in the plays because it is in some sense abnormal, a special situation that does not usually affect drama and will not often have been taken into account by a playwright. Here the musicologist, too, will recognise the usual situation in the musical world for this period: polyphonic music in mensural notation[1] – and this is basically what the notated music in the plays is – was not the norm in the Middle Ages, but something unusual and special.[2] Secular musicians performed entirely in an aural tradition, unless in an intellectually high-powered courtly context, until well into the sixteenth century, and the methods by which they turned a tune into an acceptable instrumental piece or song belonged to the same tradition. Church musicians were necessarily educated in the arts of reading and writing, including musical notation, but they too worked in a largely aural tradition. Choir boys learned the Psalter by heart; and although church singers were taught to read plainsong notation, that was largely for reference purposes. In effect, most

---

[1] 'Mensural' merely means 'measured' – that is, showing the duration of each note. The mensural system of the late Middle Ages was however very much more complex than the modern one.

[2] Indeed, written records generally were not the norm in an age that used the human memory much more than we do.

singers knew much of the huge liturgical repertory from memory by the time they had been singing it regularly for a few years; and experienced singers could improvise a polyphonic texture around the notated plainsong tunes. In this world of liturgical monody, recorded in pitch-only notation, mainly sung from memory and occasionally extended into a polyphonic texture without further notational resources, any part-music written in the more complex mensural notation was a special event. Singers had to be highly trained to cope with it, composers were almost invariably from the ranks of these singers, and the magisterial discussion of music theory at a technical notational level was a matter for those with a university education. This situation began to alter only in the second half of the fifteenth century, with a radical change making itself felt particularly in the period c.1510–40.

The answer to the first question, then, is in two parts. First, a largely memorised repertory need not be written down for dramatic use. The singers of the worldlings' obscene song in *Mankind* were perfectly capable of using a well-known tune and teaching the song to the audience by ear; Mrs Noah's gossips in **Chester 3** could use a well-known tune or make up their own – neither method is a problem; and the audience, as well as the cast, would have no difficulty in singing a well-known plainsong item such as the hymn *Veni creator spiritus*. Of course it would be sensible to have reference materials handy in case of memory lapses, and these were available. The song texts are given in the play manuscripts, where there is no point in writing the tunes, while both words and tunes of the liturgical pieces were in the service-books used by the professional singers and music director.

The second part of the answer is, then, that such written and notated materials as were necessary could be found in the normal sources used by the professional performers and directors. Any plainsong item need only be identified in the play text by a verbal incipit, and the singers could find it in their own books, if indeed they needed to do so: and the corollary to this is that the many incipits for Latin liturgical items found in the dramatic directions of the plays imply the singing of those texts to their usual chant. The performance method is however more open than this: in particular cases we may see positive reasons for thinking that the text should be spoken rather than sung (see section 2.7, above); and there is a possibility of the text being sung to improvised polyphony.

Incipits are usually verbal because words take up less space, and in any case a scribe set out his writing lines for words when copying a play text.[3] Presumably a musical incipit was demanded only if the playwright or a director wished to specify a particular musical setting. This, I believe, is the position in the case of the *Gloria*

---

[3] The Shrewsbury music is an exception to this, the manuscript being a liturgical source. Liturgical sources are of course special in the sense that they normally offer a mixture of musical settings and plain text, in both red and black ink, and with the texts disposed in various ways. Setting out a liturgical manuscript was therefore a specialised task, presenting many difficulties not present in the layout of a normal literary or musical manuscript. These difficulties were not encountered by the scribes of **York 45**, where a simple division of the writing space demanded only minimal understanding between the scribes, nor in the Coventry Shearmen and Tailors' manuscript, where the music was written out on separate sheets of paper or parchment.

in excelsis found in one copy of **Chester 7**. There must have been several settings of this text available in the music cupboard of Chester Cathedral in the mid-sixteenth century, but someone used, or intended to use, this particular setting for a particular performance. This case warns us that, while we can probably assume a chant performance for a liturgical text, it is always possible that a pre-existent polyphonic setting was intended, unrecorded in the play text because there was no need to specify the particular setting.

Nevertheless, the same point can be made about polyphonic settings as about plainsong: they were available in the singers' own sources and therefore did not need to be copied into the play manuscripts. The existence of any complete polyphonic setting in a play manuscript therefore points towards settings that were not pre-existent and so had to be notated for reference purposes in the play text. We can assume, then, that such pieces were probably composed expressly for the dramatic context in which we find them. This would be true of all the notated music in the Shrewsbury, York and Coventry plays, and it is significant (although it proves nothing) that there is not a single concordance known for any of these settings. Perhaps even more significant is the fact that the one liturgical text set polyphonically in **York 45**, *Veni electa mea*, appears in settings that make no use of the plainsong. These are non-liturgical settings, therefore, and there are very few uses to which they could have been put. It is a reasonable guess that that non-liturgical use was a dramatic one, and that these settings were composed specially for use in that play.

The repertory of notated music surviving in the plays is easily listed. The fragmentary Shrewsbury plays present settings that probably date from the 1430s or 1440s, roughly contemporary with the manuscript. The music in the Pepys fragment and **York 45** seems to date from the same two decades, although the manuscripts in which they appear are certainly later. All of this music uses a difficult late medieval notation requiring performance by highly-trained professionals. The two songs in the Coventry nativity play probably date from 1534, although they could easily be later:[4] they are in a much simpler notational style than the fifteenth-century pieces, but they were certainly composed by a professional, and would demand professional singers for their performance. Lastly, the incipit for the Gloria in **Chester 7** seems to belong to a mid-sixteenth-century setting, otherwise unknown. It is not an amateur composition, but was probably in the repertory of the Cathedral choir at Chester.

In the sections that follow I examine this music item by item in an attempt to relate it to the wider musical scene. In discussions, note-values are abbreviated as follows: L = long, B = breve, S = semibreve, M = minim, and Sm = semiminim. The transcriptions follow standard practice. In mensural notation, ligatures and coloration are shown by ⌐ and ⌐ ⌐, respectively; in chant, a ligature is shown by ⌐ and liquescence by a small note-head, ♪.

---

[4] There is some circumstantial evidence that the shepherds' song is earlier, but it is very slight. See p. 69, above.

3.2 The Shrewsbury and Pepys fragments

Shrewsbury School MS VI is a liturgical book of the early fifteenth century. Kurt von Fischer's dating of the manuscript at c. 1430 was accepted by Susan Rankin on paleographical grounds and also because of the dating between 1410 and 1420 of an isorhythmic motet, a fragment of which was used in the binding.[5] At the end of the manuscript, on ff. 38r–42v, is a single actor's part for three plays in the vernacular with interpolated Latin texts set to notated music. The plays are followed, on f. 43r, by an antiphon verse, *Unus autem ex ipsis*, which belongs to the Palm Sunday antiphon *Collegerunt pontifices*. Rankin notes, however, that this was added in a later hand, so the plays did originally form the end of the manuscript's contents. The plays are, in order, a Shepherds' play, a Resurrection, and a play of the Pilgrims to Emmaus: the actor concerned played, respectively, the Third Shepherd, the Third Mary, and one of the pilgrims, probably Cleophas. No facsimile of the Shrewsbury plays has yet been published. The standard edition is that of Norman Davis, to which is appended a discussion and transcription of the music by Frank Ll. Harrison.[6]

In the past the Shrewsbury plays have attracted attention from historians of drama for two main reasons: first, because the Shepherds' play shows a textual relationship with **York 15**;[7] second, because the apparent mixture of spoken English dialogue and sung Latin liturgical pieces was thought to exemplify an evolutionary link between the sung liturgical dramas and the spoken vernacular religious plays.[8] Although this evolutionary theory is now discredited, the Shrewsbury plays still tend to suffer from neglect of the wider issues involved. In fact, the combination of spoken English and sung Latin in the Shrewsbury manuscript is not necessarily as obvious as it seems. Although it is a reasonable assumption that the Latin text was intended to be sung, it is an assumption nonetheless for those lines not associated with a notated setting.

Susan Rankin's study of the whole manuscript demonstrated the plays' place in the context of the source rather than in that of the dramatic repertory.[9] She concluded:

— that the manuscript contains processional music;
— that the musical repertory is three-voiced polyphony, for three solo singers, the other two parts having been in similar books now lost;
— that the existing Shrewsbury tunes are related to the chants in a variety of

5 Kurt von Fischer, 'Die Passion von ihren Anfangen bis ins 16. Jahrhundert', *Gattungen der Musik in Einzeldarstellung: Gedenkschrift Leo Schrade* (Berne, 1973), 574; Rankin 'Manuscript VI', 129 and n. 2. See also Ker and Piper *Catalogue* iv, 295–6.
6 Davis *Non-Cycle Plays*. For the introduction, text, and musical commentary and transcription, respectively, see pp. xiv–xxii, 1–7 and 124–33.
7 Miller 1918.
8 Craig *English Religious Drama*, 97–8.
9 Rankin 'Manuscript VI' and *Shrewsbury Manuscript*.

ways, most importantly as counterpoints to the plainsong tunes or to 'squares' based on them.[10]

— that the range and designation 'triplex' of some items (not however in the plays) suggests that the line is the top line of the texture, not the middle line; and

— that the contents show the manuscript to have belonged to the Sarum rite as modified in the Lichfield diocese and, more specifically, in Lichfield cathedral itself.

On the last of these conclusions, Rankin quoted the late-twelfth-century statutes of Lichfield concerning the performance of a *representacio pastorum* on the night of Our Lord's birth (i.e. late on Christmas Eve), a *representacio Resurrectionis* on Easter Day and a *representacio peregrinorum* on Easter Monday. In the section concerning the succentor's duties the latter two plays are referred to as *miracula*.[11] At no other establishment is it known that plays on all three of these subjects were performed. The knowledge that the plays were part of the processional repertory of a specific establishment is very helpful to a study of the music. Whereas Harrison considered the possible reconstruction of the three-part texture on the basis of only what little information could be gleaned from the settings in the plays, Rankin discussed the whole repertory in relation to its textual concordances in other musical sources.[12]

The music is neatly written in black mensural notation on red five-line staves: full red coloration is normal, although some pieces elsewhere in the manuscript use void red coloration for triplet minims. C-clefs are used throughout, except that one piece, *Infidelis*, uses a B-flat clef.[13] The second piece in the plays, *Salvatorem Christum dominum*, exceptionally among the plays – indeed, among the pieces originally copied into this manuscript – is copied on black staves. It shares this distinction with the pieces copied at the front and the back of the manuscript by a later (but still fifteenth- or early sixteenth-century) hand. Nevertheless, *Salvatorem* is copied by the same hand as the rest of the plays' music, and does not belong to the second-layer pieces using black staves.[14] The reason must be related to the circumstances in which

---

[10] The principle of a 'square' is as follows: a polyphonic piece is composed using the chant as a basis in one voice; the bass part of this setting is then abstracted and used as the basis for a new composition. A newly-composed voice in the second setting is thus likely to be related to, but not the same as and not necessarily compatible with, the original chant. See Margaret Bent's *New Grove* article 'Square', NG 18/29–30. For some music in the Shrewsbury manuscript, though not for any contained in the plays, Rankin was able to make a stylistic reconstruction on the basis of other sources containing similar, chant-based settings of the same texts.

[11] Rankin 'Manuscript VI', 131.

[12] *Ibid.*, 135. The musical sources containing a comparable liturgical repertory are British Library MS Egerton 3307 (c.1440) and Cambridge, Magdalene College, MS Pepys 1236 (? 1474–5): for the latter, see below. As Rankin notes, although these two manuscripts share some of their repertory, 'none of the Shrewsbury musical settings exists elsewhere'.

[13] A specifically English characteristic is the joining of the ligature *cum opposita proprietate* (giving two semibreves) with notes before it: according to the theorists, and practice outside England, the c.o.p. ligature should stand alone or at the beginning of a larger ligature.

[14] Davis says that *Salvatorem* is copied 'in a different hand' (1970, 2, n. 2), but both text and music seem to me to be in the hand of the rest of the plays.

Salvatorem was copied. Although it should have appeared on f.38v it was omitted when that page was copied. Its later inclusion after the end of the *Peregrinus* play, on f. 42v, was apparently not planned in advance, nor even at the time when the scribe was approaching the end of the *Peregrinus* play.[15] By the time the scribe came to copy *Salvatorem* he was no longer in the copying habits of the preceding pieces: he did not use red ink for the staves (which saved him the trouble of making up a new batch), and he wrote the text in the same informal script that he had used for the English text of the plays, instead of the more formal 'liturgical' script used in the other musical settings (see Plate 1). That these were both an oversight is suggested by the fact that the piece nevertheless has an ornamental initial S in red.[16]

The Latin texts of the plays are in a slightly larger and more formal script than the English texts, and are in red. Most of these appear under musical notation and are certainly intended to be sung; but a few are without notation and may not have been intended for musical performance. The fact that they use the same style of script does however make it impossible to assume this, and it may even be that all the Latin texts were to be sung. Harrison states this as a fact at the opening of his section:[17]

> Music is provided for words sung by two or three characters. With the possible exception of the words at the beginning of the *Officium Nativitatis (Pastorum)*, words written in the manuscript in red are sung by the character whose part this is, though the music is not given. The possible exception is the quotation from St Luke's account of the nativity, which may have been sung to the Gospel tone.

Harrison thus explains why some Latin texts are given notated music and others are not: music for two or three voices is here composed polyphony, whereas music for a single character is sung monophonically to pre-existent chant which can either be memorised or else sung from a chant book. If Harrison was correct in this, the play as performed would have included more music than is actually notated in the manuscript.[18]

The study of music for these plays therefore demands investigation in two main areas: first, of which Latin texts are to be sung and which spoken; second, of the number of parts and the musical style of the notated pieces. What follows here is a commentary on all the Latin texts and incipits that were, or might have been, intended for singing.

[15] For the sake of simplicity I assume here that a single scribe was responsible for both text and music of this manuscript: but my argument would not be affected by the perfectly reasonable supposition that text-scribe and music-scribe were different men.

[16] The first letter of a piece is normally ornamented in this manuscript, and coloured either red or blue.

[17] Davis *Non-Cycle Plays*, 124.

[18] It is impossible to prove him wrong; but the existence of any such text as a liturgical item or as part of a liturgical play does demonstrate that the conditions are right for him to be correct – i.e. a musical setting in chant or chant style is known to exist.

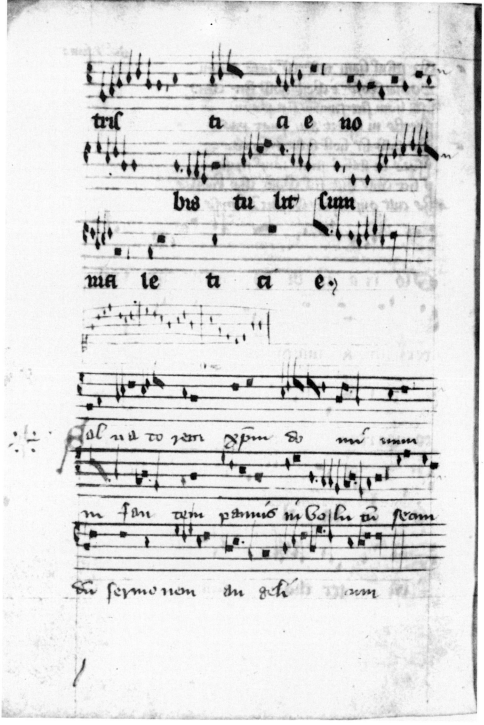

Plate 1 Shrewsbury School MS VI, f. 42v: the end of *Frater Thoma* and the setting of *Salvatorem Christum* added with informal underlay.

O ye pepull of ierusalem be holde & se — *Jeremias*
make yo respecte into the orient
a kyng is comyng of gret poste
the maker of this worlde omnipotent
renyue ye pepull y be psent
& thanke hym of his grete mercy
for he is disposyd among yo to dy

lyft vp yo yew to henyn an hey — *Ysayas*
& be holde the power of ye myzt kyng
he cometh to saue yo etnally
& fro damynacyon yo for to bryng
for yo sowle helth is hie comyng
whych is to hym but anguysth & payn
for he among yo shall be mased & slayn

O ye pepull of ierusalem whyle ye may attayn — *David*
aske mercy of this lorde for yo offence
lyft vp yo hedis ...

On a Crucifix

why not the picture of our dying Lord
as of a friend nor this nor that is adored
does not the Eternal law command that thou
shalt even as well forbeare to make as bow

ri en teret m de.lo . nav

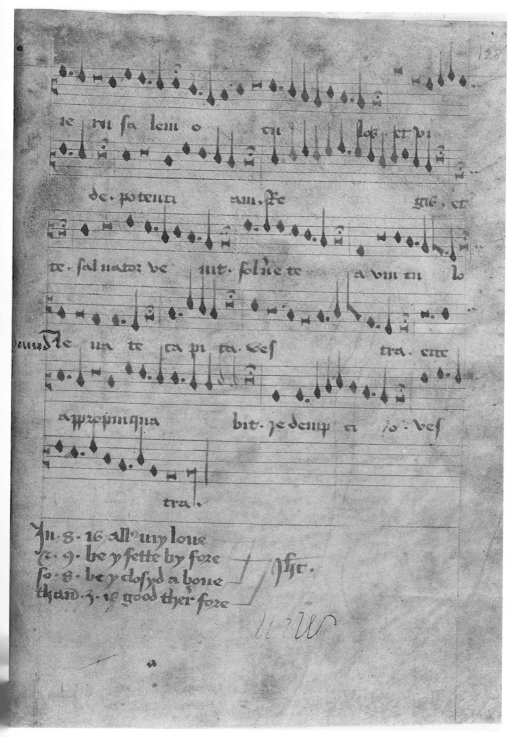

Plate 3 Magdalene College, Cambridge, Pepys MS 1236, f. 128r.

Plate 4 London, British Library, Add. MS 35290, f. 236r (Beadle 251r): the York *Veni de Libano* A setting, following the speeches of the twelve angels.

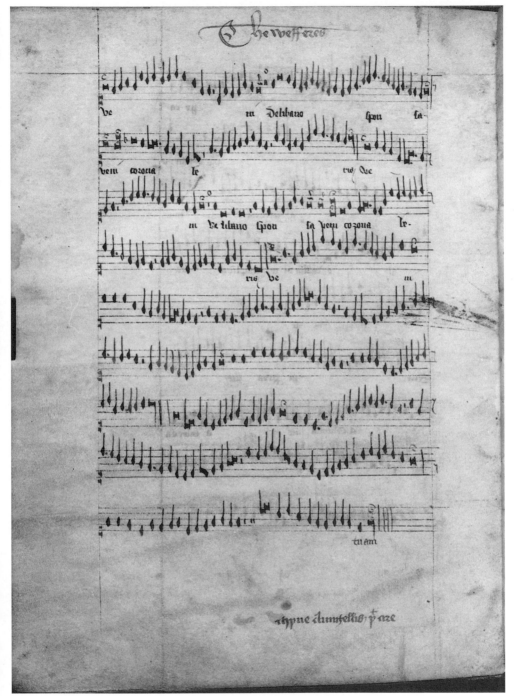

Plate 5 London, British Library, Add. MS 35290, f. 241v (Beadle 256v): the York B settings of *Veni de Libano* and *Veni electa mea*.

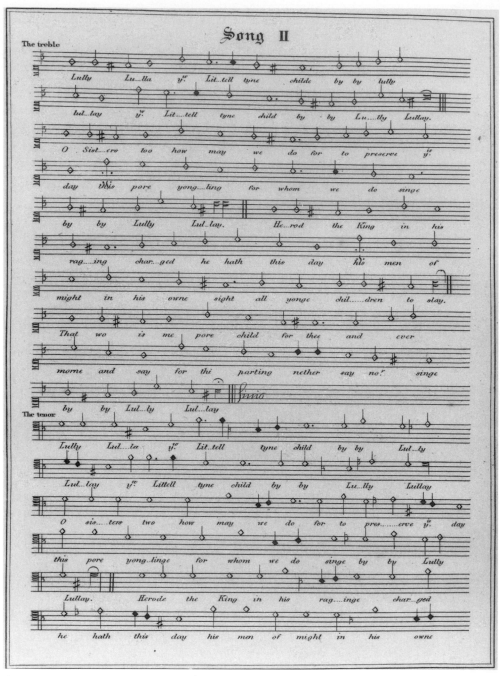

Plate 6 Thomas Sharp, *A Dissertation on the Pageants or Dramatic Mysteries Anciently performed at Coventry* (1825), p. 116: the treble and most of the tenor of the Coventry lullaby in Sharp's own copy, now British Library, Add. MS 43645.

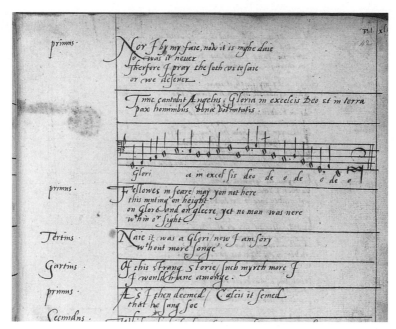

Plate 7 London, British Library, MS Harley 2124, f. 42r: music for the angelic Gloria in Chester play 7.

Plate 8 Detail of the Assumption painting *Mary, Queen of Heaven* by the Master of the St Lucy Legend, c.1485–1500. Samuel H. Kress Collection, National Gallery of Art, Washington DC.

Plate 9 *Compost et Kalendrier des Bergiers* (Paris: Guiot Marchant, 1541), frontispiece: the Houghton Library, Harvard University. The shepherds' vigil outside Bethlehem.

Plate 10 Oxford, Bodleian Library, MS Douce 88, f. 73v (detail). A late 13th-century illustration of a bell-wether leading the flock.

Shrewsbury

Play 1: Officium Pastorum

1/1–   The heading *Pastores erant . . . et timuerunt timore magno* is a rather shortened version of Luke 2/8–9. This part of the story was included in the Gospel at first Mass on Christmas Day,[19] but its presentation here is clearly not a liturgical one. In fact, although Harrison floats the possibility of it being sung to a Gospel tone (which he quotes following the quotation above), it seems to me unlikely that it was intended to be sung, or even spoken: its purpose is surely as an authority for this first dramatisation of the group.[20]

1/32+music   A setting of *Transeamus usque Bethelem* (*sic*), originally à 3. The text appears not to be a liturgical item: it is based on Luke 2/15, but it is not exactly quoted. The precise wording is however found in the twelfth-century Fleury play of the adoration of the shepherds and magi,[21] and also in the play of the shepherds found in a thirteenth-century gradual from Rouen.[22] Harrison's edition of the Shrewsbury setting is in Davis 1970, 128.

1/38+music   A setting of *Salvatorem Christum Dominum*, originally à 3. As already noted, this music was apparently omitted from f. 38v in error, for it appears on f. 42v, with an asterisk as marker for the correct position. This, too, I do not know as a liturgical piece in England, but it is in the Fleury play book and the Rouen gradual just mentioned.[23] In both plays this piece is separated from *Transeamus usque Bethleem* only by the midwives' query 'Quem queritis, pastores, dicite?'[24] Harrison's edition of the Shrewsbury setting is in Davis 1970, 129.

Play 2: Officium Resurrectionis

2/1–   *Hic incipit Officium Resurreccionis in die Pasche* is a heading of standard type for a service book and is clearly not intended to be sung.

2/1–2   The first two lines of the play, 'Heu redempcio Israel ut quid mortem sustinuit' (written as a single line in the source), are given to the Third Mary. There is no reason here to think that they should be sung, and I cannot find the text as a liturgical item. A setting of these words does appear as one of a series of speeches by the three Marys in a Resurrection play in a thirteenth-century manuscript from Tours, however,[25] so the possibility cannot be ruled out. In the Tours play

---

[19] MisS(L), 26.
[20] See the discussion in 2.7, above, for Latin material set out as an authority for dramatic representation.
[21] Orléans, Bibliothèque de la ville, MS 201; see Coussemaker DL, 144. A reduced photographic reproduction of the Fleury book appears at the end of Campbell and Davidson *Fleury*.
[22] Now Paris, Bibliothèque national, MS lat. 904: see Coussemaker DL, 237. Harrison notes that the piece is known in the liturgy of Rouen, presumably with this gradual in mind.
[23] See Coussemaker DL, pp. 144 and 237.
[24] Coussemaker DL, 144 and 237; Bailey *Herod*, 21. Both plays give the spelling 'Bethleem', which is usual.
[25] Tours, Bibliothèque de la ville, MS 927: see Coussemaker DL, 24, and Smoldon 1980, 156.

these words are sung by Maria Jacobi, who in Shrewsbury is the Second Mary. The text and music of some of these lines, including this one, also appear at the end of the Fleury Resurrection play,[26] where they may constitute an alternative opening for the play. In any case, there is a known musical setting of this text in chant style – in fact, two variant versions. There is no way of knowing how much Latin if any is given to the other Marys in this part of the Shrewsbury play, and the possibility of this text being sung is no more than doubtful.

2/8–11 This pair of couplets, beginning 'Heu cur ligno fixus clavis', is written as two lines in the source: it is the second half of a speech by the Third Mary. This appears not to be a liturgical text, and I have not found it in any other drama, so there is no evidence for it being sung. Like **2/1–2**, therefore, this text is at best a doubtful contender for sung performance, and in this case no continental parallel presents itself.

2/20+music A setting of *Iam, iam ecce*, originally à 3. Davis prints the text as two lines (21–2). The text seems not to be a liturgical one, but it occurs in both the Fleury and Tours Resurrection plays at the end of the group of speeches that includes 'Heu Redempcio Israel': in both cases it is sung by all three Marys.[27] Harrison's edition of the Shrewsbury music is in Davis 1970, 128.

Between this and the next two lines, also set to music, there is only a direction: 'Et appropiantes sepulcro ca[n]t[ent]'.

2/22+sd+ music A setting of two lines beginning 'O Deus quis revolvet nobis lapidem', originally à 3. This is of course a biblical text, Mark 16/3, and with a short narrative introduction it forms an antiphon, 'Et dicebant ad invicem'.[28] These two lines (**2/23–4**), sung by Mary Magdalene, are found in the Resurrection play in the Tours manuscript, not long after the appearance of *Iam, iam ecce*.[29] Harrison's edition of the Shrewsbury setting is in Davis 1970, 129.

2/35–6 The two lines beginning 'Surrexit Christus, spes nostra' are the opening of a speech by the Third Mary, the rest of which amplifies it in English (**2/37–44**). These lines are a verse of the Easter sequence *Victime paschali laudes*, and could therefore be sung to the normal chant of that sequence. There are precedents for the use of a substantial section of *Victimae paschali laudes* in continental Resurrection plays: large parts of it, including this verse, appear in the fourteenth-century plays from Origny and Cividale. In both cases the musical setting is that of the normal chant of the sequence.[30] It seems quite possible that the Shrewsbury play, like the continental ones, split a

---

26 Coussemaker DL 187: the line is given to the Second Mary.
27 Coussemaker DL, 25 and 187.
28 Smoldon 1980, 101: the antiphon is in LA 215 and WA 131.
29 Coussemaker DL, 26.
30 Coussemaker DL, 268–70 and 302–3. The sequence is in LU 780.

section of the *Victimae paschali laudes* between the three Marys, but that it added a (presumably spoken) vernacular amplification after each sung verse.

Play 3: Officium Peregrinorum

3/1– *Feria secunda in ebdomada Pasche discipuli insimul cantent* starts as a typical heading for a service book and then adds a stage direction. It should be neither sung nor spoken.

3/1–4 A musical setting of *Infidelis incursum populi*, originally à 3: presumably the 'discipuli' referred to in the rubric are the whole body of disciples, not just the two who travel to Emmeus. I do not know of this as a liturgical text. Harrison's edition of the music is in Davis 1970, 130.

3/23+lat Two Latin lines beginning 'Et quomodo tradiderunt'. I do not know of this as a liturgical text, but it appears in the Fleury Emmeus play (without the initial 'Et') in a speech by the Second Disciple,[31] so there was a chant setting for it.

3/32+lat A single Latin line beginning 'Dixerunt eciam se visionem'. I do not know of this as a liturgical piece or as part of a drama.

3/41+music A setting of *Mane nobiscum*. It is sung probably by the two disciples, and so may have been in only two parts originally. The text is that of a Benedictus antiphon in Easter time.[32] Harrison's edition of the music is in Davis 1970, 131.

3/61–5 A setting of *Quid agamus vel dicamus*, sung by the two disciples and presumably à 2 originally. I have not found the text elsewhere. Harrison's edition of the music is in Davis 1970, 131, and the original is reproduced as the frontispiece.

3/76–9 A setting of *Gloria tibi domine*, apparently in three parts originally. At this stage of the play the two disciples have reported their experience to the others, so the 3-part texture simply reflects the fact that this is to be sung by all the disciples. The text is that of the doxology of the hymns 'Jesu Salvator seculi' and 'Ad cenam Agni providi' (among others, probably).[33] Harrison thought that there was no clear relation between the Shrewsbury line and the chants of any of the relevant office hymns, unless the former were 'an elaboration of the faburden of the Compline hymn *Jesu Salvator seculi*.'[34] His edition of the Shrewsbury music is in Davis 1970, 132.

3/80–1 The last piece, a setting of *Frater Thoma, causa tristicie*, follows with no material intervening. It was apparently in three parts originally. I cannot find this text elsewhere. Harrison's edition of the music is in Davis 1970, 133.

---

[31] Coussemaker DL, 196.

[32] AR 476, WA 138.

[33] These hymns are in HS, 92–3 and 99–100, respectively. The latter does not have the doxology printed in HS, but see AM 459, 467, and Wieland 1982, 87–8.

[34] Davis *Non-Cycle Plays*, 127. Harrison cites his own article 'Faburden in Practice', 11, for this possibility.

This examination of the performance method of Latin texts in the plays suggests their division into three basic groups. The first group includes the headings to the three plays (**Shrewsbury 1/1–, 2/1–** and **3/1–**). Although the three headings take different forms, they are all types that need not surprise us in the context of a service book, a play, or both. There is no reason to think that any of them need be spoken, let alone sung, and they all make sense as authorities or directions intended for the reader, whether that reader be a censor, a director or an actor.[35]

The second group is those Latin texts belonging only to the character whose part this manuscript is. In these cases there is no written music, and if such a text were to be sung at all it would be a solo performance of a chant setting. Of the five examples in this group, two – **2/8–11** and **3/32+lat** – are not known to me as either liturgical pieces or items from a sung drama. This is not to say that they do not exist in one or both of these guises. The other three examples – **2/1–2, 2/35–6** and **3/23+lat** – all exist, with chant settings, in continental sung dramas, the second being in addition part of the Easter sequence the chant of which is seen to have been used in the two dramas concerned. On balance I imagine that Harrison was basically right to suggest that Latin lines given to a single character were intended to be sung to their chant settings. This in turn raises interesting questions about the precise nature of these plays, but we are unlikely to answer such questions unless a fuller text of the Shrewsbury plays can be found.

The third group is those texts for two or more (but usually three) characters for which a notated setting is provided. This group brings us to the second of our questions: what is the musical style of these pieces?

Harrison suggested various methods of performance, of which the first was as a monodic line sung in unison by all three shepherds. This is not impossible: much of the Shrewsbury music is clearly a decorated and rhythmicised version of the chants on which it is based, and such a line would have to be notated however many singers were to perform it. I shall discuss the notion of 'mensural monody' below, since it has been offered as an explanation of much of the music in Pepys 1236: but the arguments seem merely circumstantial, even for the existence of the style. The alternative, then, is some form of polyphony of which the surviving line was a part, and Harrison's alternative suggestions are for polyphonic textures. This latter view was taken by Rankin, who considered the possibility of the Shrewsbury music being a repertory of mensural monodic settings but decided that the stylistic reconstructions possible using chant-related voices surviving elsewhere on some of the Shrewsbury texts were good evidence of a polyphonic origin for the Shrewsbury pieces.[36]

---

[35] It should perhaps be noted here that the purpose of Latin in a service book, or for that matter in a playbook written for performance in an ecclesiastical institution, will not be the same as that of Latin in a civic play. The much higher incidence of literacy and the normal use of Latin in the former situations makes Latin more useful for spoken or unheard texts.

[36] Rankin's argument, which I find convincing, is in 'Manuscript VI', 136–42. The textual concordances used did not however include any items from the plays.

3.2 *The Shrewsbury and Pepys Fragments*

The principal style of composition on a chant was based on a technique for improvising a polyphonic texture, in which the given tune was sung as the middle line of a three-part texture.[37] In theory the bass line under this tune can be at the interval of a third, a fifth or a sixth below at any given moment, and indeed there are treatises surviving from the fifteenth century that show how this should be done.[38] In practice, however, this technique really works only in two parts: it is impossible to control a three-part texture with so free a bass. In a three-part texture, therefore, the range of intervals between tenor and bass was severely limited. The usual interval was the third, with a fifth at the beginning and end of each phrase: Example 1a shows the bass line that results when this technique is applied to the 'Surrexit Christus, spes nostra' section of the Easter sequence *Victime paschali laudes*. The singer of the bass line could achieve this quite simply: he would pitch his first note a fifth below that of the tenor and imagine that he was to sing the chant at that pitch; but when the chant moved he would deliberately sing a third above the chant note that he should have sung, and so on until the cadence.[39] The effect of singing a third high in a line which follows the chant at the fifth below is, of course, to produce a line actually a third below the tenor. Example 1b shows this, the open noteheads being the pitches of the transposed chant and the black noteheads being the pitches actually sung.

The singer on the top line had a simpler task, singing the chant itself a fourth higher than the tenor but with no other modification. The result was a rich three-part texture in which most chords were first-inversion triads, with an open octave and fifth at the beginning and end of each phrase. Example 1c shows the complete texture. Most chants could be performed this way, with all the singers reading from the monodic notation in the relevant service book. The technique as a whole is known as 'faburden', and the process of deriving a polyphonic texture from a single line of music as 'sighting'.

The improvising voices used whatever rhythms (if any) were in the tenor. However, a practised singer could embellish his line while keeping to the basic rhythm of the tenor tune, so that the texture became more interesting than merely a series of block chords: in this case the music was necessarily performed by three *solo* singers, which was the case for most polyphony anyway until the middle of the fifteenth century. So useful was this texture that much composed music keeps to it, even music that is not chant-based. Moreover, the texture spawned a second-generation style in that some music – perhaps considerably more than has so far been identified – was based not on the chant but on the bass line derived from it in the

---

[37] The techniques described here are discussed in Trowell 'Faburden and Fauxbourdon', *passim*; Trowell's *New Grove* articles 'Faburden' and 'Fauxbourdon'; Harrison 'Faburden in Practice', and Benham *Latin Church Music*, 102.

[38] See Meech 'Treatises'.

[39] I discuss this as if for soloists, since any embellishment would be impossible with more than one singer to a part: but the basic technique allows of no real variation and therefore could be used chorally. Pitches are of course nominal: there was no absolute pitch-standard in the Middle Ages, although local pitch-standards could be described in terms of the length of an organ-pipe.

way just described. 'The faburden' was the term used to describe such a line, which did not need to be used as the bass of the second-generation composition. This technique of composing on a 'square', as the linking counterpoint was also called, seems to be specifically English and to date from the fifteenth and sixteenth centuries.

A related technique is usually called 'fauxbourdon', although the two styles are related in complex ways that do not allow a complete distinction to be made between them.[40] As a compositional style it dates from the early fifteenth century in the works of Dufay and his contemporaries. In fauxbourdon the chant is transposed up an octave to the top line; the middle voice then 'sights' the chant a fourth below, and the bass line can be derived much as before: the aural effect of this as an improvisatory technique is the same as that of faburden, although the nominal pitch is of course a fifth higher.[41] In composed polyphony this means, in effect, that there is no basic difference between a faburden setting on a chant transposed up a fifth and a fauxbourdon setting: in both cases the middle voice is a fifth higher than the chant as it appears in the service books. One reason for using the fauxbourdon technique would be that a low-lying chant might generate too low-lying a texture in faburden style: Example 1c is a tenor-baritone-bass setting, whereas in Example 1d the fauxbourdon style produces an alto-tenor-baritone texture.

The style of any fifteenth-century piece is therefore closely bound up with the treatment of the chant, so the next stage of our examination of the Shrewsbury music concerns the relations between the existing line and the chant. As it happens, this relationship is clearest in the settings at the beginning of the section containing the plays and becomes more problematic as the plays proceed. The settings will therefore be discussed very nearly in the order in which they appear.

The first two sung items in the plays, *Transeamus usque Bethelem* and *Salvatorem Christum Dominum*, have much in common. Both occur in two continental liturgical dramas, the twelfth-century Fleury *Adoration of the Magi* and the thirteenth-century Rouen Shepherds' Play; in both French plays the two pieces are separated only by a question to the shepherds, 'Quem queritis [in presepe], pastores, dicite?'; and the musical settings are recognisably the same, with only minor variations between the two versions.[42] The Shrewsbury composer did not use either of these, for the

---

[40] The matter is discussed in Trowell 'Faburden and Fauxbourdon', and in his two *New Grove* articles; see also Harrison's discussion of the Scottish Anonymous of 1558, in 'Faburden in Practice', 12ff. It is axiomatic in these styles that the voices keep to their own pitch ranges and will not normally cross.

[41] This technique is one of those described by the Scottish Anonymous of 1558. As a compositional style in the first half of the fifteenth century the top and bottom lines were notated in a suitably decorated form, while the middle line – not notated – was sung as the top line a fourth lower.

[42] Orléans, Bibliothèque municipale, MS 201, pp. 205–6: see Coussemaker DL, 144 (edition), and Campbell and Davidson *Fleury*, plates 37–8; Paris, Bibliothèque nationale, MS lat. 904, f. 11v: see Coussemaker DL, 237. On the closeness of the musical readings of these two manuscripts, see Smoldon 1980, 204–5. In the intervening question, the words 'in presepe' are omitted from the Fleury version. Only the variants are shown here in the Fleury tune.

Example 1: Improvised textures on a chant

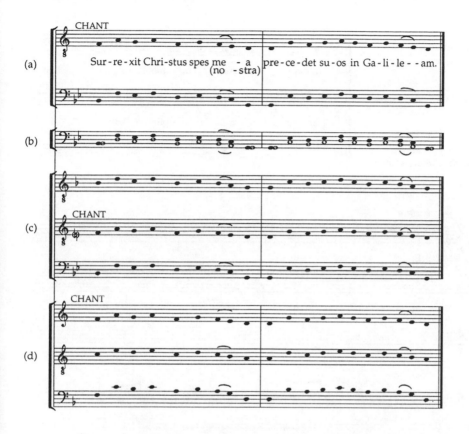

intonation of *Transeamus usque Bethelem* lacks notes that are in both: so there was presumably an English version of the chant that was simpler than either of them. In general, however, the Shrewsbury lines are clearly elaborated versions of the chant, in both pieces being closer to the Rouen than to the Fleury version. A comparison of the tunes is shown in Example 2.[43] As can be seen, the Shrewsbury line largely follows the chant in each case, but is transposed a fourth up at some of the cadences, so that the line cadences on c' or d' instead of on g. This relationship is especially clear in the case of *Transeamus usque Bethelem* (Ex. 2a). Of the various possibilities for this line, none is satisfactory unless a certain compositional freedom is accepted. If this is the middle voice and carries the plainsong, the chant actually disappears at these cadences: it cannot have migrated to the bottom voice, because

---

[43] Smoldon for some reason says that the Rouen version is notated a fourth lower than Fleury. The two versions are however plainly at the same pitch, and no transposition is necessary. The first line of *Transeamus* could be interpreted as mensural notation: but this would result in some very long notes, and Harrison is probably right to transcribe it as an unmeasured intonation in chant notation. Only variants in the Fleury tune are shown here.

Example 2 (a): Transeamus usque Bethelem

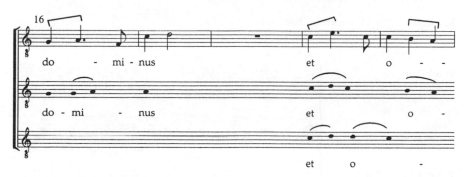

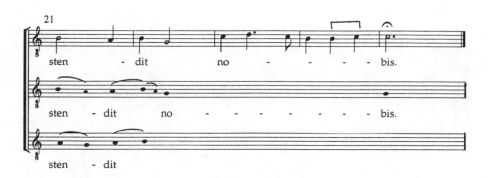

the fourths between them would be harmonically unacceptable, but it may have migrated to the top voice. It is also possible that the surviving line is the top voice. In this case some of the tune will be too low to generate the normal texture, and the piece must presumably deviate from the usual faburden practice. On balance I feel it most likely that this voice is the chant-carrying line on which a freely chant-based texture has been constructed: but we shall never know unless another voice comes to light, and even so we badly need the version of the chant used for this composition.

Salvatorem presents more problems in transcription than *Transeamus* does. One reason is that there is considerable doubt about the possibility of red coloration: while it seems likely that some of the black notes have faded to a reddish colour, it may also be that, having decided not to make up more red ink, the scribe later found it necessary to add red to some existing black notation. Another and purely musical problem is that this piece more often lies a third or a fourth above the chant than the *Transeamus* line does, arguing for either a freer chant-based line or a clearer example of a part lying above the chant in the manner of a triplex. This line is however too low to be the top voice of a three-part faburden or fauxbourdon texture, and in the absence of other evidence it is probably as well to assume that the relationship between notated line and the original chant is much the same as that for *Transeamus* but with more extensive modifications.

The next group of pieces is one in which the Shrewsbury part has an even less

Example 2 (b): Salvatorem Christum

clear relationship to one or two chants. The items concerned are *Iam, iam ecce; O Deus, quis revolvet; Mane nobiscum*; and *Gloria tibi, domine*. The first two of these are found in the Tours manuscript, which dates from the thirteenth century, and Smoldon notes that *Iam, iam ecce* is found also in several other manuscripts:[44] the twelfth-century Fleury play book;[45] Madrid, Biblioteca Nacional, MS C.132 (a twelfth-century Norman-Sicilian gradual); a Dutch Easter Play of the twelfth or thirteenth century;[46] and Oxford, Bodleian Library, MS Rawlinson liturg. d.4, which is fourteenth-century and also from France. Smoldon considered that 'the settings are all variations on some kind of common source, probably originating somewhere in Normandy'.[47]

A notational problem in *Iam, iam ecce* is that the time-signature **C** seems to refer to the breve, rather than the semibreve, as the beat. My transcription (Example 3a)

[44] Smoldon 1980, 297.

[45] Orléans, Bibliothèque de la ville, MS 201: for an edition see Coussemaker DL, 187; for a photograph of the Fleury version of *Iam, iam ecce*, see Campbell and Davidson *Fleury*, plate 56.

[46] See Smoldon 1980, 181–5; transcriptions are in Waesberghe 'Dutch Easter Play'. The play survives in two manuscripts which give essentially the same text: the Hague, Royal Library, MS 76, F.3, of the late twelfth or early thirteenth century; and MS 71, J.20, probably from the fifteenth century.

[47] Smoldon 1980, 297.

Example 3 (a): Iam, iam ecce

therefore notates the piece in 2/2 to avoid a reduction of note-values different from that in other pieces, where the semibreve is transcribed as a crotchet beat. A similar problem occurs with *O Deus, quis revolvet* (Example 3b), where there is no time-signature but the note groupings show a triple division of the long and therefore a breve beat. This interpretation is confirmed by the coloration at 'quis [revolvet]'. My transcription notates this piece in 3/2 time, using a minim beat for the same reason as in *Iam, iam ecce*.

Both Shrewsbury lines are in the tenor register and appear to be the middle part of three rather than the upper part. However, they lie mainly higher than the

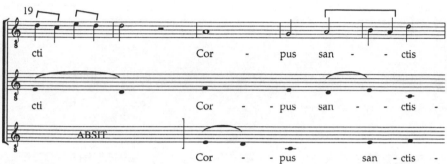

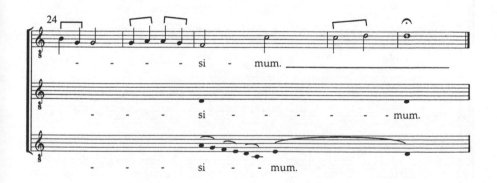

relevant chants. In the case of *Iam, iam ecce* the Shrewsbury line seems marginally more compatible with the Tours chant than with that of the Fleury play (even without the Fleury version's omission of 'dilecti'), but this is not saying very much: neither chant is closely related to the polyphonic voice. Only the range and final – authentic D mode – suggest the existence of another version of the chant to which the Shrewsbury part may be more closely related. In the case of *O Deus, quis revolvet* even this possibility seems remote: the finals are different – C for the polyphony and D for the chant – and even if the Tours chant is transposed down to the C mode the compatibility is only moderate. Transposition up a fifth does however produce considerable coincidence between the two lines, and the relationship is then more

Example 3 (b): O deus quis revolvet

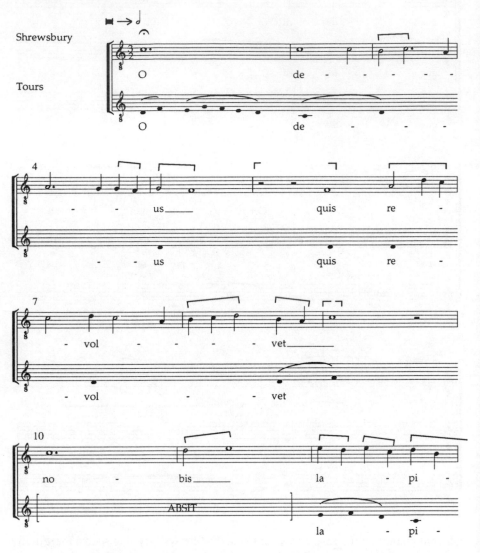

like that of *Transeamus* and *Salvatorem Christum dominum*. A possible solution is therefore that the piece is in fauxbourdon style, with the (decorated) chant in the top voice.

Mane nobiscum and *Gloria tibi domine* both revert to the metre of the first two pieces, with a semibreve beat in triple time. *Mane nobiscum* could well be compatible with the chant, but in a different relationship: the chant shares a G final with the polyphonic line but lies almost wholly above it (Example 4). If the two did go together, then the elaborated chant was in the top line, with the Shrewsbury line below it in the middle of the texture. While it would not be difficult to construct a

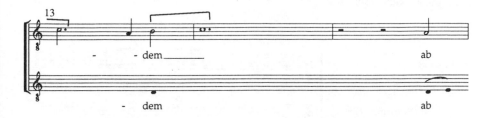

bass-line for this texture, the distance between voices would be unacceptably large at 'et inclinata' (Example 5).

Gloria tibi domine may be based, as stated above, on the doxology of either *Jesu salvator seculi* or *Ad coenam Agni*, two hymns with very similar chants. As Example 6 shows, there is little to choose between these two tunes: neither fits obviously with the Shrewsbury line, although both have important points of compatibility. Harrison's choice of *Jesu salvator seculi* as a possible basis for the Shrewsbury setting does

Example 4: Mane nobiscum

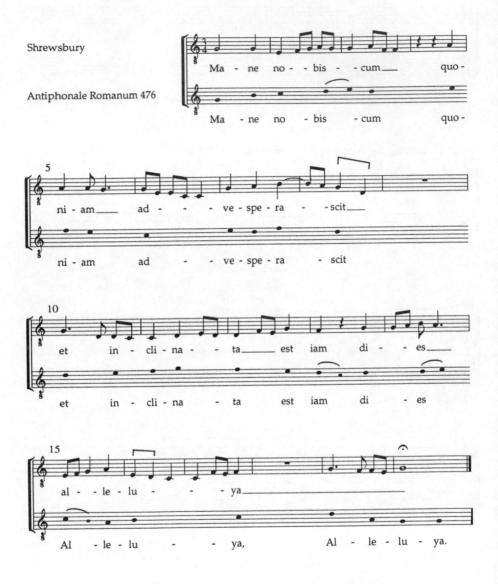

Shrewsbury

Antiphonale Romanum 476

not seem to have anything particularly to recommend it, though this is not to say that he was wrong.[48]

There remain three items for which no chant is known. *Infidelis incursum populi* looks as if it might be corrupt in several places, but it is impossible to be sure. The range of the line is from a to a', with most cadences on f' and the final cadence on

---

[48] See Davis *Non-Cycle Plays*, 127; and especially Harrison 'Faburden in Practice', 17.

Example 5: Reconstructed texture in "Mane nobiscum"

g': this suggests strongly that it was the top line of the texture, and indeed Harrison transcribed it in the treble clef. *Quid agamus* has a range of f to g', ending on d'. Although the story would suggest that it should be sung by the two disciples, the number and length of the rests in this part make it unlikely that the polyphony was in only two voices: and in addition, it is a curiously undirected line and may have been the least important of the three. Finally, *Frater Thoma* has a range of only f to e', with the final on c', and was certainly the middle voice of three.

The Shrewsbury music is tantalising in its incompleteness. The lines are generally interesting enough to suggest that the settings were of considerable intrinsic value, and the notational and musical puzzles – even without the possibility of scribal corruption in at least one piece – are such as to invite a musicologist to propose solutions. But reconstruction seems impossible, because the surviving parts are apparently free decorations of the chant and it must be assumed that the compositions are far removed from strict or simple faburden and fauxbourdon style. We shall learn no more about these pieces unless we can find at least one more voice and a closer set of chants than those currently available to us. This would obviously be very desirable, for the pieces show that there was at least one composer of considerable talent at Lichfield in the first half of the fifteenth century. Certain melodic fingerprints suggest the identity of composer for several of the pieces, although other features, such as the rather wide-ranging nature of *Infidelis incursum*, with its curious rhythmic ambience and its instantly-recognisable repeated motives, should perhaps warn us that more than one composer was probably involved.

The special relationship between liturgy and drama shown in the Shrewsbury plays is evident also, and in a more conspicuous way, in a manuscript almost exactly contemporary with the York register. Cambridge, Magdalene College, Pepys MS 1236 is a commonplace book compiled c.1460–75, probably at the Cathedral Priory of Christ Church, Canterbury: the compiler, a single scribe apparently making a personal choice of material, may well have been one of the priests of the Almonry

Example 6: Gloria tibi domine

Chapel.[49] Its contents are miscellaneous, but by far the greater part of it – 100 leaves out of 130 or so – is devoted to music. This is written in full black notation with coloration and semiminims in either full red or black void, depending on whether

[49] The manuscript is described by McKitterick and Beadle, *Catalogue*, 12–14, and by Bowers 1982, 111–14. I am indebted to Dr Beadle for drawing the dramatic fragment to my attention. The

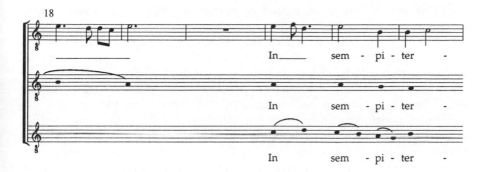

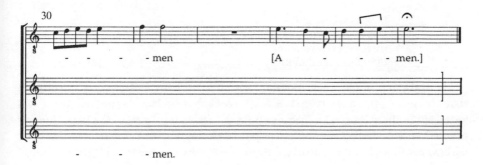

parchment or paper is in use.[50] The music has been edited by S.R. Charles, and F. Ll. Harrison has commented extensively on the musical repertory that it contains.[51]

A connection with Shrewsbury MS VI is circumstantial and general, but depends on several features. The first is that among the Pepys repertory of music for the Mass

suggestion as to the scribe's identity is due to Bowers, who also gives a slightly shorter period, c.1465–75, for the copying.

[50] Generally, the outer and centre bifolia of each gathering are of parchment, with the rest being paper. No gathering is of fewer than 8 leaves. See Bowers 1982, 111.

[51] Charles *Pepys* 1967; Harrison 'Music for the Sarum Rite'.

and Office of Salisbury Use is a good proportion of processional music, some of which will be discussed below. Second, much of the Pepys music is considerably older than the compilation, dating from the 1440s or so. Third, Pepys 1236 is in small format, very like that of Shrewsbury VI: its page size is 181 x 127 mm, as opposed to Shrewsbury's 8.2 x 5.7 inches (roughly 204 x 104 mm), and its written area 152 x 108 mm, as opposed to Shrewsbury's approximate 6 x 4 inches (roughly 152 x101 mm).[52] Fourth, its notation is similar to that of Shrewsbury VI. And last, like Shrewsbury it includes a likely dramatic item in (presumably spoken) English allied to Latin texts sung to mensural music. As I shall show, the musical style of the Pepys repertory raises problems for which reference to Shrewsbury VI may be helpful.

The possible dramatic item is even more fragmentary than the Shrewsbury plays. On the last open spread of the manuscript, ff. 127v–128r, are found three speeches in English, followed by a single line of measured music (see Plates 2 and 3). The English text, in three stanzas with speech headings for Jeremias, Ysyas and David, respectively, is set out in the manner of a dramatic text, with the speeches separated by red lines. These stanzas take up much of f. 127v, but there was room at the bottom for two staves, on which was copied the opening of the musical setting, which continues for six staves on f. 128r. The beginning of the music is however missing, because an area at the bottom of f. 127v, including the last four lines of English text and much of the music, has been cleaned off and over-written with unrelated material by a seventeenth-century hand. At the bottom of f. 128r the music ends less than half-way along the sixth staff, the rest of which is unused. In the spacious bottom margin the scribe has added a short verse on the gematria numbers of the name of Jesus:[53]

> In .8. is all my loue
> and .9. be ysette byfore
> so .8. be yclosyd aboue   Jhc
> than .3. is good therfore.

The music is a single voice underlaid with the text *Ierusalem respice ad orientem, et vide*. This is set out on the page as a single block: but, as Harrison noted, the text is found as the three Prophet's speeches from the *En rex venit* part of the Palm Sunday procession, which also appear as antiphons during Advent.[54] Harrison therefore rejected his first identification of the Pepys item, when he regarded it as a prophets' play and related it to dramatic texts known elsewhere, and treated it instead as a version of this part of the Palm Sunday procession. This section of the ceremony is already part-dramatic, for the prophecies are directed to be read by a boy 'dressed in the style of a prophet' (*ad modum prophetae indutus*). Example 7 compares the Pepys line with the chant of the relevant sections as Harrison quotes it from the 1517

---

[52] These measurements are from Bowers 1982: McKitterick and Beadle give 182 x 127 mm and 158 x 103 mm, respectively.

[53] Charles 'Provenance and Date', 62, notes that there are other versions of this rhyme, for which see IMEV, 114 (item 717).

[54] Harrison 'Music for the Sarum Rite', 126–7.

Example 7: Pepys 1236, ff. 127v-128r

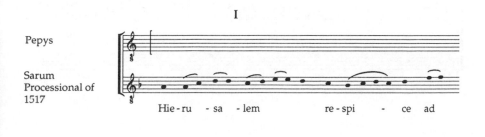

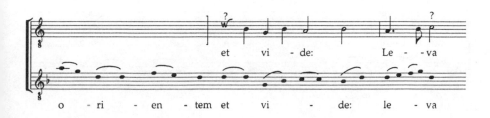

Sarum Processional: the Pepys line is a decorated version of the chant, and in this respect is comparable to the first two pieces, especially, of Shrewsbury VI.[55] It is possible to regard this music, then, as a line to be sung by a soloist taking the part

---

[55] Harrison 'Music for the Sarum Rite' gives this chant, 126–7, with a flat in the key-signature for the first two readings: however, the related chants in WA 8 and 26–7 have no flat.

II

ec - ce sal - - va - tor ve - - nit

Ec - ce Sal - - va - tor ve - nit

sol - ve - re te_____ a vin - - cu - - lo_____

sol - ve - re___ te a vin - - cu - lis:_____

David

Le - - va - te ca - pi - ta ve - - - - - - stra.

le - va - - te ca - pi - ta ve - stra.

of the prophet in the Palm Sunday procession, recognisably related to the plainchant and to be sung instead of it. The character-ascription 'David' in the gutter-margin of f. 128v, against the music, would support the notion that this version of the ceremony ascribes specific parts of the Latin text to particular prophets, and that the three spoken English texts may be further additions to the ceremony. The expansion of the liturgical text into a more dramatic form of the ceremony may therefore be seen to have three elements: the musical setting is a composed mensural monody that decorates the chant both melodically and by the kind of rhythmicisation associated with part-music; the spoken English text, starting 'O ye pepyll of ierusalem beholde and se' is a vernacular commentary on the Latin text, both expanding the ceremony and putting it on a more popular, explanatory level; and the liturgical representation of the prophet is extended to take in the dramatic representation of three named prophets, not only in the added English text but perhaps in the sung Latin as well. This last element suggests that the Latin may be performed by more than one singer: and certainly the representation of prophets

III

ec - ce ap - -pro - pin - qua - - - - bit

Ec - ce_____ ap - pro - pin - qua - - - - bit

re-dem - -pti - -o ve - - - - - - stra.

re-dem - pti - -o ve - - - - - - stra.

on Palm Sunday by more than one performer is attested in sixteenth-century London parish church accounts cited by Harrison.[56]

This explanation is not entirely satisfactory, and this section of Pepys 1236 is likely to be a separate drama in the manner of the Shrewsbury plays. The first reason for this concerns the setting-out of the text. I have said that the music is laid out as a single piece: this is not quite true, but it is certainly not set out as the three sections demanded by the Palm Sunday procession, which are as follows:

(1)   Hierusalem respice ad orientem et vide: leva Hierusalem oculos et vide potentiam regis.

(2)   Ecce Salvator venit solvere te a vinculis: levate capita vestra.

(3)   Ecce appropinquabit redemptio vestra.

In Pepys 1236 the two notes of 'Ecce' at the beginning of section 2 are divided between staves, and the 'Ecce' at the start of section 3 is similarly separated from the rest of its text: moreover, neither of these is distinguished in any way, having lower-case initials with no rubrication. On the other hand, the Pepys text does use capital initials at 'Leva', 'Regis' and 'Levate', and the last of these is at the beginning of the staff where the character heading 'David' is in the margin. Assuming that this last capital letter is more important than the others, and also that the capital for 'Regis' may be honorific rather than structural, we have a very different layout for the text:

56 Harrison 'Music for the Sarum Rite', 125: payments concerning prophets (in the plural) on Palm Sunday at St Peter, Cheap, in 1519 and 1534, and at St Mary at Hill in 1530–31 and 1534–5.

Example 8 (a): Antiphon "Ierusalem respice"

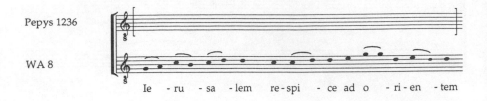

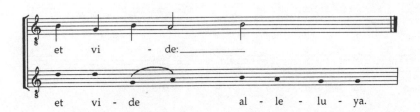

(1) (a)   [Ierusalem respice ad o]rientem: et vide.

   (b)   Leua ierusalem oculos: et vide potenciam Regis. ecce saluator venit
          soluere te a vinculo.

(2)   DAVID Leuate capita vestra: ecce appropinquabit redempcio vestra.

As Harrison mentions, this is how the text is distributed in the Advent antiphons:
'*Hierusalem respice* is the antiphon to the Magnificat at Vespers on Monday of the
first week in Advent; *Leva Hierusalem oculos* is the antiphon to the Benedictus on the
following day; and *Levate capita* is the fourth antiphon at first Vespers on Christmas
Day.' There is also a responsory *Leva Ierusalem oculos*, which has the same text as the
third antiphon. Antiphon, responsory and the Pepys version all read 'vinculo' in
section 1b, whereas the processional reads 'vinculis'.[57] The Pepys text, then, distributed as I have just set it out in sections 1a, 1b and 2, is the same as those of the three
antiphons, and 1b is also that of the responsory.

If the Pepys text is distributed in the same way as that of the antiphons, it is
reasonable to ask if the music is not more closely related to the antiphons' chants
than to the relevant section of the Palm Sunday procession. Reference to Example
7 shows that, although the correspondence between Pepys music and the processional chant is fairly good for the section 'et vide . . . regis', it is much less so for
'Ecce salvator venit' onwards – in fact, the relationship seems non-existent for

---

57 Harrison 'Music for the Sarum Rite', 127. *Ierusalem respice* is in WA 8 and LA 22; *Leva Ierusalem
oculos* is in LA 7, and in AR 220 and AM 191; *Levate capita vestra* is in WA 26–7 and LA 30, and
also in AR 260, AM 237, and LU 365. The respond *Leva Ierusalem oculos* is in AS, plate f, and
LA 9.

Example 8 (b): "Leva Ierusalem oculos" (antiphon and respond)

considerable stretches. In contrast, a comparison between the Pepys line and the chants of the antiphons and responsory shows a much closer relationship (Example 8). For the first antiphon, 'Ierusalem . . . et vide', there is too much missing from the Pepys music for any certainty, and there seems little to choose between the two chants: but it is worth noting that the A at the start of 'vide' in Pepys 1236 is supplied only by the antiphon, and that the procession chant has a B-flat in the key-signature that the Pepys line and the antiphon do not have. In 'Leva Ierusalem . . . vinculo' there is something to be said for both the processional chant and the antiphon, but little for the responsory. Here, too, the antiphon does not have the key-signature of

the processional version. On balance I think a derivation from the antiphon tune a more consistent one, in view of the pitches at the cadences: but this is only with the antiphon tune transposed up a fifth. There is a slightly surprising moment at 'oculos', where the Pepys tune is closer to the monastic version of the antiphon (as in AM) than to the secular version, although the difference between the two is so small that it is perhaps not significant. Finally, 'Levate capita . . . redemptio vestra', none of which was very close to the processional chant, is closely based on the antiphon tune transposed up a fifth. The repeated unison on the opening of 'Levate' is noticeable, as is also the preference for the secular version at the first 'vestra' where it differs from the Worcester (monastic) reading.

It seems clear that the Pepys tune is based on the antiphon chants rather than on the relevant section of the procession on Palm Sunday; that there has been some

Example 8 (c): Antiphon "Levate capita vestra"

adjustment of the finals so that the three antiphons, heard on different days in their normal liturgical position, can be performed 'end-on' without tonal gear-changes; and that this adjustment has resulted in transposition of the second and third antiphon chants.

It follows from all this that the compiler of this dramatic section – not the compiler of Pepys 1236, but the 'playwright' working some decades earlier – took the texts of the three antiphons as the verbal basis of the passage transmitted in this manuscript. It follows also that if the third antiphon text is allotted to David in the play, the first and second antiphon texts may have been intended for Jeremiah and Isaiah: that is, that the Latin text was meant to present a parallel to the English text, with the same three characters involved. A comparison of the texts bears this out:

JEREMIAS	O ye pepill of ierusalem be holde & se	[Ierusalem respice
	make your respecte into the orient	[ad orientem et vide
	a kyng is comyng of gret poste	
	the maker of this worlde omnipotent	
	reuyue ye pepill þat be present	
	& thanke hym of his grete mercy	
	for he is disposyd among you to dy.	
YSYAS	Lyft vp your yen to heuyn an hey	[Leva ierusalem oculos
	& be holde the power of þis my3t kyng	[et vide potentiam regis
	he cometh to saue you eternally	[ecce salvator venit
	& fro dampnacyon you for to bryng	[solvere te a vinculo
	for your sowle helth is his comyng	
	whych is to hym but anguysch & payn	
	for he among you shall be murdred & slayn.	
DAVID	O ye pepyll of ierusalem whyle ye may attayn	[Levate capita vestra
	aske mercy of this lorde for your offens	[ecce appropinquabit
	. . .	redemptio vestra.

In the first two stanzas, certainly, a paraphrase of the Latin lines is followed by comment on the process of salvation, so that these confirm a parallel relationship between English and Latin texts. The pattern of these stanzas, with paraphrase followed by comment, is usual in the vernacular biblical dramas. The third stanza is not on this pattern, but since five lines of it are lost it is difficult to guess what the relationship between English and Latin might be. We are perhaps fortunate to have the speech heading 'David' in the musical text, which points to the parallel sung presentation in Latin. Or perhaps that heading is in the musical setting precisely because the texts by themselves do not make their relationship clear at the beginning of David's stanza.

What sort of musical settings are these? It must be said first that the metrical structure of these pieces is impossible to determine: there are no good clues as to a regular metre for any of them. Although both *Leva Ierusalem oculos* and *Levate capita vestra* use note-groupings that strongly suggest triple mensuration, any attempt to impose O time consistently runs into difficulties over the perfection or otherwise of breves. For example, the musical phrase to 'oculos' works well in this metre (Example 9), but the next phrase is a semibreve too long, since the final breve must (in this common cadential formula) be at the beginning of a perfection: thus the phrase works only if we assume that the first five notes of it were originally a coloration group – that is, that both semibreves that start the phrase are imperfect (Examples 10a and 10b). Unfortunately this phrase does not work in C time either (Example 11), when there is a semibreve too many. The line may be a rhythmically free voice, then, which was not intended to be performed in the kind of regular metre normally used for polyphony.

Example 9: "Leva Ierusalem", second phrase

Example 10: "Leva Ierusalem", third phrase

Example 11: "Leva Ierusalem", third phrase

This circumstance probably helped to make the idea of mensural monody an attractive one to commentators on the music of Pepys 1236: another is the wide pitch range of certain pieces in the manuscript – notably the astonishing *Lamentations* setting by John Tuder – which seems to make any polyphonic collaboration with other voices very unlikely. Although this rather extreme style is not found in the dramatic music on ff. 127v–128r, there is still a good case to be made for this music, like other single-line settings in Pepys 1236, being monodic in conception. The great majority of pieces in the source are polyphonic, after all, with all voices copied: and if the compiler was collecting a selection of favourite items, why should he make incomplete copies? Charles gives an explanation for some of the 'monodic' pieces: namely, that they are counterpoints to their respective chants. If this is so, then the chants, being available in the usual service books, did not need to be copied, although we have to assume that the rhythmic interpretation of the chants is clear.

In this way, certainly, a single notated mensural line in Pepys 1236 could give rise to a piece of two-voice polyphony.

But this does not explain the pieces based on the chant itself and therefore incompatible with a performance of it. There are four of these: nos. 37, 52, 68 and 121 in Charles's edition. Of these, the last is our dramatic scene, the settings of the three antiphon texts. Charles does not offer criteria by which a monodic composition can be distinguished stylistically from a single voice of a polyphonic composition. There is in fact no obvious stylistic difference between these four pieces and no. 1 in the manuscript: but whereas Charles states that the former pieces are monophonic (no. 121), or suggests it (no. 68), or does not draw a conclusion (nos. 37, 52), he is able to explain the features of no. 1 as belonging to incomplete polyphony on the grounds that f. 2 of the manuscript is missing and the rest of the first piece was presumably on f. 2r. Yet because of the particular features of the piece as it survives, he has to explain a partial following of the chant as being due to its migration to another voice. One is tempted to make the comment (a) that f. 2r may well have contained a completely separate piece, and (b) that chant migration would be a convenient explanation of the third phrase of *Leva Ierusalem*, too.

I do not really think that this problem can be solved at present. For one thing, the whole question of 'mensural monody' seems to me very doubtful: it may be a useful concept by which certain problematic phenomena can be explained, but I see no hard evidence for even the existence of the style. Against this, it is certainly true that an acceptable explanation is needed of the copying of single lines in Pepys 1236 if those lines are in fact from polyphonic compositions. Is there any internal evidence of polyphony in the dramatic scene's music?

I would think that the transposition of the chant in *Leva Ierusalem oculos* and *Levate capita vestra* points in this direction. As far as one can see, the Pepys line for *Ierusalem respice ad orientem* is at the pitch of the antiphon chant and coincides with that chant at the cadence, although it ends on a B instead of a G (the chant being in the authentic G mode). But in the second and third pieces the chant is transposed up a fifth: why? I believe that this is a consequence of putting three antiphons together, 'end-on', that would normally have been separated. The problem arises because of their modalities, but only in a polyphonic setting.

These three antiphons have no key-signature in their chants; none of them needs one. *Ierusalem respice ad orientem* is in the authentic G mode, and ends on a G after a prominent B-natural. *Leva ierusalem oculos* and *Levate capita vestra* are both in the authentic D mode. Although there is a change of mode after the first antiphon, therefore, the change of final from G to D is a simple one: and as the second and third antiphons do not need a B-flat key-signature there is a minimum of gear-change at the border between the first and second antiphons. This situation would however be different in faburden style if the chant were in the middle voice for all three pieces. Then, *Ierusalem respice ad orientem* would effectively be in the authentic C mode, because of the top voice being pitched a fourth above the chant, with the bass line similarly aligned: but no B-flat would be required, because the note F does not appear in the chant. There would be a distinct tonal lurch into the second piece, however, in which the authentic D mode of the chant would give rise to a tonality a fourth above – that is, a G mode with B-flats. The way out of this problem would be to compose the second and third pieces in fauxbourdon style. Then the authentic D mode of the chant is retained, no B-flat is required in the key-signature, and the tonal shift from the C mode is almost as good as that from the G mode.

Despite the problems, then, I believe that the music of this scene probably was three-part polyphony, the first section being in faburden style and the second and third in fauxbourdon style; that the texts are those of three Advent antiphons, the musical setting being based on the chants of those antiphons and not, as Harrison thought, on the relevant section of the Palm Sunday procession; and that, consequently, this material must be regarded as a brief separate Prophets' play for three characters in the same spoken-vernacular-plus-sung-Latin style as the Shrewsbury plays. Whether it was performed at Canterbury Cathedral or not cannot at present be determined, although the provenance of the manuscript would make that likely: but, as the source of the music surely indicates, the season of the performance would be Christmas.

3.3 York

British Library Additional MS 35290, the York register, was copied some time in the period 1463-77, and was still in use as a check on the individual play texts of the York cycle in the mid-sixteenth century.[58] **York 45**, the Weavers' Guild's play of *The Assumption of the Virgin*, belongs to this main compilation. The play is copied in its own gathering of four parchment bifolia, giving eight leaves: these are ff. 249–56, inclusive, forming quire 32.[59] The play does not take up the whole gathering, but ends on f. 255r: despite this, the scribe wrote the guild-heading, 'The Wefferes', to the end of the quire, and rubricated the heading on all but the last two pages. Thus, of the pages that follow the end of the play, f. 255v has a rubricated heading, and ff. 256r and 256v have unrubricated headings (compare Plates 4 and 5).

A full description of the manuscript will be found in the introduction to the facsimile, Medieval Drama Facsimiles VII (1983), which also contains a colour facsimile of the music pages (following p. xlvi). The music has been edited by Ruth Steiner (in Wall 'York XLVI', pp. 698–712), by John Stevens (in Beadle 1982, pp. 465–74), by JoAnna Dutka (*Music* 1980, pp. 38–50), and by myself (*Six Songs* 1985). The music and its performers are discussed in Rastall 'Vocal Range' 1984.[60]

At three points in the play, after **York 45/104, 45/117** and **45/208**, there is angelic singing: the positioning of these music cues will be discussed below, in relation to

---

[58] Beadle and Meredith 'Dating the York Register'; Meredith 'John Clerke's Hand'.

[59] I use Beadle's numbering for the plays of the cycle (Beadle 1982), which he and Meredith adopted also for the facsimile (MDF 7); I use his foliation also, rather than Toulmin Smith's or the British Library's. (MDF 7 gives all three.)

[60] Discussions of the texts will be footnoted below. Wall used Toulmin Smith's numbering for the plays, in which *The Assumption* – she called it *The Appearance of Our Lady to Thomas* – is Play 46.

the numerological structure of the play, in 6.3. The music is written into the play text at these places, on ff. 250v, 251r and 253r. It is music for two equal voices, written in score. As is usual in fifteenth-century score notation, the text is underlaid to the lower voice only: an exception to the norm is that the word 'Surge' is written at the beginning of the top staff on f. 250v. Each piece is copied into a space presumably left for it by the main text scribe. The three pieces set texts that begin, respectively, 'Surge, proxima mea', 'Veni de Libano, sponsa' and 'Veni, electa mea'. Ruth Steiner referred to these as the 'A versions', to distinguish them from the settings of the same texts (the 'B versions') that follow the play text: this is a convenient designation that I shall follow here.

The spaces for the A versions were apparently carefully calculated when the play text was copied. In each case the music makes use of the vertical lines of the frame drawn on the page, and on f. 250v of the top line as well. On f. 251r the music takes up a little space below the frame at the foot of the page, but the margins are generous and there is ample room for this (see Plate 4). The lateral spacing is such as to allow the end of a musical phrase to coincide with the end of a system. Examination of the scribe's spacing suggests that he manipulated his material with this end in view, which also explains the decorative longs that help to fill the space on the last system of *Surge* A.[61] The music progresses in clear phrases, with the two voices largely coinciding and always cadencing together, so the line-by-line layout of these settings is sensible: indeed, it is the kind of relationship between material and layout that could be expected in the work of any professional scribe.

All the music in the A versions is on the flesh side of the parchment. If this is coincidental – and it is hard to see how the main scribe could manipulate his material from the beginning of the gathering if it was deliberate on his part – it was certainly fortunate for the music scribe, who (as we shall see) probably preferred not to use hair sides if roughnesses remained.

At the end of the play there are three more pages before the end of the gathering (ff. 255v–256v). The last two of these also contain music, f. 255v being unused. On f. 256r is another setting of *Surge proxima mea* (except that in this setting the second word is given as 'propera'), while on f. 256v are settings of *Veni de Libano sponsa* and *Veni electa mea*. As already noted, I shall follow Steiner in referring to these as the 'B versions'. These settings, like the A versions, are in two voices, although a four-part chord in *Veni de Libano* B shows that at least four singers were needed for these two voices. In the B versions the music is set out in separate parts, not in score, and for this reason both voice-parts are underlaid with text. However, the end of the text is omitted from the lower voice of *Surge* B, while *Veni electa* B has only the first word copied below the upper part and only the last word ('tuam') under the lower part. The latter word is in red.

It may be that the music scribe originally intended to copy one piece on each of the last three pages of the gathering (ff. 255v, 256r and 256v). *Surge* B, the longest of the B versions, takes up the whole of f. 256r, which has an extra, ninth, staff

61 See my discussion in MDF 7, xliii, top paragraph.

straddling the bottom frame line.[62] However, the scribe left f. 255v unused, and therefore had to copy both *Veni de Libano* and *Veni electa* on the final page of the gathering (see Plate 5). This is unsatisfactory: not only is the lateral compression of the notes greater than elsewhere, but the scribe had to increase the line-length, for which reason he drew a new frame-line near the middle of the outer margin. Even so, the available space was not increased so much as to enable each new voice-part to start on a new line, as had been possible in *Surge* B on the previous page. The lower voices of both pieces, and even the upper voice of *Veni electa*, begin in mid-line immediately after the end of the previous voice.

The problems here are caused by the non-use of f. 255v. With three available pages providing ample room for the B versions to be copied in a neat and orderly fashion (even if not quite as generously spaced as the A versions are), why did the scribe put himself into a position where this was impossible? There seems no doubt that the play was already copied when the B versions were written into the gathering, so the answer does not lie with any uncertainty about the space available.[63] A probable reason is that f. 255v is a rather roughly-prepared hair side, and that the scribe considered it unsuitable for the finer pen-work demanded by music.[64] He could not altogether avoid using a hair side, of course, since f. 256r is a hair side, as well; but f. 256r presents no problems inside the writing frame, whereas f. 255v has a considerable patch of hair-follicles in the writing area. That the scribe did not improve the preparation of this page, so that he could use it, is probably the final piece of evidence that the play text had already been copied when it came into the music-scribe's hands. Folio 255r had already received its text, and the scribe's aids to a good writing surface – pumice-stone, chalk, and a bone or ivory smoother – could not be applied to f. 255v without damaging the text-scribe's work. In the circumstances, the music scribe may well have felt that it was preferable to use the better of the two hair sides for a single piece and to squeeze the remaining two pieces onto the unproblematic flesh side.

The music and its underlaid text are written in rather blacker ink than the play text, although in some paces it has faded to the reddish-brown of the rest of the main part of the manuscript. The ink-colour suggests that a single scribe was responsible for both the music and its underlaid text, and features of the layout confirm this supposition. In most cases the text was copied before the music, as was usual.[65] In *Surge* B this is shown by the fitting of minim stems around the words 'columba' and 'columba mea' (f. 256r). In the A versions, an even clearer indication appears from comparison of the spacing of the music with that of the text: for while there are no signs that the scribe encountered spacing problems in copying the words, there

---

[62] The ideal spacing occurs on f. 250v, where *Surge* A takes the whole page, with space for text between the bottom (eighth) staff and the frame line. *Veni de Libano* A, on f. 251r, also has its last staff, the fourth, straddling the frame line (a complete thirteen-line stanza of text at the top of the page takes up so much room that there is space for only three staves above the line).

[63] I discuss this question in MDF 7, xliv.

[64] Quire 32, like the other gatherings in this manuscript, is of the usual structure with the flesh side of the parchment on the outside and also in the centre of the gathering.

[65] For the exceptions, see the comments on *Veni de Libano* B and *Veni electa* B, below.

are inconsistencies in the spacing of the music that obviously derive from the constraints of a previously-copied text.[66] Despite these features, however, the general accuracy of the spacing of the text in relation to the music shows that the scribe had a copy of this setting in front of him when he copied the text. This, in turn, reinforces the proposition that text and music were copied by a single scribe.

There is however no evidence that the music scribe was the same as the main scribe of the plays. The underlaid text is in a smaller and more formal style than the English spoken text of the plays, but this is to be expected anyway and it does not constitute evidence in either direction.[67] The different ink colour does suggest a non-identity of the scribes; and we ought not to suppose that a professional text scribe employed by the City of York to copy the register would also be a music scribe, although this is not impossible.[68] It is however clear that the music scribe worked in close collaboration with the main text scribe, or at least that the main scribe had very clear directions as to how much space to leave for the musical settings of the A versions, in which he has been very accurate. It is probable, in any case, that he had the musical settings in front of him when he copied the play.

The writing of the York music and its underlaid text is that of a clear, regular and professional hand. The A versions are neatly and accurately copied, and the scribe seems to have experienced no difficulties with the process of copying. The B versions, which were copied by the same scribe, presented more problems. Here, in pieces that are longer and more melismatic than the A versions, the relationship between text and music is more complex and the assessment of the lateral space needed for each syllable consequently more difficult. *Surge* B was copied text-first in the usual way, as already noted: but the shortage of space and the consequent need to add a ninth staff evidently upset the scribe's calculations, and he decided to play safe by leaving out the end of the text for the lower voice until he had copied the music. He therefore omitted the text of the bottom two staves of the page. Having done so, however, he then failed to return to his task, so that the text '[taberna]-culum gloria, vasculum vite, templum celeste' at the end of the piece is missing. Perhaps as a result of his experience with *Surge* B, the scribe made no attempt to assess the spacing of the text for *Veni de Libano* B and *Veni electa* B, which he realised would have to be squeezed in together. For these two pieces, therefore, he abandoned the 'text-first' principle and wrote the music in as best he could: only after the music was copied for at least *Veni de Libano* B did he underlay the text of that piece, not entirely avoiding collisions between text and minim-stems.[69] As for *Veni electa*, by the time he had copied the music he found it impossible to copy the text for some reason, or perhaps simply lost interest. The word 'Veni' is underlaid to the

---

[66] These features are described in MDF 7, xliii, second paragraph.

[67] Compare the similar circumstance in the Shrewsbury manuscript, where however the script for *Salvatorem Christum dominum* shows that the same scribe copied both dialogue and music underlay (p. 89, above).

[68] As Peter Meredith pointed out, the full title of the Scriveners' Guild was 'the Science of Tixtwryters, Lominers, Noters, Turners and Florisshers', so that it may have included music copyists in its ranks at the relevant time (see MDF 7, xlviii, n. 15).

[69] See Plate 5, third staff.

first half-line of the upper voice; but the only other text for the piece, written in red and therefore presumably an after-thought,[70] is the last word of the text, 'tuam', underlaid to the last two notes of the lower voice. It is impossible to know quite what happened, but the scribe must have been aware that he had not provided the information necessary for a satisfactory performing copy.

The music is written in full black notation with full red coloration, on red five-line staves.[71] The semiminim is usually of the full red type, but there are two instances of the black void form. The rhythm normally notated by a dotted minim and a semiminim is on one occasion displaced by the colored semibreve-minim group, for no obvious reason. The musical style uses too many short notes for ligatures to be much in evidence, but the ligature *cum opposita proprietate* occurs throughout, the descending ligature taking the oblique form in every case; a single breve-breve ligature is found in the lower voice of *Veni electa* A. Other symbols are much as expected: the C-clef is of normal form, although invariably written in red; the flat, which applies only to the B-flat above Middle C, is of the double-bulbed type; the pause and *signum congruentiae* both appear at the ends of musical phrases (they seem to be used as alternatives, although the former is more common); the direct or *custos* is present where necessary at the end of the line on all occasions but one; and a 'bar-line' is normally used at the end of a musical phrase.[72]

The use of colored notes to show rhythmic modification is itself unremarkable in this manuscript, and the music scribe wrote red pauses and *signa* over such notes, as is normal. However, he was inconsistent in his use of black and red ink in several places: dots may be of either colour, and there are examples of a mensuration-sign, a flat, four directs, part of a *signum* and a pause-sign copied in red.[73] The normal method of copying black notation with red coloration was to write the black notation first, leaving suitable spaces for the red notes, which were then fitted into the spaces later. This procedure allowed the scribe to prepare red ink for a single work-spell during which no change of the pen was necessary. The inconsistencies in the York scribe's copying suggest that he had no habits concerning the change of pens, and therefore that he was not trained to write in this notation. This in turn implies that he was working long after the period in which black notation with red coloration was normal, and therefore that the music itself was from an earlier period. The use of red for the notes sung *divisi* in *Veni de Libano* B has good precedent in the Old Hall manuscript (compiled c.1410–20) and sources contemporary with it.[74] We shall return to the question of dating the music.

The use of red ink for symbols other than notes and their associated dots and

---

[70] Whether text or music was copied first, we should expect that the black ink would be used first, the red being added later. At whatever stage he copied it, the scribe presumably wrote this word after copying something else in red, and therefore out of order.

[71] I describe the notation more fully in MDF 7, xli–xlii.

[72] Lack of space is responsible for the omission of 'bar-lines' in *Veni electa* A (f. 253r, first and third staves) and probably in *Veni de Libano* A (f. 251r, second and fourth staves) also.

[73] These are detailed in MDF 7, xlii, the top six lines.

[74] See Hughes and Bent *Old Hall, passim*. Some further notational features, which however do not concern us here, are discussed in MDF 7, xlii, second complete paragraph.

pauses may or may not reflect the scribal practices of the exemplar from which this music was copied. The clefs are written in red throughout, a procedure that would normally indicate transposition but is likely here to be merely decorative.

We have noticed a number of differences between the A and B versions of the York pieces. The A versions, carefully copied in a way that shows a clear relationship between material and layout (both of the musical items and of the play as a whole), is notated in score, while the B versions, less carefully copied, slightly corrupted, and with the original intentions for the layout apparently altered, are in separate parts. These differences are related to an important difference in musical style: for while the A versions are largely homorhythmic and progress in short, clear phrases with simultaneous cadences, the B versions are longer, contrapuntally freer, and make use of overlap at the cadences to produce a more nearly continuous texture. In effect, then, the B versions are very much more difficult to sing. In addition, it would be fair to say that the A versions are more suitable for outdoor performance, while the more rhythmically complex B versions would probably work much less well out of doors.

We shall return to these differences, but they need to be understood in the context of certain similarities that have not yet been mentioned. There is some evidence that the six pieces were planned as a group, or rather as two similar groups. Evidence for this over-all plan is provided by the arrangement of metres and tonalities in the two groups of settings. *Surge* and *Veni electa* are in perfect *tempus* and imperfect *prolatio* in both of their settings, although the time-signature O appears only in the B versions. That is, they are in triple time, best transcribed as 3/4. Both versions of *Veni de Libano*, on the other hand, are imperfect in both *tempus* and *prolatio*, with a time-signature C. That is, they are in duple metre, best transcribed as 4/4. The duple time is not used consistently, however, and one has the impression that the composer was happier in triple time: the duple metre is used fluidly in *Veni de Libano* A, which requires the occasional three-beat bar, while *Veni de Libano* B quickly reverts to triple time completely. The choice of a different metre for the middle piece of each group, then, is not carried through, although there is enough of it to show the difference. This is perhaps no more than an obvious way of creating a contrast in pieces that might otherwise sound too much alike.

In a similar fashion, the tonalities of the six pieces suggest a simple device by which variety can be achieved in a stylistically homogeneous set of pieces. In each set, *Surge* has G as its final, *Veni de Libano* has C, and *Veni electa mea* has F. The first and last notes of each voice in the six pieces demonstrate this (Example 12). Two apparent anomalies in this example do not affect my basic contention, but may suggest that the pieces were not composed at leisure. First, the difference in mode between the two settings of *Surge* is more a confusion than a contradiction. The one-flat key-signature appears in only the upper voice of *Surge* A, and it is cancelled – not to reappear – a third of the way through the piece. This is symptomatic of a slight tonal ambiguity that is something of a feature of these pieces and is particularly evident in *Veni de Libano* B and both versions of *Veni electa*. The second anomaly is the interval of a fifth on which *Veni electa* B ends. This is not merely the only fifth

Example 12: Starting and ending notes of the York music

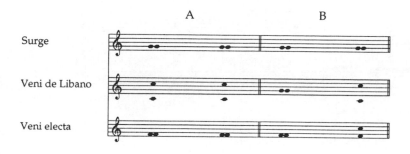

Example 13: "Veni electa" B, ending

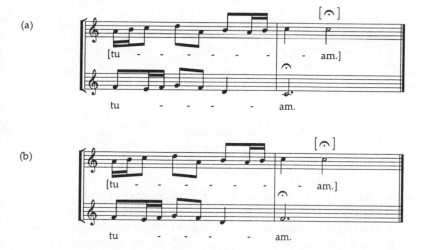

at the end of a piece: there are very few cadences anywhere in the York pieces that
do not end on the unison or octave. In this case, it is uncertain whether the key-note
of the piece is really F rather than C, for although the piece seems to struggle towards
F there is no flat in the key-signature and the constant B-naturals undermine the F
tonality.[75] The final cadence is an extraordinary affair in which an apparent move
towards C as the final is subverted at the last moment. Example 13a shows the
approach to this cadence and the ending that the ear is led to expect, while Example
13b shows what actually happens. The aural effect of this is to suggest that C, rather
than F, is after all the final of the piece, and in performance it is certainly better to

---

[75] It is possible that some B-flats should be introduced, but the melodic contours prohibit that in
several rather important places: one cannot, in fact, reasonably change enough B-naturals to
B-flats to turn the tonality firmly to F.

Example 14: "Veni electa" B, "corrected" ending

Example 15: Common cadence in A settings

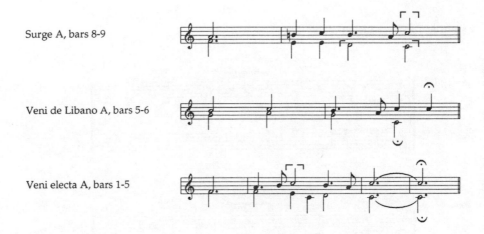

Surge A, bars 8-9

Veni de Libano A, bars 5-6

Veni electa A, bars 1-5

'correct' this passage and perform the cadence of Example 13a.[76] It is also tempting to amend the cadence in such a way as to make sense of the scribe's reading. Example 14 shows a possible solution, which assumes that the scribe omitted a note in the lower voice: but this is not a likely two-voice cadence in the fifteenth century, and certainly not in the first half, when (as we shall see) the music was composed. Besides, the over-all plan of tonalities shown in the other five pieces suggests that this F is not a scribal error but the result of a misjudgement in composition – a somewhat desperate expedient by the composer, correctly copied by the scribe, to pull the piece back to its intended final. If this is so, it seems extraordinary that the composer did not re-work the last few bars. Perhaps he had little time to complete the composition.

This plan, if it really is a plan, implies that a single composer was responsible for all six pieces and this is confirmed by other features of the music. The three A settings share a common style, with clear-cut phrases and crossing of parts that is often a device for varying the texture. They also share an obvious structural feature, a

---

[76] Steiner made this change; Dutka and Stevens retained the manuscript reading.

Example 16: Common phrase in "Surge" settings

Surge A, bars 14-16

TEXT   Vas - cu - lum   vi   - te   Templum

Surge B, bars 28-30

Example 17: The phrases of "Surge" A and B

A
phrase-lengths
(perfections)

B
phrase-lengths
(perfections)

cadence on C which is shown in its various forms in Example 15. This cadence is common enough, but its appearance here in three short pieces with different finals implies a single composer's fingerprint rather than a general stylistic feature of the time. The B settings, more decorative in style and with frequent non-simultaneous changes of syllable, show an overlapping of phrases between the two voices that has been mentioned already. Even in this relatively seamless texture, however, there are some echoes of the A version style, and this is most noticeable in *Surge* B, where there is almost no overlapping of phrases. As it happens, however, *Surge proxima mea* is a special case, with a clear structural relationship between the two versions. The most evident feature of this relationship is the use of a common phrase for 'vasculum vite', only slightly decorated in the B version (Example 16). But this turns out to be only one item in a case of structural parallelism.[77] If we define the phrases of the B version by means of the simultaneous cadences and then look at the first and last notes of each phrase, the correspondence seems much too close to be

[77] This has been discussed by both Steiner (in Wall 'York XLVI', 699) and Stevens (in Beadle 1982, 467).

Example 18: Common material in "Veni de Libano" A and B

Veni de Libano B

Veni de Libano A

accidental, as Example 17 shows. Moreover, if we ignore the fifth phrase (asterisked in Example 17, and common to the two versions), the B version is a fairly consistent phrase-by-phrase expansion of the A setting, a 3-bar phrase becoming 5 or 6 bars and a 5-bar phrase becoming 7, 8 or 9 bars. As it stands, the A version is 25 perfections (bars in the transcription) long and the B version 38 perfections (bars). Allowing for the expansion of the fifth phrase to 5 bars, the proportion would be 5 : 8 (25 : 40). There is no direct evidence that this was in the composer's mind: but whether he intended a consistent expansion by simple mathematical ratio or not, it remains something of a puzzle why the fifth phrase should be treated to minimal decoration rather than to expansion.

In the two versions of *Veni de Libano* there is again some musical material used in both (Example 18). Two melodic motives that appear in voice I (the upper voice) of the B version, bars 2–3, recur in voice II, bars 16–17: but the first of them also appears in voice I of the A version, bars 3 and 10.[78] This may be taken as evidence of a relationship between the A and B versions, although it is impossible to detect the phrase-by-phrase expansion found in *Surge* A and B. All that can be said is that *Veni de Libano* B is a new, decorated composition along the lines of the A version. Just as striking, however, is a relationship between *Veni de Libano* and *Surge*: bars 3–5 of *Veni de Libano* B appear also as bars 6–7 of *Surge* A (Example 19).

In *Veni electa*, too, the phrases sometimes coincide in the two versions: but they do not always match in pitch, and the B version seems to be a decorated recomposition. As Example 20a shows, *Veni electa* B actually incorporates material from *Veni de Libano* B in both voices, while a phrase in *Veni electa* A, bars 16–19, seems to derive

---

[78] Bar numbers refer to my own edition, *Six Songs*.

Example 19: Common material in the York music

Veni de Libano
B, bars 3-5

Surge A,
bars 6-7

from the 'vasculum vite' phrase common to the two settings of *Surge* (Example 20b, and cf. Example 16).[79]

The possible intended proportions of the two versions of *Surge* raise the question of such proportions in the cases of *Veni de Libano* and *Veni electa*, but no comparable plan emerges. In the *Veni de Libano* pair the expansion is largely due to a change to triple time in the B version after 17 semibreves, and the overall proportion of 46 : 71 semibreves seems to have no significance.[80] It is notable, however, that the most striking gesture of *Veni de Libano* B comes almost exactly half way through, after 35 semibreves, and itself takes six semibreves with pauses: this is the setting of the word 'Veni' in which both parts divide (Example 21).[81] In *Veni electa* the B version is only marginally longer than the A version – 85 semibreves, as opposed to 84 – and again the proportion seems not to be significant.

If the cadences shown in Example 15 suggest that the three A versions were the work of one composer, the structural connections between the two versions of *Surge proxima mea* and the web of motivic connections concerning all six pieces are reasonable evidence that this composer was also responsible for the B versions. We cannot put a name to him, but the music can be dated within a decade or two. I have already mentioned that the scribe's apparent unease with coloration points to the music having been composed some decades before the register's compilation in the period 1463–77, and the general style of the music confirms this. The duet style for

---

[79] This could be the other way round, presumably: it is hardly safe to assume that the order of composition was the same as that of copying.

[80] I count semibreves here because of the metrical irregularity of the piece. On all occasions I count longs as imperfect and phrase-end breves as perfect or imperfect according to the prevailing metre.

[81] The coloration of these chords indicates *divisi* performance for the second. Treating the ligatures as ordinary long + breve ligatures makes harmonic and durational nonsense of the passage.

Example 20: Common material in the York music

(a)

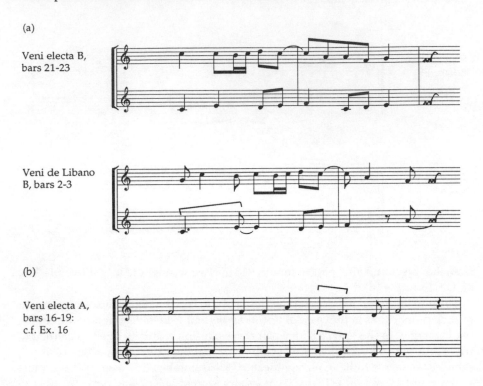

Veni electa B,
bars 21-23

Veni de Libano
B, bars 2-3

(b)

Veni electa A,
bars 16-19:
c.f. Ex. 16

Example 21: Four-part chord in the York music

Veni de Libano B,
bars 12-13

Ve - ni

Ve - ni

equal voices, which makes no apparent use of chant in any of the six pieces, was
not common in the mid-to-late-fifteenth century, when most two-part writing was
for two different voices.[82] The duet-style for equal voices is certainly found in some
English music of the fifteenth century, including the following:[83]

---

[82] Steiner and Stevens both compared the York pieces to the polyphonic carol style, while noting
the use of different voices in the duets of the carol repertory.

[83] For an example from later in the century, but for tenors and probably Flemish, see the
anonymous *Ave regina* presented in Appendix A.

Example 22: Equal-voice duet in "Cantemus domino"

British Library
MS Egerton 3307:
"Cantemus domino",
bars 1-11

— The duets of the four-part motet *Cantemus domino* in BL MS Egerton 3307. As Example 22 shows, the clarity of phrase-structure in this piece is reminiscent of the York A settings, as are the rhythms of bars 5–6 and the exchange of notes there between the parts (cf. Example 16). The more florid writing is very close to that of the York B settings, even to those near-miss consecutives (bars 3–4) that feature several times in the York pieces. McPeek dated Egerton 3307 at around 1430–44.[84]

— The equal-voice duet in the Agnus Dei of Lionel Power's Mass *Alma*

[84] McPeek *Egerton 3307*, 16.

Example 23: Equal-voice duet by Power

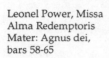

Redemptoris Mater.[85]The opening of this duet is shown in Example 23, where one can see the crossing of parts, the parallel thirds, and even a distinctive melodic motive (bar 60, and cf. Example 18) that feature in the York music. Power died in 1444, and the earliest sources of this piece date from c.1440: but the piece does not appear in the Old Hall manuscript, in which Power is well represented, so the Mass was probably composed in the 1420s or 1430s.

All of this suggests that the York music was composed in the 1430s or 1440s, some twenty or thirty years before the copy in the York register was made. Another feature of the music that suggests this dating is the setting of the word 'Veni' in *Veni de Libano* B, seen in Example 21. This special treatment, with pauses over the two syllables of what is in effect a separate phrase, is a feature of settings of texts from the Song of Songs in the middle third of the fifteenth century. It appears first in various settings by Dunstable and his contemporaries, in a style that Burstyn relates to the 1430s, and more or less comes to an end with the next generation in the 1460s.[86] Our York composer, then, was a part of the musical mainstream of the period.

In this case, why does the York music show signs of haste, and why did the composer not amend it? In what circumstances might a composer not correct such

[85] Curtis, ed., *Power: Mass Alma Redemptoris Mater*, 12–13.
[86] Burstyn *Song of Songs*, 159ff, and especially 163: among Burstyn's transcriptions, see examples on pp. 283, 315, 331 and 369; also Dunstable's *Quam pulchra es*, in Bukofzer *Dunstable*, no. 44.

Example 24: Vocal ranges of the York music

problematic features as the inconsistent use of duple mensuration in the two settings of *Veni de Libano*, the confusion of mode in *Surge* A, and the tonal confusion and impossible final cadence of *Veni electa* B? And are the omissions of *Veni de Libano* B and *Veni electa* B – which make those pieces in effect almost impossible to perform – due to the composer rather than to the copyist? We should note that no concordances for these pieces are known to survive, which tends to confirm the natural assumption that the York music was composed specifically for the York plays. Moreover, this in turn is confirmed by the fact that the one liturgical text of the three – *Veni electa*, which is a Mattins responsory for the Feast of the Assumption in the York use[87] – does not seem to have a chant-based setting in either version.[88] A freely-composed setting of a liturgical text at this date would certainly be for non-liturgical purposes.

One answer could certainly be that the music was provided for the revised version of the play, some time between the *ordo paginarum* of 1415 and the copying of the register. John Robinson thought it possible that the revision had been undertaken by the York Realist, working 'some decades before 1463' but 'probably not before 1422' – in fact, 'early in the middle third of the fifteenth century'.[89] This would seem to put the revision perhaps in the 1430s or 1440s, then. If Robinson was right, and perhaps even if he was not, the York music may have been composed in a hurry for the revised version of the play: and perhaps the B versions, which are considerably more difficult to perform, were abandoned or even never used.

The dating of this music may have a bearing on its performance. The singers would seem, from the ranges of the six pieces, to be countertenors for the A versions and trebles – or rather, second trebles or 'means' – for the B versions (Example 24). Certainly that is the case if the music should be performed at anything like modern pitch, and the clef used (C[1]) does suggest high voices. There are three possible explanations, then, for the second group of settings, the B versions: they may be

[87] BE II, 481.
[88] On the York texts, see Rastall 'Vocal Range', 197–8, and *Six Songs*, 7; and below.
[89] Robinson *Studies*, 34 and 19.

Example 25: Pitch centres of gravity of the York music

written for different voice-types, trebles rather than altos; they may be intended for more experienced or more competent singers than the A versions; and they may be for performance indoors rather than in the open air. Of these, there seems to me no doubt about the second: the B versions *are* much more difficult than the A versions, and demand more from the performers. The third possibility need not concern us here, for although arguments about indoor performance may continue, the B versions have now been performed perfectly satisfactorily in the proper outdoor conditions.[90] The first two questions do however present something of an anomaly. The countertenors for whom the range of the A versions would seem most suitable would be adult singers, or at least pubescents whose voices were already changing, and these would have sung as trebles for some years.[91] On the other hand the trebles or means for whom the range of the B versions seems most suited would have been on average less experienced than the countertenors. Thus we have a situation in which the A versions are apparently for relatively inexperienced adults and the B versions for experienced boys. This situation is impossible to reconcile with what we know of the training and professional life of singers in the Middle Ages.[92]

The ranges of the voices are however misleading. Certainly the top notes of the B versions are such that those pieces could not be sung by countertenors; but the bottom notes of the A versions are much the same as those of the B versions – a semitone lower in the case of *Veni electa* – so that the A versions could be sung by

---

[90] The question of indoor performance of the York plays was raised by Alan Nelson (1974), but has not been properly discussed again after Nelson's objections to processional performance were shown to be misplaced. Nelson made some good points that might relate to occasional indoor performance of individual plays, however, and his arguments should perhaps be reassessed.

For the 1994 performance of *The Assumption*, see n. 95, below.

[91] On voice types and the effects of puberty, see below, section 8.2. This notation would demand professional singers, and professionals had to start at the beginning, as trebles. Thus any countertenor would have several years of training behind him, which in any case was necessary for the notation used here.

[92] Note that at the relevant period we can discount the possibility of professional female church singers, while minstrels would not be able to read this notation.

lower trebles, i.e. means. In fact, a study of the tessiture of the various voices shows that the two groups of settings were written for the same type of voice, the pitch centres of gravity (PCGs) being much the same for the two versions of each text (Example 25).[93] All of the York music, then, was apparently composed for treble voices singing in the lower or 'mean' (second treble) range. As we shall see (section 8.3), it is probable that the twelve speaking angels of this play were choristers who included (or were) the singers, and this is compatible with a performance date for the music from 1425 onwards. *Veni de Libano* B demands a division of the singers into four, so in any case we should not be thinking in terms of solo singers in these pieces.

The York music has suffered in the past from the adverse remarks of the cycle's first editor:[94]

> One would have been glad to find that this music . . . were of any considerable beauty or value; but truth compels us to say that it is not so. Reminiscences of old church music, . . . they are not even so intelligible as the songs found among the Coventry Plays, nor give us a beautiful melody, like the song of Chaucer's child recently discovered . . .

But her music editor, W.H. Cummings, clearly did not understand the notation, thought that there were only five pieces, and did not attempt to transcribe the B versions. The incompetence of his transcriptions made such views almost inevitable. It is a great pleasure now to state the opposite opinion: that these are fine compositions that have now proved their worth in performances of **York 45** in the streets of York, in John McKinnell's 1988 production (when the A versions were sung) and on 10 July 1994 (the B versions).[95] We can now see and hear, despite the evident problems of composition or transmission, that the pieces are mainstream polyphony, unusual in appearing in a dramatic context, and clearly an important part of a lavish and spectacular play.

3.4 Coventry

I have already given reasons for thinking that the two song-texts in the Coventry Shearmen and Tailors' pageant date from the first half of the sixteenth century (2.6, above). The date of the musical settings is more difficult to establish, but certainly

---

[93] The method used here, and the nature of the pitch centre of gravity, is explained in detail in Rastall 'Vocal Range', 190–9.

[94] Smith *York Plays*, 517–27, and especially 524.

[95] McKinnell did not use trebles, however. In Jane Oakshott's production of nine plays on waggons, part of the 1994 York Early Music Festival, the singing angels in *The Assumption* were Ruth Holton, Deborah Roberts, Sally Dunkley and Caroline Trevor. A video recording of the 1994 production by the Centre for Medieval Studies, University of York, which has been made into films of all the plays performed, including many musical items, is commercially available: and Cathy Parnall's Yorkshire Television film *A Medieval Mystery* includes many musical excerpts (some from *The Assumption*).

the musical style could be compatible with a date contemporary with the texts: and it is surely not likely that so old-fashioned a text would be set to music much later in the century or, if it were, that the old-fashioned orthography would be retained. On the whole, I am inclined to believe that Thomas Mawdyke collected up in 1591 whatever materials he could find for this play, and that the songs, at least, dated from a long way back. It is of course a great pity that the manuscript does not survive, since details of the notation and layout would have enabled a more precise dating to be made.

As already mentioned, the two songs were published by Thomas Sharp in *A Dissertation on the Pageants or Dramatic Mysteries anciently performed at Coventry* (1825), in a quasi-facsimile engraving that was presumably intended to give the reader some idea of the manuscript's appearance. This publication was issued as a facsimile reprint in 1973. The lullaby, the famous 'Coventry Carol', has been edited and published many times, although most often in a spurious four-part version and frequently inaccurately. The shepherds' song was first brought to public notice by John P. Cutts in 1957,[96] but the first reputable commercial edition was that of Thurston Dart in 1962.[97] Dart, like many before him, believed that the music should have been in four parts, and that one voice had been lost: but it is notable that in *As I out rode* he added a voice between the top and middle of the surviving lines, whereas in the lullaby he added one between the middle and bass lines. There is good reason for this misunderstanding, in that the textures of the two songs may well lead one to Dart's conclusion. On the other hand, the layout of the source does not admit of the loss of a single voice, and Dart's conclusion implies that the layout as given by Sharp is not that of the original.

Later editions have accepted that only three voices were involved. JoAnna Dutka edited both songs,[98] and I have also published them.[99]

The music of the songs appears on four leaves in Sharp's book, but in fact takes up only four pages: as is usual with engravings, only the recto side of each leaf is printed, the verso being left blank. The four recto pages are numbered 115–118, and although there is only one number per leaf, these are part of the book's pagination series. Song I, *As I out rode*, is on p. 115; Song II, the lullaby *Lully lulla thow littell tyne childe*, takes up pp. 116 and 117; and Song III, *Doune from heaven*, is on p. 118. In each case the three voices, marked 'The treble', 'The tenor(e)' and 'The basse', are set out in order down the page. The two verses of *As I out rode* were evidently separate at an early stage, since its layout is different from that of the lullaby: all three voices are given on each of the two pages, whereas the lullaby sets out the voices spread over the two pages concerned. Table 5 shows the disposition of the voice parts on the page. Assuming that Sharp's copy bears a general resemblance to the original manuscript, this layout seems to suggest the following: that in rehearsal the singers read from a single page for each verse of the shepherds' song separately, whereas

[96] Cutts 'Second Coventry Carol'.
[97] Dart *Two Coventry Carols*.
[98] Dutka 1980, 51–6 and 59–62.
[99] Rastall *Two Coventry Carols*.

TABLE 5 : DISPOSITION OF VOICE-PARTS IN THE SOURCE OF COVENTRY 1

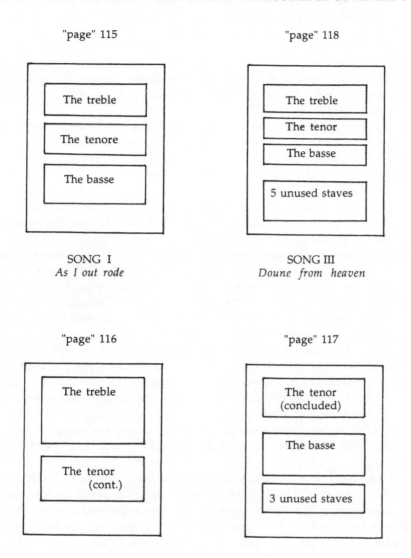

"page" 115

The treble

The tenore

The basse

SONG I
As I out rode

"page" 118

The treble

The tenor

The basse

5 unused staves

SONG III
Doune from heaven

"page" 116

The treble

The tenor
(cont.)

"page" 117

The tenor
(concluded)

The basse

3 unused staves

SONG II   *Lully Lullay yʷ Littel tyne childe*

rehearsing the lullaby demanded that they hold both pages simultaneously, and indeed that the tenor singer move from one to the other in the course of the song. Clearly the layout of the shepherds' song is rather more convenient than that of the lullaby, but on the other hand it has been responsible for the misunderstanding that *Doune from heaven* was a separate song.

The notation is void, with full black semiminims (i.e. crotchets), and is engraved on five-line staves (see Plate 6). There are a few inaccuracies, such as the wrong pitch or dots omitted, but the only notational surprise is that the flat-sign, both in the key-signatures and as accidentals, is invariably of the double-bulbed variety whether it appears on a line or in a space. The only other notational matter of interest is that the treble part of *Doune from heaven* is incomplete. However, the music of that song is of course almost note for note the same as that of *As I out rode*, and as the same refrain occurs in both verses there is certainly no problem caused by the omission of part of the second refrain. On the whole it seems likely that this omission was in the original.

Sharp, or his engraver David Jee, certainly did alter some things that they found incomprehensible or thought unimportant. Patterned minim rests, for instance, appear in the engraving as a triangle of dots. Considering that neither Sharp nor Jee was likely to have any knowledge of old notation, however, even if they knew anything about music, the engravings are surprisingly accurate. In general, although the source needs constantly to be assessed, my impression is that Sharp and Jee tried to be accurate, and that one can have confidence in their intentions even if not always in the detail of their results.

Neither song has any musical concordance. *As I out rode* is a neat little refrain song in which the refrain is actually longer than the verse. Its lively texture alternates homophony with simple imitation, the cadences are clear and invariably simultaneous in the three voices, the harmonic language is limited, and there is no modulation away from the tonic of F major. Despite these limitations the piece has a considerable charm, and must have been written by a highly-skilled composer who knew how to manipulate very limited resources in an effective way. The limitations stem from the brief that any composer must follow in writing for civic dramatic performance: to compose an interesting setting, in which the words can be clearly heard even in an outdoor performance, and which therefore incorporates a mainly homophonic texture in a sectional structure to enable the singers to get back together if they should lose control of the music. The means by which the composer maintains interest in such limited conditions is the main point of interest in the song.

It should be noted first that the metrical structure of the song is fluid: it is not possible to treat it as being in a regular metre, whether one chooses a duple or a triple mensuration. This fluidity is especially important in counteracting the effects of a three-line verse in which only one rhyme appears and in which there is no enjambement. The composer takes the initiative right at the start of the song: the chordal opening demands the listener's attention but so modifies the apparent stressing of the first line,

As I̲ out ro̲de̲ this e̲nderes ni̲ght̲,

that in retrospect one is not sure whether the first note was a downbeat or part of a two-beat anacrucis, and whether the piece is really in triple time or not (Example 26). To some extent this may have been forced on the composer, since the second verse begins with a stress:

Do̲une̲ from he̲aven̲, from he̲aven so hi̲gh̲.

140

Example 26: The opening of "As I out-rode"

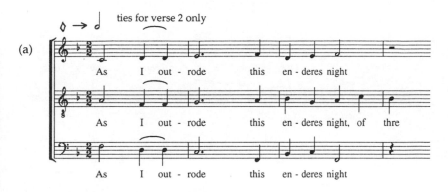

(a)

(b)

The first half-phrase needs to be ambiguous, therefore. But the listener is intrigued rather than upset, because there are deliberate stabilising features in this passage: absolute homophony, and a logical presentation of most of the harmonic repertory of the piece, with a strong dominant on the agogic accent at 'rode' and a clear harmonic cadence to the tonic chord.

At this stage the music must be moved on, and for the second text line this is done through imitation and the use of the smaller note-values required by the extra syllables (Example 27). The imitation is minimal – really only for four notes – and so are the means by which the tenor and bass voices extend their lines to the cadence at bar 5: the tenor repeats the last four syllables, while the bass returns to longer note-values. As a result, the second line is only six beats long, the same length as the first, despite the staggered entries. It is worth noting also that the bass's initial descent in bars 1–2, F-D-C, together with its associated harmonic progression, is repeated in the bass of the second line; that this repeat, with the third filled in, is related also to the inversion of this figure, seen in the treble of bars 1–2; and that the

Example 27: "As I out-rode", bars 3-5

Example 28: "As I out-rode", bars 5-7

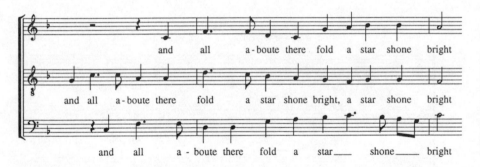

very strong opening rhythm of those bars, ♩ ♩ ♩, but in diminution, forms the basis of the rhythmic interest of the imitation.

It will be seen that these first imitative entries appear in a classic pitch-disposition for three voices – dominant-tonic-tonic, starting with the middle voice – and that they appear at intervals of a beat. This pattern is used again for the third line, with the voices entering in the order tenor-bass-treble, as before. Here, too, the point of imitation has its own rhythmic characteristic, which in this case is a dotted rhythm; and here the treble's initial rise of a fourth and fall of a third is telescoped to those two intervals (Example 28, and cf. Example 26, treble part). This line is a little longer (seven beats instead of six) because of the extra poetic foot:

And all aboute there fold a star shone bright.

The composer has been careful to let the imitation run a little longer than in the previous line, and the near-canon between bass and treble for four beats does much to give the listener the feeling of simultaneous expansion and confirmation. He is also careful not to let the cadence at bar 7 sound like the end of the piece, however. The dominant ('imperfect') cadence in bar 5, the end of the second line, did certainly

Example 29: "As I out-rode", bars 7-9

bright: they sange ter - ly ter - lo, [they sange ter - ly ter - lo]

bright: they sange ter - ly ter - lo, [they sange ter - li ter - lo]

bright: they sange ter - li ter - lo, [they sange ter - li ter - lo]

imply a tonic cadence at the end of the third line, but too firm a cadence in bar 7 would prevent further progression of the music: so the composer uses a VIIb cadence there rather than a full V-I ('perfect') cadence. This effect of non-completion is enhanced by the texture, for the crossing of the lower parts, with the bass high in its range, causes a tension that prohibits anything but further movement into the piece.

What the music moves into is a second half that simultaneously mirrors the first half's structure and presents a quite different two-part structure with repeats. This setting of the refrain broadly divides into three sections, of seven, eight and nine beats, respectively, and in that sense mirrors the tripartite structure of the verse in bars 1–7. However, the first of these sections, which treats the first refrain line, 'They sang "Terli terlo" ', divides exactly into a sub-phrase and its repeat; and the third of these sections is effectively a repeat of the second. Thus the refrain takes on the form aa'bb', where b is approximately twice the length of a. The first half of the song is mirrored also in that each section ends with a clear cadence, the first section is homophonic, and the second and third sections make use of modified material from the first half in its imitative writing. The way that this is all done continues the story of the careful structuring and motivic concentration that we have already seen in this song.

The verse had ended at bar 7 with the lower voices in reverse position. The two sub-phrases that start the refrain vary the repeat by following this layout for the first and then exchanging parts for the second, a device that alters the texture considerably even without any alteration of the notes. The more dominant of these lines, falling from middle C, is reminiscent of the tenor line at bar 3: and to give a sense of progression, the treble changes its tune for something higher in pitch (though related to much material that has gone before: see Example 29, and cf. Examples 27 and 28). After these chordal interjections, as after the initial phrase of bars 1–3, a new rhythmic character emerges in an imitative texture. The point of imitation takes up the rising scalic fourth, with the voices entering in the same order as before (Example 30): but here there is more variety in the starting-pitches used, and the more spacious proportions of the section allow the tenor to repeat the whole of the text line, which it does with a near-imitative entry in bar 10. The repeat of this

Example 30: "As I out-rode", bar 9 to the end

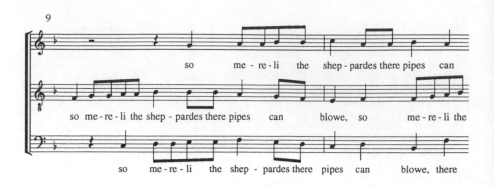

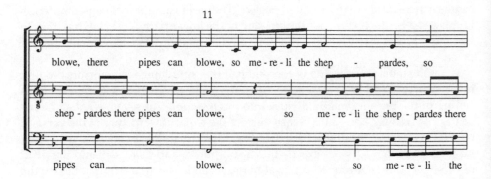

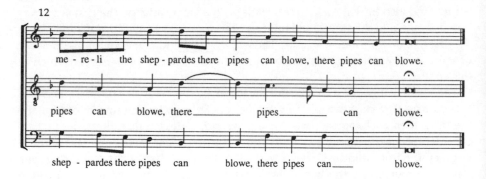

section, bars 11–13, contrives to ring the changes in the order of entries – now treble-tenor-bass, on C, G and D, but still at a beat's distance – and to contrive a higher-pitched climax before returning to the same cadence as before in treble and bass, but with a decorated tenor line (end of bar 12).

It has not been my intention to present an analysis as such of this piece, nor to suggest by this description that the composer set about his task in ways that we may

Example 31: Phrases of the Coventry lullaby

phrases: 1   2   3

verse 2:   O sis - ters two how may we do   for to pre - serve this day

4   5   6

oure pore yong - ling for whom we do singe   by by lul - ly lul - lay.

6

verse 3:   all yong chil-dren to   slay.

feel anachronistic for sixteenth-century music. I do however want to show that the composer of this song was highly skilled and able to produce a splendidly appropriate piece for the peculiarly limited circumstances of the projected performance; and that the apparently simple surface of the piece hides a motivic concentration and level of manipulation of harmonic and rhythmic resources that we might not expect in so short a work. The Coventry shepherds' song is a better piece, I think, than it has ever been given credit for.

The much better-known lullaby is justly famous, a strophic setting in homophonic style of a four-verse poem. Like the shepherds' song, it does not modulate, although its G minor tonality allows a certain flirtation with B-flat major. And, like the shepherds' song again, it has a flexible metre and cannot be thought of in either duple or triple time for long: I shall return to this.

Stanzas 2–4 have a regular six-line form, rhyming aabccb, in which the b rhyme is the same throughout: may/day/lullay/slay. This poetic form gave rise to a parallel musical structure, in which phrases 4, 5 and 6 are variations on phrases 1, 2 and 3 (Example 31). In fact, phrases 2 and 5 are identical except for small rhythmic changes demanded by the different number of syllables; phrases 3 and 6 differ only in the tendency towards B-flat major in phrase 3, except that the lower-pitched cadence in the treble of verse 3 (bars 33–34), with its third-less final chord, gives a bleak sound particularly in keeping with the grim message of that verse. The pair that differs most is phrases 1 and 4: one reason is the triple rhythm and falling scalic tune that relate phrase 4 to phrases 2 and 5; another is the bright B-flat major harmonies that initially take the place of the darker G minor of the opening. This parallelism has caused problems in the past. At some stage a copyist – perhaps

Example 32: Error in phrase 6 of the Coventry lullaby

Phrase 3, all verses

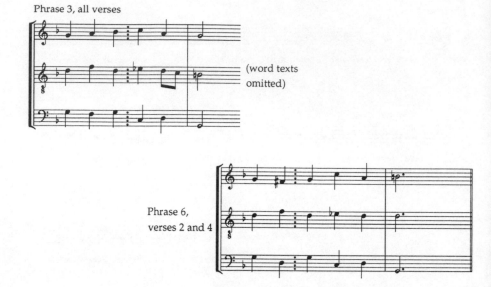

(word texts omitted)

Phrase 6, verses 2 and 4

Phrase 6, verse 3

Example 33: Phrase 6 of the Coventry lullaby, corrected

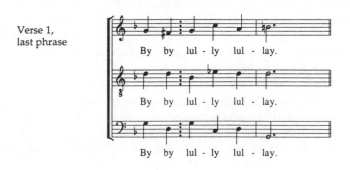

Verse 1, last phrase

By   by   lul - ly   lul - lay.

By   by   lul - ly   lul - lay.

By   by   lul - ly   lul - lay.

Example 34: Coventry lullaby, verses 1 and 2 (voice I only)

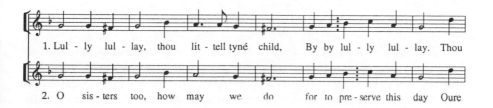

1. Lul - ly lul - lay, thou lit - tell tyné child, By by lul - ly lul - lay. Thou

2. O sis - ters too, how may we do for to pre - serve this day Oure

lit - tell tyné child, By by lul - ly lul - lay.

pore yong - ling for whom we do singe By by lul - ly lul - lay.

David Jee, perhaps the scribe of his exemplar – made an error by contamination of the last phrase of verses 2, 3 and 4, thus conflating the B-flat major and G minor versions (Example 32). Although this reading is possible (if unusual) and is attested by three examples, the extreme expressivity of this dissonance seems to me pointless in the textual circumstances, and I prefer the plainer reading of verse 1 (Example 33). It is perhaps worth pointing out (a) that any scribe copying this piece might well be in automatic pilot by the middle of verse 2, the lines being both memorable and easily confused; and (b) that Jee may have copied out the music for verses 2–4 from a single notation in which the underlay of the verses is not always obvious. In this case, of course, he would have multiplied any error by reproducing it for each verse.

The puzzles in this piece invite speculation, but in two important areas I believe that it is better to accept that the piece's rather strange features were intended by the composer. The first of these is the structure of verse 1. This verse uses the same tune as verses 2–4, but omits the fifth phrase (Example 34). It is a natural assumption that this phrase, together with its associated text, has been lost at some stage in the piece's history, but it is hard to see how this could have happened unless the piece were notated differently in the past. Only if the lullaby were in score could a complete phrase have been torn off or burnt, for instance. Even this does not seem likely, however: a situation might conceivably arise in which reconstruction of the music did not take place, but in that case it is very odd that reconstruction of the text *did* occur. For the text of verse 1 does not rhyme aabcb, as one would expect if it were like the other verses but with the fifth line missing: it rhymes bcbcb, with the b lines as 'lullay' lines and the two c lines both 'Thou littell tyne child'. If one were simply to reinstate the fifth musical phrase, making the musical structure the same as that of other verses, it would still be impossible to add suitable text in a way that would result in the aabccb rhyme-structure of verses 2–4.

Verse 1, then, for whatever reason, is different from verses 2–4. This has led to speculation that verse 1 is really the burden of a carol-form song, and that 'verse 1' should therefore be sung again after each of the other verses. The situation might have arisen in either of two ways: the composer might have composed 'verse 1' as a burden using the same texture and material as the rest of the song but with a distinct structure; or he or someone else might have rewritten the first verse of the song, originally of the same structure as other verses, giving it a distinctive structure but not altering the material or texture. Either of these is possible, but they are both, in my view, very unlikely. If the lullaby had been originally composed or later revised as a carol we should expect the then-known carol form to be followed, but this was not the case:[100]

— In the late carol repertory the burden and verse sometimes share musical material and text: but I know of no example where the burden has the same musical material as the verse but a *different* text;

— Where the music and text are shared, the sections are differentiated by texture: for instance, Burden I might be an upper-voice duet, Burden II a full three-part texture and the verse a lower-voice duet;

— The late (sixteenth-century) carol form was often modified to allow a smooth transition from the end of a verse to the start of the burden or to the beginning of a subsequent section of a multi-section burden. There is no reason to make such a modification near the *end* of the burden.

If the existing verse 1 of the lullaby was an attempt to make the burden of a carol, then it was not only extremely clumsy but was also quite without precedent. It seems to me inconceivable that a carol-burden might be composed that way, since the composer was free to use other and much more effective methods to differentiate a burden; but it is just possible that the fifth phrase was excised in a misguided attempt to create a carol out of an ordinary strophic partsong. The only possible support for this latter scenario, however, is that one cannot see in what accidental circumstances verse 1 could have acquired its present form. In any case, I think it better to leave the lullaby as a strophic song and to accept it in its perhaps mutilated state.

The other puzzle is that of the metre. Although the song is basically in triple time, the first metrical unit of each verse has four beats, while each 'lullay' line includes a unit of two (see Example 31, bars 1, 3 and 6). This has a considerable attractiveness, and may be one reason why the piece has maintained its popularity over the years: but it gives the song a curious limping character that may be felt at odds with the usual regular rocking motion of a lullaby. Successive editors have tried to explain

---

[100] For examples to illustrate what follows, see John Stevens, *Mediaeval Carols, Music at the Court of Henry VIII* and *Early Tudor Songs and Carols, passim*.

Example 35: Coventry lullaby in Caldwell's rhythmic interpretation

perfect S   altered M

would be transcribed not as

but as

this feature, especially since many of the engraving's errors are of durational values, but the 'irrational' duple metre is difficult to banish from the scene. John Caldwell has recently proposed a solution that is elegant, logical, and could well be correct: namely, that the piece is indeed in triple mensuration – in fact, in ₵ time – and uses the medieval devices of imperfection and alteration.[101] In this mensuration all semibreves are perfect, whether dotted or not, unless imperfected by a minim or minim rest following; and the odd two minims that give a short metrical unit are subject to alteration – i.e. the second is lengthened in order to make the whole into a perfection. Thus the first bar of Example 31 is actually two perfections long (Example 35, and cf. Plate 6).

The more difficult part of the solution concerns the third and sixth phrases (third and fifth in verse 1). Here the tenor's minim and two semiminims seem not to be amenable to any interpretation other than as a beat and two half-beats. Caldwell's explanation is that the two semiminims are in fact colored minims, so that they take a full minim beat each and therefore coincide precisely with the altered minims in the outer parts. I show the original notation of the tenor part, with the two interpretations, in Example 36. As is very clear from this, the coloration can have no function, its normal purpose in this context being to prevent alteration – that is, to make sure that the two minims together made up an imperfect semibreve. In this line, however, there is no doubt that they do: the dot after the semibreve on 'child' ensures that the minim at 'By [by]' is at the start of a perfection, and thereafter two groups of three minims bring us to a new perfection for the semibreve on '[lul]-lay'. These notes make no sense, then, as colored minims; but as semiminims they confirm the irregular rhythm of the outer voices.

It is the pointlessness of these notes as colored minims that makes me doubtful of Caldwell's interpretation, which is otherwise a very attractive theory. I should not go so far as to say that he is wrong; but I suggest that if he is right we must find a satisfactory explanation for these two notes – and they come both at the mid-point

---

[101] Caldwell *English Music* I, 265–6. For imperfection and alteration, see Rastall *Notation*, 70–3.

Example 36: Coventry lullaby in C

Tenor: phrases 1-3 in original notation

Lul ly lul la y[o]w lit tell ty ne childe by by lul ly lul lay

standard transcription

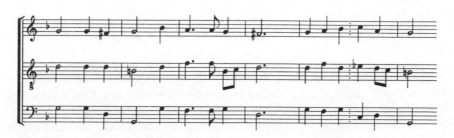

Caldwell's transcription

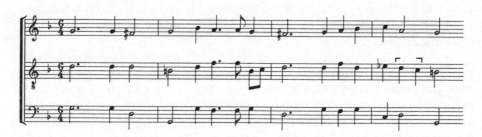

of each verse and at the end. This song is frankly an editor's nightmare, and there is much work to be done on it before we can be sure of any interpretation. Where Sharp sometimes has a semibreve and sometimes a minim, which is correct? Why do some minim tails go up and others down, in an apparently irrational manner? Why is it that even the most unlikely passages occur repeatedly, and does this tell us anything about the original from which Jee copied? And why are so many accidentals misplaced on the staff?

Whatever the problems, these two songs are fine pieces that deserve to be performed. I imagine that one composer was responsible for both, but this cannot even be demonstrated except by reference to the (perhaps doubtful?) metrical irregularities that are characteristic of both. One other matter should be noted in this connection, however. Both songs demand a group of three professional singers, and the voice ranges show them to be an alto, a tenor and a bass (Example 37a). The

Example 37: Voice ranges and pitch centres of gravity of the Coventry songs

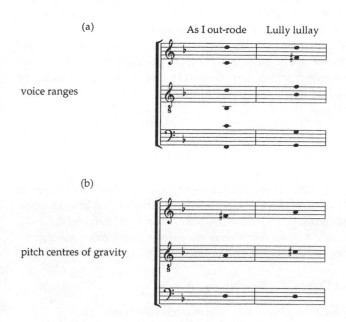

Shearmen and Tailors would certainly not employ two such groups (even if they were available in Coventry on the relevant dates), but would ask the one group to play both the shepherds and the singing mothers of the Innocents. In performance there is about half an hour between the exit of the shepherds and the entrance of the mothers of the Innocents, and this is ample time for the three singers (who are evidently accomplished actors, too) to change costumes.

The voice ranges in Example 37a are not however the same for the two songs, and the reason for this is very simple. In the first song the singers impersonate men, and in the second women: the composer (it might be two composers, but I think one more likely) would have to engineer some difference in sound between the two, therefore, even though both songs are for male-voice trio. The voice ranges suggest how this was done, those for the lullaby being narrower than those for the shepherds' song. The highest voice has the same top note in the two songs (d′), but a much smaller range in the lullaby; in the tenor parts, the lowest note of the lullaby is a full octave above that of *As I out rode*; and the bass range in the shepherds' song goes both higher and lower than in the lullaby. The pitch centres of gravity show more clearly what the composer has done (Example 37b).[102] The PCGs for the bass parts are almost exactly equal, but in both the alto and tenor parts the narrower

---

[102] See also 3.3, above, for a discussion of the voice-types used in the York pieces. I give the Pitch Centres of Gravity here to the nearest semitone, but more precise figures are shown in Rastall 'Vocal Range', 194.

pitch ranges are responsible for much higher PCGs in the lullaby – a minor third higher in the case of the alto, and a major third higher in the tenor. These differences are considerable, and do much to alter the texture to a higher and lighter sound for the lullaby: and at the same time these higher PCGs in alto and tenor effectively separate those two voices further from the bass in that song, thus attenuating the texture as a whole. I do not doubt that the contrast in texture between these two songs was a deliberate measure on the part of one composer, designed to make the same three singers sound quite different in the two songs, in which they imperson-ate quite different characters.

3.5 Chester

The latest and most fragmentary of the notated items appears in play 7 of the Chester cycle, the Painters' and Glaziers' play of the Shepherds (Plate 7). It is white mensural notation with black semiminims (crotchets), on a five-line staff with clef C^4 and a key-signature of one double-bulbed flat. This music is found only in manuscript H, which is dated 1607; there are editions in Dutka *Music* 1980, 29, and Lumiansky and Mills *Essays* 1983, 149.

The stage direction at **Chester 7/357+sd** reads:[103]

> Tunc cantabit Angelus . Gloria in excelcis Deo et in terra
> pax hominibus bonae voluntatis.

This is the text of the verse to the first responsory at Christmas Mattins, as we should expect. This piece was traditionally performed by a group of boys placed high up in the church building, but boys seem not to have been used for polyphonic performances until the middle of the sixteenth century: all earlier settings are for men, which limits the boys' performance to normal occasions when the service was sung entirely to plainsong.[104] Although the subsequent dialogue between the shepherds shows that the whole of this text was sung, the musical notation shows a setting of only the first four words (Example 38). However, this passage is an independent phrase in the chant, and polyphonic settings invariably show a firm cadence at this point, with fermate after which a new musical section begins. The Long with fermata and double bar does not mean that this is the end of the Chester piece, therefore, but merely that the scribe has given the *incipit* of the piece by copying the whole of the first musical section.

The Chester piece has been considered an example of mensural monody in the past. John Stevens referred to it as 'a snatch of plainsong' in his seminal article of 1958, but later modified his description to 'a simple monodic Gloria in excelsis

---

[103] I give here the reading in MS H: the other MSS show some small variants, detailed in Lumiansky and Mills *Chester* I, 141.

[104] Another piece traditionally sung by the boys was *Audivi vocem de caelo*, the eighth responsory at Mattins on the feast of All Saints: see Harrison *Music in Medieval Britain*, 107.

Example 38: Chester Gloria

[see also Appendix B]

Glo - - - - ri - a   in ex - cel - sis de - o de - o   de - o de - - o.

dco'.[105] To my eyes and ears the setting has all the features of a polyphonic line, a view that I put forward in 1983.[106] In reviewing that work Stevens has reiterated his belief that the music is monodic:[107] but he seems careful not to be dogmatic on this issue, presumably because he is aware – as he stated in his *New Grove* article[108] – that the Chester Gloria, which according to the shepherds' discussion in **Chester 7** ought to be florid and decorative, 'does not seem adequate to the occasion'. Indeed it does not. On the other hand this objection would disappear if the line were part of a polyphonic texture.

It will be best if we first dispose of Stevens's original view, later abandoned, that the music is plainsong. That it clearly is not, for rhythmicised plainsong sung as plainsong is always rhythmically simpler than this. The most obvious example is Merbeck's *Booke of Common Prayer Noted* of 1550, but the picture is much the same elsewhere.[109] Mother Thomas More concluded that mensural notation of chant in the late Middle Ages and sixteenth century reflected a stylised speech-rhythm, and that speech-rhythm was an important factor even in the case of the Magnificat tenors of British Library MS Royal Appendix 56, which are in white mensural notation of c.1530.[110] The tenors of Royal Appendix 56 are in simpler notation than that of the Chester Gloria, however, and the latter seems too complex rhythmically for anything less than strict mensural interpretation. Indications (but not proofs) of non-chant character are the five-line staff and the cadence from the lower leading-note. Moreover, the line cannot be identified as even an embellished version of any chant: it is impossible to prove that a given line is not chant, of course, but this tune certainly bears no relation to any of the relevant Gloria chants.[111]

With the view that the line is a non-chant monody the evidence is more difficult to assess. Apart from rhythmicised chant, mensural monodies up to the end of the sixteenth century fall into the following categories:

[105] Stevens 1958, 81; *New Grove* 12/44, in the article 'Medieval Drama'.

[106] In Lumiansky and Mills *Essays*, 147–8.

[107] In *Early Music History* 6 (1986), 320.

[108] NG 12/44.

[109] See Merbecke BCPN and Milsom 'English-texted chant'.

[110] More 'Performance of Plainsong', 127–8.

[111] This is not an important objection, however, since polphonic settings of *Gloria in excelsis* do not normally show much relationship to the chant until 'et in terra': see Harrison *Music in Medieval Britain*, 367.

(1)   The songs of the troubadours, trouvères and their successors, normally notated mensurally only when borrowed for use in polyphonic compositions;

(2)   Measured monody of the type found in Pepys 1236 (discussed in 3.2, above);

(3)   Monodic instrumental dances;

(4)   Lines extracted from polyphonic compositions for use in new works, whether written down or improvised. Such lines are usually the tenor part, occasionally the cantus; and

(5)   A tune newly composed for the purpose.

Of these, (1) can be discounted because of the parody technique involved, but in any case the line does not sound like a song. We can also discount (2) on the grounds just given, that as a monody it is inadequate to the occasion. Nor does the line bear any resemblance to dance tunes, the rhythms of which would have to be more regular than the Chester line's are: we can discount (3), therefore. In (4) the line is not monodic anyway, in that its original and proposed contexts are both polyphonic. This leaves us with (5), and a further problem. The tune is texted only as far as 'deo', leaving 'et in terra pax hominibus bone voluntatis' unset. This is not an underlay error, for there are not enough notes to accommodate the whole text. Yet if this were a specially-composed piece we should expect to find the whole of it here. It seems pointless to copy only the first section of the setting into the play text: for either it is known, in which case this copy is unnecessary, or else it is not known, and an incomplete copy is of no use.

I conclude, therefore, that this line is from a pre-existent polyphonic piece,[112] available in a place known to the dramatist and/or a director of music and/or the scribe (Scribe A). The written line is therefore a reference, an incipit that will tell a producer or director of music what piece should be performed. Working on this basis, it is possible to say something about the piece from which the line comes. It is a mid-sixteenth-century setting of the responsory verse *Gloria in excelsis*; it was probably composed in Mary's reign (1553–8), since the style is too late for a pre-Reformation date and the composition of a Mattins responsory verse would be less likely in the reigns of Edward VI or Elizabeth; and it was perhaps composed by a musician working at Chester. This last is not of course necessary for a piece found in a Chester manuscript, but the lack of concordances suggests that it was not part of the well-known national repertory of London-based composers and composing gentlemen of the Chapel Royal. That the piece has apparently not survived in

---

112 William Mahrt has suggested an alternative solution, that the second line of words ('et in terra . . . voluntatis') could be sung to the same line, the verbal repetitions of the setting bringing 'Gloria in excelsis deo' to the same number of syllables, fifteen. Theoretically elegant as this is, I must reject it on both stylistic and historical grounds. Readers can judge for themselves whether the second line fits the music as well as the first (see *Contexts*, 206); and I know of no precedent for such a proceeding anywhere in the late medieval or sixteenth-century musical repertory.

Example 39: Chant tunes for Gloria in excelsis deo

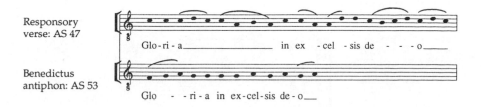

Responsory
verse: AS 47

Glo-ri-a_____ in ex - cel - sis de - - - o____

Benedictus
antiphon: AS 53

Glo - - ri-a in ex-cel-sis de-o__

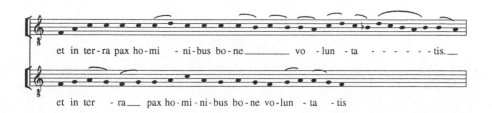

et in ter-ra pax ho-mi - ni-bus bo-ne_____ vo - lun - ta - - - - - - tis.__

et in ter - ra__ pax ho-mi-ni-bus bo-ne vo-lun - ta - tis

Al - le - lu - ia,____ al - le - lu - ia.

Chester is related to the more general problem of poor manuscript survival in that cathedral.

Nevertheless it is possible that the piece will come to light one day. David Mills has discussed the will of James Miller, the organiser and third scribe of manuscript H. The will is dated 20 July 1617 and was proved on 28 July 1618. Among the bequests was one to James Willding, who was to receive Miller's Latin books on Divinity and his song-books in Latin. Willding was evidently someone whose moral judgement Miller respected, for the bequest of his other song-books to his daughter Mary contains a qualification in respect of some of them, that she shall have those that 'James Willding shall thinke most fitt for her'.[113] The general impression left by the will is, as Mills notes, that Miller had collected books of divinity, music and history, many of them in Latin, and cared enough for them to be concerned about their disposal after his death. This indicates an antiquarian and scholarly activity unusual even in an educated clergyman.[114] If we are looking for a source for the

---

[113] Mills 'Will', 11.
[114] Mills 'Will', 12. Miller was rector of St Michael's church at the time.

Example 40: Works using material like that of the Chester Gloria

(in original note-values)

(a)   Anonymous
anthem, ?c. 1560: "If
ye be risen again with
Christ"

Gloria setting, then the chances are surely high that it was in Miller's possession when H was copied in 1607, and therefore that the setting could be found in one of the 'songe bookes in Latine' eventually left to Willding.

That Willding was also a clergyman seems almost certain, but little is known about him. Mills has found the name of James Willdinge among the eight choir boys in the cathedral accounts for the period 1587–96, and has remarked that this Willding 'seems a promising candidate, at a later stage, for Miller's will'.[115] Assuming that

[115] In a private communication.

3.5 *Chester*

(b) Anonymous
consort song,
?c. 1560-70,
"Ah silly poor Joas"

Ah sil - ly poor Jo - as

this man became a chorister at about eight years of age and that his voice changed at seventeen or so,[116] he would have been born c.1579: he was almost forty years old at Miller's death, therefore, and may be expected to have died c.1640, plus or minus twenty years. A search for Willding's will is clearly indicated, and – if successful – an attempt to trace any Latin song books mentioned.

Returning to the music, it is as well here to demonstrate that the Chester tune is unrelated to, and will not work as a counterpoint to, the obvious chants. I show the two tunes concerned in Example 39.[117] They are:

— The verse of the first responsory at Christmas Mattins, *Hodie nobis celorum rex*, which can be found in AS 47; and

— The Benedictus antiphon at Lauds on Christmas Day; this item, which is in AS 53, adds two alleluias to the text given above.

The lack of alleluias in the SD points towards the responsory verse rather than to the Benedictus antiphon. Both versions are known in liturgical drama, but the tradition of special semi-dramatic performance of the responsory verse in England suggests that it rather than the antiphon would come to an English playwright's mind – or a musical director's – as a dramatic item. The use of the responsory verse is confirmed by the fact that in England the responsory verse rather than the antiphon was given polyphonic treatment: examples are the single setting in Cambridge UL Add. MS 5943 (c.1400), the six settings in Pepys 1236 (c.1460–70), and mid-sixteenth-century settings by Sheppard, Taverner, Tallis and others.[118]

That the Chester line will not work in counterpoint with either of these chants is

---

[116] On the age at which boys' voices changed, see section 8.2, below.

[117] I give my reasons for considering only these two pieces in *Essays*, 147–8.

[118] For Cambridge University Library Add. MS 5943, see Rastall *Fifteenth-Century Song Books* and *Four Songs in Latin*; for Cambridge, Magdalene College, Pepys MS 1236, see Charles *Pepys 1236*, nos. 7, 36, 47, 71, 76 and 82.

(c) William Byrd:
anthem "Christ rising
again"

not necessarily evidence against the proposition that it is a setting of the responsory
verse, since the first section of such a setting was not normally obviously chant-
based. As Harrison noted, it is with the more recognisable intervals of the chant
from 'et in terra pax' onwards that the chant makes itself heard in most Gloria
settings.[119] On the other hand, D minor is a strange key for a piece that makes any
use at all of the Gloria chant, which is in the 5th mode. There must be a slight

[119] Harrison *Music in Medieval Britain*, 367.

possibility, then, that the piece is a post-Marian setting, not based on the chant at all: but if so it still adheres to the traditional structure, in that the words 'Gloria in excelsis deo' are set to a formally separate section of music ending with a full cadence.

With this information it is possible to make an informed guess at the style and texture of the original setting. The surviving line is one such as might have been written by any competent composer of the time: in fact, the style is like that of Robert White, who is known to have been at Chester Cathedral in the 1560s and was involved in the plays.[120] Several pieces from the middle of the sixteenth century use a similar line in D minor: among them are the anonymous anthem 'If ye be risen again', the consort song 'Ah silly poor Joaz' and William Byrd's consort anthem 'Christ rising': I give the openings of these in Example 40. These may be compared with my reconstruction of the Chester piece in Appendix B: I have not attempted to reconstruct the music for 'et in terra . . . hominibus', of course, since this would be a purely compositional task.[121]

I do not however suggest that in performances of this play the angelic Gloria was sung as a piece of four-part vocal polyphony: this would contradict **Chester 7/357+sd**, which requires the angel to sing the *Gloria in excelsis* as a solo. The solution most in line with known practice is to sing the given line as a solo for tenor voice, with an organ playing the whole texture (or perhaps playing an improvised texture from the bass line) as a supporting accompaniment. This gives a musically sensible solution which is apparently to be seen also in the Smiths' accounts, where a regals is used.[122]

[120] See Lumiansky and Mills *Essays*, 134–6, and Shaw *Succession*, 62.
[121] This reconstruction is a revision of that first published in Mills *Staging Chester*, 96.
[122] See *Essays*, 135–6, and cf. the case of James Hewitt of Coventry, discussed in 8.3, below, pp. 341–2.

4

THE DOCUMENTARY EVIDENCE

4.1 Introduction, and a note on money

The history of the study of documentary evidence in English drama studies goes back to the eighteenth century, when scholars such as Percy and Warton made some inroads into account-books and other types of documentation to illustrate their studies of early literature. Their work was useful in giving some direction to further study, but its usefulness was limited by two main factors. First, it was directed towards literature rather than drama, and especially towards building up a context for the works of Shakespeare which were the main focus of literary (not at that stage *dramatic*) study. There was only a limited impetus, therefore, towards solving – or even identifying – the problems specific to early drama. Second, the need for illustration rather than for full contextual study led the scholars concerned to trawl the material for items interesting in themselves, to search for 'plums' rather than to attempt the building up of a complete picture by collecting and assessing a huge volume of average or routine information.

This situation might have changed dramatically with the publication in 1825 of Thomas Sharp's *Dissertation on the Pageants at Coventry*. Sharp's interest in his native city focussed on the biblical drama for which Coventry had been famous, and he searched an enormous body of documentary evidence relating to the city and its trade guilds. Interestingly, and perhaps surprisingly, Sharp concerned himself primarily with the two plays that survived, being side-tracked neither by other existing cycle texts nor by parallel traditions and customs elsewhere. In editing the two surviving pageants he joined a very small body of men interested in the play texts themselves. It is as well that he did so, since the manuscript of the Shearmen and Tailors' pageant was destroyed by fire at the Birmingham Free Library in 1879. But although that century saw the setting-up of local record societies and an increased interest in the social context of literature, Sharp's lead in respect of drama was not followed. Lucy Toulmin Smith's use of record material in the introduction to her edition of the York cycle (1885) is hardly more than a nod in the right direction, containing no new research on the York records;[1] Hardin Craig's edition of the Coventry plays (1902) reused Sharp's work and added little to the material;[2] and Sir

---

[1] Smith *York Plays*.
[2] Craig *Two Coventry Plays*.

Edmund Chambers's *The Mediaeval Stage* (1903), which collected together an enormous amount of information, was too diffuse to be of immediate help in this respect, although very useful indeed as a quarry for more detailed work. Wickham's first volume of *Early English Stages*, which appeared in 1959 and marvellously supplements Chambers's work, did not materially alter this situation. It is in fact significant that all of the works just mentioned by Sharp, Toulmin Smith and Craig were re-issued between the late 1950s and the early 1970s. Only two pieces of work done at that stage were really comparable to Sharp's: one was that of J.S. Purvis on the York cycle, a study that was incidental to his translation of the cycle for performances at York from 1951 onwards; the other, first delivered as a series of lectures at Toronto University in 1954 and published the following year, was F.M. Salter's study of the financing of the Chester cycle.[3]

Sharp's lead was eventually followed by JoAnna Dutka, whose doctoral thesis (1972) impressively put together record material (much of it newly-researched by her) and the play texts in an attempt to learn more about the use of music in the civic cycles. As it turned out, this was to be part of an increasing interest in dramatic records on the part of scholars in Toronto University, and by the time Dutka published her book on the subject (1980) the activities of the REED project had made it unnecessary to publish the records section of her dissertation. Records of Early English Drama, which began publishing in 1979, aims to make available all documentary evidence of dramatic, folk ceremonial and minstrel activity in England up to 1642.[4] The first three publications in the series, on York, Chester and Coventry, reflected the general feeling of the time that the great civic centres of dramatic activity were the immediate priority, an understanding perhaps enhanced by the processional productions of the York cycle on waggons at Leeds (1975) and Toronto (1977)[5] and reflected also in the concern with waggon staging shown by the newly-founded *Medieval English Theatre*.[6] REED's first three publications, in any case, have proved crucial in the studies made since the late 1970s of the locatable civic plays: in all three cases a vast body of documentary material closely concerned with the organisation and production of civic drama could be used to elucidate

---

3 For Purvis's work, see *From Minster to Market Place*, 1969: Purvis had been custodian of the York diocesan archives and founding Director of the Borthwick Institute of Historical Research. His short version of the York cycle was prepared for the 1951 performance, and the complete cycle translation appeared in 1957. Salter's work (Salter 1955) probably marks the beginning of the Toronto involvement in dramatic records (as opposed to the study of play texts through performance).

4 Wales, Scotland and Ireland have now been added to this remit, in projects to be known collectively as Records of Early Drama (RED): see Sally-Beth MacLean's report in REEDN 18/1 (1993), 22–23. For a brief history of the REED project and its antecedents, see Johnston 'What if no texts survived?' in Briscoe and Coldewey *Contexts*, 1–3.

5 Further on these productions, see Oakshott and Rastall 'Town with Gown', and Parry 'York Cycle at Toronto'. The Toronto production was affected by adverse weather and was partly performed indoors.

6 METh, which began publishing in 1979, seems to have been partly motivated by a dissatisfaction with the results of such anti-waggon-staging work as Alan Nelson's *The Medieval English Stage*, which cast doubt on the traditional understanding of processional staging.

problems raised by some of the most important surviving play texts. This, together with the new editions produced in the 1970s, '80s and '90s, is perhaps the most important single area of progress in recent times.

Later REED volumes have moved away from the major civic centres, dealing principally with rural areas of the country where no locatable play texts can be matched with the records of dramatic activity.[7] In this, the project has followed its immediate forebear, the documentary studies published by the Malone Society, of which Giles Dawson's study of dramatic and minstrel activity in Kent and Stanley Kahrl's of dramatic records in Lincolnshire are justly famous pioneering studies.[8] In the short term this is a less fruitful side of record-collection, but long-term it may be more rewarding. A large proportion of the surviving play texts cannot be assigned to specific locations, so that the assessment of documentary evidence has little immediate effect on our understanding of them: but it is in this area of day-to-day evidence of dramatic activity away from the major centres that we now need to build up a picture of that activity. Once this picture is clearer and more detailed we shall understand better how some of the unlocated plays were performed, and in what circumstances. It will occasionally then be possible to attempt a matching of play texts with records – in other words, to locate a text. At least one proposed matching has already taken place, discussed in section 4.3, below. But in a sense this is a secondary consideration, and perhaps will never be entirely possible anyway: for we are likely to find, as in the case of the locatable plays, that the usefulness of the records is limited by a chronological mismatch between text and documentation – that the records are for an earlier or later (but anyway different) version of the play that we have.

The danger of trying to match texts and records is already a cautionary tale well illustrated by the N-Town cycle. The assigning of those plays to Coventry led to the title *Ludus Coventriae* being given to them at one time, which caused one of several bibliographical hiccups;[9] the attempt to locate the cycle in Lincoln cost much time and energy; and the proposal of Bury St Edmunds as the original home of the plays could still lead scholars in inappropriate directions. As it happens, the language of the cycle is now known to make the first two locations ineligible: only Bury St Edmunds would make a good linguistic match for that text. It is still necessary to point out, however, that to posit a specific location for a play and then to interpret the record material with that in mind is the opposite of the proper scholarly procedure and may lead to a circular argument that can be broken only by some body of evidence that is currently unknown or unavailable to us.

Before the records are discussed I must say something about English currency in the period concerned. Until decimalisation in 1971 the English pound was divided

---

7 The main exceptions to this are *REED.Cambridge* (2 vols., 1989) and *REED.Oxford* (in preparation).

8 Dawson's work forms the Malone Society's *Collections* VII (1965); Kahrl's appeared as *Collections* VIII (1974 for 1969).

9 The plays have also been known as the 'Hegge' plays from the name of an early owner, and briefly as the 'Lincoln' plays. See Epp 'Towneley Plays', 122–3. These various titles have been individually misleading, and have tended to prevent objective study of the plays.

into twenty shillings, each shilling being composed of twelve pence. Large sums of money were therefore expressed in terms of pounds, shillings, and pence: the abbreviations for these, £ s d (the first of which is still in use), are the initials of the Latin *libra, solidus* and *denarius*. The penny was itself divided into two halfpennies or four farthings (i.e. fourthings, or quarters).

Sums of money were not invariably expressed in this way, although other modes were rare by the date of most of the financial records discussed here. Business could be transacted in terms of coins that did not coincide precisely with rational units in pounds, shillings and pence. The guinea (21 shillings) remained a normal unit of currency – at least for tailors and bloodstock dealers – long after the demise of the gold coin itself early in the present century; and the half-crown (2s 6d) was still a common coin until its withdrawal in the late 1960s.[10] For much of the late Middle Ages in England transactions were often made in terms of the mark, a coin worth 13s 4d (two-thirds of a pound), or of the half-mark (6s 8d, one-third of a pound). These are both mentioned in *The Castle of Perseverance* (**Castle 2726, 2740**). The half-mark, or noble, valued at 80 pence (6s 8d) was introduced in 1344, together with its own half (3s 4d) and quarter. Its value was given to the angel in 1464, and to the George noble in 1530, coins whose names derived from their designs.[11] Although the mark and, later, the half-mark fell out of use their value remained a common accounting unit. As late as the twentieth century 6s 8d was still the normal fee charged by a solicitor for a consultation, some four centuries after the demise of the half-mark as a coin.

It is tempting, when dealing with sums of money some centuries ago, to give precise price-equivalents in terms of a factor by which a medieval price can be multiplied for comparison with the modern price. Such attempts quickly become out of date when the current inflation-rate is high, but that is not the only problem that makes this procedure inadvisable. The equivalence has varied with time anyway since inflation became a serious issue early in the sixteenth century, so that the result would depend on the precise time concerned: but, more seriously, the equivalence also depended at any particular time on the relative values in real terms of the specific commodities or services in question. That is why F.M. Salter's brave attempt to relate the expenses of the Chester plays to the average labourer's daily wage of 1d was ultimately doomed to failure.[12] The only useful way of tackling this problem is to build up as full a picture as possible of the prices of a variety of everyday commodities, and to compare these with the incomes of specific social groups.

This task is too large to be dealt with here, but a few items of income and expenditure may be helpful. For much of the later Middle Ages the value of money in England stayed fairly stable, and many prices rose very little during the fourteenth

[10] The crown itself (5 shillings) had by then long disappeared from normal currency, although commemorative crowns are still occasionally struck.

[11] See Davis *Mediaeval England*, 568–73, and for a more recent and European account Spufford *Handbook*, xix–xxvi.

[12] Salter 1955.

and fifteenth centuries. A sheep or pig might be valued at 1 shilling or so, or a horse at 2 shillings:[13] a squire of a royal household earned 7½d a day when he was in Court, in addition to his liveries and board, while a yeoman received 4½d; a group of the king's minstrels often received 6s 8d from a large town or a nobleman, but a mere 1d or 2d was an acceptable gift to a beggar.[14] With the influx of precious metals from the New World early in the sixteenth century there was a noticeable rise in most prices: but, as late as the mid-sixteenth century, as we see from some of the civic accounts for the plays, 2d would buy enough ale for several men, 12d was a suitable sum for a composer who produced a short song, and the players were rewarded with sums between 6d and 3s 4d, depending on their roles.[15]

Such everyday payments may give us some idea of costs and values, and to some extent of the relationship between income and the food and drink necessary to live. There is however another factor that must be kept constantly in mind, although dramatic records give little evidence on which a balanced view might be based: I refer to the difference between advantaged and disadvantaged groups – sometimes, but not always, the same as the rich and the poor. Although nothing in the dramatic records is as mind-boggling as some of the items in royal household records – Henry VII's gift of £30 to a girl who danced, for instance[16] – there are certainly occasional hints of a differential. If we consider the general consistency of the Chelmsford payments discussed in section 4.3, below – for example, the cost of meals that first weekend (f. 22v of the accounts) – then the payments made to the flute player and the trumpeter for their 'pains' may well refer to similar services, although the trumpeter gets three times as much as the flute player.[17] It is known that trumpeters were an exclusive and relatively highly-paid type of minstrel: this would suggest that, all else being equal, a trumpeter could command three times the fee of a less prestigious colleague.

4.2 Guild accounts and related records

Broadly speaking, the documentary evidence relevant to dramatic activity falls into five categories:

— Civic records, including financial accounts.

— Court records: that is, the documents generated by legal processes.

— Records and accounts of the trade guilds.

---

[13] See Hewitt *Cheshire*, 46, 62 and 163, for example.
[14] See Rastall *Secular Musicians* II, *passim*.
[15] For the ale and payments to individual players, see for instance *REED.Coventry, passim*; the payment for songs is discussed above, pp. 65, 74.
[16] See Ashbee 1993, 153.
[17] See below, p. 170, for the payments on f. 22r of the accounts. How this affects our view of the drum player depends on circumstances: but 'Mr Beadle's man' was presumably not the original colleague of the other two, and a different sort of differential may be in operation.

— Parish and other ecclesiastical records.

— The records, principally financial accounts, of individual households, including the royal households and ecclesiastical households.

Of these, it is undoubtedly the third that has been of most immediate benefit to early drama studies, because of the role played by the trade guilds in mounting the cyclic dramas in Coventry, Chester, York and elsewhere. In effect, the guilds' accounts in such places contain the records of the play production. These are sometimes supplemented by the civic records, since the plays were mounted under the ultimate authority and control of the city or town. Civic records would be the principal documentary evidence for plays mounted directly by a civic authority, but the texts concerned cannot be assigned to specific towns and therefore cannot be matched to town records of a production. To some extent the parish records document transactions that we might expect town records to deal with, and it is in relation to churchwardens' accounts that a possible matching is discussed in section 4.3, below. Parish and household records otherwise provide evidence of the performance of parish and domestic drama rather than of actual productions, and can be regarded as confirmatory evidence rather than primary evidence about particular plays. Finally, court records give information about individuals rather than groups or productions.

In this section, then, we shall be concerned with guild records. This evidence has challenged many presuppositions and long-held beliefs about medieval drama, its nature, its staging and its organisation. If the first three REED volumes had done nothing else – and they did a great deal more – they would have made us question the belief that each trade guild in York, Chester or Coventry financed and played its own play, bringing in professionals only to organise and sing the items of liturgical vocal music or to provide minstrelsy as demanded by the plays. In fact, though, the evidence is rarely incontrovertible.

The first reason for this is that the recording scribes did not have the enlightenment of modern scholars as a priority. As Alexandra Johnston has noted, the records that survive to the present are[18]

> enigmatic and infuriating: a payment here, a complaint there, a property list, a fine, a list of pageants, a transfer of responsibility – all written for and by men who knew exactly what they were referring to (they had just seen it, after all) and who were anxious to satisfy not our curiosity but, in the main, the sharp eyes of the auditors.

The records, in fact, are incomplete, because some of the information needed by a modern scholar was not considered relevant to the scribe. Even in a court case, where the circumstances of the misdemeanour should be relevant, many of those circumstances could be taken for granted and so are not mentioned. This situation obtains also for any more specific section of the community, such as a trade guild,

---

[18] In 'What if . . .?' in *Contexts*, 4.

where the common understandings of the guildsmen and their associates covers matters on which we now badly need information.

Nevertheless the records of a specific group, if numerous enough, can be expected to give a great deal of information. The guild records of York are rather disappointing, but only by comparison with those of Chester and Coventry. In these latter places, the financial accounts of the guilds mounting plays are full enough and run over a large enough period of time to give information for a fairly clear picture of such matters as organisation and properties, though these have little effect on the use of music. Matters concerning the personnel involved, the roles taken and fees earned do however help our study of music considerably if we can assume a certain stability of text and production method over a period of years. Among the Chester guild accounts are those for four plays that include music. These have been discussed elsewhere, and need not be presented in detail now,[19] but it will be helpful to indicate some of the issues and possible solutions. In the case of the Painters and Glaziers, who produced the shepherds' play, accounts from only three years survive: 1568, 1572 and 1575.[20] This is enough for us to see that the guild used a senior singing-man from the cathedral, usually the precentor, to provide singers and suitable music for them to perform: we have to assume that he also rehearsed them. In 1568 the singers are referred to only as 'Sheperdes Boyes'. In each year these boys were paid a sum higher than would be reasonable unless they were singers, and comparison of all the accounts for these years suggests strongly that these are the same as 'the iiij syngares' who appear in the 1572 accounts and 'the sengers' in 1575. As one version of the play (manuscript H) requires 'helpers' to sing with the shepherds at **Chester 7/447+sd**, it seems certain that that was the function of the choristers. Another sung item in this play is the angelic Gloria sung to the shepherds by the angel, but as the text shows that this is a solo song it was evidently not performed by the boys. This raises a problem, for the angel was paid the small sum of 6d for his part in the play, commensurate with his eight-line speech: Mary, with the same number of lines, received the same fee. Evidently the angel that appears in the list of fees to players took a speaking role only, but in that case, who sang the Gloria? It would have to be a professional singer, and there are only two possibilities. One is that payment to the precentor included a fee for another singing man; the other, and more likely, solution is that the precentor himself sang this role.

This kind of argument is needed elsewhere, such as in dealing with the Smiths' guild, which produced the Purification play. Here, too, a senior singing man – sometimes the same precentor – was responsible for finding singers. In two years, 1567 and 1568, a second singing-man puts in an appearance, one 'Mr White'. This is almost certainly the composer Robert White, who is known to have worked at Chester between posts at Ely and Westminster. The only way in which the high fee paid to White (4 shillings) can be explained is, I think, that he played the part of

---

[19] See my section in Lumiansky and Mills *Essays*, 132–8.
[20] This brief account follows the discussion in *Essays*, 132–4.

Simeon, a role that is not only the largest in the play but that also needs considerable skill as a singer of liturgical music.[21]

We can add a little to our knowledge of White's biography from these records, and the same is true of other singers. In some cases the records provide a considerable body of biographical information, as is the case of James Hewitt at Coventry. Hewitt, like John Genson the Chester precentor, was employed by more than one guild, and exemplifies the way in which certain useful people were available for general hire. Hewitt was a town wait and keyboard-player who possessed his own regals, and he was apparently responsible for the music in the pageants of the Weavers and the Drapers at various times during the 1550s, '60s and '70s. It is possible that he worked for both guilds in certain years, which would raise a nice logistical problem if we had the data to pose it.[22]

Apart from the kind of mismatch between text and musical resources that we have seen in the Chester records, the financial accounts do also spring complete surprises – singers and, more especially, minstrels for whom there is no apparent place in a particular play. To some extent we must assume that local guild tradition sometimes included material that did not find its way into official material such as the civic register of the texts. Such tradition may in part account for the variant versions of the Chester text, for example, although another reason for those would be the availability or otherwise of such outside professional help as singers. In a non-musical context, Peter Meredith has suggested that some rather cryptic marginal directions in **Chester 8** may show Herod indulging in various pieces of stage business including a juggling act, and also that two of the Shepherds in **Chester 7** may have been well-known as stilt-walkers and used for that purpose in the play.[23] The appearance of 'whistles' in the Painters' accounts for 1568, 1572 and 1575 – specified as 'ij wystyles for trowe' (i.e. Trowle, Garcius, the youngest shepherd) in 1572 – suggests some sort of musical business, while the Third Boy's mention of a very loud 'pipe' must presumably be a bagpipe.[24] I no longer equate these two, and it is perhaps bad luck that the bagpipe does not appear in the accounts. If a bagpipe was there in the play, could a piper resist the temptation to play on it?

Another kind of surprise is the appearance of minstrels not required by the play text. The position of minstrels in the plays is discussed in section 8.5, below: but we may note here that, in addition to the minstrels required by directions and text references, some probably had a function during the performance as entertainers at specific stations or processing with specific pageants. Some entries for payments to *bas* minstrels I can explain only with difficulty: there seems no proper function for the Chester minstrels Randle Crane and William Lutter, for instance. Crane was paid 2 shillings by the Smiths in 1554. The entry immediately follows the record of a payment to the singers for the performance that year, so that it looks as if he was

---

21 *Essays*, 134–6.

22 Hewitt's involvement with the plays is discussed in section 8.3, below.

23 Peter Meredith 'Scribes, Texts' in *Aspects*, 25–6; and 'Item for a grone' in Dutka *REED.Proceedings*, 29–31.

24 This matter is discussed in Rastall 'Some myrth' in Mills *Staging Chester*, 86–9; and in 8.4, below.

associated with them in the performance. There are similarly problematic payments by the Smiths to William Lutter in 1561: of 4½d at the general rehearsal, and of an unspecified amount 'for plleyinge', again immediately after the payment to the singers.[25] What did these two do? In the performance Lutter at least was evidently part of the costumed cast:[26] perhaps he was responsible for 'heavenly' music, either as a soloist or accompanying the singers. However, the latter does not seem likely, since professional singers and minstrels followed radically different traditions. Lutter was also working at the rehearsal. Was this simply to rehearse his own role in the play, or did he perhaps also 'fill in' for the singers in their absence?

The common factor in the material under discussion here is money. Players, singers and minstrels were paid for what they did, and on a scale that reflected their involvement and their expertise. Increasingly, commentators are emphasising this point, and noting it not only for the big civic productions on which a large budget could be spent, but also for the much smaller productions mounted in country areas, perhaps at parish expense.[27] This is an area in which there is clearly much more waiting to be learned, and it may be some years yet before much can be said about the financing of music in these smaller productions. John Coldewey's theory about drama at Chelmsford must be discussed here, however, since he has proposed specific surviving plays for a performance in which minstrels are known to have taken part in circumstances of which there is all too little evidence.

4.3 Chelmsford: the summer of 1562

In searching for dramatic activity amongst the documentary records of Essex, Coldewey may be said to have struck gold. The Chelmsford churchwardens' accounts show that in the summer of 1562 that town produced what amounts to a drama festival, in which four plays were mounted in a period of several weeks beginning at midsummer. This is a different kind of organisation from that with which we were mainly concerned in section 4.2, and the records are therefore of a different type, too. In the production of a northern processional cycle the wealth and resources of a large industrial town are used in an organisation in which the civic authority delegates financial responsibility to the guilds. The records of this activity therefore fall into two groups: the official civic records document the initiating decisions, the methods of monitoring progress and the final civic results, while the financial accounts of the individual guilds record the transactions of the bodies actually mounting the drama. In the case of Chelmsford it was the church that took financial responsibility and overall control of the venture, and we should therefore expect the parish records alone to show a detailed account of it. In fact, only the churchwardens' accounts are helpful: and although the civic records might have shown something of the support and collaboration of the city for the venture,

---

[25] These payments are discussed in *Essays*, 137.
[26] The word 'plleyinge' means 'acting' rather than 'playing music'.
[27] See, for instance, Johnston 'What if . . .' in *Contexts*, 8–9.

nothing of the sort seems to have survived. Some corroborative evidence has survived in the Maldon chamberlains' accounts, but Coldewey was unable to obtain unequivocal results by conflating the two sets of records.

In this short discussion of some of Coldewey's findings I shall refer mainly to his brief published account of his research in RORD 1975; specific accounts are quoted from the material presented in his doctoral thesis.[28]

The churchwardens' accounts are presented in chronological order, but the order in which payments were made, not the order of the events as they occurred. Thus it is possible to distinguish the records of the different plays although the sequence of events for any one of them is not always clear. Coldewey gives the following chronology for the whole 'festival':[29] Sunday, midsummer day, was a 'showday' and the following day a 'playday', both apparently in Chelmsford; the Tuesday was another 'showday', this time in Braintree, but there is no record of the play being given there. There followed a two-week period of preparation for the 'show' to be given in Maldon; again, there is no record that the play was given there. Three weeks later the second play was apparently performed at Chelmsford, and three weeks later still the last two plays seem to have been given in quick succession. If this chronology is correct, with a total period of eight and a half weeks from 21 June, the 'show' was given in Maldon around 8 July, the second play was performed around 29 July, and the final performances occurred around 19 August.

There are no records of singers being employed, and we can assume that any singers involved were local church singers for whom no extraordinary payments were needed. The presence of payments for minstrels, on the other hand, shows that professionals from outside were employed and had to be given board and lodging. The relevant payments are shown in Table 6.[30]

Coldewey's chronology of the first week depends on the second group of payments, on f. 22v, which shows the costs of the minstrels' meals. He assumes that they arrived in Chelmsford on the Saturday afternoon (20 June 1562), since they had supper that evening.[31] That they were not local is shown by the costs of pasturing their horses 'at the furst playe' recorded on f. 23r. They stayed in Chelmsford for the next two days, taking all three meals on the Sunday and both breakfast and dinner on the Monday. Sunday was the show day and Monday the play day, the minstrels' fee for these being 20 shillings in all – the first item in these accounts (f. 22r). A total of 11s 6d for food and drink in this first group of payments (f. 22r) seems excessive: certainly one would expect payments for drink, since minstrelsy is thirsty work, but this is a huge payment in addition to the three meals per day that the minstrels were

---

28 John C. Coldewey, 'Digby Plays' (1975), 103–21, and *Early Essex Drama*, 1972. I am grateful to Professor Coldewey for providing information and discussions during my study of his work.

29 Coldewey 'Digby Plays', 104–5. Coldewey says that the Saturday on which the minstrels arrived – that is, the day before the first 'showday' – was Midsummer Day: in fact, 21 June 1562 was a Sunday.

30 Chelmsford, Essex Record Office, D/P 94/5/1, f. 22r–25v, quoted from the appendices of Coldewey's thesis. Items are adjacent unless intervening items are shown by . . .; scribal abbreviations are extended in [ ].

31 Coldewey 'Digby Plays', 104.

TABLE 6 : MUSIC IN THE DRAMA AT CHELMSFORD, SUMMER 1562

f. 22r]	Inprimis paid unto the minstrell[is] for the Showday and for the play daye	20/-
	It[e]m paid unto Burtonwoode for ther meat and drink	10/-
	It[e]m paid unto the trumpetar for his paynnes	10/-
	It[e]m paid unto Burtonwoode for meate and Drink for the drumme player, the	
	fluet plaier and the trumpeter	18d
	It[e]m p[ai]d unto the fluet player for his paynes	3/4d
	It[e]m paid unto mr Beadilles man for playenge on the drom	10/-
	...	
f. 22v]	It[e]m for the mynstrells Soper a saterday at nyght	2/-
	It[e]m for ther Breakfasts on Sonday mornynge	2/-
	It[e]m for ther dynners on Sondaye	2/-
	It[e]m for ther Soper on Sonday	2/-
	It[e]m for ther brekfaste on mondaye	2/-
	It[e]m for ther dynner on Mondaye	2/-
	...	
f. 23r]	It[e]m paid unto the mynstrells for twoo daies	20/-
	It[e]m p[ai]d to the same men for goynge to Branktre	10/-
	It[em] for the breakfast on Tewsday morne	2/-
	It[e]m leide out for my parte for the plaiers Dynners at Branktre	
	at the Showe ther	7/8d
	It[e]m paid to the trumpetter ther	20d
	[items for expenses at Braintree]	
	It[e]m p[ai]d unto Mr Scotte for pasturynge the mynstrells horsse at the furst playe	2/-
	It[e]m p[ai]d unto hym more for pasturynge the said horsses for iij dayes &	
	one nyght at the last playe	3/-
	[items for food and drink]	
	It[e]m for the mynstrells dynners at branctre	2/-
f.23v]	[Payments out from receipts at the second play]	
	...	
	It[e]m paid to mr Browne for the waightes of Bristowe and ther meat, drinke	
	and horsmete	4/8d
	...	
f.24r]	It[e]m for the mynstrelles meat and Drinke at the laste playe	12/-
	...	
f.24v]	[1562: Receipts for last 2 days and hire of costumes. Payments]	
	...	
	It[e]m p[ai]d unto the mynstrells for the Showe day	
	and for the playe daye	33/4d

given. Perhaps it is mainly composed of food for their horses, who do not otherwise appear in this section of the accounts.

This first section of the accounts tells us what instruments the minstrels played: they were a drummer, a flute player and a trumpeter. The last two were paid for some special service, the trumpeter at three times the rate of the flute player if their 'pains' were comparable. These sums are so large that I suspect some occasion additional to what we already know – perhaps a social gathering with music after the 'show'. The minstrels' main fee being 10 shillings per day, both at Chelmsford and at Braintree, these extra payments could only be for something very special – certainly more than just an extra rehearsal, for instance. The drummer is left out of account here presumably because his place was taken by 'Mr Beadle's man', who received the same as the trumpeter. This may be the servant of a Mr Beadle, but he is more likely to be the servant or assistant of the town beadle. Whatever this event was, the wording of the payment to 'Mr Beadle's man' suggests that it took place at Chelmsford, as we should expect.

Going now to the accounts on f. 23r, we find, as Coldewey says,[32] that the minstrels were among the group that travelled to Braintree, some 10 or 11 miles away, to produce a 'show' there. The cost of the minstrels' next meal, Tuesday breakfast, is in this group of payments, apparently at Braintree, so they had probably been there overnight. Evidently they had travelled on Monday afternoon or evening, following the performance in Chelmsford, and no doubt took supper *en route*. The missing meal, Monday supper, may therefore be included in the 10 shillings 'paid to the [minstrels] for going to Braintree': even supposing that a meal on the road would cost more than the 2 shillings allowed for each meal in Chelmsford, 10 shillings must surely include care of the horses and several miscellaneous expenses during the journey.

The minstrels were in Braintree for two days, according to the first item on f. 23r. This group of payments is very short on meals, and the two payments for the players' dinners and the minstrels' dinners are only enough for a single meal.[33] Probably the meal costs were shared with Braintree, appearing in a set of accounts of that town that have not survived. During the two days in Braintree the trumpeter (or a trumpeter) was again used for some special service, but one only worth 20d in this case. It is unclear whether 'the trumpeter there' means 'our trumpeter, being at Braintree' or 'the local trumpeter at Braintree'.

There is no record of the first play being performed at Braintree, and it seems possible that the 'show' there was for the second play, not for the first. If this is so, it partly explains why so little money was spent on minstrelsy at the second play. In fact, the first group of minstrels disappears from the records for a while – if indeed it is the same group that returned for the last two plays – and there is no indication that they even took part in the 'show' at Maldon two weeks later. The chances are that it was convenient to them to earn some more money by performing at the 'show' at Braintree the day after the first Chelmsford play performance, but that, living at a considerable distance from Chelmsford, they decided to stay away from the second play and return only for the last two. At any rate, the only payment for minstrels in connection with the second play is the record of 4s 8d paid for food and drink for the Waits of Bristol and their horses. This is barely more than the first group of minstrels were allowed for two meals. It is hard to believe that the Waits came all the way from Bristol for so little, and it is a small payment even if they happened to have reached London, say, on their summer travels and were coming to Chelmsford from there. Had they fitted Chelmsford into their summer itinerary,

---

[32] Coldewey 'Digby Plays', 104.

[33] Coldewey reckons that there were not more than fifteen players at Braintree ('Digby Plays', 104), so the 7s 8d paid for the players' dinner represents around 8d per man per meal: this is consistent with the 2 shillings per meal for the three minstrels.

perhaps, and did they stay only long enough to perform for the one 'play day' before moving on? At present we have no information about the movements of the Bristol Waits in the summer of 1562, but some information may eventually be found.

The last two items concerning minstrels seem to relate to the last play: a payment of 12 shillings for their 'meat and drink', and what seems to be their fee of 33s 4d for the 'show day' and 'play day'. The 12 shillings fits with the 2 shillings per meal of the accounts for the first play – that is, six meals in the two days. Any interpretation of the 33s 4d must be much more speculative. If we assume that three minstrels were hired, as before, then the parallel costs shown on f. 22r might be the 20 shillings paid 'for the showday and for the play day' plus the 10 shillings to the trumpeter and the 3s 4d to the flute player for their 'pains'. This would leave a lot of costs unrecorded, however, such as those of the care of horses and incidental expenses for food and drink. It may be, of course, that these minstrels were local ones who did not need to be boarded out and who had not brought horses that must be pastured.

Although the interpretation of these accounts involves much guesswork, some results can be offered. Most certainly, and not at all surprisingly, we find that a group of professional minstrels can arrive one evening and be involved in a performance of some kind the next day, and in the main production the day after that. There is no reason to suppose that, being given a basic outline of their duties, such a group needed more than a few minutes to learn their cues and decide where to stand and what music to play. That such a group was a costly item in the play's budget is likewise not surprising, nor that a trumpeter could command the sum of 10 shillings for some special performance. Real professionals could always command a good fee, and trumpeters had a long tradition of special consideration in this respect. Nevertheless, the scale of the incidental expenses in connection with the minstrels may well have raised some eyebrows, for they are of the same order as the fees. If we consider that the total spent on the minstrels is over £7 – around a third of the sum raised from the sponsors – we see that minstrelsy was regarded as a very important element in the venture as a whole.[34]

The reason for this may become clear if we examine this use of minstrelsy in the light of Coldewey's theory that the plays performed were those now known as the Digby Plays.[35] Coldewey admits that he cannot prove his hypothesis, but it is persuasively argued and could well be correct. In any case it is worth provisional acceptance for our present purposes. Even if the plays concerned were other plays, those performed at Chelmsford in 1562 must have been similar in size, scope and staging requirements to the Digby plays suggested by Coldewey.

Coldewey proposed that the plays performed were, first, *The Conversion of St Paul*, second, *The Killing of the Children* and, finally, *Mary Magdalen* performed in two separate halves. Of these, *The Conversion of St Paul* requires no professional singers,

---

34 This sum should be compared to the £4 15s 4d paid to Burles, the 'property-player' who produced the first and second plays, and to the £3 paid in all to the various producers of the last two plays.

35 This theory is expounded in Coldewey 'Digby Plays', 108–19.

although there is an original direction for the singing of *Exultet celum laudibus* at the very end. This is a hymn of no great difficulty, and given a few members of the cast with strong voices it is a piece in which the audience could be encouraged to join. Originally this was the only music in the play: but in the mid-sixteenth century directions were added for a dance at three points of dramatic articulation, and the Belial episode and much business with gunpowder were also added. The overall effect is of a professional touring play that was adapted for amateur civic production in mid-century. The indications are that if this is indeed one of the plays performed at Chelmsford then it would have been produced there in its later, expanded, form. The minstrels have three dances to play for, then, as well as any loud music and/or dances required for the pre-performance 'show'.

Whatever 'the show' was, there seems no doubt that 'the play' was the principal production. On the other hand, all three minstrels were used for the 'show' before the first play at Chelmsford; up to fifteen players went to mount 'the show' at Braintree, and Coldewey points out that in the Maldon records 'the show' is actually referred to as a 'play'.[36] We do not have the banns for any of the Digby plays: but if they took the same form as those for other East Anglian plays (see 2.5, above), they would include minstrelsy and/or dances, with descriptions of the plot that could well have been illustrated by costumed dumb-show. These are the elements of a dramatic entertainment that would be an advertisement for the particular play – and up to a point a 'play' itself – without actually being the play in question.

The Killing of the Children of Israel and Candelmas Day (to give the play its full title in the correct order) requires minstrels and a group of professional singers who can also dance. Leaving aside the dancing for a moment, the requirement for the 'virgins' to sing *Nunc dimittis* (**Killing 484+sd**) would suggest a group of choir-boys. It is no doubt possible that choristers could have been trained to dance, if they did not already know how to do so, and I think that this is probably what happened. There is another possibility, however, since *Nunc dimittis* in its psalm-tone setting is a congregational piece of no difficulty. Perhaps in this case the 'virgins' really were girls who knew how to dance and who could be trained to sing an easy piece of chant that they would, in fact, already know. As for the minstrels, here too they have three dances to play for.

The first day of *Mary Magdalen* (up to **Mary Magdalen 924**) has only one certain music cue, where Mary and Curiosity dance together (**Mary Magdalen 533**). In the early part of the century they would perhaps have danced a *basse dance* to the music of shawms and trumpet, but this would be out-dated by 1562, when a pavan would be more likely, played by a softer consort. At that time a flautist and a drummer, or even a single player with pipe-and-tabor, would be adequate for the Chelmsford performance.[37] There is also some sense in suggesting a trumpet fanfare at the start of the play. If the King of Marseille has a trumpet fanfare at the start of Day 2 (as seems likely), then his remark about being honoured as an emperor (**Mary**

---

[36] Coldewey 'Digby Plays', 104–5.
[37] Further on this, see section 8.5, below.

Magdalen 933–4) implies that the Emperor has already had a fanfare in Day 1. A trumpeter and drummer could provide this between them, or even a trumpeter alone if necessary.

The second day of *Mary Magdalen* requires several professional singers. The priest and his boy sing the office of the day at **Mary Magdalen 1227+sd**, and although it is a performance that goes horribly wrong, very good singers are needed if the result is to be entertaining rather than distressing to the audience. The 'mery song' at the entry of the ship at **Mary Magdalen 1394+sd** is apparently sung by different singers: these need not be professionals. They sing again at **1438+sd**.[38] An angelic choir is then needed for two liturgical pieces in praise of Mary – *Assumpta est Maria* and an unspecified 'mery song' to receive Mary's soul in heaven (**Mary Magdalen 2030+sd, 2122+sd**). These must be professional singers, and the iconography of the Assumption of the Virgin, which is clearly referred to here, would suggest that the angels form a larger choir than just the two singers who played the priest and his boy earlier.[39] Finally, there must be 'clerks' to sing *Te deum laudamus* at the end of the play (**Mary Magdalen 2139**). This needs to be strong, because it is the final tableau: and in any case the audience ought to join in (see section 8.6).

There is less minstrelsy than singing, and in fact no certain occasion of minstrelsy at all. As already noted, it seems likely that the King of Marseille is announced by a fanfare at the start of Day 2 (**Mary Magdalen 925**); and there may have been soft minstrelsy when the King makes his offering (**1221**).

There is no way of telling from this if Coldewey was right to suggest these plays as the ones performed at Chelmsford in the summer of 1562. Certainly they do have the right sort of requirements for minstrels, but we can say this only in the broadest sense; certainly, too, a group of professional minstrels might be a real crowd-drawer at the riding of the banns for such plays. Whatever the minstrels did, the scale of payments made to them and for them during this summer festival of drama suggests that they did at least as much as the Digby plays would have required of them.

[38] This is an editorial placing: the direction is actually an MD that occurs between lines **1436** and **1437**.
[39] See Rastall *Repertory, passim*.

5

MUSIC AS REPRESENTATION

5.1 Introduction

Until the late 1950s scholars of early English drama tended to view music as incidental, not as an integral part of a dramatic presentation. Various circumstances contributed to this. The antiquarian impetus of early drama studies took in the recorded payments to musicians but it proved impossible to relate them to the surviving play texts, and this encouraged scholars to see music as essentially decorative.[1] Many literary scholars were interested in this drama mainly as a precursor to Shakespeare's dramaturgy, an attitude that was not conducive to serious study of music in the earlier plays. Finally, comparison between the various biblical cycles – the obvious way to build up a picture of musical usage – failed to uncover any clear principles either about where music should appear in the biblical narrative or what pieces should be used in any episode. The result was a general feeling that music in early drama was incidental and therefore unimportant. This feeling was fostered by the nineteenth-century tradition of music as essentially *emotive*.[2]

A strong tradition of performance might have helped to dispel the misapprehension: but in the early part of this century serious attempts to perform biblical cycles were frustrated by the blasphemy laws.[3] In consequence, a tradition of performance such as might have led to practical discovery of music's real role never formed. Even when changes in the law made it possible to perform the cycles, from 1951 onwards, the short versions played at York, Chester, and elsewhere were not such as to help in this respect. Important as they were for the rehabilitation of early English drama, they were travesties of the plays as they had survived, making little attempt to follow medieval taste.

At this stage John Stevens, both a literary scholar and a musicologist, offered a *rationale* for the use of music in early English drama. It is not too much to say that Stevens's contribution remains the single most important piece of work in the field. His paper to the Royal Musical Association on 15 May 1958 proposed explanations

---

[1] The pioneering work of Sharp in presenting material from the Coventry guild accounts, for instance, bore little fruit in music studies until the work of JoAnna Dutka (1972).

[2] The point that music was not emotive in the plays was made by Stevens (1958, 82–3).

[3] For the fascinating history of modern productions, see Elliott *Playing God*, and a briefer account in Robinson *Studies* 1–12.

of the role of music in medieval English drama in terms of its representational functions.[4] It did not ask all of the necessary questions, and some of his answers must be modified in the light of work done in the intervening years: but there is no doubt that Stevens set the subject of music in early English vernacular drama, for the first time, on a clear course in the right direction.

5.2 The music of Heaven

Stevens began with the proposition that 'The most frequent use of music in the plays is *to symbolize Heaven*.'[5] As we shall see, 'symbolize' is questionable; and indeed Stevens immediately turned to the idea of *representation*, which offers a much better way of understanding music's function.

The Cornish plays confirm Stevens's main point in the clearest way. In the first day of the Ordinalia, when Seth is invited to look into Paradise, his description of what he sees and hears includes 'minstrels and sweet song' (**Ordinalia 1/770**). Here it is obvious that the music is an important and integral part of the vision; that it is one of the heavenly attributes of Paradise; and, since the 'sweet song' is the only audible part of the vision mentioned by Seth, that music and the right text are the audible equivalent of what Seth sees.[6] In general, 'the Heaven' will have been a high-up location large enough to accommodate singers and sometimes instrumentalists. Such a location is referred to in the phrase 'þe hefne syngynge', for instance (**N-Town 9/227+sd**).

The first music in the dramatic history of the universe occurs as soon as the angels have been created – that is, immediately the performers are available. In each case the angels sing in praise of the Creator: sections of *Te deum laudamus* at **York** (cues 1_1, 1_2) and in the **N-Town** plays (cue 1_1), and *Dignus es domine deus* at **Chester** (cue 1_1).[7] Here, as in other cases, the angels' singing is an expression of joy as well as praise, a combination expressed also in the speech of the angels (for instance, **York 1/41–8**). Such expressions of joy and praise are very common in relation to heaven and its musical representation in the plays. No doubt partly for reasons of alliteration, 'mirth and melody' is a common phrase: but it nevertheless neatly epitomizes the widely-understood relationship of these two in the Middle Ages.

It will be useful here to note two things. First, heavenly music creates a feeling of joy in the hearts of the faithful, who in turn may express their joy in song (see 5.3). Second, many plays seem to end with a tableau in which either God gives a blessing to his Creation or the Creation gives praise to God; and this tableau is often

---

4 Stevens 1958.
5 Stevens 1958, 82. The emphasis is his.
6 This leads us to suppose that the mere mention of music was enough to conjure up the vision. For example, when heavenly music is heard at Everyman's death (**Everyman 891–3**) there should surely be a view of Heaven, with at least an angelic choir in the audience's sight.
7 Music might be expected also at **Towneley 1/76** and **Ordinalia 1/16**, but there is no evidence of it.

accompanied by music in God's praise. This music may be that of angels or of mortals.

The medieval understanding of heavenly music was of course older than the drama. Medieval pictures of the Assumption or Coronation of the Virgin, or simply of the Virgin and Child, frequently included angelic musicians;[8] and a worshipper who looked heavenward in the parish church at March, in what is now the cathedral in Manchester, in the choir of Lincoln Cathedral, or in many other churches, would see angels singing and playing musical instruments. So strong is the iconographic representation of Heaven by music that medieval man no doubt expected Heaven to be peopled with musical angels. Thus the depiction of Heaven as a musical place in the plays – specifically, as a place where the Creator is praised and joy expressed through music – is part of a widely-held belief that helps to explain the power of the dramatic use of music. When the archangel Michael concludes the N-Town Assumption play with

> Now blysid be youre namys we cry
> ffor this holy assumpcyon . alle hefne makyth melody.

(**N-Town 40/499–500**) the playwright is making use of a powerful tradition that was (to use Stevens's phrase) 'deeply ingrained in medieval consciousness'.[9]

In all this heavenly music, God himself does not join. God is the source of all joy, and need not express it; and he is the object of all praise, and does not praise himself.[10] There are three apparent exceptions to this – one in the Towneley cycle and two in the Chester cycle – when Christ sings, but in each case he does so as the incarnate Son, not as the Creator. In the Towneley play of Thomas of India Christ twice appears to the apostles after the Resurrection with the words 'Pax vobis et non tardabit, hec est dies quam fecit dominus' (**Towneley 28/83+sd, 91+sd**). This may sound like a heavenly apparition, for this text is a close relation of the angels' 'Fear not' to Mary, the shepherds and Joseph. Indeed, Jesus's translation at **28/96** makes this clear: 'peasse emangys you euer ichon! / it is I, drede you noght'.[11] It is not an appearance of the same sort, however, for Christ displays his wounds and asks for food to eat in order to prove his bodily presence (**28/98–9, 116–19**); and a few lines later he is addressing his 'dere fader of heuen' and mentioning the circumstances of his birth and death (**28/124–5**).

Of the two occasion when Christ sings in the Chester cycle, one is in the Ascension play, during the musical scene of the Ascension itself. Here, even more clearly than

---

8 This subject is treated in Meyer-Baer *Music of the Spheres*, 130-87; Hammerstein *Die Musik der Engel, passim*; and Brown 'Trecento Angels', especially 112–40.

9 Stevens 1958, 82.

10 'The fadirs voyce' is 'herde full riȝt' in the York Baptism play (**York 21/69–70**) in a musical item: but when it occurs it turns out to be two angels singing *Veni creator spiritus* (**York 21/154+SD**), so that God's speech is much less direct than it is in the biblical narrative. In fact, it is far from clear that this really is intended as the voice of God: it seems likely that a speech is missing.

11 The word 'tardabit' may come from a liturgical text, but if so I cannot find it: the translation here, in any case, follows Luke 24/36, 'Pax vobis; ego sum, nolite timere'.

in the Towneley example, Christ presents himself as the incarnate Son, not as the Creator. He first sings

> Ascendo ad Patrem meum et Patrem vestrum,
> Deum meum et Deum vestrum. Alleluya.   (**Chester 20/104+[a]**)
>
> (I go up to my Father and your Father, to my God and your God. Alleluia)

Here he is still a part of the Creation, as 'my God' shows. The other two verses sung by Jesus also refer to his work of Salvation on earth (**Chester 20/154+[e], [g]**: Isaiah 63/1, 3):

> Ego qui loquor justitiam et propinquator sum ad salvandum.
>
> (I that speak in righteousness, mighty to save)

and

> Torcular calcavi solus, et de gentibus non est vir mecum.
>
> (I have trodden the winepress alone, and of the people there was none with me)

'Mighty to save' may make us think of Christ as the all-powerful God. But the audience had just seen the act of Salvation itself, in the Passion sequence of the cycle, and Christ is displaying his wounds as he sings these verses.[12] Here, too, Christ sings as the obedient Son, not as the Creator God.

The other occasion is during the Last Judgement (after **Chester 24/452**). As explained above, pp. 81–2, Jesus apparently sings one of the *Venite benedicti* pieces before speaking the English paraphrase. The reference to 'my Father' again shows that he is speaking as the incarnate Son (Matthew 25/34):

> Venite benedicti patris mei: percipite regnum quod vobis paratum est ab origine mundi.   (Benedictus antiphon, Sarum Use: AS 158)[13]
>
> (Come, ye blessed of my Father, inherit the kingdom prepared for you from the foundation of the world.)

It is nevertheless the case that Christ is here in glory, and perhaps we should regard this item as a heavenly tableau, even though Christ is not in Heaven at this point. My distinction between the singing of Christ and the non-singing of God the Father is perhaps a fine one. It is dramatically clearer, certainly, when it is the angels who do all the heavenly singing, and this may partly explain why Christ sings so rarely in the plays.

[12] **Chester 20/121–2**: TERTIUS ANGELUS Whye ys thy cloathinge nowe so reedd / thy bodye bloodye and also head ...

[13] This text is used also for the Introit on Wednesday in Easter Week, but with Alleluias added. I discuss these texts in Lumiansky and Mills *Essays*, 153–4.

5.2 *The Music of Heaven*

To understand the music of Heaven – and indeed the representational use of music as a whole – we need to understand the theological and philosophical concepts behind it. Almost throughout the Middle Ages the teachings of Boethius (c.480–c.525) about the place of music in the universe were standard.[14] He – and others, notably Cassiodorus (c.485–c.580) and Isidore of Seville (c.560–636) – transmitted a view of the universe proposed in the ancient world. According to this view the universe was founded on simple mathematical proportions, as were the consonant musical intervals. The Creation itself produced music, the harmonious sound made by the rotating crystal spheres to which the heavenly bodies were attached. This was *musica mundana*, the Music of the Spheres. Two other categories, *musica humana* and *musica instrumentalis*, completed a framework for the whole material universe: the first governed the relationship between man's body and his soul, while the second (which included vocal music) governed music as we would now define it. More will be said of these in 5.3 and 5.4., below.

The concept of this cosmic music, along with a comprehensive cosmology to be discussed below, seems to have been initiated by Pythagoras (sixth–fifth century B.C.).[15] The commentary by Plato (c.428–357 B.C.) is basically the form in which Boethius transmitted it to the Middle Ages, but there were other ancient commentators, of whom Aristotle (384–322 B.C.) and Cicero (106–43 B.C.) were the most influential. Aristotle, for example, denied that *musica mundana* was potentially audible. The older, Platonic view, that *musica mundana* is potentially audible but that the sinful ears of mankind are incapable of hearing it, was more commonly accepted in the Middle Ages.[16]

The Music of the Spheres was not simply an incidental result of the rigorous mathematical ordering of the cosmos. 'Music' as a concept was not confined to the sounds that we now refer to as music, nor even to the theoretical and speculative aspects of that art. Music was a science, and an all-embracing one at that. Little notes that the most often-repeated definition of music was St Augustine's:[17]

Musica est scientia bene modulando,

which Little translates

Music is the knowledge of how to order things well.

Late medieval expansions of this definition show that, even when the writer confined himself to the theory of musical sounds, the important characteristic of

---

[14] This subject is discussed by several authorities. Much of what follows here is based on Little's *Place of Music*, chapter 5, which treats matters untouched by other commentators. Standard published treatments are those of Lewis *Discarded Image*; Meyer-Baer *Music of the Spheres*; Irwin 'Mystical music', 187–201; and Schueller *Idea of Music*. See also Chamberlain 'Philosophy' and Slocum 1991 (which I have not been able to consult).

[15] Little *Place of Music*, 45: the examination of *musica mundana* is on pp. 45–91.

[16] Chadwick *Boethius*, 78–81; Irwin 'Mystical music', 189.

[17] Little *Place of Music*, 38.

music is its ordering according to mathematical principles.[18] Jacobus Leodiensis cites Robert Kilwardby's definition,[19] that

> Music is the perfection of the intellectual soul, for it is the understanding of the mutual harmonic arrangement of all possible things in the appropriate order.

Music, then, is a matter of understanding by the intellect of a rational being; it is at the basis of cosmological order; and it concerns the whole material universe. It is of course susceptible to practical application, and the making of music by instrument or the human voice is in itself good.[20] At this stage we return to a very important feature of the plays: namely, angelic music.

Angelic music is not fully explained by the Boethian triad of *musica mundana*, *musica humana* and *musica instrumentalis*. These are categories of the material universe, of which the angels are not a part. Angels have no bodies, for all that they must appear to men in human likeness: and the Middle Ages understood their depiction with wings and haloes to be 'symbolic rather than genuinely descriptive'.[21]

For this reason a separate category was eventually introduced: *musica caelestis*, which appears for the first time at the beginning of the fourteenth century. It is described by Jacobus Leodiensis in Chapters XI and XII of the *Speculum Musice* of c.1330. To my knowledge, Little is alone among modern scholars in his full treatment of this subject.[22] He is careful to point out that *musica caelestis* is not merely an addition on a par with the other three but a qualitatively distinct category, concerned with the spiritual, not the material, universe.[23]

The idea of *musica caelestis* depends on the fusion of two concepts: the structure of the spiritual universe, equivalent to the spheres of the material universe, and the *laudes dei*, or praises of God.[24] God and his angels do not inhabit the material universe, because they do not live in bodily form. They are outside time and place, and cannot be thought of as even beyond the outermost sphere. They do in fact permeate the whole physical universe, for otherwise Man could have no relationship with God and angels could not visit Man. The spiritual universe, then, is outside the known dimensions of the physical one, but it was convenient to conceptualise it along similar lines. The medieval understanding of it was, therefore, of concentric spheres – nine, like those of the material universe – with God at the centre. The angels were ordered in a hierarchy which was, from highest to lowest:

---

18 Augustine's definition is discussed by Schueller, 241–2.
19 Little *Place of Music*, 40.
20 *Ibid.*, 40–41.
21 *Ibid.*, 16: see also Lewis *Discarded Image*, 71.
22 Irwin 'Mystical music' does mention *musica caelestis* (192), but she seems to regard it as equivalent to *musica mundana*; later works by Chamberlain and Slocum acknowledge it more usefully. I have formerly followed Stevens in assuming that the significance of the music around the throne of God was somehow derived from the Music of the Spheres (*Essays*, 114–15; *Contexts*, 194–5), but have stated my present position in 'Sounds of Hell', 129 (n. 36).
23 Little *Place of Music*, 45.
24 Little *Place of Music* discusses this matter fully, 125–62.

Seraphim, Cherubim, Thrones; Dominations, Powers, Virtues; Principalities, Archangels and Angels.[25] Little points out that the Cherubim have nothing to do with the *putti* or cherubs of Renaissance art:[26]

> Cherubim are among the most terrible of created beings . . . Indeed, an angel is so terrible that even for an event as important as the Annunciation it was only an archangel – the lowest order but one – which bore God's message. Even so, his first words were 'Fear not': which are the first words of almost any biblical angel.

In the plays Gabriel and Michael, both archangels, are the two named angels who deal with mortals: all the rest are simply designated 'angel' and are therefore to be supposed of the lowest rank. Higher ranks are found in the plays of the creation of the angels and fall of Lucifer, of course, but no mortals are concerned in that action.

These orders were thought of in terms of their closeness to God. The first species (Seraphim, Cherubim and Thrones) were believed to be closest, while only the lowest orders (the third species: Principalities, Archangels and Angels) had anything at all to do with Man. It might be thought an obvious organisational ploy to relate these nine orders of angels to the nine spheres, but in fact there was little attempt to do so.[27] It was however standard theory in the late Middle Ages that these spheres, like those of the material universe, revolve at speeds in harmonious proportions, and are spaced at distances making harmonious proportions, so that their 'music' is harmonious.

The concept of this essential structural harmony joined with that of the *laudes dei* to form the conceptual background of angelic music. The *laudes dei* (praises of God) are the proper activity of all angels, and of the souls of those holy men who join them. The original and influential description of the *laudes dei* is Isaiah's vision of Heaven (Isaiah 6/1–3), in which the angels are depicted as praising God:[28]

> Et clamabant alter ad alterum, et dicebant: Sanctus, sanctus, sanctus Dominus, Deus exercituum; plena est omnis terra gloria ejus.

> (And one [seraph] cried unto another, and said, Holy, holy, holy, is the Lord of hosts: the whole earth is full of his glory.) (AV Isaiah 6/3)

Their praise is ceaseless because they constantly strive to praise God adequately; and they call to one another in order to share their knowledge of God. Isaiah's vision was transferred to the opening section of *Te deum laudamus*, which follows it closely:

> Tibi omnes angeli, tibi celi et universe potestates: Tibi cherubyn et seraphyn

---

[25] *Ibid.*, 15. This is not the only order proposed in the Middle Ages, but it is a common one: see also Lewis *Discarded Image*, 71–2. In the course of a discussion of various orderings, Meyer-Baer *Music of the Spheres*, 24, deals also with the 'beautiful angels', the highest order of the original ten, which fell with Lucifer: see also *ibid.*, 81.

[26] Little *Place of Music*, 15–16.

[27] Dante's is a well-known case: see Little *Place of Music*, 16–17 and 160–161.

[28] *Ibid.*, 142.

incessabili voce proclamant: Sanctus, Sanctus, Sanctus, Dominus deus sabaoth. Pleni sunt celi et terra maiestatis glorie tue.

(*Te deum laudamus*, Sarum version of vv. 3–6)

(To thee all Angels cry aloud: the Heavens, and all the Powers therein. To thee, Cherubin and Seraphin: continually do cry, Holy, Holy, Holy, Lord God of Sabaoth; Heaven and earth are full of the Majesty: of thy Glory.)

The concept of the *laudes dei* appears again in the Preface of the Mass, together with the text of the same angelic hymn:

Et ideo cum angelis et archangelis cum thronis et dominacionibus cumque omni milicia celestis exercitus ymnum glorie tue canimus sine fine dicentes.
Sanctus. Sanctus. Sanctus. Dominus deus sabaoth. Pleni sunt celi et terra gloria tua
. . .   (MiS 220)

(And therefore with Angels and Archangels, with Thrones and Dominations and with all the host of the heavenly army we sing the hymn of thy glory, evermore saying: Holy, Holy, Holy Lord God of Hosts. Heaven and earth are full of thy glory
. . .)   (Translation from *The English Missal*, 1958)

Isaiah's was the principal biblical text to be interpreted in this way, but it has a New Testament parallel in Revelation 4/8–11:

Et quatuor animalia, singula eorum habebant alas senas, et in circuitu et intus plena sunt oculis; et requiem non habebant die ac nocte, dicentia:
Sanctus, Sanctus, Sanctus Dominus Deus omnipotens, qui erat, et qui est, et qui venturus est.
Et cum darent illa animalia gloriam, et honorem, et benedictionem sedenti super thronum, viventi in saecula saeculorum, procidebant viginti quatuor seniores ante sedentem in throno, et adorabant viventem in saecula saeculorum, et mittebant coronas suas ante thronum, dicentes:
Dignus es, Domine Deus noster, accipere gloriam, et honorem, et virtutem, quia tu creasti omnia, et propter voluntatem tuam erant et creata sunt.

(And the four beasts had each of them six wings about him; and they were full of eyes within: and they rest not day and night, saying,
Holy, holy, holy, Lord God Almighty, which was, and is, and is to come.
And when those beasts give glory and honour and thanks to him that sat on the throne, who liveth for ever and ever, The four and twenty elders fall down before him that sat on the throne, and worship him that liveth for ever and ever, and cast their crowns before the throne, saying,
Thou art worthy, O Lord, to receive glory and honour and power: for thou hast created all things, and for thy pleasure they are and were created.)

The relationship of the first of these hymns to the Almighty to that in Isaiah's vision is obvious. More important for the drama is that the second is another text (*Te deum laudamus* is the first) sung by the angels after their creation in **Chester 1** (see above).

That the angelic shouts of praise should be turned to song is partly due to the place of music in the material universe. Little notes that Jacobus Leodiensis quoted David as inciting the heavenly company to sing in God's praise:[29]

29 Little *Place of Music*, 135.

Alleluia. Cantate Domino canticum novum; laus ejus in ecclesia sanctorum.

(Psalm 149/1)

(Praise ye the Lord. Sing unto the Lord a new song, and his praise in the congregation of saints.)

Just as the audible sound of David's minstrelsy was regarded as a *speculum* (mirror) of *musica mundana* (see 5.3), so angelic music could be seen as related to the music of the spiritual universe.

For St Augustine, earthly music was a step on the way towards heavenly music, itself an understanding of God's order and virtue. Other Church Fathers discussed it, notably St Bernard of Clairvaux, writing on the *Song of Songs*. In Bernard's writing, as in that of Nicholas of Usk, audible music is regarded as a metaphor for heavenly music. For all of them, *musica caelestis* is an expression of God's goodness, indescribable by mortals except in the most inadequate critical terms used for audible music.[30]

There is a sense, then, in which Stevens's statement 'Heaven is music' would be accepted as true in the Middle Ages. Music was understood as order, and ultimately as the order of the cosmos, whether spiritual or material. Music in the plays is intended as more than a symbol of God's order: it is a *representation* of it in the fullest sense. When minstrelsy and song are heard in dramatised presentations of Heaven and Paradise, they are not merely an incidental characteristic of the state represented. Heavenly music is the only audible representation of that state, an exact parallel on equal terms with the whole iconographic representation.[31]

The importance of musical representation explains why music is heard in the plays when order is restored after a period of disorder. Vocal music indicates the restoration of order when God returns to drive the rebel angels from Heaven (**Chester 2/213+sd**); minstrelsy shows God's ability to restore order in Paradise after the Fall (**Chester 2/280+sd**) and (as Stevens pointed out) the actual restoration of it when Adam and Eve are expelled from Paradise (**Norwich A/81-sd-md**; **Chester 2/384+sd, 424+sd**);[32] minstrels play again when God returns to deal with Cain after the murder of Abel (**Chester 2/616+sd**); the archangel Michael leads the patriarchs to Heaven singing *Te deum* after the Harrowing of Hell (**Chester 17/276+sd**); and Michael sings again after the death of Antichrist as he leads Enoch and Elias to Heaven (**Chester 23/722+sd**). These last two occasions anticipate the singing at the ultimate restoration of Divine Order – to which the whole cycle has been progressing – as the Saved Souls, separated from the Damned after the Judgement, are taken to Heaven in the final working-out of God's purpose for Man (**Chester 24/508+sd**).

Angelic music can be explained satisfactorily, then, at different levels: but its incidence – or rather, its absence where we should expect it – raises some problems. Most commentators have rightly pointed out that angelic music often accompanies God's intervention in human affairs. That is, God's messengers, the angels, tend to

---

[30] Little *Place of Music*, 151–62.
[31] See Stevens 1958, 83; Robinson *Studies*, 22–3.
[32] Stevens 1958, 83.

TABLE 7 : ANGELIC APPEARANCES IN THE YORK CYCLE

Play	To character(s)	a	b	c
6	Adam & Eve	1		
7	Abel / Cain	1,2		
10	Abraham	1,2		
12	**BVM** (Annunciation)	1		
13	Joseph	1		
15	[shepherds] This part of the play missing			
16	Magi	1		
17	Simeon	1,2		
18	Joseph	1		
21	John Baptist The angels sing at Christ's Baptism	1		2
22	Tableau, in Jesus's presence Jesus	2		1
28	Jesus	1		
38	(Resurrection) Marys	2		1
42	**BVM & apostles** (Ascension: 1 and 2 perhaps not separate)	2		1
43	**BVM & apostles** (Pentecost)			1
44	BVM, **BVM** (death of BVM) (or should 2 be (b)?)	1		2
45	vision of **Thomas** BVM addressed in music			1,2,3
46	**BVM** (not separate appearances)	1	2	3
47	**Saved souls**			1

sing, or to be accompanied by other angels singing or playing, when they appear to mortals in order to deliver a specific message from God. But there are unfortunately many occasions when music might be expected but no evidence for it can be found. Is this because, for whatever reason, no cue was written in the play text although music was intended? Do later texts have music where earlier texts omit it? If so, is this a question of making explicit a production-matter that was previously implicit, or did later productions include music where earlier ones did not? Or is there perhaps a pattern which tells us of particular circumstances in which angelic appearances do or do not include music? In particular cases, I suspect, the answer might be 'Yes' to any of these questions, and each case must be examined separately. It will be helpful to consider a full list of angelic appearances in the York cycle: in Table 7 the name of the mortal concerned is in bold if the appearance includes music. The columns are for (a) an appearance with a message, (b) the leading of mortals or souls from one place to another, and (c) for a tableau of Heaven or Paradise, whether static or not.[33] The numbers in these columns refer to the order of appearances.

This list immediately pinpoints some of the difficulties. The Blessed Virgin is treated to a concert on most occasions when an angel visits her, but not every time. **12/144+md** is a late direction, by John Clerke, but in a typical Latin+English situation: we may therefore guess (but cannot demonstrate) that that cue was always a musical one, and that it was noted marginally only on some occasion when Clerke watched a performance. **Play 44** shows the anomaly more clearly. Gabriel does not sing, apparently, at the beginning of the play. This is not a Latin+English situation, since Gabriel's opening speech is apparently not a Latin text translated; yet the angels do sing to the Virgin in a tableau at the end. One may conclude, perhaps, that the opening of the play is a possible place for angelic music; that it is not an obvious one, there being no obvious text that should be sung there; that the choice – if there is indeed a choice – is one for the individual producer or musical director; but that here (as, in fact, at the beginning of the cycle) declamation may well be the way to start the play.

Before discussing the other characters it may be useful to list angelic appearances, in the same way, for the latest of the cycles: they are shown in Table 8.

The general picture here is no clearer than in the York cycle. Moreover there is little in common between them, although music for the Saved Souls at the Judgement occurs in both. Of course, much of the non-correspondence between these two cycles is accounted for by differences in the material covered: Chester has no Marian group, for example. On the other hand, Chester makes something of a feature of musical processions, and these do not necessarily occur in York, even when the same material is treated.[34]

One possibly surprising feature of these tables concerns the initial appearances of message-bearing angels. These are only rarely accompanied by music. It is not always easy to distinguish between an announcing appearance, a transportation task akin to that of Universal Aunts (which seems to be a sort of moving tableau, if that is not a contradiction in terms), and a static tableau proper. Further experience with actual performance may help to make the distinction clear in some cases. At any rate, it is in these latter types – columns (b) and (c) in Tables 7 and 8 – that music is mainly found, not in the initial announcements.

While the music is representative of Heaven, therefore, not of the recipient of the

---

[33] Tableaux are discussed in 6.2, below.

[34] For instance, **York 18**, *The Flight into Egypt*, has no music, whereas **Chester 10/458–97+lat**, which treats the same material much more briefly, ends with a musical procession.

TABLE 8 : ANGELIC APPEARANCES IN THE CHESTER CYCLE

Play	To character(s)	a	b	c
4	Abraham (no music for God's appearances, either)	1		
5	Balaham (no music for God's appearances to Moses and Balaham)	1		
6	BVM/Joseph/BVM/Salome/**Octavyan & Sybbell**	1-4		**5**
7	**shepherds**, shepherds	2		**1**
8	Magi	1		
9	Magi	1		
10	Joseph/**BVM & Joseph**/Joseph/**BVM & Joseph**	1,3	**2,4**	
11	Simeon, audience	1,2		
17	**Patriarchs**		**1**	
20	**Apostles** (Ascension) (not separate occasions)	**2**		**1**
21	**Apostles**	**1**		
23	Antichrist/**Elias & Enoch**	1	**2**	
24	**Saved souls**	**1**(Xt)	**2**	

angel's attention, it is also clear that both the occasion and the mortals concerned are factors in the use or non-use of music at these appearances. Certainly the Blessed Virgin hears music more than others. It may be useful, then, to discuss the nature of angelic song in relation to the ability or worthyness of mortals to hear it. Why are some characters treated to an angelic concert but not others?

This question is one of the most serious for a producer trying to put music in the right places in a play. Part of the answer, and perhaps all of it, can be found in the treatise *Of Angels' Song* by the Augustinian canon Walter Hilton (d.1396).[35] Hilton was very much concerned with problems of deceit, by which the devil might persuade someone, wrongly, that he or she has heard angelic song. I shall touch on this matter in 5.4: here I want to note that in order to discuss deceit Hilton has to explain what angels' song is and what it does. He writes of 'angels' song' and 'heavenly sound' together, making no distinction between them. It appears, there-

---

[35] The work was formerly thought to be by Richard Rolle of Hampole, and until very recently it was not easily available. Meyer-Baer, Little and Schueller apparently did not know of it, and it is not mentioned in the standard histories of music. Kolve cited a passage from it in his discussion of the angelic Gloria (*Corpus Christi*, 171, where he ascribed the work to Richard Rolle), but saw no general principle at work in it. Citations here refer to the edition by Kuriyagawa and Takamiya, by line-number of the edited text.

fore, that what he has to say about angelic vocal music applies also to angelic minstrelsy. He begins by describing the perfect soul: it is a soul that is close to God because of its perfect love ('charite': see lines 11–13). Such a soul is perfectly reformed, returned to its initial state (lines 13–15) – that is, to the state prior to the Fall of Man. For this to happen, the mind must be fixed on God and spiritual things, the reason must be freed from all worldly things and illuminated by grace to behold God and spiritual matters, and 'þe wyl & þe affeccion' must be purged of worldly love and inflamed with love of the Holy Spirit (lines 15–22). The soul cannot be continually in this condition in earthly life, but only in heavenly bliss: but the nearer a soul comes to this condition, the more nearly perfect it is (lines 22–25). A soul that is in this state of charity takes comfort from, and is made glad by, all around it (lines 49–66). ('Comfort' here is clearly in its original sense of 'strength' or 'support'.)

Angels' song is a specific means used by Our Lord to comfort a man's soul. What that song is, no mortal can tell, for it is beyond mortal imagining and understanding: it can be experienced in the soul, but it cannot be described (lines 67–70). The next few lines (71–6) explain this in more detail:

> When a saule es purified be luf of God, illumynd be wysdom, stabild be þe myght of God, þan es þe eghe of þe saule opynd to behalde gastly þings, & uertus, & angels, & haly saules, & heuenly thyngs. Þan es þe saule abil, because of clennes, to fele þe touchyng, þe spekyng of goode aungels.

This touching and speaking of angels is not bodily, but spiritual: and the soul may be in such condition that (lines 79–81)

> if oure lord uouchesafe, þe saule may here & fele heuenly sowne, made be þe presence of aungels in louyng of God.

The effect of hearing angels' song is considerable: a soul in the presence of angels is 'rauisched oute of mynde of al erthli & fleschly thyngs into a heuenly ioy, to here aungels sang & heuenly soun' (lines 93–95). But Hilton reiterates that no soul can truly feel angels' song or heavenly sound unless it be in 'parfit charite' (lines 96–97): and not every soul in perfect charity does hear it, but only one that 'es so pouried in þe fyre of luf, þat al erthly sauour es brent oute of it . . . ' (lines 97–100). Given those conditions, though, the soul may 'synge a new sang, & sothly may he here a blisful heuenly soun & aungels sang' (lines 102–103).

Our Lord knows that soul which, for its burning love of God, is worthy to hear angels' song. Whoever wishes to hear angels' song, therefore, must have perfect charity, which Hilton goes on to discuss (lines 104–111). Hilton's argument is much more complex than this, but for our present purpose some interesting information is gained. Angels' song and 'heavenly sound' are characteristic of the pre-Fall state; they cannot be fully comprehended by sinful Man; yet mortals may experience angelic music if the soul is in a fit state for them to do so; and angelic song is used by God to comfort the soul. In considering angelic music in the plays, therefore, some important distinctions must be made.

The first is that the singing or non-singing status of a message-bearing angel depends both on the state of the recipient's soul and on God's intention to comfort that soul or not to do so. When Gabriel is sent to the spotless virgin who is to be the Mother of God, both the state of Mary's soul and God's intentions towards her suggest that the archangel might sing to her.[36] As we have seen, it is the Blessed Virgin above all who is allowed to hear angelic song.

At the other end of the scale, there are angelic appearances where neither the state of the recipient's soul nor God's intention would suggest that music was appropriate. When Joseph is told that Mary has not been unfaithful to him, that he can take her as his wife, and that the Child is of God, he is being upbraided for his lack of faith: he did after all know the scriptural prophecies, and he had been chosen as Mary's husband in a most unusual way (dramatised in the Mary Play section of the N-Town cycle).[37] Joseph is a much-loved servant, necessary to the work of Salvation: but – in the plays more than in the scriptures – he suffers from a lack of faith and understanding, and seems in consequence never to hear angelic music in the plays.

Another case is that of Salome, the midwife whose disbelief in Mary's virginity results in the shrivelling of her hands (**N-Town 15/252+sd; Chester 6/539+sd**). Her sin is the same as Joseph's: but she, too, is set on the right path by an angelic message. Clearly, in this case also there is no question of music. It is however more than usually important that this be understood, since Salome's hands are healed: it is tempting to see angelic intervention (especially with accompanying music) as a sort of magic, a conspicuous manifestation of supernatural power. This temptation may persuade a producer to include music, as part of the 'magical' character of the appearance, at any angelic intervention, and especially where there is some miraculous content. This, of course, would be not only a misunderstanding of angelic intervention (and of God's relationship with Man) but also of the dramatic characters portrayed in the plays. Salome is not an architypal 'baddy' who must be taught a lesson and then brought back to God by some puerile sleight-of-hand: she is a sinner who has made an error through pride but who can be helped, by direct intervention, to be a true servant of God.

The importance of this principle is perhaps not so much to explain why some angelic appearances do have music as to give a reason for the non-musical nature of others. Surely Noah, Abraham and the Magi are potential hearers of angelic song? Yet apparently none is ever heard by them. Some possible reasons for this could be put forward, of course: Abraham expresses his sorrow at killing Isaac, which runs counter to his obedience in carrying out the sacrifice; and the Magi are, after all, pagans. But we should not expect these to be over-riding considerations, for Abraham *is* unquestioningly obedient, while Octavian and the Sibyl, both pagans, are allowed to hear heavenly music (**Chester 6/666+sd**). Moreover, there seems no good reason, on grounds such as these, why Noah should be deprived of angelic song. We must assume, I think, that there is another factor at work: perhaps that the

---

[36] See Table 7, play 12. The Chester Annunciation scene has no music prescribed: but as Gabriel speaks paraphrases of the relevant liturgical texts (**Chester 6/1–4, 9–14**; and cf. **York 12/144+sd-148, 152+sd-158**) it is likely that he was intended to sing those texts first.

[37] The story is not scriptural, of course, but it was well known from the *Legenda Aurea* account of the Nativity of the Virgin Mary (8 September): see LA 589, GL 524.

dramatists saw no liturgical texts as being immediately and importantly relevant to the situations in which these characters are involved, and saw no reason to engineer a musical salutation of a different sort. Unsatisfactory as this is, we must accept, I think, that some purely pragmatic considerations were as influential in the plays as the main philosophical theories.

In any case, it is not likely that dramatists knew the fine details of Hilton's treatise: *Of Angels' Song* was not widely disseminated, and cannot have been well known. Indeed, the York Realist presents us with a problem in this area, in that he either went against the principles involved or was aware of more detailed principles than are visible to us now. At **York 38/186+sd** Jesus rises from the tomb to the accompaniment of an angel singing *Christus resurgens*. The marginal direction *Tunc Angelus cantat Resurgens* is a late one by John Clerke, but it apparently corrects the defective Latin of the original direction *Jesus resurgente*.[38] Whatever the textual problems, there is no doubt that the playwright intended the angel to sing here, for the ungodly soldiers refer to the 'melodie' that they heard during their strange experience at the tomb (**York 38/383–6**). On the other hand they do not seem to have derived any message from this singing, which has had no comforting or strengthening effect on them. This is yet another kind of experience of angelic music, then: they have been allowed to hear it as a demonstration, but there are no spiritual or intellectual results.

The York Realist may not have gone against any principle concerning angelic music, then, for the soldiers' experience is not such as would be covered by Hilton's discussions. This case does not necessarily make any difference to the thesis that any medieval dramatist is likely to have been educated in at least the basic principles of angelic appearance.

A second distinction is that between angelic song forming a personal message to one or more individuals and a more general concert forming a glimpse of the heavenly kingdom. This surely took the place of the fine detail of Hilton's work in guiding playwrights and others, and it may solve some of the anomalies that arise. The distinction is seen in the biblical account of the Annunciation to the Shepherds in Luke 2/8–14. The angel of the Lord first appears to the shepherds with a personal message: 'Fear not, for behold I bring you good tidings of great joy . . .'. Then, when this message has been delivered and the shepherds know what they must do, the angel is joined by 'a multitude of the heavenly host praising God, and saying, Glory to God in the highest, and on earth peace, good will toward men'. This vision of the heavenly host bears an obvious and close relationship to that of Isaiah 6/1–3. We are accustomed to think of the first of these as a spoken message and the second as a sung vision, although in the biblical account both are spoken.[39]

[38] Even without the MD this SD seems most likely to refer to the Communion *Christus resurgens* (LU 795).
[39] If the angelic praise of God is spoken, what form would we expect it to take? Unordered shouts of praise – which is perhaps what twentieth-century people would expect, if anything – seems wrong in an ordered environment, while ordered shouting would take the form of directed choral speech. Thus for the dramatist a musical setting – and therefore usually a liturgical setting – is a practical solution as well as a philosophically acceptable one.

The distinction between a specific angelic message and a glimpse of Heaven is not always easy to make, but the staging of a play demands that a decision be made whenever the issue arises. Seth's vision of Paradise (**Ordinalia 1/766–74**) is a clear example of the second type, for he has been brought to the gates of Paradise and invited to look in: thus the location itself is not in doubt. The N-Town directions which treat 'þe hefne' as a location are also of this vision-of-Heaven type (notably **N-Town 8/147+sd, 9/227+sd, 9/259+sd**). The angelic Gloria should be another example, but in fact the plays do not always follow the biblical account exactly, presumably for dramatic reasons. In both Towneley shepherds' plays the Gloria is a solo with the angel's speech immediately following (**Towneley 12/295+**; **13/637+sd**), so that the singing is part of the message-giving. The Coventry play, on the other hand, has the heavenly choir's singing of Gloria followed only at a distance by the angel's speech, so that the Gloria is part of a heavenly vision (**Coventry 1/263+sd, 281+sd, 297–306**). The N-Town play presents a textual problem, but a likely reconstruction would have the heavenly choir singing the Gloria immediately before the angel speaks the paraphrase of it.[40] The speaking angel is perhaps part of this choir, for the word 'synge' suggests it, unless it is meant as a metaphor:

[ANGELUS]   Therefore I synge a joyful steuene   (**N-Town 16/7**)

But whether he does or not, the Gloria is clearly intended as a heavenly vision. Chester also presents us with a textual problem, since the Exemplar apparently offered alternative texts which have all been copied into the surviving manuscripts. In **Chester 7/357+sd** the Gloria is sung by a single angel, but the separation of this from the angel's speech to the shepherds (**7/464–71**) probably means that the singing is part of a vision of Heaven. However, if all discussion of the song can be omitted (as it apparently can), so that the speech immediately follows the Gloria, then the singing becomes part of the personal message.[41]

One reason why the distinction between individual message and heavenly vision is difficult to make in a dramatic context is that the results on the characters concerned are not readily distinguishable: either type could be expected to 'comfort' the soul of the hearer, and either might give information of cosmic importance. The problem is most easily seen in the vision vouchsafed to the pagans Octavian and the Sibyl in **Chester 6/666+sd**, an experience that is at quite as high a level as might be allowed to one of God's saints. Octavian is well aware of the cosmic importance of what he sees, and at a personal level the effect is also typical of the soul-comforting described by Hilton:[42]

[OCTAVYAN]   A, Sybbell, heres not thow this songe?
                            My members all yt goeth amonge.

---

[40] These problems are discussed in the relevant places in Volume 2.
[41] On the alternative passages in **Chester 7**, see *Chester* II, 118. The shepherds were obviously considered worthy to hear the angelic message, for they become the first Christian pilgrims and the first evangelists: see below, 8.4.
[42] On Octavian as a righteous ruler, see Keane 'Kingship', especially 77–8, and May 'Good Kings and Tyrants', especially 96–7.

Joy and blys makes my harte stronge
to heare this melody.   **(Chester 6/667–70)**

The distinction between heavenly vision and individual message-giving is obviously an important one for the staging of the plays, then. The situation affects the musical resources required (the number of singers, and whether instruments should be used), and the type of music to be heard. It will be helpful now to look at the evidence for the musical nature of angelic song and its performance as it appears in the arts.

Angelic song had to be clearly distinguished from mortals' music, and that was not easy when the heavenly realm could be described only in terms of the earthly one. Of all the methods available to artists for making this distinction, perhaps only one – a gold face – was exclusively non-mortal, and that was of course perfectly comprehensible in terms of paint or a mask. The visual arts normally show angels to be dressed in liturgical vestments. This is often of the very simplest type, a plain alb (i.e. *tunica alba*, white tunic) worn with an amice. Some however wear richly embroidered copes, often with significant iconographical details, and often with a handsome jewelled morse (medallion clasp). Hans Memlink's famous Najera altarpiece has angels in both kinds of vestment, perhaps indicative of their status.[43] The liturgical distinction signalled by these vestments is seen also in the angels' choice of Latin liturgical or quasi-liturgical texts for singing: certainly the sung texts quoted in the plays – all in Latin – either are or at least could be liturgical, with the exception of a very few items that cannot be identified, while liturgical texts are the rule in the visual arts. The Latin language needs to be translated or explained, so that although the form of musical utterance is recognisable the angels are seen to be the original performers of that incomprehensible and eternal hymn of which human liturgy is the pale shadow.

Moreover, the liturgical music can normally be assumed to be plainsong, for the proper medium of worship was liturgical texts sung to their own plainsong tunes. This principle is not without its exceptions, for any form of polyphony, be it improvised or composed, was an embellishment that added to the solemnity (in its liturgical sense of 'celebratory nature') of the occasion.[44] This rare embellishment was most properly used in honour of the Blessed Virgin, and it is no accident that it is the splendid set-piece performances in **York 45** that gave rise to the unusual phenomenon of composed polyphony in that cycle, nor that it is mainly in devotional pictures of the Virgin that notated polyphony is shown.[45] But it must be

---

[43] For the Memlink, see Meyer-Baer *Music of the Spheres*, 180 f; see also Jan van Eyck's Ghent altarpiece, reproduced ibid., 358, and my discussion of various paintings in Rastall 'Repertory'. Such rich vestments would be seen as exceptional in earthly terms.

[44] On these basic musical styles, see section 3.1. Polyphony – music in parts – had only a precarious place in medieval liturgy, and was disapproved of by many clergy for its obvious sensuous appeal (and for the special status and occasional antics of its performers).

[45] See Rastall 'Repertory', *passim*.

stressed that the Assumption ranked very highly indeed in medieval conscious-ness,[46] and in general we should beware of the modern supposition that splendid musical observance automatically required polyphony.

Another distinction is the use of instruments to accompany angelic singing. In the visual arts the painters often presented a whole range of musical instruments apparently taking a full part in the musical performance, and there is some evidence that the painter concerned had a clear idea of how that performance might be arranged.[47] In real life this seems not to have happened, except for performances of *Te Deum laudamus* with shawms:[48] otherwise, the traditions and repertories of minstrels and church singers seem to have been so different that the two groups did not perform together.[49] In this respect, therefore, medieval depictions of angelic song were able to show an ideal collaboration, and a larger range of musical resources, than was possible in real life. In the drama this was more difficult, because the performance actually had to happen, and I think that a compromise was effected here: for we find singing 'angels' being accompanied by a regals – instrumental accompaniment that could be performed by a church musician with a singer's training.[50]

A note must be added here about chronology. Although most fifteenth-century thinking probably favoured unaccompanied chant as the proper music of Heaven, in the last quarter of that century and into the sixteenth both polyphony and instrumental (organ) accompaniment became more normal, for reasons already noticed.[51]

A distinction should be made between civic and institutional dramatic produc-tions. As was pointed out in 1.3, above, the resources available and desirably to be used in an institutional performance were much greater than those of a civic performance. This factor must be taken into account in any discussion of an individual play, although in most cases there is too little evidence for firm conclu-sions to be drawn. We are on surer ground, probably, in proposing that antiphonal performance was regarded as typical of angels' song. This idea comes from the vision of Isaiah, already mentioned, in which the angels call to one another. There is no hard evidence that this was followed in productions of the plays, but the supposition would be a sensible one: and there is a single SD that prescribes an antiphonal performance, although only as second-best:[52]

---

46 See Gibson *Theater of Devotion*, 166–8.
47 See Rastall 'Repertory', *passim*.
48 See Rastall 'Minstrelsy, Church and Clergy', 92–4.
49 This is in reference to England only: there is some evidence of 15th-century instrumentalists playing from notation on the continent.
50 There is of course no question of instruments being needed to support the singers: it is simply that the accompaniment adds colour (ceremoniousness, solemnity, opulence, conspicuous consumption) and a significant symbolic content to the singing of the text.
51 See section 3.1, above.
52 'Cantus fractus', or 'broken song', refers to the splitting of a long note into shorter ones and therefore (in this context) to rhythmicised melody. What is intended here is presumably the kind of mensural monody found in Pepys 1236 (see 3.2, above). The translation of 'in

Tunc hee tres cantant idem, id est, Victime paschali, *totum usque ad 'Dic nobis' in cantifracto vel saltum in pallinodio. . . .*

(Then these three [Marys] sing the same – that is, *Victime paschali* – the whole as far as 'Dic nobis' in rhythmic style or at least antiphonally.)

(Resurrection 690+sd1 [part])

Various types of liturgical item were normally performed antiphonally, and it is disappointing that there is only this one piece of evidence – and concerning humans, not angels – for antiphonal singing in the whole dramatic repertory considered here.

Another matter to be considered is that of the actor-singers. In institutional performances there were no doubt enough singing-men to act the part of angels if necessary, and some of the evidence is for tenor singers:[53] but in much of the evidence that we have it is boys who sing the angels' roles. We have already noted that **York 45** used boys for the singing angels and presumably for all of the twelve speaking angels, since the music is notated for high voices. This, if it is correct, would follow the usual iconography of angels as being physically immature males, beard-less and not obviously of masculine rather than of feminine appearance. Drama presumably followed this iconography of the actors and their vestments, with boys or young men playing angelic roles and strong masculine characteristics of any sort being minimised. This depiction of angels as ageless and sexless, it must be said, seems to have little to do with the terrible nature of angels already mentioned. From the dramatic point of view this is probably just as well: no actor could be asked to portray the unthinkable and incomprehensible.

The other aspect of angelic music about which we learn from iconography is the use of musical instruments. Here it is probably not safe to assume that dramatic iconography follows the main iconographic traditions, which show that angelic singing was normally accompanied by instruments. Late medieval depictions of angels show that *bas* instruments were usual, but the groupings do not often make musically-sensible consorts, the instruments apparently being chosen more with an eye to visual variety.[54] This matter will be discussed further in section 8.5, with reference to possible consort-groupings.

5.3 The music of mortals

Enough has been said in the previous section to suggest that God's faithful servants on earth might emulate the hosts of Heaven by making music in praise of the Creator. David had proposed this idea many times,[55] notably in three great psalms

---

pallinodio' is from Stevens 1958, 90. Stevens translates 'in cantifracto' as 'polyphonically' (*ibid.*), but I doubt if polyphony is meant.

[53] The polyphony in various late-fifteenth-century paintings, for instance, and some plainsong depicted in paintings: see Rastall 'Repertory', *passim*; and see Plate 8 and Appendix A.

[54] Rastall *Secular Musicians*, I/xxx–xxxv; but see also the possible groupings discussed in Rastall 'Repertory', *passim*.

[55] The Middle Ages accepted that all the Psalms had been composed by King David.

of praise beginning 'Cantate Domino canticum novum' – 'Sing unto the Lord a new song' (Psalms 95, 97 and 149: AV 96, 98 and 149). Moreover the last of these, which mentions the chorus, tympanum and psalterium as musical instruments to be used in praise of God, is followed by the last psalm of all, in which these and other musical instruments are enlisted in God's praise, as previously noted:[56]

> Alleluia.
> Laudate Dominum in sanctis ejus;
>   laudate eum in firmamento virtutis ejus.
> Laudate eum in virtutibus ejus;
>   laudate eum secundum multitudinem magnitudinis ejus.
> Laudate eum in sono tubae;
>   laudate eum in psalterio et cithera.
> Laudate eum in tympano et choro;
>   laudate eum in chordis et organo.
> Laudate eum in cymbalis benesonantibus;
>   laudate eum in cymbalis jubilationis.
> Omnis spiritus laudet Dominum.
> Alleluia.   (Psalm 150)

This psalm was known – at least to educated people, such as a dramatist must have been – not only in its Latin version but also in a number of English paraphrases such as Robert Mannyng's, already quoted, which illustrates his story of Robert Grosseteste's approbation of music.[57] There was a general principle, then, that God should be praised in song in emulation of the heavenly host. In the plays this principle accounts for almost all of the vocal music performed by mortal characters and souls. There are ways, too, in which the music of mortals could be seen as a specific emulation of *musica caelestis*. It is in the nature of the occasion that processional singing by angels and souls (or mortals) together should signify *inter alia* some restoration of Order: singing after the Harrowing of Hell, after the death of Antichrist, and after the Judgement are just such occasions, as was mentioned in 5.2, p. 183, above. All of these are initiated by angels: but there are occasions when singing is initiated by mortals with the same (if unspoken) cosmic purpose. Noah and his family sing at various points in the story of the Flood in the different plays, partly as an expression of joy and praise:

[NOE]   Mare joie in herte never are I hadde,
         We mone be saued, now may we synge.   **(York 9/259–60)**

But their singing during the Flood itself, when everyone else has been drowned, and more particularly when Mrs Noah enters the Ark after a period of refusal, can be seen as occasions of the restoration of order. So, too, can the singing at the end of the play, although this can also be interpreted – and it is perhaps the primary interpretation intended by the playwright – as an act of praise. Kolve and Woolf both discuss Noah's Ark as a type of the Church, with entry into the Ark as a

---

56 See pp. 60–1.
57 See p. 61, above.

forerunner of Salvation through Christ.[58] Both also see Mrs Noah – at least in her more intransigent dramatisations – as the unrepentant sinner brought to Salvation. The physical salvation of Noah and his family, then, and the destruction of their world, is seen as a parallel to the Last Judgement, the ultimate restoration of Order. It is perhaps for this reason as much as any other that Noah and his family sing at this point in the Chester cycle (**Chester 3/252+sd**, not MS H); and it probably explains the singing at the entrance of the Ark in **N-Town 4/197+sd** at the height of the Flood, where Noah's speech is of sadness for the loss of men and animals.

The example of Noah and his family opens up a more general case for the singing of mortals. Only those who do the Will of God would wish to emulate the heavenly host, an issue that is dealt with in the Boethian cosmology discussed in 5.2, above. The second type of music categorised in this cosmology, *musica humana*, is as much concerned with Order as *musica mundana* is, but at a different level. *Musica mundana* concerns the macrocosm, *musica humana* the microcosm. *Musica humana* arises from the proportions governing the political and governmental aspects of society, and of individuals: in other words, the relationship of the individual parts of an organism to the whole. Most importantly, it governs man's body, his soul, and the relationship between them.[59] This relationship is harmonious when a man is in tune with God: and it is a measure of the strength of this concept that we still use the language of musical metaphor in discussing it. The consonance of this relationship, then, is another kind of harmonious music.

As in the case of *musica mundana*, the inaudibility of this music is of small importance compared to the general principle: but, again, it is to be expected that those who do the Will of God will be musical in the narrower sense. Those who sing in the plays, therefore – with some important exceptions to which we shall return in section 5.4 – are those who have been chosen by God as instruments of his Will: not just the angelic messengers and Christ himself, but the Prophets in Limbo, the Saved Souls (whose works of mercy are enumerated to them in the Doomsday plays), and a number of mortals who play crucial roles in the Salvation story – notably Noah, the Virgin Mary, the shepherds, Simeon, and the Apostles. Moses, too, is at least involved in a song of praise (at the end of **York 11**, probably, and perhaps also at the end of **Towneley 8**: the textual problem does not allow a clear answer), whether he himself sings or not: certainly the Exodus would be seen as a type of the Harrowing of Hell or the ultimate Salvation itself. As before, we may reasonably wonder why Abraham is missing from the list. It will be seen that the list largely coincides with that of mortals who hear angelic song. Again, then, there is an apparent discrepancy. Is there really a distinction to be made between those who sing, those who hear angelic song, and those who both sing and hear singing? And if so, what significance should we attach to it?

Any answer to these questions is likely to be speculative, but it is necessary to draw at least tentative conclusions because of the practical implications for

---

[58] Kolve *Corpus Christi*, 69; Woolf *English Mystery Plays*, 139 and 143.
[59] Little *Place of Music*, 103, 108–12.

performance. I have partly answered the first question (in respect of those who hear angelic song) in section 5.2. In respect of singing, one might think that such characters as Abraham, Joseph, the Magi and John the Baptist would sing, but there is certainly no evidence that they do. On the other hand there is no positive evidence that they do not. The question 'Is the distinction significant?' can be answered only tentatively, then: for we cannot be sure of the distinction itself, being uncertain of the non-singers. And, of course, the situation may be different in the various plays.

In addressing this problem we should note, first, that all those of God's servants who do sing (for evil characters see 5.4, below) make some positive contribution to the process of Salvation. Noah is responsible for the bodily salvation of men, animals and birds, so that Mankind can continue to ultimate spiritual salvation; the Virgin Mary agrees to bear the Saviour; the shepherds become the first pilgrims and then the first evangelists; Simeon announces the appearance of the Saviour; and the Apostles form the nucleus of the Church, the defender, repository and disseminator of the Good News. Of the group who do not sing, the Magi need cause no heart-searching. They do God's Will, certainly, and are in a sense active about it: but their pilgrimage affects no-one else. The charge of inactivity may seem a little hard on Joseph, and on Abraham and John the Baptist, too. The fact is, however, that the activities of these characters do not directly further the cause of Salvation in the particular episodes dramatised.

There are anomalies in this explanation, no doubt. On the other hand we need not assume that the playwrights consciously followed some detailed theological argument in deciding which characters should sing, and – as before – it is likely that factors such as the availability of an obviously appropriate liturgical item weighed heavily in the playwright's mind. Nevertheless, the principal concept was well known and continued to be so long after the centuries in which this drama was performed. As many have pointed out, Shakespeare, Milton and Dryden are among those English writers who made use of it in the late sixteenth and seventeenth centuries, and Shakespeare's plays, at least, were directed partly at an uneducated audience. We must assume that even the groundlings in Shakespeare's audience understood what was happening when, for instance, Richard II drew attention to the broken proportions of the 'sour' music representing the turmoil both at a personal level in Richard's life and at a political level in his mis-managed kingdom:

> [KING RICHARD] ... Music do I hear?
> Ha, ha! keep time: how sour sweet music is
> When time is broke and no proportion kept!
> So is it in the music of men's lives.
>> (Shakespeare, *Richard II*, publ. 1597, V/5)

Similarly, the famous exposition of *musica mundana* and *musica humana* found in *The Merchant of Venice* is quite long enough to have been catcalled out of the script if the audience was bored by it, for it discusses the 'singing' of each heavenly body, and the similarity of that singing to angelic music; the essentially harmonious nature of an immortal soul, and our inability to hear any of this music while in our sinful earthly bodies; and, in the second section, the converse proposition that an unmusical man is untrustworthy, harmful to society and to the individuals with whom he comes in contact:

> [LORENZO] . . . Look how the floor of heaven
> Is thick inlaid with patines of bright gold;
> There's not the smallest orb which thou behold'st
> But in his motion like an angel sings,
> Still quiring to the young-ey'd cherubims:
> Such harmony is in immortal souls;
> But, whilst this muddy vesture of decay
> Doth grossly close it in, we cannot hear it.
>   . . .
> The man that hath no music in himself,
> Nor is not mov'd with concord of sweet sounds,
> Is fit for treasons, stratagems, and spoils;
> The motions of his spirit are dull as night
> And his affections dark as Erebus:
> Let no such man be trusted . . .
>   (Shakespeare, *The Merchant of Venice*, publ. 1600, V/1)

No doubt there were members of that audience who did not understand the full implications of such 'Boethian' passages as these: but apparently they were not puzzled, irritated and bored by them to the extent of not attending Shakespeare's plays.

Little need be said here about the circumstances in which God's servants sing in the plays (for which see *Essays* 115–16). In the main, singing is an expression of joy and praise in particular circumstances. True, the occasions when Noah and his family sing *Save me O God* at a time of danger (**Chester 3/260+sd**) and the Apostles, waiting for the gift of the Holy Spirit, sing *Veni creator spiritus* (**Chester 21/120+sd**) do not at first sight seem to fit the pattern. But these are both petitions – the first for (spiritual) safety and the second for the gift of the Spirit – and they are addressed to a God powerful enough to grant them if it is his Will. Submission to the Divine Will is itself a form of praise: so although the Chester cycle demonstrates here, as so often, a feature that seems lacking in other cycles, it can hardly be said to break the pattern seen elsewhere.

It will be convenient to mention here the rather rare phenomenon of indirect characterisation in respect of music, which occurs only when the person characterised is not present. Two lines from the Towneley Second Shepherd's unflattering portrait of his wife take the edge off the unkind things said about her and show that her heart is in the right place – and, incidentally, that the shepherd knows it:

> [SECUNDUS PASTOR] had She oones Wett hyr Whystyll / She couth Syng full clere
>   Hyr pater noster.   (**Towneley 13/103–04**)

No one who can sing the Paternoster 'full clear' is likely to be a servant of the Devil, even if a drink is needed as preparation.[60]

---

[60] For a rather different view see Robinson *Studies*, 42–3.

Before leaving the singing of God's servants we must briefly discuss an item in the Chester cycle (at **7/447+sd+md**), when Trowle/Garcius apparently teaches the whole audience a song, much as is now done in pantomimes. Another example will be discussed in 5.4, below. This 'educational' use of music is not found elsewhere, and it may well be a late feature in the play: but it is perfectly compatible with the uses of music already discussed. The shepherds' individual views on music are all standard: a means to pray for grace, a means to personal solace, and an entertainment that must not be allowed to become an end in itself.[61] The song 'Trolly lolly lo', whatever it was, is not obviously a song in praise of God, and it is impossible to know what validity the MD may have had. But a 'merry song' is a means by which 'mirth' – that is, joy – may be passed on to others, and that in itself is a godly act. Thus the teaching of such a song may be regarded as a form of evangelising, at least to the extent that it disseminates joy – heavenly joy, if the text involved is appropriate.

At this stage it is clear that the music of mortals in the plays involves not only the actors but the audience as well, a matter that is discussed in section 8.6, below. Indeed, the audience becomes part of the cast in some plays. But even where this is not the case, participation in singing by the audience must have strengthened that audience's perception of the role played by music in the spiritual lives of mortals as represented in the drama. Several plays end with the singing of *Te deum laudamus* or some other piece in which the audience could join, led by the cast.

In a similar way, dance apparently fulfilled some of the functions of vocal music. It is used in the Cornish and East Anglian plays to celebrate the end of a performance, and in this respect its use seems similar to that of *Te deum*. Audience participation is clearest in *Beunans Meriasek*, where the dance is stated to be for everyone. In fact, there seems to have been something of a tradition of a general dance at the end of a play: this is discussed further in 8.6, below. We should recognise the features of such a dance that make it an acceptable parallel to the making of music. Whether general or confined to members of the cast, these are social dances. In addition to being a sequence of ordered steps, therefore, which makes them a *speculum* of Divine Order, they also illustrate the ordered relationship between the individual and society. They are, then, a form of *musica humana*, the relationship of individual parts to the (social) organism as a whole.[62]

It is this relationship that ultimately explains why the abuse of music is characteristic of the devil's agents. The principle of *musica humana* demands a harmonious and ordered relationship between a song, an act of praise or a dance and its various components, such as the text. This relationship is dissonant and disordered if the overall harmoniousness of the ordered structure is opposed by the disorder of out-of-tune singing or by a text that does not fulfill the required function of praise. That is why the text of a song is so important. Music, by its nature as a *speculum* of Divine Order, is an act of praise of God; an ungodly text set to the music sets up an

---

[61] This is discussed in Volume 2 under **Chester 7/436–49**.

[62] For a broader view of religious dance and its relationship to procession, see Faulkner 'Harrowing', 151–2.

opposition to this act and destroys the harmonious relationship between the parts and the whole. In doing so it negates *musica humana* in that work.

The use of music and dancing by the agents of Hell depends on their use by God's servants, then, and on the abuse of this relationship betweeen the parts and the whole of a song or dance. The music and dancing of the Devil's agents are therefore discussed in the next section.

5.4 The sounds of Hell

In Mankind the worldlings Nought, New Guise and Nowadays play a trick on the audience in the course of teaching them a song (**Mankind 331–43**).[63] Nought apparently sings a line at a time, each being repeated by New Guise and Nowadays leading the audience. This method of teaching a song by ear is quick and efficient, and no doubt had a long tradition of use: the technique is now associated mainly with a pantomime act, but was formerly much used in psalmody, where it was known as 'lining out'.[64] In the context of the drama, there is an obvious parallel with the scene in Chester 7 where Garcius leads the audience and the other shepherds in a 'merry song' (**Chester 7/447+sd**). But the whole event in Mankind is set up to deceive the audience, and it is in this that the three worldlings show their allegiance to the forces of Hell.

The substantial difference lies in the text itself (**Mankind 335–43**, quoted in section 2.6), which is obscene enough to be shocking to many of the audience and to make a vivid contrast with the earlier part of the play. Some minor indecencies have indeed already been heard: but the worldlings have been careful to present themselves as good fellows who mean no real harm – rough diamonds at worst – and have even quoted from the Psalms (see lines **324–6**) to echo the kind of language and sentiments expressed by Mankind himself in lines **310–22**. Mention of the Devil (at **325**) as the author of the psalm in question is only one of several indications of the worldlings' true allegiance: but it is easily overlooked, perhaps, in view of their cheerful promise of a 'Christmas song' in which the audience are invited to join 'wyth a mery chere' (**334**). In these circumstances, even the first line of the song, 'It is written with a coal', will seem innocuous. Only in retrospect is 'coal' significant as symbolic of hellish business. Whether it means 'coal' in the modern sense or (as seems more likely) 'charcoal' its blackness and association with fire are clearly a deliberate allusion.

---

[63] The song text is discussed further in 2.6, above: on its effects and the mechanics of staging it, see Taylor in Twycross *Evil*, 163–4, and Neuss 'Active and Idle Language', 54–5.

[64] See the articles 'Lining out' and 'Psalms, metrical' (section III.1 [iv]) in NG XI/7 and XV/362, respectively. In the latter article Nicholas Temperley cites a work of 1644 as the first evidence of lining out, but comments that the method 'may have existed earlier'. Given the examples in *Mankind* and Chester 7, it must have been in use (in the secular sphere, anyway) at least as early as the 1460s.

At the time, however, the gross indecencies of the second and subsequent lines come as a shock. In performance the audience's sense of being shamefully duped is very strong. Cajoled into singing the (apparently harmless) first line, they are committed to singing the song by the time they are asked to repeat the scatological second line, 'He hath shitten with his hole'. It is a brilliant dramatic stroke, an audience 'set-up' simultaneously entertaining and degrading.

The deceit of this event is paramount. Since mortals' songs of praise are in imitation of angelic song, the worldlings' promise of a 'Christmas song' would have borne precisely that implication. Thus the event nicely exemplifies the dangers discussed by Walter Hilton in *Of Angels' Song*, mentioned in section 5.2. There, it will be remembered, Hilton described angelic singing mainly in order to warn his readers against music that might seem angelic but is not. Some, he says, come so close to perfection that their souls are gladdened and strengthened by all created things (Hilton, lines 26–66, 108–12). 'Neuer-þe-latter,' he warns, 'sum men er de-sayued be þar awn ymaginacioun, or be illusioun of þe enemy in þis mater' (lines 112–14). Even when, by God's Grace, the soul has come so far, it is not out of danger: indeed, it seems that the danger is greater than ever. Hilton states that if at this stage a man relinquishes God's guidance and relies too much on his own intellect, his brain may be turned to the extent that he imagines heavenly sounds when there are none (lines 114–24); and then, like a man in a frenzy, he 'thynk þat he heres & sese þat nan oþer man dos, & al es bot a uanite & a fantasy of þe heued, or els it es be wirkyng of þe enemy þat feynes swylk soun in his heryng' (lines 126–9). In this last situation, when the Devil 'entyrs man be fals illuminaciouns, & fals sownes, & swetnes' he 'desayues a mans saule' (lines 130–35): and

> of þis fals ground springes errours & heresys,
> fals prophecies, presumpciouns, & fals roysyngs,
> blasphemes, & sclaunderyngs, & many other myscheues.
>
> (Hilton, lines 136–8)

This passage not only warns of the danger to the individual soul – which is the immediate message of any morality play, too – but suggests also the wider implications of the work of the Devil and of the coming of Antichrist.[65]

It would be a mistake, then, to underestimate the connection between the Devil's deceit and that of his agents. The fact is underlined by the Devil's own deceit in the Fall of Man sequences of the Cornish plays. When the Devil comes to Eve 'like a serpent' in the first day of the cycle (**Ordinalia 1/148+sd**), he tells her that he came from Heaven (**1/165**) to better her position by persuading her to eat the forbidden fruit. Eve is afraid that he is deceiving her (**1/196**), but later tells Adam that he was an angel and that he sang to her (**1/215, 229**). Whether Eve really believes this or not

---

[65] See Revelation 19/20, for instance, concerning the false prophet's deceitful miracles. In relation to the Devil's deceit, note that in **Towneley 30/285–6** Tutivillus actually quotes the saying 'Diabolus est mendax / Et pater eius' (The Devil is a liar, and the father [of lies]), for which see Whiting, p. 129, item D186.

is beside the point: at the least it is a possible excuse for plucking the fruit. Adam contradicts her, saying that

> [ADAM] . . . he was an evil bird
> Whom thou didst hear singing.   (**Ordinalia 1/223–4**)

But the possibility of a singing angel is powerful – again, it does not matter whether Adam really believes it or not – and Adam eats the fruit. As in the biblical account, he accuses Eve of deceiving him.

We are not told what the 'angel' sings to Eve, so that we have information only on the Devil's general deceit in making Eve think that she has heard angelic song. In the *Creacion of the World* the deceit is more comprehensively specified. Lucifer not only dresses up like a 'sweet angel' (**Creacion 538**) but changes his voice to sound like that of a girl (**531–2**). Moreover, Eve is impressed by the beauty of the 'angel's' face (**563–4**). The visual and vocal transformation, then, is a radical one. The Devil is not half-hearted in deceit: the rewards are too important.

No song-text is given, but Lucifer presumably sang flattering praises of Eve's beauty, 'many fair words' (**Creacion 1016**). Eve gives these 'fair words' as a reason for thinking that Lucifer was an angel from Heaven (**1017–19**), so possibly they were in the form of a song of praise such as those addressed to the Blessed Virgin.[66] Certainly the playwright has set up a context in which such a parody would be possible, for the angels have already praised God in song (at **Creacion 78**, or perhaps **68**), providing a direct model against which a parody could be understood.

Deceit of a different kind is found in the Chester play of the Flood. Mrs Noah wants her gossips to join the family in the Ark, and tells Noah that if he will not let them in he can sail off without her (**Chester 3/201–08**). The deceit may be partly self-deceit, for Mrs Noah's statement that '[My gossips] loved me full well, by Christe' (**205**) is not quite borne out by the events that follow. In a speech (or song) by a single gossip Mrs Noah is asked to 'lett us drawe nere'.[67] But immediately (and perhaps because Mrs Noah is obviously willing) the gossip(s) put forward a different suggestion: that Noah can wait while they drink a quart each. Indeed, the drink is probably poured out by the start of the third stanza. That the apparent anxiety of the gossip(s) should give way to delaying tactics like this is symptomatic of a standard deceit. Knowingly or not, the gossips are being used by the Devil to keep Mrs Noah out of the Ark – typologically, to prevent her salvation. That music should be used as an aid to this process was a well-known phenomenon.

As always, the text is the feature that identifies this song as being from the Devil. It is clearly a drinking song, but at the same time line **234** is close enough to descriptions of the effects of heavenly music to introduce an element of parody into it: 'It will rejoice [the] heart' is very much the language of holy rejoicing, including

---

[66] I suggest this because Eve is the typological forerunner of the Blessed Virgin, and a Marian text (perhaps changing 'Maria' to 'Eva' as necessary) would be understood in this way by a medieval audience.

[67] The complete song text, **Chester 3/225–36**, is quoted in section 2.6, above, where the textual problem is also discussed.

that brought on by music. Drink is being equated with (among other things) heavenly music, then. Clearly these people are not to be trusted. In addition, this is not a pre-existent drinking-song, for the text is to the immediate purpose: this, too, shows that it is no ordinary drinking-party.[68] The song must be sung so that the words can be heard, therefore.

Text audibility apart, it would be appropriate if the Gossips' song were badly sung, although there is no information on that point. The general principle that music is characteristic of God's servants has a corollary: an unmusical man is a servant of the Devil. Thus the singing of a lullaby by Mak, the sheep-stealer in the Towneley Second Shepherds' Play, is denigrated as 'clere out of toyne' by the First Shepherd (**Towneley 13/477**). Mak's wife, Gyll, is groaning at the same time, in the aftermath of 'childbirth': and the Third Shepherd cannot distinguish the singing of the one from the groaning of the other – or at least, so he pretends:

TERCIUS PASTOR will ye here how thay hak? / oure syre lyst croyne.
PRIMUS PASTOR hard I neuer none crak / so clere out of toyne.

Similar musical deficiency characterises the priest and his boy in *Mary Magdalen*. Their singing of the service is prefaced by the priest's injunction to the boy to clear his throat ('Cowff vp þi brest': **Mary Magdalen 1224**) and the boy's amateurish assurance 'I home and I hast, I do þat I may' (**1226**). Despite these preparations the music breaks down: the boy makes the performance go badly wrong, and the priest is evidently too incompetent musically to retrieve the situation. As suggested in 2.4, above, it is likely that their unmusicality results in singing that is both out of tune and out of time.

This 'service' is presumably a real one, or at least a recognisable parody of a real one. Liturgical parody is another characteristic of the Devil's agents, because it makes fun of some of the most sacred aspects of the life of the playwright and audience alike. Thus Herod gives a parody blessing at **York 31/370**, as does his herald at **Towneley 16/1**, while a left-handed blessing by Titivillus in *Mankind* is specifically identified as a curse (**Mankind 522**); the Coventry Herod misquotes the liturgical text *Qui statis in domo domini* in **Coventry 1/486** as a statement of his own importance; and Mak's 'prayer' before sleep – 'Manus tuas commendo poncio pilato' (**Towneley 13/266–7**) – is a jumble from at least two liturgical or biblical sources, all the more telling for having its own perfectly clear but perverted meaning: 'I commend your hands to Pontius Pilate'.[69] Finally, in **Chester 23/196+sd** Antichrist performs a blasphemous parody of the giving of the Holy Spirit two plays earlier, by sending his spirit to the four kings with the words 'Dabo vobis cor novum et spiritum novum in medio vestri'. Lumiansky and Mills identify this text as a

---

[68] See section 2.6, above.
[69] 'In manus tuas Domine commendo spiritum meum' is a short responsory at Sunday Compline (AS 190; AR 62, 63; LU 269, 270), based on Luke 23/46, 'Pater, in manus tuas commendo spiritum meum'; 'Pontio Pilato' is from the Nicene Creed, recited at Mass on greater feasts: 'sub Pontio Pilato passus, et sepultus est'. On the popular use of Christ's words, see Richard Proudfoot's comments in *Aspects*, 93.

modified version of Ezechiel 36/26: 'Et dabo vobis cor novum, et spiritum novum ponam in medio vestri' (AV: A new heart also will I give you, and a new spirit will I put within you).[70] Although I cannot find this as a liturgical item, Antichrist's use of it is clearly a parody of the same type.

The most concentrated and far-reaching example of this technique is found in *Mary Magdalen*, where the boy's reading of the 'Leccyo mahowndys, viri fortissimi sarasenorum' (Lesson of Mahomet, the very great man of the Saracens) is a monstrous parody filled with blasphemous and obscene allusions (**Mary Magdalen 1186–97**). Here, too, there are reversed blessings. The boy gives one in the concluding versicle of the lesson, naming two demons ('Ragnell and Roffyn ... Gravntt yow grace to dye on þe galows': **1200–01**); and the priest's final blessing is a more extended parody of the same type:

> Lorddys and ladyys, old and ynge,
> Golyas so good, to blysse may yow bryng,
> Mahownd þe holy and Dragon þe dere,
> Wyth Belyall in blysse ewyrlastyng,
> Þat ye may þer in joy syng
> Before þat comly kyng
> Þat is ower god in fere.   (**Mary Magdalen 1242–8**)

On a very similar plane, the priest's business with the relics (**1230–41**) is as disgraceful as the failure to sing the service properly.

The problem for the playwright is that of portraying pagans effectively and of making some valid distinction between them. In this scene he shows the relationship between worship of Mohamet and that of the Devil. Such gross blasphemies as we hear in this play mark out the priest and his boy as true devil-worshippers. The King and Queen of Marseilles, on the other hand, can be understood as merely misguided, since they take no active part in these parodies.

The Devil's agents on earth, and demons themselves, are quite capable of quoting Latin texts when it suits them.[71] As noted earlier, New Guise even quotes a psalm correctly and attributes it to the Devil (**Mankind 325–6**). Many of the plays show the forces of Hell speaking Latin, ranging from two words in the middle of an English sentence, through two-line legal or scriptural tags, to passages of several lines. These characters' competence with Latin varies a good deal, as we have already seen. While it is sometimes to the Devil's advantage to quote Latin correctly, this is not usually the case. Because Latin is the language of all intellectual activity (including liturgy), it is the Devil's work to make nonsense of it. That is presumably why the worldlings in *Mankind* use nonsense mock-Latin to upset Mercy and Mankind, even using garbled vernacular words with Latin endings (e.g. Mischief's 'Corn seruit bredibus, chaffe horsibus, straw fyrybusque': **Mankind 57**). It is for similar reasons that Titivillus uses a similar technique in **Towneley 30/251–2** ('ffragmina verborum / tutiullus colligit horum, // Belzabub algorum / belial belium

---

[70] See *Chester* II, 338.
[71] See above, section 2.7.

doliorum'). In *Mankind* the worldlings go further and use Latin for verbal indecencies, baiting Mercy by using a Latin translation of an indecent expression (142: 'Osculare fundamentum' = 'Kiss my arse') and by challenging him to translate an indecent couplet:

> [NOWADAYS]   I prey yow hertyly, worschyppull clerke,
>   To haue þis Englysch mad in Laten:
>   'I haue etun a dyschfull of curdys,
>   Ande I haue schetun yowr mowth full of turdys.'
>   Now opyn yowr sachell wyth Laten wordys
>   Ande sey me þis in clerycall manere!   **(Mankind 129–34)**

Such uses of Latin are only indirectly associated with musical matters, but it is a factor worth noting because it gives an idea of the strength of liturgical/scriptural influence on the writing of the individual play. It may be surprising to find characters such as Cain speaking Latin, and indeed the dramatists' rationale for using the language is not entirely obvious. But two results of the use of Latin are inescapable: first, that a flexible use of Latin fulfils a number of dramatic functions concerned with both characterisation and the articulation of action; and second, that it provides a context for matters such as parody.

Another matter raised by this discussion is that of scatological speech. Indecent language is also a mark of the Devil and his agents, and a brief study of it may help in the understanding of hellish attitudes to music and other sounds. Some examples from *Mankind* have already been mentioned in relation to their use of Latin, but this was only one of the worldlings' ploys in trying to upset Mercy. Nought tries to shock him with the line 'Yf ʒe wyll putt your nose in hys wyffys sokett' **(Mankind 145)**, which Mercy describes as 'idle language'. By this he presumably means the kind of loose speech warned against by St Paul, symptomatic of an unclean mind and negative, undirected thinking.[72]

It is partly with this destructive attitude in mind that variants of the ancient insult 'Kiss my arse' should be read. Two occurrences in *The Castle of Perseverance*, both in a medieval version, are spoken by the Bad Angel in contemptuous speech to the Good Angel:

> Þerfore, goode boy, cum blow
> At my neþer ende   **(Castle 813–4)**
>
> Goode Syre, cum blowe myn hol behynde   **(Castle 1276)**

Cain's opening remark to Abel in Towneley 2 is just as direct: 'Com kis myne ars, ...' **(Towneley 2/59)**; and, in the same speech, 'Com nar, ..., / and kys the dwillis toute' ('the Devil's arse': **63**). Further examples at **266** ('Yei, kys the dwills ars

---

[72] See, for example, Colossians 3/8: 'But now ye also put off all these; ... filthy communication out of your mouth'. This subject is fully discussed in Neuss 'Language'; but see also the essays by Lester and Chaplan in Twycross *Evil*, 129–39 and 140–49, and Taylor's comments, *ibid.*, 164.

behynde') and **287** ('Com kys the dwill right in the ars') are related to Caiaphas's exasperated wish on Jesus in **Towneley 21/170–1**

> weme! the dwillys durt in thi berd,
> vyle fals tratur!

Cain's dismissive command to Abel 'Go grese thi shepe vnder the toute' (**Towneley 2/64**) is also closely related.

Such ideas are part of a common stock of insult and threat, the very gratuitousness of which is indicative of Hell's influence. It is in this light that we should view the lewdness of the priest's boy in *Mary Magdalen* – for instance at **Mary Magdalen 1149** – and of the shipman's boy in the same play. Both are beaten for their vulgarity. In the latter case the boy uses an expression, 'I ly and wryng tyll I pysse' (**1409**), that belongs to a strong scatalogical tradition. *Mankind* uses this tradition more concentratedly than other plays, and in the couplet just noticed as being offered by Nowadays to Mercy for translation,

> I haue etun a dyschfull of curdys,
> Ande I haue schetun yowr mowth full of turdys.
>
> $\qquad$ **(Mankind 131–2)**

expresses the idea articulated by Wentersdorf.[73]

A distinction must be drawn, however, between the behaviour itself and the mention of it. The active nature of the lines from *Mankind*, like the imperative 'Kiss my arse', demonstrates hellish allegiance; and Caiaphas' reference to Christ as 'peewee-ars' (**Chester 16A/150**: glossed as 'pissy-arse' in *Chester* II, 250) does so, too. However, one similar usage evidently works the other way, the hoydenish language of one of the Chester mothers of the Innocents apparently being an accurate characterisation of the soldier she is addressing and striking:

> Have thou this . . .
> . . .
> . . . and thou this,
> though thou both shyte and pisse. $\qquad$ **(Chester 10/353, 357–8)**

Here the indecency seems to be a true reference to the nature of the person addressed, not indicating hellish allegiance in the person speaking. A more difficult example is Colle's description of his master as

> Þe most famous phesycyon
> Þat euer sawe vryne. $\qquad$ **(Sacrament 535–6)**

This certainly indicates the allegiance of the doctor. That of the boy is less obvious, but it is presumably similar.

This discussion may explain Lucifer's farting in **N-Town 1**. Lucifer, as an angel, must originally have been musical, but when pride overtakes him he stands aloof

---

[73] Wentersdorf *'Figurae Scatologicae'*, 10–12.

from the angels' singing of praise to the Creator (**N-Town 1/4**). Subsequently deprived of 'merth & joye', he is presumably deprived of music also (**1/71**). His statement 'Ffor fere of fyre a fart I crake' (**1/81**) therefore emphasises his fall from grace: he now cracks a fart, whereas he formerly cracked musical notes.[74] This is not a parody of angelic music but a substitution for it, and it becomes a normal reaction of demons under stress. When Satan fails to tempt Christ he, too, 'lets a crack' (**N-Town 22/195**). This textual evidence of farting is too thin to allow much speculation on its own, but it is possible that farting was a not unimportant feature of the devils' stage-business. On the basis of a wide range of iconographic and literary evidence, Wentersdorf came to the conclusion that devils were depicted as breaking wind as part of their technique in attacking angelic virtues or humanity.[75]

This behaviour is funny to a modern audience, and may have been so to a contemporary one.[76] Its main effect was perhaps threatening, however, and it is backed up by other noise-making expedients that are certainly not funny. Perhaps undirected energy is itself hellish. Hell is certainly a noisy place, and a book on music in the drama cannot ignore the necessary sound effects such as thunder and shouting. Thunder occurs at **Mary Magdalen 691+sd** at the Bad Angel's entry into Hell; a devil enters with thunder and fire in **St Paul 411+sd**; the devil Mercury enters 'wyth a fyeryng' in the same play (**St Paul 432+sd**); and, again in that play, Belyal and Mercury vanish together 'wyth a fyrye flame and a tempest' (**St Paul 501+sd**). The three examples from *The Conversion of St Paul* all come from the mid-sixteenth-century section of the play, but the ideas must be much older; and the tempest of the last-cited is presumably staged with the sound of thunder. Wentersdorf's review

---

[74] For 'cracking' in this sense see 2.4, above.

[75] Wentersdorf *'Figurae Scatologicae'*, 8.

[76] Among other factors, there is a long history of farting as entertainment. St Augustine mentions entertainers who could 'make musical notes issue from the rear of their anatomy, so that you would think they were singing' (*The City of God*, Book 14, Chapter 24: see Welsh and Monahan (1952), 403). One Roland le Pettour, later also called 'Le Fartere', was rewarded by Henry II for his service – apparently a special trick of his – of making 'a leap, a whistle and a fart' (*saltum, siflum et pettum*) before the king on Christmas Day (Southworth *Minstrel*, 47; Bullock-Davies *Register*, 174). Although this sounds like an isolated instance, farting as entertainment was certainly known elsewhere in the later Middle Ages: as Andrew Taylor notes (1988, 138–40), farting is one of the minstrels' accomplishments listed by Haukyn in *Piers Plowman*.

In an episode in Cantos XXI and XXII of the *Inferno* Dante relates how the demon Malacoda ('Evil-tail') 'made a trumpet of his arse' to sound the signal for ten demons to start a raid on a group of the damned. 'I have seen the starting of raids, the onset of tournaments, and the running of jousts, now with trumpets and now with bells, with drums and castle-signals . . . but never to so strange a pipe have I seen horsemen or footmen set forth . . .'; Dante *Inferno*, Canto XXI/139-Canto XXII/12.

Finally, Le Petomane (Joseph Pujol, 1857–1945) appeared at the Moulin Rouge 1892–4 and elsewhere in Paris until 1914 with an extraordinary farting act: see Jean Nohain and F. Caradec, *The Master Farter*, trans. Warren Tute (London, New English Library, 1981). It is however quite clear that Pujol had no knowledge at all of previous farting acts; that his talent manifested itself to him quite by accident; that for many years he made no use of it; and that he developed his act entirely *ab initio*. The nineteenth-century phenomenon, then, was unconnected with the work of earlier farters and cannot be regarded as in any sense part of a tradition. It remains to be seen if the two earlier examples cited are isolated instances of a continuing form of entertainment at that time: *prima facie*, they seem to be.

of the use of farting and the ancient insult 'Kiss my arse' convincingly associates this general picture with the use of fireworks by demons in the plays: that is, the scatalogical background, farting, fireworks, and the noise of thunder are all related in the dramatic presentation of evil in these plays.[77]

Stage directions for and text references to the shouting of demons hardly need to be listed here. It is however worth pointing out that this shouting is semantically meaningless. A direction such as 'Clamant' does not imply the transmission of a message by the devils, but loud undirected noise-making.[78] This is of course the opposite, the total negation, of the angelic use of suitable texts.

The direction for shouting at Christ's coming in the Chester Harrowing of Hell play introduces another noise-making expedient: it reads, in part,

Tunc venit Jesus et fiat clamor vel sonitus magnus materialis

(Chester 17/152+sd)

(Then Jesus comes and there shall be shouting, or a great 'material' noise: translation by David Mills)

The 'material noise'[79] is a parallel to the shouting, then: it may signify thunder, but what can this wording mean? The Harrowing of Hell play at Chester was performed by the Cooks, and it seems likely that this direction indicates how the Cooks made the necessary noise – by banging on pots and pans.[80] There is a whole area here, I suspect, that is understood only imperfectly: the idea of Hell as a kitchen; marginal grotesques in manuscripts playing a pair of bellows like a stringed instrument, with a pair of tongs as a bow; and the famous misericord in Great Malvern Priory in which a monk punishes the Devil by sticking a bellows in his backside and pumping.[81] There is a practical side, too, of course: the Cooks were the right people to make and control fire, and therefore to play hellish scenes successfully and safely. The noise-making of 'material' might also explain the payment for a rattle in the

---

[77] Wentersdorf '*Figurae Scatologicae*', 8–11. For the use of fireworks, see Butterworth 'Hellfire'.

[78] Martin Stevens expresses this idea well in his discussion of musicality and the 'vice' figure Mak in the Towneley *Secunda Pastorum* (*Four Cycles*, 177–78). Although he confuses the issue by using 'discord' in a non-technical sense, Stevens clearly contrasts the shepherds' musicality and the unordered and meaningless shouting that results from Mak's behaviour towards them.

[79] Translation by David Mills, from *Chester Cycle Modernised*. It has occasionally been suggested that the sound referred to is the noise of Hellgate breaking down: but this cannot be correct, since Christ has not yet declaimed the 'Attollite portas' text. I take it that in practice shouting and 'physical din' (or 'noise of material') are likely to occur together.

[80] This suggestion is from John Stevens (1958, 85, n.16a), who cites the more specific direction in the *Jeu d'Adam* requiring the banging of 'caldaria et lebentes' (i.e. cauldrons and pans) at the entry of Adam and Eve to Hell: see Noomen, 54. Barbara Palmer points out the use of flesh-hooks by devils, another item of kitchen equipment that the cooks could supply: see Davidson and Seiler *Hell*, 25.

[81] For grotesques playing bellows and tongs, see Remnant, 71 and 114. The Great Malvern misericord (rather coyly described in Edminson, 15, and not illustrated) is on the south side of the chancel, back row, the sixth stall from the east.

play-accounts of the Coventry Cappers for 1544, as the Cappers seem to have played (among other episodes) the Harrowing of Hell.[82]

As these uses of unstructured noise would suggest, the Devil and his agents often dislike music, finding it annoying or distressing. In the York and Towneley Harrowing of Hell plays (which are parallel at this point) the demon Rybald hears the singing of *Salvator mundi* by the Souls in Limbo and describes it first as a 'dyn' (**Towneley 25/90**) and then as an 'vggely noyse' (**York 37/101, Towneley 25/95**). It is perhaps the text rather than the music itself that is so offensive to the demons, for Rybald complains that the Prophets 'crie on Criste full faste / And sais he schal þame saue' (**York 37/107–08, Towneley 25/101–02**). The offensive message need not be verbal, either: in the Towneley Judgement play the devil Tutivillus shows a strong aversion to church bells calling the faithful to worship:

> Then deffys hym with dyn
> the bellys of the kyrke,
>   When thai clatter;
> he wishes the clerke hanged
> ffor that he rang it.   (**Towneley 30/344–7**)

This aversion to meaning, whether expressed verbally or otherwise, also shows itself in Caiaphas's slighting references to singing the services in the Towneley Buffetting play. 'As ever syng I mes' is not an oath that we should expect from a priest (**Towneley 21/159**), while there is a positive anti-liturgy thrust to his curse on the man

> that fyrst made me clerk / and taght me my lare
> On bookys for to barke / . . .   (**Towneley 21/307–8**)

In these circumstances it is hardly surprising that Christ's Hell-shattering cry of 'Attollite portas' is described as calling 'hydously' (**York 37/138, Towneley 25/119**).

We have seen that music can be a part of the armoury of the Devil and his agents: but on what principles, precisely, do the plays use song, minstrelsy and dancing to characterise the forces of evil? From what has gone before, two clear positions can be identified:

(1)   The Devil and his agents use music – even good music – to beguile a potential victim. This might be called the 'seduction' or 'deceit' position. The deception is usually, but not invariably, contained in the message transmitted through a text;

(2)   They use loud unstructured noise, etc., the antithesis of meaning and directed communication. In this case, which might be called the 'force of arms' position, the corollary is that the forces of Hell actually dislike order and clarity of structure, and therefore music.

[82] See Butterworth 'Hellfire', *passim*, and *REED.Coventry*, 167. Rattles and other noise-makers were used in the Towneley *Harrowing* at Wakefield in 1980, and demonstrated the very frightening effect that such simple properties can have.

There are positions between these, but they are not easily identified. The Chester gossips, for instance, might belong to the first position as far as we can tell from the evidence; but it is unlikely that their drinking-song would be given a fine, musical performance, if only because it is a drinking song and the deceit involved in its use by the gossips depends on its acceptance as 'normal' of its type. Thus the position of the gossips is presumably nearer to (1) than to (2) but definitely somewhere between them. Of course, in practice *all* performances resulting from position (1) will be less than perfect: but it seems to me clear that the Chester gossips do not sing with the same intention as, say, the Serpent in the Cornish Fall sequences discussed above.

It will be useful to examine the position adopted by most of the Church Fathers: namely, that however good music may be in itself as a *speculum* of Divine Order, it is harmful to the soul if one gives way to an appreciation of its beauties at a purely sensual level. Here it becomes not a gateway to understanding of the Eternal but the path to carnal vice.[83] There is a particular danger that the sensuous enjoyment of music may take the place of spiritual exercises, of which church attendance is the one most easily identified. This is the message of Robert Mannyng's warnings against minstrelsy:

> . . . entyrludes, or syngynge,
> Or tabure bete, or oþer pypynge,
> Alle swyche þyng forbodyn es,
> Whyle þe prest stondeþ at messe.
>
> (Mannyng *Handlyng Synne*, 8995–8)

Elsewhere it is clear that Mannyng views dancing in the same light. This warning against such entertainments in the time of Mass is echoed by Accidia (Sloth) in *The Castle of Perseverance*, who describes his followers as men

> Þat had leuere syttyn at þe ale
> Thre mens songys to syngen lowde
> Þanne toward þe chyrche for to crowde.   (**Castle 2334–6**)

In *Wisdom* the worldlings put this into practice, celebrating their vicious powers by singing a song in three parts, presumably a three-men's song (**Wisdom 620+sd**). As with all vocal music, in performance the text itself no doubt underlined the difference between godly and ungodly mirth.

The dangers of misuse are seen in the realm of minstrelsy, too. The Reynes *Delight* fragment associates 'Swet musyciauns in dyuers melody' with dangerous worldly pleasures (**Delight 49–54**), and this is clearly the allusion intended when in *Wisdom* Will tells a group of carnal sins that their accompanying minstrel is

> . . . a hornepype mete
> Þat fowll ys in hymselff but to þe erys swete.   (**Wisdom 757–8**)

---

[83] For St Augustine's views on this, see Schueller *Idea of Music*, 255–6.

In particular, sweet music was associated with seduction, a connection that is common enough in iconography and to which we shall return in respect of dancing. It is not inappropriate, either, that Nought should play a pipe to bring out Titivillus, the devil responsible for collecting all 'idle words' spoken for presentation at the Judgement (**Mankind 453+**).[84]

The ambivalent attitude to music shown by the Church Fathers and retained throughout the Middle Ages was inherent in the dichotomy between the nature of *musica instrumentalis* (i.e. sounded music, the third type of music in the Boethian triad) and the place that music held in society.[85] As we have seen (5.2), the audible result of musical philosophy, *musica instrumentalis* ('music' in the modern sense), descended directly from *musica mundana* (the Music of the Spheres) through *musica humana* (the smaller-scale order of the universe) and could therefore be regarded as the practical expression of the Divine Order that these represented; and, more precisely, it was the mortal equivalent of *musica caelestis*, the music of the heavenly host. On the other hand, as the only kind of music that could be manipulated by Man, *musica instrumentalis* could be used badly or even misused deliberately. In other words, *musica instrumentalis* was the only kind of music open to perversion. This caused a problem for dramatists: the distinction between *musica caelestis* and *musica instrumentalis* could not be shown in the plays, where the former must be represented by the latter. The anomaly in Lucifer declining to sing at **N-Town 1/39+sd** but singing to Eve at **Ordinalia 1/148+sd** and **Creacion 538+sd** is thus a practical one only: there is no *philosophical* anomaly. Lucifer's pride makes him ineligible to join in *musica caelestis*, but as the Serpent he can use *musica instrumentalis* in any way he chooses in the cause of Evil.

The dangers of music are entirely reliant on the uses to which humans can put it, therefore, and the confusion in St Augustine's thoughts about it stem not only from the subjective nature of his assessment[86] but also, presumably, from the difficulties attendant on self-analysis. Commentators in the later Middle Ages were really no more successful in finding an objective viewpoint, and the result was some controversy and no single clear direction to those who needed it. On the one hand monks and others welcomed the recreation offered by 'minstrels of honour' who would sing the deeds of the saints; on the other, the authorities were always aware that minstrels could be vicious and highly undesirable socially. Thomas of Chabham's famous categorisation of minstrels is simply an attempt to make sense of a difficult situation. In the same way the larger churches used music as an embellishment of the services in praise of God, yet there were many warnings against the dangers of

---

84 For Titivillus, see Neuss 'Language', 55–68. In view of the worldlings' indecent play on the idea of Christ as 'head', involving parodic references to the penis (see Gibson *Theatre of Devotion*, 111), the use of a 'flute' might well have an indecent meaning at this stage of the play.

85 See Rastall 'Minstrelsy, Church and Clergy', *passim*; and in *Contexts*, especially 194–5 and 197–8. See also 5.3, above.

86 Schueller *'Figurae Scatologicae'*, 255–6.

polyphony and musical instruments in church and even against the antics and morals of lay singers.[87]

This philosophical position makes it unnecessary to look for technical characteristics of hellish music other than out-of-tuneness or a lack of rhythmic precision. There is no need to postulate very dissonant music or the use of specific dissonant intervals (such as the tritone) as distinguishing features of music-making by the forces of evil.[88] In dealing with humans such music would be useless to further the kind of deceit which is the Devil's aim in using the 'seduction/deceit' method; and, as we have seen, the sounds of Hell itself in the 'force of arms' category are disordered noise. Dissonant music, and specifically music deliberately using 'Mi contra Fa', would certainly be disordered in the sense that it made less use of the simple mathematical proportions: but it would not be disordered in the sense of being *unstructured*, so that the style would become a rather heavy-handed type of perversion.[89]

It is also unnecessary to suppose that music showing an evil character's social position was automatically subject to the type of conditions governing singing by one of those characters. While Mak, Mrs Noah's gossips or the priest's boy must show their allegiance through unmusicality, a social position entitling a character to music is itself a situation susceptible to perversion. Thus in *The Castle of Perseverance* Mundus uses the showy music of worldly pomp (**Castle 455+sd, 574+sd**). He expects to be served at table with 'mynstralsye and bemys blo' (**Castle 616–7**), and holds out this lifestyle as a temptation to Mankind. Herod has this lifestyle, too, and misuses the power that goes with it: his demand for the minstrels to

> blowe up a good blast
> Whyll I go to chawmere & chaunge myn array
>
> (**N-Town 17/19–20**)

not only emphasises the essential shallowness of his lifestyle but also serves as a showy event intended to impress the Magi at their arrival. The frivolousness and waste are there also in the Coventry cycle, where Herod orders 'Trompettis, viallis,

---

87 For Thomas of Chabham's categories, see Tydeman *Theatre*, 187–8; and my own comments in *Contexts*, 197.

88 These have been suggested by several writers: in particular, Dutka (1980, 11–12) makes out a good case for such technical means of showing hellish allegiance through music. However, for the reasons given here I do not think that it is likely to be correct in these plays. As for the idea (not cited by Dutka) that the 'devil in music' suggests the dissonant tritone as an interval to be used for this purpose ('Mi contra Fa / diabolus est in musica'), Smith points out (*Jacobi Leodiensis*, 116) that no medieval theorist used the term 'diabolus in musica' for the tritone, the eighteenth-century theorist J.J. Fux being the first to do so. In fact, the tritone is not the only interval produced by 'Mi contra Fa', and earlier theorists did discuss the extreme dissonance that arises when Mi in one voice coincides with Fa in another: see Toft *Aural Images*, 26–7.

89 There is of course a great difference between the normal contrapuntal dissonance of passing-notes and suspensions that results from the ordered movement of individual voices (on which most music depends for its life), and the textural dissonance of 'Mi contra Fa' intervals that add a second, largely chordal, layer of dissonance. It is the second that the listener mainly hears as something harsh, unwelcome, or ugly.

and othur armone' when he goes to rest (**Coventry 1/538**). The misuse of power is put in close proximity with Herod's music in the N-Town Massacre play, where Herod orders minstrelsy for the banquet that immediately follows the killing of the Innocents (**N-Town 19/153–4**); and later in the same play the minstrelsy emphasises the empty show of his life by taking place at the moment when Herod and his soldiers are killed (**N-Town 19/232+sd**).

In *The Castle of Perseverance* trumpets are used both at Detraccio's crying of his message (**Castle 646+sd**), an event that parodies the beginning of the banns for the play itself, and on three occasions for an attack on the castle (**Castle 1898+, 2198+, 2377+**).[90] This is again the showy music of wordly pomp – specifically, of those who can afford to make war.

Dancing in the plays is governed by the same philosophical considerations as music: indeed, since music accompanies dancing that is bound to be at least partly the case. The dancing of the worldlings in *Mankind* is the equivalent of their 'idle talk'; Mercy is moved to protest at it (**Mankind 81+sd**) and then declines to dance himself (**90–97**). Curiosity's dancing with Mary Magdalene is the beginning of his seduction of her (**Mary Magdalen 533+**), a well-known connection of dance and lust echoed elsewhere.[91] Magdalene's dancing with Curiosity would fall into the same category as music resulting from the first philosophical position discussed earlier: that is, it is a 'seduction/deceit' situation, and the dancing is a real social dance, properly done. The iconography of the occasion shows this to be the case.[92] In *Wisdom* dancing is made into a special feature – the forces of evil at **Wisdom 685**, the Devil's dance at **700–08**, and dancing by the Quest of Holborn ('an evyll entyrecte') at **730–34**. Here, too, we must assume (for want of precise information) that this dancing and the music accompanying it constitute a good performance with no deliberate hint of incompetence.[93] These uses of dancing by the forces of Hell are clear enough for us to assume that use of the metaphorical phrase 'dance in þe devil way' in the York cycle (**York 7/52, 29/395** and **31/423**, for instance) is intended to show the speaker's allegiance to the forces of Hell.[94]

A more difficult matter is the direction at **N-Town 31/753+sd**, which requires the executioners to dance around the Cross:

here xule þei leve of & dawncyn a-bowte þe cros shortly.

There are two basic possibilities here. First, it could be an actual dance, with or without music of some kind. In this case it might have some ritual purpose (now unknown to us) or it could be an occasion of mockery. Second, the direction could

---

90 Here, too, note Dante's story of Malacoda making 'a trumpet of his arse' to sound the signal for a raid by ten demons on a group of the damned: see n. 76, above.

91 See, for instance, *Everyman* 360–2, where Kindred's description of a 'nyse' (i.e. wanton) girl includes her love of feasting and dancing.

92 See Slim 'Mary Magdalene', especially plates 4 and 5a.

93 This would also apply to Herod if he were shown to be dancing in a play: he does appear to be shown dancing in a roof boss illustrated in Anderson *Drama and Imagery*, 89.

94 There are proverbial sayings concerning the dancing of the Devil: see Whiting *Proverbs*, 129–30, item D191.

refer metaphorically to an informal capering having mockery and humiliation of Christ as its sole or main purpose. JoAnna Dutka regards it as an actual dance, as does Meredith.[95] Meredith notes that the executioners' dancing relates to all the 'game' implications of the torturers' treatment of Christ, both in drama and in iconography.[96] It is true that this direction separates the nailing of Christ to the Cross from the scene of mocking that follows, so it may well be correct to see the dancing as an extension of the 'game' element rather than as a mere letting-off of high spirits. This need not imply that the dance is an ordered event with its own structure, however, as the 'game' element could result in mere capering.[97]

In order to make sense of this dance, Dutka attempted to show a tradition of such dancing, by relating it to various pieces of evidence:[98]

(a)   an English alabaster carving of the Scourging in which one of the torturers wears a rope of bells round his waist;

(b)   morris dancers wear bells;

(c)   Hugh Gillam, a noted morris dancer, was paid by the Chester Coopers for appearing in their play, and may therefore have played one of the executioners;

(d)   in Matthias Grünewald's 'Christ Mocked' of 1503, one of the onlookers plays pipe-and-tabor; and

(e)   three dances are performed by the virgins in *The Killing of the Children*.

Some of these are potentially less useful than others. Item (e) can immediately be dismissed as evidence, since the virgins are not evil characters and there is a clear relationship between music/dancing that is good in itself and that which is perverted. Item (a) is of considerable interest, since the illustration cited certainly does seem to show bells.[99] The scene depicted is however that of the Scourging, not the Crucifixion, so that its relevance to the N-Town direction is only indirect. The same may be said of item (d), the Grünewald painting, which concerns the Mocking, not the Crucifixion.[100] There is no hint that the onlookers behind the torturers are dancing: on the contrary, they are fairly clearly static. The minstrel, too, is after all easy enough to explain, for torture and execution were occasions of public spectacle

---

[95]   Dutka 1980, 151; Meredith *Passion Play*, 208–9.

[96]   Meredith *Passion Play*, 208–9 and 197, discusses the nature of such games as 'Hot Cockles' and relates it to the text of the play. In this context it is easy to see the dance as being in the nature of a *ritual*, children's games being played according to strict procedures.

[97]   As we shall see, the iconography does not suggest more than this. We should note, however, that the dancing has a structural function in the play, as it separates scenes: see below, 6.2.

[98]   Dutka 1980, 151.

[99]   Hildburgh 1949, plate 17b.

[100] Grünewald's painting has often been reproduced: see, for instance, Nikolaus Pevsner and Michael Meier, *Grünewald* (London: Thames and Hudson, 1958), plate 43; and, for a colour reproduction, Giovanni Testori and Piero Bianconi, *Grünewald* (Milan: Rizzoli Editore, 1972), plate 1.

at which minstrelsy was usual.[101] Whatever the painter's reason for including a taborer in his composition, then, there is no necessary connection with the Crucifixion and its dramatisation in the N-Town plays.

Items (b) and (c) do however require some explanation. Morris dancers did indeed wear bells: at least, some depictions of the *moresca* show bells on the dancers' costumes.[102] There may therefore be some connection between the *moresca* and the torturer in the Hildeburgh alabaster. However, the connection cannot be demonstrated by reference to Hugh Gillam, for the Chester records show only that Gillam was paid for dancing on occasions nothing to do with the plays.[103] Moreover, it is likely that in the Coopers' pageant of the Trial and Flagellation Hugh Gillam played the doubled roles of Herod and Pilate, not a torturer.[104] There is of course the possibility that Herod and/or Pilate danced in the Coopers' pageant as part of the tradition for which we are searching, but there is no evidence for that either.

In all, the evidence for dancing at the Crucifixion is weak. Much of it relates to the Mocking and Scourging, and not to the Crucifixion at all, and its significance is in any case questionable; and the relationship between the *moresca*, bells, the dancing of Hugh Gillam, and the Chester Coopers' play is quite unable to support any hypothesis. This is not to say that the N-Town direction cannot be taken as an indication of real dancing in that particular play, that dancing did not take place in any other Crucifixion play, or that there is no possibility of evil characters dancing in any one of several other episodes in the Passion sequence: indeed, Dutka's evidence seems to suggest that a tradition of some sort, perhaps relating to the Mocking and Scourging, did exist. But what the tradition and the precise significance of the evidence might be, we are really in no position to discover at present.[105]

As with singing, it is worth asking if any observable characteristics distinguish the dancing of evil characters from that of the good. Ingrid Brainard has suggested two features that would characterise dancing by these two categories:[106]

(1) First, good characters will perform social dances, whereas evil characters will dance the *moresca*. Social dancing, certainly, would be a deliberate and observable *speculum* of *musica humana* in showing an ordered relationship between the individual and society, while the *moresca* had connotations of

---

101 This picture was no doubt a political statement by the painter: but reference to fifteenth-century politics does not alter the fact that Christ, having been tried by civil authority, was tortured and executed, as a criminal of Grünewald's day would be. Only the method of execution was different. On minstrelsy at the punishment of lesser criminals in London, see Taylor 'Pagyn of þe Devyl', 168.

102 See Alan Brown's article 'Moresca' in NG XII.572–3.

103 *REED.Chester* 70, 74 and 96.

104 Marshall 'Players', 21.

105 Dutka's general thesis could indeed be supported by the twelfth-century evidence of the *Ordo Representationis Ade*. There, when Adam and Eve are taken to Hell, the demons welcome them with *magnum tripudium*, which certainly might indicate dancing. I think, however, that the more general meaning of the term – Muir 'Adam', 183, translates it as 'noisy rejoicings', and other translators do similarly – is perhaps intended.

106 In discussion during session 133 at the 24th International Congress on Medieval Studies, Western Michigan University, Kalamazoo, on 5 May 1989.

anarchy and pagan power. It is nevertheless notable that it is precisely the first category that would be perverted; and that Mary Magdalene and Curiosity perform a social dance before her seduction (see above) because that is a vital element in the deceit of the situation.

(2)   Second, dancing by good characters will proceed clockwise, that by evil characters anti-clockwise (widdershins).

The musical and aural representation of evil in the plays was clearly not the result of a single, unified view by the dramatists. On the contrary, the philosophical and social contexts were far too complex for the playwrights to take any simple approach to the problems of characterising the inmates and agents of Hell aurally, even in a single play. It is no doubt true that characterisation was effected primarily – and is now understood primarily – through iconographic and literary traditions: but there obviously were some widely-understood aural conventions, too, and clearly these have to be taken into account when the characterisation of evil roles is discussed.

5.5   Realism and representation

In earlier sections of this chapter I have tried to show that the theory of representation as proposed by Stevens can be extended beyond the examples that he offered. I believe that it can be made to explain all occurrences of music in the plays, but at this stage some problems remain. In particular, an overall view of the repertory shows some possible anomalies in the use of music, contradictions that seem inexplicable in terms of the philosophical background as I have discussed it so far. In this situation there is a temptation to look for some other reasoning on the dramatists' part, some principle other than representation that will explain the remaining uses of music.

Stevens proposed realism to explain those musical items that were not obviously governed, directly or indirectly, by Boethian cosmology. After noting the joy that is the main feature of angelic music and its mortal imitation, he wrote that it is 'rare indeed to find songs sung in a time of tribulation', citing Noah and his family singing in the Ark (**Chester cue 3₂**), the lamentations of the three Marys at the tomb (**Ordinalia cue 3₃**), and the singing of Adam and Eve after their expulsion from Eden (**Norwich cue A₂**).[107] Stevens felt able to say that such scenes as these

> may reflect nothing more than the desire of the dramatists to depict certain characters and actions 'from life'. The mystery plays are rooted firmly in the ground, in solid, contemporary, English ground. Naturalism, not symbolism, certainly accounts for some musical scenes ...

He then cited the Entry into Jerusalem and certain scenes in Herod's court as examples in which 'naturalism' was a primary factor in the dramatic presentation.[108]

[107] Stevens 1958, 87.
[108] *Ibid.*, 88.

In the past it has seemed reasonable to assume that the playwrights might well have 'naturalism' or 'realism' as a basic tenet, and the appeal to common sense is an attractive one. But this recourse to 'naturalism' has its dangers in any attempt to understand the plays. In drama studies it has now become clear that all sorts of 'unnatural' features were normal in the plays. In the field of costume the Virgin Mary's wearing of a crown and God's wearing of a golden mask are obvious examples. But similar developments have taken place in our understanding of other arts, which in turn have illuminated drama studies. Pamela Sheingorn articulates a well-known phenomenon when, in relation to the visual arts, she states that the medieval artist[109]

> does not attempt to reproduce what he sees, but, aiding the process of intellectual vision, creates forms that reveal their origin in number – proportion, geometric shape, symmetry. Since the goal of intellectual vision is to gain knowledge of divine wisdom, rather than of the mutable world, the medieval artist correctly refuses to focus on nature as a model or to accept the limitations of physical sight.

This statement could be applied to late medieval drama, and indeed Sheingorn's paper is concerned to compare the iconographic composition of paintings and plays. But it also summarizes much of what has been said earlier in this chapter. The assumption of naturalism, far from being common sense, is on the contrary not at all what we should expect in the plays.

Nor is it what we find. Looking back at Stevens's first three examples we should ask to what extent they show a 'naturalistic' use of music. Has it ever been normal for people to sing if they are caught on water in a storm? Do they sing of their sorrow when they visit the grave of a loved one or find themselves dismissed from their post? Only in a musical or opera is such behaviour acceptable: in real life the singer would be considered in need of psychiatric treatment.[110]

Moreover, the scenes at Herod's court cited by Stevens as those in which 'Herod has music wherever a king or duke would in real life' are not really 'naturalistic' at all. The scene in **Chester 8/144+sd**, for instance, is a royal audience-chamber, which Herod enters to interview the Magi. Although the music of actual royal audiences may inform the use of music in this scene, few of the play's spectators would have attended a royal audience and thus know by experience that it was 'real.' Rather, the music is part of the representation of Herod's character as an earthly king, informed by the bystanders' common knowledge that when nobility or royalty entered their city (for example) they did so with the ceremonial music of shawms and trumpet. This distinction between reality and representation in Herod's music may seem a fine one, but it is vital.

Disregarding the distinction would actually destroy the moral representation discussed above. For example, because Octavian and the Magi are kings there is a great temptation, on a 'realism' basis, to allow them trumpets at their entrance:

---

[109] *Contexts*, 176.

[110] Occasions are known when pilgrims sang hymns or psalms when in danger at sea, but they were passengers: Noah and his family were sailing the ship.

Herod has them, so surely these kings should, as well? As we have noted, however, the use of pompous, showy music is a sign of an unjust worldly ruler, such as Octavian (and the Magi even more) are not shown to be. The plays, then, take a moral stance which is *not* that of everyday life, denying the possibility of 'natural' or 'realistic' presentation in favour of a more sophisticated system of representation that allows a consistency of dramatic and spiritual integrity not available in realistic terms.

The basis of musical 'naturalism' is certainly a shaky one. Stevens also attempted to explain the relationship between music and vice in the plays, on historical grounds, as stemming from this 'naturalistic' use. This explanation does not, in fact, depend on the validity of the 'naturalistic' argument, but Stevens used it as a foundation:[111]

> It is not difficult to see how music, from being a naturalistic detail of background in the presentation of earthly pomp, becomes through its association with the more seductive courtly pursuits, feasting, dancing, and dalliance, itself a symbol of seduction.

Stevens continued by pointing out that in the morality plays 'music is no longer on the side of the angels; it is almost invariably associated with such characters as Pride, Riot, Hypocrisy, Fellowship and Abominable Living'.[112] This is an attractive idea, but it is untenable. To begin with, the chronology of the cycles and moralities does not allow any progression in the use of music to be traced from one to the other. Herod's music in the N-Town, Coventry and Chester plays cannot be a forerunner of the uses of music in *The Castle of Perseverance, Mankind,* and *Wisdom.* Second, music as a symbol of seduction is much older than any of the extant plays: again, 'realistic' use in drama is too late to have any originating role in the relationship between music and seduction. Finally, the resort to 'naturalism' brings to bear something of a quite different nature from the concept of representation: and however difficult the details of a representational use of music may be, a second and completely different concept in operation alongside that of representation is highly unlikely.

It is nevertheless useful to discuss the matter a little further, because it may throw some light on various aspects of the plays' musical usage. This is especially so if we consider the Entry into Jerusalem, another event that Stevens saw as essentially realistic, calling to the spectator's mind the various royal entries that he would have seen. Here the argument of non-experience does not apply as it does in the case of Herod's audience-chamber: most spectators probably *had* seen an entry and would recognise such an event in a play modelled on it. But if royal entries are indeed the model for the Entry plays, where is the loud ceremonial music, the fountains running wine, and the singing virgins dressed as angels?[113] Stevens notes that the

---

111 Stevens 1958, 89.

112 *Ibid.*

113 There is good reason to omit the last of these in a drama where actors represent angels, for the spectacle of actors playing the part of people dressed as angels would be unacceptably confusing in plays that require characters and their functions in the drama to be clearly

'extravagant pomp and display that characterized the street-shows' are missing, but passes over it.[114] This is however a crucial difference between a royal entry and the Entry plays: for Christ was not an earthly king and deliberately did not enter Jerusalem as one. The audience is not allowed to confuse Christ's heavenly kingship with the rule of such as Herod.

To claim royal entries as the model for the Entry plays, moreover, turns the whole question on its head. For, as any late medieval dramatist knew, the royal entry was itself modelled on Christ's entry into Jerusalem. The singing of 'Benedictus qui venit in nomine Domini' at Henry V's triumphal return to London after the Agincourt campaign of 1415 is a good instance of this fact: and it is not the blasphemy that we might think it, but the proper expression of the role that medieval people expected their monarchs to play.[115] But this modelling is also indirect, through the liturgy: for, as Clifford Davidson has pointed out,[116] the biblical narrative is the basis of the Palm Sunday procession, and it is this procession that provides certain distinguishing features of both the Entry play and the late medieval royal entry (see 7.5, below). In view of this it is surely inconceivable that a cycle dramatist should confuse exemplar and copy when writing an Entry play.

Nor is realism on safer ground when it is proposed for the drinking song performed by the Chester gossips. This is not a real drinking song, as the text clearly shows: and the primary aim of the gossips (as discussed in section 2.6, above) is to detach Mrs Noah from her family and ultimately from salvation. However great the incidental realism may be, therefore, its function is not to promote a realistic event but to identify the character of the gossips. As we have already seen, the function of the music is representational.

It is ironic, perhaps, that Stevens's own function of representation should be used as a weapon against his argument for realism. But his paper was a ground-breaking exercise in which there was little time for detailed explorations; the work on texts, records and iconography of the intervening period has made clear to us much that was hardly to be guessed at in 1958; and the theory of representation, I suggest, has turned out to be a larger subject than Stevens could have suspected at that time. Most importantly, perhaps – although it is not relevant to my present purpose – Stevens's work on realism or 'naturalism' still demands that the idea be explored, although perhaps in a different form. Realism of a sort permeates all drama – in the repertory studied here most obviously, perhaps, in the shepherds' plays; equally obviously, that realism is considerably modified and/or limited for various (mainly purely dramatic) reasons. The question is, at what point does realism of detail give

defined. The conceptual problem involved is, of course, the general case of that already mentioned – the representation of *musica caelestis* by *musica instrumentalis*.

114 Stevens 1958, 88.

115 On the reception of Henry V to London after Agincourt, 1415, see Withington I, 132–5, and Bent 'Sources of Old Hall', 23; for settings of *Hosanna to the Son of David* written for entries of James I and VI, see Brett 'Scottish Progress', 223; on royal personages shown as Christ-like in entries on the continent, see Kipling 'Civic Triumph', *passim*.

116 Davidson *Creation to Doom*, 89–90.

way to something that is no longer primarily realistic? The subject has exercised many scholars, and will no doubt continue to do so: we have touched on it here in relation to the use of instruments to accompany angelic singing, for instance. Its relevance to music is very limited indeed, however, and it is time to summarize our findings in this chapter and to attempt to see our way to solving the problems that remain.

5.6 Conclusion

An initial reading of the plays leaves the impression that different types of drama use music in different ways. In particular, it seems that in the historical plays music is a heavenly attribute while in the moralities it is a tool of the Devil. Two things would follow from this general situation. First, it would mean that two separate and irreconcilable philosophical approaches were in use, one for the historical plays and the other for the moralities. Second, it would be clear that a number of anomalies exist, such as the Devil's singing in the first day of the *Ordinalia*.

This chapter shows, I hope, that the situation is not the one just outlined. A single philosophical approach is used which, despite its intricacies (compounded by our ignorance in some areas), explains all of the musical events in the plays. Undoubtedly individual plays lay more emphasis on particular parts of the range of musical usage available. But the very concentrated range of ploys used by the worldlings in *Mankind*, for instance (and here I am thinking not only of the uses of music, but also of Latin, liturgical parody, and obscenity), tends to confirm recent thinking about the nature of different types of play: for while it loosely underlines the distinctions between 'morality' and 'historical' play it also firmly emphasises the considerable differences among the moralities themselves.

Moreover, the concentration of certain features is not confined to particular kinds of play. The Towneley cycle, which among the historical plays shows the widest range of usage for the powers of Hell, shares this distinction with the moralities (and especially with *Mankind*) rather than with the other cycles. In this respect it is probable that Chester, which also provides much information on hellish behaviour without aligning itself particularly with the East Anglian group, is simply the best-annotated of the northern plays.

We must also remember not to regard the biblical cycle as a unit. Towneley's use of obscene speech is largely concentrated in a single play, that of Cain and Abel; and it is in two particular plays of the N-Town cycle that we find a deliberate distinction between the singing of angels and the speaking of mortals (that is, where the non-singing of mortals is a feature that distinguishes them from angels.[117] Even when particular features are spread more widely, they may not cover a large enough proportion of the cycle to be counted as generally characteristic. The Towneley cycle makes a feature of showing how Hell's agents dislike music, liturgy and things

---

[117] See **N-Town 13** (especially **13/105–07**) and **N-Town 41**.

associated with them, for instance, but the examples cover only three plays altogether: Caiaphas's anti-liturgy comments are in **Towneley 21** (The Buffetting), Rybald's description of the Souls' singing as 'ugly' in play **25** (The Harrowing of Hell), and Tutivillus's disparaging comments about church bells in play **30** (The Judgement). It is probably significant that the first of these plays is one of the Wakefield Master's group and that the other two are probably reworkings of early York pageants. When dealing with a cycle whose pageants are from different places it is obvious that the provenance (and no doubt date) of the individual plays is of importance in assessing the musical characterisation of various roles. This must apply also to the more 'homogeneous' cycles as well, however – York and Chester – so that even there the unity of the cycle must not be assumed. There may also be a question of geography. The dancing which seems to connect the Cornish plays with some of the East Anglian ones is not as clear-cut a connection as it might be, since the probable audience participation in the *Ordinalia, Creacion of the World* and *St Meriasek* is not certainly echoed elsewhere.[118] On the other hand, there are features of the Chester cycle – the teaching of an audience song and the use of unsuitable words – which might suggest a Chester/East Anglia connection in addition to that already supplied by Chester's textual relationship with the Brome *Abraham*.[119]

This section raises several questions, some of importance outside the field of music. It is now essential, for instance, that we tackle the question of interrelations between plays, particularly in relation to the transmission and adaptation of texts: and when this brings a better understanding of the repertory as a whole we shall also learn something more about the uses of music. Similarly – although this does not directly affect the material discussed in the present chapter – the question of pre-existent lyrics in the plays needs to be opened up, as was noted in 2.6, above. Most importantly, perhaps, from the musical point of view, we need to know still more about the staging methods of the various plays: and this is a need that will become more apparent in the discussion of the dynamic functions of music in the next chapter.

[118] I would however make a case for this: see 8.6, below.
[119] On this matter, see Davis 1970, lxiii–lxv.

6

MUSIC AND DRAMATIC STRUCTURE

6.1 Introduction

Stevens discussed only the representational functions of music in early English drama, and there is no indication in his article that music might ever be a structural element. The first hint of such functions had already been given by Nan Cooke Carpenter, however, in her article on music in the Towneley *Secunda Pastorum*.[1] There she noted that music marks the main structural divisions of that play, separating the introductory scene of the shepherds from the main farce and the farce from the short nativity scene at the end; and that music also marks the end of the pageant as a whole. But Carpenter's interest in this was restricted to its foreshadowing of features characteristic of later drama:[2]

> Music serves, first of all, as a structural element in the play in a way which foreshadows its use a little later in the interludes and still later in the academic comedies, the parts of which were often outlined by musical insertions.

In declining to see the structural function of music in this play as a feature in its own right, Carpenter failed to understand that it might be a feature of the entire repertory. The reason for this may lie in her attitude to the whole subject: 'musical insertions' suggests that music appears in the drama only as an afterthought rather than as something planned by the playwright.

It is obvious from Carolyn Wall's discussion of **York 45** that music occurs at the major divisions of that very symmetrically-structured play, but Wall did not in fact call attention to it.[3] The structural importance of music in the plays was therefore not recognised until Dutka's discussion in her doctoral thesis (1972) and subsequently, in a shorter form, in her published book (1980). Dutka's chapter on the 'Dramatic Functions of Music' in her thesis begins with a discussion of the inadequacy of much previous work on music in the plays, and laments the misunder-

---

[1] Carpenter 1951: R/1972, 213.

[2] *Ibid.*

[3] Wall 1970, especially 172–3. The play called 'The Appearance of our Lady to Thomas' and numbered XLVI in Toulmin Smith's edition of the York Cycle is numbered XLV by Beadle and entitled 'The Assumption of the Virgin'. Further on the relationship between music and structure in this play, see section 6.3, below.

standing of music as an interruption to the dramatic action.[4] Dutka made her own views absolutely clear, and at the same time introduced the bulk of her chapter, with an impressive forthrightness:[5]

> In my view, music in the cycles is essential to the production, and it is deliberately included for its utility as well as for its beauty. Its use is in conjunction with the three components of drama: to delineate character, to establish setting, and to advance action.

Of these three functions, the first is that discussed in chapter 5, above, while the second – which Dutka treats as providing 'realism' – is mainly concerned with the liturgical scene-settings of the N-Town cycle.[6] It is the third component with which we are concerned here, discussion of which forms the major part of Dutka's chapter.[7]

Dutka approached her 'action-advancing' functions through that of establishing the setting. Her list of functions therefore begins with Carpenter's scene-divisions, although Carpenter's name is not mentioned:

(1) Music marks 'changes in the place being depicted' in two circumstances:[8]
(a) 'where the same characters must be in different localities in adjoining scenes'. In this case, of course, at least some of the characters must move from one location to another.
(b) '. . . where the shift from one locality to another includes, in addition, a change of characters.' She later makes it clear that a *complete* change of characters is intended:[9] that is, no movement of characters is involved.

(2) Music marks the passage of time.[10] Dutka's examples are all from the Chester cycle. Her concern throughout being with music that 'advances the action', she does not confine herself here to *considerable* passages of time, but includes brief tableaux in which music underlines a dramatic situation.

(3) Music can 'facilitate stage business'.[11] Under this heading Dutka includes
(a) the starting of a play;
(b) the ending of a play;
(c) the exit of characters at the end of a play;
(d) entrances and exits within a play;
(e) ascents and descents;
(f) other movements about the stage: here Dutka is particularly concerned with liturgical processions;[12] and
(g) revelation or disclosure: Dutka cites the angels' singing immediately

---

4 Dutka 1972, 130–1.
5 Dutka 1972, 131.
6 Dutka 1972, 132–4.
7 Dutka 1972, 134–51.
8 Dutka 1972, 134.
9 Dutka 1972, 136.
10 Dutka 1972, 139.
11 Dutka 1972, 142.
12 Dutka 1972, 148–9.

after their creation, the angelic *Christus resurgens* at the Resurrection, and Christ's *Pax vobis* at his appearance to the apostles.

These categories are presented again, in the same order, in Dutka's later publication:[13] but this short version (which is merely a commentary on the presentation of reference data) does not do justice to her work in this area, which is illuminating and well worth reading in full. In her dissertation the material is treated comprehensively, and the categories used clearly work well as a basis for the descriptive discussion of examples from the English cycles. There are however two related problems in the details of her categories. First, in discussing these ideas in terms of their dramatic purpose she makes the music seem more provably structural than it is. We do not know that a dramatist would demand music in a particular structural situation (although in 6.3, below, I shall discuss some special examples where I believe that this was the case); we know only that it is in the nature of the drama that music used for representational purposes will often occur at important structural moments. Dutka does indeed try to redress the balance in this respect, in a final paragraph in which she warns against any assumption that the dramatic situation invariably dictates the appearance of music:[14]

> Did . . . every ascent, descent, entrance, exit, play beginning, or play ending have music? Most likely not: the demands of a particular play and performance, the finances available for musicians in certain years, the constantly changing notions of production – all these factors would ensure that the use of music would not follow rigid patterns . . .

Almost any analysis of the dramatic situations in which music appears will tend to give the opposite impression:[15] but this is probably less the case if the structural functions are discussed in terms of the individual dynamics of the drama rather than of the dramatic situation as a whole. I shall return to this in 6.2.

Second, there is a serious possibility of confusion in discussing a complex dramatic situation if one or more elements of it are uncertain. It is therefore best to isolate the individual features that articulate the drama. For example, Dutka's categories 3 (b) and 3 (c) beg the question of what was in the dramatist's mind by putting together two essentially different types of structural function: the end of the play is structural in the articulative sense, while the exit of a character is a matter of iconographic motion. The end of the play is structurally the same in either case: it is the iconographic motion that varies. The characters must leave the acting area

---

[13] Dutka 1980, 7–8.

[14] Dutka 1972 150–151; 1980, 8.

[15] See, for instance, in John Stevens's review of my own discussion of 1983: 'In the interesting discussion of structural functions . . ., there seems to be an underlying assumption . . . that all dramatic occurrences of music . . . are structural in the proper sense. But characters would move about the "place" or pageant, would enter and "exit", and so on, whether music accompanied them or not. . . .' (EMH 6 [1986], 319). I actually wrote that 'Whenever a musical item can be categorized as having one of the [structural] functions . . ., it also marks a structural division of the play' (*Essays*, 122). This does not mean that every structural division is marked by music.

anyway at the end of a play, but if they do not do so to music two questions arise: What *is* the music's function? and How do the characters remove themselves from the acting area? The answer to the first question is presumably that the music is part of a tableau: this is Dutka's functions 2 and 3 (g), so that the confusion grows. The answer to the second question is presumably that they walk off, but of course this may be no longer a musical matter (see below).

This problem arises also when the dramatic situation is unclear because the theatrical or other conventions are unknown. In this case, too, reducing the functions to individual units helps to isolate the difficulty. To take one of Dutka's examples, it will be useful to consider **Coventry 2₆**, in which, she says, an anthem is sung while the procession to the altar takes place.[16] She may well be right in this, but the direction does not in fact show it:

> *There the all goo vp to the awter and Iesus before. The syng an antem.*
>
> **(Coventry 2/805+sd)**

It would be wrong to assume that the two parts of this direction happen simultaneously, however strongly twentieth-century dramatic instincts suggest it. A modern mind may certainly regard it as somehow wasteful to have a non-musical procession followed by a static musical event: but this relies on the assumptions (a) that a silent procession is unacceptable, (b) that a static musical event is unacceptable, and (c) that putting them together is more satisfactory because it saves time. It is hardly necessary here to question whether the one is really silent, the other really static, or for what reasons either might be considered unacceptable; nor need we give much time to considering whether the audience begrudges the time spent (see, however, p. 232, below). The point is that the dramatist had other considerations to take into account, in this case liturgical ones. We should not ask what would be most effective theatrically, therefore, but what the dramatist intended.[17] Should the anthem be sung at the altar, or was it a processional piece? Only a knowledge of the liturgy involved will tell us that. If the anthem was sung at the altar, was it normal to process without music? Only a general knowledge of the liturgy will provide the answer.[18] If it was normal to process without music, do the *plays* show non-musical processions? If we are to understand the mental conditions in which the dramatist worked, it will be best to separate out the various strands.

It is for these and other reasons that my categories are simpler than Dutka's. At the same time, there have to be more of them – and more, in fact, than it was

---

16 See 2.3, p. 27, above, for this SD.

17 This is not to say that early English drama is untheatrical, of course, nor that dramatists did not on the whole think in terms of effective drama. Modern productions have demonstrated the quality of the repertory often enough. It would however be unfruitful to approach these problems in the light of nineteenth/twentieth-century theatrical traditions rather than through what we know (and can find out) about fifteenth/sixteenth-century concepts of drama.

18 For a consideration of what can and cannot be learned in this area, see chapter 7, below.

necessary to use in respect of the Chester cycle alone.[19] Those discussed in this book are examined in the section that follows.

6.2 The dynamic functions of music

Those functions that Dutka saw as 'advancing action' I have here and elsewhere called 'structural functions' (above, and in *Essays*, 120–2). Examination of the non-representational functions in the whole repertory, however, shows that not every occurrence is structural in the strict sense. On the other hand, as Dutka noted, every occurrence does affect the forward movement of the drama in some way. It does this either by assisting iconographic change (movement of characters, change of location) or by forming a punctuation in the dramatic action. The latter is often at a structural division but occasionally at some non-structural point of iconographic stasis, such as a numerically-important point of the kind discussed in 6.3, below. These non-representational functions may therefore best be referred to as *dynamic functions*, a term that acknowledges Dutka's definition without negating their largely articulative effects on the drama.

It is convenient to give a check-list of these functions before discussing them in detail. They are:

(a) Movement of character(s) around the acting areas;
(b) Entrance of character(s);
(c) Exit of character(s);
(d) The passage of time;
(e)   Change of location;
(f) Start of play;
(g) End of play;
(h) Scene-division; and
(i) Tableau.

In the cue-lists of Volume 2 these functions are identified by the letters allotted to them here.

(a) A musical item often covers the movement of characters about the acting areas. Some of these are processions of one sort and another, and therefore imply movement between locations. In cases such as that of Christ's entry into Jerusalem the movement is from an ill-defined location to a well-defined one, the latter being the city gate; in the case of liturgical processions the movement may be towards (or away from) an altar. The locations concerned may be those of adjacent scenes, so that functions (e) and (h) are also involved: the song performed by the shepherds while they travel to Bethlehem is such a case. In a similar way, a quasi-procession may be an entrance or exit, as discussed under (b) and (c), below. However, it is not always possible to identify an entrance or exit as such. For instance, the movement of the Holy Family with the singing angel at **Chester 10/288+sd** may be an exit: but in view of the fact that they appear also in the last scene of the play I assume that they remain in the audience's sight throughout the intervening scene. This movement, then, is a quasi-exit (from 'on-stage' to 'off-stage-but-in-sight') rather than an exit proper (which ends with the characters out of the audience's sight). This is not a distinction that need worry us, I think, and indeed it may have been a matter for directorial decision then, as it would be now.[20] Clearly, however, a quasi-exit presupposes a later quasi-entrance, and this will be mentioned again below.

It should be emphasised here that although one talks of 'covering' movement with music the function is less vital from a practical point of view than that would suggest. This applies also to entrances and exits. Movement without music is perfectly possible and apparently took place often enough. Only where there is a hiatus that seems to destroy the dramatic impetus and thus damage the play – as in the case of the foot-washing in Last Supper plays discussed in section 7.6 – is music felt as vitally necessary.

(b) Music is sometimes used at the entrance of a character: the singing entrance of the Coventry mothers of the Innocents is an example. Entrances are a special case of (a) and, for reasons discussed there, must be taken to include quasi-entrances as well. Quasi-entrances, however, usually involve a change of location at the start of a new scene, so that functions (e) and (h) may also be operative.

(c) Music for exits is probably more common than for entrances. Some of them are processions, such as those in which angels lead souls to Heaven after the Harrowing of Hell and the Last Judgement. The case of a possible quasi-exit in **Chester 10** has been mentioned above, but in fact there is a certain case of an exit at the end of that play when the angel sings again. Not surprisingly, musical exits (and quasi-exits, for that matter) often occur at a scene-division, so that function (h) is also involved: and, more specifically, they occur also at the end of a play, in which case function (g) is in operation. Not all music at the end of a play is an exit, however. The more one considers musical play-endings, the more one is drawn to the idea of a tableau in many instances, a matter discussed under (i), below.

(d) The passage of time is sometimes marked by music. The considerable periods of time that occur in the course of individual plays are as follows: between the Expulsion of Adam and Eve from the Garden of Eden and the manhood of Cain and Abel; the forty days of the Flood; and the twelve years between Christ's infancy and the episode with the doctors in the Temple. In most texts the first and last of these are in separate pageants or – in the non-processional cycles – in separate sections that seem not to assume continuous action. No music occurs at these places in the relevant Cornish plays. Only in the Chester and Coventry plays are these time-lapses in a single pageant, and the junction between the Purification and Doctors sections is now lost from Coventry 2. The Chester cycle, then, provides the only extant examples: **Chester 2/424+md** is for minstrelsy at the end of the Expulsion section, which also marks the passing of thirty years before the Cain and Abel

---

[20] But see Mary Loubris Jones in *American Notes and Queries* 16/8 (April 1978), 118–19, and in *Theatre Notebook* 32 (1978), 118–26; and Alan C. Dessen, *Elizabethan Stage Conventions and Modern Interpreters* (Cambridge: Cambridge University Press, 1984), chapter 7.

TABLE 9 : MUSIC AND THE PASSAGE OF TIME IN CHESTER 3

Line	Group MSS	MS H
247 251	NOE Aha, marye, this ys hotte; ... Over the land the water spreades; God do hee as hee will.	(as in the Group MSS)
	Then the singe ...	(no stage direction)
253 -260	NOE Ah, great God ... ... bee slaked through thy mighte.	(as in the Group MSS)
	Then shall Noe shutt the windowe of the arke, and for a little space within the bordes hee shalbe scylent: and afterwarde openinge the windowe and lookinge rownde about sayinge:	(different SD, for closing the window, singing "Save mee O god" and opening the window again)
		NOE Now 40 dayes are fullie gone. (The Raven and Dove scene: 48 lines in all)
261	NOE Lord God in majestye ... [etc.]	(as in the Group MSS)

episode; as for the junction between Purification and Doctors episodes at **Chester 11/206+**, where there is a time-lapse of twelve years, it is not certain that music should occur there.

The other case, that of the Flood, is also marked musically only in Chester. It is, however, a particularly interesting case, as Table 9 shows. After Noah and his family have entered the Ark and the water is spreading over the land, the Group MSS give a SD (marginal in A) requiring the family to sing (**Chester 3/252+sd**). Noah's next speech shows that time has passed and the flood is at its height; the 8-line speech itself (**3/253–60**) gives the relative time-scale for the period during which the flood covers the earth; and this is followed by a short space during which Noah shuts up the Ark and is silent (**3/260+sd**). When he speaks again (**3/261**), the water has receded. In this version, then, there are three periods of time: in the first, the flood rises; in the second, Noah looks out and sees no recession of the water; and in the third, the water recedes. Of these, the first (after **3/252**) is probably the longest, the dramatic time being marked by the song.

The version transmitted by MS H has quite a different time-scale because of the inclusion of the Raven and Dove scene. Here there is no SD after **Chester 3/252**, the whole of **3/247–60** being a single speech during which the flood-water covers the earth. The space that follows is not a short one: in fact, it is forty days long, as Noah states immediately afterwards. In H, then, it is here that the music comes, with a SD requiring Noah to shut up the Ark, the family to sing *Save mee, O God*, and Noah then to open the window and look out. By means of the music here, H gives an impression of the periods of dramatic time quite different from that of the Group's version.

There are a number of smaller time-periods in which music occurs with no obvious dynamic function, and it is possible to argue that these are examples of music used for the passage of time. In no case does this seem to me likely: but the matter is discussed in (i), below. In general, in any case, dramatists evidently did not feel it necessary to mark small periods of time by music. There is none between the various days of the Creation, for instance, where dramatists seem to have felt that the dramatic time was not an inappropriate representation of real time.

(e) Music can be used to change the location of the dramatic action. Such change is often necessary in drama that allows two or more locations to be alternated for a series of scenes: the audience's attention has to be directed to the one where the action is about to happen. Depending on the dramatic situation, this might be done musically by a procession moving from one location to another or by the (music-heralded) entry of a character: but both of these involve physical movement that is itself an attention-catcher, and in the second case a loud pomping entry is just as effective – and, incidentally, rather more common. Nor is the music at a scene-division normally associated with the scene to follow: more often it belongs to the previous scene, of which more will be said under (i), below. This situation is spelled out in **N-Town 9/259+sd**, where the minister enters and speaks only after the singing of *Jesu corona virginum* in Heaven, which belongs to the previous scene:

> *hic osculet [Maria] terram . here xal comyn Allwey An Aungel with dyvers presentys goynge & comyng and in þe tyme þei xal synge in hefne þis hympne. Jhesu corona virginum . And After þer comyth A minister fro þe busschop with A present & seyth*

While most true examples of music for location-changing occur at the beginning of a scene, this is not invariable. When Trowle/Garcius sings at **Chester 7/164+sd** the First Shepherd has previously referred to him (at **7/163**) as 'Yonder lad that sittes on a lowe', so he has probably been in the audience's sight for some time already. This is not wholly clear, however, and the possibility remains that he enters with his song: for Garcius speaks of himself as walking, not sitting (**7/167**). Is the First Shepherd making an assumption about Garcius, or is Garcius speaking generally about his work? This may well be a directorial decision. However, it makes no difference to the fact that Garcius draws the audience's attention to himself by means of his song, and that this is the start of his 32-line soliloquy.

(f) That music sometimes starts a play is beyond doubt, although it is not common. Indeed, the surprise is that it happens so rarely. JoAnna Dutka cited the single example of **Chester 2**, with its marginal direction for minstrelsy, and pointed out that only one of the five manuscripts included the direction.[21] Thinking it likely

> that the numerous minstrels and waits hired by the guilds earned their wages, and played wherever the producers felt the dramatic situation required music

she then suggested that the beginning of Passion Play II (**N-Town 28/1-sd**), with its 'processyon' of powerful people (Herod, Pilate, Annas, Caiaphas), would be a very suitable place. Dutka admitted that there was no proof, but made a general suggestion that music was probably used to begin plays more often than the play texts tell us.

In this she may well be right, though the criterion involved will not be the need of the 'dramatic situation' but that of the *representation* required, as discussed in Chapter 5, above. The problem will not be resolved without more evidence, however, for the guild records showing apparently unused minstrels do not coincide with plays of which the openings might be thought suitable for minstrelsy.[22]

(g) Evidence is more frequent for music at the end of a play. In most cases this is clearly a tableau, a matter that is discussed in (i), below. Even where it appears to be a procession, however, with characters leaving the acting area with music, it is still quite possible that a tableau is intended. At the end of **York 37**, for example, it seems that Michael will lead the released souls away from the acting area following the Harrowing of Hell:

> MICHILL   Lorde, wende we schall aftir þi sawe,
> To solace sere þai schall be sende.   (**York 37/397–8**)

But before going he asks Christ's blessing (**399–400**): this is given (**401**), and Jesus adds that he will be with the blessed ones (**402**) and that they will be eternally blessed by him (**404**). This implies that he will join them all in their movement towards Heaven. In the final four lines (**405–8**) Adam gives praise to Christ and initiates the singing of *Laus tibi cum gloria*. While it might seem sensible to use this to let the actors process away from the station, it is by no means certain that that was how it was done. It is something of a 'blessing' ending, with a present blessing and the promise of eternal blessings to follow, so that a static tableau would also be effective. And, of course, as in all the processional plays, the whole cast must process away from the station within the next few minutes anyway. By taking the 'static' option for *Laus tibi* we do not lose the procession but gain a set-piece performance of the piece.

(h) The point has already been made that music often coincides with a major structural articulation of the drama. It is in the nature of this type of drama that the

---

[21] Dutka 1972, 142.

[22] These 'spare' minstrels are discussed in the studies of individual plays in Volume 2. The problems are noted in *Essays*, 132–8, and see also section 8.5, below.

entrance or exit of a character, the passage of time, or the change of focus from one location to another will usually occur at the end of a scene or other important structural subdivision. I have used the word 'scene' because it is convenient to do so. It is anachronistic, of course, but its meaning is hardly controversial. As in much drama from Shakespeare to eighteenth-century opera, 'scene' is taken to denote a part of the action that takes place in a single location, on a single occasion, with little or no change of cast, and dealing with a single idea or recognisable group of ideas. The division between scenes in this case is usually marked by a change in the characters present and sometimes, though by no means always, by a change in the location. Carpenter discussed the musical items in the Towneley *Secunda Pastorum* in these terms, and I have done the same with **Chester 7**.[23]

The question of scene-divisions is especially interesting in those plays where it seems possible that two or more relatively small plays have been put together, whether or not that is in fact the case. The resulting structure may involve a linking Expositor scene (as in **Coventry 1**), but may go directly from one to the other (as in the cases of **Chester 2** and **Chester 11**, in both of which several years pass).

(i) Music often takes part in a tableau that is neither more nor less than a set-piece performance. There is normally no over-all movement of characters in such a case, although that does not preclude some movement around fixed points. For example, when the angels praise God in **York 1** we may surely take it that there is no necessity for either God or any of the angels to move from one place to another during the singing. The same is probably true in **Chester 1**, although there **1/125+sd** (H only) gives the possibility of God moving away during the singing rather than after it: 'Tunc cantant et recedet Deus' (Then they sing, and God goes away). The angelic Gloria sung to the shepherds is such a tableau, and here it is worth mentioning a special factor that operates here and in one or two other tableaux: namely, that the audience can identify with the shepherds as the total audience for the piece. Heavenly musical tableaux occur also in the York and N-Town Assumption plays and elsewhere.

Occasionally it is difficult to decide whether a musical event is a tableau or a procession, as we have already noted. The spectacular Ascension scene in **Chester 20** is, I suspect, a tableau, so that Christ and the angels remain static in mid-air during the musical scene. The same must surely be the case in **York 45**, where the whole central scene, with its polyphony, takes place during the Blessed Virgin's assumption. These are both waggon plays, of course, and therefore demand a particular kind of staging. Only plays with much more space available could have the music performed while characters were actually on the move: the floor-to-ceiling mechanism of the Elche play comes to mind. Among the English plays perhaps the N-Town Assumption – however it was staged – is the most obvious candidate for the possibility of continuous movement through the musical performance. At this stage it is however worth saying again that very difficult music cannot be processional. An actual procession requires music that is rhythmically and texturally simple: this

23 Carpenter '*Secunda pastorum*', 213; Rastall 'Some myrth', 82–4.

is quite different, in practice, from a 'moving tableau' such as is still staged at Elche, where the musicians are static on the moving *mangrana*.[24]

In this respect the Entry plays should perhaps be reconsidered. It is easy to assume that the singing children are part of Christ's procession, but that is probably not the case, since they discuss the procession and obviously wait for it to come – in other words, they start the play in a different location. In any case the liturgical model, the Palm Sunday procession, has the choristers taking part in a separate procession from Christ's and at one point singing from a separate location in a high place. It is possible, therefore, that in some plays the boys sang from a high and fixed location, perhaps the top of the gate of Jerusalem. This matter is discussed in section 7.5, below.

Finally, it seems that a number of plays end with a tableau. As already noted, it is tempting to assume that the music would be used to get the cast off-stage in procession, but a separate tableau seems often to have been intended. Certainly in many plays a set-piece ending, a closer in the grand style, would be a more fitting climax to a play. The end of the York cycle is surely like this, a not-quite-static tableau, as discussed in section 2.3, above. Here, as in various other plays, there is a 'blessing' ending, which presupposes a tableau whether it is musical or not.

It is in fact sometimes difficult to decide when a 'blessing' ending is musical: each has to be examined in its own right, a general conclusion being impossible. To a large extent it depends on who is doing the blessing: if God the Father or Christ is the blesser then a heavenly vision is usually in the offing and there is a possibility of angelic music. In all, however, the question of music in play-endings is often not a clear one.

It is instructive to compare the endings of the various plays of the Flood. **Towneley 3** ends with a prayer from Noah, to which all, I imagine, respond 'Amen' (see 8.6, below). **York 9** ends with a blessing from Noah that prepares the audience for the cast's withdrawal:

[NOE]   And wende we hense in haste
           In Goddis blissyng and myne.   **(York 9/321–2)**

In **Chester 3**, a blessing ending from God also prepares for withdrawal, but whether God's, the rest of the cast's or both is not clear:

[GOD]   My blessinge nowe I give thee here,
           to thee, Noe, my servante deare,
            for vengeance shall noe more appeare.
           And now farewell, my darlinge dere.   **(Chester 3/325–8)**

Some directors have tended to feel embarrassed at having the cast move off, as it were, out of the play: but this is surely unnecessary. **N-Town 4**, the only one of the four Flood plays to end with music, must certainly use a tableau, even if the cast eventually goes off while they are still singing – there is too much to be sung for it

---

[24] On the Elche staging, see King and Salvador-Rabaza 1986.

to happen otherwise. They may sing while processing around the playing area, of course, but there is really no need to do this. As in the case of **Coventry 2/805+sd**, discussed in 6.1, above, the pitfall of seeking to save time should be avoided. The song is an interesting musical event that needs no accompanying physical movement, while the exit of the ship and players is a procession that needs no music: Indeed, the ordering of elements in the SD seems to mean that the psalm-singing should be complete before the ship moves off:

> *Hic decantent hos versus* . ¶ Mare vidit et fugit . jordanis conuersus est retrorsum . Non nobis domine non nobis . sed nomine tuo da gloriam . *Et sic recedant cum naui.*
>
> **(N-Town 4/253+sd)**

In the interpretation of this direction much depends on the meaning of the word 'sic'. The usual meaning, 'in this way' or 'in these circumstances', may well suggest that music and procession do happen simultaneously.

One of the problems in defining the various functions of the musical items is that there is much overlapping of functions. An item may have a representational function and also two or more dynamic functions. In that case it is difficult to speak of any of them as a clearly-defined function of that piece of music: different commentators may propose different functions as the primary one. An example is the music that accompanies the Chester Adam and Eve's dismissal from the Garden of Eden (**Chester 2/424+sd**). It represents the restoration of Divine Order in Eden; covers the departure of the four angels from the playing-place, probably back to the waggon; denotes the passage of the thirty years in which Cain and Abel are born and grow up; helps to redefine the location of Heaven and thus to distinguish it from earth, now being used for the first time; and prepares the audience for a new scene.

It is not easy to rank these functions in order of importance, although there are certain criteria that can be used. First, the representational functions presumably come before the dynamic ones: that is, music is not used for a dynamic purpose unless a representational purpose has first required it. Second, we can probably assume (and it is surely obvious here) that the purely practical considerations of covering processions, exits and journeys from one location to another take precedence over academic matters of scene-division. Although music is clearly a help in staging a play with several scenes in different locations, there is no doubt that the problems – such as they were – often had to be overcome without it. Nevertheless, I think that the question of music was taken seriously by the playwrights, and that the conventions at work perhaps gave a more consistent use of music than the surviving evidence has allowed us to discover. In the next section we shall explore one particular type of convention for which this may be true.

6.3 The music of numbers: structure and proportion

We noted in 6.1 that **York 45**, *The Assumption of Our Lady*, is structured symmetrically, with three scenes of exactly equal length. Further, the use of music at the divisions of that play is part of the evidence supporting the proposition, made in 6.2, that music cues often occur at scene-divisions. We should now try to answer two questions, therefore. First, is there a general case for thinking that plays were structured according to numerological principles? Second, is there evidence that music was used deliberately to enhance articulations created by this structuring? Considering also that some apparently equally important musical performances happen in places that are not scene-divisions or other obvious structural articulations, a third question arises out of these two: can we demonstrate a numerological and/or symbolic purpose behind music that seems not to be related to the principal structural articulations? I shall address these questions in relation to plays from the York cycle.

It will hardly be surprising if we can answer 'Yes' to one or more of them.[25] From ancient times until the seventeenth and eighteenth centuries educated men had, in any one time and place, a common understanding of numerology and its symbolic meanings. The concept of Divine Order, by which the universe was thought to run by means of simple, harmonious proportions, was part of this understanding. In these circumstances one might expect poets, playwrights, composers, architects and others to take numerological considerations seriously and to make use of numerology in designing poems, plays, musical works, cathedrals, and so on. On the other hand, none of these people has ever, to my knowledge, told us what they were doing in this respect. There is no reason why they should: their audience is required only to perceive the proportions of the work of art as pleasing and harmonious in the most general way. Nobody watching a play will count lines to see if the play divides exactly in the middle, and nor need they do so. The result of a good numerological construction is good construction such as might have been achieved without the aid of numbers, and will be perceived as such.[26]

This interest in numbers was transmitted from the Greek mathematicians of late antiquity to the Middle Ages by Boethius and others. Another strand of significance, starting in ancient Babylon, stems originally from the relationship between written numbers and letters. The immediate result of this relationship is that many numbers acquired symbolic meanings, and these became an important tool in biblical exegesis.[27]

---

[25] John Robinson discussed numerological construction in the Towneley cycle: see *Studies*, 87–8, 114–5, 178–9, 173 and 236. His examination is the most cogent that I know of in drama studies, but he certainly underestimated the extent to which the York Realist had used numerology: *Studies*, 34–5.

[26] In discussing **Towneley 13** Robinson was careful to state that the numerology was 'a private guide to the playwright': *Studies*, 115.

[27] On numerology in ancient times see Wilson 'Jabirian numbers'; on the history and uses of numerology generally, Hopper *Medieval Number Symbolism*, Butler *Number Symbolism* and

Numerological considerations relevant to the design of a play must be discussed, then, under the two main headings of structure and symbolism. A little more must be said about these before we turn to the York cycle. In general, the proportions of the sections of the work concerned will be simple, but the actual numbers chosen may depend on their mathematical properties, a subject that has always fascinated mathematicians and philosophers. Pythagorean number-theory categorised individual numbers as perfect, deficient or abundant, for example, according to whether the sum of its divisors is equal to, less than or more than the number itself. The divisors of 6 (other than itself) are 1, 2 and 3: 1+2+3=6, so 6 is a perfect number (the first, in fact); 14 is a deficient number because its divisors – 1, 2 and 7 – add up to only 10; 12 is an abundant number because the sum of its divisors, 1+2+3+4+6, is more than 12 (16). The perfect numbers are the rarest of these categories: the second perfect number is 28. Another way of categorising numbers was as triangular, square or oblong. A triangular number is the sum of successive terms: 1+2=3; +3=6; +4=10; +5=15; +6=21 gives the series 1, 3, 6, 10, 15, 21, . . .; a square number is the sum of successive numbers of the odd series: 1+3=4; +5=9; +7=16; +9=25, which in fact is the succession of squares, 1^2, 2^2, 3^2, 4^2, 5^2, . . .; an oblong number is the sum of successive even numbers (2, 6, 12, 20, 30, 42, . . .), which is twice the triangular numbers.

Some of these numbers have a less purely theoretical importance, too, sometimes of very ancient standing. Four elements, four humours, four seasons and four corners of the earth, for instance, led to the number 4 being associated with the earth and the physical universe in general. 10 was a complete unit (fingers), and so associated with perfection; hence 9 was all-but-complete or just-less-than-perfect. 3 also signified a form of perfection: since 1 was unity and 2 distinction between entities, 3 was the superlative, or numeral of completeness; and as such it came to be associated with the spiritual universe. 28 was the number of the lunar month, and the second perfect number. 7 was important probably as a quarter of the lunar number, but perhaps also because the sum of the first seven terms, 1+2+3+4+5+6+7, is the lunar number, 28. In the Middle Ages 7 was regarded as the virgin number because it did not generate nor was generated within the decad (1–10): that is, no manipulation of squaring, cubing nor summing of series produces 7. It was significant also as a prime number – it has no divisors other than 1 and itself – and as the sum of the spiritual and physical numbers, 3 and 4. The Middle Ages also regarded even numbers as feminine and odd numbers as masculine.[28] The sum of the first

Curtius *European Literature*. Butler continues the story into the post-medieval periods, a subject treated also in works by Alastair Fowler (see Bibliography). Fowler's work concentrates on literature, as does McQueen *Numerology* and other works. Some very useful work has been done on music, too, including Trowell 'Dunstable' and Slocum 'Speculum Musicae'. My principal authority for the common interpretations of various numbers is Hopper, whose work is indispensable in this kind of study.

[28] Hopper explains this in terms of power. Adding an odd number to any number changes the nature of the result, which the addition of an even number does not; odd plus odd is even, but odd plus even remains odd. Similarly, if an even number is divided by two it is merely diminished, while an odd number divided by two leaves a remainder. On the early history of the male-female question, see Wilson 'Jabirian numbers', 7–9.

two real numbers, 2 and 3, gives the masculine marriage number, 5; their product is the female marriage number, 6; the sum of these two marriage numbers, 11, symbolised marriage between a man and a woman, although it could also signify sin, being the transgression of (that is, one more than) perfection (10) and the Decalogue (the Ten Commandments).

It will be seen from this that a number might attract not only a symbolic significance, but even two or more different symbolisms that were not necessarily mutually compatible. The second heading, symbolism, under which numerology must be studied is therefore a more complex subject than that of mathematical properties. When numbers have two or more meanings the interpretation of any particular number may be difficult: certainly, in the absence of any direction from the person using the number, any interpretation must be speculative, although external evidence may give a clear lead. For example, Christ died in his 33rd year, which is normally understood in a particular way: 33 = 11x3 – the principal marriage number (which incidentally is also a prime number) multiplied by the trinitarian number of perfection. It is also clear that the three years of Christ's Ministry should be understood to be of trinitarian significance, however (like his three days in the tomb), which leaves 30 years before his Ministry started: and 30, as 3x10, is the product of two numbers of perfection, the one trinitarian and the other signifying the Decalogue that Christ came to confirm and elucidate.[29] Consideration of numbers in this way was certainly important to medieval thought, and, whatever the dangers of misinterpretation, we cannot ignore it in our study of medieval culture. Two examples may suggest the kind of study in which number considerations can be helpful. In 1993 Lan Lipscomb suggested that the Wilton Diptych might have been painted on the occasion of Richard II's betrothal or marriage to Anne of Bohemia, noting that the eleven angels accompanying the Virgin and Child were perhaps significant.[30] These angels – five on the Virgin's right and six on her left – are indeed likely to signify a marriage: and it might be added that Richard's three sponsors in the Diptych would suggest a wholly unsurprising devotion to the Trinity on his part. Such interpretations probably explain other numbers in various paintings: I have elsewhere suggested that the angels in the painting of the Assumption and Coronation of the Virgin by the Master of the St Lucy Legend have precisely this kind of significance, with powers of 4 in the nearer part of the picture, on the earthly side of the gate of Heaven, and numbers signifying the Trinity and marriage (again, 5+6=11) within the gate.[31]

In addition to such symbolisms are the various systems of *gematria* by which numbers are assigned to letters and hence to names or concepts. The oldest known system, the Babylonian, was used also by the Jews: the first nine letters stand for

[29] See Matthew 22/37–40 and 5/17.
[30] At a special session of the Society of the White Hart, 28th International Congress on Medieval Studies at Western Michigan University, Kalamazoo, on 7 May 1993.
[31] See Rastall 'Repertory', 180 and 194 (n. 69).

units, the next nine for tens, and the rest for hundreds.[32] This system was still in use in the early Christian era: Gnostics used 801 ('dove') or 888 ('Jesus') for 'Christ'; 91 for both 'Amen' and 'God' ('Jahveh Adonai'); 358 for Messiah; and 13 for 'love of unity', since 13 stands for both 'love' and 'unity' separately. The Latin natural-order alphabet is the one that we most often meet in medieval usage, with a=1, b=2, c=3, and so on as far as z=23:[33] a sixteenth-century version used and perhaps invented by John Skelton additionally uses 1–5 for the vowels while the consonants have their normal places.

The texts of many individual York pageants seem to have been corrupted very little since revision or rewriting in the mid-fifteenth century, and it is therefore possible to analyse them numerically with a reasonable chance of success. Moreover, the scenes in this cycle tend to be a whole number of stanzas, and the stanzas tend to be regular.[34] In all, the survival-state of the cycle is such as to eliminate the worst doubts as to the integrity of the text being analysed and its relationship to possible numerical structures.

We may begin with **York 14**, *The Nativity*. The dramatist chose to write in 7-line stanzas, itself a significant choice since 7 is a sacred number and specifically the virgin number. In choosing also to write the play in twenty-two stanzas, he created the option of dividing the play into two equal halves of 11 stanzas. The division is created by the light that signifies the birth of Christ after line 77. Thus each half of the play consists of 11 stanzas of 7 lines each, and these are significant numbers: 7, as the sum of 4 (the material universe) and 3 (the spiritual universe), represents the whole Creation – Heaven and earth in little space, as the carol *There is no rose* has it; 11 is symbolic of marriage. Moreover, the product of these two, which is 77, the number of lines in each half, symbolises the Forgiveness of All Sins. Thus the numbers of this play presumably refer, at least in the author's mind, to the Incarnation of God as Man, in the context of the marriage of the Virgin Mary to Joseph, for the purpose of Redemption.

The structure is however a little more complex than that. The play falls into seven well-defined scenes, another obviously deliberate choice of numerological significance,[35] disposed symmetrically. Thus the centre of the play is disguised to the extent that the light appears in the middle of the two-stanza speech by Joseph that constitutes scene 4:

[JOSEPH] Now gud God þou be my bilde
          As þou best may.

---

32 The most usual number-alphabets are conveniently listed in Tatlow *Bach*, 130–38. The Hebrew milesian alphabet is on p. 130.
33 In this system i=j and u=v: a number of variants treat k, o and w in different ways, but in the principal version k=10, o=14, u/v=20 and there is no w (Tatlow *Bach*, 132).
34 This may be one result of numerical construction, of course: but in any case it removes one of the problems of such analysis, that the analyst cannot always be sure of the unit (syllable, line, stanza) that is relevant to the analysis.
35 Scenes 5–7 are defined by subject-matter rather than by changes of personnel or location, but this is so obvious a gear-shift that it has a similar articulative effect.

TABLE 10 : YORK 14

The Nativity   in 7-line stanzas

scene	1	2	3	4	5	6	7
lines	1-28	29-49	50-70	71-84	85-105	106-33	134-54
	28	21	21	14	21	28	21
stanzas	4	3	3	2	3	4	3
	J solo	M+J	Birth	J solo LIGHT	M+J	Adrtn	M+J

> A, lord God, what light is þis
> Þat comes shynyng þus sodenly?   **(York 14/76–9)**

The 'sudden' appearance of the light, then, takes Joseph unawares between lines 77 and 78, so that the stage effect, although it does not need a direction, forms a dramatic articulation that is separate from those of the stanzas and scenes. Those of the scenes are a much clearer pattern to the watching audience, although the symmetry of the seven scenes will not be perceived through the ear alone. As the table shows, the three central scenes form a completely symmetrical pattern, while the outer two scenes on either side form a 4+3 balance of stanzas that prevents the play from being too obviously symmetrical in an artificial way.

A different structure, but also dividing into two equal halves, is **York 11**, *Moses and Pharaoh*. This play consists of 34 regular 12-line stanzas dividing into four unequal scenes.[36] In the first, stanzas 1–7, Pharaoh hears that the captive Jews are a potential danger and decides what to do about it; in the second, stanzas 8–17, Moses is commissioned by God and determines to speak to Pharaoh; in the third, stanzas 18–32, God sends the plagues and Pharaoh allows the Jews to leave; and in the final scene, stanzas 33–34, the Egyptians follow the Jews and are drowned in the Red Sea. This last and very brief scene is considerably extended by the performance of *Cantemus domino* at **11/408**, which enhances the 'praise' ending. This hymn of praise sung by the Israelites after the overthrow of Pharaoh's forces, Exodus 15/1–19, appears in the York liturgy, the first two verses being used as the tract for the Vigil of Easter and a slightly different selection of verses being the third responsory at mattins of Quadragesima.[37] This text also appears as the final piece in Egerton 3307.[38]

Music makes no difference to the structure of the play, then, except to enhance

---

[36] Beadle 'York Hosiers' Play', 4–6, identifies ten scenes. His extra divisions are obviously minor compared with the four used here, but a more detailed numerological analysis than mine may well be possible.

[37] MisE, and also the Sarum version in GS, 111; BE I, 330, and the Sarum version in AS, 183.

[38] See p. 133, above.

TABLE 11 : YORK 11

Moses and Pharaoh in 12-line stanzas

scene	1	2	3	4
lines	1-84	85-204	205-384	385-408
	84	120	180	24
stanzas	7	10	15	2
	17		17	
proportions	1		1	

the final scene, and especially the ending. As a table of the lines and stanzas shows, however, the play is carefully structured, with 17 stanzas on either side of a central division. The number 17 symbolised the life well lived, being the sum of the Ten Commandments and the 7 Gifts of Grace of the Holy Spirit that enabled men to keep them. Moses was of course the man to whom the Commandments were entrusted, which may be why the scene of his commissioning, scene 2, is ten stanzas long; and the Chosen People were those required to live by the Commandments.

York 35, *The Crucifixion*, has a symmetrically-structured pair of central scenes with slightly asymmetrical pairs of scenes at beginning and end. It is in 25 regular 12-line stanzas, or 300 lines. In the introductory section the four soldiers discuss the forthcoming crucifixion for four stanzas, after which Christ addresses God for a single stanza. The central part of the play consists of two equal sections, each eight stanzas long. The first of these concerns the nailing of Christ to the Cross, and the second the raising of the Cross: the division between them is just past the mid-point of the play, after thirteen stanzas. The end of the play consists of one stanza in which Christ addresses the multitude and three in which the soldiers dice for Christ's garment. This slightly-off-centre structure is very obvious when the lines and stanzas are tabulated.

There is no obvious interpretation of the various scene-lengths, although the structure of this play is, as it happens, highly satisfying. It is notable that the soldiers' scenes consist of 4 or 8 (=2x4) stanzas, which may signify their earthly allegiance and is certainly in distinction from the single-stanza speeches of Christ: but the significance of the single stanzas, and that of the three-stanza scene of the dicing, is less clear. What does seem more obvious, perhaps, is the total length of 300 lines: this number is represented by the letter Tau in the Greek milesian alphabet, and is therefore a common *gematria* symbol for the Cross.[39] Whatever else this playwright did, he had to calculate the length of the play precisely.

---

[39] For the Greek milesian alphabet, see Tatlow *Bach*, 131.

TABLE 12 : YORK 35

The Crucifixion   in 12-line stanzas

scene	1	2	3	4	5	6
lines	1–48	49–60	61–156	157–252	253–264	265–300
	48	12	96	96	12	36
stanzas	4	1	8	8	1	3

These three plays, I suggest, demonstrate the kind of numerological and symbolic considerations that playwrights took into account in laying out the proportions and numerical lengths of their plays and the constituent scenes of those plays. I repeat that an audience would not be aware of these numbers in performance, although clear structuring does help audience comprehension, and a sense of satisfaction with the play may result as much from this as from the proportions themselves. A play's structure can be clarified by various staging techniques, however, as we saw with **York 14**: and I turn now to plays in which one or more structural articulation points are confirmed by music cues.

The structurally simplest play in which this can be seen is **York 46**, *The Coronation of the Virgin*. Its metrical scheme is not entirely regular,[40] for although it is based on 4-line stanzas these are sometimes grouped into 8-line stanzas and some 6-line stanzas are also used. The play certainly divides into two exactly equal parts, however. In the first half, lines **1–80**, Jesus sends his angels to bring his mother to him, and they greet her; in the second half, lines **81–160**, Christ greets Mary, rehearses her Five Joys, and crowns her Queen of Heaven.

There is music at the end of each half. After line **80** the marginal direction *Cantando* is written in red by the main scribe. The opening of the speech following, 'Jesu, lorde and heueneis kyng', is reminiscent of certain Middle English lyrics,[41] and it may translate or paraphrase a Latin text sung after line **80** – perhaps something like the hymn *Jesus rex regum omnium*.

The second musical item takes place at the end of the play. There is no direction, but it is a 'blessing' ending and Christ's words leave no doubt that music is heard:

[JESUS]   Myne aungellis bright, a songe 3e singe
             In þe honnoure of my modir dere.   (**York 46/157–8**)

There is no indication of what item is involved, although we can probably assume a Marian text: there are many possibilities, including texts from the Canticum Canticorum such as *O quam pulchra es*.

The first of these cues, at least, covers movement. Three different locations are

---

[40] Beadle 1982, 462.
[41] See, for instance, IMEV, 272.

TABLE 13 : YORK 46

The Coronation of the Virgin

scene	1	2	3	4	
lines	1-36	37-80	81-104	105-160	
	36	44	24	56	
	Xt & angels	Mary & angels	Xt & Mary	Xt speaks to Mary	
proportions	9	11 song	6	14 song	

implied by the text: one where Mary is to begin with, a second where she is brought for her meeting with Christ, and a third where she will spend eternity in bliss. It is however not clear that all three are represented on the waggon, and the play could be staged with only the first two. That a vertical distinction is made between at least the first and last of these is clear from Christ's words early in the play:

[JESUS]   Vnkindely thing it were iwis,
            Þat scho schulde bide þe hire allone
            And I beilde here so high in blis.   (**York 46/14–16**)

It is possible that Christ is in Heaven at the beginning of the play, and that he moves down to some middle place where he will meet Mary: or perhaps Christ is in that middle place at the start of the play. It does however later become clear that Mary must ascend for her meeting with Jesus, so that there is certainly a vertical distinction between the first and second locations:

[II ANGELUS]   Come vppe nowe lady, meke and mylde.   (**York 46/56**)

This ascension must take place after line **80** ('Go we nowe', says the Fifth Angel at line **73**, and there is no place for the movement to occur before the end of the scene): it may be, therefore, that the marginal direction *Cantando* refers to the movement of Mary and the angels. There may even have been an original direction in the exemplar, omitted by the scribe (perhaps as unnecessary): in this case the marginal direction would certainly have been needed, since nothing in the text suggests singing there, although with the main direction now absent the remaining one is grammatically incomplete.[42] We may take it, therefore, that after line **80** Mary and the angels ascend to Christ, the angels singing as they go.

[42] 'Cantando' is an ablative gerund meaning 'by means of singing': it ought, therefore, to refer to a grammatically complete SD such as 'Ascendit Maria ad Jesum' or 'Ascendent angeli cum Maria'.

The end of the play is more problematic. Near the beginning of the second scene Jesus seems to be saying that the final ascension, into Heaven itself, is about to take place:

JESUS   Come forth with me my modir bright,
                  Into my blisse we schall assende   (York 46/101–02)

The ascension apparently takes place at the end of this stanza, after line **104**. Christ immediately turns to the enumeration of the Five Joys, the last of which is Mary's eternal bliss 'Full high on highte in mageste' (line 133), and the coronation itself then takes place (lines **155–6**). There is no indication of any movement between line **105** and the end, so if the final ascension has not taken place after line **104** it must happen at the end of the play. The end is however a 'blessing' ending with a musical item, which is likely to be a static tableau: and in any case if Mary is to be queen where Christ is king (line **156**) then the coronation should take place in Heaven (which is what the contemporary iconography shows), not at an intermediate point.

It seems, then, that the angels bring Mary up to Christ with singing at the central division of the play after line **80**; that Christ meets her at a mid-point but takes her up to Heaven after line **104**, apparently without music; and that the musical ending of the play is a static tableau in Heaven, the highest of the three locations. If this is correct, it follows that the dramatist regarded the music's dynamic function of covering movement as less important than the scene-division function, since there is no music at the second ascension, after line **104**, although music is needed for the final, static, tableau. It may equally be said, however, that if the playwright expected three musical items, after lines **80**, **104** and **160**, it is perfectly possible that the middle one was not regarded as needing a direction.

Perhaps more important for our present purpose is the fact that the proportions made by a division at line **104** are probably not such as needed to be enhanced by music. With divisions for movement at lines **80** and **104** the proportions come to 80 : 24 : 56 (i.e. 10 : 3 : 7) or, combining the first two, 104 : 56 (13 : 7). These figures do not seem significant, and perhaps only the principal ratio, 1 : 1, is. In this play, that ratio may symbolise the unity, if not the equality, of Christ and his mother, the king and queen of Heaven.

York 9, *The Flood*, is similar to *The Crucifixion* in having a symmetrical main structure. The play is in twenty-three regular 14-line stanzas and falls into five unequal sections: Noah's soliloquy takes the first three stanzas; another three are devoted to persuading Mrs Noah into the ark; after the forty-day period, the next seven stanzas treat the arguments concerning the Flood, and the end of this section marks the family's understanding of what has happened and why; a section of six stanzas is devoted to praise of God, the episode of the raven and the dove, and the sighting of the hills of Armenia; and finally, a four-stanza section concerns the rainbow and the family's future life.

Noah's preliminary remarks give 'the story so far' and form a prologue: the content of this section marks it out from the rest and justifies us in regarding the play proper as starting at line **43**, when Noah begins to address his family. Treating it this way, the play is seen to divide at the centre point. All the play up to line **182**

TABLE 14 : YORK 9

The Flood in 14-line stanzas

scene	1	2	3	4	5
lines	1-42	43-84	85-182	183-266	267-322
	42	42	98	84	56
stanzas	3	3	7	6	4
		3 | 7		6 | 4	
		10		10	
proportions		1		1	

concerns the period of disharmony, while in the second half, from line **183** ('O barnes, it waxxes clere aboute'), the new harmony is in operation. It is probably for this reason that the two equal halves of the play (scenes 2–3 and 4–5) are made up differently. Counting stanzas, the first half brings together the sacred numbers 3 and 7, while in the second the sum of the numbers 6 and 4 gives the same result. Thus the first half is made up of odd numbers and the second half of even numbers, symbolising discord and concord, respectively. Moreover, the proportions involved are inharmonious for the first half – 3 : 7, which gives a musically unusable interval – and harmonious for the second – 6 : 4 or 3 : 2, *sesquialtera*, which gives the musical interval of a (Pythagorean) perfect fifth.

Although scene 1 constitutes a separate prologue, it was apparently not a late addition. As the table of lines and stanzas shows, the sum of scenes 1 and 2 is balanced by scene 4 (42+42 = 84 lines), while the sum of the outer scenes balances the large central scene (42+56 = 98 lines). This play is in fact a good example of overlapping structures binding the whole together. The use of regular 14-line stanzas automatically makes the number 7 an important one, since it is a factor of the number of lines in any scene (as usual, scenes are in whole stanzas). The number 7 is an important number in any case, as already stated, and here represents the whole Creation, carried in the ark to salvation.[43] We should probably see the 56 lines of the last scene as $2^3 \times 7$, especially as the central scene of the play has 7 stanzas. As for the bipartite structure of the play in 140+140 lines, there is so obvious an avoidance of a structure of (5+5)+(5+5) stanzas that it must be deliberate.[44] Probably

---

43 The ark is a type of spiritual salvation through Christ, so both the dramatist and his audience would have in mind the salvation of souls in this play, not just the protection of human and animal life against physical destruction. See Kolve, 69.

44 The playwright could have made scenes 2 and 3 into 5+5 stanzas without destroying the odd/even distinction between the two halves of the play, but the proportion 5 : 5 is a very simple and harmonious one, and unsuitable for replacing the discordant proportion 7 : 3.

each half should be regarded as 2x10x7, where the 10 symbolises the perfection of the whole Creation (7) saved in the ark.[45]

The playwright probably intended scenes 1, 2 and 4 to be understood as multiples of 21, therefore, this being the product of the sacred numbers 3 and 7. The sum of these numbers has already been seen as significant in the length of the first half of the play (scenes 2 and 3). This also gives a higher-level *sesquialtera* structure cutting across the stanzas of these scenes, since two of these 21-line units cover three stanzas: i.e. (2x21)=(3x14)=42. The other two scenes are anomalous in not having 3 as a factor, but they share the property of being expressible in terms of 2 and 7 only: for the third scene, $98=2x7^2$; for the fifth, $56=2^3x7$.

If music were to play any part in **York 9** we might expect it to be at the mid-point (after **9/182**) to mark the turning-point between (metaphorical) discord and harmony, the old order and the new. There is no original direction for music in this play, however: that for singing after **9/266**, at the division between the fourth and fifth scenes, is a late marginal direction confirming the reference at **9/260**: 'We mone be saued now may we synge'.

There are many good reasons for having the music after **9/266**: the family's procession out of the ark onto dry land can be a musical one, and a performance here confirms their allegiance to God at the start of their new life. The position is however a significant one structurally. The cue comes at the end of 19 stanzas out of the play's 23, which provides adjacent prime numbers. More importantly, perhaps, if we ignore the initial soliloquy (scene 1), the music comes after 16 of the play's 20 stanzas, and therefore divides the play proper into the simple proportions of 16 : 4 (4 : 1, the double octave in music). However, we ought probably to view this division in lines rather than stanzas. The music comes after 224 lines of the play proper: this is 2^3x28. 28, the 'lunar' number, is a multiple of 7, but it is important for other reasons, as noted earlier. It is the seventh triangular number (1+2+3+4+5+6+7) and the second perfect number (1+2+4+7+14=28).[46]

There are two major divisions in this play then, both distinguished by their content. The first, following scene 1, separates the prologue from the main dramatic narrative, the play proper beginning at **9/43**: the second divides the play proper into two exactly equal parts, after scene 3, where the discord of the old life gives way to the harmony of the new. The playwright may have thought the division after scene 4 to be the most significant one, however, on grounds of its symbolism, for all that it is relatively unimportant structurally. The music signals the stepping-off – the literal stepping-off, onto dry ground – of the saved Creation at the start of its new life.[47]

In this second group of plays, then, the music cues confirm existing structural articulations and sometimes distinguish certain of them as symbolically more

---

[45] Compare the structure 2x11x7 in **York 14**, already discussed.

[46] See above, p. 234.

[47] Or the later addition of the MD may have been for representational purposes only: it is possible that **9/260** was intended as a metaphorical reference, although it does not seem likely.

TABLE 15 : YORK 12

The Annunciation and Visitation

scene	Prologue 12-line stanzas	Annunciation 8-line stanzas	Visitation 8-line stanzas
lines	1-144	145-192	193-240
	144	48	48
stanzas	12	6	6
		* 1 * 5	
lines	152	88	

* = music cue

important than others. My final group consists of plays in which music cues may actually create articulations in places that would otherwise have no such importance. In the tables for these plays, a music cue is indicated by an asterisk.

It will be convenient to discuss the simplest case first, which is that of **York 12**, *The Annunciation and the Visitation*. This play is in three parts. A doctor's prologue, lines 1–144, is in twelve 12-line stanzas; the Annunciation, lines 145–192, and the Visitation, lines 193–240, consist of six 8-line stanzas each. The prologue may have been added to an existing Annunciation and Visitation play.[48]

This structure shows very simple proportions of 144 : 48 : 48, or 3 : 1: 1. If the prologue was indeed a late addition, then the original play consisted of two exactly equal halves, the same space being given to the Visitation as to the Annunciation. But in that case the dramatist who wrote the prologue was certainly aware of the existing structure, since his addition gives two simple ratios: in stanzas, of 1 : 1; in lines, of 3 : 2. The division between the Annunciation and the Visitation, after line **192**, is in the middle of a speech by Mary, and is not marked by music: but the more important division, between the prologue – actually longer than the play – and the play itself has a late marginal direction by John Clerke for the angel's singing.[49] The speech following, lines **145-8**, is an English paraphrase of the biblical speech beginning 'Ave gratia plena, Dominus tecum' (Luke 2/28), so the angel was presumably intended to sing one of the liturgical pieces on the *Ave Maria* text. There is also music after one stanza of the Annunciation episode. The stage direction is again marginal, and by Clerke: *Ne timeas Maria* is specified, and the angel speaks an

48 This basic information is taken from Beadle 1982, 423–4. Beadle notes that the 8-line stanzas are of two types, corresponding to the two scenes, and that the first type overlaps briefly into the Visitation scene. It is probably safe to assume that the Visitation dramatist started with the versification of the Annunciation episode and then changed to a verse-form that he found more congenial.

49 **York 12/144+md:** see MDF 7, f. 46r.

TABLE 16 : YORK 1

The Fall of the Angels   in 8-line stanzas

scene	1		2	3	4
lines	1-40		41-80	81-120	121-160
	40		40	40	40
stanzas	5		5	5	5
	God		Discssn of angels	Fall of bad angels	Good angels & God
	3 angels	* 2 * earth	lack of harmony in heaven		harmony restored

English paraphrase of it immediately afterwards. Music does not have an obvious structural function here, but it does divide the play into a proportion of 152 : 88, or 19 : 11. These latter are prime numbers, and important for that reason. But the real significance is in the numbers of lines: 152 is the Greek *gematria* number for MARIA, while 88 factorises as $2^3 \times 11$, where 11 symbolises marriage, relevant to both Mary and Elizabeth.[50]

The second music cue, then, creates an articulation of great significance, quite as important symbolically as the 300 lines of the *Crucifixion* play, **York 35**. In the opening play of the York cycle the structure created is on a smaller scale and adds to an already extensive symbolic structure that coincides (thus far) with the division of the play into scenes.

York 1, *The Fall of the Angels*, is in regular 8-line stanzas. It has a symmetrical structure, dividing into four scenes each of 40 lines in five stanzas. In the first scene God creates the nine orders of angels, creates the earth, and commissions Lucifer as chief angel. The angels sing after their own creation (following the third stanza) and again at the end of the scene. In the second scene the angels present differing opinions of their situation, and in the third the rebellious angels transgress and fall to Hell. The final scene shows the good angels confirming their love of God. The four scenes thus demonstrate a symmetrical structure of order and disorder, harmony and discord: the first scene is the creation of the ordered universe, the second and third show disorder, and the fourth confirms Divine Order in the altered situation. The symmetrical pattern of order, disorder and restored order in this play presents the simple proportions 1 : 2 : 1, the simplest of all proportions after equality (1 : 1). The first and dramatically most important division is marked by music, and this incidentally also divides the play in the proportion of 1 : 3. The first scene is itself divided by music, however, in the proportion 3 : 2. Thus the play's structure presents the proportions corresponding to the musical intervals of the unison

---

[50] The Greek milesian alphabet is in Tatlow, 131.

(order/disorder *in toto*), the octave (order:disorder:order), the twelfth (scene 1/ scenes 2–4, divided by music) and the fifth (the parts of scene 1, divided by music).

The dramatist certainly thought of the first scene as a separate and important unit with its own structure. The first five stanzas of this play are about the creation of the perfection that is immediately lost, to be regained only in the last eight lines of the cycle. The unity of this scene, as well as the concept of Order, is enhanced by the use of two sections of a single musical item, the hymn *Te deum laudamus*, of which verses 1–2 and 5–6 are highly suitable for these two occasions:[51]

> 1. Te deum laudamus te dominum confitemur.
> 2. Te eternum patrem omnis terra veneratur.
>
> (We praise thee, O God: we acknowledge thee to be the Lord.
> All the earth doth worship thee, the Father everlasting.)
>
> 5. Sanctus, sanctus, sanctus dominus deus Sabaoth.
> 6. Pleni sunt celi et terra majestatis glorie tue.
>
> (Holy, holy, holy Lord God of hosts,
> Heaven and earth are full of the majesty of thy glory.)

In such a regular structure the number of lines in the stanza is almost certain to be a deciding factor: 8 is the first cube (2^3). The number of scenes in the play is the first square ($4=2^2$), but the real significance of this number is probably that, as the number of elements and humours, it symbolises the material universe, which God creates in the fourth stanza (itself presumably a deliberate choice). The 40 lines in each scene should probably be regarded as 4x10, for 10 is the number of perfection and the lines of each scene therefore presumably symbolise the perfect physical Creation. The total number of lines in the play, then, 4^2x10=160, is an enhancement of the basic 4x10, perhaps because Divine Order is restored in Heaven during the last scene. Since there are five stanzas in each scene there is something to be said for interpreting 160 as 2^5x5, but this seems less important than the 4-based interpretation.

Finally, I return to **York 45**, *The Assumption of the Virgin*, which is musically the most important play in the cycle. The notated music for this play is discussed in 3.3. As Carolyn Wall noted, the play divides into 8+8+8 regular stanzas of thirteen lines:[52] the first and last musical items occur at the two main divisions. In the first scene the apostle Thomas wanders alone in the Vale of Jehoshaphat; in the second, he sees and has a conversation with the Blessed Virgin as she is assumed into Heaven, surrounded by angels; and in the third Thomas tells the other apostles what he has seen and shows them the girdle given to him by the Virgin. The beginning and end of the middle scene, a vision of Heaven, are therefore marked out by the angelic music that characterises Heaven.

This middle scene is itself structured symmetrically. Of its eight stanzas the first

---

[51] Verses 3–4, 'To thee all angels cry aloud . . . continually do cry', are introductory of verses 5–8, and were presumably not sung after stanza 3. **1/40+sd** specifies the text starting at 'Sanctus sanctus sanctus . . .'.

[52] Wall 1970, 172.

(stanza 9 of the play) is marked off by music on both sides. It forms a separate sub-scene which, together with the music, makes an integral unit for performance by the twelve choirboys who play the angels. Each angel has one line, with the eighth angel returning at the end of the stanza to deliver the thirteenth line. This stanza, in each line of which the Virgin is addressed, is carefully patterned: each of the first nine lines begins with the word 'Rise', and each of the last four with 'Come'.[53] The third, sixth and eighth stanzas of this middle scene are similarly patterned: the words 'Haile' (twelve lines of stanza 11), 'I thanke þe' (nine lines of stanza 14), and 'Gramercy' and 'Farewele' (four lines and nine lines, respectively, of stanza 16) give a similarly ritualistic feel to the conversation between Mary and Thomas. It is in the first and last stanzas of this scene, stanzas 9 and 16, that the line-openings are entrusted to two words. Even this sub-pattern is symmetrical – 9+4 lines in stanza 9, and 4+9 lines in stanza 16 (i.e. 4^2).[54] In the middle scene the stanzas marked with a 'x' are those not using an initial word or words regularly. The overall symmetricality of the play has a clear parallel in the structuring of the middle scene. It will be safe to assume that the tripartite overall structure was intended as a reference to the Trinity, and it is possible that the number of lines in a stanza, the number of stanzas in a scene, and the overall number of stanzas had some significance for the playwright. For the first of these, perhaps Mary+12 angels=Christ+12 apostles=13.[55]

It remains to say something about the second musical occasion, after stanza 9. This has a representational function in marking the end of the angels-only sub-scene, which in effect is a heavenly vision, and it also has a dynamic function in that it covers Mary's raising from the tomb to some point in mid-air from which she can speak to Thomas. Although the music also divides the middle scene into 1+7 stanzas I am not sure that the proportion 1 : 7 should be considered significant here. Of much more importance, and surely intended by the playwright, is the division of the play as a whole at this point into 9+15 stanzas, a proportion of 3 : 5.[56] The proportion of 3 : 5 may have had some symbolic significance for the playwright: but it is also close to the Golden Section proportion of 0.618 : 1.[57]

I have concentrated on structural issues in this section, using symbolism only to suggest interpretations of observable features of the plays. Such symbolisms as I

---

[53] These translate the Latin 'Surge' and 'Veni' with which the sung texts of this play begin, suggesting that in this case the playwright himself chose the texts to be set. See Plate 4.

[54] The stanza-numbers do not appear in the manuscript, but of course the playwright would be aware of them if he were structuring a play in the kind of way I suggest. See above, for instance, concerning the fourth stanza of **York 1**.

[55] The 13 might have been intended as the sum of 6 (the female marriage number) and 7 (the virgin number), but the line-lengths and rhyme-scheme divide the stanza into 4+4+5 lines, which suggests that this was not in the playwright's mind.

[56] This is the proportion that the composer apparently failed to attain in expanding *Surge* A into *Surge* B (see 3.3, above), but there is no evidence that the playwright knew of the composer's supposed intentions. Although this is a simple proportion, and no doubt desirable for that reason, it has no particular musical significance.

[57] The Golden Section is that division of a length into two parts such that the proportions between the larger and the whole are equal to those between the smaller part and the larger.

TABLE 17 : YORK 45

The Assumption of the Virgin   in 13-line stanzas

scene	1	2	3
lines	1-104	105-208	209-312
	104	104	104
stanzas	8	8	8
	Thomas alone, disconsolate	Vision of Assumption	Thomas and Apostles
	* 1 *	7	*
proportions	9	15	
	3	5	

* = music cue

stanzas 9-16

	angels	Thomas and BVM : girdle						
stanza numbers	9	10	11	12	13	14	15	16
	* Rise Come	* x	Haile	x	x	I thanke	x	Gram'y * Farewell
lines	9+4							4+9

have mentioned may well affect aspects other than structure, however. To take an obvious and important example, the numbers of characters in a play may depend at least partly on numerological considerations. Both **York 35**, *The Crucifixion*, and **York 38**, *The Resurrection*, have four soldiers doing the sinful work of their earthly masters; and in the latter case this is in clear distinction from the three Maries who act as a group on the spiritual side of the cosmic conflict.[58] So far so good: but there are only three soldiers in **York 34**, *The Road to Calvary*, so that the situation is not as simple as might at first appear.[59] This needs investigation, for when the dramatist had to make such a decision he was likely to draw on his knowledge of exegetical writings. He would know, for instance, that 2 is an evil number (because God apparently did not consider the second day's creation to be good: Genesis 1/6–8) and that the separation of the sheep from the goats at the Judgement is prefigured

---

[58] Three magi and three shepherds also represent this spiritual side of mankind in various plays (not just at York), as do the three Children of Israel in **York 11**, *Moses and Pharaoh*.

[59] This is true also of **Towneley 22**, *The Scourging*.

by Adam's two sons.[60] We should undoubtedly understand, then, that when we find that Pharaoh's henchmen are two Consolatores and two Egiptii in **York 11**, *Moses and Pharaoh*, their evil character is presented to us at the outset by the playwright. Again, there are problems with the number 2 in various parts of the repertory, and careful interpretation is needed: but we can probably accept the most basic hypothesis, that numbers of characters do sometimes act as a key to their moral state and therefore to their affiliation in the cosmic battle.

There is undoubtedly more to learn about the York cycle through studies of its numerology. There are several other plays that exhibit features similar to those of plays studied here, and a fuller mathematical investigation of these is needed. Meanwhile my brief examination has attempted to demonstrate something of the range of considerations taken into account by some fifteenth-century playwrights in structuring a play, the way in which the provision of music may affect that structure, and – most important of all, I think – the use of music *by the playwright* as a means of creating a structure that would otherwise not exist.

---

[60] See Butler *Number Symbolism*, 73.

7

MUSIC AND LITURGY

7.1 The liturgical background

Biblical drama, by its nature, dramatises narratives found in the Scriptures. It is therefore natural to assume that the biblical plays are primarily dramatisations of the scriptural texts themselves. To a large extent this is true, and the relations between biblical narrative and drama are often close. There are however two important qualifications to this general statement. The first is that the fleshing-out process, by which the biblical narrative is given the necessary dramatic detail not found in the Scriptures, involves the assimilation of material from a variety of sources such as biblical commentaries and glosses, homiletic writings, and so on – the kind of material in which the main biblical narratives are explained, amplified and presented for the edification of the relatively unlearned. The second is that even the biblical plays use narrative material that is not found in the Bible at all, such as the events surrounding the death of the Blessed Virgin: and here we find a similar use of non-biblical material such as the *Golden Legend* and the martyrologies. These two qualifications are of course very closely related: they are really versions of one another. In this matter, too, there is really no substantive difference between the biblical plays and the other religious plays: some saint plays use biblical narrative that has to be expanded, and all types of play use non-biblical material that has to be found in other sources. Indeed, all the religious plays include episodes that must be composed *ab initio*, such as *diableries* and – especially in the moral plays – the working-out of abstract theological ideas. In this chapter, therefore, no further distinctions will be made between biblical, hagiographic and moral *genres*, even though certain discussions may be more relevant to some than to others.

An important source of material is liturgy. The textual relations between the Bible and the Liturgy are complex. The great majority of liturgical texts are, of course, biblical in origin: but they do not always correspond to the texts of the main Latin bible of the Middle Ages, St Jerome's Vulgate translation, being derived from earlier Latin versions. At the same time the liturgical texts, being divorced from their biblical context, are sometimes compiled from two or more sources; the wording may be slightly changed in order to make them immediately relevant to the liturgical context; and Alleluias or other additional text may be incorporated. It is not enough to identify the biblical source for a Latin text in the plays, therefore, which may itself be a difficult process: one also needs to know if the quotation is a biblical one in the narrowest sense or a liturgical one; and if the latter is the case the text must be fully identified. The primary reason for this is simple: the Vulgate was usually spoken, the liturgy usually sung, so that the identity of any Latin quotation in the plays has an immediate bearing on its method of performance in the play. In addition, however, any one text-incipit may be shared by several liturgical items, often with their own chants, so that a full identification is needed before one can make a proper choice of musical setting; and, finally, any liturgical item may exist in several slightly different versions, according to different liturgical uses.

What makes a search for liturgical content relevant in the first place? The immediate answer is that there are so many examples of Latin *incipits* to be sung in the plays (usually appearing as SDs or text references) that we should think in terms of liturgy for them even without the occasional identification of the text as an antiphon, hymn, or other liturgical type. The Bible very rarely says that a particular text was sung, so the singing of a Latin text is likely to signal the use of a liturgical item. In addition, the precise wording may be that of the liturgy, not the Vulgate. As we shall see in section 7.3, the angelic Gloria is a rather special case, with a semi-dramatic liturgical form that no doubt made it an obvious choice for musical treatment in the plays: but it is not a unique example of a liturgical text appropriated for use in a narrative dramatic context.

Not all Latin quotations are to be sung, however, and part of the reason for identifying each one accurately is to ensure the correct distribution of singing and speech. Leaving aside those quotations that are prescribed to be sung and/or are described as a particular liturgical type, Latin quotations can still present problems that effectively preclude a firm decision. As we have already seen, it is sometimes hard to know whether a Latin quotation should be heard at all, since some were almost certainly included as theological justification for the play's content, or perhaps a note of the way the dramatist went to work: in either case, these are in the nature of scholarly footnotes, and are there for the reader to read, not for the actor to speak. This problem is discussed by Lumiansky and Mills in their work on the Chester Cycle but has not been solved for other plays. Lumiansky and Mills also identify a category of Latin quotations in which the actor does indeed speak the line, apparently giving his audience the relevant text – much as a text is given at the beginning of a sermon – as authority for that part of the play. These categories sometimes overlap, in situations which seem deliberately to offer a producer alternative choices. This is clear in places in the Chester Cycle, but it therefore demands a *caveat* in other plays: if alternative options can be seen in the Chester plays, where several sources exist, some such indication of alternative options may be lost in those cases where only one play-text survives.

Biblical narrative, then, the ostensible source for a dramatic episode, is often not the real source at all. In such a case the dramatic details of the narrative presentation may be wholly dictated by the form and content of the liturgical item concerned. As a general statement this is of course very uneven in its provability, and some surprising examples even turn out not to be based on liturgy. For instance, the general theory would suggest Christ's breaking of bread and offering of wine at the Last Supper as an episode likely to be decisively influenced by liturgy, the institution of the Eucharist being actively commemorated in every celebration of Mass. But, as

I shall show in section 7.6, this episode is not obviously based on the liturgical celebration. On the other hand the episode of the washing of the disciples' feet does seem to be based on liturgy in at least some of the plays.[1]

The liturgical background that can be seen in so many plays is hardly surprising. Anyone capable of writing a play in the fourteenth or fifteenth centuries could be counted a well-educated man: certainly all the plays dealt with here are the work of highly trained and educated playwrights. Such education was largely the preserve of an environment in which the full daily round of the liturgy was an integral part of life – monastic schools and the like – so that clerics and religious form the basis of the class in which dramatists would be found. Thomas Binham, the Dominican who composed the Beverley banns in 1423, and William Peers, the Earl of Northumberland's secretary responsible for the revisions to the same cycle in 1520, both belonged to that category.[2] Only around the latter date, well into the sixteenth century, would bourgeois and secular education probably be sufficient for the purpose: Robert Croo, who revised plays at Coventry in 1534, may have been an example of such education, although too little is known about him for certainty. It is perhaps hard for us to realise how little even educated men read the Bible itself: certainly there was a general move towards Bible-reading and a wider knowledge of the Scriptures long before Croo's time, but in practice most men, however well educated, gained their most direct knowledge of scripture from the liturgy. We should remember, too, that even the liturgical readings (which are generally short in any case) included passages from the saints' lives and from sermons and other homiletic material. In these circumstances it is hardly surprising that scripture, liturgy, saints' lives and other material were not always clearly distinguished, nor that the Scriptures should often be seen, as it were, through a liturgical filter.

The use of biblical and liturgical texts by the dramatists may usefully be categorised as follows:

(1)   A biblical text is accurately quoted. The quotation may be for purposes of authority, and may or may not be spoken in the play.

(2)   A biblical text is quoted inaccurately, being contaminated by a liturgical text that the dramatist remembers subconsciously.

(3)   The dramatist deliberately uses a liturgical text. In Latin, this must be chosen in preference to the Vulgate version, in which case the dramatist presumably intended the text to be sung in performance. In English, it may be a translation or (expanded) paraphrase; or the quotation of a part of the liturgy normally performed in the vernacular.

(4)   A liturgical text that derives from the biblical narrative (e.g. *Magnificat*) is used at the relevant place in the drama. Here, too, the text may be intended for sung performance in the play.

---

[1]   See 7.6, below. 'Liturgy' is here used in a loose sense, of ritual and ceremonial carried out in the church building.

[2]   See Wyatt *Beverley*, l–li; for Binham, see also Lancashire *Dramatic Texts*, 82. These matters are discussed also in Volume 2.

(5)   A liturgical ceremony takes the place of the biblical narrative on which the ceremony is based (see sections 7.6 and 7.7, for instance).

(6)   An actual liturgical ceremony is part of the drama, and its text, perhaps altered to suit the dramatic context, is performed as part of the drama (see section 7.3).

All of the above situations are met with in the plays. A dramatist could look for a Latin text in the Vulgate, but this was probably unusual: it is more reasonable to assume that when he needed a quotation from the scriptures, or the incipit of a liturgical item, he would search first his memory and then the liturgical books to hand. Thus if he was a secular cleric we may expect liturgical quotations to belong to the relevant diocesan use; if a religious, then the use of his order. The Latin quotations in a play therefore act as possible indicators of the liturgy of the dramatist's education and/or of his location at the time. This matter is discussed further in section 7.9.

7.2 The Presentation in the Temple

The Presentation of Mary in the Temple at the age of three is treated in only one English play, the fifteenth-century *Mary Play*. The text survives as N-Town pageant 9, which becomes **Mary Play 224–593** in Meredith's edition. Joachim and Anna, who have vowed to present their first-born child to the Lord, decide that Mary is now old enough to be taken to the Temple. They approach the chief priest, Isakar, and explain their purpose. Mary asks her parents for their blessings, which they give, and then climbs the fifteen steps of the Temple. She is welcomed by Isakar, who explains the two commandments that replace the Decalogue and introduces her to the five maidens and seven priests who will help and teach her. After bidding her parents farewell, Mary prays briefly and is ministered to by an angel. When food is brought to her from Isakar Mary, having no need of it, gives it to the poor.

The identifiable liturgical material in this play falls into three categories:

(1)   The blessings given by Joachim and Anna separately to Mary, and by Isakar to the assembled company;

(2)   The incipits of the fifteen gradual psalms, which Mary briefly explains; and

(3)   The angelic singing of the hymn *Jesu corona virginum*.

Of these, (1) will be discussed in section 7.8, below.

The feast of the Presentation of the Blessed Virgin in the Temple is a recent innovation in the western church, having been introduced to the West on 21 November 1372 in the church of the Friars Minor at Avignon. The acceptance and celebration of the feast was organised by Philippe de Mézières, who also wrote the office for the feast and a drama that was performed on that first occasion.[3] By early

---

[3] The office and drama can be found, with a brief but very useful introduction, in Coleman

in the sixteenth century the feast was celebrated in England, on 21 November. This play seems to take nothing from the liturgy of the new feast, however: the hymn *Jesu corona virginum* is set for the Common of a Virgin and Martyr and not for the feast of the Presentation, and the gradual psalms as such have no place in that feast either.[4] Perhaps in the late fifteenth century the feast was still not sufficiently established in England for liturgical material to be an obvious source for a dramatic presentation.[5]

It has been suggested that the Vespers lessons for the feast in the Sarum rite played some part in the composition of the play,[6] and certainly the *Gesta de praesentatione beatae Mariae* read at Second Vespers could have been used by the playwright.[7] Another possibility was put forward by Raymond St-Jacques, who suggested that the office of the Consecration of Virgins was a source for the play.[8] St-Jacques based his theory on the many 'interesting parallels, too numerous to be simply coinciden-tal' that emerged when he compared the play to the office. These can be grouped as follows:

(1) The blessing at the end of the ceremony, which likens the postulants to the Virgin Mary;

(2) The 'calls' to Mary in the drama (**N-Town 9/57, 94: Mary Play 310, 347**), which St-Jacques relates to those in the liturgy;

(3) Mary's white clothing in the play (**N-Town 9/17+sd: Mary Play 270+sd**), which parallels the white vestments of the postulants in the liturgical ceremony;

(4) (a) The names of the five maidens who are to look after Mary, which St-Jacques relates to the specific virtues that in the ceremony the abbess is directed to maintain in the postulants; and
(b) The names of the seven priests who are to instruct Mary, which St-Jacques relates to the seven Gifts of the Holy Spirit as enumerated in the blessing at the end of the liturgy;

(5) The reference to Mary as God's wife (**N-Town 9/33: Mary Play 286**), which can be compared with the 'wedding' of each postulant to Christ in the liturgy; and

(6) The bishop's words to Mary, reminding her of the Commandments, and her duties to hate evil and to serve God, which St-Jacques compares to the list

---

Philippe de Mézières' Campaign. Information on the history of the feast in this paragraph is taken from Coleman's work.

4 The Sarum office for the feast of the Presentation is in BS II, 330–52; for the hymn see BS II, 448.

5 On the probable sources of the play, see Meredith *Mary Play*, 16 and 95; Spector *N-Town* II, 441–3; and St-Jacques 'Mary in the Temple'.

6 Marjorie Downing, *The Influence of the Liturgy on the English Cycle Plays* (dissertation, Yale University, 1942), 211, cited in St-Jacques 'Mary in the Temple', 295 and n. 1. Unfortunately I have not been able to consult Downing's work.

7 BS II, 345–9, and especially 348–9.

8 St-Jacques 'Mary in the Temple' (1980).

of duties and virtues to be maintained by the postulants and enumerated by the bishop in the liturgy.

The theory that N-Town 9 is partly based on, or at least significantly informed by, the liturgy for the Consecration of Virgins is a credible one that deserves further analysis. I shall not undertake this here, for no music is involved in the play, but there are certainly other parallels to be drawn between play and liturgy. One of these is Anne's question to Mary 'Wole 3e be pure maydyn . . .' and her reply (**N-Town 9/33–6: Mary Play 286–9**), which could derive directly from the bishop's question to the postulants in the liturgy, 'Vultis in sanctae virginitatis proposito perseverare?' (response, 'Volumus', and that to each postulant individually, 'Promittis te virgini-tatem perpetuo servare?' (response, 'Promitto').[9] Another point that must be ex-plored is Mary's answer to the second part of this question, ' . . . and also Goddys wyff?' (**N-Town 9/33: Mary Play 286**), to which she replies that she is unworthy (**N-Town 9/37ff: Mary Play 290ff**). This reply is the fore-runner of Joseph's response when he is asked if he will marry Mary herself in the next play (**N-Town 10/304–5: Mary Play 877–8**), a matter that we shall discuss in section 7.8.

It must be said that all of the similarities cited by St-Jacques could easily be explained in terms of standard theological ideas and the normal textual relation-ships that they engendered. It nevertheless seems to me that he was probably right in this matter, and that there is room for a fuller comparison between the play and the Latin liturgy of the Consecration of Virgins. But St-Jacques invoked a more specific correlation, between the play and the English version of this liturgy in the Russell pontifical (c.1480?), and this raises a second layer of questions. Does a correlation of wording suggest a direct connection between play and English liturgy (taking into account the changes demanded by versification and the different presentational circumstances), or can we realistically suggest only that an indirect use of the Latin liturgy by the playwright would anyway result in a similar wording to that of the English liturgy? This is an impossible question to answer (although it will arise again in section 7.8), and at present I wish only to offer St-Jacques's comparisons as possible evidence for my main thesis in this chapter, that play-wrights quoted, translated and paraphrased the liturgy often when it suited their need for dramatic material.

The question of the fifteen gradual psalms in N-Town 9 is a less important matter liturgically, although it has a greater bearing on musical performance in that play. These psalms, numbers 119–133 (AV 120–134), are all – as *The Catholic Encyclopedic Dictionary* has it – 'expressive of trust in God'.[10] In the Sarum use they were not recited straight through as a set, and nothing in the play connects these psalms with a liturgical context.[11] Meredith notes, however, that they appeared in primers as a

---

[9] I take this from a Pontifical in my possession published by Plantin at Antwerp in 1627 (p. 139), but this part of the office was probably standard.

[10] Attwater *The Catholic Encyclopaedic Dictionary*, 229–30. A more detailed commentary on the individual psalms as applied to Mary's situation is given by Meredith in *Mary Play*, 16.

[11] It is possible that the gradual psalms were considered as a group earlier in England, however:

group taking up a separate section, which is in accordance with their use in this play by a young learning person.[12]

Mary deals with the psalms, one at a time as she ascends the steps: there are fifteen steps and one psalm for each. In every case she gives a brief explanation of the psalm, followed by a paraphrase of its opening, after which the first verse (or, when the first verse is long, the first half of the first verse) is presented in Latin. As we should expect, the Latin lines are copied in a more formal, liturgical, script with decorative rubricated initials.[13] It is not made explicit that Mary recites the Latin lines, although they are in the text area used by the English speeches. While it is possible that the Latin is intended as an authority only, and not to be spoken, therefore, one can hardly avoid the inference that it was meant to be heard. This matter is discussed further in Volume 2.

7.3 The angelic announcement to the shepherds

The story of the angel's announcement to the shepherds at the Nativity is one of the best-known scriptural passages: it is quoted below, in section 8.4. The angel of the Lord appears to the shepherds and gives them the specific message that the Messiah is born and tells them where to find him. The message given, the heavenly host praise God in a hymn which has found its way into various parts of the liturgy:

> Gloria in altissimis deo,
> et in terra pax hominibus bone voluntatis. (Luke 2/14)

This is the Vulgate version: the wording used in the liturgy is an older version that has 'excelsis' for 'altissimis'. In all of the plays (and in most other contexts, such as the scrolls in painted windows) it is this earlier version that is used.[14] The implication of this is, not surprisingly, that those responsible for the texts used in plays, windows, and so on, were more conversant with the liturgy than with the Vulgate version of the Bible, at least in regard to such well-known texts as this.

'Gloria in excelsis deo . . . voluntatis' appears with no additions in only one place in the liturgy, namely as the verse of the first responsory, 'Hodie nobis celorum rex', at mattins on Christmas Day:[15]

Hughes *Medieval Manuscripts*, 374 (under n. 17), gives a reference for these psalms being distinguished in English psalters of the tenth and eleventh centuries.

12 Meredith *Mary Play*, 16 and 95.

13 See the facsimile, MDF 4, ff. 44r–45r.

14 Further on this, see Rastall 'Musical Repertory', 166–8.

15 This version is taken from AS 47: BS I, clxxiv, has 'caelestia regna' (and modern orthography throughout). The Benedictus antiphon *Gloria in excelsis deo* sets the same text, but with two Alleluias: see AS 53. There is no evidence that the Benedictus antiphon affected the biblical plays.

7.3 The Angelic Announcement to the Shepherds

R   Hodie nobis celorum rex de virgine nasci dignatus est: ut hominem perditum
     ad regna celestia revocaret: gaudet excercitus angelorum. Quia salus eterna
     humano generi apparuit.

V   Gloria in excelsis deo: et in terra pax hominibus bone voluntatis. Quia.

In the York use the repeat is from 'Gaudet', which emphasises the element of
heavenly rejoicing.[16]

In the Salisbury use this verse was performed in a particularly dramatic fashion
by five choristers, as the rubric shows:[17]

Iste Versus subsequens cantetur a quinque Pueris in superpelliciis et amictis albis
capitibus velatis, cereosque accensos singulis deferentibus in loco eminenti, scilicet
ultra magnum altare: ad chorum conversi cantent similiter hunc Versum.

The three important elements here are the white vestments, the lighted candles that
the boys hold, and the positioning of the boys 'in a high place' above the high altar.
White vestments are common for the lowest orders of angels in medieval iconography, and they perhaps have a second function here in being a better reflector of
light than the richly-coloured copes sometimes worn by the more senior orders.[18]
Light is an important symbolism in the Nativity, and the first reading of Christmas
mattins, immediately preceding this responsory, is Isaiah's prophecy of the Messiah's coming (Isaiah 9/1–8),[19] which includes (verse 2)

Populus qui ambulabat in tenebris vidit lucem magnam. Habitantibus in regione
umbre mortis, lux orta est eis.

(The people that walked in darkness have seen a great light: they that dwell in the
land of the shadow of death, upon them hath the light shined.)

In St Luke's account of the nativity (2/9) it is the *claritas Dei* – 'the glory of the Lord'
– that 'shone round about' the shepherds. In dramatic presentation this glory is
represented by light. Mention of light in a shepherds' or nativity play does not
necessarily imply that the Star of Bethlehem is visible, therefore, as we noticed in
section 6.3.[20]

Putting these elements together with the placing of the boys high up above the
altar, it seems clear that, whatever the theological justifications put forward for this
performance-method, there is a strong element of representation. The visual impact

---

[16] BE I, 78: this also reads 'regna celestia'.
[17] This version is from BS I, clxxiv: the version in AS 47 is substantially the same, although the
vestments are not specified as white. A more elaborate ceremony, with seven boys, was enacted
at Exeter, but the plays do not seem to take anything from that version: see Harrison *Music in
Medieval Britain*, 107.
[18] On angelic vestments, see Rastall 'Musical repertory', 173–84, *passim*; and also, in the same
volume, Clifford Davidson's comments on pp. 17–18.
[19] This is so in both the Salisbury and York uses: see BS I, clxxiii, and BE 78.
[20] Concerning the division at the mid-point of **York 14**. In this play and in **N-Town 15** the light
seems to be transferred to the figure of Christ himself, however: see especially **N-Town
15/162–77**. **N-Town 15/178–9** identifies this light as 'The might of the Godhead' that 'will not
be hid'.

257

of a group of candle-bearing choristers, wearing white, appearing high up in the gloom of a dimly-lit cathedral around midnight on Christmas Eve must have been very great: and their singing of the angelic *Gloria in excelsis deo* must surely have been perceived by the congregation as a dramatic representation of the event narrated by St Luke.

Medieval composers tended to set solo sections of the liturgy to part-music, and there are several polyphonic settings of the verse *Gloria in excelsis*. Because it is not the start of the piece – the respond itself is sung as the first section of the responsory – the polyphonic verse does not have a solo intonation and the polyphony starts straight off with the word 'Gloria'. This is quite different from settings of the Gloria of the Mass, where the 'Gloria . . . bone voluntatis' text is the opening of the piece: in that case the words 'Gloria in excelsis deo' are sung as a plainsong intonation, the choral monody or the polyphony beginning at 'Et in terra pax'. Polyphonic settings of the responsory-verse are nearly always based on the chant, but this is not usually noticeable until the words 'Et in terra', where the chant tune becomes more individual. In the opening phrase the chant is not characterised by easily-recognisable intervals or direction, and composers probably felt that they had a free hand to write interesting polyphony independently of the chant, as long as the piece was in the right mode. The tune was shown as the first part of Example 39, in section 3.5.[21]

'Gloria in excelsis' is the only unchanging feature in the English shepherds' plays. The plays vary in whether the angel speaks to the shepherds before or after the Gloria, but the Gloria itself is invariably the responsory-verse text. It is reasonable, then, to suppose that the liturgy may well offer us some guidance as to how the Gloria was performed dramatically. We may guess that the singer or singers stood in a raised place, on a waggon or high-level stage (according to the main form of staging being used), costumed in white vestments, probably in gold masks, and brightly illuminated by artificial light. Although dramatic requirements might have demanded some methods not used in liturgy, we should expect the visual and audible effect of this scene to be recognisably related to that of the singing of the first responsory at mattins on Christmas Day.

7.4 The Purification

The Jewish rite of purification is set out in Leviticus 12/1–8. This requires that on the birth of a male child a woman shall be deemed unclean for seven days; that the child shall be circumcised on the eighth day; that on the fortieth day after the birth she shall bring to the temple a lamb for a burnt offering and a pigeon or a turtle-dove for a sin-offering; that these shall be brought to the door of the temple, and offered by the priest; and that if, on account of poverty, she cannot bring a lamb, then she shall bring two doves or pigeons, one for the burnt offering and the other for the

---

[21] See my comments on the Gloria setting in Cambridge Add. MS 5943 in section 2.4, above. On the polyphonic setting of *Gloria in excelsis*, see Harrison *Music in Medieval Britain*, 367.

sin-offering. This law is cited by Joseph and Mary in all of the Purification plays: and all show that, being poor, they bring two birds rather than the larger sacrifice. The Law in fact requires only the mother to attend, but the plays need Joseph there as well. The requirement of the Law is modified by heavenly decree on this occasion, therefore:

> [GABEREEL]   But leyve nott ye wold Josoff at whome
> For nedely, lade, he mvste be won
> In this sacrefyce doyng.   (**Coventry 2/380–2**)

But probably it was quite normal for the father to be present at the offering. St Luke gives no explanation for Joseph's presence, presumably because none was required:

> Et postquam impleti sunt dies purgationis eius secundum legem Moysi tulerunt illum in iherusalem, ut sisterent eum domino: sicut scriptum est in lege domini. Quia omne masculinum adaperiens vuluam, sanctum domino vocabitur.
> (**Luke 2/22–3**)

> (And when the days of her purification according to the law of Moses were accomplished, they brought him to Jerusalem to present him to the Lord; (As it is written in the law of the Lord, Every male that openeth the womb shall be called holy to the Lord) . . .)

This passage also shows that Christ himself was an offering. The scripture cited is Exodus 13/1–2 and 11–12, which prescribes how the first-born male – of either beast or man – shall be the Lord's. The phrase used in Exodus 13/12 is 'consecrabis domino', which clearly means (verse 13) a burnt offering of the beast concerned. Our modern understanding of the Authorized Version's 'present' in Luke 2/22 is weaker than 'ut sisterunt eum domino' suggests: the verb *sisto* implies some mutual obligation, as in a lovers' tryst, or a compulsion on one side, as in an appearance in a court of law. The second of these is in operation here. In the Coventry Purification play Gabriel speaks of the Child as one of three offerings, the doves being the other two:

> [GABEREEL]   Unto the tempull thatt þou schuldist goo,
> And to whyt turtuls with the also,
> And present the chyld and them to,
> All iij of them in offeryng.   (**Coventry 2/375–8**)

In the York Purification play Joseph explains the Law which makes it possible for them to offer two doves instead of a lamb and a dove, and continues:

> [JOSEPH]   And yf we haue not both in feer,
> The lame, the burd, as ryche men haue,
> Thynke that vs muste present here
> Oure babb Jesus, as we voutsaue
> Before Godes sight.
>   He is our lame, Mary, kare the not,
>   For riche and power none better soght;
>   Full well thowe hais hym hither broght,
> This our offerand right.

He is the lame of God I say,
That all our syns shall take away
    of this worlde here.
He is the lame of God verray
That muste hus fend frome all our fray,
. . .
                                                            (York 17/254–67)

The offering of the Christ-child, the Lamb of God, is actually a sacrifice, then. In the N-Town play Mary's speech of offering is made explicit by a direction that 'Mari leyth þe childe on þe Autre' (**N-Town 19/176+sd**), by Joseph's subsequent payment of five pence to redeem the child (**19/177–80**), and by the priest's insistence that the other sacrifices be made (**19/181–3**).[22] Since the play ends with the sacrifice of the two birds on the altar, the offering of the Child would probably be understood by a Christian audience as a type of the Mass.

In the Jewish rite the offerings were accepted by the priest at the Gate of Nicanor and taken by him to the altar to be offered on the woman's behalf. Women were not allowed beyond the Court of the Women: but standing at the Gate, at the top of the Levites' Steps, the woman could see her offering being made on her behalf.[23] After the sacrifice had been made, the priest returned to the woman and effected the purification by sprinkling her with the blood of the offering. The medieval Christian office of Purification apparently derives from this, but was modified in various ways. The priest and his ministers met the woman at the church door, where two psalms were recited and some prayers read:[24] but then the woman was sprinkled with holy water and the priest led her by the right hand into the church, saying:

Ingredere in templum dei vt habeas vitam eternam et viuas in secula seculorum. amen.

In a version of the Salisbury *Ordo ad Purificandum Mulierem* published at Douai in 1604 the woman is required to hold a lighted candle. The Douai print is said to be a reprint of earlier Salisbury offices, *secundum antiquam Angliae consuetudinem –* 'according to the ancient custom of England'.[25] If that is correct, this feature of the office of Purification was perhaps a late medieval one, which would partly explain why Joseph offers a candle 'of virgin waxe' in the Chester Purification (**Chester 11/144**). The explanation given there is however that the purity of the wax symbolises the purity of Mary.

Thus far the action of the plays seems to follow the liturgical structure, at least in so far as the Christian office of Purification contains features of the Jewish rite. There are however two major modifying factors. First, the biblical narrative shows that the liturgical ceremony was interrupted by Simeon, an elderly and good man who

---

[22] The redeeming of the Child by the offering of five coins is explained in LA 161, GL 150.
[23] It was at the fifteen Steps of the Levites that the Levites sang the gradual psalms during the Feast of Tabernacles: see Edersheim *The Temple*, 48–50 for the topography of the Court of the Women, and 344–5 for the office of purification.
[24] The *Ordo ad Purificandum Mulierem* . . . of the Sarum use is in MS 43–4.
[25] MS xxiii and 44, n. 1.

had been told that he would not die until he had seen the Messiah (Luke 2/25–35), and by the prophetess Anna, who also gave thanks for the coming of the Christ (Luke 2/36–38). In the plays too, therefore, the liturgical structure of the office of Purification is invaded – indeed, apparently replaced – by the episode with Simeon and Anna, in which the former sings the *Nunc dimittis*. Some of the dramatists evidently found it convenient to amalgamate roles by having Simeon be the priest in charge of the temple, an easy change to make in view of the importance of Simeon's intervention in the narrative as a whole. Second, neither the psalms nor the prayers associated with the occasional office of Purification are to be found in the plays. Rather, there are texts and references pointing to the liturgy of Candlemas, the feast of the Purification of the Virgin (2 February), and in particular to the procession before Mass on that day.[26] The procession on the feast of the Purification had the special feature that 'the whole choir – and the people when the procession was public – carried lighted candles'.[27] It is this feature that gave the name of Candlemas to the feast.

There are six Purification plays: York 17, N-Town 19, Towneley 17, Digby, Coventry 2 and Chester 11. Of these, the York, N-Town and Coventry plays have no title; Towneley 17 has the heading *Purificacio Marie*, and Chester 11 is entitled *De Purificatione Beatae Virginis*. The composite Digby play is however headed *Candelmas Day & the Kyllyng of þe Childre[n] of Israell*, which indicates an association with the liturgy of the feast of the Purification. Of all the plays it is the Digby one that shows the most obviously liturgical content: on taking the Child in his arms Simeon recites *Nunc dimittis* in English (**Killing 445–60**), Anna brings the virgins of the temple to worship the Child, bearing wax tapers (presumably lit) in their hands (**Killing 461–4**), and then there is a procession about the temple while *Nunc dimittis* is sung by the virgins. This last element is unusual, in that it is elsewhere Simeon who sings *Nunc dimittis*, just as it is he who recites it in the biblical narrative.

This procession apparently includes all present, although that is not stated clearly. Simeon states his intention to 'go procession' in worshipping the Child (**Killing 470**) and Mary and Joseph both agree, Joseph apparently including them all:

JOSEPH   In worshippe of oure child with gret devossion,
         Abought þe tempille in ordire let vs go.   (**Killing 475–6**)

'In order' seems to imply a degree of formality and the use of a known procedure. Simeon calls on the virgins to be prepared to sing, states his intention of carrying the Child in procession, and finally tells the virgins to sing *Nunc dimittis* (**Killing 477–84**). This text is followed by an equivocal direction:

here shal Symeon bere Jhesu in his armys goyng a procession rounde aboute þe tempill & al þis wyle þe virgynis synge nunc dimittis . . .   (**Killing 484+sd**)

This cannot be taken at face value, since it leaves Mary and Joseph out of account

---

[26] The procession is in PS(P) 134v–140v and in PS(H) 139–44.
[27] Bailey *Processions of Sarum*, 115.

and has Simeon processing alone with the Child in his arms. Equally, there seems no sense in having Mary and Joseph in the procession with Simeon and the Child if the virgins are static while they sing *Nunc dimittis*. If we put together the various elements – the procession, the choir singing *Nunc dimittis* and the lighted tapers – we surely have the liturgical procession of Candlemas Day, which would be a good reason for the play bearing that heading. Moreover, Simeon explains the symbolism of the wax, wick and flame of the tapers, so that the candles (which they clearly are, therefore) have an important role to play and must surely have been in the procession.

The Digby play does not say that Simeon is the priest of the temple, but certainly the cast includes no priest otherwise to accept the offerings. The N-Town Purification play, on the other hand, shows Simeon to be what Luke 2/25 states, a just and devout man of Jerusalem, and the play includes a *capellanus* who receives the offerings. Here, too, it seems that Simeon is not the singer of *Nunc dimittis*, in contravention of the biblical narrative:

> *Nunc dimittis seruum tuum Domine et cetera.*
>
> *The psalme songyn every vers and þerqwyl Symeon pleyth with þe child . . .*
> (N-Town 19/146+sds)

He does however recite an English version of the canticle immediately after this (**N-Town 19/147–54**).

Another liturgical item is named rather earlier in the play, soon after Simeon has accepted the Child in his arms (**N-Town 19/136+sd**). The play text does not say that this is sung, but it is hard to see why the *incipit* is given otherwise. *Suscepimus Deus misericordiam tuam* is a text found in different guises: it is a short antiphon used at Christmas and the feast of the Circumcision,[28] but it is also, more relevantly, and with longer texts, both the introit and the gradual at Mass on the feast of the Purification.[29] Of these, the text of the gradual is translated in the speech that Simeon makes immediately after the presumed singing of *Suscepimus Deus*, whereas the extra text found in the introit is not translated there:

> [SYMEON] Lord God in mageste,
> We haue receyvyd þis day of þe
> In myddys of þi temple here
> Thy grett mercy, as we may se.
> Therfore þi name of grett degre
> Be wurchepyd in all manere
> Over all þis werde, bothe fer and nere,
> 3evyn onto þe vterest ende. (N-Town 19/137–44)

Suscepimus Deus misericordiam tuam in medio templi tui [end of antiphon text] secundum nomen tuum domine ['deus' in the introit] ita et laus tua in fines terre [end of the gradual text, followed by the psalm verse 'Sicut audivimus'] iusticia plena est dextera tua [end of introit].

[28] AS 48 and 77.
[29] See GS plate j. The introit is used also for the 8th Sunday after Trinity: GS 149.

It seems clear from this that the gradual is the version translated, and therefore presumably the item sung at **19/136+lat**. It should be noted here that the psalm verse is a formally separate item to which the text in question is an antiphon with a musically independent setting.

We can go further in identifying the liturgical position of Latin items in this play. *Nunc dimittis* occurs twice in the liturgy of the Purification. During the distribution of the candles before the procession it is sung under the antiphon 'Lumen ad revelationem gentium', which is not the case in any of the plays.[30] The only occasion when it is sung straight through is as the tract during Mass. In fact, when the tract is sung (rather than the Alleluia), the gradual and tract will be sung in immediate succession, as the texts are in this play.[31] It may be that the dramatist, deliberately giving such prominence to the subject of sacrifice in this play, wanted Mass chants here as a reference to the Mass recognisable to the audience.

Neither the gradual nor the tract is a congregational chant, and both demand a trained choir. A production of the N-Town play therefore needs a group of singers that does not appear in the named cast and is not mentioned in the text. The virgins who sing in the Digby play must be a trained choir: and in fact we should expect that these roles would be taken by boy choristers, who would be trained in plainsong. The Digby play does presumably show that strict liturgical propriety is not necessary, however, if the tract *Nunc dimittis* was sung in procession. It may be that the absence of a specified antiphon should not be taken as positive evidence in this case, and that the musical director of the Digby play was free to choose the processional version, with the antiphon, if he so wished.

Of the other Purification plays, the York one has least liturgical content. Simeon does recite an English version of *Nunc dimittis* (**York 17/415–24**), but there is no indication that a liturgical item is sung: and in fact if the Latin were sung immediately before the English text it would have to be in mid-stanza, which seems unlikely. The Towneley play is unfortunately incomplete, a gap of two leaves occurring just before the meeting of Simeon with the Holy Family, with the loss of the rest of this play as well as the opening of the next. What we have uses some business with the temple bells, which ring of their own accord to welcome the Christ, and has angels singing *Simeon justus et timoratus* for the second angelic appearance to Simeon (**Towneley 17/102+sd, 132+sd**). It is not clear whether there is a separate angelic choir in the heaven or the piece is sung by the two angels who speak to Simeon. *Simeon justus et timoratus* is set as both a responsory and an antiphon in the liturgy of the Purification: either would be musically self-sufficient, with a choice in the case of the responsory of singing the complete responsory or only the respond itself, finishing before the verse.

The Coventry Weavers' play is also affected by a missing leaf. The lacuna occurs just as Simeon has taken the Child to the altar, where he may be about to sing *Nunc dimittis*. In this play Simeon is the priest – Joseph addresses him as 'gentill

---

[30] PS(P) 138r.
[31] GS plates j and k.

bysschope' (**Coventry 2/650**) – and he has an unspecified number of clerks to help him: only one of these is a speaking role. The clerks are responsible for ringing the bells to welcome Christ (**Coventry 2/624, 633**), and they also sing twice (**2/636+md, 694+md**). Both occasions of singing are either immediately before or during a procession: the first, the procession of priest and clerks to meet the Holy Family; the second, Simeon's move to the altar – presumably a procession – with the Child in his arms. These could be liturgical items, and perhaps were so at some stage in the play's history. As the play has come to us, however, there are two song texts at the end which, *prima facie*, are to be associated with the play and could arguably be intended for these two occasions. As discussed in section 2.6, above, however, there is a question of directorial amendment over the placing of the first song, while the second song text seems not wholly suitable for this play. For the present, this problem may be insoluble.

Finally, in the Chester Purification play Simeon apparently sings *Nunc dimittis* before speaking an English version of it (**Chester 11/166+sd, 167–174**). There is no indication of movement around the acting area, however, so that it is impossible to know where the dramatist expected any processions to take place. In addition, part of Simeon's speech shortly before this seems a clear reference – it is hardly a translation – to the opening of the liturgical text *Senex puerum portabat*, which occurs both as the Benedictus antiphon and (in the monastic use of Worcester) as a responsory in the liturgy for the Purification.[32]

> [SIMEON]   Though I bere thee nowe, sweete wight,
> thou rulest mee as yt is right;
> . . .   (**Chester 11/159–60**)

Senex puerum portabat; puer autem senem regebat . . .

This seems quite insufficient evidence for suggesting that one of the *Senex puerum portabat* pieces was performed after **11/158**, and it is probable only that the playwright merely found it convenient to think in terms of one of the liturgical texts for the occasion. A similar consideration, and perhaps not even a conscious one on the dramatist's part, may inform the direction before this speech:

> *Tunc Simeon accipiet puerum in ulnas.*   (**Chester 11/150+sd**)

This has echoes of several liturgical items from the Purification: the antiphons *Adorna thalamum tuum* ('quem accipiens Simeon in ulnas suas'), *Responsum accepit Simeon* ('accepit eum in ulnas suas'), *Hodie Beata Virgo Maria* ('et Simeon . . . accepit eum in ulnas suas') and *Accipiens Simeon puerum in manibus*. With such a concentration of similar texts as occurs in the liturgy of the feast of the Purification it is perhaps to be expected that some common phrases would find their way into a dramatist's work.

---

[32] AS 404, WA 270. The text is also known as an alleluia verse, but not in the Sarum use.

7.5 The Entry into Jerusalem

The biblical episode of Christ's entry into the city of Jerusalem is recounted in all four gospels. Christ and the apostles made their way from Jericho, and as they approached Jerusalem many people heard of it and came to meet them outside the city. According to St Matthew,

> Plurima autem turba straverunt vestimenta sua in via. Alij autem cedebant ramos de arboribus: et sternebant in via. Turbe autem que precedebant et que sequeban-tur, clamabant dicentes. Osanna filio dauid: benedictus qui venit in nomine domini: osanna in altissimis. Et cum intrasset iherosolimam: . . .
>
> (Matthew 21/8–10)

(And a very great multitude spread their garments in the way; others cut down branches from the trees, and strawed them in the way.

And the multitudes that went before, and that followed, cried, saying, Hosanna to the son of David: Blessed is he that cometh in the name of the Lord: Hosanna in the highest.

And when he was come into Jerusalem . . .)

St Mark gives a very similar account of the proceedings, but with some additional text:

> Multi vestimenta sua strauerunt in via. Alij autem frondes cedebant de arboribus: et sternebant in via. Et qui preibant, et qui sequebantur clamabant dicentes. Osanna benedictus qui venit in nomine domini: benedictum quod venit regnum patris nostri dauid: osanna in excelsis. Et introiuit iherosolimam . . .
>
> (Mark 11/8–11)

(. . . Hosanna! Blessed is he that cometh in the name of the Lord: Blessed be the kingdom of our father David, that cometh in the name of the Lord: Hosanna in the highest. . . .)   (AV verses 9–10)

St Luke's narrative offers a different text again, although it has some of the same elements:

> Eunte autem illo substernebant vestimenta sua in via. Et cum appropinquaret iam ad descensum montis oliveti: ceperunt omnes turbe descendentium gaudentes laudare deum voce magna super omnibus quas viderant virtutibus dicentes. Benedictus qui venit rex in nomine domini: pax in celo et gloria in excelsis.
>
> (Luke 19/36–38)

(And as he went, they spread their clothes in the way.

And when he was come nigh, even now at the descent of the Mount of Olives, the whole multitude of the disciples began to rejoice and praise God with a loud voice for all the mighty works that they had seen;

Saying, Blessed be the King that cometh in the name of the Lord: peace in heaven, and glory in the highest.)

St John as usual puts a different emphasis on certain matters, and in this case has the events in a slightly different order: but the proceedings are recognisably the same, and so is the text:

In crastinum autem turba multa que venerat ad diem festum cum audissent quia
venit ihesus iherosolimam acceperunt ramos palmarum: et processerunt obuiam
ei et clamabant: osanna, benedictus qui venit in nomine domini rex israhel.

(John 12/12–13)

(On the next day much people that were come to the feast, when they heard that
Jesus was coming to Jerusalem,
　Took branches of palm trees, and went forth to meet him, and cried, Hosanna:
Blessed is the King of Israel that cometh in the name of the Lord.)

Christ and his disciples form a procession along the road to Jerusalem, and the first
three of these accounts suggest only that the crowd lined the way or joined in this
procession in front of or following Christ and his friends. Only St John makes
explicit the processional quality of the people's actions in '[going] forth to meet him'.
There were two processions, then, with Christ's being intercepted by the procession
of the people. It is this idea of one procession intercepting another that gives the
Palm Sunday procession one of its distinguishing features.

　The procession before Mass on Palm Sunday was one of the most elaborate of the
church year. In its general conformation it can be seen as a ritualisation of the biblical
accounts of Christ's entry into Jerusalem: the main body of the clergy, choir and
people processed around the outside of the church; a second, smaller procession
with the Host (the Body of Christ) joined it, usually on the north side of the church
building;[33] and the main procession made a ceremonial re-entry into the church
through the west door (at Worcester, apparently the north door). The procession's
texts refer constantly to the biblical narrative, many of the antiphon-texts sung being
sections of the biblical story. More specifically, branches and flowers were blessed
before the procession and these were put to some use which is unspecified in the
rubrics; and the processional re-entry into the church is marked with the antiphon
Ingrediente Domino in sanctam civitatem, showing that the church here represents
Jerusalem. In two uses, in fact – at Christ Church, Canterbury and at Hereford – the
procession actually went outside the city walls and the second station (at which
Gloria laus was sung) was at one of the city gates, the third station being at the church
door.[34]

　The Palm Sunday procession varied considerably from one use to another. This
was bound to be the case, perhaps, for a procession in which the actual topography
of the church, its associated buildings and its surroundings were a major factor in

---

33 The rubrics are unclear about this for the Sarum use, and there is even a doubt as to the
direction of the procession's movement.
34 Tyrer *Holy Week*, 57 and 62: Tyrer's work is an excellent introduction to the Holy Week liturgy
and ceremonies. There was an interesting variation at the Benedictine nunnery in Chester,
where a location called 'Jerusalem' was visited as the first station. The antiphon 'Cum
appropinquaret Dominus' was sung between the church door and the station; then the
Prioress, two nuns (the cantors) and the priests entered 'the cyte of Ierusalem' (which was
apparently an enclosed space) and sang 'En rex venit', after which there was an exchange of
antiphons between those within and the main body of the procession outside. The location of
'Jerusalem' is however unknown: see Chaplain-Pearman *Palm Sunday Procession*, Map II and
p. 76.

the way the proceedings developed. Even among the Benedictine houses, there is a surprising lack of uniformity, as if each church had decided its own order of events.[35] It is difficult to see precisely what these variations are, for a number of reasons: few relevant service books survive that can be identified as coming from specific churches; the material might be in the relevant processional or the missal, or split between them, so that surviving books often lack texts or rubrics; and some widely-used details of the ceremonies do not appear in the service books anyway, and have to be studied through other types of source.

One of the most important sources is 'A Potation for Lent' by Thomas Becon, written perhaps in the 1540s. Becon explains a number of liturgical ceremonies performed in earlier times – ceremonies that he, born c.1511, must have experienced as a child and a young man. For our present purpose it is the section entitled 'Of the Ceremonies that are used in the Procession of Palm-Sunday, and What they Signify' that concerns us. Here Becon describes the Palm Sunday procession and offers theological explanations of many of its features, producing a theological construct of considerable intellectual interest which may be understood as a justi-fication for the ceremonies themselves. The incidental descriptions of details of the procession are very helpful, because they include elements that do not appear, or appear only in incomplete references, in the service books. It will therefore be useful to discuss briefly the main outlines of the procession and to add to this such details of the ceremony as can be abstracted from Becon's account. My brief description of the procession will use the Salisbury version as its basis, but it must be remembered that other uses varied in the number and placing of stations and in the precise repertory and ordering of pieces.

The preparations for the procession began with a reading, Exodus 15/27 to 16/10: here the hungry Israelites are promised bread from the Lord, a promise later fulfilled by the appearance of manna. This was followed by a Gospel reading, John 12/12–19 (part of which is quoted above). This passage describes the manner of Christ's coming, gives the reason for the people's coming to him (their interest in the raising of Lazarus), and mentions the resulting anger of the Pharisees. The connection of the gift of manna with the coming of Christ (the Bread of Life, symbolised in the Host) seems to be made directly here. This is not discussed by Becon, but presum-ably it is the reason for the throwing down of wafers during the procession. The blessing of the flowers and branches followed: the palms were then distributed, and two antiphons were sung before the procession left the choir. Tyrer mentions that the most common substitute for palm in England was the willow with its 'catkins'.[36] The Palm Sunday rubrics in the Sarum Processional variously mention 'flowers and leaves' (flores et frondes) and 'branches with leaves' (ramis cum frondibus), while

---

[35] These variations among the different uses have been studied in Chaplain-Pearman *Palm Sunday Procession*. It seems that the printed Sarum processionals present a generalised version of the ceremony, not that of Salisbury Cathedral or any other specific church.

[36] Tyrer *Holy Week*, 55–6. Tyrer also mentions yew and box as possible substitutes, and perhaps these were used when willow was not available. Becon confirms the use of branches of the 'sallow-tree' (i.e. willow), however: 'Potation', 112.

'flowers and leaves' were blessed (flores et frondes). Eventually 'palms' were distributed (palme).[37]

Presumably willow catkins might be described as 'flowers', although it is possible that flowers of other plants were used. The distinction between flowers and leaves is made in the diagrams of the positions for the blessing of the palms: the 1502 text shows two bunches of material, one of which seems to be of long leaves and the other of a more delicate and interesting shape. If these are 'frondes' and 'flores' respectively, the flowers might well be catkins or something similar. The 1508 woodcut is different, but just as clear in this distinction. In any case, it seems that the flowers are distinct from the leaves/branches, and that it is the leaves/branches that are distributed.[38] The flowers must have played a part in the proceedings, or it would be pointless to bless them: as we shall see, they were used during the procession.

The procession left the choir at the west end, preceded by a covered cross ('sine imagine'), left the church and made its way round to the north side while several antiphons were sung. One of these, *Cum appropinquaret Dominus*, is based on St Mark's account of the Entry, but with an important variation. I give here part of the text, corresponding to part of the quotation given above:[39]

> . . . et qui sequebantur clamabant osanna benedictus qui venit in nomine domini benedictum regnum patris nostri dauid osanna in excelsis miserere nobis fili dauid.

These extra four words of text, 'Have mercy on us, thou Son of David', are referred to in the N-Town play of the Entry:

[PRIMUS CIUES]　Thow sone of Davyd, þu be oure supporte
　　　　　　　　At oure last day whan we xal dye!
　　　　　　　　Wherefore we alle atonys to þe exorte,
　　　　　　　　Cryeng mercy! Mercy! Mercy!
　　　　　　　　　　　(N-Town 26/454–7: Passion Play I/411–14)

The first station was at the eastern end of the cemetery on the north side of the church, and there the Gospel, Matthew 21/1–9, was read. Although this Gospel does not deal with the healing of the blind men (which had happened on the road from Jericho), Becon associates this station with the prophecies that at the coming of Christ the blind shall see, the dumb speak, and so on.[40] This is probably why the healings that in the Gospel accounts take place on the road from Jericho or in Jerusalem itself were transferred in the plays to the scene outside the city walls. At this first station the main procession was joined by the smaller one in which the Host and relics were carried under a canopy. An antiphon was sung – *En rex venit*

---

37 PS(P) 37r–39v; PS(H) 45–7.
38 It was normal to keep the unused branches until the following year, when they were burned to provide the ashes for Ash Wednesday.
39 See PS(P) f. 41v; PS(H) 48.
40 Becon 'Potation', 113.

in the Sarum use and *Dignus es, Domine* in the York use – during which the priests, choir and people genuflected to the Host and kissed the ground.[41] In the Sarum use the procession with the relics and Host then joined the main procession in its movement to the second station; at York, the relics and Host were taken back into the church.

In the Sarum use the second station was on the south side of the church: two antiphons and two responsories were provided for the procession from the first station to the second. At the second station seven boys 'in a high place' (in eminenti loco) sang the verses of the processional hymn *Gloria laus et honor*, the rest of the choir singing the refrain. Although the rubrics usually do not mention it, the boys threw down wafers and flowers on the procession below. Becon observes that 'At the end of every verse the children cast down certain cakes, or breads, with flowers'.[42] He explains this performance of *Gloria laus* as follows: the children represent 'the faithful christian men in the world, which ought to be simple and humble in heart as a child is'; their singing signifies the 'giving of glory and praise to Christ for his innumerable benefits shewed unto us'; the flowers that the children cast down signify 'an honest conversation and the continual exercise of godly virtues'; and the cakes signify mercy toward the poor, the 'needy members of Christ', mercy that 'ought diligently to be exercised of all christian men which have the goods of the world in their possession, or else they shew themselves unworthy the benefits of God.'[43] Concerning the high place in which the children stand, Becon explains that 'they which give praise unto God, and practise an honest conversation, and shew mercy to the poor people, should not do it for vain-glory nor for the praise of men, but only for the glory of God, setting their minds, seeing they are come to Christ, no more upon earthly things, but upon things celestial and heavenly; in token whereof they ascend and go up into such an high place from the earth.' One might also note that the wafers signify God's provision of manna to his people, while flowers were almost certainly intended to represent Heaven.[44]

Another antiphon sung on the way through the cloisters took the procession to the west door of the church, where the third station was observed. Pieces sung in procession and at this station reflect the evil of the enemies of Christ, but the subsequent entrance into the church symbolises the attainment of heavenly bliss. The identity of the holy city with the New Jerusalem is made clear in the responsory sung at the entrance, and the processional entrance underneath the Host and relics

---

[41] In the printed Sarum processionals of 1508 and 1517 this scene (for one thinks of it in dramatic terms) is expanded by the inclusion of the prophecies beginning *Jerusalem, respice ad orientem* (discussed in section 3.2, above), sung by a boy 'dressed as a prophet'.

[42] Becon 'Potation', 114. It is a great pity that the service books do not mention the throwing down of flowers.

[43] Becon 'Potation', 115.

[44] See the contributions of J.T. Rhodes and Clifford Davidson in Davidson's *The Iconography of Heaven*, especially pp. 73–4 and 110–11.

held high over the doorway is a reminder that entry into heaven comes only through the redeeming work of Christ:[45]

> *His finitis intrent ecclesiam per idem ostium sub feretro et capsula reliquiarum ex transverso ostii elevatis cantantes, cantore incipiente, responsorium:*
> Ingrediente Domino in sanctam civitatem, Hebraeorum pueri resurrectionem vitae pronuntiantes. Cum ramis palmarum, Hosanna clamabant in excelsis. . . .

> This ended, let them enter the church by the said door under the feretry and the reliquary, [held] up across the doorway, singing this responsory, the cantor beginning:
> While the Lord entered the holy city the Hebrew children, proclaiming the resurrection of life with palm branches, cried out 'Hosanna in excelsis . . .'

At this point Becon tells us something that is not in the rubrics and which confirms this interpretation: namely, that the priest symbolically opened the door of the church by means of the cross, an action reminiscent of the bishop's entry to consecrate a church (see below, section 7.7). He also says that on the arrival of the procession at the church door a choir of children sings inside the church:[46] there are several variants in which a group inside the church sings in alternation with the main body outside. This is something that did not happen at Salisbury, and offers a clue as to the location of the ceremonies that Becon described. Another piece of evidence is that Becon apparently says that at the end of the procession the priest sang a piece of which the text is *Dignus es, Domine*, an item that comes much earlier in the procession in most uses.[47]

Inside the church, the procession came to a stop for the fourth and last station in front of the Cross in the nave. Following the singing of antiphons here, the procession re-entered the choir, and after a short prayer Mass was begun.

There are four Entry plays extant, those of the York, N-Town, Cornish and Chester cycles. Of these the most obviously liturgically-based is **N-Town 26**, which is part of **Passion Play I**. As Entry episodes go, this is a short one: John makes a statement about the approach of Christ (**N-Town 26/418–41: Passion Play I/375–98**), and the four citizens decide to 'don hym honour and worchepe' and to 'welcome hym with flowrys and brawnchis of þe tre' (**N-Town 26/445, 448: Passion Play I/402, 405**). The citizens go to meet Christ, spreading their clothes out before him.

> . . . *And þei xal falle downe upon þer knes all atonys, þe fyrst þus seyng:*

[45] PS(P), 47v; PS(H), 53: the translation of *Ingrediente Domino* is taken from Chaplain-Pearman, Appendices II and III.
[46] Becon was born in Norfolk, educated at Cambridge and held his first living as the vicar of Brenzett, near Romney in Kent: see Ayre's introduction to Becon, *The Early Works*, vii–viii. The use described here may be from Norwich, Ely or Canterbury, therefore. Using the foot of the cross to demand entry was widespread outside England, and in some books it is specified that the archbishop, if he is present, uses his staff for this purpose: see Tyrer *Holy Week*, 59–64.
[47] See Becon 'Potation', 116. The text of *Dignus es, Domine* is only part of the text that Becon quotes, however, and he may be drawing on material from outside that particular section of the liturgy.

7.5 The Entry into Jerusalem

PRIMUS CIUES   Now blyssyd be he þat in oure Lordys name
                To us in any wyse wole resorte.
                And we beleve veryly þat þu dost þe same,
                For be þi mercy xal spryng mannys comforte.

*Here Cryst passyth forth. Þer metyth with hym a serteyn of chylderyn with flowrys,
and cast beforn hym. And they synggyn 'Gloria laus', and beforn on seyt:*

Thow sone of Davyd, þu be oure supporte
        At our laste day whan we xal dye.
        (N-Town 26/449+sd–455: Passion Play I/406+sd–412)

This fairly obviously follows the biblical narrative, although it incorporates the kind of modification of chronology that is common enough in the plays. The liturgical elements (as opposed to the biblical ones) are:

(1)   The genuflexion at Christ's coming (**26/449+sd: Passion Play I/406+sd**);

(2)   The text 'Benedictus qui venit in nomine Domini' (**26/450–1: Passion Play I/407–8**);

(3)   Possibly a second section of text (**452–3: Passion Play I/409–10**) concerned with mercy;

(4)   The meeting with children, who throw flowers and sing *Gloria laus*; and

(5)   Perhaps, another section of text (**454–5: Passion Play I/411–12**).

Of these, (1) belongs to the first station in the Sarum use, where the second procession joins the first; (2) is in several liturgical items, but (2) and (3) together appear only in *Cum appropinquaret Dominus*, one of the pieces used during the procession to the first station; and the events of (4) take place at the second station. Item (5) is more difficult: the address 'Son of David' occurs in the Gospel, read at the first station, but in association with 'supporte' – or more specifically, *redemption* – it occurs in the Antiphon *Ave, rex noster, fili David, redemptor mundi*. This piece follows the entry to the church with *Ingrediente Domino* in the uses of three secular cathedrals (Salisbury, York and Lichfield) and one Benedictine house (the Chester nuns).[48] This is not to say that the use of any of these informed the composition of the N-Town play, of course, which is more likely to have followed an East Anglian use.

These various elements, then, admittedly partly in an efficient disguise, may well belong to the procession, and in the order in which they occur in the play. Clearly the relationship between liturgy and play is not a very direct one: yet if I am right about these five items the playwright undoubtedly had the liturgy in mind when writing this scene – not the Sarum use, presumably, but an East Anglian one. If that use could be identified we might be able to see that the liturgical items concerned are more clearly related to the play text.

[48] See Chaplain-Pearman *Palm Sunday Procession*, 112; PS(P), f. 48r; PS(H), 53.

7.6 The Last Supper: Maundy and Mass

The biblical account of the Last Supper, Christ's final meal with the disciples on the night before the Crucifixion, gave rise to two particular liturgical ceremonies that fed back into the biblical drama: the Mandatum and the Canon of the Mass. The Mandatum – in English, 'Maundy', Christ's command to his followers to serve one another – was a foot-washing ceremonial based on the episode in which Christ washed the feet of his disciples as a model of what that service should be: it was celebrated on the evening of Thursday in Holy Week. The Canon of the Mass has at its centre the words of Christ as he distributed the bread and wine on that occasion, the statement that what he was actually giving them was his own body and blood.

These two ritual re-enactments of Christ's actions led to quite different types of ceremony and to very different dramatic uses.

The Mandatum

The scriptural account of Christ's act of humility is narrated only by St John (13/4–15). It is essentially quite simple, and can be broken down into three phases:

(1)   Christ wrapped a towel round himself, filled a basin with water, and washed his disciples' feet, drying them on the towel.

(2)   Peter protested, and in the ensuing conversation Christ explained his actions.

(3)   After sitting down again Christ made a more general statement about Christian service.

We are here concerned with phase (1) only, in which the Gospel provides no dialogue at all.

N-Town 27 includes this episode in lines **511+sd–535**, which is also **Passion Play I/824+sd–848**. The playwright modified the biblical narrative in important ways, making Christ approach Simon Peter first, so that the conversation with Peter precedes the washing of the other disciples' feet. The SD concerned makes this inescapable:

> *Here Jesus takyth a basyn with watyr and towaly gyrt abowtyn hym and fallyth beforn Petyr on his o kne.*   **(N-Town 27/511+sd: Passion Play I/824+sd)**

A further very important modification is shown in the second SD of this episode:

> *Here Jesus wasshyth his dyscipulys feet by and by, and whypyth he[m], and kyssyth hem mekely, and sythy[n] settyth hym down, . . .*
> **(N-Town 27/527+sd: Passion Play I/840+sd)**

The kissing of his disciples' feet after the washing is an extra-biblical feature of this event, for St John gives no hint of it. It is not an error on the part of this particular playwright, however, for it appears in a closely-related event, that of the anointing of Christ's feet by Mary Magdalene. This is reported by St John (John 12/1–3), who describes an occasion when Christ was eating supper in the home of Mary, Martha and Lazarus at Bethany. Mary took a pound of spikenard, with which she anointed Jesus's feet, afterwards wiping his feet with her hair. In the Middle Ages this story was conflated with the rather different version of St Matthew and St Mark (Matthew 26/6–7, Mark 14/3), in which Jesus was eating a meal at the house of Simon the leper at Bethany when an un-named woman brought an alabaster box of precious ointment (identified by Mark as spikenard) which she broke open, pouring the contents on Jesus's head. These stories were further conflated with St Luke's account (Luke 7/36–8), in which Jesus is eating at the house of a Pharisee named Simon, and the woman bringing the box of ointment is a known sinner who now repents, weeping. She washes his feet with tears, wipes them with her hair, kisses his feet and anoints them with the ointment. These conflations can be seen in both of the English dramatisations of which we know. At York, the Ironmongers' play of *Jesus in the House of Simon the Leper* was never registered, but John Clerke's description of it shows that it included 'Maria Magdelena lauans pedes Jesu lacrimis et capillis suis tergens'.[49] In the Chester cycle, the existing play of Mary Magdalene dramatises this event in **Chester 14/40+sd-56+sd**. The anointing is dealt with in this second SD, which reads

> *Tunc aperiet pixidem, et faciet signum unctionis, et rigabit pedes Jesu lachrymis et tergebit capillis suis.*
>
> (Then she will open the box, and will pretend to anoint him, and will moisten Jesus's feet with tears and will wipe them dry with her hair.)

This whole episode is based on St Luke's narration, but there are two matters in which the SD differs from St Luke's account: the order of her actions is that of St John, and – as in St John's account – she does not kiss Christ's feet. However, in a later speech of the play, when Jesus rebukes Simon for his attitude towards the woman, we find that not all of her actions were described in the SD:

[JESUS]	Into thy house here thou me geete;
	no water thou gave mee to my feete.
	Shee washed them with her teares weete
	and wyped them with her heare.
	Kisse syth I came thou gave non,
	but syth shee came into this wonne
	shee hath kyssed my feete eychon;
	of weepinge shee never ceased.
	With oyle thou hast not me anoynt,
	but shee hat donne both foot and joynt. **(Chester 14/101–10)**

Despite what the SD says, therefore, Mary's actions here both follow the order of St Luke's account and include the kissing of Christ's feet that only Luke describes.

---

[49] Beadle 1982, 198; MDF 7, f. 107r: 'Maria Magdalena washing Jesus' feet with her tears and wiping [them] dry with her hair'. I read 'Magdalene'.

To return to Christ's washing of his disciples' feet at the Last Supper: what does the Mary Magdalene episode tell us about that extra-biblical kissing in **N-Town 27**? It is tempting to suggest that it arose through narrational contamination from the Mary Magdalene story, or that the playwright deliberately engineered a cross-reference between the Last Supper episode and the Mary Magdalene episode that is so obviously a fore-runner of it. In proposing a different solution, that both dramatisations derive from the liturgical ceremony of the Mandatum, I would point to two circumstances of very different kinds. First, the Mandatum itself is undoubtedly based upon both biblical episodes, for it amalgamates the Mary Magdalene episode with the Last Supper to produce a ritual version of the story in which the officiant kisses the foot that he has just washed. Second, the dramatisations are almost completely lacking in dialogue during the action of washing, which makes it seem that the washing of the feet must take place in silence.[50] I came to this problem first in a practical situation, as musical director for a performance. I was aware of the great embarrassment sometimes shown by producers, who tended to shorten the washing as much as possible, telling Christ to give a wipe and dab to one foot only of each disciple.[51] But even this took too long for a silent ceremony, and in any case this token washing seemed quite alien to what I understood as the medieval sense of drama. My empirical solution was to have the disciples sing some of the antiphons from the Mandatum ceremony while the washing was going on, since those texts were clearly very suitable for the occasion. Only much later did it occur to me that this was the real solution, and that the Mandatum ceremony, originally derived from the biblical accounts of both episodes in Christ's life, had itself been appropriated for the medieval dramatisations of those episodes. Once it becomes clear that that section of the Last Supper can be staged as a Mandatum ceremony, problems disappear.

The medieval Mandatum ceremony existed in many variant forms.[52] Leaving aside the Mandatum performed by the king (which apparently included gifts for the poor people concerned), the ceremony consisted of a ritual washing of the feet of a lay congregation by the priest in charge or (in a cathedral) a senior cleric, or of a congregation of religious by their abbot, abbess or prior. In some places there was a double ceremony, in which the washing of the brothers' feet followed a similar ceremony for a lay congregation of poor people.[53] The Mandatum was one of the ceremonies performed after the evening meal on Thursday in Holy Week ('Maundy Thursday', from Christ's Mandatum, or command to his disciples to serve one another in the same way). It was preceded by the washing of the altars and followed

---

[50] The quotations already given show this clearly, but see also **York 27/46–60+sd**, where the whole washing must be done with no more dialogue than the brief exchange between Peter and Christ.

[51] See my comments in 'Some myrth', 60–1: this practical solution can now be confirmed theoretically.

[52] See Tyrer *Holy Week*, 109–12, who discusses the ceremony as it happened at Rome, Salisbury, York, Canterbury and elsewhere.

[53] See *The Gilbertine Rite* I (London: Henry Bradshaw Society 59, 1921), 33–5, and MisE I, 101.

TABLE 18 : THE MANDATUM PSALMS AND ANTIPHONS

Antiphon	Psalm		Length
Mandatum novum	66	Deus misereatur nostri	6 verses
Diligamus nos invicem	132	Ecce quam bonum	4 verses
In diebus illis	50	Miserere mei Deus secundum	20 verses
Maria ergo unxit	118	Beati immaculati in via	16 verses
Postquam surrexit Dominus	48	Audite hec, omnes gentes	12 verses

by Compline.[54] In the Sarum use the procession went after the washing of the altars to the Chapter house, where a deacon read the Gospel (St John 13/1–15) and a sermon was preached to the people. Two priests then washed the feet of the congregation, taking half each: neither the Sarum nor the York books mention that the feet should be kissed, but the kiss is prescribed by the Roman *Rituale Monasticum*.[55] While this washing was happening the choir, seated, sang five appointed psalms, each of them all the way through but without the doxology, and each under an antiphon that was repeated after every verse. The antiphons, the psalms and the number of verses in each psalm are shown in Table 18. The last two psalms are multi-sectional: I assume that only the first section was sung, and the number of verses shown is for that section only. The total of 58 psalm verses sung is more than doubled by the antiphons, especially since *In diebus illis* is itself a long piece. The actual time taken for the performance of these psalms would differ considerably with the size of choir and of the acoustics of the building: but at a rough estimate they could hardly be sung in less than 20 minutes, and in most circumstances could take considerably longer. The liturgy nevertheless takes account of the possibility that the washing will not be completed by the time these psalms end, and provides another four antiphons to be sung should the need arise.

Following the washing the love-cup (*potus caritatis*) was passed around and some versicles and responses and a prayer were said. The ceremony ended with a reading of the continuation of the Gospel already heard, John 13/16–14/31, after which Compline was recited in the church.

It may be said that any dramatisation of the foot-washing episode at the Last Supper is itself a dramatisation of the Gospel readings that frame the Mandatum ceremony. Certainly the N-Town play is careful to include the statements that Christ made at the end of that Supper, apparently deliberately fulfilling that ceremonial function as well as completing the Gospel narrative (**N-Town 27/528–71: Passion Play I/841–84**). It is, therefore, impossible to prove that the dramatisations follow

[54] St John is clear that Christ's washing of the disciples' feet took place after the meal was over: the anointing of Christ is variously reported as before or during the meal. The Mandatum is in PS(P) 56v–60r and PS(H) 63–9.

[55] For the York version, see MisE I, 101; also *Rituale Monasticum* (Collegeville, Minnesota. Abbey of St John the Baptist, 1942), 215.

the liturgy of Maundy Thursday. It is nevertheless worth noting that the correctly-placed SD for Christ approaching Peter to wash his feet refers to the previous SD as a 'rubric', as if the scribe is copying a service book rather than a play book:[56]

> *Here he takyth þe basyn and þe towaly and doth as þe roberych seyth beforn.*

These SDs are not rubricated, in fact, although in common with other SDs in the manuscript they are underlined in red. But the use of the word 'roberych' does perhaps confirm a 'liturgical' attitude of mind in the playwright and/or the scribe.

The Eucharist

On the face of it the dramatic scenes in which Christ distributes the bread and wine at the Last Supper provide close parallels to the Eucharist but offer no evidence that they derive from it. The Gospel accounts of this episode are, after all, quite detailed in their descriptions of what happened and what was said on that occasion. It is true that we have no clue to the small-talk that one imagines might occur between so many friends sharing a special meal: but when such a momentous occasion is concerned we can easily suspend our disbelief to the extent of thinking that there might have been no place anyway for small-talk. Did not the whole occasion centre on Jesus? And was anything worth recording done or said that did not find its way into the Gospel accounts? We shall never know, of course, but from a dramatic point of view the limitations of the Gospel account merely provide a concentration of material that gives the episode the sharp focus necessary to the presentation of such an important part of the story.

The relationship between Mass and drama has been explored by Lynette R. Muir, who takes a more comprehensive view than I shall do here.[57] Muir identifies three groups of plays dealing with the Mass in one way or another:

(1)   Sacramental plays, 'where the essential element is the Corpus Domini and the exegesis of the doctrine of Transubstantiation'. This is a group of only four plays – one Italian, one Dutch, one French and one English – which have little in common dramatically speaking. The English example, the Croxton *Play of the Sacrament*, deals with the Host as the Body of Christ, and indeed dramatises the transformation of the consecrated wafer to the wounded Body of Christ: the Host bleeds when the Jews stab it, the cauldren bubbles blood when they boil it, and when they bake it in an oven the oven bleeds and bursts, and the person of Christ appears from it. But although the Jews rehearse Christ's institution of the Eucharist in his own words (**Sacrament 397–404**), the play owes little to the actual liturgy.[58]

---

[56] As Meredith points out (*Passion Play*, 188), **N-Town 27/511+sd**, which is **Passion Play I/824+sd**, is misplaced.

[57] Muir 'Mass'.

[58] The use of the antiphon *O sacrum convivium* (**Sacrament 840**) confirms this play's alignment with the feast of Corpus Christi (the antiphon being that for the Magnificat at second Vespers on that feast) rather than with the Mass: see BS I, mlxxiv–mlxxv.

(2)   The biblical plays dealing with the Last Supper and Christ's institution of the Eucharist. This is the group with which we shall be concerned in this section.

(3)   Three plays, none of them English, that include 'an actual on-stage re-enactment of the Mass'.

Muir very properly points out that in a Last Supper play the words of Institution are certain to appear, as are the bread and wine. For her, therefore, the signs of liturgical content, the 'additions to the biblical data', are references to the paten, the Host, wafer, communion, transubstantiation and priests.[59] Not many of these feature in English biblical plays. She notes the reference to an 'oble' in **N-Town 27/372+sd**, but indeed the rest of the SD and the speech following show a relationship to the liturgy rather than to the biblical accounts alone:[60]

Here xal Jesus take an oble in his hand lokyng vpward into hefne, to þe Fadyr þus seyng:

[JESUS]   Wherefore to þe, Fadyr of Hefne þat art eternall,
Thankyng and honor I ȝeld onto þe,
      . . .
Thankyng þe, fadyr, þat þu wylt shew þis mystery;
And þus þurwe þi myth, fadyr, and blyssyng of me,
Of þis þat was bred is mad my body.

(N-Town 27/372+sd–374, 378–80:
Passion Play I/686+sd–688, 692–4)

Jesus's 'looking upward into Heaven' is non-biblical, and translates the 'oculis elevatis' (with raised eyes) of the liturgical rubric. As for his prayer, the Gospels certainly do say that he gave thanks but do not transmit his exact words. In the liturgy this thanksgiving is transformed into the prayer that starts the Canon of the Mass, 'Te igitur clementissime pater', and this N-Town speech does owe something to the prayer.[61] The continuation of Christ's speech, too, makes much of the Paschal Lamb and the Agnus Dei, actually using the Latin phrase that appears in the Mass soon after the Consecration of the Host.

As so often, the N-Town play suggests a liturgical approach that seems missing in other plays, a point noted by Peter Meredith: 'More than any of the other vernacular English plays this one emphasises the institution of the sacrament of the eucharist, not only by using the sacramental wafer (*oblé*), but also by keeping close to the actions and in some cases words of the mass. . . .'[62] Muir cites the mention of a Host in the Cornish cycle, but this underlines the special position of the N-Town play in this respect: for the Cornish *Passio Domini* has little eucharistic content, and indeed the SD *hic Jhs dat hostiam apostolis* (**Ordinalia 2/760+sd**) is a late addition, presumably the work of a director rather than of the playwright. As such, of course,

[59] Muir 'Mass', 319–20.
[60] The synoptic Gospels narrate the institution of the Eucharist; St John does not.
[61] See MisS(L), 221.
[62] Meredith *Passion Play*, 183.

it may result from a more eucharistic *production* than the text alone allows us to assume.

In the English plays the lack or playing-down of eucharistic content may in some cases be due to reforming ideas. One would give much to know the contents of the leaf missing from **York 27**, and Beadle suggests that it is precisely because of the 'doctrinally sensitive issue of Transubstantiation' that the leaf is now missing – in other words, that it was removed.[63] **Towneley 20** is no help in filling this gap, for the institution of the Eucharist makes no appearance in that play. **Chester 15**, however, includes the episode, and not only adds brief thanksgivings for the bread and wine (**Chester 15/89, 97–8**) but also uses the liturgical phrase 'oculis elevatis' at the giving of the cup:

> *Tunc accipit calicem in manibus, oculis elevatis, . . .*
>
> **(Chester 15/96+sd)**

The Chester play, as Muir points out, was stated in the Late Banns to be eucharistic:[64]

> And howe Criste our Savioure at his laste supper
> gave his bodye and bloode for redemtion of us all,
> yow Bakers see that with the same wordes you utter
> as Criste himselfe spake them, to be a memoriall
> of that deathe and passion which in playe after ensue shall.
>
> **(Chester Late Banns, 131–5)**

Not for the first time, we find that the Early Banns and the Late Banns are complementary: in this case, the Early Banns mention 'the Maunday' but are entirely silent about all other events of the Last Supper.[65]

7.7 The Harrowing of Hell

The dramatic episode of the Harrowing of Hell derives ultimately from the statement of the Creed that Christ 'descended into Hell' after his death on the Cross. No canonical scriptures expand this statement, although references to 'Abraham's bosom' (Luke 16/22) and 'Paradise' (Luke 23/43) were taken to refer to the Limbo of the Fathers, a place where 'the souls of the just who died before Christ's ascension were detained until he opened Heaven to them'.[66] Dramatic presentations of the Harrowing of Hell depend on the so-called Gospel of Nicodemus, an apocryphal writing that its editor considers to have been written 'in order to document, by the official authority of the Roman Empire, the main tenets of the Christology in the

[63] Beadle 1982, 230–1.
[64] Muir 'Mass', 327: I have quoted the Late Banns from Lumiansky and Mills *Essays*, 291.
[65] See *Essays*, 281, lines 96–9.
[66] Attwater *Catholic Encyclopaedic Dictionary*, 309. Attwater notes that Ephesians 4/9 and I Peter 3/18–20 were also taken to refer to Limbo and Christ's descent to it. The second type of Limbo, the Limbo of Children, does not concern us here.

Apostle's Creed.'[67] There appear to have been several stages of compilation, but by the thirteenth century the story existed in the complete form from which the Harrowing of Hell was retold by various commentators, including Jacobus de Voragine in the *Legenda Aurea*.[68]

An important element in this story is the dialogue that takes place at Christ's demand for entry. The anonymous author had a ready-made dialogue in Psalm 23 (AV 24), verses 7–10 of which read as follows:

> 7   Attollite portas principes vestras:
>   et eleuamini porte eternales:
>   et introibit rex glorie.
> 8   Quis est iste rex glorie?
>   dominus fortis et potens:
>   dominus potens in prelio.
> 9   Attollite portas principes vestras:
>   et eleuamini porte eternales:
>   et introibit rex glorie.
> 10   Quis est iste rex glorie?
>   dominus virtutum ipse est rex glorie.

> (Lift up your heads, O ye gates; and be ye lift up, ye everlasting doors; and the King of glory shall come in.
> Who is this King of Glory? The Lord strong and mighty, the Lord mighty in battle.
> Lift up your heads, O ye gates; even lift them up, ye everlasting doors; and the King of glory shall come in.
> Who is this King of Glory? The Lord of hosts, he is the King of glory.)

The Gospel of Nicodemus and the Legenda Aurea both use the form 'Tollite portas', which is found as the incipit of a responsory verse, an antiphon, an offertory and a gradual. Possibly this (presumably older) version came more naturally to the author of the Gospel of Nicodemus because he was used to hearing it in the liturgy; and perhaps Jacobus de Voragine used it for the same reason, or simply because he derived his story from the Gospel of Nicodemus; perhaps, too, many medieval clerics used the alternative forms 'Attollite' and 'Tollite' more or less interchangeably. The use of 'Attollite' in the York, Towneley, Chester and N-Town plays nevertheless suggests that the material of those plays was not derived solely from the obvious sources. While it is possible that the plays drew on the psalm directly, this does not solve the problem: for the dramatic narrative could have come ultimately only from the Gospel of Nicodemus. Whatever the truth of this, the wording – which is not hard evidence of any source for the plays – suggests the possibility that some source other than the Gospel of Nicodemus or the Legenda Aurea had been involved in the composition of the plays of the Harrowing of Hell.

The most obvious possibility would be a different liturgical source, and this is

---

[67] Kim *Gospel of Nicodemus*, 2.

[68] See LA 242–5; GL 221–3. The Gospel of Nicodemus tells the story in the last few chapters (except the very last): see Kim *Gospel of Nicodemus*, 36–49.

supported by the red *versus* sign that accompanies the first verse of this dialogue in the N-Town version:

The sowle goth to helle gatys and seyth
V   Attollite portas principes vestras et eleuamini porte eternales et introibit rex
      glorie.   **(N-Town 33/23+sd: Passion Play II/1016+sd)**

While the first line of this is underlined in red, like other SDs, the text line is not underlined and must therefore be assumed to be spoken in the Latin, as the *versus* sign suggests:[69] Christ's next two speeches both identify himself as the King of Glory and make clear his intention to release the imprisoned souls 'out of here purcatorye' **(N-Town 33/25–32, 41–8: Passion Play II/1019–26, 1035–42)**. This scene not only accommodates the demon Belial but itself gives way to the scene at the Cross. While the *versus* sign may signal a liturgical source, therefore, the brevity of the scene at the gates of Hell prevents the introduction of any structure that might be identified as liturgical.

The dialogue is used much more extensively in the York cycle. Here Jesus delivers the opening verse in a mixture of Latin and English, Satan asks the question and the answer is delivered (appropriately enough) by David, who is one of the imprisoned prophets:

JESUS   Attollite portas, principes,
               Oppen vppe, ȝe princes of paynes sere,
           Et eleuamini eternales,
               Youre yendles ȝatis þat ȝe haue here.
SATTAN   What page is þere þat makes prees
               And callis hym kyng of vs in fere?
DAUID   I lered leuand, withouten lees,
               He is a kyng of vertues clere,
               A lorde mekill of myght
               And stronge in ilke a stoure,
               In batailes ferse to fight
               And worthy to wynne honnoure.   **(York 37/121–32)**

There follows a passage, lines 133-180, in which the demons discuss the situation. This is followed by a repeat of the process just quoted, with Christ's macaronic statement, Satan's question and David's answer **(York 37/181–92)**.

This double statement and interrogation follows the form of Psalm 23/7–10 as quoted earlier: that is, the two stanzas correspond to verses 7–8 and 9–10, respectively, of the psalm. There is however a difference. While the two pairs of verses in the psalm are adjacent, a dramatic scene separates the relevant stanzas in the play. This is seen also in the related play in the Towneley cycle, where Jesus speaks the entire Latin verse, 'Attollite portas . . . rex glorie' **(Towneley 25/115)** and then, after a long demons' scene in which David joins, does so again **(25/184)**. This follows the plan of this part of the Gospel of Nicodemus.[70] The plan is slightly modified in the

[69] See MDF 4, f. 185v.
[70] See Kim *Gospel of Nicodemus*, 40–1.

Chester play, for Jesus speaks the Latin only once. **Chester 17/152+sd** includes the psalm verse that clearly has to be spoken, and this is followed by the English version in the next four lines ('Open up hell-gates . . . the kinge of blys': **17/153–6**): but after a scene between the demons, with King David once more, Jesus speaks a more precise English version of the psalm verse, apparently without speaking the Latin first:

JESUS   Open up hell-yates yett I saye,
                 ye prynces of pyne that be present,
                 and lett the kinge of blys this waye
                 that he may fulfill his intent.   **(Chester 17/193–6)**

Finally, the Cornish cycle presents the dialogue twice through with nothing between, as the psalm does, but entirely in Cornish **(Ordinalia 3/97–124)**.

The evidence suggests, then, that the psalm and the *Gospel of Nicodemus* (or the *Legenda Aurea*) were both sources for the Harrowing of Hell plays. But the evidence is not unequivocal, for both the use of 'Attollite' and the appearance of the *versus* sign in the N-Town version militate against it. These are both of unknown but probably doubtful value, and more work must be done on the subject: but they suggest that we should search for another and liturgical source.

There are two liturgical occasions on which the 'Attollite portas' text was used in conjunction with a ritual entry, demanded with a show of force and eventually granted. In both cases the show of force is the use of the foot of a bishop's staff or a crucifix to knock on a church door. The first, which we noticed in section 7.5, above, is at the re-entry into the church during the Palm Sunday procession: it is true that the English service books seem not to include it, but in view of the presence of this ceremonial entry in several continental uses we need not disbelieve Thomas Becon, the only authority for it in English uses.[71] On the whole this does not seem to be a forced entry of the type required by a Harrowing of Hell, and of the ceremonies described by Tyrer only that at Toledo seems to make use of the psalm dialogue to a substantial degree.[72] Unless further evidence comes to light, therefore, it seems unnecessary to consider the Palm Sunday procession further as a source for the dramatisation of the Harrowing of Hell.

The second occasion, the pontifical office of the consecration or dedication of a church, has been suggested as a source for the Harrowing of Hell by Daniel

---

[71] See section 7.5, p. 270, and Tyrer *Holy Week*, 59–60 (Becon, location unknown) and 63–4 (modern Roman rite). See also the next note.

[72] According to Tyrer *Holy Week*, 64, the procession's entrance to the cathedral at Toledo was preceded by a ceremony in which the Archbishop knocked on the closed door with his staff (or the Dean with the cross). There followed the dialogue taken from Psalm 23, starting with the Archbishop's 'Attollite portas', the other side being taken by two canons who have previously entered the church. The canons' first response was 'Quis est iste rex glorie', so the Archbishop had recited the whole of verse 7. Neither the Sarum nor the York book includes this item.

Sheerin.[73] This office included just such a use of the dialogue of Psalm 23 as we have noted, at the point where the bishop demands entrance to the building for the purpose of dedicating it. A seventeenth-century Roman Pontifical in my possession gives the text of the dialogue as follows:[74]

> . . . *Pontifex, accepta mitra, ad ostium Ecclesiae appropinquans, percutit illud semel cum inferiore parte baculi pastoralis super liminare, dicens intelligibili voce:*
> Attollite portas principes vestras, & eleuamini portae aeternales; & introibit Rex gloriae.
> *Diaconus intus existens dicit alta voce:*
> Quis est iste Rex gloriae?
> *Pontifex respondet:*
> Dominus fortis, & potens: Dominus potens in proelio.

The Bishop had already made a circuit of the church before this exchange, aspersing the building while the choir sang a responsory. At this stage he made another circuit and eventually approached the church door again, when the same dialogue ensued. A third circuit of the church then took place, and when the Bishop returned to the church door the dialogue was that of Psalm 23/9–10 instead of 7–8:[75]

> *Tum, accepta mitra, appropinquans tertio ad ostium Ecclesiae, percutit iterum super liminare cum baculo pastorali, dicens:*
> Attollite portas principes vestras, & eleuamini portae arternales: & introibit Rex gloriae.
> *Diaconus intus existens, dicit:* Quis est iste Rex gloriae?
> *Pontifex, & vniuersus Clerus respondet:* Dominus virtutum ipse est Rex gloriae.
> *adijcientes:* Aperite, Aperite, Aperite.
> *Pontifex facit Crucem super liminare in ostio cum inferiore parte baculi pastoralis, dicens:*
> Ecce Cru+cis signum, fugiant phantasmata cuncta.

The door was then opened to him. The significance of the reference to putting 'phantasmata' to flight will be obvious.

The ceremony contained in the pontifical of Christopher Bainbridge, Bishop of Durham 1507–08 and Archbishop of York 1508–14, is rather different in its details, not all of which need concern us here.[76] Again, the dialogue occurred three times, although the bishop's verse started 'Tollite portas', a single 'minister' replied from inside the church, and the bishop's answer was different each time: 'Dominus fortis et potens'; 'Dominus potens in praelio'; and 'Dominus virtutum, ipse est rex gloriae'. The bishop was to strike the door three times on each occasion; and after the third exchange the bishop said 'Aperite portas', on which the door was opened to him.

---

[73] ' "Signum victoriae in Inferno": An Allusion to the Harrowing of Hell in Late Medieval Dedication Rituals', at the 21st International Congress on Medieval Studies, Western Michigan University, Kalamazoo, in May 1986.
[74] *Pontificale Romanum* (Antwerp. Plantin, 1627), p. 214.
[75] *Pontificale Romanum*, 216–8.
[76] *Liber Pontificalis Chr Bainbridge Archiepiscopi Eboracensis*, ed. W.G. Henderson (Surtees Society 61, 1875), 55–7. As Henderson notes, English pontificals do not belong to a 'use', but can only be regarded as 'English'.

This is clearly not particularly close to any of the dramatic versions of the Harrowing of Hell that we have, but it is certainly a ceremony that could be an important source for the plays and in any case offers some important possibilities for staging:

(1)   Although the play texts seem to show that Christ simply goes away out of the audience's sight while the demons' scene takes place, the office of dedication of a church suggests that he might make a circuit of Limbo, sanctifying it (as it were) before breaking into it.

(2)   The office would also suggest that the heavenly choir might sing while Christ makes this circuit, and the Bainbridge pontifical provides suitable items.[77]

(3)   Christ could well use his Agnus Dei staff to strike the gates of Hell three times to make them fall down.

These are all speculative, of course, although the evidence is good enough, I feel, for them to need careful consideration. It may of course be argued that very few of the audience would normally have seen a church dedication performed, and certainly not often enough for the actions just suggested to be instantly recognisable. I am not sure that that is a relevant argument, however: it is more important that those writing the plays, overseeing their doctrinal content, and staging them should be aware of the relationship between the plays and the liturgy, and that, I think, would be so.

7.8 Miscellaneous sacraments and offices

Scattered through the plays are a number of sacraments and offices, sometimes celebrated out of the audience's sight but usually 'on stage', that are intended as representation of actual services. There must of course be differences between a dramatic representation and the real thing, but equally there must be features, or a structural outline, that can be recognised as belonging to the sacrament or office concerned. In this section we shall examine some of these dramatised ceremonies and their relation to the originals.

Baptism

The baptism of Christ is dramatised in York 21, where the ceremony takes up only three lines of text:

---

[77] This would be especially effective in the York and Towneley plays, where the singing of the Souls in Limbo has already upset the demons, who refer to it as an 'ugly noise' (**York 37/101: Towneley 25/95**). This is not a good reason for choosing the dedication office as a source of the play, of course: but on the other hand the general attitude of demons to music would make heavenly singing here appropriate in any case.

[JOHANNES]   Jesus, my lord of myghtis most,
              I baptise þe here in þe name
              Of the fadir and of the sone and holy gost.   **(York 21/148–50)**

This precisely follows the wording of the *Ritus Baptizandi* in the York and Sarum manuals, adding only 'my lord of myghtis most' for the specific dramatic situation and 'here' for metrical reasons: 'N, Et ego baptizo te in nomine Patris; et Filii; et Spiritus Sancti. Amen',[78] where N is the name of the baptised person. The manuals show in addition that the person being baptised is dipped into the water three times, at the mention of each Person of the Trinity. Any producer of the play would know this, presumably, and would therefore stage a three-fold immersion of Christ during these lines.

The more expansive Towneley play of John the Baptist uses both the Latin words, modified for metrical reasons, and a translation that minimises the problem of the Son being baptised in his own name:

[IOHANNES]   I baptyse the, Ihesu, in hy,
              In the name of thi fader fre,
              In nomine patris & filii,
              Sen he will that it so be,
              Et spiritus altissimi,
              And of the holy goost on he.   **(Towneley 19/185–90)**

Immediately following the baptism, the manuals show that the baptised person is anointed with oil in the form of the Cross during a prayer that is effectively a blessing: 'N, Deus omnipotens, Pater . . . ipse te liniat chrismate + salutis in Christo Jesu Domino nostro in vitam aeternam. Amen'.[79] Both blessing and anointing appear in the Towneley play, although in this case it is John who asks the blessing of Christ, presumably given silently after **19/192**:

[IOHANNES]   I aske the, lord, of thi mercy,
              here after that thou wold blys me.

            . here I the anoynt also
              with oyle and creme, . . .   **(Towneley 19/191–4)**

The beginning of the ceremony, in which the person's name is established and the sponsors renounce the devil and all his works, is omitted in these plays, since Christ is an adult and sinless. All the plays find it sufficient to follow the biblical account in this, since John's protestation that Christ does not need baptism and he, John, does is enough to establish that this part of the *Ritus Baptizandi* need not be followed. The latter part of the ceremony, in which the baptised person is given a symbolic candle, is likewise unnecessary in the plays, although the Towneley play again makes reversed use of this idea when Christ delivers the Agnus Dei to John **(19/209–16)**.

---

[78] MPE 17; MS 36.
[79] MPE 17. The wording of the Sarum manual (MS 37) is essentially the same.

Of the other cycles, Chester and the Cornish cycle do not dramatise the Baptism. The N-Town cycle has a Baptism play, in which the text makes no use of the *Ritus Baptizandi*: the baptism takes place during the events of **N-Town 22/92+sd**, where the Holy Spirit descends to Christ. Here, one assumes, a three-fold immersion is staged: but we need not assume that it takes place in silence, since John could recite the words of baptism as set out in the manuals.

Peter's baptism of the King of Marcylle in *Mary Magdalen* follows parts of the service not referred to in the Baptism of Christ plays. When the king tells Peter of his wish to be baptised (**Mary Magdalen 1826**), Peter responds in the terms of the interrogation in which the sponsors renounce the works of the Devil, although his statement is very positive and includes material not in the service:

PETYR   O, blyssyd be þe tyme þat 3e are falle to grace,
               And 3e wyll kepe yower beleve aftyr my techeyng,
               And alle-only forsake þe fynd Saternas,
               The commavndmenttys of God to have in kepyng.

                                           (Mary Magdalen 1827–30)

Line **1829** is a clear reference to the interrogation:[80]

               Abrenuncias sathane?
               Abrenuncio.
               Et omnibus operibus eius?
               Abrenuncio.
               Et omnibus pompis eius?
               Abrenuncio.

In the next four lines the king makes an affirmation of faith:

REX   Forsoth, I beleve in þe Father, þat is of all wyldyng,
               And in þe Son, Jhesu Cryst,
               Also in þe Holy Gost, hys grace to vs spredyng.
               I beleve in Crystys deth, and hys vprysyng.

                                             (Mary Magdalen 1831–4)

This affirmation is normally made by the sponsors, where the priest asks them if they believe in the various articles of the Creed and they respond 'I believe' to each.[81]

         Credis in deum patrem omnipotentem creatorem celi et terre?
         Credo.
         Credis et in iesum christum filium eiusvnicum dominum nostrum natum et passum?
         Credo.
          Credis et in spiritum sanctum, sanctam ecclesiam catholicam, sanctorum communionem, remissionem peccatorum, carnis resurrectionem et vitam eternam post mortem?
         Credo.

---

[80] MS 36.
[81] MS 36. MPE 16 gives a slightly different disposition of the text.

Peter's next question, 'Syr þan whatt axke ʒe?' (line **1835**) is the priest's question 'Quid petis?' that follows this affirmation, and the king's reply is an amplified version of the response 'Baptismum' in the service:

> REX   Holy father, baptym, for charite,
> Me to save in eche degre
> From þe fyndys bond.   (**Mary Magdalen 1836–8**)

Peter omits the question that confirms this response and continues with the baptism itself, in rather modified wording:

> PETYR   In þe name of þe Trinite,
> Wyth þys watyr I baptysse þe,
> Þat þou mayst strong be
> Aʒen þe fynd to stond.   (**Mary Magdalen 1839–42**)

This section of *Mary Magdalen* follows much of the baptism service, then, in order and with very clear references that a medieval audience would follow. It should be said that although the Sarum manual (and the York manual, too) gives very little of the service in English, either language could be used, and in many parishes no doubt an English version was preferred.

Marriage

The only dramatisation of a marriage is in **N-Town 10**, often known as The Betrothal of Mary but in fact following the medieval marriage service in many particulars. This is the section that starts at **Mary Play 594**, but at this place the amalgamation of pageant material and the original Mary Play begins.[82] This section begins with the choosing of the unwilling Joseph to be Mary's husband. Joseph himself contrasts his old age and infirmity with the youth and vivacity of Mary, whom the bishop has described as 'buxum' (defined by Spector as 'gentle, humble, submissive'); and to the bishop he insists that 'in bedde we xul nevyr mete' (**N-Town 10/275, 295: Mary Play 848, 868**).[83] This wording echoes that of the woman's vows in the Sarum *Ordo ad faciendum Sponsalia*, where in taking her husband the bride promises 'to be bonere and buxum in bedde and atte borde'.[84] In the York version, too, the woman is asked first if she will 'be buxum to hym' and promises to look after him 'at bedde and at borde'.[85] The alliteration of these questions and vows, heard at every wedding and repeated by every bride and bridegroom, makes them so memorable that we can almost certainly assume a deliberate reference in the N-Town play. Similarly, when Pilate says that his wife 'In bedde is full buxhome and bayne' (**York 30/52**) he is surely making a direct reference to the marriage vows: Procula takes her wifely

[82] Meredith *Mary Play*, 3 and 100.
[83] Spector's gloss is in *N-Town* II, 567.
[84] MS 48.
[85] MPE 26, 27.

duties seriously, and the sexually-provocative conversations between them show that their marriage is a passionate one.

In the late Middle Ages the interrogation and vows of the man and woman to be married took much the same form that they do now. The Sarum and York manuals give the full Latin text but note that this part of the service should be in the mother-tongue (in lingua materna): both give an English version, which could vary slightly in its wording.[86] The order of events is as follows:

Interrogation of the man (I give the York version here, because there is no translation of the question 'N, Vis habere hanc mulierem . . .?' in the Sarum manual): 'N, Wylt thou haue this woman to thy wyfe and loue her and keep her, in syknes and in helthe, . . . and holde the only to her to thy lyues ende[?]'
Answer: 'I wyll.'

Interrogation of the woman (York version, for the same reason as above): 'N, Wylt thou haue this man to thy husbande, and to be buxum to hym, serue hym and kepe hym in sykenes and in helthe: . . . and holde the only to hym to thy lyues ende[?]'
Answer: 'I wyll.'

Vows of the man to the woman (this and the woman's vows are given in the Sarum version): 'I N take the N to my wedded wyf to haue and to holde fro this day forworde for bettere for wers for richere for pouerer: . . . and therto y plight the my trouthe.' (The priest says this phrase by phrase for the man to repeat.)

Vows of the woman to the man: 'I N take the N to my wedded housbonde to haue and to holde fro this day forwarde for better for wors: for richer: for pouerer: in sykenesse and in hele: to be bonere and buxum in bedde and atte borde tyll dethe vs departe if holy chyrche it wol ordeyne and therto I plight the my trouthe.' (The priest says this phrase by phrase for the woman to repeat.)

In the play this part of the service is modified in various ways, in the first place because certain changes are demanded by the need to versify it. The interrogations are also shortened to a mere two lines, as Joseph's shows:

[EPISCOPUS]   Joseph, wole ʒe haue þis maydon to ʒoure wyff
           And here honour and kepe as ʒe howe to do?
                      (N-Town 10/302–3: Mary Play 875–6)

Then follows the worst nightmare of every mother of the bride and most brides:

JOSEPH   Nay, sere, so mote I thryff!
                      (N-Town 10/304: Mary Play 877)

This unexpected answer gives rise to a short passage in which the bishop persuades Joseph that God wishes him to marry Mary. At this stage the interrogation of Mary should follow, but it is dramatically neater to let the bishop lead Joseph in saying

---

[86] The interrogations and vows are in MPS 47–8 and ME 26–27.

his vows. As Meredith points out, the layout (in fact, the punctuation) shows the sections in which this speech is spoken and repeated.[87]

> *Episcopus et idem Joseph:*
> Here I take þe, Mary, to wyff
> To hauyn, to holdyn : as God his wyll with us wyl make.
> And as longe as bethwen us : lestyght oure lyff
> To loue ȝow as myselff : my trewth I ȝow take.
>
> **(N-Town 10/310–13: Mary Play 883–6)**

I have added colons to show where the bishop breaks mid-line (these replace the manuscript's tick-and-comma signs). We can safely assume that breaks occur also at the line-ends.

This change of order would be obvious to the audience. It may have been intended as humorous, and it could certainly be played that way, the bishop taking the opportunity to get Joseph to make his vows before he can change his mind again. It demands a further change of order, and Mary's deferred interrogation now occurs:

> [EPISCOPUS]   Mary, wole ȝe haue þis man,
> And hym to kepyn as ȝoure lyff?
>
> **(N-Town 10/314–15: Mary Play 887–8)**

Mary's vows do not follow, as one might expect: instead, Mary itemises some of the promises (and one, that of chastity, that does not occur in the marriage service) in a speech that ends the service as depicted in this play:

> MARIA   In chastyte to ledyn my lyff
> I xal hym nevyr forsake,
> But evyr with hym abyde.
> And, jentyll spowse, as ȝe an seyd,
> Lete me levyn as a clene mayd;
> I xal be trewe, be not dysmayd,
> Both terme, tyme, and tyde.
>
> **(N-Town 10/324–30: Mary Play 897–913)**

But before this the final part of the marriage service occurs, the giving of the ring. In the manuals the ring is first blessed, but in the play the bishop merely tells Joseph to 'wedde þi wyff' with the ring. Joseph's form of words is very brief compared with the wording of the manuals, and there is no indication here that the bishop leads him in this speech:

> JOSEPH   Sere, with þis ryng I wedde here ryff,
> And take here now here for my make.
>
> **(N-Town 10/320–1: Mary Play 893–4)**

The full version of this is hardly required: we know by now that Joseph will honour Mary, and the promise to endow her with his possessions is hardly relevant or

---

[87] Meredith *Mary Play*, 104; see MDF 4, f. 55r.

appropriate in the play. This is not the end of the liturgical content, however: the bishop ends the ceremony with the singing of the Pentecost hymn *Alma chorus Domini*, also sung on the feast of the Name of Jesus (**10/334+: Mary Play 907+**),[88] and finally gives his blessing (**10/342–3: Mary Play 915–16**). These two liturgical items signal the end of the marriage service in the play. In fact, the play is framed by 'set-piece' liturgical items, because the beginning of it is signalled by the singing of the sequence for the Commemoration of the Holy Trinity, *Benedicta sit beata Trinitas*:[89]

EPISCOPUS   This holyest virgyn xalt þu maryn now.
                     3oure rodde floreschyth fayrest þat man may se.
                     Þe Holy Gost, we se, syttyht on a bow.
                     Now 3elde we all preysyng to þe Trenyte.

Et hic cantent Benedicta sit beata Trinitas
                               (N-Town 10/298–301+sd: Mary Play 871–4+sd)

Meredith points out the particular appropriateness of this piece, and indeed of *Alma chorus* at the end: for the 'Sarum Use contains a Trinity mass as the nuptial mass but substitutes *Alma chorus domini* for *Benedicta* as the sequence ... York however retains it ...'[90]

Burial

There are various offices for the occasions of death and burial, and most of the dramatisations make only passing reference to some identifiable liturgical item that serves to define the occasion. The *Creacion of the World* does not even do this in the scene of Adam's burial, but makes it clear that appropriate music would be heard:

Lett Adam be buried in a fayre tombe with som churche songys at hys buryall

SEYTHE   Ow thas pan ewa marowe   Since my father is dead
            Me a vyn y anclythyas   I shall bury him.
            Dun a lebma heb falladow;   Let us come away without fail;
             Gorryn an corf in gweras   let us set the body in the ground
            Gans solempnyty ha cane.   with ceremonial song.
                                   (Creacion 2078+sd–2083)

The last line literally means 'with solemnity and song', and therefore refers (as **2078+sd** does) to liturgical items sung at an inhumation. It may be assumed that the producer would know what was appropriate, although if he were not a cleric he presumably might ask advice.

---

[88] Dutka 1980, 19–20, identifies this piece and gives the reference to BS II, 236 and III, 618. It is variously called a hymn or a sequence, depending on its liturgical function.

[89] Identified by Dutka 1980, 23, and found in BS II, 502.

[90] Meredith *Mary Play*, 103, with references. See MisS 416 (and MS 51–2); MPE 30. MisE I, 213, gives *Benedicta sit beata Trinitas* as the sequence for Trinity Sunday; MisE II, 191, gives no sequence at a nuptial mass.

The order for the burial of the dead follows the Mass for the Dead in the Sarum manual,[91] and includes the procession from the church to the cemetary as well as the burial itself. The processional psalm is *In exitu Israel* (Psalm 113: AV 114 and 115), sung under the antiphon *In paradisum* and without the *Gloria patri*.[92] This psalm is sung during the procession to bury the body of the Virgin in the N-Town Assumption play:

> *Hic portabunt corpus versus sepulturam cum eorum luminibus.*

PETRUS   Exiit Israel de Egypto, domus Jacob de populo barbaro. Alleluia!
APOSTOLI   Facta est Judea sanctificacio eius, Israel potestas eius. Alleluia!

> *Hic angeli dulciter cantabunt in celo,* Alleluia.   **(N-Town 41/368+sd–370+sd)**

It is an unusual performance of this psalm, not least because the angels in Heaven join in the Alleluias, themselves an unusual feature. In fact, the use of the incipit 'Exiit Israel' instead of the expected 'In exitu Israel' may point to some usage that I have not been able to discover; and it does not appear that the psalm is being sung under an antiphon. The play does however follow the *Legenda Aurea* in these particulars.[93] How much of the psalm is sung is not clear: but the bishop and princes hold an indignant meeting about it for the next thirty-nine lines before they break into the procession physically, so the apostles presumably continue to sing the psalm until about **41/409+sd**, when the princes attack the procession. When the procession continues there is no indication that the apostles resume the psalm, although if there is any way to go one assumes that the producer would not let the procession continue in silence.

When the procession has arrived at the place of burial, the apostles place the body in the sepulchre, censing it and singing:

> *Hic ponent corpus in sepulcrum insensantes et cantantes.*

JOHANNES   De terra plasmasti me et carne induisti me;
                      Redemptor meus, Domine, resuscita me in novissimo die.
                                                (N-Town 41/452+sd–454)

The events of the office are here telescoped somewhat: according to the Sarum manual, when the body has been placed in the grave the psalm *Quemadmodum desiderat cervus* is sung under the antiphon *Ingrediar in locum,* and only after various prayers and another psalm (*Memento domine dauid,* under the antiphon *Hec requies mea*) is the psalm *Domine probasti me* sung under the antiphon *De terra plasmasti me* while the body is sprinkled with earth by all present.[94] In the play the service ends with the blessing of the body in the usual form:

> *Hic vnanimiter benedicent corpus in nomine Patris, et Filii, et Spiritus Sancti.*
>   **(N-Town 41/455+sd)**

---

91 *Inhumatio defuncti*: see MS 152–62.
92 MS 155. The omission of the *Gloria patri* is confirmed in the *Commendatio Animarum,* MS 119.
93 See LA 508; GL 453.
94 MS 157–8.

This takes the place of the commendation that immediately follows the final singing of *De terra plasmasti* in the Sarum manual:[95]

> Commendo animam tuam deo patri omnipotenti: terram terre: cinerem cineri: puluerem pulueri: in nomine patris [et filii et spiritus sancti]

> (I commend your soul to God the omnipotent Father: earth to earth, ashes to ashes, dust to dust: in the name of the Father, and of the Son, and of the Holy Spirit.)

Curiously, I think, there is little element of the burial service in the various deposition scenes in the cycles, although a producer may well have added material that does not appear in the script. In the York *Death of Christ*, for instance, Joseph and Nicodemus agree 'To dresse hym with dedis full dewe' (**York 36/385**) and proceed to wrap Christ in a sudary (shroud), to lay him in the grave and to anoint the body with myrrh and aloes (**36/387–403**). This follows St John's Gospel (John 19/38–42), which is the only account of the burial to include Nicodemus or the spices: the synoptic Gospels all say that Christ was wound in a shroud and laid in the tomb by Joseph of Arimathea, and that the women prepared spices to be used on the body after the Passover. St John says specifically that Christ's body was wound in the linen cloth 'with the spices, as the manner of the Jews is to bury' (AV John 19/40). The York play's reversal of these actions, leaving the anointing until last, means that only a token anointing of the body – already wrapped and laid in the tomb as it is – could be staged. This may reflect the playwright's wish to present a burial in a form convenient for dramatic presentation: the whole action takes place in these nineteen lines.

In other circumstances one would suspect a ceremony in which a sung liturgical text might be added to the written script, but that is probably not the case here. There is certainly a ceremony in the Sarum manual that covers all these actions: in the preparation of the body of a dead monarch, the body is washed, anointed with balsam and aromatic spices and wrapped in a waxed linen cloth, a procedure that no doubt owes much to the biblical account of Christ's burial.[96] It is however not accompanied by any liturgical ceremony. The preparation of any other body is accomplished by washing it and wrapping it in cloth, after which it is placed on the bier during the recitation of Vespers:[97] but there is no reason to think that any Vespers material should be included in the staging of this play.

The Towneley Crucifixion play ends with Joseph and Nicodemus wrapping the body and taking it 'vnto the kyrke' on a bier (**Towneley 23/655–60**), an intention that is stated in a single six-line stanza. The remaining stanza of the play begins with Nicodemus's agreement to this and ends with a conventional commendation of the audience, so the action of wrapping Christ either does not happen on stage or occurs briefly enough for the body to be removed on the bier at the end of the play. The Chester Crucifixion, similarly, ends with a statement of intent in the very last stanza

---

[95] MS 158–9.
[96] MS 121. These details do not appear in the York manual.
[97] MS 122. These details do not appear in the York manual.

(**Chester 16A/472–9**), and it seems that no preparation of the body takes place, even though Nicodemus gives the biblical details that he has brought myrrh and aloes of a hundred pounds weight. The N-Town Burial gives two lines each to the grave-clothes and the 'oyntment', and it is clear that Christ has been wrapped, anointed and laid in the tomb before the next line (**N-Town 34/138–42: Passion Play II/1180–4**). The Cornish cycle dramatisation was originally as simple, the entombment being undertaken by Joseph and Nicodemus after Mary has been dismissed:

NICODEMUS   Leave me now to embalm him,
Before wrapping him in cloth,
With aloes, myrrh also.
And they shall preserve his body,
That it do not decay ever,
Though it be in the grave a thousand years;
Nor shall his skin be once broken;
Well embalmed he is indeed,
Now wrap him in linen.   (Ordinalia 2/3196–3204)

After this, Joseph takes one line to wrap the body and two lines to lay it in the tomb. As it stands this scene includes no ceremony. At some stage a producer has decided to make the anointing more ceremonious, however, and a later, additional direction after **2/3201** requires Mary to anoint Christ's head (she has evidently ignored the attempt to dismiss her), Mary Magdalene to anoint his feet, and 'the other' Mary to anoint his heart. One would like to know whether this SD was intended to add to the action of the play or simply to make explicit something that had always been staged anyway. I suspect that the former is the case: Mary must ignore her dismissal from the scene if she is to take part in the anointing; the presence of the three Maries in any case contradicts Nicodemus's stated intent to anoint Christ himself; and the SD is misplaced, the proper place for it probably being after **2/3202**. This does not however say anything about the possibility of liturgical ceremony informing the anointing and wrapping as originally undertaken by Joseph and Nicodemus alone.

Any liturgical ceremonial would apparently not involve singing in any case: but the plays are so consistent in the brevity of this scene that I am inclined to take the texts at face value. One reason for this brevity may be that the scenes with Longinus, Pilate and Mary, necessary for the biblical story, leave little room for ceremonial expansion; another may be that in the circumstances of Christ's deposition and burial very few people were involved (Joseph, Nicodemus, the Blessed Virgin; and two other Maries in the *Ordinalia*), so that the forces for singing or even saying a burial service are not available. I suspect that the first of these reasons is the more important one, however, for even the Digby Burial play, which is institutional not civic, offers only the briefest of entombments:

JOSEPHE   Now in his grave, lat vs ly hym down,

Sepelit[ur]

And then resorte we agayn to the town,
To her what wille men saye.   (Christ's Burial 833–5)

In this case there has been a long *pietà* and a scene in which Mary cannot bring herself to be parted from Christ's body, so the playwright may well have felt (correctly, no doubt) that a burial service would be too slow an end to the play. But for a religious house there would be another reason. On the evening of Good Friday the brothers would celebrate the office of burial in which the Cross was placed in an Easter sepulchre, not to be removed until the morning of Easter Day.[98] The Digby *Burial of Christ* was written to be performed on the afternoon of Good Friday, so that a burial service in the play would pre-empt the ceremony of the same evening.[99]

One more burial should be mentioned – that of Pontius Pilate at **Ordinalia 3/2084–6** and again at **3/2110+sd**. Here again no detail is given, and there is no indication of a service or ceremony of any sort. In this case the reason is, probably, that Pilate is not only a very wicked man but one who has committed suicide, so that his body is disposed of in the simplest and quickest way possible.

Sacrifice and blessing

Sacrifice, being no part of a Christian service, is represented textually by only a plain statement of intent:

> [ABRAHAM] That pereles prince I praye
> Myn offerand heretill haue it,
> My sacryfice þis day
> I praye þe lorde ressayve it. **(York 10/297–300)**

Blessing is likewise signalled by a statement of intent, but is usually given in the name of the three persons of the Trinity. This follows the standard liturgical form, where the specifics of the blessing are delivered *In nomine patris, et filii, et spiritus sancti* (In the name of the Father, and of the Son, and of the Holy Spirit). When the intent to bless is known, in fact, this formula is all that is required to make a stage blessing, as when Joachim and Anna give their daughter Mary their blessing (**Mary Play 323, 325; N-Town 9/53, 55**), to which Mary replies 'Amen' on each occasion. The plays have many blessings in complete form – that is, with specific intention expressed – but it is unnecessary to give more than one example. When the King and Queen of 'Marcylle' decide to go together to Jerusalem to be baptised by Peter, Mary Magdalene blesses their project:

> MARY Syth 3e ar consentyd to þat dede,
> The blyssyng of God gyff to yow wyll I.
> He xall save yow from all dred,
> *In nomine Patrys, et Filij, et Spiritus Sancti.* Amen.
> **(Mary Magdalen 1712–15)**

---

[98] On the Easter sepulchre in England see Sheingorn *Easter Sepulchre*, especially Chapter 1. The ceremony is discussed in Tyrer *Holy Week*, 140–1.

[99] See the statement about the play following line **55+heading**. The play dates from c.1520, was apparently written by a Carthusian, and may come from the Charterhouse at Kingston-on-Hull: see Baker, Murphy and Hall, lxxxi–lxxxii.

This format is recognisable even when, as occasionally happens, the wording is modified:

[REX]	Yower pvere blyssynd gravnt vs tylle,
	Þat, feythfully, I crave.

PETRUS	Now in þe name of Jhesu,
	Cum Patre et Sancto Speritu,
	He kepe þe and save.

(**Mary Magdalen 1858–62**)

Elias's blessing of the bread in the Chester Antichrist play uses the correct form of words but with asides:

[HELIAS]	Have here breadd both too.
	But I must blesse yt or yt goe,
	that the fyend, mankyndes foe,
	on hit have no power.

This bread I blesse with my hand
in Jesus name, I understand,
the which ys lord of sea and land
and kinge of heaven on hie.
In nomine Patris, that all hath wrought,
et Filii virginis, that deare us bought,
et Spiritus Sancti, ys all my thought,
on God and persons three.

(**Chester 23/565–76**)

A blessing was accompanied by the sign of the Cross for each person of the Trinity, and although this is not in the Chester text it is clear that Elias has made the sign of the Cross: *Primus Mortuus* cannot look at the bread, and is afraid of 'That prynt that ys uppon hit pight' (**Chester 23/579**).

7.9 Questions of provenance

The liturgical content of any early English play may be difficult to track down, as this chapter shows. In many cases, fortunately, it is hardly necessary: but if we start from the premise, stated in section 7.1, that the playwright, the producer and the director of music are all likely to have been educated in a clerical tradition, and in most cases were clerics themselves, the liturgical content of the plays immediately becomes potentially important. Even if the influence of liturgy in a play is not immediately obvious, it may still be vital, affecting the use of music, of gesture, even of properties. This chapter has, I hope, demonstrated the possible importance of the liturgical content of various plays.

I suggested earlier that the precise nature of the liturgical content would depend on the playwright or musical director – that a secular cleric would introduce liturgical quotations from his own diocesan use, while a religious would quote from the use of his order. It is not likely that there will be a simple correlation between the playwright's or music director's use and the liturgical content of a play, however, for a variety of reasons concerning the circumstances of his life; and there are particular problems around the time of the Reformation, as the following example demonstrates.

In the Chester play of Moses there are three Latin texts that should probably be declaimed by the characters in whose speeches they occur.[100] The second of these is a prophecy of Christ's coming, recited by Balaham:

Orietur stella ex Jacobb et exurget homo de Israell et consurget omnes duces alienigenarum et erit omnis terra possessio eius.   (**Chester 5/319+sd** [part])

Lumiansky and Mills noted that this text is not close to the biblical source, Numbers 24/17–18:[101]

Orietur stella ex Jacob. et consurget virga de israhel: et percutiet duces moab. vastabitque omnes filios seth: et erit ydumea possessio eius.

(There shall come a star out of Jacob, and a sceptre shall rise out of Israel, and shall smite the corners of Moab, and destroy all the children of Sheth. And Edom shall be a possession . . .)

The Chester version, they pointed out, 'excludes the application to the immediate situation of the Jews and makes [the text] more clearly Messianic'. In fact, the Chester version is liturgical, the text of a responsory set in the Sarum Antiphoner for the third week in Advent, feria iv:[102]

Orietur stella ex iacob et exurget homo de Israel et consurget omnes duces alienigenarum. Et erit omnis terra pocessio eius.
Et adorabunt eum omnes reges terre omnes gentes servient ei. Et erit . . .

The version given in MS H, which presents a rather different text of the play, substitutes 'confringet' for 'consurget', a reading that is found also in the Sarum breviary and in the Worcester antiphoner.[103]

What are we to make of these different readings? Much hinges on the reasons of James Miller, the antiquarian scribe of MS H, for copying a reading different from that of the Group. If the Exemplar read only 'consurget', then we must postulate that Miller knew the other reading (presumably from a service book), preferred it, and chose to write it in his copy of the plays even though it had no authority in the play texts. Lumiansky and Mills's examination of Miller's work does not rule out the possibility that Miller might make this kind of change:[104] but they seem more convinced that his priority was to make sense of the material that he had in front of him:[105]

---

[100] This matter is discussed fully in Volume 2.
[101] *Chester* II, 72; *Essays*, 100ff.
[102] AS plate j. The spelling 'pocessio' is not significant; AS reads 'alienigenorum', which is clearly an error.
[103] BS I, cxvii; WA 5. The Worcester responsory has a different verse, 'De iacob exiet'.
[104] See *Essays*, 71–6.
[105] *Essays*, 76.

We acknowledge Miller as the first editor of the Chester cycle. We strongly suspect an idiosyncratic element in his text and doubt whether Chester was ever performed in the words that he supplies. But we recognize also that Miller was intent on making sense of a difficult Exemplar and was alert, as other scribes were not, to the possibilities of choice, the existence of error, and the desirability of completeness and coherence in his text.

I therefore prefer an alternative situation, in which Miller was faced with two available readings in the Exemplar and, alone of the Chester scribes, chose 'confringet' rather than 'consurget'.

What is the significance of these two readings? 'Confringet' appears in the liturgy of a cathedral priory, Worcester, and may therefore be the version preferred in Benedictine houses. A search of Benedictine service books is needed to establish that, although such a search would probably not be conclusive.[106] On the other hand it cannot be said that 'confringet' and 'consurget' represent the monastic and secular readings, respectively, since both appear in the Sarum books.[107] Furthermore, churches in Chester would have followed the Use of Lichfield up to 1542, when the Convocation of Canterbury prohibited all but the Salisbury breviary in the southern province, so that there is a third possibility for the derivation of these readings.[108] Even if Chester churches clung to the Lichfield use, which was probably almost indistiguishable from the Salisbury one, they would have changed after the Act of Uniformity of January 1549, when the Salisbury use was followed in both provinces. Roughly, the situation in Chester at different times was as follows:

(1) In St Werburgh's Abbey, the monastic use was followed until the suppression (1539–40), and perhaps until the prohibition of 1542; thereafter the Sarum use was required, and a change presumably occurred, although at what stage we do not know.[109]

(2) In secular churches in the city of Chester the use of Lichfield would be followed until the prohibition of 1542; thereafter, as in the Abbey, a change to the Sarum use should have occurred.

(3) The Act of Uniformity of 22 January 1549 required both provinces to follow the Sarum use: in fact, the introduction of the Book of Common Prayer in June that year changed the situation considerably in any case, but the Act

---

[106] Very few English Benedictine antiphoners survive, and in some respects the difference between the uses of individual Benedictine houses was as great as that between monastic and secular uses.

[107] AS plate j is not from the Barnwell antiphoner, an Augustinian book, but from Bodleian Library, MS Bodley 948, 'a Sarum Antiphonal of *circ.* 1400 from the Church of St Mary Axe, London' (AS, Introduction, p. 78); the edition of the Sarum breviary is based on the Chevallon print of 1531.

[108] Ratcliff *Book of Common Prayer*, 9.

[109] St Werburgh's continued as a place of worship after the suppression of 1539–40, becoming a cathedral in 1541. I assume that a place so far from the centre of government might not find it necessary to spend money on new books, whatever was officially required.

ensured that the Sarum use was available to be followed throughout the kingdom during Mary's reign (1553–8).

We know from the documentary evidence that St Werburgh's was involved in the plays in the 1550s and 1560s, and at that time the cathedral music presumably used Sarum service books if Latin services were sung at all. In theory the cathedral might have used Lichfield books between the suppression (1539–40) and the Canterbury prohibition (1542), or even later, but in practice the monastic books would surely have continued in use until the advent of English services. Thus any plays written, revised or musically-directed by St Werburgh's staff up to 1542 would probably have taken liturgical material from the monastic use; after that date the material might have been from the Sarum use; and only in Mary's reign, it seems to me, could we be fairly sure that the Sarum use was followed. Any writing, revision or musical direction from secular churches in Chester would be from the Lichfield use up to 1542 and perhaps to 1549 as well: but there is no evidence that the plays ever used musicians from churches other than St Werburgh's.

There are several possible reasons for the occurrence of two readings in the Exemplar, then. One, or even both, might be a monastic reading; one or both might be a Sarum reading; and presumably one or both might be a Lichfield reading. Since the scribes of the Group manuscripts all chose one reading, however, with Miller choosing the other, we might speculate that Miller's choice – the older reading and therefore to him the more interesting one – had been cancelled in favour of the other, later and to the Group scribes more authoritative reading. In that case it is most likely that 'consurget' is the Sarum reading that was substituted for the monastic 'confringet' some time in the middle of the sixteenth century.

Of course there are other perfectly reasonable ways in which these two readings might have come into being in the Chester texts. My speculation is unprovable: and even to make it a likelihood would require some firm evidence of preference for each of these readings in the different uses. Unfortunately, such is the dearth of Lichfield and Chester books that such preferences are very unlikely ever to be demonstrated.

I wish nevertheless to state briefly what I believe might eventually lead us to a greater knowledge of the plays' origins. If it is possible to identify the liturgical content of a play to the extent that it can be located in a particular use (even better, to a particular church), then we have gone most of the way towards locating the play itself. This is of limited importance for plays of known provenance. In the case of the York and Chester cycles, for instance, there is the question whether the liturgical items are from the secular or monastic use: but while identification of the use involved would allow a proper choice of liturgical items to be made, ignorance on this point will hardly make a vital difference to a production. It is with plays of unknown origin, where the practical application of such knowledge is of less immediate interest, that a theoretically more important issue arises. In particular, the identification of the use involved could eventually shed light on what I might describe as The East Anglian Problem. A large proportion of the English drama of the late fifteenth century comes from the area of the Norfolk-Suffolk border around

Thetford and Bury St Edmunds, and the area of Cambridgeshire to the immediate west of that: but the documentary evidence is not helpful, and it has proved difficult to build up a picture of dramatic activity.[110] That this activity was important is shown by the textual remains: The Castle of Perseverance, Mankind, Wisdom, The Play of the Sacrament, The Conversion of St Paul, Mary Magdalen, The Killing of the Children, the various components of the N-Town Cycle, and some earlier plays which, although now fragmentary, show that the tradition of dramatic activity in that area was a long one. The question arises, therefore, whether the specific identity of the liturgical content of these plays can provide any clues as to their provenance.

Some years ago I made a search in various East Anglian service books (necessarily cursory, for time was limited) for the specific wordings of various play-text appearances of liturgical material. I chose certain textual features that were apparently unusual or specific to particular plays and tried to match them with texts from various liturgical books of identifiable uses. Some of these features have been discussed in this chapter – the 'Attollite portas' of the N-Town Harrowing of Hell, for instance – and all are discussed in Volume 2. I shall not detail here the texts, the books that I searched and the results: the results (such as they are) will be found in volume 2.[111] It will be enough to say that the results were all negative and inconclusive. On the evidence it did seem probable that the N-Town Purification play did not originate at Crowland (or, by extension, at another Benedictine house); that the Passion Play probably did not come from Ely, Lincoln or Peterborough; and that the Assumption does not belong to Bury St Edmunds, Ely or Lincoln.

None of these rather arbitrary results is a surprise: in fact, a positive result in any of these cases would have been almost incredible. My only regret is that the N-Town Assumption cannot be located at Ely, for a performance of that play on a sunny 15 August under the great lantern of St Etheldreda's cathedral would have been a wonderful experience. But Ely was never a strong contender anyway for that play, and there is no evidence that drama ever took place under the lantern there. Nor is the provisional elimination of Benedictine houses for some of these plays of any importance, for I do not see the Benedictines as a major sponsor of drama, however important they may have been at Chester. Given the known involvement of the Dominican Thomas Binham, the black-and-white symbolism in Wisdom and the emphasis on (and considerable skill shown in) sermons in the plays,[112] the Dominicans (Friar Preachers) are surely the most probable order to invest energy and intellectual resources into the initiation of dramatic activity.[113]

---

[110] The most important work on this question is still Richard Beadle's doctoral thesis, *The Medieval Drama of East Anglia* (The University of York, 1977)

[111] I reported my methods, material and results in a paper, *Eastern England: Liturgy in the N-Town Cycle*, in session 194 at the 22nd International Congress on Medieval Studies, Kalamazoo MI, 8 May 1987.

[112] This matter is dealt with further in Volume 2.

[113] Given the linguistic locations of much of the East Anglian drama, an investigation of the Dominican House at Thetford is needed: see Norton, Park and Binski *Dominican Painting in East Anglia*.

7.9 Questions of Provenance

In all, the problems concerned with the identification of liturgical material in the plays are as yet very far from a solution. Here, more than anywhere else, perhaps, is room for some carefully-designed research: but it must be said that the risk of getting nowhere is considerable.

8

THE PERFORMERS

8.1 Professional and amateur

Close examination of the evidence enables us to answer some of the questions posed at the beginning of this book, but by no means all of them. Questions on the precise nature of the musical performances, in particular, are impossible to answer on the basis of the types of evidence discussed so far. When known performers are singing a piece of music of which the title is known, the next stage is to ask some detailed questions about the performance itself: is the music polyphonic, are the singers supported by one or more instruments, and is any practice such as antiphony in use? When such questions cannot be answered by recourse to the evidence of the text and external records – as is usually the case – it is necessary to study the performers themselves: what was their status, what were the directorial expectations of them, and what were the traditions that they brought with them to the performance?

Examination of these issues must begin with a consideration of the concepts of the professional and the amateur as they applied to musicians in the fifteenth and sixteenth centuries. To a large extent these concepts were bound up with the issue of musical literacy. The situation was not a static one and did not present the same features in all places simultaneously, so any examination must take account of both date and place. For this reason the discussion will be restricted to the two centuries of the play texts and records studied here, and to England.

Late twentieth-century definitions of 'professional' and 'amateur' depend largely on the receipt of financial reward.[1] The distinction is one of quality of services rendered, the professional being held worthy of payment where the amateur is not. Two further considerations tend to confuse this picture. The first is that the individual may have a choice, with the result that some retain an amateur status even though the quality of their work is better than that of some professionals. Although this is rare, amateurs and professionals have certainly met to work together on equal terms in the past – for instance, in various sporting activities. One reason why it is rare for amateurs to do exceptionally well in a partly professional field, however, is that doing something well demands a considerable commitment of time and

---

[1] See, for example, the discussion of the rise of professional players of interludes in Wickham *Medieval Theatre*, 181–99.

resources. Hence the second consideration: on the whole, we think of amateurs as spending only part of their time on the activity concerned, whereas professionals make it their life's work. These various distinctions did all play a part in the musical life of fifteenth- and sixteenth-century England, but there were some vital differences. These were decided, in effect, by the matter of training. The situation is most unfamiliar to the late twentieth century in the realm of the professional lay singer trained in sacred music: so it will be useful to start there, moving on to discuss other types of singer and, finally, minstrels.

A singer trained in a collegiate, cathedral or monastic choir school of the late Middle Ages was a professional in the strictest modern sense of the term.[2] As a boy chorister, he would learn the psalter by heart and would also learn the rest of the plainsong repertory. Some of this huge body of music he would come to know by heart because of frequent repetition, but much of it is sung only rarely and would be read from a book. The singer, then, was taught to read the Latin texts, and also to read the plainsong notation in which the chants of the various services were written. This notation may include considerable subtleties in showing expressive features: but it is basically a pitch-notation, and does not show the strict durations necessary for the organisation of metrical and rhythmic units.

The most promising choristers were also taught to play keyboard instruments. One reason for this was the use of the organ to support the singers: but that instrument was also used in *alternatim* performance, in which singers and organ took alternate verses,[3] and to provide introductions to certain sung items, giving the pitch and mode of the piece. Much of this was no doubt improvised over the plainsong tunes, but increasingly it was composed: and such compositions are of course polyphonic.[4] A boy who learned the organ was likely to work with, or join, a select group of singers trained in vocal polyphony, a type of music in which the notation was quite different from that of plainsong. In late medieval measured music, it is the notation of rhythms that is the most difficult aspect, and it still gives most trouble to students learning musical paleography. One problem is that the possibility of triple mensuration, in which three, rather than two, of any duration make the next duration up, makes rhythmic interpretation contextual; the other is that this rhythmic complexity was matched by a variety of notational resources – coloration, various uses of the dot, imperfection by remote values, and so on – that are difficult to learn.[5] To some extent, too, the difficulty of late medieval notation

2 For the singers and their establishment in the secular cathedrals (principally Lincoln), see Edwards *Secular Cathedrals*, 159–75; for Wolsey's statutes for the Augustinians, 1519, see Gasquet *Henry VIII*, 73–5; and for the indenture of 1534 between the Abbot of Glastonbury and a singing man, see Gasquet *Glastonbury*, 107–10.
3 This was a form of antiphony, but it meant that the text was not heard in those verses played on the organ.
4 It is sometimes difficult to distinguish between vocal and instrumental polyphony: but the preludes in Paumann's *Fundamentum Organisandi* (mid-fifteenth century, and in continental sources) are certainly for organ, as are *alternatim* settings in the Mulliner Book, an English collection of about a century later.
5 See, for instance, Rastall *Notation*, chapter 6.

was used by musicians to keep their group exclusive. This attitude can be seen in such features as the late medieval use of canon and the complex notation of the Eton, Caius and Lambeth choirbooks, which inhabit a tradition of learned complexity needed to maintain the special status of its initiates.

By the time these choirbooks were produced, however, c.1500–10, notation had already simplified in general, coming into line with the further simplification of musical style in the latter part of the fifteenth century. The ability to read the notation of complex mensural music had previously set the choir-school-trained professional apart from all others.[6] Late in the century a general simplification of musical style made the worst notational complexities redundant, and at that stage mensural music became more accessible to amateurs as both performers and composers. It is only in the last two decades of the century that we find amateur composers – Sir William Hawte (c.1430–1497) and John Tuder (fl. 1466–96), both career administrators from Kent – taking their place alongside the professionals on more or less equal terms.[7] That there was a general move towards increased accessibility is suggested by the experiments with orthochronic notations, in which duration is simply and unambiguously shown; and at the same time the main features of triple mensuration began to fall into disuse.[8] From the earliest years of the sixteenth century musical and notational styles were such that musical amateurism became a worthwhile possibility. The period c.1500–40 in England saw a very interesting change in the technical and sociological aspects of musical life: the breakdown of elitism and exclusivity, the blurring of borders between professional and amateur, and the emergence of a new class of 'musicians' who destroyed the distinctions between singers and instrumentalists and earned for themselves (in some cases) the right to be called 'gentlemen'. This change will be discussed later.

To return to the fifteenth century, we have seen that the trained singer, able to read mensural notation and therefore to sing polyphony – that is, music in parts – was a very special case, with abilities that marked him out as a true professional in an area where amateurs could not compete. That part of their training that involved plainsong, however, long and arduous as it was, did not require the technical knowledge demanded by mensural notation. The training required for the singing of plainsong, therefore, was available to a much larger body of men and (in this case) women. These were the monks and nuns, friars, canons regular and secular, secular priests and clerks in minor orders whose lives consisted of the daily round of worship in the religious, collegiate and major secular churches.[9] We must

---

6 The only exceptions to this rule are truly exceptional – royalty. We know that Henry IV or Henry V was a composer, the 'Roy Henry' of the Old Hall Manuscript. Only royalty would have the opportunity to undergo such training without needing to use it for a livelihood. It is possible that Henry VI also had some skill at music; but by the time of Henry VIII it was already the period of amateur music-making, as we shall see, and although he was exceptional as an amateur musician he was not unique.

7 See the articles by Sydney Robinson Charles in NG 8/316 and 19/248, respectively.

8 On orthochronic notations and their use, see Rastall *Notation* and Benham 'Salve Regina'; also Bent 'New and Little-Known Fragments'.

9 'Religious' and 'secular' here have their strict meanings: 'religious' concerns the communities

remember that throughout the period concerned polyphony was not the normal music of worship but an exception. Plainsong was the normal method of performing the liturgical and ceremonial texts of the Church's daily life. Some chants, certainly, demanded more skill than others, while certain types of liturgical piece required the use of soloists or small hand-picked groups to sing chant that is usually more difficult than the main body. Thus any religious community might make use of members who had more natural ability as singers than others, and so spend more time in training them; but this is a difference of ability and commitment in undertaking the same kind of task – the singing of chant – not a difference of function. These singers are therefore professionals in a different sense: the daily round of worship is part of their religious or clerical vocation, their 'profession' in the true sense of that which they have professed. This is not a musical professionalism, then, and should not be confused with the professionalism of lay singers capable of performing polyphony from mensural notation.

A large part of the liturgical and ceremonial repertory is congregational. This music is relatively simple, uses a narrow pitch-range, and sets the text syllabically or nearly so. This part of the repertory includes those items, such as the hymns, in which repetition increases the chance of untrained singers to learn the music and sing effectively. Most religious were probably at least partly literate, so that the learning and performance of congregational items in a monastery could be accomplished partly by use of the written word (if not of the music), although memory and learning by ear must have been at least as important for most members of the community. The best-educated members might form a large choir, the training of which included a higher degree of reliance on reading. The average secular congregation must have been less literate, however, and we should assume that in secular cathedrals congregational items were normally learned by ear and sung from memory. In so far as members of such a congregation joined in, then, they did so as part of an oral tradition, not as part of a tradition of literacy, and it may be that they did not do so with much success.[10] On the other hand, we should not underestimate the memories and aural abilities of illiterate folk, who were probably much better than we should be at learning and performing by ear. As we shall see in section 8.6, it is possible to guess at the minimum abilities of a dramatic audience in the fields of music and liturgy.

The singers of secular polyphonic songs belonged to the first of these groups:

---

living under the vows of a monastic or other order, such as the friars or canons regular (under a 'rule'); 'secular' concerns the diocesan and parochial organisation of clergy providing worship, instruction and the sacraments to society at large.

[10] I ignore parish churches here, because the chances are that much of the service would be read or recited, not sung to plainsong. The situation in cathedral priories is different from that in monasteries and secular cathedrals, in that the singing at the 'cathedral' (as opposed to the 'monastic') services was led by the monks: but even in this case the greater part of the secular congregation was probably only passively involved.

The change to increased musical literacy that started in the very late fifteenth century and through the first half of the sixteenth was overtaken, in the field of English liturgy, by the reformed services of the 1540s onwards.

whenever singers performed polyphony in fifteenth-century England they were trained chapel singers. The singers of monophonic secular songs, on the other hand, belonged to the minstrel tradition, however indirectly. In England the minstrel tradition was a wholly oral – or rather, aural – one. Iconography is the only evidence that can be cited for this, but it seems consistent enough to be taken at face value: although singers of plainsong and polyphony are invariably depicted reading from notation,[11] no depictions of instrumentalists earlier than the late sixteenth century show the players doing this. This is not to say that minstrels could not read plainsong notation, and indeed one assumes that they may have done so in rehearsal: but in *performance*, it seems, they played from memory even when written music was available. This fact concerns not only the plainsong repertory, in fact, of which only a small part ever concerned minstrels: the few surviving books of basse dance tunes, written or printed in a non-rhythmic notation very like that of chant, could no doubt have been used in performance if the players so wished. The evidence – admittedly meagre, especially for England – suggests that they did not so wish.

It is true that we do not know what minstrel-music would look like if we saw it written down, but it is clear, I think, that no surviving piece of apparently instrumental music from the fifteenth or earlier centuries in England is likely to have been minstrels' music. Our information on the instrumental repertory is in fact non-existent: we have to assume that minstrels improvised over well-known tunes that they had memorised, and that the methods of training advocated by Al Farabi (d.950) continued in operation: namely, that the novice minstrel chose a tune, decided on a method of treatment, and played the tune many times in that way; then, choosing another method of treatment, repeated the process; and eventually, having exhausted the possibilities with that tune, chose another tune and went through the same process.[12] Learning to be a minstrel, then, took the apprentice minstrel through a number of fairly obvious stages: learning technical proficiency on the instrument; learning a repertory of tunes which, however they were picked up in the first place, were fixed in the minstrel's mind by repetition; and learning from his master a variety of possible treatments, which no doubt depended on the particular characteristics of his instrument[13] and which could then be applied to any given tune in the repertory to provide a set of varied presentations of that tune.

Many minstrels were singers, performing songs to an instrumental accompaniment provided by themselves or another minstrel. Of this repertory, too, we know very little, although a few song-titles have come down to us. There is no doubt that a minstrel-singer in a noble household could be an artist of very high

---

11 Occasionally singers seem to be reading plainsong only from a verbal text (facial expressions and concerted declamation suggest singing rather than speaking in such cases).

12 For Al Farabi (d.950) and his writing on minstrelsy, see D'Erlanger *La musique arabe*.

13 Some of the most exciting and rewarding work on medieval instrumental practice in the last twenty years or so has been concerned with finding out the capabilities and characteristic techniques of various instruments and making use of them in specific playing styles.

quality.[14] It is in this area, however, that amateur minstrels could go furthest: while an amateur instrumentalist would usually show his status by a greater or lesser degree of technical competence on the instrument, no exclusive technique prevented the amateur singer from following the profession successfully, given a good voice, a musical ear, and a memory for songs. Of course a professional minstrel-singer, like other professionals, had the advantage of a greater commitment available to a task on which his livelihood depended: but it was a matter of degree, not of kind. We may take it, then, that amateur singers performing a monophonic repertory might be quite successful and even rival a professional in his performance.

In the first half of the sixteenth century this situation changed considerably, for reasons that I have outlined above. The oral tradition remained strong in the field of amateur singing, and also maintained an unchanged role in liturgical singing. Professional church singers remained the principal users of complex notation for the performance of polyphony, although 'complex' denotes something on average less formidable than before. Although this properly remained a matter for 'professionals', the field nevertheless opened up to some extent to amateurs, and by the end of the century the rising merchant class, as well as the nobility, had bought considerable musical knowledge. This affected instrumental performance, as well: minstrels became musically literate, and made use of suitable music in a new style of relatively simple composed polyphony.[15] In this process the new invention of printing played a considerable role, although not to the same extent as in the field of literature. At the same time, the new accessibility of polyphony coincided with a breakdown of the demarcation between singers and instrumentalists. It now became normal for a musician to read notation and to be a proficient singer and instrumental player. Because the merchant classes now wished to learn music, there arose a new type of music teacher, conversant with instrumental and vocal music, who could teach the merchants' wives and daughters – and sometimes the merchants themselves – to play the lute, keyboard or other instruments and to sing partsongs – in short, to take part in a more general musicality available to all with the time and money necessary for its pursuit.

This new professional had pretensions to a new status, no longer a servant but a 'gentleman'. In the middle of the sixteenth century the chapel singers in royal service became *gentlemen* of the Chapel Royal, and the aspirations of both a freelance and a household musician in this direction can be seen in the autobiography

---

14 I think that these singers were usually harpers and went under that title. For harpers as singers, and for the titles of songs, see Rastall 'Minstrelsy', 90–1; for the instruments used as accompaniment, see Rastall 'Consort-groupings', 184–6.

15 The first indication of minstrel-literacy in England dates from 1533–4, when the Norwich waits were given 3s 4d to learn to read mensural notation: see G.A. Stephen, 'The Waits of the City of Norwich', *Norfolk Archaeology* 25 (1933), 7f. England had nothing to compare with the printed instrumental works of Attaingnant, Phalèse, Gervaise and others in mid-century, but by the end of the century several collections suitable for the London waits were available. Morley recommended his *Consort Lessons* of 1599 to the London waits, which gives us an idea of the quality and standards of the group.

of Thomas Whythorne.[16] Whythorne was a typical all-rounder of the better sort: something of a poet, a composer, singer and performer on the lute, harpsichord and organ. This diversity of talents can be seen also in the town waits, an institution that had previously been much more limited. From being, as far as we can see, a loud band of shawms and trumpet in the fifteenth century, they became a much more flexible group in the sixteenth, learning to read notation and to play a variety of instruments, soft as well as loud.[17] Moreover, this flexibility enabled such men to become 'musicians' rather than 'minstrels', and in the middle of the century we find versatile groups such as the Coventry waits in James Hewitt's time, who doubled the duties of town waits with those of singers in Holy Trinity Church.[18] This versatility, bringing together the activities of what would formerly have been two completely different types of musician, would have been unthinkable in the fifteenth century. By this time 'professional' had certainly changed its meaning slightly, for the opportunities for amateurs to do well in music had surely increased. The difference between amateur and professional, then, was no longer wholly one of training and capabilities, but largely of proficiency in activities that were open to both.

At this stage we shall discuss the musical performers in the plays under various headings. Since the majority of play texts and surviving records date from the sixteenth century we shall have to concentrate our attention in that period: but we shall nevertheless find that some useful inferences can be made also for fifteenth-century performances of texts surviving in an older form. Before discussing some roles in which musical competence is an important issue, however, it will be useful to look briefly at the kind of role that I believe could have involved singing by actors with no professional competence in music.

In several plays the singing of a congregational item is required. Although a single character or a small group of characters is sometimes specified for this – and it may be apparent that one or more professional singers were involved – in some cases the group of characters is a large one. In this case we must assume that, rather than professional singers being drawn in, the cast members themselves had to perform the musical item. I have in mind such cues as those at **Chester 21/120+sd**, where the Apostles sing the hymn *Veni creator*, and **York 9/266+md**, where Noah and his family sing in thanksgiving for their deliverance after the Flood. In cases like this second one, where the text is not specified and we therefore have no evidence of the kind of piece to be performed, we must assume that the item chosen would have been a congregational piece, simply because it is inconceivable that such a large proportion of the cast would have been trained singers drafted in from a local church – for which, in fact, there is no evidence anywhere.[19]

In preparing the music for cycle performances I have found no real problem with

---

[16] See Whythorn *Autobiography, passim*.

[17] See Rastall *Secular Musicians, passim*; Woodfill *Musicians*, especially chapter 4.

[18] Further on Hewitt and his colleagues, see section 8.3, below.

[19] I except from this, of course, the use of a group of singers for angelic roles or as shepherds,

this. Producers have sometimes cast actors who cannot sing, but this is infrequent, and we should assume that medieval producers did not make this mistake. In general, anyway, a competent amateur actor – then as now – has a strong usable voice and a reasonably good ear (even if an untrained one), so that learning to sing a piece of music is not too difficult. A modern cast faces two related difficulties that did not confront its medieval counterpart. First, modern actors tend to rely on notated music, but the unfamiliarity of plainsong notation is a real block to the learning process, at least in the early stages. Second, a modern actor does not have as highly-developed an aural sense, nor as well-trained a memory, as a medieval one had. In the event I have always provided the text and the notation for a cast learning a sung item, but have nevertheless concentrated on teaching the music and the words by ear. In a piece like *Veni creator*, which has a memorable, metric and repeated tune, learning the first verse is easy enough, although there is considerable difficulty as additional verses are learned which have to be fitted to the tune. Modern actors do not feel confident when relying wholly on their memories for a sung item, and this is of course especially so when it is a Latin text being sung. Not surprisingly, the trained musicians find this more nerve-wracking than those who have not been trained to work principally from notated music.

The actors playing the Apostles or the Noah family, then, can be taught to sing a plainsong piece, in unison, and to perform it with some aplomb: but the confidence with which the performance will happen, and ultimately the success of the performance, does depend on the amount of material that they have to learn. One verse of *Veni creator* (as given in MS H, as it happens), is no problem: in the 1983 production at Leeds I made the Apostles learn all seven verses, but in the end they decided to sing fewer than that to reduce the strain involved.

This strain, if one is to be practical, must be taken into account in choosing an item where it is unspecified in the text. In the 1994 production of nine York plays in York I made the Noah family learn the whole of Psalm 112 (AV 113), *Laudate pueri dominum*, to one of the simpler tones: this psalm is only eight verses plus the doxology, but again the cast did not feel able to cope with it under the required conditions. The solution to the problem in this case was not to cut down the amount of singing but to have the words of the psalm painted on a cloth, where the actors could see it but the audience could not.

In both of these cases it is clear that a modern cast labours under certain disadvantages compared with a medieval one. None of the modern actors already knew the Latin text, nor the music, while in the case of the psalm the performance-practice, too, had to be learned from first principles. In all cases of 'congregational' singing by the actors, I have felt that the demands would not have been excessive for a group of medieval citizens, who already knew the texts and music of the items concerned through hearing them many times, even if they had not learned them by heart and were not sure of the text's meaning.

which are discussed later in this chapter: I am here discussing the roles of historical mortal characters in general.

To some extent this capability – or rather, its assumed limitations – has to be taken into account in choosing a plainsong item to be sung by the actors. Where there is a choice, a more obviously 'congregational' item should be chosen and an item suitable for a choir rejected. In practice, the difference is usually between items in syllabic style on the one hand, and items in neumatic or melismatic style on the other. Where a piece in neumatic style is chosen, actors may cope with an easier example but are likely to find a more complicated one too difficult to learn. In 1994 I chose two items for the citizens to sing at the Entry into Jerusalem, **York 25/287+md** and **544+md**. For the first of these the antiphon *Osanna filio David* is the most likely candidate according to the internal evidence of the text. It is also short, mainly syllabic, of a fairly narrow pitch-range and with some melodic repetition, so it is an obvious congregational piece, and it worked very well. For the end of the play the processional responsory *Ingrediente domino* seemed to fit the occasion, as this is the item sung during the processional entry into the church at the Palm Sunday procession. This turned out to be much harder for the cast, however: it is longer and in neumatic style, and the cast found it very much more difficult both to learn and to sing. In the end we had to omit it, and the cast repeated the antiphon *Osanna filio David* at the end of the play, instead.

These experiences cannot tell us that one piece of music is possible in a play while another is not: we know far too little about the knowledge and capabilities of a medieval citizen for that. They do however suggest the kind of criteria that we should bear in mind when choosing and rehearsing musical items with the cast, and that may have been in operation in late medieval times. And as we cannot now enter fully into the minds of medieval people, the lessons learned in modern production are helpful, if we take account of the circumstantial differences, in our decisions about repertory and rehearsal in 'congregational' music.

8.2 The problem of female roles

Many late medieval plays on the Continent used female actors for the female roles, but this was never the case, as far as we know, in the English plays. The evidence is of course incomplete: no records survive for the East Anglian or Cornish plays, for instance, and it is therefore entirely possible that females played female roles in those dramas. Where we have records, however, for the northern cycles organised civically through the trade guilds, the plays were performed by all-male casts. The adjective 'all-male' is carefully chosen: the frequently-made assertion that in these plays female roles were taken by *men* is seriously misleading and begs the most important question of the whole subject of casting. Recent experiments in playing Shakespeare with young adult males in female roles would have bewildered that playwright considerably, just as the use of young adult males to play the young Eve or the young Virgin Mary would have bewildered a medieval audience.

This is not to say that mature males with changed voices never played female roles, for the records show that they did. But while they were perfectly satisfactory for older roles, such as the Virgin Mary at the end of her life or the prophetess Anna at the Purification, mature males would not have been suitable for younger roles. These were played by males who had not yet reached puberty – boys. In this section I shall attempt to show that the situation then was not at all what it is now; that a whole class of actors existed, suitable for playing female roles, which we have now lost; and that recent discussions about the effects of having 'men' play young female roles, and the supposed problems presented, are largely irrelevant.[20]

The misunderstanding has arisen from assumptions that seemed authorised by common sense but were in fact erroneous:

(1) Male actors are of two types: 'men' and 'boys'.

(2) 'Boy' indicates a male who has not yet reached puberty. By implication it therefore means *'small* boy', not above fourteen years old, or fifteen at the most. Such an actor is small of stature, with a small vital capacity (lung volume). He therefore has a small, piping voice which has not yet broken. He is emotionally immature and, being in his very early teens, is too young to have much experience as an actor.

(3) 'Man' indicates a mature, adult male with a broken voice. If he can be categorised as a 'young' man the implication is that he is not many years past puberty: not less than seventeen years old, but perhaps in his early twenties at most.

(4) There is a state between these two that can more or less be ignored because it is generally thought unsuitable for an actor. At puberty there is a period when the voice cannot be controlled closely enough for special uses such as drama or music.

The first of these assumptions, partly supported by the last, has led to an anachronistic polarisation of possibilities. Directors wishing to use an all-male cast now think only in terms of the present-day situation, where a female role must be played by a fifteen-year-old (at most) boy or a young (broken-voiced) man. Assumption (3) leads in two directions. The first is that an older man can indeed play the more dignified roles, as the records show. The second is that a young man may be considered to play a variety of role-types: at one end of the spectrum is the young attractive female, for which the actor must hide his masculinity as best he can, while at the other is a series of roles in which the actor's masculinity, clearly at odds with the role, can be exploited in various ways. Here a discussion is made easier by the use of recognisable modern concepts, such as 'pantomime dame' and 'drag queen'. Between these extremes there is an area where the physical qualities of the male actor can be used in a more realistic presentation – Mrs Noah in her quieter versions, and the Mothers of the Innocents.

The second assumption has had serious consequences in denying boys much participation in biblical drama: this subject, which is my main interest here, has received no real discussion in the past. It is in critical writings on the choirboy

---

[20] The ideas presented in this section first appeared in Rastall 'Female roles' (1985), which followed a series of articles in *Medieval English Theatre* 5/2 (1983) about 'transvestite' or 'cross-played' roles. I have shortened some parts of my argument for present purposes.

companies of the sixteenth and early seventeenth centuries that the principal results of the assumption are found. On the one hand a number of scholars who have studied the choirboy plays have concluded that the texts themselves demand considerable expertise on the part of the actors, and that that expertise must therefore have been available:[21] on the other, the assumption that choirboys were *small*,[22] and that a boy's emotional, physical and experiential limitations generally ended in failure to create a serious female role, has led other writers to argue that the choirboy companies showed little acting ability,[23] that the actors' inadequacy in love-scenes was responsible for such scenes being played as comic,[24] or that the actors must have been 'consciously ranting in oversize parts'.[25] This latter view implies that the dramatist's intention was unrealisable by the choirboys, a position that clearly needs to be resolved. Even Maurice Charney's thoughtful and largely credible analysis of what boy actors could reasonably be expected to accomplish sounds a little like special pleading: and his difficulty is made explicit only when he remarks that Pandora's temperamental condition under the influence of Saturn is 'easily within the grasp of a twelve- or thirteen-year-old boy'.[26] Undoubtedly there were few boys of that age in the top rank of actors, and most commentators on the choirboy companies are unhappy with the rather limited range of experience, physique and emotional maturity that an age-range of eight to thirteen implies. Fortunately we do not have to work within these limitations.

The primary assumption which leads to those noted earlier in this section is a simple one: that puberty in boys has always taken place at the age of fourteen or so, as it does now. David Wulstan has noted, however, that puberty in males has grown progressively earlier during the present century, and that at the beginning of the century it was not unusual to find an eighteen-year-old still singing treble, 'whereas now such a boy would be regarded as something of a freak'.[27] The age of puberty has probably always varied slightly in earlier centuries with such factors as climate and nutrition,[28] but not to an extent that is significant for the present discussion. It

21 For example Brian Gibbons, *Jacobean City Comedy* (London: Hart-Davis, 1968), especially 26–8; E.J. Jensen in *Comparative Drama* 2 (1968), 100–11.
22 See, for example, J. Reibetanz in *Renaissance Drama* n.s. 5 (1972), 89–121; and Michael Shapiro in *Comparative Drama* 3 (1967), 42–53, and *Research Opportunities in Renaissance Drama* 18 (1975), 13–18.
23 See A. Caputi, *John Marston, Satirist* (Ithaca NY: Cornell University Press, 1961), especially 96–110.
24 J.I. Cope, 'Marlowe's *Dido* and the Titillating Children', *English Literary Renaissance* 4 (1974), 315–25: see 316 *et passim*.
25 R.A. Foakes, 'John Marston's Fantastical Plays: *Antonio and Mellida* and *Antonio's Revenge*', *Philological Quarterly* 41 (1962), 228–39, especially 236.
26 M. Charney, 'Female Roles and the Children's Companies: Lyly's Pandora in *The Woman in the Moon*', *Research Opportunities in Renaissance Drama* 22 (1979), 37–43, especially 38.
27 Wulstan 'Vocal colour', especially 25–7; Tanner *Growth at Adolescence*, especially 153.
28 Weiss 'Pubertal Change', 126–59 and 132–3; Tanner, *op. cit.*, Chapter V, especially 121. The only historical period for which there is evidence of maturation occurring as early as in the present century is that of the later Roman Empire: see Marcel Durry, 'Le mariage des filles impubères chez les anciens Romains', *Anthropos* 50 (1955), 432–34. See Tanner 154, however, for the possibility that girls matured at around 14 in medieval times, which would be correct for the

will not be far wrong to take seventeen or eighteen, rather than thirteen or fourteen, as the normal average age for the beginning of male maturation in earlier centuries. Historical work has also indicated that the onset of puberty in girls (shown by the menarche) has always occurred a year or more earlier than that in boys (shown by the voice-change).[29]

Before discussing some of the evidence for this, it will be useful briefly to review the process of pubertal development in the male. D.A. Weiss has distinguished three phases of the overall transformation that he refers to as 'puberty'. In the first phase, which he calls 'pubescence', the changes begin: here 'signs of disorganization are most conspicuous'.[30] In the second phase, the main period of 'pubertal develop-ment', 'the transformations become most apparent'. I shall refer to this as the 'transitional' phase. In the third phase, 'adolescence', 'the functions continue on a newly organized level'. However, adolescence is not the same as maturity, for in this phase 'transformations continue to occur but at a slower and more orderly pace'. Vocally, this last phase includes the 'settling down' period for the singing voice, in which the voice finds its eventual bass, baritone or tenor register. Puberty does not necessarily include a 'breaking' of the voice, with 'sudden and involuntary changes in its pitch and quality': in fact, Weiss rejects the breaking of the voice as a common symptom of pubescence, believing that in the majority of cases the voice simply descends gradually during puberty, allowing a treble singer to become an alto before further vocal transformation to the eventual tenor, baritone or bass register. Tanner also notes this, adding that the deepening of the voice takes place fairly late in the maturing process.[31]

I shall not try to deal consistently with the changing states of the pubescent, transformational or transitional, and adolescent actor. A role best played by a prepubescent male will not be ruined by a pubescent one (as long as his voice is stable), and even a transitional actor may be able to play the role successfully. Similarly, an adolescent may well be able to play a role that would be best played by a mature, postpubertal actor. Puberty affects individuals in different ways, at different rates.

The order of events in the maturation process follows a standard sequence, however, and this common pattern formed the basis for Daw's investigation of J.S. Bach's choir at Leipzig in the year 1744. This work is important for my present argument because Daw showed that the average age of the boys at the onset of

---

BVM's conception of Christ: in this case the difference in age at puberty between girls and boys was apparently greater than the two years or so that was general thereafter.

I do of course confine my argument to Western Europe, for the situation certainly has been very different elsewhere.

[29] Wulstan 26; Tanner 1 and 149.

[30] Weiss, 129. Weiss probably had in mind the sometimes rather dramatic onset of the growth-spurt: the start of menstruation in girls and seminal emission in boys, the development of the breasts in girls and the genitalia in both sexes, and the voice-change in boys. For the sequence of events in both sexes, see Johnson and Everitt *Essential Reproduction*, especially Figure 6.7 on p. 151.

[31] Weiss, 134; Tanner, 34.

pubescence was probably a little over seventeen years.[32] Daw noted that Bach's choir consisted entirely of schoolboys, so that the distribution of trebles, altos and tenors/basses must coincide with that of unchanged, transitional, and changed voices, respectively. On this basis he made a statistical analysis which led him to the following conclusions:[33]

— Few voices began to change (Daw used 'break') under the age of sixteen;
— Hardly any were completely changed by the age of seventeen;
— Most had begun to change by the age of eighteen;
— Most had completed the change by the age of 17½ to 18½; and
— Unusually late development resulted in trebles and altos aged nineteen and even twenty years.

Such evidence as exists for other centuries before the present one suggests that the age of puberty remained broadly constant.[34] That it was on average three or four years later than now puts a different complexion on some well-known evidence. John Rainoldes, who played Hippolyta at the age of seventeen in 1566, was presumably still prepubertal, with a treble voice: certainly there is no reason to think that he was transitional or adolescent, much less that he was postpubertal with a changed voice.[35] It must be emphasised, too, that seventeen to eighteen is a rough *average* estimate for male puberty in earlier times: the actual age at which the onset of puberty occurred was a little more variable than now. While voices did change as early as fourteen or so,[36] it was not unduly remarkable for a boy to remain a treble until the age of twenty. There were no doubt thirteen-year-olds playing demanding female roles, for child actors must usually have started their careers before the age of ten, and some fifteen-year-olds must have had changed voices: but as some males retained their treble voices even until they were nineteen or twenty, we can consider unchanged and transitional voices at that sort of age, as well as changed voices. Some evidence from continental plays shows, in my view, the casting of prepubertal males in their late teens,[37] and there is one item concerning a young actor of around twenty years old. This *pulcerrimus iuuenis circa xx. annos sine barba* played Ecclesia in the Avignon *Presentation* of 1372: he was apparently prepubertal or at an early pubescent stage, for he was not yet growing facial hair ('sine barba'); at 'around twenty years' ('circa xx. annos') his age was worthy of remark; and he brought very

---

32 Daw, 89.
33 Daw, 89 and Johnson and Everitt, 149–50.
34 See, for instance, the musical evidence discussed in 8.3, below, and the quotation from the *Liber Niger* of Edward IV, p. 320, below.
35 For Rainoldes, see Twycross 'Transvestism', 138, and the *Dictionary of National Biography*. Sidney's fictional Pyrocles, successfully playing the Amazon Zelmane at the age of 18, would seem to be good evidence, since Sidney does not appear to be presenting something unusual: see Twycross, *op. cit.*, 144.
36 For instance, the composer Henry Purcell, who as a child was a chorister in the Chapel Royal, was about fourteen when his voice changed in 1673 and he became assistant to John Hingeston. See NG 15/458.
37 Twycross 'Transvestism', 133–4.

good looks to the role.[38] A reason for the use of a prepubertal actor emerges in the text, for he is required to sing a substantial solo; and his age evidently implies considerable stature with commensurate vital capacity (he needs good 'stage presence' for the role in any case) because he must sing 'alta voce' – that is, in a loud voice.[39]

What physical qualities did an older prepubertal actor bring to the playing of a female role? In general, the sexes are not easily distinguishable before puberty: the overall physical conformations are very similar, as are the voices, skin-textures, and so on. Thus the prepubertal male and female can usually impersonate one another quite easily by the simple expedient of changing their clothes for those of the other sex. The same is largely true of the prepubertal male and the postpubertal female: only the growth of the female's hips and breasts is an added circumstance that must be taken into account, and this, of course, is easily dealt with in drama by the judicious use of padding.

While the prepubertal male can relatively easily impersonate a female, the physical developments of the sexes at puberty are such as to increase the distinction between them:[40]

(1) The hair-line, which in the female and the prepubertal male is well forward and roughly straight across the forehead, recedes a little at the temples in the postpubertal male.

(2) The male begins to grow facial hair, starting on the upper lip, and there is later some coarsening of the complexion. This normally affects females only very slightly and a considerable time after puberty.

(3) The body composition of males and females is virtually identical before puberty, but a great divergence takes place early in pubescence. In mature individuals, the lean body mass and skeletal mass of the male are both about 1.5 times that of the female: this is reflected partly in the greater height of the male and partly in the larger number of muscle-cells. Against this, the female normally has about twice the body-fat of the male.[41]

(4) The male's shoulders broaden and become much heavier in the years following puberty: in the female, a similar development takes place in the hips. A related effect concerns the male's hands and feet, which become proportionately larger than those of the female.

(5) The pitch of the male voice drops an octave or more: that of the female drops about a major third.

---

[38] 'Pulcerrimus iuuenis' need not mean 'a very beautiful youth' in a feminine sense: 'very handsome' is possible or, most likely here, the more neutral 'very good-looking'.

[39] Coleman *Presentation*, 88 and 101.

[40] These are all secondary sexual characteristics, for which see Johnson and Everitt, 145. The primary characteristics, the reproductive systems, are not relevant to this discussion; nor are such secondary characteristics as pubic hair and the development of the genitalia.

[41] Johnson and Everitt, 149.

The first of these is no problem to the actor and director. A female role in early drama demands headgear and/or a wig in any case, so that there is no question of the actor's receding hairline being visible. To some extent this is also true of (3) and (4), in that contemporary costuming is likely to reduce the effects of the physiological changes concerned, although hands and feet remain something of a give-away for the mature actor. A more pervasive problem is the different developments of shoulders and hips which, together with the different body-fat distributions, cause mature men and women to move quite differently. This is most obvious in the ways that the two sexes walk, a characteristic that an actor must always attend to very carefully when playing a female role. One cannot be dogmatic, but in general there are distinct difficulties in mature males and females impersonating one another, or even impersonating a prepubertal member of either sex. While such an impersonation is by no means impossible, a seventeen- or eighteen-year-old prepubertal male would have had definite advantages over an adolescent male of the same age in playing the pre-Fall Eve or the young Virgin Mary.

The actor has less control over (2), although it should go without saying that a mature actor will shave carefully when playing a female role. As for the coarsening of the skin-texture, this often results in a lack of softness in the complexion, leading to the rather brassy good looks of a man playing a young woman.[42] Even in very elderly women the skin texture does not normally approach that of a mature male. At that age a certain amount of facial hair is not unusual in women, though it approximates to the relatively soft and downy growth of an adolescent male. In no case is the female complexion like that of the mature male: there is no parallel to the tough stubble of a five-o'clock shadow. Though one can make no firm generalisation, it seems to me that a mature male will not necessarily be suitable to play the prophetess Anna, say, or the Virgin Mary at the end of her life, and that in general elderly women may have been best played by adolescents or men not far past puberty.

The third of these developments raises another important general question. Writers on the physical development of children are unanimous in regarding puberty as a chronological consequence of the growth-spurt.[43] The sudden speeding-up of growth in a child's teens occurs simultaneously with, or only very shortly before, the beginning of the maturation process: thus in a better-nourished age, such as ours, the growth-spurt happens earlier and in consequence so does puberty. The corollary to this is that in an age when puberty occurred later than now, we must assume that the growth-spurt happened later as well. Thus Wulstan is wrong to suppose that a prepubertal male in his late teens was necessarily approaching the size of a mature male: in fact, a prepubertal teenage male would on average be noticeably smaller than a postpubertal male of the same age. Thus, while a postpubertal male will always be affected by the growth that normally gives him a lean

[42] Twycross 'Transvestism', 143.
[43] See, for instance, Johnson and Everitt, 144 and 165; Tanner, 1 and 143; and Tanner in John O. Forfar and Gavin C. Arneil, eds., *Textbook of Paediatrics* (Edinburgh and London: Churchill Livingston, 1973), 239.

body-mass much greater than that of a female, a prepubertal male may be affected by it very little, if at all. To put this another way, a teenage male who is not noticeably larger than a young female will normally be prepubertal. There are two probable consequences of this: first, that a prepubertal male of seventeen, say, would be smaller than we should now expect a seventeen-year-old to be;[44] second, that such an actor would often be the right size to play a nineteen- or twenty-year-old female.

Of all the changes in the list above, however, it is perhaps the last that for most of us clearly distinguishes the adolescent or postpubertal male. Yet the use of a changed voice does not of itself make the speech in a female role necessarily unfeminine. While the male speaking voice is in general recognisably lower in pitch than that of a female, there is wide divergence among the members of both sexes, with considerable overlap. Moreover, it is not the fundamental pitch that distinguishes the male speaking voice from the female so much as its *quality*: and it is possible for a man so to modify his speech that with a little practice he can produce a passable imitation of female speech. In general this is probably easier in the adolescent state.[45] But it is possible, in my view, only because the female voice deepens slightly with age, allowing the use of a deeper-voiced actor for older female roles.[46]

I therefore do not think that a postpubertal actor was or is ideal for a young female role such as the pre-Fall Eve or the Virgin Mary of the Annunciation: for this, an older prepubertal player, one in his late teens, perhaps, would surely be best. We shall presumably never know from direct experience the effect of such a casting, but if we are to understand the conditions of early production in order to reproduce the same effect, we must make the best-informed guess that we can. Such an actor would be rather larger than a present-day fourteen-year-old, with a marginally better vital capacity;[47] he would have the skin textures, body-fat distribution and treble voice characteristic of the prepubertal state in both sexes, and without the shoulder development of a post-pubescent male; he would have a good vital capacity, though smaller than that of a postpubertal male because of the narrower

[44] This should be borne in mind when iconographical evidence is used. For example, depictions of the Chapel Royal, such as that of Queen Elizabeth's funeral procession in BL Add. MS 353245, f. 31v, show the children as significantly smaller than the gentlemen, but the children may not be as young as we suppose. There may be another reason for this, however. If Tanner, 149, is right to think that males did not reach their full size until 26 or so, the gentlemen would show a range of sizes, contiguous with the greater height-range of the children: and as the illustrator's purpose was largely documentary, he may have found that depicting the children as consistently smaller than the 'full-size' gentlemen was the best way of showing which were which. (The generally smaller size of sixteenth-century people does not affect these arguments.)

[45] Weiss, *passim*, especially 131 and 137–8.

[46] This accounts for the operatic convention by which the young heroine is sung by a soprano and an older woman by a mezzo-soprano or contralto. As already noted, the female voice does in fact deepen slightly at puberty (Weiss, 131 and 137–8); and there is also a slight deepening with age later on. Two convincing recent examples of cross-dressing from the cinema concern the roles of 'women' well into middle age: Dustin Hoffman's performance as Tootsie and Robin Williams's as Mrs Doubtfire.

[47] As already noted, Wulstan, 15–16, overstates his case here in saying that such an actor would be full-grown or nearly so.

shoulders; he would be approaching the peak of his intellectual and memorising abilities; he would have the emotional maturity of his age; and, according to his experience and training, he might well have been acting regularly for ten years or so. In the case of a trained chorister, the years of regular daily training in voice-production, liturgical ceremony and behaviour generally in the public eye would then (and still do) constitute an excellent training for dramatic activity.

Speech sound-qualities vary enormously with the individual, and so the pitch-ranges for any type of voice also appear to do so. Thus there is no standard to which the sound of a prepubertal male of, say, eighteen can be assumed to have approximated. All we can say, I think, is that its pitch, quality and power are likely to have been broadly similar to those of a girl of the same age. Even here we must specify a *clear* female voice, however: because the quality of female speech is affected by puberty, we cannot take the sound of a *modern* eighteen-year-old girl as the standard, since such a girl is further advanced towards maturity than a sixteenth-century girl would have been at the same age.

As regards the singing voice, we may guess that in some respects it could be likened to that of a castrato or of a modern countertenor, but these comparisons may well be misleading rather than helpful. Only one castrato was ever recorded, and he could not be mistaken for a female or prepubertal male voice;[48] and the modern countertenor voice has a wide range of quality and power (as the castrato voice did, no doubt) that seems to depend very much on the individual singer. What these two voice-types have in common is a vital capacity that, by modern standards, is far too large for the type of voice involved. The effect in both cases can be instructive, but the actual sound-quality must be quite different from that of our lost class of late-teenage trebles. Recent audiences may however gain a glimpse of what was once possible by recalling the sound of the treble soloist Aled Jones, who retired in 1986. His voice changed slowly, beginning to deepen when he had already turned sixteen, so that at the end of his career as a treble his vital capacity was larger than trebles usually have and he had been for some years a highly experienced performer. His voice-quality was very individual, but it may be helpful to off-set it against the sound of a 'boyish' young female singer – that is, one with a clear voice using minimal vibrato.[49]

On the specific question of vital capacity and its musical effect I shall say more in considering the role of boys as singers in the next section. For the moment it will be enough to point out that the higher average age of choirboys in the sixteenth century certainly resulted in a more powerful treble line than we have now. We should no longer think in terms of thin, weak, piping voices when choirboys were

[48] Alessandro Moreschi (1858–1922), probably best known for his recording of the Bach-Gounod *Ave Maria* in the Sistine Chapel in April 1904. On the sound of his singing, see Eric Van Tassel's review of his recordings, *Early Music* 13/2 (1985), 326–8. A large vital capacity was a feature of many famous castrati, but it is a rather special characteristic that would not apply to a prepubertal teenage male.

[49] The field of early music offers the most likely comparison with the boys of an earlier period: many recordings by singers such as Tessa Bonner and Caroline Trevor may well approximate to the sound of a good sixteenth-century boy in his late teens.

used in the plays, in either speaking or singing roles. I do not mean that all members of a group of choristers were eighteen-year-olds, of course, for that is most unlikely. But a normal spread of ages would include some boys in their late teens as well as some younger ones: and, that being so, both speaking and singing voices must have been stronger and more audible than we should expect those of modern boys to be.[50]

The same arguments will apply to late-teenage males who were not choirboys. Those that concern us here, because they played female roles in the civic biblical plays, are the young males found in the trade guilds of the West Midlands and the North.[51] Here, however, there are problems in usng the terms 'child', 'boy' and 'man', which do not now have quite the meanings that they had in the fifteenth, sixteenth and seventeenth centuries. That is why I have so far preferred cumbersome terms like 'prepubertal male' and 'postpubertal male'. The next step, therefore, is to consider some definitions.

In the centuries concerned, 'child' meant a prepubertal person of either sex: this was its general, physiological definition. The documentary use of the term does not therefore of itself tell us the age of the person concerned, only that he or she had not yet reached pubescence. With girls, the boundary between 'childhood' and 'womanhood' is not clearly marked for the onlooker,[52] so that the use of 'child' may be less precise than for boys, for whom the voice change is a clear indication of the onset of pubescence.

'Child' also had a more specialised technical usage in music and drama. Here 'child of the Chapel [Royal]', or of any other church establishment, meant a prepubertal male. Again, the term did not depend on the age of the subject; a male person ceased to be a 'child' at fourteen if his voice changed then, or he might remain a 'child' into his late teens. The 'childir' who sing in the York Entry into Jerusalem, at **York 25/264–5**, were almost certainly prepubertal, therefore, although the text does not show whether they were trained choristers or not.

'Boy' was synonymous with (male) 'child' in the context of a musical establishment.[53] The 'boys' of a choir, under the jurisdiction of a 'Master', were by the nature of their job also 'children'. This was therefore true also of any 'boys' in the plays if the roles concerned are known to have been acted by *choir*boys: the boys of Chester 7, who were in the care of 'master Chaunter' of the cathedral, are obvious examples.[54]

The use of 'boy' is rather different in the context of the trade-guilds, however,

---

[50] I do not forget that modern boys are larger than sixteenth-century boys, mainly for nutritional reasons. Nevertheless, I imagine that the four-year average age-difference might give the sixteenth-century boys a vocal advantage.

[51] I do not ignore other plays here: but the financial and other records for them are missing, so that the question cannot be pursued.

[52] It is always clear when a boy's voice is changing or has changed, but the onlooker cannot tell quite when a 'girl' becomes a 'young woman'. For a female, therefore, 'child' may have been used rather further into the maturation process than for a male.

[53] See Dobson 'Etymology . . . of *Boy*', 121–54.

[54] For these choristers, see *REED.Chester*, 81; *Essays*, 246; and 8.4, below.

where the classification was social and professional. Here, 'boy' probably signified the status of an apprentice. Thus the 'shepherds' boys' of Chester 7 are the roles of the shepherds' apprentices, while the 'pueri' that appear in Chester 14, similarly, must have been played by actors of the right age to be apprentices. This usage presumably stems from the late medieval use of *garcio* and *puer* to signify a groom or page in a household – that is, the ranks below *valletus* or yeoman.[55] There is some evidence that the royal households, at least, tended to place several grooms under the care of a *scutifer* (squire) given the style of 'Master',[56] providing a parallel with the organisation in the guilds and in choirs.

Thus the 'boys' in the plays are not necessarily also 'children', unless they are known to have been played by choirboys: for although the majority of apprentices probably were prepubertal, this cannot be assumed. Among the dramatic roles concerned there are a number of rebellious apprentices who are clearly more mature and in a position to challenge the authority of their masters. The fourth shepherd of Chester 7, called Trowle but referred to as Garcius ('boy') in the SHs, is apparently married (**Chester 7/590**); he is strong enough to throw all his masters in a wrestling bout, and although they address him affectionately as 'lad' he is cheeky enough to address them (less politely) in the same way (**Chester 7/195, 254–280**). He is therefore in a different position from the other, non-speaking, 'boyes' in the play, although he has the same substantive rank. Iak Garcio, the shepherds' apprentice in Towneley 12, is similarly rebellious, as is the apprentice of the N-Town Noah play: Lameth addresses this latter as 'boy' and he addresses Lameth as 'master', but the SH *Adolescens* shows him to be at least obviously past the prepubertal stage.[57] Lastly, Cain's *garcio* Pikeharness in Towneley 2 has a curiously near-equal relationship with his master, although he does address him as 'master' occasionally: Cain strikes him when provoked, and suggests releasing him from his apprenticeship as the price of his silence about Abel's murder (**Towneley 2/385–7, 406–8**). Abel refers to Garcio, in speaking to his brother, as 'thi man', however. This may be mere politeness, but it is in fact the term to be expected for a journeyman rather than an apprentice. In any case it does suggest that Pikeharness is older and more mature than the average apprentice would be.

A brief digression on the subject of apprentices and journeymen in the London companies will be useful here, for the overall picture was far from standardised.[58] Most companies required apprentices to serve at least seven years, a longer term (up to ten) being decided according to the boy's age and the financial agreement involved; most also prohibited the bestowal of freedom in the trade before the age of twenty-two or twenty-four (a rule of 1555 imposed the age of twenty-four on all London companies); some guilds imposed a three-year minimum period between

---

55 There was however no equivalent to 'page' in a guild organisation, and the use of *garcio* and *puer* seems to be indiscriminate in the present situation.

56 Rastall *Secular Musicians* I, 97f. and 143f.

57 I do not suggest that the playwright used the same definitions as Weiss, of course, but 'adolescent' must signify a state well on in the process of pubertal development.

58 Unwin *Gilds*, 91–2 and 265–6, on which I draw for much of this paragraph.

the end of an apprenticeship and the attempt to become a master, so that a three-year period as a journeyman was unavoidable; and the cost of obtaining mastership often prohibited applications for it from those who were eligible. In addition, there is some evidence that journeymen had not necessarily served an apprenticeship – that is, that some were untrained labour. Since the normal age for starting an apprenticeship was between ten and fourteen, we can conclude that apprentices might normally be of any age between ten and 21, while most journeymen (who might conceivably be of any age) would normally be between seventeen and 24, with a peak in the distribution at about 21–23. From this we can draw two vital conclusions about young guild actors: namely, that at any given time

— Some apprentices would have transitional or changed voices, though around two-thirds of them would be prepubertal; and

— While a few journeymen would have unchanged voices and a significant proportion would be pubescent, transitional or adolescent, those at the postpubertal stage were likely to be in the majority.

'Man' is a general term, though it is often exclusive of 'boy' or 'child'. In the context of a choir it means 'postpubertal male': that is, a 'singing-man' is no longer a 'child'. This often implies a degree of maturity, in fact, because there was sometimes a period of time after a singer's voice ceased to be a treble voice before it settled into its mature range (but see above, p. 311, and below, at p. 324). Between times, the singer very often remained in the charge of the Master of the Children, but without the status of a 'child'. This situation is illustrated in the case of the composer Peter Philips, born in 1560 or 1561, who is known to have been a choirboy at St Paul's in 1574. When Sebastian Westcote, the Almoner and Master of the Children, died in 1582, he left £5 to each of four choirboys 'now remayninge in my howse' and £5 13s 4d to Peter Philips 'likewise remayninge withe me'.[59] Philips was twenty-one or twenty-two by this time.

Probably Philips had an arrangement with Westcote by which he made himself useful as Westcote's assistant in return for board and lodging, no doubt playing the organ, taking some rehearsals, and perhaps copying or even composing music for the choir.[60] This was of course the best kind of post-choirboy training for the career of a singing-man and organist.[61] William Hunnis, Master of the Children of the Chapel Royal at this time, was also concerned about choirboys whose voices had changed. When he petitioned in 1583 for increased allowances he stated, among other things, that 'there is no allowance nor other consideration for those children whose voices be changed, who only do depend upon the charge of the said master

[59] NG 14/654.

[60] His earliest known composition dates from 1580: NG 14/654.

[61] Those composers who took up organists' posts early, such as Byrd (Lincoln Cathedral, at the age of nineteen or twenty) and Purcell (Westminster Abbey, also at nineteen or twenty), must have had this sort of training. See NG 3/537 and 15/458: Byrd was Tallis's protégé; Purcell (as already noted) served under the royal musician John Hingeston before becoming Blow's assistant at Westminster. Philips, as Westcote's star pupil, was probably close to such a position, but he went abroad soon after Westcote's death because of his Catholicism.

[that is, Hunnis] until such time as he may prefer the same with clothing and other furniture, unto his no small charge'.[62] The monarch apparently no longer 'preferred' such boys as a matter of course, as her father had certainly done.[63] The possible types of preferment are listed in Edward IV's *Liber Niger* of c.1471–2:[64]

> Also when [the boys] be growen to the age of xviij yeres, and than theyre voyces be chaunged, ne can nat be preferred in this chapell [Royal] nor within this court, the numbyr beyng full, then, if they wull assent, the king assigneth euery suche child to a college of Oxenford or Cambridge, of the kinges fundacion, there to be in finding and study sufficiauntly tyll the king otherwise list to avaunce hym.

These alternatives seem to be more or less in order of desirability.[65] For our present purpose it will be useful to note the implication that the voice will not necessarily have changed at the age of eighteen.[66]

In the context of a trade-guild, 'man' probably meant 'journeyman': in this case, therefore, it did not have the exact connotation of postpubertal state. As we have already noted, an apprentice might well find himself a journeyman before he lost his treble voice. I think we may be sure that 'Ryngolds man Thomas þat playtt pylatts wyff' and 'rychard ye capper borsleys man that playth ane' in the Coventry plays of 1496 and 1544, respectively, were journeymen and therefore in the seventeen to twenty-four age-group:[67] but we cannot assume that 'man' implies maturity here, for that is not necessarily the case.

Finally in this section, I shall look at types of female role and, bearing in mind the wider range of options available to an early producer, try to suggest what sort of actor was considered most suitable for each. This is an area prone to subjective argument, and I shall confine myself as far as possible to factual evidence – musical, as well as the type of documentary evidence already used.

Here I must set down a series of *caveats* that will serve not only as warnings but also as some guide to the criteria used in attempting to make decisions in this section. First, I work on the assumption that in at least *some* roles alternatives were always possible. For example, it may be that in a certain role an eighteen-year-old adolescent male would be a good second-best to a prepubertal male of the same age, and preferable to a weaker prepubertal actor of any age. Second, casting

---

62 Cited in Woodfill *Musicians*, 171.
63 Woodfill, 173.
64 Myers *Household of Edward IV*, 137; cited by Woodfill, 172–3, in modernised spelling.
65 A suitable musician would wish for a singing-man's post in the Chapel, and if he were prevented by vocal inability or lack of vacancy, a paid post as one of the two Yeomen of the Chapel was probably acceptable. (For the Yeomen of the Vestry, or Chapel, see Myers *op. cit.*, 70 and 136. The latter reference shows that the two yeomen were children of the Chapel whose voices had changed.) Failing this, some other musical place at Court would be useful: see above, n. 36, for training under royal musicians. Only if these places were unavailable was an ex-choirboy sent to university, and then only with his agreement.
66 A second implication is, I think, that the king did not normally find preferment until the boy had reached 18, which is why Hunnis had to maintain those whose voices had changed earlier.
67 *REED.Coventry*, 86 and 168.

probably depended very much then, as it does now, on the size, shape and experience of the individual actor.[68] Third, it would be wrong to be exclusive in cross-referring any precise personal details of an actor from one play to another, because circumstances can decide such things. If a twenty-year-old takes a certain role in one cycle, for instance, we dare not assume that that is the age required for the same role in other cycles.

Lastly, I am sure that we should expect some broad dramatic coherence in the performance of a cycle. While it would clearly be wrong to assume a detailed standardisation between cycles, therefore, in the matter of voice-types, actors' ages or anything else, it is equally wrong to treat each play as a dramatic unit having no reference to other plays in the performance. This is why, ultimately, I reject the notions of Mrs Noah as a pantomime dame or Procula as a drag queen: it is not that one cannot read the plays in that way,[69] but that such interpretations disrupt a dramatic coherence in the cycle as a whole.

We have now reached a stage when it will be possible to discuss what the evidence can tell us about the main female types and roles in the plays.

1 *The Blessed Virgin Mary as a small child*

Only one relevant play, N-Town 9, includes this role. Mary is presented in the text as a child of three years old (**N-Town 9/9, 17+sd; Mary Play 262, 270+sd**). In the Avignon *Presentation* of 1372 the little girl playing this role really was three or four years of age,[70] but that is almost a non-speaking role: in the N-Town play Mary has a speaking part of 135 lines, and so young an actor is obviously out of the question. A realistic representation of a three-year-old is hardly possible, therefore, but the role could be taken by a young choirboy, especially if he were small for his age. In the position of a late fifteenth-century producer, I should look in the local church choir for an intelligent but undergrown eight-year-old.[71]

---

[68] This is particularly noticeable in some continental records of a kind not available for English drama. Twycross 'Transvestism', 133–4, cites examples of comparability or interchangeability between males and females. At Mons in 1501 the four daughters of God were played by a female and three males, which suggests comparability between them. At Metz the daughter of Dediet the glazier, then aged about eighteen, played St Catherine in 1468; but a fifteen-year-old boy named Lyonnard played St Barbara in 1485, and St Catherine the following year. Dediet's eighteen-year-old daughter and the fifteen-year-old Lyonnard seem to be broadly comparable, then: and Lyonnard was not a great success as St Catherine mainly because his voice had begun to change (at the age of 16, NB). Clearly, Metz preferred a prepubertal actor for its young female saints.

The examples cited by Twycross are taken from Cohen *Mons*, c–cv; Petit de Julleville II, 32, 48, 52 and 147–9.

[69] For the view that they can or should be so played, see Twycross 'Transvestism', 135.

[70] Meredith and Tailby *Staging*, 208; Coleman *Presentation*, 85.

[71] There is some question of Mary singing the gradual psalms in this play, which would make it a much more demanding role: but I am sure that she was not intended to sing.

2 *The Virgin Mary as a young girl*

Only N-Town 10 has the role of Mary at her marriage: she is fourteen years old (**N-Town 10/6-19; Mary Play 599-612**). There would be no difficulty in casting a prepubertal boy in this role, and no reason why the guilds should ever have done otherwise.

3 *A young but almost fully-grown girl: a young wife*

The young Eve is the first female in the cycles: she must be attractive, and credible as a female. Her relationship with Adam is not a passionate or overtly sexual one, for the whole point of their pre-Fall state is that it is innocent and unpassionate. But this does not mean that Eve is unfeminine. In fact, it is precisely her femininity – shown through her curiosity in the face of potential novelty and excitement, and in her ability to win Adam over by her charm – that enables the Fall sequence to happen credibly.[72] An unfeminine Eve simply will not work, and it seems to me out of the question to have used a postpubertal or even adolescent male: a 'child' of the right size and personality would surely be the obvious choice.[73]

It is worth noting that in the Norwich plays of the Fall Adam and Eve are required to sing (**Norwich A/88+sd; B/153+sd**, discussed in 2.6, above), and in these circumstances Eve could hardly be played by a postpubertal male. In discussing the potential overlap in sound-quality of the male and female voices earlier, we were concerned only with speech: the overlap is much less evident in singing, when the male and female voices can be confused only in rather special circumstances. The two high voices, soprano and tenor, are about an octave apart; similarly, the two low voices, alto and bass; and the two pairs are about half an octave apart. There is a pitch overlap between tenor and alto in which these two can be confused, so that a mature male singer might actually make himself sound like an alto; or he might sing in a countertenor (male alto) voice: but these are not sound-qualities that one expects from a female in the present category. In these late Fall plays there can be little doubt that Eve was played by a treble.

The case of the Virgin Mary at the Annunciation and Visitation is, I think, very much the same. Here, too, the need for singing clinches the argument in two of the relevant plays – **York 12** and **Chester 6** – for sixteenth-century performances, at least.[74] In these, Mary must surely have been played by a prepubertal boy. In the others, a transitional male would presumably be possible, although the Annunciation was considered to have taken place very soon after Mary's marriage. This is

---

[72] The winning-over happens after Eve has eaten the apple, however, and she is no longer innocent. See 5.4, above, on the deceit involved.

[73] Here and in similar roles I would not wholly rule out a pubescent or even transitional actor: but this would depend very much on the individual, and seems to me in general much less likely to be successful. Success would certainly depend on the physical changes being slow and the voice remaining stable.

[74] **York 12/240+sd**: 'Tunc cantat Magnificat'; **Chester 6/64+sd**, discussed in *Essays*, 128. The 'Tunc cantat' of the York SD is a mid-sixteenth-century addition in John Clerke's hand.

hardly a separate role from (2), then, and on the whole I think that Mary must have been played by a prepubertal boy in all the Annunciation plays.

4 *The Virgin Mary as a young mother*

A range must be considered here. Mary at the Purification is less than a year older (nine months and forty days, in fact) than at the Annunciation, so she would have been cast as in (3), above, and therefore probably as in (2). Between the Purification and the episode of Christ with the Doctors some twelve years pass, and it is reasonable to assume that Mary could be played as an older type in the latter. Mary does not have to sing, so that an adolescent need not be ruled out. However, the Coventry Weavers' play puts the Purification and Christ with the Doctors together, and so does Chester 11, requiring the same actor throughout.[75] In these two plays, at least, a prepubertal actor is likely even for the Doctors episode, therefore.

As already noted, the Coventry Weavers' play includes a stage direction (**Coventry 2/805+sd**) that could be interpreted as requiring Mary to sing.[76] However, I am sure that the singing was performed by a group of professional singers, so this SD is not evidence for the actor playing Mary.

5 *The mothers of the Innocents*

Here, too, we must consider a range of types. This category is not the same as (4), since in this case the youth of the Innocents does not necessarily indicate youth in their mothers, who might well be assumed to have other, older children. In York 19 the mothers hardly depart from truly lady-like speech, as is the case also in N-Town 19; those of Towneley 16 are rather more outspoken, reminding us of Mrs Noah and probably displaying the same kind of physical reaction; those of Chester not only fight the soldiers physically, but use language stronger than ever Mrs Noah allowed herself:

> PRIMA MULIER]   Have thou this, thou fowle harlott
> and thou knight, to make a knott!
> And on buffett with this bote
> thou shalt have to boote.
> And thow this, and thou this,
> though thou both shyte and pisse!   (Chester10/353–8)

Prepubertal or transitional boys might be most suitable for the York and N-Town plays, while the Chester play might be thought to demand the physical and vocal

---

[75] According to the Chester Blacksmiths' accounts for 1553–4 and 1571–2, a single actor was paid for the role of Mary: *REED.Chester*, 53 and 91. In other years the list of characters is missing or incomplete. In the Coventry Weavers' accounts the payments seem to be for only the Purification part of the play, no Doctors being mentioned: *REED.Coventry, passim.*

[76] See above, section 2.3, p. 27.

presence of postpubertal males. This is however quite subjective reasoning on probably anachronistic grounds.

Fortunately, we have some guidance in the Coventry pageant of the Shearmen and Tailors, where the speech and behaviour of the mothers are somewhere between those of the Towneley and Chester versions. The music surviving for their lullaby is set for alto, tenor and bass, which suggests that vocal quality, rather than pitch-range, was what decided the 'female' characteristics of the music. How the trio of male voices was made to sound like females is discussed in 3.4. above: it is a rather special effect, and it has no bearing on, for example, the singing of Eve at Norwich. But it does tell us that at Coventry at least two of the mothers were played by post-pubescent males.[77]

We are not necessarily justified in assuming *mature* singers, however. Although there is no discernible tradition in England of using immature voices for the lower singing parts, such a tradition is known in Germany (where there has been much support for the view that singers should continue to sing during puberty)[78] and elsewhere. At the Thomasschule in Leipzig, for example, the lower parts are still sung by boys who have only recently reached adolescence, giving a distinctive (and distinctively immature) sound.[79] It is quite possible that such voices were used in sixteenth-century England. However, if the mothers of the Innocents were played by mature singers, here presumably is an example of men modulating their speaking voices in order to sound like women. The roles do not need to be burlesqued – indeed, should not be – for the text gives us no reason to doubt the essential credibility of the mothers and the horror of the slaughter enacted before us.

If there is any validity in my rough-and-ready division in Massacre plays requiring pre-pubescent males and those requiring post-pubescent or mature males for the mothers, the evidence of Coventry certainly strengthens my suggestion that the latter should be used for the Chester play, but it does not help us over the Towneley one, where either might be seen as acceptable.

6 *Older women: Elizabeth, Anna, Mary at the end of her life*

Here a deeper voice is appropriate and a coarser skin-texture not out of place. Probably no singing is needed.[80] Such a role need not be played by a mature male,

[77] The tenor and bass would be at least adolescent and could be mature; the alto might have been at any stage, although the pitch-range of the part suggests that a prepubertal singer is unlikely: and considerations of vocal consistency and musical texture in the group also suggest that the alto would be at a similar stage to the other two – that is, at least transitional. See 3.4, above.

[78] Weiss, 127, 134 and 140.

[79] I am grateful to Simon Lindley for this information: cf. Daw's work.

[80] In the N-Town Assumption Mary is given versicles that would normally be sung (**N-Town 41/320–29**: Spector's edition does not show the *versus* signs to be seen on f. 219r and elsewhere in the manuscript, for which see MDF 4). While there is no indication that these are sung rather than spoken, so that the use of a post-pubescent actor for the role is possible in the play as we have it, the situation is potentially less simple. The play is an interpolation in the collection, and was originally not a civic drama. We must therefore bear in mind the possibility that the role of Mary was spoken and sung by a choirboy in pre-N-Town performances.

although it clearly can be performed that way with considerable success.[81] Originally, a transitional or adolescent male might have been used, and as noted earlier Richard the Capper, 'Borsley's man that plays Anna', may well have been at that stage.

7 *Procula*

Procula's language in York 30 is closest in aggressiveness to that of the Towneley mothers of the Innocents, but it also reflects that of Pilate, with whom she carries on a decidedly sex-oriented dialogue. It would be possible to play the relationship between them, and therefore Procula herself, in various ways, but the obvious one is surely intended: she is an attractive young wife, capable of a provocative dialogue with Pilate, whom she vamps when possible. Pilate is obviously besotted with her, and remarks that his wife 'In bedde is full buxhome and bayne', which Beadle and King translate as 'most willing and eager'.[82] I think that she was probably played by a prepubertal actor. As noted above, Procula is that role in the Coventry Smiths' play acted by 'Ryngold's man, Thomas' in 1496. 'Man' to a guild accounting clerk must certainly have meant 'journeyman', so it is quite possible that Thomas was prepubertal or pubescent.

N-Town 31 does not develop the relationship between Procula and Pilate: their brief exchange neither contradicts nor supports what I have said here.

8 *Mrs Noah*

Mrs Noah is a complex character that varies from one cycle to another: there is a great difference between the character portrayed in the N-Town plays, for example, and that found in the Chester cycle. The latter could certainly be played basically as in category (6), above, but I do not feel that the role should be played as anything approaching a pantomime dame.[83] The fact that the role is enjoyable and seems to work as a farce character does not mean that she was *intended* to be played that way. On the contrary, we should not confuse the traditions of farce and biblical drama. Recent performances using female actors suggest that a non-farce approach is perfectly acceptable, and even gives Mrs Noah a necessary dignity lacking in a farce-like production.[84] I find it interesting that a generally perceptive scholar like

---

[81] Twycross 'Transvestism' discusses this and other cross-played roles in her own productions: see also the contributions of Peter Happé, Sarah Carpenter, Henrietta Twycross-Martin, Diana Wyatt and Carl Heap on these and other productions in *Medieval English Theatre* 5/2 (1983), 110–22.

[82] **York 30/52**; Beadle and King, 156.

[83] See Twycross 'Transvestism', 135.

[84] In Twycross's own demonstrations for the 1983 METh meeting at Salford; the Towneley cycle at Wakefield, 1980; the Chester cycle at Leeds, 1983; and the York plays in York, 1994, among others.

John Robinson should become almost incoherent in his attempts to reconcile the various positions into which his assumptions on this subject led him:[85]

> Characters like Noah's wife ... are rare in the religious plays but not in proverbial lore. She is comic, especially if she is played by a female impersonator as it is reasonable to assume, but the playwright has taken pains to make her a credible woman. The player is perhaps a cross between the pantomime dame and the modern drag artist skilled at womanly mannerisms.

Leaving aside the question of how reasonable it is to make any such assumption, and ignoring the undefined 'female impersonator', Robinson's statement almost beggars belief. If one can imagine a 'cross between [a] pantomime dame and [a] modern drag artist' the result will not, I suggest, have the appearance of 'a credible woman'. And if the playwright has indeed 'taken pains to make [Mrs Noah] a credible woman' why talk in terms of a more recent type of impersonator whose element of *incredibility* is precisely what makes the entertainment what it is?[86] Robinson's reading of the play (and the playwright) was correct, but he did not have the nerve to follow the train of thought to its logical conclusion: that the playwright was not wasting his time in attempting the impossible; that comedy and dignity (indeed, femininity) are not incompatible; and that the type of 'female impersonator ... skilled at womanly mannerisms' is neither of the types that he suggested but something quite different and able to fulfill the playwright's (correctly-identified) expectations.

The factor of dramatic coherence is relevant here, too, for the real danger of playing Mrs Noah as a pantomime dame is not its unsuitability in a single play but its effect in the cycle as a whole. In the Chester cycle Mrs Noah is the second female role, only Eve coming before her: and as the same actor must play Eve throughout Play 2, which starts before the Fall, the possibilities for making Eve into a significantly older woman in the Cain and Abel section of the play are limited. Even if this were done, the difference between Eve and a pantomime dame in the next play would be so great as to overstretch our capacity of belief in the role. Broadly speaking, the same argument obtains in other cycles.

Mrs Noah's gossips (Chester 3) must be played by pre-pubescent or transitional males, I think, if they sing the drinking song (for which no music survives). However, the Chester manuscripts seem to offer speech and singing as alternatives (pp. 72–3, above), allowing a producer to play a version in which the lines are spoken if he should prefer it. The possibility of using transitional or changed voices would be one reason for the need of a choice. Granted that both possibilities were there, the choice made for Mrs Noah presumably applied also to the gossips, and *vice versa* – that is, that they should be comparable voices as a group. If they were not required

---

[85] Robinson *Studies*, 130. Robinson placed Mak's wife, Gill (Towneley 13), in the same category as Mrs Noah, which is reasonable.

[86] What would be our reaction if told that Barry Humphries ('Dame Edna Everidge') *actually is a woman*?

to sing, this might mean all changed voices, or some mixture of prepubertal and transitional voices.

Other female roles in the cycles, and indeed in other plays too if they were thought to use male actors for female roles, can be categorised in this way. Some are unlikely to be controversial: the wives of Noah's sons, for instance, must certainly have been played by pre-pubescent boys; the Sibyl of the Chester Nativity, described as a 'well fayre maye' in **Chester 6/179**, was presumably played by a prepubertal or at most pubescent actor. Other roles are more difficult to categorise and, as shown in the case of Mrs Noah, might involve a range of types demanding directorial choice.[87] In all cases, of course, the whole range of evidence must be brought to bear on the problem.

It may be useful, before leaving this subject, to list the main conclusions that can be drawn for the playing of female roles:

— Because males were older at the onset of puberty in previous centuries, a whole category of young males existed then that no longer exists: namely, boys in their later teens, and even as old as twenty, who had not yet reached puberty.

— Most apprentices and some journeymen belonged to this category.

— Members of this category, in general, had the right size, shape, skin-texture and voice for the impersonation of women.

— Such an actor might have a long experience of acting – much longer than boys can now achieve before the onset of puberty.

As regards the female-role categories listed above,

there is factual evidence for the use of adolescent or postpubertal males only in my category (5);

there is possible, but minor, circumstantial evidence that category (8) was sometimes played by a postpubertal male;

category (6) works well when played by postpubertal males, although there is no evidence of such playing; and

there is *no evidence* that roles in categories (1), (2), (3), (4) and (7) were ever played by postpubertal males.

---

[87] It is worth remembering that when choirboys were hired for a specific dramatic purpose the producer was not presented with any problem: they *were* boys – prepubertal males – and the question of their maturity did not arise. The producer knew what he was getting, as he did in the case of mature professional singers. But when a guildsman or apprentice was chosen for a role the producer had vocal and physical factors, acting ability and personality to juggle with, as well as different stages of maturity. It is in these circumstances that directorial choices (perhaps unwelcome choices) had to be made.

8.3 The Angels

Angels sing in the plays more than any other type of role. For some plays there is evidence to show that the angels were played by choirboys, and elsewhere we may suspect it; in other plays the angels were probably played by mature males. In some places angelic roles may, of course, have been played by female actors, although – as in the case of female roles considered in the previous section – the information is not available for performances in England because records survive only for the all-male civic plays. The main question of the previous section recurs, then: in any play, at any particular time, were the angels played by boys, adolescents, or mature men?

I shall consider principally the angelic roles taken by professional singers, whether men or boys: that is, trained singers working regularly in a church, and hired out for the occasion with the agreement of the church authorities. I assume that a mature singer would be responsible for learning any lines necessary, for learning the music needed, and for rehearsing his role in advance of final rehearsals with the guildsmen. In the case of boys, the training, rehearsals and welfare of the singers would be in the hands of the Precentor, Master of the Children, or some other singing man acting as deputy.

Some music, such as popular songs and the best-known congregational chants, could no doubt be sung by guildsmen (see 8.1, above). In this category, of course, I include any suitable boys and adolescents among the guild's apprentices and journeymen. It is now impossible to distinguish firmly between singing that demands professionals and that possible for amateurs, since the evidence is simply not available. In the discussion that follows I shall therefore begin with the clearest possible evidence for professional singers, and proceed to gain some idea of the singing forces needed for the whole York cycle.

The earliest good evidence for English plays is provided by the music of **York 45**, discussed earlier in section 3.3. As noted there, the music seems to have been written for boys singing in the mezzo-soprano range. The play has speaking parts for twelve angels, but two particular features mark these out as unusual roles. First, each angel has only a single line, apart from Angelus VIII, who returns with a second line at the end; second, these thirteen lines constitute a single stanza, which gives the impression that these twelve small roles are somehow connected together. The stanza is in fact ideal for a group of twelve bit-part players who were not members of the main acting group but would be able to rehearse together.

This seems to answer the main questions about the singing angels: how many of them were there, and are they – or some of them – the same as the speaking angels? The nature of **York 45/105–17** seems to show that the answer must be 'Yes' to the second of these questions, because one cannot imagine other circumstances in this play in which so many actors might come together with such small speaking parts. These lines could easily have been given to a single angel, after all, and it would be strange to rehearse twelve guildsmen where one would serve. Thus it seems to me quite obvious that the twelve angels were twelve choirboys; and, given this, that some or all of them were the angels who sang the notated music.[88] This is not a matter of convenience, then, but of necessity: a waggon that can be pushed through the narrow streets of York is simply not large enough to accommodate twelve men and at least four singers as well.[89] Having the same players both speaking and singing seems an obvious dramatic intention.

The survival of the financial records of the trade guilds at York is unfortunately poor. No relevant accounts for the Weavers' guild survive, but the proclamation found in Roger Burton's *Ordo paginarum* of 1415 does give information of the type found in banns.[90] The entry for Play 45 does not mention the musical concert given to Thomas, but this is not perhaps surprising: the surviving music had not been composed by 1415,[91] so that the play as Burton knew it may have been much less ambitious musically than the extant text shows. The list does however show that Mary's Assumption was accomplished with 'a crowd of angels': 'Maria ascendens cum turba angelorum'. For the staging of this play it is important to know how many angels constitute a 'crowd', not least because of the limitations of space on a waggon. It need not have been as many as twelve, probably.

If the angels were indeed played by choirboys by 1463–77, when the Register was copied,[92] then, there were twelve of them at that time. Twelve boys together could only come from a major choir, unless they were drawn from several institutions: but this latter possibility would lessen the opportunities for rehearsal as a group. On the whole, it seems likely that the twelve angels were from a single institution, and probably only York Minster could boast so many boys in its choir. In fact, the choir at York had seven boys until 1425, when Thomas Dalby, the Archdeacon of Richmond, paid for the number to be increased to twelve.[93] If the boys remained at that number, the play text may have been revised to take advantage of the increase. This is not to say that all twelve boys sang the York 45 pieces, however, for even the A versions would be beyond the capacity of a very young choirboy at the start of his singing career. On the other hand, all twelve were required to speak, so they must all have had a certain training. Did the Minster, perhaps, not train boys from the beginning but, like the Chapel Royal, recruit trained boys by transfer from other establishments? If that were the case, all twelve of the Minster boys might well be capable of singing polyphony as well as having the stage experience – small enough, after all – to speak a line.[94]

---

[88] The question also arises how many angels could be accommodated in the Heaven. If the twelve speaking angels were guildsmen, the Heaven would still have to contain extra angels to do the singing.

[89] I specifiy four singers as a minimum here because of the four-part chord in *Veni de Libano* B (see section 3.3). Performance of the A versions would apparently not demand more than two singers, of course.

[90] *REED.York*, 16–26; MDF 7, following p. lxi.

[91] The musical style is too late: see 3.3, above.

[92] Beadle and Meredith 1980.

[93] See See L.W. Cowie, 'Worship in the Minster', in P.M. Tillott, ed., *A History of Yorkshire: The City of York* (Victoria County History. London: Oxford University Press, 1961), 345.

[94] There is of course no real evidence that the musical settings were ever performed. My argument is however valid even if we take the notated settings to be a statement of intention

In the context of the York cycle as a whole, the last two plays provide a problem. Play 46 (The Coronation of the Virgin) has speaking parts for six angels and also requires angelic singing; play 47 (The Last Judgement) requires 'cantus angelorum' at the Judgement and 'melodia angelorum' to end the play (and the cycle: **York 47/216+sd, 380+sd**), while there are three speaking angels, two of whom play the Last Trump. Were any of these angels boys? And if so, what establishment provided them? Clearly, if the Minster had made its boys available to the Weavers for Play 45, those boys were denied to several plays on either side. In fact, if Margaret Dorrell's timings for the York cycle are at all accurate (and the evidence suggests that they are not far out)[95] the singers in Play 45 had to be ready to start at the first station around 4.56 p.m., so that the singers could not be part of any play that ended too late for them to return to the starting point for that performance. The latest of the previous plays for which that would be possible was Play 24 (The Woman Taken in Adultery and the Raising of Lazarus), which finished at the last station at 3.55 p.m. (There is in fact no angelic music in that play.) Dorrell's timings, then, show that the singers of Play 45 could not have been involved in Play 25 (The Entry into Jerusalem), in which eight singing boys are involved, not as angels but as children.[96] I think, therefore, that another whole choir of boys was needed for Play 25. From there until Play 45, professional singers were needed in smaller numbers. The plays concerned are as follows:

38 *The Resurrection* requires one angel. The singer is a boy, for **38/225** describes him as 'a ₃onge childe'. The evidence is sixteenth-century, but probably reflects earlier performance-practice.

42 *The Ascension* probably requires one singing angel, although there is a doubt about this. **York 42/176+sd** is a sixteenth-century direction, but this too may reflect earlier practice.

43 *Pentecost* requires two singing angels (see **York 43/96+sd, 133–6**).

44 *The Death of the Virgin* has four speaking roles for angels, who sing *Ave regina celorum*. The angels speak the last twelve lines of the play (2, 2, 4 and 4 lines, respectively), which is their only speech: as in Play 45, this suggests that they are a self-contained non-guild group able to rehearse on their own. After Angelus IV's final line, 'A semely song latte vs sing' (**York 44/194**), the SD

on the guild's part, since the registered play text must have been performed (i.e. with twelve angels).

95 Dorrell's timings for the York cycle in *Leeds Studies in English* 6 (1972), 102–07, formed the basis of the projected timetable for the Leeds performance of 1975, and were found to correlate with the actual timings in performance quite well.

96 Eight are specified in the 1415 *Ordo paginarum*: the play might well have changed by the time of the Register, but this number fits with the eight citizens, whose 'childur' the boys are (**York 25/264**) in the play as we have it. For the singers and music of this play see above, section 8.1: the singers might have been guild-members, but if so they probably did not sing the obvious items.

Et cantant antiphona[m] certainly suggests that all four sing. Four men would have been very expensive, and it is perhaps more likely that the singers were boys.

44A *The Funeral of the Virgin* does not appear in the Register of the plays, and information on its possible performances is thin.[97] It would probably have required some singing by the apostles, which could be done by the guild's own actors; it *may* have included angelic singing or the need for a professional singer in another role, but this seems unlikely.

In this final group of plays in the York cycle, then, where singers cannot be shared between plays, the minimum requirement of professional singers is as follows: three groups of boys, numbering eight, twelve (almost certainly from the Minster, and the full complement of its choristers, even if they did not all sing) and four; and smaller groups, likely to be men or at least the most senior boys, numbering one (certainly a 'child'), probably one, two and perhaps one. To summarise a little: the total is two dozen choirboys in three groups, a solo boy, and between two and four other soloists, probably men.

Earlier plays could perhaps share these singers, in which case this would be the cycle's sum minimum requirement of professional singers. Those required for the rest of the York cycle are as follows:

1   In *The Fall of the Angels* the angels sing, but the piece is the *Te deum*, (**1/24+sd, 40+sd**) which in a chant setting is a congregational piece and could therefore be sung by amateurs. In fact, only two sections of the hymn are sung, not the whole piece. This, and the lack of music elsewhere in the play, may suggest that the services of professional singers were avoided. Also, the speeches of Angelus Cherubyn and Angelus Seraphyn need too much integration with other actors' parts for it to be likely that they were played by outsiders.

12 *The Annunciation and Visitation* includes both a singing angel and a singing Mary. The former may well have been a man, but the latter is one of the roles that I should expect a choirboy to take.

15 *The Shepherds* probably used guildsmen actors for the singing shepherds: but the missing passage near the opening of the play must have included the angelic *Gloria in excelsis*, and I should therefore expect a professional singer to have taken part.

18 *The Flight into Egypt*. The angel may have been a singer: his 19-line part shares a scene with Joseph but needs little rehearsal-time for putting the scene together. Although Joseph's remarks about the angel's voice could apply to singing (**York 18/42–4**) they are equally applicable to speech and there is no real evidence that this angel sings.

21 *The Baptism of Christ*. Two angels sing *Veni creator spiritus*: they have a speech each, which would be easy to fit together with John's part. This suggests that

---

[97] See Beadle 1982, 391 and 460.

the two angels were professional singing-men, but as the hymn is a congregational piece it is also possible that they were guildsmen.

22 *The Temptation*. Angels sing *Veni creator*: again there are two speaking roles, of one speech each, and either professionals or guildsmen are possible. **York 22/91+md** is a late marginal direction by John Clerke, however, and may therefore be of limited application.

The first half of the cycle, then, uses rather fewer professional singers than the second half, but may have required at least two professionals, probably three, and perhaps as many as eight or more. As we have already noted, any professional singers in these plays could in theory be doubled with singing roles in the second half of the cycle, and apparently such doublings did happen: for the city ordinance of 3 April 1476 allowed players to play twice on the day, but not more often.[98] To take one of several possibilities, then, the boy singing Mary in the Annunciation play would have started at the first station at 6.41 a.m., according to Dorrell, finishing the performances of that play more than five hours later, at 11.57 a.m. There would then be plenty of time for him to have a meal, relax and return to the starting point in time to take the singing role in Play 38 (The Resurrection), starting at 3.14 p.m., or that in Play 42 (The Ascension), starting an hour later. Whether this would have been wise or not is another matter: The Resurrection would have finished its last performance at 10.22 p.m., and The Ascension at 11.12 p.m., according to Dorrell.[99] In the case of the York cycle much depends on the number of plays being given, the number of performances of each, and the exact method of performance. Recent scholarship certainly favours the traditional view that a more or less complete cycle was normally played entire at something like twelve stations, all in the one day.

From what has just been said, then, the musical demands of a performance of the York cycle would be such as to stretch the resources of even so large a city. Unfortunately, the records are too sparse to show what doublings, if any, occurred. The evidence of the better-recorded Chester and Coventry cycles suggests that doubling did not normally take place, despite the fact that resources were fully stretched, although from the 1530s or so some versatile musicians did work for more than one guild in any one year. It will be worth our while to examine the Chester records for the deployment of such forces, therefore, since the texts survive. The plays concerned are:

1 *The Creation and Fall of the Angels* requires the singing of two antiphons. These are both possible for amateur singers, although one would perhaps expect professionals to be used for such important angelic performances. However, all nine orders of angels have speeches – presumably each is represented by a single being – and the provision of nine singers seems unlikely, even if they were boys. While professionals are a possibility, therefore, I suspect that the

---

[98] REED.*York* I, 109.
[99] This would be a long day, but perhaps not impossibly long for an older child.

Tanners were able to field a group of their own members who could do justice to these two pieces. (In this case they provided, directly or by borrowing from other guilds, all nine angels: but not all of these nine needed to be singers.)

6   *The Salutation and Nativity* needs two singers. Granted that Mary must have been played by a boy, I think that a choirboy is likely, for Mary apparently sings the whole Magnificat. This is not certain, however, and the Magnificat is in any case a congregational piece, so that it could be sung by an amateur.

The angel has a speaking role of four stanzas – eight if Gabriel is the same role[100] – in addition to singing 'Haec est ara dei caeli'. The direction here, *Fiat notam secundum arbitrium agentis* (6/666+sd), seems to suggest that the performer must provide a musical setting. This, and the size of the role, may indicate a mature professional singer: but on the other hand the Angel's role demands rehearsal with several members of the cast in different parts of the play, which would create problems for an outsider.

7   *The Shepherds*. This play needs a good singer to perform *Gloria in excelsis*, according to the Second Shepherd's admiring description (7/406–7: see above, 2.4). The Angel has a single stanza of speech, and the role can be rehearsed wholly with the shepherds. This would seem to be a a role for a professional singing man or a senior choirboy.

The Painters' play is one of those for which accounts survive, but this additional evidence raises as many problems as it solves. The accounts are for the years 1568, 1572 and 1575.[101] They seem to show that the guild hired the services of four boys to play the shepherds' boys, and that these four sang; thus they can be identified with some certainty as the 'helpers' who sing with the shepherds at 7/447+sd.[102] These are however the only professional singers identifiable in the accounts: who, then, sings the *Gloria in excelsis*? In each year the accounts show that the Angel received only 6d, which is a small wage entirely commensurate with his small speaking role. There are only two possibilities: first, that a guildsman had a good enough voice to sing the Gloria, at no extra payment, without making a complete nonsense of the Second Shepherd's assertion that he had a fine voice; second, that a singer, either a professional or a good amateur borrowed from another guild, who did not take the speaking role, sang the Gloria either from behind the waggon or – as seems more likely – as a costumed actor in the Heaven. If this second theory is the correct one, then the singer concerned no doubt appears in the accounts, unrecognised for the part he played or perhaps even for having played any part.

There is the very slightest piece of evidence for this latter view, in that the

---

[100] This does not seem to be the intention, however: see *Chester* II, 84 (note to **Chester 6/159+sh**).

[101] These accounts and their possible interpretations are discussed at length in *Essays*, 132–34, and above, 3.2. For the accounts themselves, see *REED.Chester* under the relevant dates, and *Essays*, 246–53.

[102] This is not the only possible interpretation, and Peter Meredith has suggested that the 'helpers' of **Chester 7/447+sd** (MS H only) were non-costumed extra singers off-stage (at the METh meeting, Leeds University, 23 March 1991).

1575 accounts record the payment of the 6d 'to oure Angell', which may suggest a distinction between the Painters' angel and another one.

10   *The Innocents*. This play has two occasions for singing by an angel. The first piece, *Ecce dominus ascendet*, is unidentified as a liturgical piece; the second, *Ex Egipto*, is a Magnificat antiphon, set syllabically. The Angel's speaking role is of 36 lines: this could be rehearsed entirely with Mary and Joseph only, but seems too large a speaking role to be given to an outsider. The role could have been played by a professional singing man, then, but there is no evidence that the *music* demanded it and the spoken text suggests otherwise.

11   In *The Purification* Simeon sings *Nunc dimittis*, and nothing in the text suggests singing angels. There are however two places in the play, at **11/40+sd** and **11/71+sd**, where angelic music would be suitable. These have to be considered because the Smiths' company records show that a variety of singers were paid for performances in the play during the 1550s, 60s and 70s. It is not easy to make sense of the extant records,[103] but as far as the angels go the situation seems to have been as follows. A group of professional singers from the cathedral was involved in the play in 1554 and again in 1561: in the latter year they are specified as five boys. In 1567 there were no boys, but someone – presumably the precentor, who is named in the accounts – played a regals. As he is listed among the actors we can assume that he was costumed, presumably as an angel, and played in full view. It is known that the Painters hired boys in 1568 (see above, under Play 7): if they did so in 1567 as well, the Smiths' use of a regals in that year must mean that the supply of suitable singing boys was strictly limited.

The following year, 1568, the situation is unclear. The precentor was running the music for the Painters, and took boys with him for the purpose, and the music for Play 11 was again in the hands of the singing man Randle Barnes. Barnes seems to have provided more lavish music than had been available in 1567, for he was paid more: perhaps he was able to supply a small group of boys, or perhaps he gave a more substantial recital or even brought a colleague to sing. In 1572 there were 'songes' provided by 'the Clergy', but no indication of who sang them; in 1575 there was again a group of singers, apparently four or more, so perhaps the Smiths were again able to hire the boys.

Uncertain as much of this information is, the records seem to show that the Smiths hired a group of choirboys when they could, and that the 'songs' sung by them were a performance separate from Simeon's singing of *Nunc dimittis*. This angelic music may have occurred at the two places in the play where Simeon's 'correction' of holy scripture is erased and the original reading reinstated by the angel.

14   There are no angels in the Shoemakers' play of *Mary Magdalene and the Entry into Jerusalem*, but boys are needed to sing 'Hosanna filio David' at **14/208+sd**.

---

[103] See *Essays*, 134–6.

17 No professional singers are required for *The Harrowing of Hell*. The archangel Michael intones *Te deum*, but this is a congregational piece and the intonation could be managed by a competent amateur.

18 In *The Resurrection* two angels sing *Christus resurgens* at **18/153+sd**. This is a long and difficult piece requiring professional singers.

20 *The Ascension* has three cues for angelic music, the first of which is an extended musical scene between Christ and a group of angels. The first angel has a speaking role of two four-line stanzas, while three more angels have a single four-line stanza each. For the singing roles, most manuscripts specify two angels and a chorus, but MS H gives the chorus section to a third angel: there is no singing role specifically for the fourth angel. The textual variant may reflect a range of possibilities, then: (i) the first, second and third angels sing solos, but the fourth angel is not a singer (MS H only); (ii) the first and second angels sing solos, the third joining in the chorus with them, the fourth not being a singer (other MSS); and (iii) the first and second angels sing solos, the third and fourth joining them in the chorus (other MSS). A fourth possibility exists, although it is not shown in the manuscripts: namely, (iv) a variant of (ii), in which there is no fourth angel, his speaking role being taken over by one of the others.

The singing of *Exaltare domine* and *Viri Galilei* in succession (**20/152+sd1, 2**) imposes a restriction on the mode of the former that demands the singing of the neumatic/melismatic responsory rather than the syllabic antiphon with that incipit.[104] Although the rest of the music is syllabic and could in theory have been performed by amateurs, therefore (although the quantity of music to be sung suggests that amateurs would not be used), *Exaltare domine*, at least, must have required that the angels be played by professional singers. The role of Christ, which involves only a small amount of singing of syllabic chant, could have been played by a competent amateur.

23 The archangel Michael ends the *Antichrist* play by singing *Gaudete justi* as he leads Enoch and Elias in procession to eternal bliss. Both pieces with this *incipit* are set to neumatic/melismatic chants,[105] so that Michael is likely to have been played by a professional singer. His speaking role, although important, is small, and rehearsals should not have created problems.

24 In *The Judgement* two angels sing *Letamini in domino* and/or *Salvator mundi domine* (**24/508+sd**) while they come to collect the blessed souls and lead them to bliss. Each of the angels has a four-line speech immediately before-hand. MS H gives the two pieces as alternatives, which would suggest different production circumstances (time needed for the procession, professional or amateur singers, etc.); but Lumiansky and Mills seem to prefer the majority reading in which, apparently, both pieces are sung.[106] If the angels do sing *Letamini in domino*, which has a neumatic chant, professionals are more likely although really good amateurs would be possible.

---

[104] For an explanation of this, see *Essays*, 152.
[105] The likely choice is the communion from the common of martyrs (GS 218): see *Essays*, 153.
[106] *Chester* II, 371.

I have assumed that the 'angeli' of the SD refers to the two angels who have just spoken: the Latin does however allow other angels to be referred to, although this is not likely. The identity of the angels in this play is an important issue, however, because the First and Second angels appear earlier in the play, as the angels who blow the Last Trumpet, with an eight-line stanza each to speak. Again, the SD would allow angels other than those who have spoken to blow the trumpets, but this seems unlikely. A strict interpretation of the text, then, would require two angels only, who both blow the Last Trumpet and sing at the separation of the blessed from the damned. Leaving aside the possibility of the trumpet-blowing angels miming to the actual playing of trumpeters behind the set, this does seem unlikely. Lumiansky and Mills point out, too, that additional angels seem to be needed to display the instruments of the Passion.[107] In practice the guild no doubt preferred to be flexible in this matter, fielding as many angels as was possible and convenient for the purpose. From a musical point of view it might be sensible to assume that at least four musicians were necessary: two trumpeters and two singers, at least the latter being costumed.

The trumpet-players would certainly be professionals; the singing angels would have been difficult roles for amateurs, even if *Letamini in domino* were not sung, and professional singers seem probable.

The Chester cycle was apparently performed on a single day at its transfer from Corpus Christi to Whitsunday in or before 1521, but by 1531 the plays had been spread over the Monday, Tuesday and Wednesday of Whitsun Week: nine plays were performed on each of the first two days, and seven plays on the third.[108] A further change took place for the last performance only, in 1575, when the plays were performed on four days just after midsummer. Lumiansky and Mills consider that a statement near the end of Play 5 indicates that the first day ended with that play.[109]

The 1575 performance was unusual, then, and in earlier years for which relevant guild records have survived a three-day performance was in operation. Assuming that the three days dealt with plays 1–9, 10–17 and 18–24, respectively (Lumiansky and Mills's plays 16 and 16A being separate pageants), it would be possible for an actor playing anywhere in one group to play also anywhere in another group. In 1568, then, the shepherds' boys of Play 7 could have returned the following day to sing as angels in Play 11, and it is a pity that the Smiths' accounts for that year leave the matter unresolved.

Doubling singers' roles within the group of plays on any one day is another matter. The situation is less complex than at York, because the Chester plays were normally played at only four stations, albeit rather more widely separated than those at York. Table 19 shows approximate timings for the Chester cycle. The timings for individual plays are based on my calculations for the 1983 performance in Leeds, which turned out to be fairly accurate; I have allowed one minute for a waiting play

---

[107] *Chester* II, 353.

[108] *Essays*, 176 and 182.

[109] *Essays*, 193 and n. 20.

TABLE 19 : TIMING OF THE CHESTER CYCLE

play	length (mins)	station 1 Abbey gates	station 2 Pentice	station 3 Watergate St	station 4 Bridge St
Day 1					
1	18	0.00-0.18	0.23-0.41	0.46-1.04	1.09-1.27
2	42	0.19-1.01	1.06-1.48	1.53-2.35	2.40-3.22
3	23	1.02-1.24	1.49-2.12	2.36-2.59	3.23-3.46
4	29	1.25-1.54	2.13-2.42	3.00-3.29	3.47-4.16
5	27	1.55-2.22	2.43-3.10	3.30-3.57	4.17-4.44
6	43	2.23-3.06	3.11-3.54	3.59-4.42	4.47-5.30
7	42	3.07-3.49	3.55-4.37	4.43-5.25	5.31-6.13
8	25	3.50-4.15	4.38-5.03	5.26-5.51	6.14-6.39
9	16	4.16-4.32	5.04-5.20	5.52-6.08	6.40-6.56
Day 2					
10	30	0.00-0.30	0.35-1.05	1.10-1.40	1.45-2.15
11	20	0.31-0.51	1.06-1.26	1.41-2.01	2.16-2.36
12	19	0.52-1.11	1.27-1.46	2.02-2.21	2.37-2.56
13	29	1.12-1.41	1.47-2.16	2.22-2.51	2.57-3.26
14	26	1.42-2.08	2.17-2.43	2.52-3.18	3.27-3.53
15	22	2.09-2.31	2.44-3.06	3.19-3.41	3.54-4.16
16	24	2.32-2.56	3.07-3.31	3.42-4.06	4.17-4.41
16A	29	2.57-3.26	3.32-4.01	4.07-4.36	4.42-5.11
17	20	3.27-3.47	4.02-4.22	4.37-4.57	5.12-5.32
Day 3					
18	26	0.00-0.26	0.31-0.57	1.02-1.28	1.33-1.59
19	17	0.27-0.44	0.58-1.15	1.29-1.46	2.00-2.17
20	12	0.45-0.57	1.16-1.28	1.47-1.59	2.18-2.30
21	23	0.58-1.21	1.29-1.52	2.00-2.23	2.31-2.54
22	20	1.22-1.42	1.53-2.13	2.24-2.44	2.55-3.15
23	43	1.43-2.26	2.31-3.14	3.19-4.02	4.07-4.50
24	42	2.27-3.09	3.15-3.57	4.03-4.45	4.51-5.33

to be ready to begin after the exit of the previous play. The estimate of 5 minutes between stations may be a little generous, especially between stations 2 (the Pentice) and 3 (Watergate Street), where the distance is short and there are no narrow corners to turn. Conditions would certainly have been very variable, however, depending on the density of the crowd. All timings for each day begin from the time at which the first play of the day begins playing at the first station (0 hrs 00 minutes).

As always in processional performance, a play that is considerably longer than the preceding play will find that each station has already been vacated by the time it arrives there, while a relatively shorter play has to wait at each station for the previous play to end. In theory, a run of shorter plays held up by a longer one could result in a total of seven plays being in the circuit simultaneously – one at each station and three waiting at stations 2, 3 and 4. This probably never happened at Chester, although six plays in the circuit may have occurred on all three days, notably on Day 2, when Play 15 started at the first station before Play 10 had finished at the fourth station. The possibilities for doubling on any one day are therefore limited, and specific consideration shows that doubling was virtually impossible for the professional singers. Those apparently needed for each day are as follows:

Day 1   probably a boy and a man in Play 6, four boys and a man in Play 7.

Day 2   five boys in Play 11 (and/or an organist in 1567), a group of boys in Play 14 (as boys, not as angels).

Day 3   two singers in Play 18, three or four in Play 20, one in Play 23, and two in Play 24.

As Table 19 shows, no doublings are possible between plays in Day 1 or Day 2, so that the requirement for Day 1 is probably five boys and two men, and for Day 2 two groups of boys. We should probably assume that any group of boys was in the charge of a singing man who was present, so that in practice we can add another two men into the total for Day 2: the additional man for Play 11 would presumably be the organist, however, if organist and boys performed on the same occasion – that is, the man in charge of the choristers was the one who accompanied their singing on the regals.

The boys of Day 1 could in theory sing again in Day 2. I suspect that for a busy cathedral choir the problems of rehearsing for two or more plays might be considerable, however, and the need for two groups of boys in Day 2 may suggest that the plays had other sources of singers apart from the cathedral. It is however important to know how many boys the cathedral could supply at any one time, and we shall return to this question.

One doubling is possible in Day 3: the two singers of Play 18 could perhaps have returned to the start in time to sing in Play 24. The margin is however too small to allow for much variation in the timings given, and I should not like to assume that it was possible in practice: it must be remembered, too, that the uphill climb from station 4 in Bridge Street back to the Abbey gates takes time, especially in a crowd, and a singer who arrives hot and breathless is in no fit state to perform. Day 3, then, does not really allow of any doubling of singers, and therefore demands eight or nine professionals.

At this stage it becomes important to address a question that arose in connection with both cycles: how many men and boys could we expect in a cathedral choir?

In the late fifteenth and sixteenth centuries, as now, boys were normally admitted to choirs at the age of eight or nine. The average age of the choristers in any choir was presumably higher than now, however. As we have seen (8.2, above), a treble could continue singing to a greater age because of the later onset of puberty, and this implies some further physical development before the voice change, and on average a greater vital capacity. Since a choirboy was on average closer to the stature of a mature man – and also because, as previously noted, men did not attain their full stature until later – the vocal power of a boy was then greater, compared with that of a grown man, than it is now. That being so, we should expect that the part-for-part ratio of boys to men was then less than it is now: that is, fewer boys on a musical line would be needed to balance a single mature singer on another line.

Nowadays, when an all-male church choir is assembled primarily with four-part SATB music in mind – that is, for the soprano/alto/tenor/bass disposition – the balance is maintained by the full complement of about twenty boys against a dozen or so men. This is a ratio, part for part, of 20/4:4:4, or boys/men = 5/1 in single parts. (I am assuming here the normal disposition, where the alto part is sung by falsettists.) A wide variety is however possible: St Paul's cathedral choir in London, for instance, currently numbers around 24/6:6:6, a boys/men ratio of 4/1 in single parts, but on weekdays the full complement of boys sings with only half the men, who work on a rota basis, giving a part-to-part ratio of 8/1. It has also been pointed out to me that in a building where there is an acoustical disadvantage to the altos (as in Westminster Cathedral) the number of boys and altos must be increased.[110] A choir of such size can of course divide in other ways (e.g. into five or six parts) without the texture becoming too unbalanced. Division into two choirs, as for instance for antiphonal singing, does not affect this balance: two choirs singing with a ratio of 12/3:3:3 gives the same balance as 24/6:6:6, whether they sing together or separately.

Numbers of choristers and singing men in the late Middle Ages are often difficult to pin down,[111] and in any case it is not always easy to see that they were intended to form a balanced choir for part-music. Their main business was, after all, the singing of chant, a situation that changed only with the Reformation. Where the provision of boys to sing polyphony seems deliberate, however, choral establishments of the early sixteenth century show that a choir consisting of ten boys and six men was normal.[112] While this seems to give the same ratio of 10/2:2:2, or 5/1 in single parts, this is misleading: in the early sixteenth century any well-established choir was for at least five parts, the boys being divided. Thus the real ratio is 5:5/2:2:2, or 5/2 in single parts. Some of the best choirs, too, were constituted for six-part music. The Northumberland Household Books give a list of the Chapel, undated but c.1510, as two basses, two tenors, four countertenors and five children, viz., two trebles and three means.[113] Here the countertenors divided,[114] giving ratios

---

[110] I am grateful to Simon Lindley for discussion on this issue, and for the information on St Paul's and Westminster cathedrals.

[111] See, for instance, Harrison *Music in Medieval Britain*, 11–12.

[112] Harrison *op. cit.*, 14.

[113] Percy *Northumberland*, 40.

[114] 'Countertenor' here means a higher male voice, not (as it would now) a male alto. In fact a countertenor probably had what we should now call a tenor voice, although the controversy continues as to whether the higher men's parts were intended for falsettists or not.

of 2:3/2:2:2:2. This seems to have been a year in which the choir was under strength, and later lists increase the children to six (3+3) and then the countertenors to the same number. The Northumberland choir at full strength, then, seems to have been six children and ten men, distributed as 3:3/3:3:2:2.[115] That this is so different from the constitution of a modern choir says much for the relative power of a boy's voice at that time.

A similar ratio can be found in J.S. Bach's choir at St Thomas's, Leipzig, constituted as an SATB choir. Daw's figures for the unchanged, transitional and changed voices (trebles, altos and tenors/basses) in 1744 were 8:5:16.[116] Even allowing for the weaker tenor and bass voices of adolescents (presumably eight of each, or thereabouts), it seems that the trebles could hold their own well against the other voices.

This information is too unstandardised for us to draw detailed conclusions about the singers in York and Chester in the fifteenth and sixteenth centuries, but some useful points can be made. First, York Minster was unusual in having as many as twelve boys after 1425. These would be six trebles and six means, presumably, and perhaps it was even this special feature that suggested the two-part music in York 45. In fact, a further special feature would have been that the choirboys could divide evenly into four parts, which is what happens in *Veni electa* B. A second point is that against so many boys we might expect a larger-than-usual group of men, at least three of each voice, or nine altogether: this would give a ratio of 6:6/3:3:3, or 2:1 part-for-part. Throughout the period under discussion here, then, it would not be unreasonable to think of the York choir as consisting of twelve boys and about nine men.

If the choir at York Minster was exceptional, what might be a normal choir elsewhere? We have seen that a ratio of ten boys to six men was usual, disposed as 5:5/2:2:2, and it might be unwise to assume that the Chester choir was any larger than this in the 1560s. Even the best-established parish churches in York and Chester could perhaps call on rather fewer singers than that; and although there is obviously a possibility of singers coming from other churches, it seems noticeable that the Chester records do not seem to mention singers from anywhere but the cathedral.

We have seen that York plays 25–47, the final group of the cycle in which no doublings are possible, had already used twelve boys (which I have assumed to be those of the Minster choir) and another two groups of boys (twelve in all) in addition. Even were there another church which maintained twelve boys in the choir, the remaining needs of these plays would demand the whole complement of its choristers. Large as it was by medieval standards, York cannot have had many churches with large choirs. We must therefore conclude that at least two of the York

[115] Percy *Northumberland*, 46, 88, 253 and 324. In my article 'Female Roles', p. 34, I tried to make sense of these figures in terms of a five-part choir, but several friends have since pointed out the size of the six-part repertory for such choirs in the first two or three decades of the century.

[116] Daw, 87. As noted in section 8.2, Daw did not consider that some of the tenors might also be transitional. The small number of altos relative to the other parts may suggest, however, that Bach could not always maintain the ideal constitution for his choir.

city parish churches were needed to supply singers for the cycle; that the city's musical resources were considerably stretched by the plays; and that it may well have been necessary to double singing roles between the earlier and later plays.

The Chester plays, similarly, must have stretched the city's musical resources. Probably at least one parish church, St John's, maintained a fair-sized choir, but there will have been none too many singers for the task. The maximum number of boys needed in any one day is probably those demanded by Day 2: these are a group of five and another group. If the cathedral had ten boys, therefore, probably the whole contingent would be required for Day 2. If members of the cathedral choir were the only singers, five of these boys would already have performed in the plays of Day 1, and some at least would have to perform in Day 3 as well (for it would be surprising if the majority of Day 3's eight or nine singers were not boys). Clearly, if the individual boys were not to be involved in two if not three days, some of the singers must have been drawn from at least one other choir.

I have concentrated on the boys because they present the clearest index of singers and their disposition. Their use is relatively inflexible (both in the plays and in terms of their attendance for church services) because of the numbers involved. The men, singing usually as individuals, could have been much more flexible in all respects – attendance at rehearsals, the possibility of doubling roles, the demands of the cathedral, and so on. On the whole, then, it seems that a greater number of churches were involved in providing singers, and/or more doubling of roles went on among singers, than the records have so far revealed.

Before leaving this question it will be worth while examining what we know of James Hewitt and his colleagues at Coventry, since there we seem to have a versatile group of individuals who made themselves useful in various ways.[117] The Weavers paid singers (probably two of them) regularly in the 1550s, '60s and '70s, and, as already noted (2.6, above), for much of that time James Hewitt is named as the player of the regals: presumably he accompanied the singers, and probably the latter were two of his colleagues in the waits, who were also church singing men. Hewitt is named in 1554, 1556–7, and 1561–73, and it is entirely possible that he played in some intervening years when payment was made for the regals but no player named. The Drapers also paid professional singing men in the 1550s, '60s and '70s, with regals being paid for from 1561 or perhaps 1560. Hewitt is named as the owner in 1563, and 1565–8: again, he may have been involved before and/or after these dates. Here, too, the regals were used in conjunction with two professional singers. Ingram considered that Hewitt did not perform for the Drapers but merely hired out his instrument to them, on the grounds that his work for the Weavers made him unavailable to the Drapers' play.[118] The Weavers' accounts are certainly unequivocal, and show that Hewitt was the performer, while the Draper's accounts do not

---

[117] Items from the Coventry guild accounts will be found in *REED.Coventry* under the relevant dates and guilds.
[118] Ingram 1979, 76–7.

say so.[119] But if Hewitt had been 'unavailable' to the Drapers because of performing for the Weavers, so was his instrument. There is a possibility, of course, that he owned two instruments and so could hire out one while he played the other, but this is highly improbable. For what reason would Hewitt own two pairs of regals (i.e. two instruments)?[120] It seems so improbable that someone else played as second instrument belonging to Hewitt that I shall not entertain it further. The Drapers' payments for Hewitt's regals might have covered his playing, or alternatively he might have been paid as one of the singers. Interesting as the question is, it is immaterial to the point at issue here – namely, that a doubling must have been possible, whether it concerned the man, the regals, or both.

Hewitt performed in both pageants, then, in all the years when he is named in the Drapers' accounts, 1563 and 1565–8 inclusive. The Coventry cycle consisted probably of ten pageants, all of New Testament material, played at several stations.[121] We do not know how long most of the pageants were, all but two of the plays having been lost, nor how many stations were involved. But the surviving pageants are long by the standards of other cycles – 900 lines (about 55 minutes) for the Shearmen and Tailors' play and 1192 lines (about 75 minutes) for the Weavers' play. It is notable that Hewitt performed in an early play, the Weavers', which was probably played second, and then in a late play, the Drapers' play of Doomsday, which must have been played last.[122] It is a great pity that we cannot make up for the Coventry cycle the kind of timetable that has been constructed for York and Chester, because then we should be able to check the timetable against the fact that Hewitt played twice. Of one thing I do feel quite certain: it is highly unlikely that any doubling could have taken place if ten stations had been in use for any performance.

Table 20 shows the timings for Coventry plays 1 and 2 over a five-station route, with estimated times at station 1 only for the rest of the plays. I have estimated the average length of plays 3-10 inclusive as one hour. As before, I have allowed one minute for a pageant to prepare for the performance after the exit of the previous play, and five minutes between stations. With these timings Hewitt would have had no difficulty, after Play 2 finished at the fifth station, in returning to the first station in time to perform in Play 10. On these estimates Play 2 finished at 7.31, while Play 10 did not begin until 9.19, allowing Hewitt an hour and 48 minutes for the return to station 1. This is none too long, considering that the regals must be transported, but the time available would expand, of course, if the average length of the plays were more than the hour that I have allowed. With a sixth station, Play 2 would finish at 8.51, which probably leaves too little time to transport the regals back to the first station; and with a seventh station, Play 2 ending at 10.11, it becomes quite

---

[119] The items in the Drapers' accounts are in the form 'Item paid to (James) Hewitt for his/the regals'.

[120] Regals, like some other keyboard instruments (organs, virginals), were referred to in the plural and occasionally as 'a pair'.

[121] On the number of stations, see Craig *Coventry Plays*, xiii–xiv, and Ingram 1979, 98.

[122] For the list of probable plays, see Lancashire, 115–6.

TABLE 20 : THE COVENTRY CYCLE AND JAMES HEWITT'S DOUBLING

Play	Length	station 1	station 2	station 3	station 4	station 5
1	55 mins	0.00-0.55	1.00-1.55	2.00-2.55	3.00-3.55	4.00-4.55
2	1 hr 15	0.56-2.11	2.16-3.31	3.36-4.51	4.56-6.11	6.16-**7.31**
3	1 hr (est)	2.12-3.12				
4	1 hr (est)	3.13-4.13				
5	1 hr (est)	4.14-5.14				
6	1 hr (est)	5.15-6.15				
7	1 hr (est)	6.16-7.16				
8	1 hr (est)	7.17-8.17				
9	1 hr (est)	8.18-9.18				
10	1 hr (est)	**9.19**-20.19				

impossible on this timing. The seventh station might be accommodated for this purpose if the average length of plays 3–10 was as much as 70 or 75 minutes, but this is surely stretching things a little; more importantly, we should note that if this doubling were to be possible with a full ten stations in operation, the average length of these plays would have to be around 110 minutes. We should also note that, apart from assuming that Hewitt could transport his regals back to the first station in a reasonable time – on the waggon of Play 2, presumably – I am also assuming that he required no costume change. This is reasonable enough: he would be dressed as an angel in both plays. Incidentally, the two singers in Play 10 could be the same men as in Play 2, so that Hewitt, his colleagues and the regals could all travel together in Play 2 and then back for Play 10. Although the logistics of this are not difficult, I think on balance that only five or so stations could have been in use.

It would not however have been possible for Hewitt to perform in the Smiths' pageant in any year if he were in both of these other plays. The records show that the Smiths hired the city waits in 1549, and perhaps also in 1555 and 1561.[123] 1549 antedates the appearance of Hewitt's name in the records, so we do not know that he was involved in any play; and he is not named in the Weavers' or Smiths' accounts for 1555. 1561 is the year when Hewitt was paid by the Weavers 'for hys Rygoles & synggyn' in the pageant, but the Drapers' accounts do not name 'the Syngyng men' nor the Smiths' accounts 'the mynstrelles':[124] so although this year is in a period when Hewitt was known to have been employed by all three companies in the plays, there is no evidence that he performed in the plays for more than one guild in 1561. Indeed, we should perhaps assume that one or both of the Drapers' and Smiths' companies found a substitute because he was not available (or, in the case of the waits, perhaps the others performed without Hewitt).

---

[123] *REED.Coventry*, 184, 205 and 218. In the last two, payment is made to 'the minstrels', which could refer to the waits but need not.
[124] *REED.Coventry*, 216–18.

*

Two other matters should be mentioned here. The first is that, as the Coventry records show, it was not unusual there for a group of guildsmen to play angels – presumably speaking but not singing angels, according to the payments – while two professional singers (also presumably costumed as angels) were engaged to sing. Here, then, we have evidence of a mixed group of singing and speaking angels, as we have already postulated in the York and Chester cycles. Second, minstrels were presumably costumed as angels if their business was heavenly minstrelsy. Minstrels are discussed below, in section 8.5.

8.4 The Shepherds

The Shepherds have always been among the most popular characters in the English biblical plays.[125] They are whole men, humorous and serious; they have the generosity of normal, salt-of-the-earth human beings such as we are glad to have as neighbours; they are chosen for a special commission, to be both the first Christian pilgrims and the first evangelists; they show their joy in this privilege in an honest, homely way, by singing; and they indulge in a critical discussion of the angelic concert put on for them, a temptation that few of us could resist.

The reasons for their musicality are those discussed in 5.3, above. However much bickering goes on among them, and whatever the state of industrial relations between the Chester shepherds and Garcius, there is never any doubt that the shepherds will act as God's agents by carrying out the angel's instructions. As a result, the shepherds' plays have an above-average occurrence of musical stage directions; a share of the notated music; and more musical cues than any but a very few other plays in the cycles. But it is not only in terms of quantity that the shepherds' plays are musically important: for they include sections of dialogue in which musical matters are discussed – sometimes at length and in some cases with considerable technical detail – and they are the only plays to do so. It is not surprising that commentators have always mentioned the musical content of the shepherds' plays.

The musicological interest of the plays was recognised long ago,[126] yet the subject has thrown up little argument or critical discussion. It is time, then, to ask some questions about the shepherds: How musical are they? How knowledgeable are they really in their critical discussion of the angelic *Gloria in excelsis*? And – a vital question for performance of the plays – what sort of music did they perform? If these questions can be answered, even incompletely, we shall certainly learn

[125] The shepherds plays have most often been used as examples of medieval English drama, and especially in relation to comedy. They are discussed in detail by Kolve, 151–73, and by Woolf, 182–93.

[126] See especially Carpenter '*Secunda Pastorum*'.

something about the performance of English shepherds' plays: but we may also learn something more generally about the musical expectations of an audience in the late fifteenth and sixteenth centuries.

There are shepherds' episodes in all of the surviving English cycles, including the Coventry plays, but not in the Cornish *Ordinalia*. The story is more or less closely based on the Nativity story transmitted by St Luke 2/8–20:

(8) Et pastores erant in regione eadem vigilantes, et custodientes vigilias noctis super gregem suum. (9) Et ecce angelus domini stetit iuxta illos, et claritas dei circumfulsit illos, et timuerunt timore magno. (10) Et dixit illis angelus: Nolite timere. Ecce enim euangelizo vobis gaudium magnum quod erit omni populo: (11) quia natus est vobis hodie Saluator qui est Cristus dominus in civitate David. (12) Et hoc vobis signum: inuenietis infantem pannis inuolutum, et positum in presepio. (13) Et subito facta est cum angelo multitudo milicie celestis, laudantium deum et dicentium:

(14) Gloria in altissimis deo, et in terra pax hominibus bone voluntatis.

(15) Et factum est ut discesserunt ab eis angeli in celum, pastores loquebantur adinuicem: Transeamus usque Bethleem, et videamus hoc verbum quod factum est quod fecit dominus et ostendit nobis. (16) Et venerunt festinantes, et inuenerunt Mariam et Ioseph et infantem positum in presepio. (17) Videntes autem cognouerunt de verbo, quod dictum erat illis de puero hoc. (18) Et omnes qui audierant mirati sunt, et de hijs que dicta erant a pastoribus ad ipsos. (19) Maria autem conseruabat omnia verba hec, conferens in corde suo. (20) Et reuersi sunt pastores glorificantes et laudantes deum in omnibus que audierant et viderant, sicut dictum est ad illos.

Much of this story is clear, although some of it is ambiguous and raises a number of questions. Is verse 18 a reference to the shepherds' evangelising activities after their return from Bethlehem; or is it that they told Mary, Joseph and others about their strange experience with the angels, and that it is this 'marvellous' story that Mary 'kept in her heart' (verse 19)? And are we to assume that the shepherds' 'glorifying and praising God' (verse 20) involved evangelising, or is that idea due to the first reading of verse 18? Certainly the Authorised Version does not make explicit the second reading, which on the face of it is the correct one: and the plays all seem to follow the first reading, for the shepherds do not tell Mary and Joseph about the angels, but they do go away at the end of the play to make known the Saviour's birth. Perhaps more importantly for our immediate purposes, St Luke's interest in the shepherds' story was selective. He took no interest in the detail of their vigil in the fields, for instance, nor in their precise reaction to the sight of the Christ-child in the manger; nor was it any part of his purpose to present the shepherds as characters important in their own right.

Any dramatist would have had other purposes in mind, however. If he was to set the scene properly for the angelic annunciation to the shepherds he must use his imagination to fill out that first bald statement of St Luke's, 'There were shepherds abiding in the fields, watching over their flocks by night'. Here the plays vary considerably in their material, but we should note that in the two Towneley plays and the Chester play the musical characters of the shepherds are already set in this first scene. Luke was not much interested, either, in details of the shepherds' visit to the stable, which might have detracted from his main purpose to show that the shepherds saw, recognised the truth of the angel's message, and went away to tell others. But in the plays they must say something, do something, present their reactions to the Child as part of a scene in the stable, and act out this role that they are destined to play. Here a parallel with the Magi presented itself. If the kings made gifts, as specified in the Bible,[127] could not the shepherds do the same? By the time of the plays it was common for illustrators and commentators to show the shepherds offering gifts to the Christ-child in an adoration-scene that mirrors that of the three kings. In the Coventry and Chester shepherds' plays a musical instrument, a 'pipe', is among the gifts offered. What sort of instrument this might be I shall discuss presently.

St Luke's account of the story mentions no music at all: but, quite apart from the derivation of the *Gloria* from the liturgy, the audience of a shepherds' play must have understood the musical implications of the play by the end of the first scene, and to have been prepared for the singing of an angel. Here dramatic traditions are an important factor. In almost every case the plays depart from the biblical narrative in having a single angel sing the *Gloria* first, before any spoken announcement. This allows the angel's singing to fulfill a necessary dynamic function in redirecting the audience's attention at the beginning of the new scene, while the usual representational function of the fine singing emphasises the importance of what the angel then says to the shepherds.

Similarly, the possibility that the shepherds will sing, even in those plays where there is no introductory scene before the *Gloria*, is prepared for by the angel's singing. In all of the shepherds' plays the shepherds sing at some time after the angelic *Gloria*, whether they have done so before or not: and in each case the discussion shows that the singing is either a deliberate attempt to imitate the *Gloria* itself, or else at least a practical recognition that the angelic *activity* of singing should be imitated. The primary reason for this is that singing is a suitable way to offer praise to the Christ-child; but a second reason is that singing is bound up with the idea of mirth. Thus the shepherds' singing after the *Gloria* brings joy and praise together:

GARCIUS To Bethlem take wee the waye,
for with you I thinke to wend,
that prince of peace for to praye
heaven to have at our ende.

And singe we all, I read,
some myrth to his majestee,
for certayne now see wee it indeede:
the kinge Sone of heavon is hee.   (**Chester 7/472–9**)

It is natural that this association should be continued when the shepherds leave the stable 'praising God' (Luke 2/20: 'glorificantes et laudantes deum'), with the

127 Matthew 2/11.

result that in all the plays the shepherds sing after the adoration scene. This argument applies also to their journey towards Bethlehem, since the angel has told them the significance of what they are going to see there.

Before this happens, however, the shepherds have to learn the message given to them by the angel. The reason for this is the connection made by medieval commentators between the statement that the Good News is for 'all people' (v. 10) and the shepherds' subsequent work in telling what they have seen and heard (vv. 18–19). As Kolve argued, the Middle Ages saw the shepherds as a new priesthood, the shepherds of sheep becoming shepherds of men. Commissioned by the angel to spread the Good News of what they had experienced, they became preachers, with a new pastoral responsibility.[128] They are, in fact, the first evangelists, and it is therefore vital that they learn the message. The shepherds of **York 15**, in a discussion now made incomplete by the loss of a leaf, decide that they have understood the message and can sing it, which they do: it is impossible to tell if they have discussed the Latin. The shepherds of **Towneley 12**, whose accomplishments include a knowledge of Virgil and the scriptures, and those of **Towneley 13**, who are musically knowledgeable, rehearse the gist of the message but do not need to do more: in fact, they are more interested in matters of musical criticism. Those of **Coventry 1** find it necessary to repeat some of the Latin text to make sure that they have it right, but find that they are agreed. The shepherds of **N-Town 16** twice fail to decline the opening noun ('gle glo glory' and 'gle glo glas glum') but get the basic meaning right anyway; and the Chester shepherds, who do not understand Latin at all, thrash the text out bit by bit from beginning to end.[129] The shepherds' interest in the music varies, too, but all of them (with the possible exception of the York shepherds) make at least some comment on the music as opposed to the verbal content of the message.

This scene in which the shepherds memorise the message that they are to transmit gave the dramatists an excuse for a scene of thematic seriousness in which comedy could nevertheless be a large ingredient: and a part of this was the attempt by the shepherds, having worked the message out, to repeat it to their own satisfaction before carrying out the commission. The song in which the shepherds imitate the angels, before they visit the stable in Bethlehem, therefore, is sometimes apparently an attempt to repeat the *Gloria*, although this is not invariably the case.

We can see from this that the dramatists worked around to a play-structure in which the scenes, some of them directly biblical/liturgical and some largely imaginative, were punctuated by music. Table 21 summarises the structure of the plays. Of the scenes tabulated, (3) is additional to those described in the biblical narrative. Individual plays show modifications of the pattern, but this scheme basically holds for all the plays I shall discuss. These are York 15, N-Town 16, Towneley 12 and 13, Coventry 1, and Chester 7.[130]

---

[128] Kolve, 154–5 and 171–2; and see also Woolf, 184.

[129] **Chester 7. Shrewsbury 1**, being a single actor's part, is not informative enough for a conclusion to be drawn on this matter.

[130] The shepherds in N-Town 8 (*Joachim and Anna*) are also musical: see **N-Town 8/211–12** and **Mary Play 211–12**; also the next note.

TABLE 21 : SHEPHERDS' PLAYS

	Yk	N-T	Ty 12	Ty 13	Cov	Ch	
1 Shepherds' meeting		1-295	1-189	204-41		1-299 *	
"howe" (hn /voc)			horn	voice		v/hn	
meal			yes		sd only	yes	
song			268	189			
				Mak *			
2 star appears	36-[55]		450-2		242-6	300-57	
Gloria in excelsis	[ ]	-1, 61+ *	[295]	637	263 | 281	357	
3 Verbal message	[ ]	1-13	296-304	638-46	297-306	464-71	
disc'n of messages *	[56]-78	14-25, 78-88	305-31	647-64	264-73	358-75	376-447
disc'n of prophecies	1-36	26-61	332-430	674-84	247-63		
song	64		430	664			447
4 Decision to go to	79-85	89,	431-49,	665-73,	274-7	472-9	448-63
Bethlehem		63-77	453-7	685-709			
song (journey)	85	89			277	479	
stable/Nativity					278-96		
5 Adoration		90-154	458-502	710-54	307-31	480-95	
						496-551	
gifts	86-151		yes	yes	yes	552-696	
song	yes		yes	yes	yes	yes	

* Notes

Section 3   The messages discussed are both the *Gloria* and the verbal message.

N-Town   There is a textual problem in this play, concerning the ordering of material.

Towneley 13 Mak's section, 190-637, includes his "lullaby".

Coventry   278-81 is a stable scene with Joseph, but including the second *Gloria*; 282-96 is the Nativity itself.

Chester   This scene includes the wrestling match.

*

All this music must presuppose a tradition of musicality among shepherds, a matter that has been explored by Kolve.[131] Evidence of this musicality in the drama falls into practical, theoretical and philosophical categories. There are at least two instruments that shepherds must often have made and used. The first of these, the horn, is not strictly a *musical* instrument, but must be considered here nevertheless. It consisted literally of an ox-horn with a mouthpiece cut in the closed end. It was widely used for making noise, particularly by beaters in hunting and by soldiers, especially in battle. But its principal use was for signalling, with a sophisticated usage devised for communication between hunters in the field. No formal system of horn-calls was used by shepherds, probably, but some recognised code of signals was perhaps in use. At any rate, the aims were no doubt very simple – the announcing of one's whereabouts to a colleague. In Chester 7, for instance, the First Shepherd calls a 'howe' to the Second, and the Second to the Third; but then the First Shepherd *blows* a 'howe' on his horn to attract the attention of Garcius.[132] As Table 21 shows, horn and voice 'howes' appear in Towneley 13 and the Coventry Nativity play, respectively, as well.

The other instrument always associated with shepherds is the bagpipe. The English-speaking world is mainly aware of the Scottish bagpipe, which is a war-pipe.[133] In fact, pastoral pipes are and were much more common than war-pipes all over Europe, and in several countries one can still buy a pastoral bagpipe, often not much different from a medieval instrument. To make a bagpipe one needs a whole animal skin (sheep or goat), turned wood if available (but a hollowed wooden limb otherwise), cane, tallow and twine – all of it material easily accessible to a shepherd. Although modern pipes tend to use metal or ivory for decoration and strengthening, true pastoral pipes use animal horn, although decoration is not obligatory in any case. It is difficult to know the extent to which medieval shepherds made and played the pipes: there was perhaps a significant percentage that did. Certainly in iconography there is no doubt that the bagpipe was the badge of the shepherd. The more one looks at the shepherds in late medieval and renaissance pictures, the more one is aware of the pipes (see Plate 9). Fifteenth-century books of hours often include the pipes in depictions of the angelic annunciation to the shepherds: and although English examples are again missing, continental practice is so consistent in this that

[131] Kolve, 171. See also Woolf, 182, who notes a pastoral tradition of rustic innocence, to which Joachim's shepherds in N-Town 8 are the only ones fully to conform in the plays. Woolf cites the shepherds' intention to react musically to the angelic message to Joachim, but without relating their cheerful song to the music of the shepherds of the Nativity.

[132] **Chester 7/45, 61, 69,** and **159–62.** For 'howe' as a noun with this meaning, see OED under 'how, howe' 1.

[133] The purpose of war-pipes is to make stirring sounds to hearten one's own men and frighten the enemy: horns were used for the same purpose. There is plenty of medieval evidence for this, and the tradition is still with us in the Highland regiments. When the Argylls made their surprise (NB) attack on the Crater area of Aden on 3 July 1967 they did so with the pipes playing: I am grateful to Lt Col. G.P. Wood MC for information about this event.

the tradition must have been well known in England. Besides, several continental books of hours are known to have been commissioned for the English nobility.

So strong a tradition must reflect some general understanding of the shepherds' musicality, even if these depictions of the angelic announcement do not truly constitute independent evidence. There is, in addition, another reason why the bagpipe might feature so regularly in these illustrations. The bagpipe was an instrument particularly associated with pilgrims in the late Middle Ages, and it is perhaps in connection with their position as the first Christian pilgrims that the shepherds are given the instrument so often. While their status as the first Christian pastors and preachers has been explained in the past, their function as pilgrims, as far as I know, has not. Yet that is what they are in the middle of the shepherds' plays when they travel to Bethlehem. For the medieval traveller, pilgrimage and the bagpipe did go together: Chaucer's miller brought the Canterbury pilgrims out of Southwark with his pipes, though there, admittedly, there is another association at work, connecting the bagpipe with the viciousness in the miller's character.[134] The orthodox view was put by Archbishop Arundel during his interrogation of the Lollard William Thorpe, who had spoken against the use of bagpipes and singing by pilgrims, in 1407:[135]

> . . . it is right well done, that pilgrims have with them singers, and also pipers: that when one of them that goeth bare-foot striketh his toe upon a stone and hurteth him sore and maketh him to bleed; it is well done, that he or his fellow begin then a song or else take out of his bosom a bagpipe for to drive away with such mirth the hurt of his fellow . . .

One of the shepherds' boys in Chester 7 makes a gift of his 'pipe' to the Christ-child, and by his description it must, I think, be a bagpipe:

THE THYRD BOYE	O noble chyld of thy Father on hye
	alas, what have I for to give thee?
	Save only my pype that soundeth so royallye
	elles truely have I nothinge at all.
	Were I in the rocke or in the valey alowe,
	I could make this pipe sound, I trowe,
	that all the world should ringe
	and quaver as yt would fall. (Chester 7/625–32)

A pipe that could make the earth shake, even if some acoustical help would be needed from its surroundings, is something special. We must allow for some exaggeration, of course, but this is certainly an impressive instrument.

Another instrument to be found with the shepherds, but needing a more careful search because of its size, is the recorder. In a number of depictions of the shepherds,

---

134 See Block 'Chaucer's Millers' (1954) for an explanation of the bagpipe as a symbol of gluttony and lechery. The frequent depiction of the bagpipe as the shepherds' instrument in Nativity scenes in books of hours must, I think, mean that the pilgrim connotation was stronger, at least in that context.

135 Cited in Block 'Chaucer's Millers', 240f.

both in the fields and at the stable, the recorder can be seen. Apart from the obvious fact that the recorder can easily be made by anyone with access to small timber, there is little that can be said about this at present, except that there is clearly a strong tradition in late-fifteenth- and sixteenth-century illustration (see Plate 9).[136] The Coventry First Shepherd probably offers a recorder to the Christ-child: 'hold, take it in thy hand', he says, which shows it to be small enough for the baby to grasp it (**Coventry 1/310**).

The guild accounts for the Chester shepherds' play mention 'whistles', for which there are occasional payments in the 1560s and '70s. There is no mention of whistles in the play text, and they were presumably a piece of extra-textual 'business'. Shepherds have long used whistles to control dogs, and this must be the purpose of the whistle mentioned in an English ballad dating from the 1550s, although the dog is not mentioned:[137]

> I raigne and I rowll my flocke at my wyll
> my whestell wyll make them to go or stande styll.

It is possible that the shepherds in the centre and on the left of Plate 9 have whistles in their belts, for the purpose of controlling the dogs sitting by them. One would expect a dog-whistle to have a certain durability, and perhaps that it would have been made of wood, but traditional methods may have included alternatives. In an English song of around 1400 the shepherd Wylkyn makes 'goodë pypis' out of 'rye-strawys twyn',[138] so a more perishable product may have been usable: compare the opening of Spenser's 'mournfull Dittie for the death of Astrophell', printed in *England's Helicon* (1600):[139]

> Sheepheards that wunt on pipes of Oaten reede,
> Oft-times to plaine your loues concealed smart;

The whistles paid for by the Chester Painters were very inexpensive, and may have been of the throw-away type: for the performance of 1568 they cost 1d, and in 1575, 2d.[140] No doubt there are many ways of making such an instrument, according to the resources available in the place and at the time of making. Froissart mentions the making of a straw whistle (c.1363, but in relating his boyhood, c.1350), while the novelist Nevil Shute describes the making of a whistle from a hazel twig.[141] Other materials could presumably be used.

---

[136] An earlier version of this illustration, from the edition published in Paris by Guiot Marchant on 18 April 1493, sig. a iiiʳ, is reproduced in Rastall 'Some Myrth', 87.

[137] Peter J. Seng, ed., *Tudor Songs and Ballads* (Cambridge, Mass., and London: Harvard University Press, 1978), 55f. The poem was set in folk style for Garcius to sing in the Chester production at Leeds, 1983: the setting is in Rastall 'Some Myrth', 95.

[138] 'Ye have so longe kepyt schepe', in Oxford, Bodleian Library, MS Douce 381, f. 20v: see the facsimile in Rastall *Two Fifteenth-Century Song Books*, Ob381 f. 20v, and the edition in Dobson and Harrison *Medieval English Songs*, 205f.

[139] Facsimile printed by Scolar Press (London and Menston: 1973): see sig. G[1].

[140] *REED.Chester*, 82 and 106, respectively.

[141] For Froissart, see Edith Rickert, compiler, *Chaucer's World* (New York and London: Columbia

These instruments in the Chester play – bagpipe and whistles – suggest some musical business not in the play texts, in which the bagpipe appears only as a gift and the whistles not at all. Indeed one is perhaps justified in wondering if perhaps in some particular performance the shepherds brought on a favourite dog as part of the entertainment: it is perfectly possible. Similarly, we should bear in mind the possibility that in some performance (perhaps even quite regularly over the years) someone played the bagpipe in Chester 7. The instrumentalist, of course, must have taken the role of Third Boy. It is also possible that Coventry 1 included some unscripted business with a recorder.

The use of such instruments is however far removed from the technical knowledge of professional singing that is found in some plays in scene 3 of my plan. I want now to review the shepherds' discussion, play by play. The century between 1450 and 1550 saw important changes in musical style and in the musical capabilities of various classes of musician, so that it will be best to study the plays in chronological order.

York 15, in a manuscript of around 1470, is the earliest play that we have to consider, the Shrewsbury shepherds' play being fragmentary. The York shepherds are not initially characterised as musical, there being no mention of music in the first, incomplete, scene, which is concerned with the prophecies of Christ's birth. The loss of a leaf in the manuscript before the end of the scene is responsible for the loss of the angelic *Gloria*. When the text resumes, the shepherds are discussing the angel's verbal message to them. They break off from this, however, to interpolate a brief discussion of the music. In all, the York shepherds discuss three musical performances (**15/60–4, 65, 67, 71** and **82–5**): first, that of the angelic *Gloria*; second, their attempt to repeat the angelic music; and third, their performance of another song to honour the Christ-child while they journey to Bethlehem. The second and third of these are shown by original SDs.

The implications of the missing leaf are discussed by Beadle,[142] who concludes that the angelic sung *Gloria in excelsis deo* and the angel's message to the shepherds about going to Bethlehem are among the material lost. The missing passage partly overlaps with the Shrewsbury play, which is textually related to York 15: but Beadle believes the precise relationship to be impossible to determine.[143] We can however learn something of the angel's song. Since the First Shepherd says that he 'can synge itt alls wele as [the angel]' (**15/60**) it must have been a solo song. His need for help in singing it (**15/63**) does not imply part-music, then, although admittedly the *Gloria* might have been accompanied by instruments: he is one of those amateur singers (one comes across them often enough) who can sing a tune only if others are singing

University Press, 1948; paperback edn. 1962), 97, and Scheler, ed., *Oeuvres de Froissart: poésies* I, 88–95 ('L'Espinette amoureuse'); for Nevil Shute, see *Pied Piper* (1942), chapter 2.

142 Beadle 1982, 427–8.

143 Beadle 1982, 428. In any case, it would be unwise to attempt a reconstruction of the York musical content by reference to the Shrewsbury text, since the Shrewsbury play is institutional, not civic, and the text liturgical.

with them. After the shepherds have sung it (**15/61+sd**) the Second Shepherd says that he has so 'crakkid' in his throat that his lips are 'nere drye' (**15/67–8**). This has been a serious and energetic attempt at repeating the angelic song, appropriate to a performance described by the Third Shepherd as a 'noble noyse' (**15/71**).

Of the shepherds' attempt to repeat the angelic song, then, it would seem that the three sing in unison, but we can only make an assumption about the accuracy of their imitation.

The shepherds sing again on their way to Bethlehem (**15/85+sd**). As has already been suggested on the evidence of line 63, it is unlikely that the First Shepherd would be able to join in part music, so that this song is probably sung in unison. It is a song in honour of the Child (**15/83**), and presumably cheerful, since they 'make myrthe and melody' (**15/84**), but there are no further clues as to its nature.[144]

Of the gifts made to the Child by the three shepherds, that of the First Shepherd is a child's broach, fashioned as a tin bell (**15/103–4**). It is unreasonable to think that the shepherd would have such a thing about his person, and the likelihood is that what he offers is really a bell with a fastening that allows it to be worn as a broach. A shepherd would tie a bell round the neck of the leading wether – the bell-wether – to help in keeping track of the flock, so it is not surprising that he should have a bell on his person. Plate 10 shows a late thirteenth-century English depiction of a bell-wether.

N-Town 16 may come from the last decade of the fifteenth century. These shepherds, too, are not initially characterised as musical: there is no scene of the shepherds' meeting in this play, and the discussion of the angelic *Gloria* concentrates on the words. When the shepherds themselves sing it is the antiphon *Stella celi extirpavit*. We may find it surprising that they choose a Latin piece, and especially one that had 'no official place in the liturgical books of the principal rites', but this does not presuppose any particular musical knowledge. We should assume that the shepherds sing a plainsong setting.[145]

Towneley 12 and **13**, perhaps dating from the beginning of the sixteenth century, are justly famous for their musical content. A passage from Play 12 will give an idea of the natural way in which music is introduced.

[2 PASTOR]	Who so can best syng	
	Shall have the begynnyng.	
1 PASTOR	Now prays at the partyng	
	I shall sett you on warke;	
	We have done oure parte	
	and songyn right weyll,	
	I drynk for my parte.	(**Towneley 12/265–70**)

---

[144] The frequent connection of mirth and music in the plays is one reason why the 'mirthe' of the play's last line (**15/131**) may be taken to imply singing.

[145] On *Stella celi extirpavit*, its chant tunes and polyphonic settings, see Bent 'New and Little-Known Fragments', especially 145–8.

It is obvious that the shepherds sing during this passage, the song occurring (as Cawley places it) after line **268**.[146] I do not, however, accept Cawley's interpretation of **12/265–6**, which he regards as meaning that the best singer shall start the song:[147] since the word 'sing' in **12/265** is the first mention of their intention to sing, the idea comes out of the blue with this reading, a complete *non-sequitur* to the matter previously under discussion. To make better sense of it, we must go back a few lines. In **12/260–1** it is clear that the Second Shepherd has just emptied the bottle of ale that the three were sharing, to the consternation of the other two. The Second Shepherd, however, immediately discovers another bottle (**12/262–3**), and goes on to propose that the shepherd who sings best shall drink from it first (**12/265–6**, just quoted). In fact, it is a singing competition, the prize being the first pull on the new bottle of ale. **12/267** is a proverb meaning 'Do not give praise too soon', or 'Do not praise until the entertainment is over',[148] a warning in this case to save praise until the singing is finished. The First Shepherd is aware that the Second Shepherd will have the first drink anyway if he can, and is simply warning the Second Shepherd not to anticipate the result of the competition. He therefore starts the singing without more ado (**12/268**: I shall set you to work), but when it is finished he nevertheless takes the first pull at the bottle himself (**12/270**: I drink for my part in the singing). As it happens, the Third Shepherd is again unlucky with the drink, since the other two take so much of it between them.

The second musical event is the angelic *Gloria*, which gives rise to some technical discussion: in fact, Towneley 12 is the earliest play in which this happens to any useful extent. In this play, as in most others, the singing of *Gloria in excelsis deo* departs from the biblical account in being sung by a single angel. The shepherds do discuss the text of the angel's song, but the immediate interest for us here is in their comments on the music, which falls under three heads. First, the song was unusual. It was 'wonder curiose', according to the First Shepherd (**12/306**), and such as the Second Shepherd had never heard before (**12/326–7**). Second, the angel sang many small notes: it was a florid and complex piece, which may be part of the reason why they thought it so unusual. The First Shepherd twice remarks on the number of small notes sung (**12/306, 416–8**), and the Third and Second Shepherds both describe the song as 'mery' (**12/326, 413**), which implies the same thing. The Second Shepherd tries to be much more specific about this, although there is an element of enthusiastic inaccuracy about it. The angel, he thinks, may have sung as many as 24 notes to the long: 'I dar say that he broght / foure & twenty to a long' (**12/414**).[149] Third, there is no doubt that it was a very fine performance. To begin with, the angel apparently had an excellent voice, this being the implication of the Second Shepherd's remark that the angel was recognisable by his voice as a heavenly messenger (**12/408–10**). The comments about the small notes and the fact that the song was 'mery' also imply

---

[146] Cawley *Wakefield Pageants*, 36.

[147] Cawley *Wakefield Pageants*, 102.

[148] See G.L. Apperson, *English Proverbs and Proverbial Phrases* (London: Dent; New York: Dutton, 1929); 509; and Whiting, *passim*, but especially 211.

[149] The possible mensurations for this music are discussed in section 2.4, above.

this to some extent. The First Shepherd does add more specific comments to these, remarking that the notes 'throng / on a heppe' by the angel were 'gentyll and small / And well tonyd withall' (**12/416–9**). The last part of this must mean what it seems to, 'sung in tune', but 'gentyll' and 'small' are not so easy. 'Gentyll' usually means 'soft' or 'low', 'not harsh' and therefore 'pleasing': thus in this case 'small', which can also mean 'soft' or 'low', must have its more general meaning ('not large') if it is not to be tautologous.[150] This is in any case the inference that we should draw from the various uses of 'small' in this passage.

Having discussed the song and its performance, the shepherds turn to more practical matters. The Third Shepherd wants to repeat the angel's song (**12/415**), and boasts that he can remember it and will immediately sing it (**12/420–1**). In this he is encouraged by the First Shepherd: 'Brek outt youre voce / let se as ye yelp' (**12/422**). At this invitation, however, the Third Shepherd finds that he cannot do it alone, and pleads a cold:

> I may not for the pose / but I have help.   (**Towneley 12/423**)

Nan Cooke Carpenter interpreted his request for help as meaning that the shepherds would sing in three-part improvised polyphony,[151] but this is clearly wrong. The Third Shepherd knows the tune, or he would not have offered to sing it, while a polyphonic texture would come way behind the words and the plainsong tune in importance. The problem is that he does not have the confidence to sing it by himself and needs someone else to sing it with him *in unison*. It is a common situation. The Second Shepherd is scornful, and the First begins to be angry in case the song is forgotten (**12/424, 425**), but in the end the Third Shepherd does start the singing (**12/430+**). They make some sort of attempt at the *Gloria*, then, singing in unison.

Finally, the shepherds sing again at the very end of the play:

> [PRIMUS PASTOR]   Amen, to that worde / syng we therto on hight;
> To joy al sam
> With myrth and gam
> To the lawde of this lam
> Syng we in syght.   (**Towneley 12/497–502**)

The shepherds evidently do sing in honour of the Christ-child after taking their leave of the Holy Family. What the song should be they do not say, although it may be their first attempt to evangelize – to spread their knowledge of the Christ-child whom they now praise. The Second Shepherd has, in fact, just stated their intention to 'this [i.e. their visit] recorde / where as we go' (**12/495**). The 'syng' of **497** is nevertheless metaphorical, I think – 'sing "Amen" to that' – since a literal singing of the word 'Amen' is not consistent with singing 'lawde' (praises) to the Lamb.

Much has been made in the past of the phrase 'Syng we in syght', which

---

[150] OED *sub* 'gentle' A.6.c: soft, low; not loud or harsh. See also Carter *Dictionary*, 163 and 452–3 (*sub* 'small').

[151] Carpenter *'Secunda Pastorum'*, 217.

Carpenter interpreted as a reference to improvising polyphony by a system of 'sighting' on a written melody.[152] This technique is important,[153] but I do not think that the words 'in sight' imply its use here. The method presupposes that the singers read from the written music: and although one can imagine a purely aural use of such a technique, it seems unreasonable to suppose that the word 'sight' would be used when the written page was not there. Certainly it is unlikely that the shepherds carried the music around with them. On the whole, I feel that 'in sight' means 'in the sight of this company', that is, the audience: the Bishop uses the term in this sense in the N-Town play of Mary in the Temple (**N-Town 9/145**).[154] If we remember that , as just noted, the shepherds are going out to tell the world of what they have seen and heard, then a song of praise to the Christ-child at this stage must be a rehearsal of their story to those present. That being so, the shepherds no doubt sing in unison, as before.

Carpenter's influential work on the more famous alternative play, the *Secunda Pastorum*, made the mistake of conflating much of the information to be gained from the two plays. One of the unfortunate results of this is discussed in 2.4, but the procedure did in fact colour her discussion throughout, with serious consequences for our understanding of the shepherds' capabilities. Closely as these two plays run in parallel, the differences between them are important. I shall therefore discuss **Towneley 13** in the same terms as **Towneley 12**. One difference is that Towneley 13 has more SDs, which help to avoid some of the interpretative problems of Towneley 12.

The first aural cue, as in Towneley 12, is not a strictly musical one. When the Second Shepherd, on meeting the First, asks him if he has seen anything of Daw, the Third Shepherd, the answer shows that Daw has been heard some time ago, blowing his horn not very far away:

> PRIMUS PASTOR   yee, on a ley land
> > hard I hym blaw / he commys here at hand,
> > Not far.   (**Towneley 13/11–13**)

Once the Third Shepherd has joined them the three decide to sing a song after only a short discussion about food. Here there is no doubt that they sing in parts. The First Shepherd asks to be allowed to sing the Tenor, the Second the Treble, and the Third Shepherd remarks that that leaves *him* with the Mean. This allotting of parts may certainly indicate a method of improvisation such as I discussed in 3.2, p. 95. This is associated with trained singers, of course, and is therefore not a 'popular' technique such as one might associate with shepherds. If we are looking for a measure of realism in the shepherds' capabilities (which we are not, necessarily), then a technique using strictly parallel intervals is more likely – a technique that

---

152 *Ibid.*

153 See above, section 3.2.

154 Robinson *Studies*, 76, offers a different meaning: 'very clearly', 'in his presence', 'with my own eyes' or 'in the face'.

actually happens anyway when a group of people including a 'groaner' sing in unison.

The shepherds, at any rate, are proud of their musical abilities, and they are very rude about Mak's dismal efforts to sing. Their arrival at Mak's house at **13/475** is Mak's cue to begin singing a lullaby. He sings this alone (**13/441**), because his wife Gyll needs to groan as if in the aftermath of childbirth: but the Third Shepherd cannot tell the difference between Mak's singing and Gyll's groaning – or so he pretends – and assumes that they are both singing:

TERCIUS PASTOR   will ye here how thay hak? / oure syre lyst croyne.
PRIMUS PASTOR   hard I never none crak / so clere out of toyne.
                                                                  (Towneley 13/476–7)

'Crak' seems to have its usual sense of telling out loud, pronouncing something briskly; 'hak' implies the splitting of a long note into short ones, and therefore florid music that is difficult to sing,[155] but in the present case may carry something closer to non-musical meanings, of careless or indiscriminate division.

The shepherds certainly have a different opinion of the angel's *Gloria*, which is sung at **13/637+sd**. Here, as in Towneley 12, the song has a quality that marks it out as special – a 'qwant stevyn / that euer yit I hard' (**13/647**) – and the experience is a frightening one (**13/648**). They immediately discuss the meaning of the message, though, and only after the First Shepherd's recommendation that they visit the Child in Bethlehem do they turn their attention to the song itself:

SECUNDUS PASTOR   Say, what was his song? / hard ye not how he crakyd it?
                      Thre brefes to a long. /
TERCIUS PASTOR   yee, mary, he hakt it.
                      was no crochett wrong / nor no thyng that lakt it
                                                                  (Towneley 13/656–8)

This technical discussion leaves us in no doubt of the triple metre of the music, nor of the fact that, again, there were a lot of small notes in it, which the angel sang very well.[156] Nothing daunted, these shepherds, too, reckon that they can also sing it, and apparently do so (**13/659–64**). How successful this is, it is hard to say. The First Shepherd leads off, and the others apparently join in: it seems that either the First Shepherd or the Third get a little carried away, because by the time the Second launches into a discussion of the relevant prophecies he still finds it necessary to tell one or both of them to keep quiet:

SECUNDUS PASTOR   we fynde by the prophecy – / let be youre dyn –
                      Of dauid and Isay / ...   **(Towneley 13/674–5)**

---

[155] For 'hak' and 'crak' see pp. 36–7, above. This may mean that Mak was singing in an uninhibited way, and there is a suggestion that his own opinion of his singing is not the same as that of the shepherds listening to him. As noted above, p. 202, Mak is clearly singing out of tune.

[156] Further on this discussion, see pp. 39–43, above. As already noted there, the dramatist had considerable musical knowledge and expected it in some of his audience, too.

As in Play 12, Mary asks the shepherds to evangelize (**13/744**: 'Tell furth as ye go'), and the shepherds depart singing at the end of the play. Starting as they mean to go on, they begin the song loudly, for all to hear:

SECUNDUS PASTOR	Com furth, now ar we won.
TERCIUS PASTOR	To syng ar we bun:
	let take on loft.

(**Towneley 13/752–4**)

That the song should be specifically about the the Christ-child is, I think, made clear by line 752: the singing is part of their evangelism, for they have understood that the means of redemption has come to them – 'now are we redeemed'.[157]

The shepherds in Towneley 13 must surely have been played by professional singers, though there is certainly no hard evidence. When we come to the Coventry play, however, there is no doubt about it: for the composed polyphony, even taking into account the simpler musical style and the increased musical literacy of the 1530s, would be beyond the capabilities of amateur musicians. The song 'As I out rode', sung during the shepherds' journey to Bethlehem, makes concessions to the conditions of outdoor performance – in the chordal opening, for instance (see 3.4) – but blossoms into effective, if short-winded, imitative part-writing. It is a model of its type, in every way worthy to stand beside the much better-known lullaby.[158]

The Coventry play has the main ingredients of the shepherds' episode seen elsewhere, but it is briefer than other versions. The First Shepherd calls a 'howe' to his colleagues, who recognise his voice and come to him (**Coventry 1/217–21**), but there is no indication that any of them has a horn. Following their meal they see the star, and this causes a discussion of the prophecies of Christ to come before the angelic announcement, rather than after it as happens in most other plays (York 15 is the exception). Unusually, the shepherds do not signal their allegiance to God by singing until after the angelic *Gloria* (which occurs at **1/263+sd**).

Their discussion of the *Gloria* is brief, but it contains the elements seen elsewhere. The song is unusual, for the Third Shepherd remarks that he had never heard 'soo myrre a quere' singing (**1/265**). The First Shepherd notes that the song brought 'myrth and solas' (**1/268**), and remarks on 'the swettnes of ther songe' (**1/269**). The fact that 'the syng abowe in the clowdis clere' (**1/264**) is enough to show the singers to be angels, presumably: but the shepherds also understand the angelic message, because they not only quote various parts of the Latin but also state that 'Goddis Sun ys cum' (**1/270**). There is however a considerable textual problem here, since the angels tell the shepherds that 'Godis Sun ys borne' (**1/301**) only after an intervening scene of the Nativity with Mary and Joseph, and the angels sing the *Gloria* twice. It seems that Croo conflated two alternative versions, or perhaps failed to realise that some material had been added out of order.[159] Joseph's brief speech about a 'noise' that has 'gretly amendid . . . [his] chere' (**1/278–81**) comes between

---

[157] This is the gloss in Meredith *Towneley Cycle* I, 98.
[158] See 3.4, above, for a discussion of this music.
[159] **1/278–96** may be an alternative to **264–77**.

the shepherds' song as they travel to Bethlehem (before being told to do so by the angels) and the second performance of the *Gloria* at **1/281+sd**. It is not clear, then, whether Joseph is speaking of the angels' singing or the shepherds'.

Admiring as the shepherds are of the angelic song, we learn little technical information from them: that the Third Shepherd describes it as 'armony' (**1/267**) is not unequivocal proof of polyphony.[160] There are apparently two angels involved, however, since both directions for the *Gloria* use the plural 'angelis'/'angellis' (**1/263+sd, 281+sd**) and there are two speaking parts (**1/297–306**): but this too does not necessarily imply polyphony. Besides, the two speaking angels may not be the singers, although the provision of only a ten-line 'patch' between them does suggest small speaking roles for professionals brought in from outside, as it does in other plays (see above, 8.3). The *Gloria* could still be sung in plainsong, then.

Having decided to go and worship the Child, the shepherds sing 'As I out rode'. The SD naming this song cannot be proved to be part of Croo's text (rather than a later addition) and therefore to date from 1534 at latest; nor is it possible to show that the surviving setting of 'As I out rode' is the one intended in the SD. The surviving song is however a unique source for the text, and until a concordance is found the presumption must be that this is the only *written* setting that the words ever had. As it seems unlikely that this music would be composed specially in anticipation of a hoped-for performance in 1591 (see 2.6, above), its composition can probably be assigned to the period 1534–75. I do think that the later part of this period is likely, however, not only because of the probability of the songs in the Weavers' play being composed in the 1560s, but because of the dating of the famous lullaby in Coventry 1. This is not named in the relevant direction (**1/829+sd**), unlike the shepherds' first song, and therefore may not have been fixed, may not have been decided on, or may simply have been unknown to Croo, at the time of his revision.

As noted earlier, the First Shepherd gives the Child his pipe, an instrument small enough to be held by the baby:

[FIRST SHEPHERD]   I haue nothyng to present with thi chylde
But my pype; hold, hold, take yt in thy hond.
(Coventry 1/309–10)

It is a 'pipe', not a 'whistle', and so ought to be a recorder.

The shepherds sing again after the adoration scene (**1/331+sd**), in the place which in other cycles is the end of the shepherds' play.[161] We are not told what the song is, but they must sing the *Gloria* here, since the First Shepherd has stated their intention to worship the Child and to 'syng in his presence / "Et in tarra pax omynibus" ' (**1/276–7**). This agrees with the First Prophet's later account of the events when he states that after the shepherds left the stable they sang a joyful song (**1/466–9**):

---

[160] The word could be used of the pleasant consecutive conjunction of notes: Carter *Dictionary*, 14–15.

[161] Here, the play continues with a prophets' scene providing the link to the Herod section: since the two prophets now discuss the Salvation issue and the whole matter of the Nativity, there is an obvious reason for the omission of any but a brief discussion earlier.

I PROFETA   Forthe the went and glad the were
               Going the did syng;
               With myrthe and solas the made good chere
               For joie of that new tything.   **(Coventry 1/466–9)**

Although this is the end of the biblical narrative about the shepherds, it is not quite the end of their story in this play.[162] The First Prophet goes on to say that Christ rewarded the shepherds with a place in Heaven, where they now sing in praise of the Incarnation:

               In ar the gon with joie and myrthe,
               And there songe hit ys 'Neowell'.   **(Coventry 1/473–4)**

'Nowell' means 'news' – that is, the Good News of the Saviour's redemption of the world.

We have already noted in connection with the two part-songs that the three singers who played the shepherds also played the mothers of the Innocents.[163] At this time we are clearly dealing with professional singers, although guildsmen may have been used in an earlier period when polyphony was not sung.

Finally, the three Chester shepherds do not seem either to sing part-music or to have much technical knowledge. They are however musical: the problem seems to be that they do not understand that music should be used in God's praise, and they have to be taught this by Garcius.

In the first scene of the play, as elsewhere, the shepherds use both voice and horn to call one another. The First Shepherd uses his horn after discovering that he cannot make the Second hear by calling a 'howe' with his voice:

[PRIMUS PASTOR]   Howe, Harvye, howe!
               Drive thy sheepe to the lowe.
               Thow maye not here excepte I blowe,
               as ever have I heale.
Hic flabit Primus Pastor   **(Chester 7/45–48+sd)**

The Second Shepherd hears and comes, and after a few lines they decide that they want the Third Shepherd with them. The First Shepherd gives instructions:

[PRIMUS PASTOR]   Crye thow must lowd, by this daye;
               Tudd is deafe and may not well here us.
Secundus Pastor vocat submissa voce:
               How, Tudd; come, for thy fathers kyn.
PRIMUS PASTOR   Naye, faye; thy voyce is wonders dym.   **(Chester 7/59–62)**

With another vocal 'howe' the Second Shepherd makes the Third hear (**7/69**), and the three eventually settle down to a meal. Once they are satisfied they think about

---

[162] See 2.4, above, pp. 33–4, for the shepherds' exit and subsequent movements.
[163] Above, pp. 150–1; see also *Contexts*, 204.

their herdsman, Trowle, known as Garcius in SHs and therefore presumably of apprentice status.[164] The First Shepherd tells the Second to summon Trowle:

[PRIMUS PASTOR]   Blowe thy horne and call after Trowle   (7/151)

who, the Second thinks, may be looking for them (7/154: 'that shrewe I suppose us seekes'). The Second states his intention of blowing his horn for Trowle (7/155–6), and is encouraged by the Third:

[TERTIUS PASTOR]   Blowe a note for that meetinge
                   whyle that horne nowe in thy hand ys.   (Chester 7/159–60)

For some reason it is the First Shepherd who replies to this:

PRIMUS PASTOR   With this horne I shall make a 'Hooe'
                   that hee and all heaven shall here.
                   Yonder lad that sittes on a lowe
                   the lowd of this horne shall here.   (Chester 7/161–4)

Presumably it is the First Shepherd who blows, or perhaps two or more of them do. They apparently keep this up at intervals for some time, since Garcius does not acknowledge their presence for another thirty lines (7/195).

Attention switches to Garcius after **Chester 7/164**, when he sings a song. However Garcius is presented by the shepherds – and he is certainly a rough diamond – this song marks him out as an agent of God. This play, unlike the two Towneley plays, does not have the shepherds singing soon after they have all met up: this is deliberate on the dramatist's part, for Trowle emphasises the fact, pouring scorn on them for 'sittinge withowt any songes' (**7/205**). Trowle is no respecter of his masters, and he is persuaded to join them only by the promise of a wrestling match with the Third Shepherd (**7/228–31**).

After this tournament, in which Garcius throws all three shepherds in turn, they see the star and discuss its significance. The singing of *Gloria in excelsis deo* by a single angel (**Chester 7/357+sd**) causes a long discussion, elements of which are familiar from other plays. The shepherds find it strange that they did not see the singer (**7/362–3**), but eventually it is the quality of his voice that enables them to recognise the singer as Gabriel:

[SECUNDUS PASTOR] He had a mych better voyce then I have,
                   as in heaven all other have soe.   (Chester 7/406–7)

The greater part of their discussion is taken up, as it is in the N-Town version, with a discussion of the text (**7/361–35**, *passim*).[165] Here, too, the shepherds' reaction to

---

[164] See above, p. 318. The First Shepherd also refers to Trowle as a 'knave' (**7/289**), i.e. boy. But Trowle is married, for his gift to the Child is an old pair of his wife's hose (**7/591**): so the 'boy' status is probably that of a guild, not that of a choir or the community at large.

[165] Lumiansky and Mills point out, *Chester* II, 118, how the text at **7/358–495** seems to offer alternative texts here. In Table 22, above, I have followed their suggestions for the two paths from **358** to **495**, only one of which includes the song during the journey to Bethlehem.

the *Gloria* is to sing. The First Shepherd makes a direct connection between prayer and singing;

> PRIMUS PASTOR   Nowe pray wee to him with good intent,
> and singe I wyll and me [unbrace]:
> that hee will lett us to bee kent,
> and to send us of his grace.   (Chester 7/4356–9)

But the Second Shepherd turns it to a more selfish purpose:

> SECUNDUS PASTOR Nowe syth I have all my will,
> never in this world soe well I was.
> Singe wee nowe, I rede us, shryll
> a mery songe us to solace.   (Chester 7/440–3)

Garcius then states his intention of starting a song for everyone to sing, since they can all learn from him:

> GARCIUS   Singe we nowe; lett see,
> some songe will I assaye.
> All men nowe singes after mee,
> for musicke of mee learne yee maye.   (Chester 7/444–7)

'All men' seems to mean more than just the shepherds: as suggested in 5.4, above, Garcius apparently teaches the song to the audience as well as to the shepherds, presumably by lining it out. The direction in MS H specifies all the shepherds and 'other helpers' in addition. We have already noted (see 8.3, above) that these helpers (*adjuvantes*) were perhaps the shepherds' boys played by choirboys from the cathedral. What sort of song this was originally, we cannot tell: the term 'mery songe' (7/443, just quoted) would not rule out a song of praise to God. At some stage, however, a producer decided to use a secular and perhaps rather frivolous song with a 'Trolly lolly lo' start or refrain. The marginal nature of this direction shows that the song may have been used in only a single performance.

After the journey to Bethlehem the shepherds are addressed by the angel (7/464–71), and then the shepherds decide to go to Bethlehem all over again. The song sung here (7/479+) is in honour of the Christ-child:

> GARCIUS   And singe we all, I read,
> some myrth to his majestee,
> for certayne now see wee it indeede:
> the kinge Sone of heavon is hee.   (Chester 7/476–9)

Lumiansky and Mills's proposals for variant alternatives in this scene make sense of much that is puzzling about the text at this point. Specifically, the song at 7/479+ is seen to be an alternative to the 'mery songe' at 7/447+sd.

The variant versions come together again at 7/480, which starts the adoration scene. The first part of this is taken up with a discussion of the marriage of Joseph and Mary, Joseph's doubts, and the Virgin Birth: only after they are satisfied on this issue do the shepherds move on to the adoration itself. They offer gifts in order of rank and age: the three shepherds, Garcius, and the four boys.[166] Of the various gifts, only two concern us here. The First Shepherd, like the First Shepherd in the York play, offers a bell (7/559). The other relevant gift is the pipe offered by the Third Boy, already discussed.

The element of evangelism is not explicit in this play until the shepherds have left the stable and are about to part company. In fact, Garcius intends to become an anchorite, the First Shepherd a hermit; only the Second and Third Shepherds say that they will travel about preaching the Good News. It is the Second Shepherd who mentions singing before and after his statement of intent:

> SECUNDUS PASTOR   Brethren, lett us all three
> singinge walke homwardlye.
> Unkynd will I never in noe case bee,
> but preach all that I can and knowe,
> as Gabryell taught by his grace mee.
> Singinge awaye hethen will I.   (Chester 7/651–6)

Clearly the shepherds do sing as they go off at the end of the play.

Of all the plays discussed in this section, Chester 7 is the only one for which we have supporting evidence in the form of financial records. What they tell us about the angelic *Gloria* and the roles taken by the cathedral choristers has already been discussed (8.3). It is also important to say that Garcius and the three shepherds figure in the accounts apparently as guildsmen and not as professional singers. We can take it here, I think, that the shepherds are amateurs: they certainly need a considerable competence as singers in this play, but there is no question of them singing polyphony, I think.

It remains to say something about the character of Garcius and the place of music in the philosophy of the dramatist. To many, the wrestling match is a puzzle, not only because of its violence but also because Garcius seems so contemptuous of his masters. (This last is true also of Jak Garcio in Towneley 12.) Kolve has explained this episode – convincingly, I think – in terms of the humble being exalted over the mighty in the *Magnificat* and as an allusion to the circumstances of Christ's birth.[167] But this does not seem to be quite the whole story, and as I have already suggested Garcius's musicality seems to be designed to allow him to be recognised as an agent of God, whereas the three shepherds have not yet reached that stage. Rosemary Woolf put this into a wider context by noting that 'each step forward in religious understanding is taken first by the boy'.[168] The 'moral distinctiveness' of Garcius from his masters is emphasised throughout by the dramatist's manipulation of their ethical stances as demonstrated by their musical lives. Garcius is shown as singing

---

[166] There is some doubt about the number of boys: the Third Boy says (7/607) that he will make his offering last, but in the event the Fourth Boy makes the last offering. The Painters' Company paid four boys in 1568 and three in 1575, so the confusion may well reflect changes in the casting during particular late performances.

[167] Kolve, 155–8.

[168] Woolf, 187. This is not wholly true, probably, but the textual problems make it difficult to be sure.

from the first, while the shepherds are not; when the shepherds do use their musical abilities they do so for their own solace, whereas Garcius persuades them to do it for God's sake; and it is Garcius who can teach music to 'all men' and lead the singing.[169] The Chester shepherds recognise that the angel had a very fine voice, restrict their discussion of the *Gloria* to the words and a rather vague expression of admiration for the performance, and do not attempt to imitate the *Gloria*. Instead, they sing a different kind of 'mery song', named in a marginal direction as 'Trolly lolly lolly lo'.

The shepherds' plays, then, show considerable diversity although there is a discernible pattern common to all of them. The wide diversity in usage of musical understanding, it seems to me, reflects the different philosophies of the dramatists. It is the Chester playwright who shows himself most aware of the use of music as an attribute of God's agents, even if the textual problems in the middle of the play tend to obscure this a little. The Coventry play also considers a wider context than the biblical narrative, using the shepherds' musicality both directly in the play and indirectly through their reported actions. The Towneley plays show a rather different kind of interest on the part of the playwright: here the technical knowledge is important for its own sake, but at the same time the playwright clearly has a good understanding – more so than the Chester dramatist, probably – of the practicalities and the psychology of getting people to sing. Lastly, there are indications that at Chester, at least, the only shepherds' play for which we have any financial records, there was a certain amount of extra-textual 'business' with whistles, and possibly also with a bagpipe. Peter Meredith has suggested places in the Chester cycle where special skills were probably used,[170] notably the Magi play, where Herod seems to have done a sort of juggling act; and this very shepherds' play, where stilt-walking may have been a feature. Perhaps such skills were more often used than the texts at any rate allow us to see, and certainly it would be possible for both amateurs and professionals to entertain an audience with a substantial 'party-piece' such as playing the bagpipes or handing out whistles to the children.

8.5 Instrumentalists

As we have seen in various discussions so far, it is difficult to find data that show how minstrels worked in dramatic productions. No notated instrumental music survives for the plays, no details of who the minstrels were, what instruments they played on, or what tunes they performed; no contracts or records of agreement are known. If we consider only the strictly dramatic evidence, leaving aside what we can infer from outside sources, we are left with a single painting, the Chelmsford

---

169 It is only fair to add, however, that David Mills does not agree with my view, expressed earlier, that Garcius is an early (and literal) example of Muscular Christianity (in conversation, 1983 and subsequently).

170 In Mills *Staging Chester*, 58; Dutka *REED.Proceedings*, 29–31; and *Aspects*, 25–6.

records of payments to and for minstrels during the dramatic festival of 1562, and the records of a very few northern guilds that paid minstrels in their productions. Whatever its limitations, this evidence does not require us to make assumptions about the relationship between dramatic production and other aspects of late medieval life, and must be assessed carefully. What can we learn from it?

The picture concerned is Fouquet's famous miniature of the martyrdom of St Apollonia. This is not even English, unfortunately, but it is indisputably an illustration of a staged drama and it dates from the middle of the fifteenth century, when French religious drama was already on a large scale.[171] The miniature shows a playing-place on the edge of which are scaffolds for the actors. What seems to be the Heaven on the left of the picture includes a positive organ. The organ is not large – in fact, it could not be if used in a temporary scaffold, for which a certain portability is needed – and is presumably intended to support angelic singers in the Heaven.

This usage can be identified in records and play texts. Organ support for singers was certainly required in **N-Town 41** (The Assumption of Mary) at **41/313+sd** (*Hic cantabunt organa*) and **521+sd** (*Et hic assendent in celum cantantibus organis*); and, as already noted, this seems to have been the function of the organists James Hewitt at Coventry, John Bakyn at Norwich, and probably also John Genson at Chester. In Hewitt's case we know that a regals (reed organ) was used, and not a pipe organ as Fouquet shows: but of course the Coventry plays were mounted on waggons, the organs had to be that much more portable, and probably the penetrating tone of the regals made up for the instrument's relatively small size. The organists would have been trained church singers, performing in the tradition of vocal church music (including composed polyphony) that was the province of musicians who had learned the rules of late medieval mensuration and the notation of measured music.

On the scaffold next to the Heaven is a loud band of two shawms and three folded trumpets. These minstrels are shown as playing, so *prima facie* the picture is of a loud band accompanying an execution. This may be correct, or perhaps the appearance is due to the compression of two events – the execution of Apollonia and the performance by the loud band – that could be expected to occur separately. There was a tradition of loud minstrelsy at executions, although not necessarily including this particular grouping of instruments.

We know that in the drama minstrels were required in some places at the readings of the banns, and also for the general dance that follows many of the Cornish and East Anglian plays (for which see 8.6, below). As we have seen (section 2.5, above), the minstrels in the Cornish plays were 'pipers' where they are identified at all, and most likely formed the standard four-man band consisting of a single trumpet with three or four shawms. The minstrels for the banns of *The Castle of Perseverance*, however, are required to 'trump up': this suggests that the band is either a

---

[171] Etienne Chevalier, who became Treasurer of France in 1452, commissioned Jean Fouquet to illustrate a book of hours probably between 1452 and 1456. The illustration of the Martyrdom of St Apollonia has been reproduced many times: it can be seen in colour in Jean Fouquet, *The Hours of Etienne Chevalier* (London: Thames and Hudson, 1972), plate 45. The original is in the Museé Condé, Chantilly.

homogeneous group of trumpeters, such as we know from various royal and noble households, or at least a mixed group of shawms and trumpets in which the latter predominate. This last, of course, is the case in the group depicted by Fouquet.

It cannot be stressed too much that the two traditions concerned here – the notated-music tradition of the church singers and the aural tradition of the minstrels – were quite distinct until the middle third of the sixteenth century. In English drama only one performer does not clearly fit into one of these categories, and that is the actor who played King David in **Towneley 7** (The Procession of Prophets). As the discussion in volume 2 will demonstrate, King David does apparently sing the 'fytt' that he promises in **Towneley 7/104**, and presumably accompanies himself on the harp as he states his intention of doing in **Towneley 7/110**. This would normally be an entertainment in the aural tradition, and indeed King David refers to it as 'mynstrelsy' (line **105**). Although it is tempting to suppose that a trained church singer might take this role in the late fifteenth century, it is much more sensible to assume the participation of a respected household harper-singer, whose career would usually fit him to be a competent actor as well as to accompany his own singing on the harp. At this stage of our speculation it becomes a serious disadvantage that we do not know the original auspices under which that play was performed. As we see from the example of Chester, a civic guild might employ a harper, and for all that we can tell from the records of the Chester Smiths it is possible that Randle Crane was a singer as well.[172]

The Chester records, which are our second primary source of evidence for minstrelsy in drama, are indeed as unhelpful as this would suggest.[173] The rather inconsistent payments to minstrels by the Painters over the years suggest that the Guild used them in procession rather than as a dramatic resource in the play itself. A 'mynstrelle to the plase' who was paid a mere 2d for the last performance in 1575 perhaps entertained the audience at one of the stations.[174] If this was indeed his function then he presumably made most of his money direct from the audience. There is really no place in the Painters' play (The Shepherds) for soft music – nor for loud music, for that matter.

The payments for minstrelsy in the Smiths' Guild accounts are almost as unsatisfactory as those in the Painters' records. Here, I think, there were two groups of minstrels.[175] One group, as in the case of the Painters, seems to have been involved with the waggon and its procession rather than with the play as such. This was presumably a group of loud minstrels. There are also occasional payments to individual minstrels. With one of these, William Lutter, there is a considerable doubt about his identity and whether he was a minstrel or not. On the whole, I am less inclined than formerly to think that he was a minstrel rather than simply an actor.[176] With Randle Crane the matter is different. JoAnna Dutka identified Crane as a

---

172 For Randle Crane and his work with the Chester Smiths, see *Essays*, 137.
173 I have discussed the Chester records in *Essays*, 132–8.
174 *Essays*, 133–4.
175 *Essays*, 136–7.
176 *Essays*, 137. William Lutter is connected to music only circumstantially.

minstrel:[177] again, it is not easy to see what a solo minstrel might have done in the Purification play. As always, I think it unlikely that a minstrel would have worked with singers. It is however possible that he stood in for singers absent at the early rehearsals: he would not need to perform the same music, and it would be cheaper to employ a single minstrel for this purpose than to bring one or more singers from the Cathedral, even supposing that they could be available. Since they would not need to rehearse with the other actors until a late stage, bringing the singers in for the early rehearsals would be a great waste of finances. I confess, though, that I do not know what Crane did.

The Chester Shoemakers employed minstrels for their play of Mary Magdalene and the Entry into Jerusalem in 1550.[178] There were probably two minstrels, judging by the size of the payments. Their function would be one of two. As in other cases, they may have been loud minstrels going with the waggon and entertaining the crowd between stations; or they may have provided soft music for the banquet at the house of Simon the Leper. There is no way of telling which was the case.

There is an obvious mismatch of evidence in these cases, where documentary records of minstrel activity do not coincide with clear data about minstrelsy in the play texts. The mismatch is as obvious in the other direction, unfortunately: there are play texts which tell us of the requirement for minstrelsy but for which no financial records survive. These must be rehearsed here, although a detailed listing is unnecessary. Soft music is used for purposes of 'heavenly' representation in **Chester 2**, in **N-Town 41** (including the music of 'cithare' at **41/116+sd** to cover the angel's journey to visit Mary), and in **Ordinalia 1** (at around **753–822**, when Seth looks into Paradise and describes to the cherub what he has seen and heard). Other than the mention of 'cithare', which must be harps, presumably, there is no help given by the texts as to the kind of instruments used.

When instruments are mentioned, as in **Coventry 1/538**, they are rather puzzling. 'Trompettis, viallis, and othur armone' do not sound like instruments that could sensibly play simultaneously, and the 'othur armone' in any case leaves us wondering what are the instruments that have not been named. While loud music would be suitable for Herod's exit (which happens after line **539**), it is perhaps as unnecessary as it is unsuitable to give him soft music that might be confused with heavenly music. Since the next scene concerns the three kings, perhaps Herod's soft music can be dispensed with, at least at this stage of the play.

All the cues mentioned so far require professional minstrels, performers of considerable technical skill. The same will be true of the trumpet fanfares required by the Last Judgement plays, where one or two trumpeters were normally needed. As in the case of singers and 'soft' minstrels, I assume that the professionals involved could costume in the role (in this case, angels) and perform in full view. It would also be possible for the actors to mime the fanfares, with professional trumpeters playing behind the scene out of sight of the audience: this might be a good solution

---

[177] Dutka 'Use of Music', 2–3.
[178] *Essays*, 138.

if (as was perhaps sometimes the case) the minstrel concerned was no actor and did not take a speaking role, so that considerations of space forced the alternative solution.

Strictly speaking, there could be little or no place for an amateur minstrel in a dramatic production. However, I should hesitate to be dogmatic about the professional status of those ringing the bells in **Towneley 17** and **Coventry 2**, or even about the playing of pipes by the shepherds; and the blowing of horns is certainly not a matter of professional minstrelsy. In this sort of instrumental usage, as in singing, there was no doubt a place for non-professionals to participate.

Finally, what can we learn from the Chelmsford records discussed in section 4.3? Here we have the evidence of a group of minstrels coming into the operation at a very late stage and being involved fully from then onwards. This situation need not surprise us, since the group's repertory would not be prescribed by the playwright or the organisers, and earlier communication need be only minimal. The minstrels for the first play were certainly not local men: this we know for reasons stated in section 4.3. We should however be wary of assumptions that may seem to follow from this. We cannot assume, for instance, that the minstrels were not costumed and did not take part as actors in the audience's view. Though this would seem a dangerous undertaking at very short notice, it is quite likely that preliminary work had been done on the part to be played by the minstrels.

On the other hand it is probable that the minstrels were not a regular group, such as town waits. The combination of drum, flute and trumpet, though admirably flexible for dramatic needs, is not a likely combination for any pre-existent band of minstrels. Although town waits might have been able to field this particular combination of instruments by 1562, it seems more likely that the organisers hired freelance minstrels with specific dramatic needs in mind. In this case, of course, the minstrels could have consulted with the organisers about costumes, repertory, and so on, well in advance of the plays.

The rather curious combination of instruments is reminiscent of the group mentioned in the Chester Late Banns for the Blacksmiths' play of the Purification – 'pype, tabrett, and flute'. As I have stated elsewhere, there is no very obvious place in the play where minstrelsy would be appropriate, although soft minstrelsy would not be out of place at **Chester 11/40+sd**, **71+sd**, where the angel actively intervenes to reverse Simeon's 'correction' of the prophecy. The 'pipe' may be a recorder, but could also be a bagpipe, which would be loud; and tabrett, too, is a loud instrument. On the whole I still incline to think that these minstrels went with the waggon to entertain the crowds, rather than performing during the play itself.

8.6 The audience

The nature of the audience's role depends on the kind of audience that it is. A seated audience is more captive than a standing one, and therefore tends to fill a more passive role; and an audience standing in a confined space is easier to make reactive with the cast than one that has plenty of space to move around in and can therefore move away. This phenomenon is well known to those who have played in medieval drama and can recognise the different situations: and it is not surprising, therefore, that it is in the realm of late medieval vernacular drama that the true role of the audience has been recognised in the last few years. In non-processional performance the precise type of audience-participation depends on the play. At one end of the scale *Wisdom* demands relatively little interaction between cast and audience: it is the most ceremonial of plays, a drama to be watched and listened to rather than to be participated in, and although the audience is addressed directly no demands are made of it. At the other end, the quasi-popular *Mankind* includes sections where the worldlings make a direct demand to the audience for money, bring it into the 'game' of making Titivillus appear, and get it to sing a song with them.[179] In processional drama, especially in a confined place like a York city-centre street, the whole range of participation can be observed.[180] Those furthest away are least involved in the drama, whereas those very close to the waggon and hemmed in by other members of the audience can be very involved indeed in the events being enacted.[181]

One result of this is that in certain circumstances the audience becomes part of the cast. **York 35**, *The Crucifixion*, for instance, actually uses the audience as the onlookers at the Crucifixion itself: the listeners milling around in the narrow York street become the actors playing the part of the crowd surrounding the execution of Christ. The scripted cast for that play consists of only Christ and the four torturers, but a large unscripted cast, the audience, is also required, and the play does not make sense without it.[182] The shocking graphic detail of the York Realist's dialogue strengthens the strategy by which the audience is drawn into the events enacted. For whose benefit is all the soldiers' detailed commentary on their work? Observation of the British workman shows us that the back-chat and funny comments are for the benefit of the passers-by – at least, for the female ones, especially if they are

---

[179] On the song, see 2.6, above: on audience involvement and the wordlings' manipulation of it, see section 5.4 and Chaplan's comments in Twycross *Evil*, 146–7.

[180] Those members of the medieval audience that had a private and (largely if not wholly) non-interactive view from first-floor windows could watch both the actors and the greater part of the audience, the latter standing in the street and involved in the action. The role of the 'audience' might be more complex than we normally assume, therefore, although my general statement about interaction is probably valid.

[181] The phenomenon of close audience involvement was first studied after Oakshott's 1975 production of the York cycle at Leeds, where the photographic and video records showed clearly how the audience was moved, emotionally and physically, by events being enacted before them. Since then, various productions in Yorkshire, Toronto and elsewhere have provided similar evidence. But producers and actors generally want a photographic record of their production, and this is generally what interests scholars, too. Consequently, although it was noted early on that different stations cause different audience responses (Oakshott and Rastall 'Town and Gown', 225) and reviewers of productions have tended to say something about audience reaction, no serious study of the subject has appeared in print.

[182] This was demonstrated some years ago by an Open University film of the play, in which the five members of the cast acted out their grisly business in complete isolation, to very strange effect. On the actor-audience relationship generally, see Diller *Mystery Play*, especially chapter 7; on this particular play, Mills "Look at Me" and Butterworth 'The York Crucifixion'.

young. This understanding should radically change our view of the York Crucifixion which, like many other pageant plays, demands a live, and close, audience.

A different cast-audience relationship is seen in those plays in which sermons are preached. *Mankind*, for instance, starts off with two sermons preached by Mercy. Of these, the first is preached with no other cast apparently on stage, so that Mercy is almost fulfilling the role of an expositor: but this sermon is wrecked by the three worldlings, who have evidently heard at least some of it. On their exit Mercy preaches another sermon, but abandoning the first he now preaches on the theme of the worldlings who have just behaved so badly. Again, there is no indication of any audience until Mankind speaks, some 26 lines on. The actual audience is at least most of the audience for Mercy, and perhaps all of it.

Other sermons, and such episodes as Lazarus's hair-raising description of his visit to Hell in **Towneley 31**, suggest strongly that the actual audience is also the stage audience. In some cases the relationship may well have been uncomfortably close: the exposition of the Ten Commandments in **Towneley 18** may have allowed the actor playing the young Jesus to fix his own townsmen with a beady eye and suggest all sorts of things that the script alone could not accommodate. Indeed, in the 1980 performance of the Towneley cycle in Wakefield the effect of this was quite rivetting – much more exciting than 'exposition of the Ten Commandments' would lead us to expect. Some scholars have for long tended to criticise early drama as 'dull' or 'boring' because it is didactic, forgetting that medieval sermons were intended to be entertaining and that the best preachers used many methods to hold the attention of their listeners. The range of dramatic roles used for expository functions – doctor, prophet, Contemplacio, poet, emperor, and so on – suggests that the playwrights took this same didactic responsibility very seriously – that is, entertainingly.

When this principle is taken into account, many dramatic scenes take on a new perspective. The plays that start with a herald or page shouting for room for the entry of his master – Herod or Pilate – presuppose a situation in which those members of the cast have physical contact with the audience, pushing their way through to get to the main playing area, with all the interaction that that implies. Although modern actors do not usually expect such interaction, it has always been a part of popular entertainment, and still is.[183]

Audience participation was hardly unusual in medieval drama, then, and it is reasonable to suppose that the playwright and actors could assume a not wholly passive audience and that this assumption led to the audience being treated as actors in the drama when that was appropriate. Indeed it is likely, in the age of relatively uninhibited audiences not trained in the proscenium theatre, that a medieval street audience was even more willing to take part than a modern street audience is. It is

---

[183] Witness the way an entertainer such as Frankie Howerd would use a live audience, for example. In medieval drama the skills needed for such interaction can be learned if necessary, but many townsmen (now as then) are already adept at it. A memorable occasion in the 1980 Towneley cycle saw one of the shepherds bidding good-afternoon in a perfectly natural way to a town delinquent who invaded the stage mid-scene.

easy to attribute to a medieval audience the kind of reticence that we generally feel in cast-audience relations, and the kind of embarrassment that ensues when we are made to take an interactive part in the show. The shepherds' attempt to sing the angelic Gloria at the Nativity, for example, is a non-biblical episode appearing in several plays that might well have been used to get the audience actively involved. The arguments between the shepherds, with 'glo glas glum's thrown around while they try to work out the words, are on the modest side in comparison with what good actors could ad-lib in front of a passive audience. Should we not assume, then, that the audience joined in? One can imagine how the shepherds might milk an audience already predisposed to have a go themselves at repeating the song, especially if they had heard it last year, and the year before that.

Not only the playwright and the cast might see the audience as participants in the drama then: the audience themselves might have perceived this as the role that they were playing. And once the audience accepts that – not necessarily at a conscious level – the boundary between drama and reality is soon blurred. It is instructive to watch the reaction of an audience in a narrow street around a pageant-waggon when the devils at the Harrowing of Hell begin to be unpleasant, or the soldiers start roughing up the mothers of the Innocents prior to killing the children. Such occasions bring the audience into the action by their mere proximity, making them the witnesses of street violence: and although the suspension of disbelief is only partial (at least in the adults, although the children may be affected more completely) the effects of such enactment can be considerable. People have been known to faint at the king's murder at the end of Marlowe's *Edward II*. In a recent e-mail exchange Alan Knight told of seeing a Passion play in Ohio in which the Resurrection itself was greeted by the audience with spontaneous expressions such as 'Praise God!', 'Halleluia!' and 'Thank you, Jesus!'[184] We can rationalise these as the expression of faith sparked off by the perceived truth behind the drama, but to do so would perhaps be to underestimate both the power of the drama and the strength of the audience's faith. We are gradually becoming accustomed to the power of much medieval drama: and if most modern audiences do not have the faith of the Ohio audience witnessed by Knight, medieval audiences certainly did.

If the audience felt able to be part of the cast, and if the playwright, producer and actors could rely on them to fill this function, what appropriate knowledge and skills could the audience be assumed to have? First, it could be assumed that they knew the appropriate response (verbal or behavioural) to a liturgical situation. When the parish priest or the bishop pronounced a blessing, a common enough situation for a medieval person, that person would have the knowledge to be able to make the correct response, 'Amen', at the correct time. Blessings vary in their precise wording, but the basic form is unchanging and would easily be recognised: so in the Mary Play the audience would know the bishop's blessing at the presentation of Mary in the Temple for what it is:

---

[184] On the list PERFORM, 1 February 1995.

[EPISCOPUS]   And 3e, serys, knelyth and I xal gyve
                3ow Goddys benyson:
                In nomine patris et Filij et Spiritus Sancti.
                                    (N-Town 9/216–17, Mary Play 499–500)

Who are the 'sirs' being blessed here? The stage direction that immediately follows is for the bishop to withdraw, with his ministers, and for the virgins of the Temple to say 'Amen': so 'sirs' may be the bishop's ministers, but it also includes the virgins. On the other hand, the ministers go out with the bishop, and the specifying of the Virgins seems to preclude the ministers from saying the 'Amen': and apart from Mary and the virgins of the Temple, only Joachim and Anne are left. Are the audience to be left out, or should we assume that they, too, might kneel (or stand) and accept a blessing? That is surely the point of the stage direction requiring the Virgins of the Temple to respond: they will lead the audience.

This raises the question whether the actor playing the bishop might not actually be a priest, a question that is difficult to answer with our present knowledge. Most such blessings in the drama are less formal than this, but an audience would surely recognise the blessing implications of such a place as the end of **York 46**, The Coronation of the Virgin, where Jesus finally addresses the angels and gives a blessing:

[JESUS]   Myne aungellis bright, a songe 3e singe
            In the honnoure of my modir dere.
            And here I giffe you my blissing
            Haly nowe, all in fere.   **(York 46/157–60)**

The audience would have to feel very uninvolved not to respond 'Amen' to such an ending.

There is no 'Amen' written into the text here, but in many such cases there is. The 'Amen' is always extra-stanzaic, however, and should not be regarded simply as part of the actor's text: it acts as a cue for the leading of the audience, and is not restricted to the character specified in the last speech-heading. A cue is especially necessary when the response is not to a blessing but to an exhortation to praise God, a less formalised type of religious expression, as at the end of **Towneley 8**:

MOYSES   heuen, thou attend, I say, in syght,
           And erth my wordys; here what I tell.
           As rayn or dew on erth doys lyght
           And waters herbys and trees full well,
           Gyf louyng to goddeys mageste,
           hys dedys ar done, hys ways ar trew,
           honowred be he in trynyte,
           to hym be honowre and vertew.
                               Amen.   **(Towneley 8/424–31)**

In the similar 'praise' ending to Towneley 3 the 'Amen' is taken into the text as part of a specific invitation to the audience:

[NOAH]   / I pray hym in this space,
                In heven hye with his / to purvaye vs a place,
                      That we,
                  with his santis in sight,
                And his angels bright,
                May com to his light:
                      Amen, for charite.   **(Towneley 3/552–8)**

A medieval audience would surely make the proper response here and echo the 'Amen'. How many of them actually did so is another matter, but not really an important one. The actual numbers would depend on circumstances, including the extent to which the cast had drawn the audience into the action. The only important fact is that joining in saying 'Amen' at the end of the play would be natural to all concerned, not unnatural. This principle would hold at the end of *Mankind*, where Mercy ends his final speech, addressed to the audience, with an 'Amen'; at the end of *Wisdom*, even though Anima is not there specifically addressing the audience; and in many other places in the repertory.

Such occasions provide a context for the otherwise slightly surprising audience participation at the end of other plays, where singing or dancing is involved. The end of the Towneley cycle, for instance, although not addressed specifically to the audience, surely invites them to join in: that is the point of 'all' (line 619), which would otherwise be a meaningless rhetorical device.

[PRIMUS BONUS]   Therefor full boldly may we syng
                On oure way as we trus;
                Make we all myrth and louyng
                With te deum laudamus.   **(Towneley 30/617–20)**

Here we come to the second useful attribute of a medieval audience: its members knew certain liturgical items. Perhaps most could not read and very few knew any Latin, but they had all learned the commonest items aurally, and in any case there would usually be some educated people in the audience. *Te deum* was so well known that it is difficult to imagine a medieval audience not joining in.

The audience also knew how such pieces were performed. At the end of *Mary Magdalen* the priest addresses the'clerkys':

[PRYST]   Now, clerkys, wyth woycys cler,
            'Te Deum lavdamus' lett vs syng!   **(Mary Magdalen 2138–9)**

This does not mean that the clerks, the professional liturgical singers, are to perform *Te deum* by themselves. The Priest has been addressing his 'frendys' in direct speech to the audience:

[PRYST]   Allemythty God, most of magnyfycens,
            Mote bryng yow to hys blysse so brygth,
            In presens of þat Kyng!
            Now, frendys, thus endyt thys matere –
            To blysse bryng þo þat byn here!
                  ['Amen', presumably]   **(Mary Magdalen 2133–7)**

The invitation to sing *Te deum* is to everyone, then: the Priest addresses the clerks separately because they are responsible for intoning the hymn and giving support to the main body of singers; and perhaps to signal the presence of the professionals to the 'congregation'. To a church-going nation this means business as usual, even if not in a church building. In a similar way, the invitation to sing *Te deum* at the end of *The Castle of Perseverance*, where God the Father has stepped out of his role to address the audience, must surely have resulted in a performance in which the audience was led by the cast.

Nor was it only *Te deum* that made this sort of audience participation possible. At the end of *The Conversion of St Paul* the whole audience is invited by Poeta to sing the hymn *Exultet celum laudibus*:[185]

> [POETA]   Thys lytyll pagent thus conclud we
> As we can, lackyng lytturall scyens,
> Besechyng yow all, of hye and low degre,
> Owur sympylnes to hold excusyd and lycens,
> That of retoryk haue non intellygens,
> Commyttyng yow all to owur Lord Jhesus,
> To whoys lawd ye syng: 'Exultet celum laudibus'!
> **(The Conversion of St Paul 656–62)**

This hymn was used on the feasts of apostles and evangelists,[186] and was therefore sung quite frequently. Evidently a medieval audience could join in without rehearsal.

Audiences in at least some places had knowledge of a tradition of social dancing at the end of a play. This is seen in all of the Cornish plays and in one of the East Anglian ones, *The Killing of the Children*. In the final speech of *The Killing* the Poet addresses the whole audience, and only in the last four lines speaks specifically to some of the cast:

> [POETA]   Wherefor now, ye virgynes, er we go hens,
> With alle your cumpany, you goodly avaunce!
> Also, ye menstralles, doth your diligens;
> Afore oure departyng, geve vs a daunce!
> **(Killing of the Children 563–6)**

The virgins have only just danced, in fact (at **550+sd**), so the direct speech to them implies that they are to lead the dance that follows. Who their 'cumpany' is, I am not sure. However, the dancers are a 'cumpany' that includes the Poet, or at least includes a body with which he identifies, and hence the 'give *us* a dance' of line **566** (my emphasis). At the least, then, the 'us' here is the body whose departing is alluded to in the same line. But 'departing' must here carry its then usual meaning of 'separation', so that the Poet refers not to any particular group of people leaving the playing-area, but one group (the cast) parting company with another (the

---

[185] Again, note the 'all' of lines 658 and 661.
[186] AS 66, 67, plate Q; LH 270–1. Paul counted himself as an apostle, and in this last scene of the play he appears 'in hys dyscyplys wede' (**502-sd**).

audience). Thus the 'us' of the last line is likely to include the audience as well as the cast. Again, it does not matter how many of the audience join in: participation will vary with different circumstances. The important thing is to recognise the improbability of the cast having a dance all to themselves here while the audience stand and watch.

It is hardly in doubt that the audience should join in the dance at the end of *The Life of Meriasek*, in the final speech of which the Count of Vannes steps out of character to address the audience on practical matters:

> The peace of God be with all who are gathered here. . . . Before you leave, we urge you to take something to drink for the benefit of the play.
> Now, pipers, blow, and let everyone join the dancing. Go home if you must, but if you can stay on, you'll be welcome though you were with us a week!
> **(The Life of Meriasek 4548–68**: trans. Harris, pp. 121–2)

Here again, we see the address to the audience interrupted by speech to a specific section of the cast (in this case, the minstrels), with a return to the larger body afterwards. There seems little doubt that the audience is intended to dance. In the less clear case of *The Creacion of the World* the similar circumstances of Noah's address to the audience almost certainly means that here, too, the invitation is a general one:

> [NOAH]   Come tomorrow on time:
> you will see very great matters,
> and redemption granted
> through the mercy of God the Father,
> to save whoever is lost.
>
> Pipe up for us, minstrels,
> that we may dance together,
> as is the manner and the custom.   **(Creacion of the World 2542–9)**

Here it is tantalising not to know what 'the manner and the custom' were, and yet the simplest answer is probably the correct one: we should take this passage at face value and accept that it was normal for the cast and audience to enjoy a general dance before dispersing.

The end of the Ordinalia presents a similar context:

> [EMPEROR] . . . may the Lord's blessing descend upon each of you present here today and go with you as you turn your steps toward home.
> Now, musicians, strike up a brisk tune that we may dance.
> **(Ordinalia 3/2643–6**: trans. Harris, p. 247)

It is to be expected that the ends of the first and second days of the Ordinalia would be different, and so they are: but in fact they follow the same pattern of address to the audience, and at the end of the first day the music is intended to be understood in a particular way by them:

> [KING SOLOMON]   . . . The play is ended, but, in order to see the Passion which

Christ suffered for us, return tomorrow in good time. And now let us all go
home. Play, good musicians, in honor of the Father on high.
(Ordinalia 1/2839–46: trans. Harris, p. 77)

The minstrels, then, play (presumably loud) music while the audience disperse. At
the end of the second day music is unsuitable to the subject matter concerned, and
so the audience are sent away in silence:

> [NICODEMUS] . . . Depart for your homes; the play is ended. But I ask that you
> return early tomorrow that you may see how Christ rose, radiant
> and gentle, from the grave.
(Ordinalia 2/3237–42: trans. Harris, p. 175)

To sum up thus far, it seems that an audience watching a fifteenth- or sixteenth-
century religious drama could be expected to be able to fulfill a number of functions
as a sort of unwritten cast: to be the crowd in appropriate dramatic situations; to
respond with an 'Amen' when appropriate, usually with a prompt from the cast; to
join in the singing of *Te deum* or such other piece as ended a play where congregational singing was suitable, with the performance intoned and supported by a
cantor and/or professional singers; and to join in a social dance with the cast after
the play was ended. There was, then, a general context of audience participation
and interaction in late medieval drama such as may suggest that other places in the
plays, too, would encourage and elicit audience participation that might be used
interactively by the cast. Finally in this chapter I must discuss briefly a rather
specialised form of audience participation seen in the Chester Shepherds' play and
in *Mankind* – the songs that have already been discussed for other reasons in this
book.

In Chester play 7 there is considerable competition between the rebellious apprentice shepherd, Trowle, and the three senior shepherds. This competition is partly
worked out in the famous scene in which Trowle wrestles with each of his masters
in turn and throws them: but it is worked out also in terms of music. As we have
already noted, Trowle claims to be the most musical of the shepherds, a claim which
automatically implies moral superiority. It is in the context of this situation – a
statement of both Muscular and Musical Christianity – that when the Second
Shepherd suggests that they sing a cheerful song to keep themselves happy, Trowle
makes known his intention to teach a song to the audience:

> GARCIUS Singe we nowe: lett see,
> some songe will I assaye.
> All men nowe singes after mee,
> for musicke of mee learne yee maye.   (Chester 7/444–7)

And then they sing, according to 447+md, a song 'Trolly lolly lolly lo'.[187]
How would 'all men' – that is, the audience – learn this song from Trowle? Here

---

[187] On this refrain, see section 2.6, above.

we come to a general skill – and, I think, a specific one, too – that a late medieval audience had to a greater extent than we do: the ability to learn music (and indeed other things) by ear alone. As far as the general skill is concerned, I make only a broad statement that in a relatively illiterate age people were more used than we are to presenting information orally and taking it in aurally. What of the specific skill?

From the early seventeenth century we have documentary evidence of a method of singing metrical psalms in church that we call 'lining out'.[188] Although it is known only from too late a period for our purpose, the sixteenth century must have had some such system: how else could a congregation learn a metrical psalm? Since the system of 'lining out' is probably the most obvious way of teaching a psalm to a congregation, and since it is also very efficient, it seems sensible to take as a working hypothesis the proposition that 'lining out' was used also in the sixteenth century if not earlier. Someone, usually the parish clerk, who could read both words and (probably) music would sing the psalm one line at a time, the congregation repeating each line after him as it came. Note that this was the performance during the church service, not a rehearsal: so it seems reasonable to speculate that the parish clerk first made use of one or two singers with good voices and taught *them* the psalm, so that in the Sunday service they would be able to lead the congregation in the singing. In the event, if I am right about this, the parish clerk would then sing the first line, which would be repeated by the congregation led by our two singers; then he would sing the second line, which also would be repeated; and so on.

The Chester example gives us no information about how *Trolly lolly lolly lo* was taught and sung, but we can gain some information from the other, similar, event in *Mankind*. In section 2.6 I suggested that the pattern of text-repetitions and speech headings in the indecent song 'Yt ys wretyn wyth a coll' showed that the worldlings taught the song to the audience in a specific manner worked out in advance. Nought sings a line, in which the text is repeated: it is not clear if this would be to a single tune or if the repetition is a text-and-music repeat, the whole line being sung twice to fix it in the audience's mind. However that may be, Nought takes the part of the parish clerk in the lining-out process that I have just described. New Guise and Nowadays then repeat what Nought has just sung, but as I said in 2.6, they apparently lead the audience. New Guise and Nowadays, then, take the part of the parish clerk's two assistants. Interestingly, the 'Hoylyke!' refrain is not performed in this way, all three worldlings leading the singing together from the start of the line. This may be because the playwright knew that no members of the audience would still be singing by then, but this seems unlikely: more probably, the refrain was so well known (perhaps in a form of which this is an obvious parody) that a concerted introduction of this last line was an obvious and cheerful way to finish the song.

This song underlines what is at once a problem in the religious drama of late medieval England and a fascinating challenge to those of us trying to explore the

---

[188] See the article 'Lining out' in NG 11/7.

original methods of its performance. At every turn we find ourselves facing situations that tell us of a piece of knowledge that we need but do not have; and each time we must set out to discover what that knowledge is and how to use it. In this book I have tried to explain something of the problems and solutions surrounding the use of music and other aural effects in the religious drama of late medieval England, and this process is taken further in Volume 2.

APPENDICES: EDITIONS AND RECONSTRUCTIONS

In these three appendices are editions and reconstructions of music that belongs to a play (Appendix B) or could be used in a play (Appendices A and C, neither of which has any known dramatic connection). The editorial apparatus is kept to a minimum: in the music itself, ligatures are shown by ⌐, and editorial accidentals appear above the notes to which they refer. Material in square brackets is editorial.

In the commentaries, references are to bar, voice, and symbol in the bar (or to the beat, or to a word in the verbal text): dots, tied notes, pauses, etc., do not count as separate symbols. What follows the colon is the source-reading or a comment on it. Pitches are normally referred to by letters only, and note-values by the original duration-names.

APPENDIX A

The Washington *Ave regina celorum ... Mater*

The painting of *The Assumption of the Virgin* by the Master of the St Lucy Legend was discussed in detail by Emanuel Winternitz, who reproduced the painting, together with very clear detailed illustrations of the music.[1] A study by Sylvia Kenney had been more specifically musicological, but she did not edit the music complete.[2] In fact, some of the musical text is so corrupt that it is probably impossible to reconstruct the piece with any hope of realising the composer's intentions throughout.

The discussions by Kenney and Winternitz now seem rather dated in a number of ways, although they remain basic authoritative statements. More recently I have discussed the painting and its music ('The Musical Repertory' in Davidson *Iconography of Heaven*, 178–84), dealing with such matters as the numerological symbolism of the angels depicted and the nature of the music sung by the choirs in Heaven, and providing a transcription of the music to demonstrate the difficulty of making sense of the musical text. It is unnecessary to repeat my discussion in full here, but a resumé of part of it may be helpful as an introduction to the edition that follows.

The Assumption of the Virgin was painted c.1485, probably in Bruges: it is now part of the Samuel H. Kress Collection in the National Gallery of Art in Washington, D.C. It shows the Blessed Virgin during her Assumption into Heaven, supported by eight angels and with another eight – four instrumentalists and four singers – surrounding her. Above her, four more instrumentalists flank an opening in the clouds through which Heaven can be seen. The Throne of God is surrounded by more angels: three support the hangings behind the Throne, while there are six instrumentalists to the right and two choirs of angels to the left. The music sung by the choirs in Heaven cannot be identified, but that being sung behind Mary's shoulders is a two-part anonymous setting of the *Ave regina ... Mater* text: see Plate 8.

The notated music is held by the two angels nearest to Mary, with each of the others reading the music over the shoulder of his partner. Each voice-part, then, is sung by two angels. It does not appear that any of the instrumentalists is involved in this performance. The music is notated on single parchment membranes, of which some 50–60% is visible: there appears to be no writing on the dorse of either membrane. It seems that the whole of a voice-part of the *Ave regina* is written on each membrane, for the visible notation consists of a setting of the first two text-lines and the hidden portion could accommodate the remaining four. The music is in white mensural notation with black semiminims and a few ligatures *cum opposita proprietate*. The Tenor part, on the right, is so labelled under the large coloured initial

---

1 In *Musical Instruments and Their Symbolism in Western Art*, pp. 145–9 and plates 66, 67.
2 'Four Settings', in which Kenney transcribed only the opening of the Washington piece.

A that starts the verbal text; the Cantus also has an initial A, but no voice-name, as we should expect.

The artist has made some errors, and there is at least one place where he seems to have made a correction. In several places the relationship between note and staff-line is uncertain. The transcription below is as near as I can get to a faithful representation of what the source seems to show, and clearly it does not make musical sense. In the Commentary I detail the problems. (However, I now see fewer problems than I did: some of the notes marked with a ? in my original transcription – Davidson *Heaven*, 182 – now seem correct, and these do not appear in the Commentary below.)

Although I have referred to the upper voice as the Cantus that part could in fact be either the Cantus or the Contratenor of a three-voice setting. While this setting presents a perfectly satisfactory two-part texture (or would do, if the source were not so corrupt), nothing in it precludes the possibility of a third voice: and it is worth noting that Walter Frye's famous three-voice setting of the same text appears iconographically with a part missing.[3]

However impossible it is to make even a reasonable guess at the composer's intentions, it happens that the notation of this piece presents a complete setting of the first two lines of the text in a section that is very nearly free-standing musically. Although the setting has no known connection with drama, it may be useful as a short independent piece for plays in which an *Ave regina celorum* setting is specified or needed. I have therefore adapted the piece slightly, altering as little as possible consistent with making musical sense of it. This reconstruction, which was sung at the end of **York 45** during the performance in the streets of York on 10 July 1994, is given at the end of this Appendix.

---

[3] See my essay in Davidson *Heaven*, especially 172–8. The texture of the fifteenth-century chanson is essentially a two-voice texture with a third voice (the Contratenor) perhaps altering the harmonic content but not necessary for the music to make harmonic and contrapuntal sense: as Frye's *Ave regina* is written in chanson style it demonstrates this feature, being perfectly satisfactory as a two-part piece without the Contratenor.

Transcription

Critical Commentary

Note-values are divided by four: the original semibreve beat appears here as a crotchet beat.

Original clefs: C3, C4

Original time-signature: O in I only

7 II 3–4: the consecutive fifths may be due to the artist's change of mind about where the staff-line should go / 8 I 4: probably a C / 8 II 2: this B-flat is clearly what the painter intended, although it does not make musical sense. See the note to the previous bar / 9 I 4: perhaps an E / 9 II 1–2: apparently the correction of an error, perhaps associated with a change of staff-line. See note for bar 7 / 10: all the note-pitches are clear in this bar, so the non-sense must be an error, perhaps associated with possible corrections to II earlier in the line. See the note to bar 7 / 11–15 I text: the text-area is not shown, the membrane being depicted as folded immediately below the staff / 12 third beat: the consecutive 2nds are clear in the source / 12–15 II text: the text-area is not shown, the membrane being depicted as folded immediately below the staff / 14 I 1: minim /

Performing Edition

APPENDIX B

The Chester *Gloria in excelsis*

As noted in 3.5, above, the setting of the Gloria transmitted in MS H of the Chester cycle (copied in 1607, mainly by James Miller) may be the incipit of a mid-sixteenth-century polyphonic setting: and, if so, it will be possible to reconstruct only the first section of the piece, covering the text 'Gloria in excelsis deo'.

In preparing for the Chester cycle at Leeds in 1983 I made such a reconstruction, assuming a four-part texture with an imitative opening. Although this was not performed, it was published in the appendix to my essay 'Some myrth to his majestee' in Mills's *Staging Chester* (p. 96). The present reconstruction follows that one, but makes some amendments. As there are no close models to work from, the reconstruction is of course entirely speculative. The given line is a baritone or low tenor, so other possibilities include a men-only setting (TTBarB or ATBarB) and a five-voiced setting (perhaps ATTBarB). In both of these cases the given line would have to be placed next to the bass line (i.e. as a baritone line).

The play shows that the angelic Gloria was a solo. The best way of achieving this in a polyphonic piece, and one for which there is some evidence, is to perform the given line as a vocal solo with an accompaniment on regals. For this purpose an organist would no doubt read from the open score, but I have provided a short score for those whose score-reading is not strong. (There is no reason why a fully vocal performance of this piece should not be supported by an organ, and the short score could be used for that purpose, too.)

Critical Commentary

The original notation is available in MDF 8, f. 42r: see also Plate 7. The line that here appears as the Tenor part is written with a C4 clef and one flat in the key-signature; there is no time-signature. The original underlay is approximate, although probably close to what would have been sung, and I have amended it as little as possible. The details of my underlay are however speculative, and other solutions are possible.

5 III 1: minim, with stem crossed through /

APPENDIX C
Wee happy heardsmen here

In 1984 John P. Cutts suggested that a shepherds' song in Bishop Smith's part books, then in Carlisle Cathedral Library, might be a song from a shepherds' play.[1] Cutts considered that this song, copied into the part-books c.1637, 'invites comparison' with both the notated shepherds' song in the Coventry Nativity play and the shepherds' performance in Towneley 13, and developed a rather generalised discussion about the shepherds and their songs in English vernacular drama, as well as mentioning the place of the shepherds in liturgical drama.

The song's first four verses deal with the angel's message to the shepherds and their subsequent decision

> ... with ioy
> in heart to Bethleem trudge,
> To see that blessed boy
> which once must bee our judge.

Thus far, the song could be for performance in a shepherds' play, followed by discussion of the angelic Gloria and the actual journey to Bethlehem. It is true that the last line given here suggests a wider application for the song, with a less specific purpose than the dramatic one, but this does not make the song ineligible for inclusion in a drama. The Chester shepherds' play also alludes to Christ's future role as Judge:

> [GARCIUS] That prince of peace for to praye
> heaven to have at oure ende.   **(Chester 7/474–5)**

The last two verses of 'Wee happy heardsmen' take place at the manger, for the shepherds are addressing the Child,

> All Haile ô Christ our kinge
> All Haile ô virgins sonne:

with a request to bring them to Heaven, where they can glorify the three Persons of the Trinity. Clearly, these two verses, if performed in a play, would have to be sung at the stable during the shepherds' adoration of the Child. Cutts himself made this point, and noted that the Coventry song, too, is sung on two occasions, as a response to the angelic song and after the shepherds have visited the Child in the stable.[2] Cutts's identification of the song as a possible item from a biblical play, then,

---

1 John P. Cutts, ' "Wee happy heardsmen here": A Newly Discovered Shepherds' Carol . . .' (1984). Cutts had previously described the part books in *Roger Smith his booke* (1972).
2 Cutts 1984, 267–8. In fact, Cutts thought that the first stanza of the Coventry song was sung *before* the angelic Gloria.

386

depended on the old misunderstanding about the Coventry song's two verses being performed on two separate occasions in the play (see 2.6), and must in that case fail.

To this should be added that nothing else about the Carlisle song and its source suggests a dramatic purpose. The source does contain music from seventeenth-century plays, certainly, but if the song belongs with them it was too late in date to come from a 'medieval' biblical play; and, despite the rather vague datability of the style, which could indeed be a sixteenth-century one, there is no reason to doubt that this song belongs with the rest of the non-dramatic repertory, which is basically a seventeenth-century one also.[3]

The song is nevertheless worth considering here, because the first four verses, at least, could well be used in a shepherds' play, before the shepherds go to Bethlehem. The Carlisle part books are an incomplete set, consisting of altus and bassus only, so as Cutts presented it the song is in two parts.[4] It is however in that section of the source devoted to three-part music. Cutts seems to have believed that it lacks a treble part, although it is hard to see what he means in the passage in question:[5] but the musical texture makes it certain that a middle, tenor, part is missing.

I had already constructed a tenor part when, in the course of a search for a quotation from a mumming play nothing to do with the present study, I came across another version of the song in the *Journal of the Folk-Song Society*.[6] This version, contained in British Library Add. MS 38599 (the Shann MS), not only gives all three vocal parts but adds two more stanzas to the text between verses four and five. The new text relates how the shepherds worshipped the Child, filling in the narrative missing from the Carlisle version. It thus becomes clear that the text is all of a piece; that the shepherds are looking back in time over the whole series of events of that day; and that the only dramatic use of the complete song would be at the very end of the play, when the shepherds have left the stable. It would of course be possible to sing certain stanzas at different points in the play, but I know of no evidence for this practice in any play.[7] On balance, I do not think that the song could have come from a biblical drama.

Minor variants in the verbal text may partly reflect differences in language and modes of speech at different dates: the songs in the Shann MS were compiled in 1611, a quarter of a century before the Carlisle copy was made. The musical text of the Shann MS holds no major surprises, although several of its readings are dubious and can probably be regarded as corruptions of a superior text. I therefore give the song in its two written versions, without attempting to collate them into a single 'authoritative' version. It is newly edited from the sources.

---

3 Cutts 1972, 6–10, dates much of the repertory well into the seventeenth century.
4 Cutts 1984, 271–2.
5 Cutts 1984, 266.
6 A.G. Gilchrist, 'Note on two early MS. copies of the Manx traditional carol "We happy herdsmen here" ', *Journal of the Folk-Song Society* 8/3 (1929), 153–8. Cutts can hardly be blamed for not knowing about this.
7 The two sections of *Te deum laudamus* in **York 1** are a case in point: but this is a liturgical item, not a vernacular song, and the two verses occur in the same scene of the play.

The first version given here is that from Bishop Smith's part books, c.1637, formerly in Carlisle Cathedral Library and now kept in the Cumbria Record Office (Carlisle) (Altus, pp. 8–9; Bassus, pp. 8–9). The surviving voices (I, III) make perfectly good sense together. I have constructed a tenor part that largely follows the Tenor of the Shann MS but avoids the obvious errors, such as the Shann version's consecutive octaves in bar 5 and the awkwardness of the last phrase (part of which was surely copied a third too high).

The version below it is that of the Shann MS, British Library Add. MS 38599, f. 136v. The collection of songs of which this is part was made in 1611 by Sir Richard Shanne, priest, of Methley in Yorkshire. The voice-parts are written in order on single staves at the top of the page, one staff per voice, but the parts are not aligned in score.

Critical Commentary

The original note-values are retained, where the semibreve is the (slowish) beat.
Original clefs: C2, C3, F4
Original time-signature: ₵ Carlisle only
Original key-signatures: b-flat (Carlisle I, Shann II), b-flat and b'-flat (Shann I), no k-s (Carlisle III, Shann III). All flats are double-bulbed.

The verbal texts vary slightly between voices, but there are no major discrepancies. In the edition the underlay to verse 1 follows the sources as closely as possible. The Shann MS gives verses 2 onwards only once, but the second and subsequent verses appear in both Carlisle part books. I have not attempted a full edition of the words, but collate the Carlisle versions. Orthography is not modernised, so u/v and i/j/y are as in the original; I have substituted th for thorn in the underlaid text, but not otherwise. Where abbreviations are expanded, the expansions appear as italics in the full text but are not shown in the text underlaid to the music.

5 I, II: consecutive octaves in Shann *sic* / 9 II 3: sharp cancelled before this note (Shann) / 10 II 2: flat-sign started and cancelled before this note (Shann) / 10 III 3: semiminim with stem crossed through (Carlisle) / 10–11: consecutive octaves in Shann I, II *sic* / 11 I 4–5: consecutive octaves in Shann *sic*, but see the Carlisle version, which shows that these notes are a third too low /

Text, verse 4, last line: Carlisle Bassus has 'shall' for 'must' / verse 7, first line: Carlisle has 'our kinge' written above 'of blysse', cancelled, in both parts /

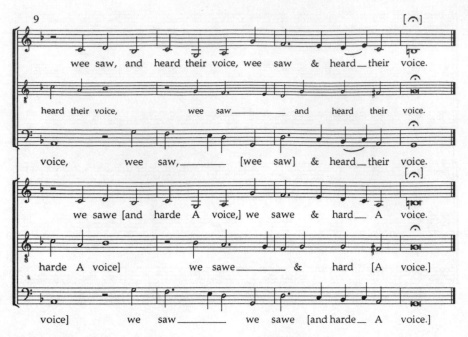

Shann

1   We happy hird*e*smen heere
     maye singe and eke reioice
     for Angells bright & cleare
     we sawe and harde A voice.

2   Gladd tiding*es* they vs toulde
     the kynge of all mankynde
     Newe borne & in clothes sould
     they saie saie we shall him fynde

3   At Bethlem in A staull
     and eke his mother free,
     Great comforth to vs all,
     Oh blissed maie he be.

4   Nowe let vs with much joie
     In haist to Bethlem trudge
     To se that blissed boie
     That once must be our judge.

5   When we to Bethlem came
     We sawe as it was saide
     That child of glorious fame
     In maunger he was laide

6   We sheperd*es* downe did fall
     And songe with voice on hie
     The Angells said we shall
     Singe glorie in excelsie.

Carlisle

Wee happy heardsmen here,
may singe & eke reioyce;
 for Angells bright & cleare,
wee saw & heard þ^r voice.

Glad tidings they vs told;
þ^e King of all mankind
is borne & in cloathes fold,
They say wee may him find.

In Bethleem in a stall,
 & eke his mother free:
Glad tidings to vs all;
yea blessed may hee bee.

Come let vs all with ioy
in heart to Bethleem trudge,
To see þ^t blessed boy
which once must bee o*u*r judge.

390

7 All haile O christ O kynge   All Haile ô Christ our Kinge
  All haile O virgins sonne   All Haile ô virgins sonne:
  We praie the vs to bringe   wee pray þe vs to bring
  In heaven with the to won   In Heauen with þee to wonne.

8 Wheere we the father may   Where wee þe Father may
  See with the holye goest   See with þe Holy ghost
  him magnifie all waie   & glorify alway
  with all the heavenlie hoste.   Him þt of might is most.

BIBLIOGRAPHY

This Bibliography is of works consulted, not only of those cited in this and the second volume. A list of abbreviations for frequently-cited works is on pp. xvi–xvii, above.

Anderson, J.J., ed. *Records of Early English Drama: Newcastle upon Tyne*. Records of Early English Drama. Toronto: Toronto University Press; Manchester: Manchester University Press, 1982.

Anderson, M.D. *Drama and Imagery in English Medieval Churches*. Cambridge: Cambridge University Press, 1963.

Antiphonale Monasticum. Tournai: Desclée, 1934.

Antiphonale Romanum. Paris: Descleé, 1924.

Antiphonale Sarisburiense, ed. Walter H. Frere. London: Plainsong and Mediaeval Music Society, 1901–15; repr. Farnborough: Gregg Press, 1966.

Antiquaries, Society of. *Illustrated Catalogue of the Exhibition of English Medieval Alabaster Work*. London: Society of Antiquaries, 1863.

Ashbee, Andrew. *Records of English Court Music VII*. Aldershot: Scolar Press, 1993.

Attwater, Donald. *The Catholic Encyclopaedic Dictionary*. London: The Waverley Book Co., 1931.

Axton, Richard. *European Drama of the Early Middle Ages*. London: Hutchinson, 1974.

Bailey, Terence. *The Fleury Play of Herod*. Toronto: Pontifical Institute of Medieval Studies, 1965.

————. *The Processions of Sarum and the Western Church*. Toronto: Pontifical Institute of Medieval Studies, 1971.

Baker, Donald C., and J.L. Murphy. *The Digby Plays: facsimiles of the plays in Bodley MSS Digby 133 and e Museo 160*. Medieval Drama Facsimiles 3, 1976.

————. and Louis B. Hall, Jr, eds. *The Late Medieval Religious Plays of Bodleian MSS Digby 133 and E Museo 160*. Early English Text Society, o.s. 283. 1982.

Bakere, Jane A. *The Cornish Ordinalia: A Critical Study*. Cardiff: University of Wales Press, 1980.

Beadle, H. R[ichard] L. *The Medieval Drama of East Anglia*. D.Phil. dissertation. University of York [UK] Centre for Medieval Studies, 1977.

————, Richard. 'Plays and Playing at Thetford and Nearby, 1498–1540'. *Theatre Notebook* 32/1, 1978. 4–11.

————, ed. *The York Plays*. London: Edward Arnold, 1982.

————. 'The York Hosiers' Play of *Moses and Pharaoh*: A Middle English Dramatist at Work'. *Poetica* 19, 1984. 3–26.

————, and Pamela King. *York Mystery Plays: a selection in modern spelling*. London: Oxford University Press, 1984.

————, and Peter Meredith. 'Further External Evidence for Dating the York Register (BL Additional MS 35290'. *Leeds Studies in English*, new series 11, 1980. 51–8.

————, intr., [with] a note on the music by Richard Rastall. *The York Play*. Medieval Drama Facsimiles 7, 1983.

Becon, Thomas. *The Early Works of Thomas Becon, S.T.P.*, ed. John Ayre. Cambridge: Parker Society, 1843.

Benham, Hugh. *Latin Church Music in England*. London: Barrie and Jenkins, 1977; repr. New York: Da Capo Press, 1980.

———. ' "Salve Regina" (Power or Dunstable): A Simplified Version'. *Music & Letters* 59/1, 1978. 28–32.

Bennett, Jacob. 'The *Mary Magdalene* of Bishop's [now King's] Lynn'. *Studies in Philology* 75, 1978. 1–9.

Benson, Edwin. *Life in a Mediaeval City*. London: Society for the Propagation of Christian Knowledge, 1920.

Bent, Margaret. 'Sources of the Old Hall Music'. *Proceedings of the Royal Musical Association* 94, 1968. 19–35.

———. 'New and Little-Known Fragments of English Medieval Polyphony'. *Journal of the American Musicological Society* 21/2, 1968. 137–56.

———. 'The Transmission of English Music 1300–1500' in H.H. Eggebrecht and M. Lütolf, eds. *Studien zur Tradition in der Musick: Kurt von Fischer zum 60. Geburtstag*. Munich: 1973. 65–83.

Bevington, David. *From Mankind to Marlowe: the growth of structure in the popular drama of Tudor England*. Cambridge, MA: Harvard University Press, 1962.

Bilson, John. 'On a Sculptured Representation of Hell Cauldron, Recently found at York'. *Yorkshire Archaeological Journal* 19, 1906–07. 435–45.

Bishop, E. 'Holy Week Rites of Sarum, Hereford, and Rouen Compared' in *Liturgica historica: Papers on the Liturgy and Religious Life of the Western Church*. 1894; repr. Oxford: 1918. 276–300.

Blackburn, Ruth H. *Biblical Drama under the Tudors*. The Hague: Mouton, 1971.

Block, Edward A. 'Chaucer's Millers and their Bagpipes'. *Speculum* 29, 1954. 239–43.

Block, K.S., ed. *Ludus Coventriae, or The Plaie Called Corpus Christi*. Early English Text Society e.s. 120. 1922.

Bonniwell, Wm R. *A History of the Dominican Liturgy, 1215–1945*. New York: Joseph F. Wagner, 1944; 2/1945.

———. *The Martyrology of the Sacred Order of Friars Preachers*. Westminster, Md: Newman Press, 1955.

Boulton, Helen E. *The Chester Mystery Plays*. Chester: Chester Corporation, 1962.

Bowers, Roger. 'Prowett, Stephen'. *New Grove*, 1980. 15/317–18.

———. 'Magdalene College, MS Pepys 1236' in Fenlon 1982. 111–14.

Bowles, E.A. 'The Role of Musical Instruments in Medieval Sacred Drama'. *Musical Quarterly* 45, 1959. 67–84.

———. '*Haut* and *bas*: the grouping of musical instruments in the Middle Ages'. *Musica Disciplina* 8, 1954. 115–40.

Breeze, Andrew. 'The Girdle of Prato and Its Rivals'. *Bulletin of the Board of Celtic Studies* 33, 1986. 95–100.

Brett, Edward Tracy. *Humbert of Romans: His life and views of thirteenth-century society*. Studies and Texts 67. Toronto: Pontifical Institute of Medieval Studies, 1984.

Brett, Philip. 'English Music for the Scottish Progress of 1617' in Ian Bent, ed. *Source Materials and the Interpretation of Music*. London: Stainer and Bell, 1981. 209–26.

Breviarium ad usum insignis ecclesie Eboracensis, ed. Stephen W. Lawley. Durham: Surtees Society 71 and 75, 1879 and 1883.

Breviarium ac usum insignis ecclesiae Sarum, ed. Francis Procter and C. Wordsworth. Cambridge: 1879–86; repr. Farnborough: Gregg Press,1970.

Breviary, The Hereford, ed. Walter H. Frere and L.E.G. Brown. London: Henry Bradshaw Society, 1904–15.

Briscoe, Marianne G., and John C. Coldewey, eds. *Contexts for Early English Drama*. Bloomington, IA: Indiana University Press, 1989.

Brown, Carleton. 'An Early Mention of a St Nicholas Play in England'. *Studies in Philology* 28, 1931. 594–601.

Brown, Howard Mayer. 'Trecento Angels and the Instruments they Play' in Edward Olleson, ed. *Modern Musical Scholarship*. Stocksfield: Oriel Press, 1978. 112–40.

Brunne, Robert Mannyng de. *See* Mannyng.

Bukofzer, Manfred, ed. *John Dunstable: Complete Works*. Musica Britannica 8. London: Stainer and Bell for the Royal Musical Association, 1953; 2/rev. by Margaret Bent, Ian Bent and Brian Trowell, 1970.

Bullock-Davies, Constance. *A Register of Royal and Baronial Domestic Minstrels, 1272–1327*. Woodbridge: Boydell, 1986.

Burstyn, Shai. *Fifteenth-Century Polyphonic Settings of Verses from the Song of Songs*. Dissertation. New York: Columbia University, 1972; Ann Arbor, MI: University Microfilms, 1975.

Butler, Christopher. *Number Symbolism*. London: Routledge and Kegan Paul, 1970.

Butterworth, Philip. 'Hellfire: Flame as Special Effect' in Davidson and Seiler, *The Iconography of Hell*. 67–101.

———. 'The York Crucifixion: Actor/Audience Relationship', *Medieval English Theatre* 14, 1992. 67–76.

Cabrol, Fernand. *The Books of the Latin Liturgy*. London: Sands and Co., 1932.

Campbell, Thomas P., and Clifford Davidson, eds. *The Fleury Playbook*. Early Drama, Art, and Music monograph series 7. 1985.

Caldwell, John. *The Oxford History of English Music* I. Oxford: Clarendon Press, 1991.

Cargill, Oscar. *Drama and Liturgy*. New York: 1930.

Carpenter, Nan Cooke. 'Music in the *Secunda Pastorum*'. *Speculum* 26, 1951. 696–700. Repr. in Taylor and Nelson 1972. 212–17.

———. 'Music in the Chester Plays'. *Papers in English Language and Literature* 1, 1965. 195–216.

——197. 'Music in the English Mystery Plays' in John H. Long, ed. *Music in English Renaissance Drama*. Lexington: University of Kentucky Press, 1968.

Carter, Henry Holland. *A Dictionary of Middle English Musical Terms*. Bloomington, IA: Indiana University Press, 1961; repr. Millwood, NY: Kraus, 1980.

Cave, C.J.P. *Roof Bosses in Medieval Churches*. Cambridge: Cambridge University Press, 1948.

Cawley, A.C. 'The Sykes Manuscript of the York Scriveners' Play'. *Leeds Studies in English*, new series o.s. 7–8, 1952. 45–80.

———, ed. *Everyman and Medieval Miracle Plays*. London: Dent, 1956; 2/rev. 1977.

———. *The Wakefield Pageants in the Towneley Cycle*. Manchester: Manchester University Press, 1958.

———. 'Medieval Drama and Didacticism' in [Rastall] *Drama* 1975. 3–12, and discussion, 13–21.

———. 'Middle English Metrical Versions of the Decalogue with Reference to the English Corpus Christi Cycles', *Leeds Studies in English*, new series 8, 1975. 129–45.

———, and Martin Stevens, eds. *The Towneley Cycle: A Facsimile of Huntington MS HM 1*. Medieval Drama Facsimiles 2. 1976.

———, Jean Forrester and John Goodchild. 'References to the Corpus Christi Play in the Wakefield Burgess Court Rolls: the originals rediscovered'. *Leeds Studies in English*, new series 19, 1988.

Chadwick, Henry. *Boethius*. Oxford: Clarendon Press, 1981.

Chamberlain, David S. 'Philosophy of Music in the *Consolatio* of Boethius'. *Speculum* 45, 1970. 80–97.

Chambers, E.K. *The Mediaeval Stage*. 2 vols. Oxford: Oxford University Press, 1903.

Chaplain-Pearman, Nicole. *The Music and Ceremony of the Late Medieval Palm Sunday Procession in England*. M.Phil. dissertation. The University of Leeds, 1993.

Chaplan, Rosemary E. "Farewell, jentyll Jaffrey': speech-act theory and *Mankind*' in Twycross *Evil on the Medieval Stage*. 140–49.

Charles, S.R., ed. *The Music of the Pepys MS 1236*. Corpus Mensurabilis Musicae 40. Rome: American Institute of Musicology, 1967.

———. 'The provenance and date of the Pepys MS 1236'. *Musica Disciplina* 16, 1962. 57–71.

Cheetham, Francis. *English Medieval Alabasters, with a Catalogue of the Collection in the Victoria and Albert Museum*. Oxford: Phaidon-Christie's, 1984.

Clopper, Lawrence M. 'The Rogers' Description of the Chester Plays', *Leeds Studies in English*, new series 7, 1975. 63–94.

———. 'The History and Development of the Chester Cycle'. *Modern Philology* 75, 1978. 219–46.

———, ed. *Records of Early English Drama: Chester*. Records of Early English Drama. Toronto: Toronto University Press; Manchester: Manchester University Press, 1979.

Cohen, Gustave, ed. *Le livre de conduite du régisseur . . . à Mons en 1501*. Strasbourg: Faculté de Lettres de l'Université de Strasbourg, 1924; 2/Paris: Champion, 1925.

Coldewey, John C. *Early Essex Drama: A History of its Rise and Fall, and a Theory Concerning the Digby Plays*. Ph.D. dissertation. University of Colorado, 1972.

———. 'The Digby Plays and the Chelmsford Records'. *Research Opportunities in Renaissance Drama* 18, 1975. 103–21.

———. 'Plays and "Play" in Early English Drama'. *Research Opportunities in Renaissance Drama* 28, 1988. 181–8.

Coleman, William E., ed. *Philippe de Mézières' Campaign for the Feast of Mary's Presentation*. Toronto: Pontifical Insitute of Medieval Studies, 1981.

Cornell, Henrik. *The Iconography of the Nativity of Christ*. Uppsala: Uppsala Universitets Arsskrift, 1924.

Coussemaker, E. de. *Drames liturgiques du moyen âge*. Rennes: Vatar, 1860; repr. New York: Broude Brothers, 1964.

Craddock, Lawrence. 'Franciscan Influences on Early English Drama'. *Franciscan Studies* 10, 1950. 383–417.

Craig, Hardin. *English Religious Drama of the Middle Ages*. Oxford: Clarendon Press, 1955.

———, ed. *Two Coventry Corpus Christi Plays*. Early English Text Society e.s. 87. 1902; 2/1957.

Craigie, W.A. 'The Gospel of Nicodemus and The York Mystery Plays' in *An English Miscellany Presented to Dr Furnivall*. Oxford: Clarendon Press, 1901. 52–61.

Cross, Frank L., and Elizabeth A. Livingstone, eds. *The Oxford Dictionary of the Christian Church*. Oxford: Oxford University Press, 1957; 2/1974.

Cunningham, John. 'Comedic and Liturgical Restoration in *Everyman*'. *Comparative Drama* 22/2, 1988. 162–73.

Curtis, Gareth, ed. *Lionel Power: Mass Alma Redemptoris Mater*. Newton Abbot: Antico Edition, 1982.

Curtius, E.R., trans. W.R. Trask. *European Literature and the Latin Middle Ages*. Bollingen Series 36. New York: 1953.

Cutts, John P. 'The Second Coventry Carol'. *Renaissance News* 10, 1957. 3–8.

———. *Roger Smith his booke: Bishop Smith's Part-Song Books in Carlisle Cathedral Library*. Miscellanea 4: American Institute of Musicology, 1972.

———. "Wee happy heardsmen here': A Newly Discovered Shepherd's Carol Possibly Belonging to a Medieval Pageant'. *Comparative Drama* 18/3, 1984. 265–73.

Dante Aligheri. *The Divine Comedy: Inferno*, trans. Charles S. Singleton. London: Routledge and Kegan Paul, 1970.

Dart, Thurston, ed. *Two Coventry Carols*. London: Stainer and Bell, 1962.

Davenport, W.A. *Fifteenth-Century English Drama: The Early Moral Plays and their Literary Relations*. Cambridge: D.S. Brewer; Totowa, NJ: Rowman and Littlefield, 1982.

Davidson, Audrey Ekdahl. 'The Performance Practice of Early Vocal Music'. *Early Drama, Art, and Music Newsletter* 4/1, 1981. 3–8.

Davidson, Clifford. *From Creation to Doom: The York Cycle of Mystery Plays*. New York: AMS Press, 1984.

———, ed. *The Saint Play in Medieval Europe*. Early Drama, Art, and Music monograph series 8. 1986.

———. 'The Middle English Saint Play and its Iconography' in Davidson *Saint Play* 1986. 31–122.

———. *Illustrations of the Stage and Acting in England to 1580*. Early Drama, Art, and Music monograph series 16. 1991.

———, and Nona Mason. 'Staging the York *Creation, and Fall of Lucifer'*. *Theatre Survey* 17/2, 1976. 162–78.

———, and David O'Connor. York Art. Early Drama, Art, and Music monograph series 1. 1977.

———, and Thomas Seiler, eds. *The Iconography of Hell*. Early Drama, Art, and Music monograph series 17. 1992.

———, ed. *The Iconography of Heaven*. Early Drama, Art, and Music monograph series 21. 1994.

Davis, H.W.C., ed. *Mediaeval England*. Oxford: Clarendon Press, 1924.

Davis, Norman, ed. *Non-Cycle Plays and Fragments*. Early English Text Society s.s. 1. 1970.

———, ed. *Non-Cycle Plays and the Winchester Dialogues*. Medieval Drama Facsimiles 5. 1979.

D'Avray, D.L. *The Preaching of the Friars: Sermons diffused from Paris before 1300*. Oxford: Clarendon Press, 1985.

Daw, S.F. 'Age of Boys' Puberty in Leipzig, 1727–49, as Indicated by Voice Breaking in J.S. Bach's Choir Members'. *Human Biology* 42, 1970. 87–9.

Dearmer, Percy, ed. *The Oxford Book of Carols*. London: Oxford University Press, 1928.

Deimling, Hermann, and [Albert] Matthews, eds. *The Chester Plays*. EETS e.s. 62 and 115, 1892 and 1916.

Denny, Neville, ed. *Medieval Drama*. Stratford-upon-Avon Studies 16. London: Edward Arnold, 1973.

Dictionary of National Biography, ed. Sir Leslie Stephen and Sir Sidney Lee. 1885–1900.

Diller, Hans-Jürgen. *The Middle English Mystery Play*. Cambridge: Cambridge University Press, 1992.

Dobson, E.J. 'The Etymology and Meaning of "Boy" '. *Medium Aevum* 9, 1940. 121–54.

Dorrell, Margaret. 'The Mayor of York and the Coronation Pageant'. *Leeds Studies in English*, new series 5, 1971. 35–45.

———. 'Two Studies in the York Corpus Christi Play'. *Leeds Studies in English*, new series 6, 1972. 63–111.

———. 'The Butchers', Saddlers', and Carpenters' Pageants: Misreadings of the York *Ordo'*. *English Language Notes* 13, 1975. 1–4. [*See also under* Johnston, Rogerson, below.]

Douglas, Audrey, and Peter Greenfield, eds. *Records of Early English Drama: Cumberland, Westmorland, Gloucestershire*. Records of Early English Drama. Toronto: Toronto University Press, 1986.

Downey, Peter. 'The Renaissance slide trumpet: Fact or fiction?'. *Early Music* 12/1, 1984. 26–33.

Downing, Marjorie. *The Influence of the Liturgy on the English Cycle Plays*. Dissertation. Yale University, 1942.

Dunn, E. Catherine. 'The Medieval "Cycle" as History Play: an Approach to the Wakefield Plays'. *Studies in the Renaissance* 7, 1960. 76–89.

————. 'The Saint's Legend as *Mimesis*: Gallican Liturgy and Mediterranean Culture'. *Medieval and Renaissance Drama in England* 1, 1984. 13–27.

Dunn, F.I. 'The Norwich Grocers' Play and the Kirkpatrick Papers at Norwich'. *Notes and Queries* 19/6, 1972. 202–3.

Durbin, P.T., and Lynette Muir, eds. *The Passion de Semur*. Leeds Medieval Studies 3. Leeds: University of Leeds Centre for Medieval Studies, 1981.

Dutka, JoAnna. *The Use of Music in the English Mystery Plays*. Ph.D. dissertation. Toronto: University of Toronto, 1972.

————. 'Music and the English Mystery Plays'. *Comparative Drama* 7/2, 1973. 135–49.

————. 'Mysteries, Minstrels, and Music'. *Comparative Drama* 8/1, 1974. 112–24.

————. 'Mystery Plays at Norwich: Their Formation and Development', *Leeds Studies in English*, new series 10, 1978. 107–120.

————, ed. *Records of Early English Drama: Proceedings of the First Colloquium at Erindale College*. Records of Early English Drama. Toronto: Toronto University Press,. 1979.

————. *Music in the English Mystery Plays*. Early Drama, Art, and Music reference series 2. 1980.

————. 'The Fall of Man: the Norwich Grocers' Play'. *Records of Early English Drama Newsletter* 9/1, 1984. 1–11.

————. 'The Lost Dramatic Cycle of Norwich and the Grocers' Play of the Fall of Man'. *Review of English Studies* n.s. 35, 1984. 1–13.

Eccles, Mark, ed. *The Macro Plays*. Early English Text Society 262. 1969.

Edersheim, A. *The Temple: Its ministry and services as they were at the time of Jesus Christ*. London: The Religious Tract Society, n.d.

Edminson, Vera L. *Ancient Misericords in the Priory Church of St Mary and St Michael Great Malvern*. Worcester: Ebenezer Baylis & Son, n.d.

Edwards, Kathleen. *The English Secular Cathedrals in the Middle Ages*. Manchester: Manchester University Press, 1949; 2/1967.

Elliott, John R. Jnr. *Playing God*. Toronto: Toronto University Press, 1990.

Emden, A.B. *A Survey of Dominicans in England . . . (1268–1538)*. Rome: Instituto Storico Dominicano, 1967.

Emminghaus, J.H. *Mary Magdalene*. The Saints in Legend and Art 5. Recklinghausen: Aurel Bongers, 1964.

England, George, and Alfred W. Pollard, eds. *The Towneley Plays*. Early English Text Society e.s. 71, 1897; repr. Millwood, NY: Kraus Reprint Co., 1978.

English Missal for the Laity, The. London: W. Knott & Son Limited, 1933; 3/1958.

Epp, Garrett P.J. 'The Towneley Plays and the Hazards of Cycling'. *Research Opportunities in Renaissance Drama* 32, 1993. 121–50.

Erlanger, R. d'. *La musique arabe*. Paris, 1930–59. 6 vols.

Farmer, Oscar G. *Fairford Church and its Stained Glass Windows*. Bath: 8/1968.

Faulkner, Ann. 'The Harrowing of Hell at Barking Abbey', in Davidson and Seiler *The Iconography of Hell*. 141–57.

Feasey, Henry John. *Ancient English Holy Week Ceremonial*. London: 1897.

Fenlon, Iain, ed. *Cambridge Music Manuscripts 900–1700*. Cambridge: Cambridge University Press, 1982.

Fletcher, Alan J. "Covetyse Copbord Schal be at the Ende of the Castel be the Beddys Feet': Staging the Death of Mankind in *The Castle of Perseverance*'. *English Studies* 68, 1987. 305–12.

Ford, Alvis E., ed. *La Vengeance de Nostre-Seigneur*. Toronto: Pontifical Institute of Mediaeval Studies, 1984.

Forrester, Jean. *Wakefield Mystery Plays and the Burgess Court Records: A New Discovery*. Ossett: 1974.

————, and A.C. Cawley. 'The Corpus Christi Play of Wakefield: A New Look at the

Wakefield Burgess Court Records'. *Leeds Studies in English*, new series 7, 1975. 108–15 and appendices following.

Fortescue, Adrian, and J.B. O'Connell. *The Ceremonies of the Roman Rite Described.* London: 1930; 5/1934.

Fowler, Alastair. *Triumphal Forms.* Cambridge: 1970.

———. *Silent Poetry: Essays in numerological analysis.* London: Routledge and Kegan Paul, 1970.

Fowler, David C. 'The Date of the Cornish *Ordinalia*'. *Mediaeval Studies* 23, 1961. 91–125.

Frere, Walter H, ed. *Graduale Sarisburiense.* London: Plainsong and Mediaeval Music Society, 1891–4; repr. Farnborough: Gregg Press, 1966.

———, ed. *The Use of Sarum.* Cambridge, 1898–1901; repr. Farnborough: Gregg Press, 1969.

———. *Bibliotheca musico-liturgica.* 2 vols. London: Plainsong and Mediaeval Music Society, 1901–32.

———. *Walter Howard Frere: A Collection of his Papers on Liturgical and Historical Subjects.* London, 1940.

———, and L.E.G. Brown, eds. *The Hereford Breviary.* London: Henry Bradshaw Society, 1904–15.

Galloway, David, ed. *Records of Early English Drama: Norwich 1540–1642.* Records of Early English Drama. Toronto: Toronto University Press, 1984.

———, and John Wasson. 'Records of Plays and Players in Norfolk and Suffolk, 1330–1642'. Malone Society *Collections* 11, 1980–1.

Gardiner, Harold C. *Mysteries' End.* New Haven: Yale University Press, 1946.

Gardner, John. *The Construction of the Wakefield Cycle.* Carbondale and Edwardsville: Southern Illinois University Press, 1974.

Gasquet, Francis Aidan. *The Last Abbot of Glastonbury and other Essays.* 1908; repr. Freeport, NY: Books for Libraries Press, 1970.

———. *Henry VIII and the English Monasteries.* 1887–8; repr. Freeport, NY: Books for Libraries Press, 1972. 2 vols.

George, David, ed. *Records of Early English Drama: Lancashire.* Records of Early English Drama. Toronto: Toronto University Press, 1991.

Gibson, Gail McMurray. 'Bury St Edmunds, Lydgate, and the N-Town Cycle'. *Speculum* 56/1, 1981. 56–90.

———. *The Theater of Devotion: East Anglian Drama and Society in the Late Middle Ages.* Chicago, IL: University of Chicago Press, 1989.

Gilman, Donald, ed. *Everyman and Company: Essays on the Theme and Structure of the European Moral Play.* New York: AMS Press, 1989.

Golden Legend, The. See Jacobus de Voragine.

Grace, Mary. *Records of the Gild of St George in Norwich, 1389–1547.* Norfolk Record Society 9, 1937.

Gransden, Antonia, ed. *The Customary of the Benedictine Abbey of Bury St Edmunds in Suffolk.* London: Henry Bradshaw Society, 1973.

Greene, R.L. *The Early English Carols.* Oxford: Oxford University Press, 1935; 2/1977.

Grove. *See* New Grove.

Gutenberg, Johann. [42-line Bible]. Maintz: Gutenberg, c. 1455; facsimile repr. New York: Brussel and Brussel Inc., 1968. 3 vols.

Hammerstein, Reinhold. *Die Musik der Engel.* Berne and Munich: Franke Verlag, 1962.

Handbook of British Chronology, by Maurice Powicke and E.B. Fryde. London: Royal Historical Society, 1941; 3/rev. by Fryde, D.E. Greenway, S. Porter and I. Roy, 1986.

Handbook of Dates, by C.R. Cheney. London: Royal Historical Society, 1945; corr. repr. 1978.

Handefull of pleasant delites, A. (1584). Facsimile. Ilkley: Scolar Press, 1973. *See* also Rollins, Ward 1957.

Happé, Peter. *English Mystery Plays.* London: Penguin Books, 1975.

——. *Song in Morality Plays and Interludes.* Lancaster: Medieval English Theatre, 1991.

Harris, Markham, trans. *The Cornish Ordinalia: A Medieval Dramatic Trilogy.* Washington, DC: Catholic University of America Press, 1969.

——, trans. *The Life of Meriasek: A Medieval Cornish Miracle Play.* Washington, DC: Catholic University of America Press, 1977.

Harris, Phyllis Pier, ed. and trans. *'Origo Mundi', First Play of the Cornish Mystery Cycle, the Ordinalia: A New Edition.* Ph.D. dissertation. The University of Washington, 1964.

Harrison, Douglas. *The First and Second Prayer Books of Edward VI.* London: Dent, 1910.

Harrison, F.Ll. *Music in Medieval Britain.* London: Routledge and Kegan Paul, 1958; 2/1963.

——. 'Faburden in practice'. *Musica Disciplina* 16, 1962. 11–34.

——. 'Music for the Sarum Rite'. *Annales Musicologiques* 6, 1958–63. 99–144.

Hartnoll, Phyllis, ed. *Shakespeare in Music.* London: Macmillan; New York: St Martin's Press, 1966.

Hector, L.C. *The Handwriting of English Documents.* London: Edward Arnold, 1958; 2/1966.

Henderson, William G. *Liber pontificalis Christopher Bainbridge archiepiscopi Eboracensis.* Surtees Society 61, 1875.

Hereford Breviary. See Breviary.

Hewitt, Herbert James. *Mediaeval Cheshire: an economic and social history of Cheshire in the reigns of the three Edwards.* Manchester: Chetham Society n.s. 88, 1929.

Hieatt, Constance B. 'A Case for *Duk Moraud* as a Play of the Miracles of the Virgin'. *Medieval Studies* 32, 1970. 345–51.

Hildburgh, W.L. 'English Alabaster Carvings as Records of the Medieval Religious Drama'. *Archaeologia* 93, 1949. 51–101.

Hilton, Walter. *Two Minor Works of Walter Hilton* ['Eight Chapters on Perfection' and 'Of Angels' Song'], ed. Fumio Kuriyagawa and Toshiyuki Takamiya. Tokyo: privately printed, 1980. [Line references in this book are to the second work.]

Hinnebusch, William A. *The Early English Friars Preachers.* Rome: Historical Institute of the Friars Preachers at S. Sabina, 1951.

——. *The History of the Dominican Order: origins and growth to 1500.* New York: Society of St Paul, 1966.

Hoffman, C. Fenno, Jr 'The Source of the Words to the Music in York 46'. *Modern Language Notes* 10, 1950. 236–39.

Homan, Richard L. 'Two Exempla: Analogues to the *Play of the Sacrament* and *Dux Moraud*'. *Comparative Drama* 18, 1984. 241–51.

Hopper, Vincent Foster. *Medieval Number Symbolism.* 1938; repr. New York: Cooper Square Publishers Inc., 1969.

Hughes, Andrew. *Medieval Music: The Sixth Liberal Art.* Toronto: University of Toronto Press, 1974; rev. edn. 1980.

——. *Medieval Manuscripts for Mass and Office: a guide to their organization and terminology.* Toronto: University of Toronto Press, 1982.

——, and Margaret Bent, eds. *The Old Hall Manuscript.* Corpus Mensurabilis Musicae 46. American Institute of Musicology, 1969–73.

Hulme, Wm Henry. *The M-E Harrowing of Hell and Gospel of Nicodemus.* Early English Text Society, 1907.

Hunt, J. Eric. *Cranmer's First Litany, 1544, and Merbecke's Book of Common Prayer Noted, 1550.* Facsimile. London: Society for Promoting Christian Knowledge; New York: Macmillan, 1939.

Hussey, Arthur, M.M. Hardy and Arthur Finn. *Records of Lydd*. Ashford: 1911.
Hymnarium Sarisburiense. London: James Darling, 1851.
Idley, Peter. *Instructions to his Son*, ed. Charlotte D'Evelyn. London: Oxford University Press, 1935.
Index of Gregorian Chant, by John R. Bryden and Anthony G. Hughes. Cambridge MA: Harvard University Press, 1969. 2 vols.
Index of Middle English Verse, The, ed. Carlton Brown and Rossell Hope Robbins. New York: Columbia University Press for the Index Society, 1943. *Supplement to the Index of Middle English Verse*, ed. Rossell Hope Robbins and John L. Cutler. 1965.
Ingram, Reginald W., ed. *Records of Early English Drama: Coventry*. Records of Early English Drama. Toronto: Toronto University Press; Manchester: Manchester University Press, 1981.
Illing, Robert. 'The English Metrical Psalter of the Reformation'. *Musical Times* 1735, 1987. 517–21.
Irwin, Joyce L. 'The mystical music of Jean Gerson'. *Early Music History* 1, 1981. 187–201.
Jacobus de Liège. *Speculum Musicae*, ed. R. Bragard. Corpus Scriptorum de Musica 3: 4 vols. Rome: 1955–65.
Jacobus de Voragine. *The Golden Legend*, trans. Granger Ryan and Helmut Ripperger. 1941; repr. New York: Arno Press, 1969.
——. *Legenda Aurea*, ed. Th. Graesse. Vratistlavia [Breslau]: 3/Koebner, 1890.
James, M.R., ed. and trans. *The Apocryphal New Testament*. Oxford: 1924.
Jarrett, Bede. *The English Dominicans*. London: Burns Oates and Washbourne Ltd, 1921.
Jeffrey, David L. 'English Saints' Plays' in Denny 1973. 69–89.
——. 'Franciscan Spirituality and the Rise of Early English Drama'. *Mosaic* 8/4, 1975. 17–46.
Johnson, Martin H., and Barry J. Everitt. *Essential Reproduction*. Oxford: Blackwell, 1980.
Johnson, R.W. 'Noah at Hull'. *The Dalesman*, 1963. 105–7.
Johnston, Alexandra F. 'The Plays of the Religious Guilds of York: the Creed Play and Pater Noster Play'. *Speculum* 50, 1975. 55–90.
——. 'The Procession and Play of Corpus Christi in York after 1426'. *Leeds Studies in English*, new series 7, 1975. 55–62.
——. 'What if no texts survived? External Evidence for Early English Drama' in Briscoe and Coldewey *Contexts*, 1989. 1–19.
——. 'Evil in the Towneley Cycle' in Twycross *Evil*, [1992 for 1989]. 94–103.
——, and Margaret Dorrell. 'The York Mercers and their Pageant of Doomsday, 1433–1526'. *Leeds Studies in English*, new series 6, 1972. 11–35.
——. 'The Procession and Play of Corpus Christi in York after 1426'. *Leeds Studies in English*, new series 8, 1975. 55–62.
—— and Margaret Rogerson [i.e. Dorrell], eds. *Records of Early English Drama: York*. Records of Early English Drama. Toronto: Toronto University Press; Manchester: Manchester University Press, 1979. 2 vols.
Jungmann, Josef A. *Pastoral Liturgy*. London: 1962.
Kahrl, Stanley J. *Traditions of Medieval English Drama*. London: Hutchinson, 1974.
Keane, Ruth M. *The Theme of Kingship in the Chester Cycle*. MA dissertation. University of Liverpool, 1977.
——. 'Kingship in the Chester Nativity Play'. *Leeds Studies in English* new series 13, 1982. 74–84.
Kenney, Sylvia W. *Walter Frye: Collected Works*. Corpus Mensurabilis Musicae 19. American Institute of Musicology, 1960.
——. 'Four Settings of "Ave Regina Coelorum" ' in [Albert Vander Linden, ed.] *Liber Amicorum Charles Van Den Borren*. Anvers: Lloyd Anversois, 1964.

————. *Walter Frye and the Contenance Angloise*. New Haven, Conn: Yale University Press, 1964; repr. New York: Da Capo Press, 1980.

Ker, Neil R. *Medieval Manuscripts in British Libraries*. Oxford: Clarendon Press, 1969–92. 4 vols.

————, and A.J. Piper. [volume 4 of the above]

Kim, H.C., ed.*The Gospel of Nicodemus*. Toronto Medieval Latin Texts 2. Toronto: Pontifical Institute of Mediaeval Studies for the Centre for Medieval Studies, University of Toronto, [1973].

King, Archdale A. *Liturgies of the Religious Orders*. London: Longman, 1956.

————. *The Liturgy of the Roman Church*. London: 1957.

————. *Liturgies of the Primatial Sees*. London: 1957.

————. *Liturgies of the Past*. London: 1959.

King, Pamela. Introduction to *Medieval Drama Facsimiles* volume of Coventry 2 (forthcoming).

Kipling, Gordon. 'The Idea of the Civic Triumph: Drama, Liturgy and the Royal Entry in the Low Countries'. *Dutch Crossing* 22, 1984. 60–83.

Kircher, Athanasius. *Arithmologia*. 1665.

Klausner, David N., ed. *Records of Early English Drama: Herefordshire, Worcestershire*. Records of Early English Drama. Toronto: Toronto University Press, 1990.

Knight, Alan E. *Aspects of Genre in Late Medieval French Drama*. Manchester: Manchester University Press, 1983.

Knowles, David, and R. Neville Hadcock. *Medieval Religious Houses: England and Wales*. London: Longman, Green and Co., 1953.

Kolve, V.A. *The Play Called Corpus Christi*. Stanford, CA: Stanford University Press, 1966.

Krummel, D. W. *English Music Printing 1553–1700*. London: The Bibliographical Society, 1975.

Lamb, H.H. *The Changing Climate*. London: Methuen, 1966.

Lancashire, Ian. *Dramatic Texts and Records of Britain: A Chronological Topography to 1558*. Studies in Early English Drama 1. Toronto: University of Toronto Press, 1984.

Legenda Aurea. See Jacobus de Voragine.

Lester, Geoff. 'Idle words: stereotyping by language in the English mystery plays' in Twycross *Evil*. 129–39.

Lewis, C.S. *The Discarded Image*. Cambridge: Cambridge University Press, 1964.

Liber Hymnarius. Solesmes: Abbaye Saint-Pierre de Solesmes, 1983.

Liber Pontificalis Chr Bainbridge Archiepiscopi Eboracensis, ed. W.G. Henderson. Surtees Society 61, 1875.

Liber Usualis, The, with introduction and rubrics in English, edited by the Benedictines of Solesmes. Tournai: Desclée, 1938.

Liège, Jacobus de. *See* Jacobus.

Little, A.G. *Franciscan History and Legend in Mediaeval Art*. Manchester: Manchester University Press, 1937.

Little, P[atrick] L. *The Place of Music in the Medieval World-System*. Ph.D. dissertation. Dunedin: The University of Otago, 1975.

Longsworth, Robert. *The Cornish Ordinalia: Religion and Dramaturgy*. Cambridge, MA: Harvard University Press, 1967.

Lumiansky, R.M., and David Mills. 'The Five Cyclic Manuscripts of the Chester Cycle of Mystery Plays: A Statistical Survey of Variant Readings'. *Leeds Studies in English*, new series 7, 1975. 95–107.

————————. *The Chester Mystery Cycle: Essays and Documents, with an Essay, 'Music in the Cycle', by Richard Rastall*. Chapel Hill, NC: University of North Carolina Press, 1983.

——————, eds. *The Chester Mystery Cycle: A Facsimile of MS Bodley 175*. Medieval Drama Facsimiles 1. 1973.

——————, eds. *The Chester Mystery Cycle*. Early English Text Society s.s. 3 and 9, 1974–86.

——————, eds. *The Chester Mystery Cycle: A Reduced Facsimile of Huntington Library MS 2*. Medieval Drama Facsimiles 6. 1980.

Machyn, Henry. *The Diary of Henry Machyn*, ed. John Gough Nichols. London: Camden Society, 1848.

McKitterick, Rosamund, and Richard Beadle. *Catalogue of the Pepys Library, V.i: Medieval Manuscripts*. Cambridge: D.S. Brewer, 1993.

McPeek, Gwynn S. *The British Museum Manuscript Egerton 3307*. London: Oxford University Press, 1963.

Malone Society *Collections*.

    III *A Calendar of Dramatic Records in the Books of the Livery Companies of London, 1485–1640*, ed. Jean Robertson and D.J. Gordon. 1954.

    VII *Records of Plays and Players in Kent, 1450–1642*, ed. Giles E. Dawson. 1965.

    VIII *Records of Plays and Players in Lincolnshire, 1300–1585*, ed. Stanley J. Kahrl. 1974 [for 1969].

    IX [Various records]. 1977 [for 1971].

Maltman, Sister Nicholas. 'Light In and On the Digby *Mary Magdalene*' in Margot H. King and Wesley M. Stevens, eds. *Saints, Scholars and Heroes: Studies in Medieval Culture in Honor of Charles W. Jones*. Collegeville, Minnesota: Hill Monastic Library, 1979.

Mannyng, Robert, of Brunne. *Handlyng Synne*, ed. Idelle Sullens. Medieval and Renaissance Texts & Studies 14. Binghamton NY: Center for Medieval & Early Renaissance Studies, State University of New York at Binghamton, 1983.

Manuale et processionale ad usum insignis ecclesiae Eboracensis, [ed. William G. Henderson]. Durham: Surtees Society 63, 1875.

Manuale ad usum percelebris ecclesiae Sarisburiensis, ed. A. Jefferies Collins. London: Henry Bradshaw Society, 1960.

Marshall, John. 'The Chester Coopers' Pageant: "Selles" and "Cathedra" '. *Leeds Studies in English*, new series 8, 1976. 120–8.

——————. 'The Chester Whitsun Plays: Dating of Post-Reformation Performances from the Smiths' Accounts'. *Leeds Studies in English*, new series 9, 1977. 51–61.

——————. 'Players of the Coopers' Pageant from the Chester Plays in 1572 and 1575', *Theatre Notebook* 33, 1979. 18–23.

Maskell, William. *The Ancient Liturgy of the Church of England according to the Uses of Sarum, Bangor, York, and Hereford*. London: 1844; 2/1846.

——————. *Monumenta ritualia ecclesiae Anglicanae*. Oxford: Clarendon Press, 1846; 2nd edn 1882; repr. Farnborough: Gregg Press, 1970.

May, Stephen. 'Good Kings and Tyrants: a re-assessment of the regal figure on the medieval stage'. *Medieval English Theatre* 5/2, 1983. 87–102.

Maydeston, Clement. *See Ordinale Sarum*.

Medieval Drama Facsimiles. Leeds Texts and Monographs. Leeds: The University of Leeds School of English, 1973– . Individual volumes are listed here by editor:

    1. Lumiansky and Mills (Chester. 1973).

    2. Cawley and Stevens (Towneley. 1976).

    3. Baker and Murphy (Digby. 1976).

    4. Meredith and Kahrl (N-Town. 1977).

    5. Davis (Non-Cycle. 1979).

    6. Lumiansky and Mills (Chester. 1980).

7. Beadle and Meredith (York. 1983).

8. Mills (Chester. 1984).

Medieval Latin Word-List, The, ed. J.H. Baxter and Charles Johnson. London: Oxford University Press, 1934. Revised by R.E. Latham as *The Revised Medieval Latin Word-List.* London: Oxford University Press for the British Academy, 1965.

Meech, Sanford B. 'Three Musical Treatises in English from a Fifteenth-Century Manuscript'. *Speculum* 10/3, 1935. 235–69.

Merbecke, John.*The Booke of Common Prayer Noted (1550).* Facsimile. London: Nottingham Court Press in association with Magdalene College, Cambridge, 1979.

Meredith, Peter. 'A Reconsideration of Some Textual Problems in the N-Town Manuscript (BL MS Cotton Vespasian D VIII)'. *Leeds Studies in English,* new series 9, 1977. 35–50.

———. 'The *Ordo Paginarum* and the Development of the York Tilemakers' Pageant'. *Leeds Studies in English,* new series 11, 1980. 59–73.

———. 'John Clerke's Hand in the York Register'. *Leeds Studies in English,* new series 12, 1981. 245–71.

———. 'Scribes, texts and performance' in Neuss *Aspects.* 13–29.

———. 'Stage Directions and the Editing of Early English Drama' in A.F. Johnston, ed. *Editing Early English Drama.* New York: AMS Press, 1987. 65–94.

———, ed. *The Mary Play From the N.Town Manuscript.* London: Longman, 1987.

———, ed. *The Passion Play From the N.Town Manuscript.* London: Longman, 1990.

———. 'Manuscript, Scribe and Performance: Further Looks at the N.Town Manuscript' in Felicity Riddy, ed. *Regionalism in Late Medieval Manuscripts and Texts.* Cambridge: D.S. Brewer, 1991. 109–28.

———, ed. *The Towneley Cycle.* Leeds: The University of Leeds School of English, 1989; 2/1991.

———, and Stanley J. Kahrl, eds. *The N-Town Plays.* Medieval Drama Facsimiles 4. 1977.

———, and John E. Tailby, eds. *The Staging of Religious Drama in Europe in the Later Middle Ages.* Early Drama, Art, and Music monograph series 4, 1983.

Meyer, Robert T. 'The Middle-Cornish Play *Beunans Meriasek*'. *Comparative Drama* 3, 1969. 54–64.

Meyer-Baer, Kathi. *Music of the Spheres and the Dance of Death.* Princeton NJ: Princeton University Press, 1970; repr. New York: Da Capo Press, 1984.

Meyers, Walter E. *A Figure Given: Typology in the Wakefield Plays.* Pittsburg, PA: Duquesne University Press, 1970.

Miller, Frances M. 'Metrical Affinities of the Shrewsbury *Officium Pastorum* and its York Correspondent'. *Modern Language Notes* 33, 1918. 91–5.

Miller, John H. *Fundamentals of the Liturgy.* Notre Dame: 1959.

Mills, David. 'The Stage Directions in the Manuscripts of the Chester Mystery Cycle'. *Medieval English Theatre* 3/1, 1981. 45–51.

———. *The Chester Mystery Cycle: A Facsimile of British Library MS Harley 2124.* Medieval Drama Facsimiles 8, 1984.

———. 'James Miller: the will of a Chester scribe'. *Records of Early English Drama Newsletter* 9/1, 1984. 11–13.

———. ' "Look at Me When I'm Speaking to You": the "Behold and See" Convention in Medieval Drama', *Medieval English Theatre* 7/1 (1985), 4–12.

———, ed. *Staging the Chester Cycle.* Leeds Texts and Monographs, new series 9. Leeds: The University of Leeds School of English, 1985.

———. ' "The Towneley Plays" or "The Towneley Cycle"?'. *Leeds Studies in English,* new series 17, 1986. 95–104.

———. 'Chester's Mystery Cycle and the "Mystery" of the Past'. Transactions of the Historic Society of Lancashire and Cheshire 137, 1988. 1–23.

————. *The Chester Mystery Cycle: a New Edition with Modernised Spelling*. East Lansing: Colleagues Press, 1992.

Milsom, John. 'English-texted chant before Merbecke'. *Plainsong & Medieval Music* 1/1, 1992. 77–92.

Missal, The Sarum, ed. J. Wickham Legg. Oxford: Clarendon Press, 1916; repr. 1969.

Missale ad usum insignis ecclesie Eboracensis, ed. William G. Henderson. Durham: Surtees Society 59 and 60, 1874.

Missale ad usum insignis et praeclarae ecclesiae Sarum, ed. Francis H. Dickinson. Burntisland, 1861–83; repr. Farnborough: Gregg Press, 1969.

More, Mother Thomas [Mary Berry]. 'The Performance of Plainsong in the Later Middle Ages and the Sixteenth Century'. *Proceedings of the Royal Musical Association* 92, 1966. 121–34.

Muir, Lynette R., trans. 'Adam, a Twelfth-Century Play'. *Proceedings of the Leeds Philosophical and Literary Society, Literary and Historical Section* 13/5, 1970. 149–204.

————. *Liturgy and Drama in the Anglo-Norman Adam*. Medium Aevum Monographs, new series 3. Oxford: Basil Blackwell for the Society for the Study of Mediaeval Languages and Literature, 1973.

————. 'The Mass on the Medieval Stage'. *Comparative Drama* 23, 1989. 314–30.

Myers, A.R. *The Household of Edward IV: the Black Book and the Ordinance of 1478*. Manchester: Manchester University Press, 1959.

New Grove Dictionary of Music and Musicians, The, ed. Stanley Sadie. 20 vols. London: Macmillan, 1980.

Nelson, Alan. *The Medieval English Stage: Corpus Christi Pageants and Plays*. Chicago and London: Chicago University Press, 1974.

————, ed. *Records of Early English Drama: Cambridge*. 2 vols. Records of Early English Drama. Toronto: Toronto University Press, 1989.

Neuss, Paula. 'Active and Idle Language: Dramatic Images in "Mankind" ' in Neville Denny, ed. *Medieval Drama*. Stratford-upon-Avon Studies 16. London: Edward Arnold, 1973. 41–67.

————, ed. and trans. *The Creacion of the World*. Garland Medieval Texts 3. New York and London: Garland, 1983.

————, ed. *Aspects of Early English Drama*. Cambridge: D.S. Brewer; and Totowa, NJ: Barnes and Noble, 1983.

Nichols, Ann Eljenholm. 'The Croxton *Play of the Sacrament*: A Re-Reading'. *Comparative Drama* 22/2, 1988. 117–37.

Noomen, Willem, ed. *Le Jeu d'Adam*. Paris: Champion, 1971.

Norris, Edwin, ed. and trans. *The Ancient Cornish Drama*. 2 vols. Oxford: Oxford University Press, 1859.

Norton, Christopher, David Park and Paul Binski. *Dominican Painting in East Anglia*. Woodbridge: The Boydell Press, 1987.

Oakshott, Jane, and Richard Rastall. 'Town with Gown: an Account of the York Cycle of Mystery Plays at Leeds, 1975' in David Teather, ed. *Toward the Community University*. London: Kogan Page, 1982. 213–29.

Ordinale Exoniense, ed. J.N. Dalton. 4 vols. London: Henry Bradshaw Society, 1909–40.

Ordinale Sarum sive Directorium Sacerdotum, by Clement Maydeston, ed. William Cooke and Christopher Wordsworth. London: Henry Bradshaw Society 20 and 22, 1901–2.

Osborn, James M., ed. *The Autobiography of Thomas Whythorne*. London: Oxford University Press, 1962.

Oxford English Dictionary, The. Oxford: Clarendon Press, 1884–1987.

Owst, G.R. *Literature and Pulpit in Medieval England*. Cambridge: Cambridge University Press, 1933; 2/Oxford: Basil Blackwell, 1961.

Palmer, Barbara. ' "Towneley Plays" or "Wakefield Cycle" Revisited'. *Comparative Drama* 21, 1987–8. 318–48.

———. 'The Application of Hildburgh's Theory to Northern Art and Drama'. Unpublished paper given in session 189, 6 May 1988, at the 23rd International Congress on Medieval Studies, Western Michigan University, Kalamazoo MI.

———. 'Corpus Christi "Cycles" in Yorkshire: The Surviving Records'. *Comparative Drama* 27/2, 1993. 218–31.

Parry, David. 'The York Mystery Cycle at Toronto, 1977'. *Medieval English Theatre* 1/1, 1979. 19–31.

Percy, Thomas. *Reliques of Ancient English Poetry*. London: 1765.

Petit de Julleville, L. *Les Mystères*. 2 vols. Paris: Hachette, 1880.

Petti, Anthony. *English Literary Hands from Chaucer to Dryden*. London: Edward Arnold, 1977.

Pfaff, Richard W. *Medieval Latin Liturgy*. Toronto: University of Toronto Press, 1982.

Phelps Brown, E.H., and Sheila V. Hopkins. 'Seven Centuries of Building Wages'. *Economica* 22, 1955. 195–206.

———. 'Seven Centuries of the Prices of Consumables'. *Economica* 23, 1956. 296–314.

Pollard, A.W., ed.*English Miracle Plays, Moralities, and Interludes*. Oxford: 1890; 2/1927.

Potter, Robert.*The English Morality Play*. London: Routledge and Kegan Paul, 1975.

———. 'The Unity of Medieval Drama: European Contexts for Early English Dramatic Tradition' in Briscoe and Coldewey *Contexts*, 1989. 42–55.

Processionale ad usum insignis ac praeclarae ecclesiae Sarum, ed. William G. Henderson. Leeds: M'Corquodale and Co., 1882; repr. Farnborough: Gregg Press, 1969.

Processionale ad Usum Sarum 1502. Facsimile. Originally published by Richard Pynson. The Use of Sarum 1. Kilkenny: Boethius Press, 1980.

Prosser, Eleanor. *Drama and Religion in the English Mystery Plays: A Re-evaluation*. Stanford, CA: 1961.

Purvis, J.S. *The York Cycle of Mystery Plays. A complete version*. London: Society for the Propagation of Christian Knowledge, 1957.

———. *From Minster to Market Place*. York: St Anthony's Press, 1969.

Ramsey, Peter. *Tudor Economic Problems*. London: 1963.

Rankin, Susan. 'Shrewsbury School, Manuscript VI: a Medieval Part Book?' *Proceedings of the Royal Musical Association* 102, 1976. 129–44.

———, S[usan] K. *Shrewsbury School, Manuscript VI: a Study and Transcription*. MMus dissertation. King's College, London University, 1976.

Rastall, G. R[ichard]. *Secular Musicians in Late Medieval England*. 2 vols. Ph.D. dissertation. Manchester University, 1968.

———, Richard. 'Minstrelsy, Church and Clergy in Medieval England'. *Proceedings of the Royal Musical Association* 97, 1971. 83–98.

———. *A Fifteenth-Century Song Book*. Leeds: Boethius Press, 1973.

———, ed. *Two Coventry Carols*. Newton Abbot: Antico Edition, 1973.

———. 'Some English Consort-Groupings of the Late Middle Ages'. *Music & Letters* 55/2, 1974. 179–202.

[———], ed. *The Drama of Medieval Europe*. Leeds Medieval Studies 1. Leeds: Graduate Centre for Medieval Studies, University of Leeds, 1975.

———. 'Music for a Royal Entry, 1474'. *Musical Times* 1612, June 1977. 463–66.

———, ed. *Four Songs in Latin*. Newton Abbot: Antico Edition, 1979.

———. 'Alle hefne makyth melody' in Neuss *Aspects*, 1983. 1–12.

———. *The Notation of Western Music*. London: Dent; and New York: St Martin's Press, 1983.

———. 'Music in the [Chester] Cycle' in Lumiansky and Mills *Essays*, 1983. 111–64.

———. 'The [York] Music' in Beadle and Meredith 1983 (Medieval Drama Facsimiles 7). xli–xlv.

———. 'Vocal Range and Tessitura in Music from York Play 45'. *Music Analysis* 3/2, 1984. 181–99.

———. ' "Some Myrth to his Majestee": Music in the Chester Cycle' in Mills *Staging Chester* 1985. 77–99.

———. 'Female Roles in All-Male Casts'. *Medieval English Theatre* 7/1, 1985. 25–51.

———, ed. *Six Songs from the York Mystery Play 'The Assumption of the Virgin'*. Newton Abbot: Antico Edition, 1985.

———. 'Music in the Cycle Plays' in Briscoe and Coldewey *Contexts* 1989. 192–218.

———. *Two Fifteenth-Century Song Books*. Aberystwyth: Boethius Press, 1990.

———. 'The Sounds of Hell' in Davidson and Seiler *Hell*. 102–31.

———. 'The Musical Repertory' in Davidson *Heaven*. 162–96.

Ratcliff, Edward C. *The Book of Common Prayer of the Church of England: its making and revisions*. London: Society for the Propagation of Christian Knowledge, 1949.

Records of Early English Drama. Toronto: Toronto University Press. The first four titles were published simultaneously by Manchester University Press.

REED.York: Johnston and Rogerson, 1979. 2 vols.

REED.Chester: Clopper, 1979.

REED.Coventry: Ingram, 1981.

REED.Newcastle upon Tyne: Anderson, 1982.

REED.Norwich 1540–1642: Galloway, 1984.

REED.Cumberland, Westmorland, Gloucestershire: Douglas and Greenfield, 1986.

REED.Devon: Wasson, 1986.

REED.Cambridge: Nelson, 1989. 2 vols.

REED.Herefordshire, Worcestershire: Klausner, 1990.

REED.Lancashire: George, 1991.

Remnant, Mary. *English Bowed Instruments from Anglo-Saxon to Tudor Times*. Oxford: Clarendon Press, 1986.

Revels History of Drama in English 1: Medieval Drama, ed. Lois Potter. London and New York: Methuen, 1983.

Riggio, Milla Cozart, ed. *The Wisdom Symposium*. New York: AMS Press, 1986.

Ritchie, H. 'A Suggested Location of the Digby "Mary Magdalene" '. *Theatre Survey* 4, 1963. 51–8.

Robbins, Rossell Hope. 'Middle English Versions of "Christe qui lux es et dies" '. *Harvard Theological Review* 47, 1954. 55–63.

Robinson, J[ohn] W. *Studies in Fifteenth-Century Stagecraft*. Early Drama, Art, and Music monograph series 14, 1991.

Rogerson [i.e. Dorrell], Margaret. 'The York Corpus Christi Play: Some Practical Details'. *Leeds Studies in English*, new series 10, 1978. 97–106.

Rolle, Richard, of Hampole. *English Writings of Richard Rolle*, ed. Hope Emily Allen. Oxford: Oxford University Press, 1931; repr. Gloucester: Alan Sutton, 1988.

———. *The Psalter, or Psalms of David*. ed. H.R. Bramley. Oxford: Clarendon Press, 1884.

Rollins, Hyder E., ed. *A Handful of Pleasant Delights (1584)*. Cambridge, MA: Harvard University Press, 1924; repr. New York: Dover Publications, 1965.

Roston, Murray. *Biblical Drama in England from the Middle Ages to the Present Day*. London: Faber and Faber, 1968.

St-Jacques, Raymond. 'The Hegge "Mary in the Temple" and the Liturgy of the Consecration of Virgins', *Notes and Queries* 225, n.s. 27 (1980), 295–7.

Salter, F.M. 'The Banns of the Chester Plays' in *Review of English Studies* 15, 1939. 432–57; and 16, 1940. 1–17, 137–48.

———. *Mediaeval Drama in Chester*. Toronto: University of Toronto Press, 1955.

Sandler, Lucy Freeman. *The Peterborough Psalter in Brussels and Other Fenland Manuscripts*. London: Harvey Miller, 1974.

Schueller, Herbert M. *The Idea of Music*. Early Drama, Art, and Music monograph series 9, 1988.

Sharp, Thomas. *A Dissertation on the Pageants . . . at Coventry*. Coventry: 1825; repr. Wakefield: EP Publications, 1973.

———. *The Presentation in the Temple*. Edinburgh: 1836.

Shaw, Watkins. *The Succession of Organists of the Chapel Royal and the Cathedrals of England and Wales from c.1538*. Oxford: Clarendon Press, 1991.

Sheingorn, Pamela. *The Easter Sepulchre in England*. EDAM reference series 5: Kalamazoo, MI. Medieval Institute Publications, 1987.

Sheppard, Lancelot C. *The Liturgical Books*. New York: Hawthorn Books, 1962.

Slim, H. Colin. 'Mary Magdalene, Musician and Dancer'. *Early Music* 8, 1980. 460–73.

Slocum, Kay Brainerd. '*Musica Coelestis*: a Fourteenth-Century View of Cosmic Music'. *Studia Mystica* 14, 1991. 3–12.

———. 'Speculum musicae: Jacques de Liège and the Art of Musical Number' in Surles 1993, 11–37.

Smalley, Beryl. *English Friars and Antiquity in the Early Fourteenth Century*. Oxford: Basil Blackwell, 1960.

Smith, F. Joseph. *Jacobi Leodensis Speculum Musicae II: A Commentary*. New York: Institute of Mediaeval Music, [1970].

Smith, Lucy Toulmin, ed. *York Plays*. Oxford, 1885; repr. New York: Russell and Russell, 1963.

Smoldon, William L., ed. Cynthia Bourgeault. *The Music of the Medieval Church Dramas*. London: Oxford University Press, 1980.

Southern, Richard. *The Medieval Theatre in the Round*. London: Faber, 1957; 2/1975.

Southworth, John. *The English Medieval Minstrel*. Woodbridge: Boydell, 1989.

Sparks, Edgar H. *Cantus Firmus in Mass and Motet 1420–1520*. Berkeley, CA: University of California Press, 1963; repr. New York: Da Capo Press, 1975.

Spector, Stephen. 'The Composition and Development of an Eclectic Manuscript: Cotton Vespasian D VIII'. *Leeds Studies in English*, new series 9, 1977. 62–83.

———, ed. *The N-Town Play*. 2 vols. Early English Text Society s.s. 11–12. Oxford: Oxford University Press, 1991.

Spufford, Peter. *Handbook of Medieval Exchange*. London: Royal Historical Society, 1986.

Staley, Vernon. *The First Prayer Book of King Edward VI*. London: Alexander Moring, 1903.

Stephen, G.A. 'The Waits of the City of Norwich through Four Centuries to 1790'. *Norfolk Archaeology* 25, 1933.

Sternhold, Thomas, and John Hopkins. *The Whole Booke of Psalmes*. London: John Day, 1579. [Version with music in four parts and the notes supplemented by sol-fa syllables.]

Stevens, John. *Mediaeval Carols*. Musica Britannica 4. London: Stainer and Bell for the Royal Musical Association, 1952; 2/1958.

———. 'Music in Mediaeval Drama'. *Proceedings of the Royal Musical Association* 84, 1958. 81–95.

———. *Music and Poetry in the Early Tudor Court*. London: Methuen, 1961; corr. and rev. edn Cambridge: Cambridge University Press, 1979.

———. *Music at the Court of Henry VIII*. Musica Britannica 18. London: Stainer and Bell for the Royal Musical Association, 1962.

———. 'Medieval drama' in *New Grove*, 1980. 12/21–58.

Stevens, Martin. 'The Staging of the Wakefield Plays'. *Research Opportunities in Renaissance Drama* 11, 1968.

———. 'The Missing Parts of the Towneley Cycle'. *Speculum* 45, 1970. 254–65.

————. 'The York Cycle: From Procession to Play', *Leeds Studies in English*, new series 6, 1972. 37–61.

————. 'Postscript [to articles on the York cycle]', *Leeds Studies in English*, new series 6, 1972. 113–15.

————. *Four Middle English Mystery Cycles: Textual, Contextual, and Critical Interpretations*. Princeton, NJ: Princeton University Press, 1987.

Surles, Robert L., ed. *Medieval Numerology: A Book of Essays*. Garland Medieval Casebooks 7. New York: Garland, 1993.

Svövérffy, Joseph. ' "Peccatrix quondam femina": A Survey of the Mary Magdalene Hymns'. *Traditio* 19, 1963. 79–146.

Swete, Henry B. *Church Services and Service-Books before the Reformation*. 1896; 3/London: 1914.

Tanner, J.M. *Growth at Adolescence*. Oxford: Blackwell, 1955; 2nd edn, 1962.

Tanner, Norman P. *The Church in Late Medieval Norwich, 1370–1532*. Toronto: Pontifical Institute of Mediaeval Studies, 1984.

Tatlow, Ruth. *Bach and the Riddle of the Number Alphabet*. Cambridge: Cambridge University Press, 1991.

Taylor, [John] Andrew. *Narrative Minstrelsy in Late Medieval England*. Dissertation. University of Toronto, 1988

————. ' "To pley a pagyn of þe devyl": *turpiloquium* and the *scurrae* in early drama' in Twycross *Evil*, 1992. 162–74.

Taylor, Jerome, and Alan H. Nelson. *Medieval English Drama: Essays Critical and Contextual*. Chicago: Chicago University Press, 1972.

Texts and Calendars, by E.L.C. Mullins. 2 vols. London: Royal Historical Society, 1958 and 1983.

Thibault, Geneviève. 'L'Oratoire du Château de Montreuil-Bellay. Ses anges musiciens – son motet polyphonique' in [Giuseppe Vecchi, ed.] *Memorie e contributi alla musica dal medioevo all'età moderna offerti a F. Ghisi nel settantesimo compleanno (1901–1971)*. Bologna: Antiquae Musicae Italicae Studiosi (Università degli Studi di Bologna), 1971. 209–13.

Toft, Robert. *Aural Images of Lost Traditions*. Toronto: Toronto University Press, 1992.

Tolhurst, John B.L, ed. *The Customary of the Cathedral Priory Church of Norwich*. London: Henry Bradshaw Society, 1948.

Toulmin Smith, Lucy. *See* Smith.

Trowell, Brian. 'Faburden and Fauxbourdon'. *Musica Disciplina* 13, 1959. 43–78.

————. 'Proportion in the Music of Dunstable'. *Proceedings of the Royal Musical Association* 105, 1979. 100–41.

————. 'Faburden'. *New Grove*, 1980. 6/350–54.

————. 'Fauxbourdon'. *New Grove*, 1980. 6/433–38.

Twycross, Meg. ' "Transvestism" in the Mystery Plays'. *Medieval English Theatre* 5:2, 1983. 123–80.

Tydeman, William. *The Theatre in the Middle Ages: Western European Stage Conditions, c.800–1576*. Cambridge: Cambridge University Press, 1978.

Tyrer, John W. *Historical Survey of Holy Week, its Services and Ceremonial*. London: Alcuin Club, 1932.

Tyson, Cynthia H. 'Property requirements of *Purificatio Marie*: Evidence for stationary production of the Towneley Cycle' in John R. Sommerfeldt and E. Rozanne Elder, eds. *Studies in Medieval Culture* 8 and 9. Kalamazoo MI: The Medieval Institute, Western Michigan University, 1976. 187–91.

Unwin, George. *The Gilds and Companies of London*. London: Methuen, 1908.

Vogel, Cyrille. *Medieval Liturgy: an introduction to the sources*. Washington, DC: Pastoral Press, 1986.

Waesberghe, Jos. Smits van. 'A Dutch Easter Play'. *Musica Disciplina* 7, 1953. 15–37.

Walker, D.P. *Spiritual and Demonic Magic from Ficino to Campanella*. London: 1958.

Wall, Carolyn. 'The Apocryphal and Historical Background of "The Appearance of Our Lady to Thomas" (Play XLVI of the York Cycle)'. *Medieval Studies* 32, 1970. 172–92.

———. 'York Pageant XLVI and its Music'. *Speculum* 46, 1971. 689–712.

Ward, John M. 'Music for *A Handefull of Pleasant Delites'*. *Journal of the American Musicological Society* 10/3, 1957. 151–80.

Warner, George. *Queen Mary's Psalter*. London: British Museum, 1912.

Wasson, John M. 'Corpus Christi Plays and Pageants at Ipswich'. *Research Opportunities in Renaissance Drama* 19, 1976. 99–108.

———. 'The Morality Play: Ancestor of Elizabethan Drama'. *Comparative Drama* 13, 1979. 215–20; repr. in Clifford Davidson, C.J. Gianakeris, and John H. Stroupe, eds. *Drama in the Middle Ages*. New York: AMS Press, 1982. 321–26.

———, ed. *Records of Early English Drama: Devon*. Records of Early English Drama. Toronto: Toronto University Press, 1986.

Wehrle, William O. *The Macaronic Hymn Tradition in Medieval English Literature*. Washington, DC: The Catholic University of America, 1933.

Weiser, Francis X. *Handbook of Christian Feasts and Customs*. New York: Harcourt, Brace and World, Inc., 1952.

Weiss, D.A. 'The Pubertal Change in the Human Voice'. *Folia Phoniatrica* 2, 1950. 126–59 and 132–3.

Welsh, Gerald G., and Grace Monahan, eds. *St Augustine: The City of God*. Washington: Catholic University of America Press, 1950; repr. 1977.

Wentersdorf, Karl P. 'The Symbolic Significance of *Figurae Scatologicae* in Gothic Manuscripts' in Clifford Davidson, ed. *Word, Picture, and Spectacle*. Early Drama, Art, and Music monograph series 5, 1984. 1–19.

White, Eileen. *The York Mystery Play*. York: Yorkshire Architectural and York Archaeological Society, 1984.

Whiting, B.J. *Proverbs, Sentences, and Proverbial Phrases from English Writings Mainly Before 1500*. Cambridge, MA: Belknap Press of Harvard University Press; and London: Oxford University Press, 1968.

Whythorne, Thomas. *See* Osborn.

Wickham, Glynne. *Early English Stages 1300–1660*. 3 vols. London: Routledge and Kegan Paul, 1959–81; Volume 1, 2/1980.

———. 'The Staging of Saint Plays in England' in Sandro Sticca, ed. *The Medieval Drama*. Albany, NY: State University of New York Press, 1972. 99–119.

———. *The Medieval Theatre*. London: Weidenfeld and Nicholson, 1974.

Wieland, Gernot R., ed. *The Canterbury Hymnal*. Toronto: Pontifical Institute of Mediaeval Studies, 1982.

Wilson, C. Anne. 'Jabirian Numbers, Pythagorean Numbers and Plato's *Timeus'*. *Ambix* 35/1, 1988. 1–13.

Wilson, R.M. *The Lost Literature of Medieval England*. London: Methuen, 1952; 2/1970.

Withington, Robert. *English Pageantry*. 2 vols. Cambridge, MA: Harvard University Press, 1918; repr. New York: Benjamin Blom, 1963.

Woodfill, Walter L. *Musicians in English Society from Elizabeth to Charles I*. Princeton NJ: Princeton University Press, 1953; rpt. New York: Da Capo Press, 1969.

Woodforde, Christopher. *The Norwich School of Glass-Painting in the Fifteenth Century*. London: Oxford University Press, 1950.

Woolf, Rosemary. *The English Mystery Plays*. London: Routledge & Kegan Paul; and Berkeley, CA: University of California Press, 1972.

Woolley, Reginald M. *The Benedictional of John Longlonde, Bishop of Lincoln*. London: Henry Bradshaw Society, 1927.

[Worcester Antiphoner] André Mocquereau. *Antiphonaire Monastique . . . de Worcester.* Paléographie Musicale 12. Tournay: Desclée, 1922.

Wordsworth, Christopher. *Notes on Medieval Services in England, with an Index of Lincoln Ceremonies.* London: Baker, 1898.

———. *Ceremonies and Processions of the Cathedral Church of Salisbury.* Cambridge: Cambridge University Press, 1901.

———, ed. *Horae Eboracenses: The Prymer or Hours of the Blessed Virgin Mary, according to the Use of the Illustrious Church of York.* Surtees Society 132, 1920.

———, and H. Littlehales. *The Old Service Books of the English Church.* London: Methuen, 1904.

Wright, Stephen K. *The Vengeance of Our Lord: Medieval Dramatizations of the Destruction of Jerusalem.* Toronto: Pontifical Institute of Mediaeval Studies, 1989.

Wright, T., and J.O. Halliwell, eds. *Reliquae Antiquae.* London: Pickering, 1841–3; facs. repr. New York: AMS Press, 1966.

Wulstan, David. 'Vocal colour in English sixteenth-century polyphony'. *Journal of the Plainsong and Mediaeval Music Society* 2, 1979. 19–60.

Wyatt, Diana K.J. *Performance and Ceremonial in Beverley before 1642.* Ph.D. dissertation. The University of York [UK], 1983.

Yates, Frances. *French Academies of the Sixteenth Century.* London: 1947.

———. *Giordano Bruno and the Hermetic Tradition.* London: 1964.

INDEX

A/Y Memorandum Book (York) 55
Abel 183, 204–5, 226, 318
Abraham 188
Accipiens Simeon puerum in manibus 264
Acle 12
Ad cenam Agni providi 93, 105
Adam and Eve 183, 200–01, 207, 226, 232, 322
Adorna thalamum tuum 264
Agnus dei (Power) 133–4
'Ah silly poor Joas' 157, 159
Al Farabi 304
Alma chorus Domini 289
altars, washing of 274–5
amateur performers 300–08 *passim*
angels, actors and singers for 193, 328–44
angels, orders of 180–1
angels' song, singing, minstrelsy 176–93, 180–4, 186–8, 189, 191, 200, 215, 219, 237–49, 283
Anna, prophetess 53, 261, 308–09, 314, 320
Anne of Bohemia 235
Antichrist 183, 194, 200, 203
antiphony 14, 192–3
Apostles' Creed 279
appearances, angelic 184–6, 188
apprentice
    see: boy
Argylls 349
Aristotle 179
Ark, as type of the Church 194
Arundel, Thomas 350
'As I out rode' 32, 67–70, 138–9, 140–5, 358
Ascendo ad patrem meum 25, 82–3, 178
Ascension 25
Ashley, Kathleen 53, 59
Assumpta est Maria 174
Attaingnant, Pierre 305
Attollite portas 207–8, 279–82, 298
Attwater, Donald 278
audience 173–4, 368–77
    as actors 369–70
    dancing of 374–6
    interaction with cast 369–71
    reactions of 371
    responses of 371–3
    singing of 373–4, 376–7
    skills of 371–6, 377
Augustine, St 179, 183, 206, 209

aural tradition 85
authority of play material 55, 78, 81, 251, 256
Ave Maria 83, 244
Ave regina celorum 330
    (Ryman) 77
Ave regina . . . mater 77, 132, 380–3
Ave rex noster fili David 271
Avignon, Friars Minor of 253
    Presentation play 253–4, 321

Babwell Mill 51
Bach, J.S., choir 311–12, 324, 340
bagpipe 167, 349–50, 352, 364, 368
Bainbridge, Christopher 282–3
Bakyn, John 74–5, 365
Bale, John 5
banner-bearers 50–3
banns and proclamations 50–7, 82, 173–4, 329, 365–6
baptism 283–6
Barnes, Randle 334
Barnwell antiphoner 296
Beadle, Richard 47, 48, 108, 325, 352
Becon, Thomas 267–70, 281
Bedford, William 21
'Beholde, now hit ys come to pase' 63, 65
Belial 173, 206, 280
bell 363
    as broach 353
    as ornament 213
bell-wether 353
Bellin, George 21
bellows 207
bells, ringing of 63, 220, 263–4
    worn by morris dancers 213
Benedicta sit beata Trinitas 289
Benedictus qui venit in nomine domini 34, 218, 271
Bernard of Clairvaux 183
Beverley cycle 252
    banns of 252
Binham, Thomas 252, 298
blasphemy laws 175
blessing 176, 231, 253, 284, 289, 290, 293–4, 371–2
    parody 202–3
Bloomfield, Lesley ix
Blow, John 319

Bible 79
'Biblical' texts 78–9
Bodley plays
    Burial 13, 292–3
    Resurrection 13, 14
Boethius 179, 215, 233
Bonner, Tessa 316
'Borsley's man', Richard 320
Borthwick Institute of Historical Research
    161
Bowers, Roger 19, 75, 109
'boy', meaning of 317–19
Brainard, Ingrid 214–15
Braintree 169–71, 173
Bristol, waits of 171–2
burial 289–93
Burles, 'property-player' 172
Burstyn, Shai 134
Burton, Roger 55, 329
Bury St Edmunds 51, 162, 298
    St Edmund's Abbey 4
Butler, Christopher 234
Byrd, William 63, 158–9, 319

Caiaphas 205
Cain 45, 183, 204–5, 226, 318
Caldwell, John 19, 149–50
Candlemas, Feast of 18, 261
    see: Purification
canon (musical) 302
Cantate domino canticum novum 194
Cantemus domino 133, 237
Canterbury, Christ Church Cathedral
    Priory 19, 107, 266
cantus fractus 192–3
Carlisle, Cathedral Library 386, 388–91
carol form 148
    style 132
Carpenter, Nan Cooke 41, 221–2, 230,
    355–6
Carter, H.H. 42, 49
Cassiodorus 179
castrato voice 316
Cawley, A.C. 84, 354
censorship 19, 20
Chabham, Thomas of 210–11
Chambers, Sir Edmund K. 160–1
Chaplan, Rosemary 59
Charles, S.R. 109
Charney, Maurice 310
Chaucer, Geoffrey 350
Chelmsford 164, 168–74, 364–5, 368
Chester, Benedictine nunnery, use of 266,
    271
Chester Cathedral, St Werburgh's Abbey
    (Benedictine) 87, 295, 297, 298, 334,
    341

Chester, High Cross x
Chester guilds 165–6
    Blacksmiths 3, 57, 323, 334, 366, 368
    Brewers 21
    Cappers and Pinners 21
    Coopers 3, 21, 213–14
    Drapers 167, 342
    Ironmongers 21
    Painters and Glaziers 3, 56, 166, 333,
        351, 363, 366
    Shoemakers 3, 367
    Weavers 167, 342
Chester music 152–9, 201, 384–5
Chester plays 5, 10, 20–1, 185–6, 219–20,
    225–6, 336
    banns 56–7, 81, 82, 278
    evidence 2–3, 16, 351
    manuscripts 21, 26
    proclamation 21
    stations of 337–8, 343
    timing of 336–9
    1 Fall of Lucifer (Tanners) 182, 230,
        332–3
    2 Adam and Eve, Cain and Abel
        (Drapers) 183, 226, 229–30, 232, 367
    3 Noah's Flood (Waterleaders of Dee)
        71–2, 73, 86, 195, 197, 201, 209, 215,
        227–8, 231, 326
    5 Moses and the Law (Cappers) 295,
        336
    6 Annunciation and Nativity
        (Wrights) 83, 188, 190–1, 322, 327, 333
    7 Shepherds (Painters and Glaziers) 3,
        23, 56–8, 87, 152–3, 166–7, 190, 198,
        199, 228, 230, 317–18, 333–4, 336, 344,
        346–8, 349–52, 360–4, 376–7, 386
    8 The Three Kings (Vintners) 31, 167,
        216
    10 Slaughter of the Innocents
        (Goldsmiths) 185, 205, 225–6, 323–4,
        333
    11 Purification, Doctors (Blacksmiths)
        3, 56–7, 82, 166, 227, 230, 261, 264,
        323, 334, 367–8
    12 Temptation, Woman Taken in
        Adultery (Butchers) 22
    14 Christ at the House of Simon the
        Leper (Shoemakers) 3, 270, 273, 318,
        334, 367
    15 The Last Supper (Bakers) 278
    16 Trial and Flagellation (Coopers) 3,
        213–14
    16A Passion (Ironmongers) 292
    17 Harrowing of Hell (Cooks) 183,
        207, 281, 335
    18 Resurrection (Skinners) 3, 335

20 Ascension (Tailors) 25, 177–8, 230, 335
21 Pentecost (Fishmongers) 80, 82–3, 197, 306
22 Prophets of Antichrist (Clothworkers) 81
23 Antichrist (Dyers) 3, 31, 80, 183, 202, 294, 335
24 Last Judgement (Websters) 57, 82, 178, 335–6
Chester, St John's Church 341
Chevalier, Etienne 365
'child', meaning of 317
choice, directorial 72
choirbooks 302
choirboy companies 309–10
choirboys, training of 301–03, 316
choirs, size and balance of 339–41
'Christ rising again' (Byrd) 158–9
'Christmas song' 199–200
Christus resurgens 189, 223, 335
church, circuit of 282
    demand for entrance to 281–2
Cicero 179
Circumcision, Feast of the 262
civic plays 10–15, 192
Cividale play 92
claritas Dei 257–8
Clerke, John 23, 24, 25, 185, 189, 244, 273, 322, 332
Clopper, Lawrence M. 56
coal 199
coins 163
    see also: money
Coldewey, John C. 168–74
Colle 205
Collegerunt pontifices 88
Common clerk (York) 20, 24
    see also: Burton, Clerke, Newton
Common Prayer, Book of 295
Community plays 10–15
competition, singing 354
Consecration of Virgins, Office of 254–5
Cornish plays 3–5, 54, 200–01, 226, 365, 374
    Creacion of the World 4, 201, 210, 220, 289, 375
    Life of Meriasek 4–5, 7, 54, 198, 220, 375
    Ordinalia 4–5, 10, 21, 25, 54, 60, 176, 190, 200–01, 209–10, 215, 219–20, 270, 277–8, 281, 292, 293, 345, 367, 375–6
Cornish, William 58
Corpus Christi, Feast of 55, 56
countertenor voice 316, 339
Coventry guilds 165–6, 175
    Cappers 65, 208
    Drapers 64, 65, 341

Shearmen and Tailors 19, 36, 67
Smiths 64, 325, 343
Weavers 19, 27, 62, 64, 69, 341, 343
Coventry music 137–52, 359
    voice-ranges 150–2
    pitch centres of gravity 151–2
Coventry plays 62, 226, 252, 320, 342, 345
    last performance of 67
    music in 32, 66, 67, 87, 386–7
    stations of 342
    1 Nativity (Shearmen and Tailors) 19, 32–4, 69, 86–7, 139, 190, 202, 211–12, 230, 324, 347–9, 351–2, 358–60, 367
    2 Purification (Weavers) 19, 27, 64, 224, 226, 232, 259, 261, 263–4, 323, 368
Cox, Captain 58
crack 36–7
Craig, Hardin 32, 63, 160–1
Crane, Randle 167, 366–7
Creed 83–4
Croo, Robert 62, 63, 66, 68–9, 252, 358–9
cross-comparison 16, 175
crotchet 37, 39
Crowland 298
Croxton 52
Cum appropinquaret Dominus 266, 268, 271
Cummings, W.H. 137
Curiosity 173, 215
currency 162–4
Cutts, John P. 138, 386–7
cycle, concept of 7

Dalby, Thomas 329
dancing 53–4, 164, 173, 198–9, 208–9, 212–15, 220, 365
    as metaphor 46–7
    social 214–15, 374–6
    see also: bells, morris dancers
Dante 206, 212
Dart, R. Thurston 158
Daughters of God, Four 10, 321
David, King 60, 112, 117–18, 182–3, 193, 280–1, 366
Davidson, Audrey Ekdahl 35–6
Davidson, Clifford 17, 28, 218
Davis, Norman 52, 74–6, 89
Daw, S.F. 311–12, 340
Dawson, Giles 162
De terra plasmasti me 290–1
Decalogue 84, 235, 238, 254
deceit, Hellish 73, 186, 199–200, 208–9, 211, 215
Dediet the glazier, daughter of 321
Deimling, Hermann, and [Albert] Matthews 72
Denny, Neville ix
diabolus in musica 211

Digby plays 172–4
Dignus es domine 176, 269–70
directions, dramatic 22–31, 76
  Chester 25
  marginal 22–4, 26, 31, 46, 58, 78, 189
  N-Town 26
  York 26
Divine Order
  see: Order
Domine probasti me 290
Dorrell, Margaret 330, 332
doubling of roles 330–2, 336, 340–3
'Downe from Heaven' 33, 67–8, 138–9
drinking song
  see: gossips (music)
Dryden, John 196
Dunkley, Sally 137
Dunstable, John 134
Dutka, JoAnna 1, 70, 72, 75–6, 121, 128,
    138, 175, 213–14, 221–5, 229, 366–7
dynamic functions of music 225–32

Ecce appropinquabit redemptio 113
Ecce Dominus ascendet 334
Ecce salvator venit 113
editorial procedures 379
Edward II (Marlowe) 371
Ego qui loquor justitiam 178
Elche Assumption play 230–1
Elias 183, 335
Elizabeth, Queen, funeral of 315
Ely 298
En rex venit 110, 266, 268–9
Enoch 183, 335
Entry into Jerusalem 265–71
Eucharist 251, 276–8
Eve, casting of 308, 315, 322, 326
Ex Egipto 334
Exaltare Domine 335
Exemplar (Chester) 20, 26, 59, 71, 72, 78,
    82, 190, 295–7
Exeter, Christmas mattins at 257
Exiit Israel 290
Exultet celum laudibus 173, 374

faburden 95–6
farting 36, 205–7
fauxbourdon 96
female roles, casting of 308–27
fictional drama 9–10
fireworks 206–7
Fitch, Robert 75
Fleury plays 91–3, 96–7, 101, 103
flowers 266–9, 271
flute (possibly indecent) 210
Fouquet, Jean 365–6
'four-and-twenty to a long' 38, 41, 354

Fowler, Alastair 234
Frater Thoma causa tristicie 93, 105
Froissart, Jean 351
Frye, Walter 381
Fux, J.J. 211

Gabriel, Archangel 83, 181, 185, 188, 259,
    361
gam 48
Gammer Gurton's Needle 60
Garcio, Jak 318, 363
Garcius 58, 167, 198, 199, 228, 318, 344,
    349, 360–4, 376–7, 386
Gaudete justi 335
gematria 110, 238, 245
'general rehearse' 11
Genson, John 167, 365
'gentleman' as style for singer 302, 305
Gervaise, Claude 305
Gesta de praesentatione beatae Mariae 254
Gillam, Hugh 213–14
Glasney, College of 21
Glastonbury Abbey, musicians at 301
Gloria in excelsis deo 25, 32, 41, 43, 57, 79,
    86, 154, 157–9, 186, 189–90, 230, 251,
    256–8, 331, 333, 344–8, 352–5, 357,
    358–9, 371, 386
  Cambridge setting 39–40, 157, 258
  Chester setting 87, 152–5, 384–5
Gloria laus et honor 266, 269, 271
Gloria patri 82
Gloria tibi domine 93, 101, 104–5, 108–09
Gnostics 236
Golden Legend
  see: *Legenda Aurea*
Golden Section 247
Goldston, wait 65
gossips (Chester) 86, 201, 209, 211, 326
  song 72, 201–2, 209, 218, 326
Grace, Seven Gifts of 238
Greene, Richard L. 63, 69, 71
Gregorie, Edward 21
Grossteste, Robert 194
'Group' MSS (Chester) 21
Grünewald, Matthias 213–14
guilds 317–19, 318–19
  accounts 164–8
  and see: Norwich Grocers
Gussenhoven, Frances 23
Gyll 37, 202, 326, 357

hack 36
Haec est ara dei caeli 333
'hail' lyrics 77
Handfull of Pleasant Delites 59
Happé, Peter 28, 30
harmony 36, 212

harp, as metaphor 49–50
Harrison, Frank Ll. 89, 94, 105, 107, 109, 121, 158
Harrowing of Hell 278–83
Hawte, Sir William 302
healing miracles 268
'Heaven, The' 176, 329, 333
Hec requies mea 290
'Hegge' plays (N-Town) 162
Hell, gates of 280–3
    sounds of 199–215
Henderson, W.G. 282
Henry II 206
Henry IV 302
Henry V 218, 302
Henry VI 302
Henry VII 164
Henry VIII 302
Hereford 266
Herod 202
Hewitt, James 27, 64–5, 159, 167, 306, 341–2, 365
hexachord system 43, 48
    see also: tonic sol-fa
Hilton, Walter 186–7, 189–90, 200
Hingeston, John 312, 319
historical drama 5–9
Hodie beata virgo Maria 264
Hodie nobis celorum rex 157, 256–7
Hoffman, Dustin 315
Holton, Ruth 137
Holy Innocents, Feast of the 14
Holy Spirit, Gifts of 254
Holy Trinity Church, Coventry 65
Hopkins, John 73
Hopper, V.H. 234
horn 349, 358, 360–1, 368
Hosanna filio david
    see: *Osanna*
'Hosanna to the Son of David' 218
hours, books of 349–50
'howe' 348–9, 360–1
Howerd, Frankie 370
Humphries, Barry 326
Hunnis, William 319–20

Iam, iam, ecce 92, 101–3
'If ye be risen again with Christ' (Anon.) 156, 159
improvised polyphony 86, 97, 355–7
    see also: sighting
In exitu Israel 290
In manus tuas domine 202
In paradisum 290
indenture: *see* York, Mercers
Infidelis incursum 89, 93, 106, 107
inflation 163

Ingram, Reginald 62, 64–5
Ingrediar in locum 290
Ingrediente Domino in sanctam civitatem 266, 270–1, 308
institutional drama 13, 10–15, 192–3
instruments, musical 47, 49–50, 60, 192, 210–11, 352
    see also: loud, still, Last Trump, bagpipe, flute, horn, organ, pipe, recorder, regals, whistles
interludes, Tudor 4
Isaac 188
Isaiah 118, 182
    vision of Heaven 25, 181, 192
Isidore of Seville 35, 179
'It is written with a coal' 59–60, 199–200, 369, 377

Jacobus de Voragine 279
Jee, David 140, 147, 150
Jeremiah 118
Jerome, St 79, 250
'Jerusalem' (location in Chester nunnery) 266
Jerusalem respice ad orientem 110, 111–14, 118, 269
Jesu corona virginum 228, 253–4
Jesu Salvator seculi 93, 105
Jesus rex regum omnium 239
John the Baptist 284, 331
Johnston, Alexandra F. 165
Jones, Aled 316
journeyman
    see: 'man'
Judgement 30, 226

Kahrl, Stanley 162
Keane, Ruth 56
Kenney, Sylvia 77, 380
keyboard instruments, boys taught to play 301
Kilwardby, Robert 180
Kindlemarsh, Francis 63, 75
King, Pamela 62, 63, 64, 66, 325
Kingston on Hull 13, 293
Kirkpatrick, John 75–6
kitchen, equipment, etc. 207–8
Kolve, V.A. 186, 194, 347, 349
knack 36–7
Knight, Alan 8, 371

Lameth 318
Lancashire, Ian 62
Laneham, Robert 58
Last Supper 251, 272–8
Last Trump 53, 55, 336

Latin, use of 78–84, 204
  by demons 203
  Latin-plus-English 81, 244–5
Laudate pueri Dominum 307
laudes dei 180, 182
Laus tibi cum gloria 229
Lay Folk's Mass Book 83
Legenda Aurea 7, 250, 279, 281, 290
Leodiensis, Jacobus 180, 182
Letamini in Domino 335–6
Leva Jerusalem 114–16, 118–20
Levate capita 114, 117–18
Lichfield Cathedral 13, 18, 19, 89, 107, 295
  statutes of 89
Liège, Jacobus of
  see: Leodiensis
Limbo 278
  see also: souls
Lincoln 298
  Cathedral 177
'Lincoln' plays (N-Town) 162
Lindley, Simon 324, 339
'lining out' 199, 377
Lipscomb, Lan 235
literacy
  see: musical literacy
Little, Patrick 179–82, 186
liturgical manuscripts 86, 267–8
liturgical provenance 294–9
liturgical texts 78–80, 87, 191, 250–99
  passim
liturgical vestments
  see: vestments
Longinus 292
loud music, instruments 47, 51, 365
Lucifer, fall of 181
'Lully lulla thow littell tyne childe' 33, 67,
  71, 138–9, 145–50
  metre of 148–50
Lumen ad revelationem gentium 263
Lumiansky, R.M., and David Mills 20, 26,
  56, 71, 78–81, 202–3, 251, 295, 335–6,
  361–2
Lutter, William 167–8, 366
Lydgate, John 49
Lyonnard 321
lyrics and song-texts 57–78, 137, 264

McKinnell, John 137
MacLean, Sally-Beth 161
McPeek, Gwynn S. 133
Maddrell, J.E. 28
Magi 188, 211, 216–17, 346, 367
Magnificat 24, 25, 27, 252, 322, 333, 363
Mahrt, William 154
Mak 37, 41, 45, 202, 207, 211, 357
Malacoda 206, 212

Maldon 169–73
Malone Society 1, 162
Malvern Priory, Great 207
'man', meaning of 319–20
Manchester Cathedral 177
Mandatum 226, 252, 272–6
Mane nobiscum 93, 101, 104, 106–7
Manly, J.M. 75–6
manna
  see: wafers
Manning, Robert, of Brunne 61, 194, 209
manuscripts
  Cambridge, Magdalene College, Pepys
    1236 19, 39, 89, 94, 107, 117, 154, 157,
    192
  Cambridge, University Library, Add.
    5943 39, 157
  Dublin, Archbishop Marsh's Library
    Z4.2.20 18
  The Hague, Royal Library, 76.F.3 101
  The Hague, Royal Library, 71.J.20 101
  London, British Library, Add. 10305 21
  London, British Library, Add. 31922 58
  London, British Library, Add. 35290 23,
    35, 48, 107, 121–26, 329
  London, British Library, Add. 38599
    387–91
  London, British Library, Add. 353245
    315
  London, British Library, Egerton 3307
    133, 237
  London, British Library, Harley 2103 21
  London, British Library, Harley 2124 21
  London, British Library, Royal
    Appendix 56 153
  Madrid, Biblioteca Nacional, C.132 101
  Oxford, Balliol College 354 70
  Oxford, Bodleian Library, Bodley 175 21
  Oxford, Bodleian Library, Bodley 791 21
  Oxford, Bodleian Library, Bodley 948
    296
  Oxford, Bodleian Library, Douce 381
    351
  Oxford, Bodleian Library, Eng. poet.
    e.1 70
  Oxford, Bodleian Library, Rawlinson
    liturg.d.4 18, 101
  San Marino, CA, Huntington Library
    HM 1 20, 39
  San Marino, CA, Huntington Library
    HM 2 21
  Shrewsbury School VI 18, 24, 88,
    109–11, 124
  York, Yorkshire Museum, Sykes MS
    19–20
  see also: choirbooks, Mulliner Book
March (Cambridgeshire) 177

Marlowe, Christopher 371
marriage 255
  of Mary and Joseph 255, 286–9
  numbers 235–6
Marseille, King, Queen of 173–4, 203, 285, 293
Mary, the Blessed Virgin 6, 8, 71, 177, 308–09, 314, 321–2, 333
  Five Joys of 77
Mary Magdalene 6–7, 173, 273–4, 292–3
masks 258
Mass 251, 276–8
'master', meaning of 317
master of the St Lucy Legend 235, 380–1
Mawdyke, Thomas 62, 66–9, 138
mean 44, 45, 356
Medieval English Theatre ix, 161
Medwall, Henry 4
Memento Domine David 290
Memlink, Hans 191
mensural monody 119–20, 152–4, 192
mensurations 37–42, 354
Merbeck, John 153
Merchant of Venice (Shakespeare) 196–7
Mercy 203–5, 370, 373
Mercy, seven corporal works of 84
Meredith, Peter 12, 21, 26, 53, 62, 124, 167, 213, 255, 276–7, 288, 289, 333, 364
'merry song' 58, 174, 198, 199, 200, 362, 364
metaphorical references 44–50,
Methley, Yorkshire 388
Meyer-Baer, Kathi 186
Mézières, Philippe de 253–4, 312
mi contra fa 211
Michael, Archangel 177, 181, 183, 229, 335
Miller, James 21, 155–7, 295–7
Mills, David 21, 25, 155–6, 207, 364
Milton, John 196
minstrels, minstrelsy 33, 47, 51–3, 57, 136, 164–5, 167, 169–74, 176, 183, 192, 208–9, 211–12, 213–14, 226–7, 229, 304, 344, 364–8, 375
  see also: dancing, instruments
miracula 89
mirth, heavenly 45
  see also: 'merry song'
misericord 207
money 162–4
More, Mother Thomas 153
moresca 214–15
Moreschi, Alessandro 316
Morley, Thomas 305
morris dancers 213–14
mortals, music of 193–9
Mothers of the Innocents 71, 226, 309, 323–4, 360, 371

Muir, Lynette 12, 276–8
Mulliner Book 301
musica caelistis 183, 194, 210, 218
musica humana 179–83, 195–6, 198–9, 210, 214–15
musica instrumentalis 179–83, 210, 218
musica mundana 179–83, 195–6, 210
musical literacy 300, 303, 305–06
musical settings 66, 74

Najera altarpiece (Memlink) 191
Ne timeas Maria 244
Nelson, Alan 136
Newton, Miles 24, 25
Nicholas, Thomas 65
Nicholas of Usk 183
Nicodemus, Gospel of 278–81
Noah 54, 188, 375
  and family sing 46, 194, 197, 215, 227–8, 306–07
Noah, Mrs 309, 321, 323, 325–7
noise, as unstructured sound 207–8
Northumberland Household Books 339–40
Norwich
  A text 46, 74, 215, 322
  B text 74, 322
  Grocers' records 74, 76
notation, musical 17, 68, 85, 87, 89, 108, 125–6, 139, 152, 305
  coloration 125
  mensural 85, 301, 365, 380–3
  plainsong 85–6, 301, 307
  and see: Nicholas, Wotton
notated music 85, 87, 191, 329
  and see: polyphony
'Nowell' 33–4
N-Town plays 5–6, 11, 21, 162, 298
  banns of 50, 52–3, 55
  proto-cycle 53
  1 The Creation, and Fall of Lucifer 53, 205–6, 210
  4 Noah 195, 231, 318
  8 Joachim and Anna 83, 190, 349
  9 the Presentation of Mary in the Temple 190, 228, 253–6, 293, 321, 356, 371–2
  10 The Marriage of Mary and Joseph 286–9, 322,
  13 The Visit to Elizabeth 14, 219
  14 The Trial of Mary and Joseph 46
  15 The Nativity 53, 188, 257
  16 The Shepherds 347–8, 353
  18 The Magi 211
  19 The Purification 261–3, 298
  20 The Slaughter of the Innocents 45, 49–50, 212, 323

22 The Baptism 285
23 Temptation 206
26 The Conspiracy, and the Entry into Jerusalem 268, 270–1
27 The Last Supper 272–4, 275–6
28 The Betrayal 229
32 The Crucifixion 212–13, 325
33 The Harrowing of Hell I 280, 298
34 The Burial 292
41 The Assumption of the Virgin 6, 14, 21, 77, 177, 219, 230, 290–1, 298, 324, 365, 367
42 The Last Judgement 45
see also: plays (individual: Mary Play)
numbers, numerology 232–49, 380
Nunc dimittis servum tuum 57, 82–3, 173, 261–4, 334

O Deus, quis revolvet 101, 102–5
O quam pulchra es 239
O sacrum convivium 35, 276
'O ye pepyll of ierusalem' 112
Oakshott, Jane ix, 81, 137
see also: productions (modern)
Octavian 188, 190, 216–17
offering 258–60
Order, Divine 183, 194–5, 198, 232, 233, 245–6
Ordo paginarum (York) 34, 35, 55, 135, 329–30
organ, organist 159, 301, 338, 365
see also: Bakyn, Hewitt, regals
organum, strict 44, 356–7
Orietur stella ex Jacob 295
'original' 19
Origny play 92
Osanna filio David 35, 308, 334
out-of-tune singing 37, 42–4, 198, 211, 357

Palm Sunday 35
procession 110, 112–13, 121, 218, 231, 266–71, 281, 308
Palmer, Barbara 207
palms 267–8
Parliament of Heaven 10
Parnall, Cathy 137
Pascha nostrum 13
Passion Play (N-Town) 21, 229, 268–71, 272–3, 275–6, 280, 292, 298
Pater noster 197
Paul, Saint 6
Paumann, Conrad 301
Pax vobis 223
Peers, William 252
Pepys 1236: see Manuscripts
music in 107–21
Percula
see: Procula

Percy, Thomas 160
performances
monitoring of 19, 20
starting-time of 51, 53
Petomane, Le 206
Phalèse, Pierre 305
Philips, Peter 319
Pikeharness 318
Pilate 292, 325
see also: Procula
pilgrims, Canterbury 350
pipe 210, 346, 359, 368
see also: bagpipe, flute, recorder, whistles
Piran Round ix
Pixley, Richard 63, 65
plainsong, styles of 307
Plato 179
plays, individual
Adam 3, 207, 214
Beunens Meriasek: see Cornish plays
Brome *Abraham* 220
Castle of Perseverance 4–5, 10–11, 50–2, 163, 204, 209, 211–12, 217, 298, 365–6, 374
Conquest of the Danes 67
Delight 209
Destruction of Jerusalem 65, 67
Dux Moraud 18, 24
Elckerlijc 5
Everyman 4–5, 10, 53, 176
Fulgens and Lucres 4
Killing of the Children 14, 53, 172–3, 213, 261–3, 298, 374
King Edward IV, History of 67
Mankind 4–5, 10–11, 59, 86, 199–200, 202–4, 210, 212, 217, 219, 298, 369–70, 373 376–7
Mary Magdalen 5, 7, 43, 172–4, 202, 203, 205–6, 212, 285–6, 293–4, 298, 373–4
Mary Play 6, 12, 14, 21, 49, 83, 188, 253–6, 286–9, 293, 321–2, 347, 371–2
Meriasek, Life of: see Cornish plays
Nature 4–5
Sacrament, Play of the 5, 7–8, 35, 51, 205, 276, 298
St Paul, Conversion of 5, 7–8, 53, 172, 206, 298, 374
Seinte Resureccion 3
Wisdom 4–5, 10–11, 209, 212, 217, 298, 369, 373
see also: Bodley plays, Cornish plays, Passion Play
polyphony 85, 87–8, 95, 191, 193, 209, 258, 301, 303–04, 329, 359, 365
see also: improvised polyphony, sighting
pontifical 255, 282–3
pots and pans 207

Power, Lionel 133
Presentation in the Temple 253
    see also: Mézières
prices 163–4
priests, seven 254
printing 305
procession 27, 224–5, 231, 261–2, 264, 266, 290
    music in 18, 34–5, 88, 110, 185, 194, 230
    see also: Palm Sunday procession
processional 18
proclamation
    see: banns
Procula 286–7, 320, 321, 325
productions, modern 175
    Ordinalia: Denny 1969 ix
    York: Oakshott 1975 ix, 161, 330, 369
    York: at Toronto 1977 161
    Towneley: Oakshott, Bloomfield and Smith 1977 ix
    Towneley: Oakshott 1980 ix, 325, 370
    Chester: Oakshott 1983 x, 81, 307, 325, 336, 351, 384
    York 1988, 1992 x, 137
    York: Oakshott 1994 x, 137, 307, 325, 381
professional performers 300–08 *passim*
prophet, choirboy dressed as 110
proportions 179, 233–49
Proudfoot, Richard 202
Prowett, Stephen 74–5
psalms 82, 194, 199
    gradual 253, 255–6, 260, 321
    for Mandatum 275
    metrical 377
    Psalm 23 279–82
    Psalm 95 194
    Psalm 97 194
    Psalm 112 307
    Psalm 144 76
    Psalm 149 183, 194
    Psalm 150 60–1, 194
psalter 85
puberty, age of, in boys and girls 310–13
    development at 313–15
Pujol, Joseph 206
Purcell, Henry 312, 319
Purification of the Blessed Virgin 258–64
Purification, Feast of the 14
purification, office of 258–60, 263–4
Purvis, J.S. 161
Pythagoras 179, 234

Quemadmodum desiderat cervus 290
Quid agimus vel dicamus 93, 107

Rachel 71

Rainoldes, John 312
Rankin, Susan 18, 88–9, 94
realism 215–19
recorder 350–2, 359, 368
Records of Early English Drama ix, 1, 161–2
regals 64, 167, 192, 334, 338, 341, 343, 365, 384
register 19, 20, 35, 48, 107, 329
    see also: manuscripts (London BL 35290)
'Rejoyce, rejoyce, all that here be' 63, 65
'Rejoice, rejoice, with heart and voice' 63
Representatio pastorum 89
Representatio peregrinorum 89
Representatio Resurrectionis 89
representational functions of music 176–220, 221, 232
Responsum accepit Simeon 264
Richard II 235
Richard II (Shakespeare) 196
'Richard the Capper' 320, 325
Roberts, Deborah 137
Robin Hood plays 4
Robinson, John ix, x, 77, 135, 233, 326
Roland le Pettour 206
Rolle, Richard 77, 83, 186
Rouen gradual 91, 96–7
royal entry 217–18
Russell Pontifical 255
Rybald 208, 220
'Rychard' 62, 65
Ryman, James 77
'Ryngold's man, Thomas' 320, 325

Sacerdotes domini 83
sacraments 282–94
Sacraments, the Seven 84
sacrifice 293–4, 258–62, 293
Sadler, Richard 65
saints, offices for 79
St Anne's Day 14
St Anne's Guild, Acle 12
St-Jacques, Raymond 254–5
Salome 188
Salter, F.M. 72, 161, 163
Salvator mundi 208, 335
Salvatorem Christum dominum 89–91, 96, 99–101, 104, 124
Satan 280
'Save mee O God' 73, 197, 228
scene-division, music for 221–3, 225, 233, 236–49
Schueller, Herbert M. 186
Scottish anonymous 96
seduction 210, 215, 217
    see also: Curiosity
Senex puerum portabat 264

sesquialtera 242–3
service-books
  see: liturgical manuscripts
set piece, musical 34, 329, 335
Seth 176, 190
Shakespeare, William 3, 160, 175, 196
Shann manuscript 387–91
Shanne, Richard 388
Sharp, Thomas ix, 1, 66, 68–9, 138, 140,
  150, 160, 175
  Dissertation ix, 1, 66, 138, 160
  edition of Weavers' play 66
shawms 192
Sheerin, Daniel 281–2
Sheingorn, Pamela 17, 216
Shepherds 36–43, 344–64
shouting 207
Shrewsbury plays 13, 113
  music 86–7, 88–107
  1 Shepherds 88, 91, 94, 347, 352
  2 Resurrection 88, 91–4
  3 Pilgrims 88, 93–4
  see also: manuscripts
Shute, Nevil 351
Sibyl 188, 190, 327
Sidney, Sir Philip 312
sighting 95–6, 355–6
Simeon 12, 57, 63, 82, 167, 260–64, 334, 368
Simeon justus et timoratus 263
singers, professional 27, 166, 173, 192–3,
  328–44, 352, 358, 360
  see also: professional
Sins, the seven deadly 84
Skelton, John 236
Smith, Lucy Toulmin 28, 121, 137, 160–1
Smith, Roger ix
Smith, Thomas 386, 388
Smoldon, William 97, 101
soft music, instruments 47, 49
Solomon, King 54
Song of Songs 183
  settings of 134
song-texts
  see: lyrics
Songs of Sundrie Natures (Byrd) 63
souls, in Limbo 208, 220, 278, 280–1, 283
  saved 183–5, 335
sources and evidence
  play manuscripts 17, 17–22
  documentary 17
  iconographic 17
Spector, Stephen 49
speech headings 22
Spenser, Edmund 351
spheres, crystal 179–80
  music of 179–81
  see also: *musica mundana*

squares 89, 96
stage directions 17
Star of Bethlehem 257
stave-lines, coloured 42
Steiner, Ruth 121, 128, 132
Stella celi extirpavit 353
Sternhold, Thomas, and John Hopkins
  see: Hopkins
Stevens, John 14, 58, 67, 121, 128, 132,
  152–4, 175, 183, 193, 207, 215–18, 221,
  223
Stevens, Martin 50, 207
Stiff, Richard 65
structure, numerical 233–49
structural functions of music 221–32,
  239–49
style, musical 94, 120–21, 132, 140–1
Surge proxima [propera] mea 122, 123,
  129–31
Suscepimus Deus misericordiam tuam 262
Sykes Manuscript
  see: manuscripts (York)

tableau 30, 178, 185, 224–5, 229–31
Tallis, Thomas 319
Tanner, J.M. 315
Tau 238
Taylor, Andrew 206
Te deum laudamus 174, 176, 181–3, 192, 198,
  246, 331, 335, 373–4, 376, 387
technical information on music 35
Temperley, Nicholas 199
Temple 260
  singers in 27, 261
  virgins of 53, 173, 213, 261–2, 374
tenor 45, 356
text references 31
'There is no rose' 236
Thetford 51, 298
Thomas, 'Ryngold's man' 320
Thorpe, William 350
'three breves to a long' 37, 41–2
time, passage of 222, 225–8
Titivillus 202, 208, 210, 220, 369
Toledo 281
Tollite portas 279, 282
  see also: *Attolite portas*
tongs 207
tonic sol-fa 42
Torcular calcavi solus 178
Tours plays 92, 101
Towneley plays 5, 10, 20, 219
  banns of 50
  descent from early York cycle 25
  1 The Creation 48, 176
  2 Cain and Abel 45, 204–5, 219, 318
  3 Noah 48, 231, 378–9

7 Procession of Prophets 366
8 Pharaoh 45, 195, 372
12 The Shepherds, first pageant 37, 41–2, 77, 84, 190, 318, 345–6, 347–8, 353–6, 358, 363
13 The Shepherds, second pageant 37, 39, 41–2, 45, 77, 190, 197, 207, 230, 233, 326, 345–6, 353–8, 386
16 Herod 202, 323–4, 325
17 The Purification 261, 263, 368
18 The Doctors 370
19 The Baptism of Christ 284
20 The Conspiracy 278
21 The Buffeting 44, 47, 205, 208, 220
22 The Flagellation 47, 248
23 The Way to Calvary 45, 291
25 The Harrowing of Hell 208, 220, 280, 283
28 Thomas of India 177
29 The Ascension 25, 82
30 The Last Judgement 29, 44, 45, 203–4, 208, 220, 373
31 The Raising of Lazarus 370
Transeamus usque Bethelem 91, 96–9, 104
Transubstantiation 276–8
treble 43, 44, 45, 356
    see also: triplex
Trevor, Caroline 137, 316
trial, legal 30
triplex 89
'Trolly lolly lo' 58–9, 198, 362, 364, 376–7
Trowle
    see: Garcius
Tuder, John 119, 302
tuning 355
    see also: out-of-tune
Tutivillus
    see: Titivillus
Twycross, Meg x, 321, 325
Tyrer, J.W. 281
'Tyrly tyrlo' 69

Uniformity, Act of 296
Unus autem ex ipsis 88

Van Tassel, Eric 316
Vannes, Count of 54
Veni creator spiritus 23, 82, 86, 177, 197, 306–07, 331–2
Veni de Libano 122, 125, 130–2, 137, 329
Veni electa mea 122, 125, 127–8, 340
Venite benedicti 57, 82–3, 178
versus sign 280–1, 324
vestments, liturgical 191, 254, 257
Vetus Latina 79
Vexillatores
    see: banner-bearers

Victimae paschali laudes 13, 14, 92–3, 95, 193
Virgil 84
virgins
    see: Temple, Consecration
Viri Galilei 82–3, 335
Virtues, the seven principal 84
voice
    'breaking' of 311–12
    castrato 316
    countertenor 316
Voragine
    see: Jacobus
Vulgate Bible 79, 250–1

wafers 267, 269, 277
Wakefield 10
'Wakefield Master', the 41, 43, 45, 220
waits 64–5, 167, 171, 306, 341, 343, 368
    of London 305
Wall, Carolyn 121, 221, 246
Warton, Thomas 160
Washington, D.C., National Gallery of Art 380
'Wee happy heardsmen here' 71, 386–91
Weiss, D.A. 311, 318
'Welaway' 45
Wentersdorf, K.P. 205–6
whistles 351–2, 364
Wickham, Glynne 161
Willding, James 155–7
willow 267–8
Winternitz, Emanuel 380
'With hart and voyce' 74, 76
White, Robert 12, 159, 166–7
Whythorn, Thomas 306
Williams, Robin 315
Wilton Diptych 235
Wolsey, Thomas 301
Wood, Lt Col. G.P. 349
Woolf, Rosemary 13, 194, 349, 363
Worcester, use of 264, 266, 295–6
worldlings 59, 86, 199–200, 203, 205, 209, 219, 370, 377
Wotton, Thomas 65
wrestling 361, 363, 376
Wulstan, David 310, 314

York Early Music Festival x
York guilds 55, 165–6
    Mercers, indenture of 29–30
    Scriveners 19
    Weavers 329
York Minster choir 329–31, 340
York music 87, 121–37
    A versions 122
    B versions 122–3
    dating of 134

four-part chord in 122, 132
pitch centres of gravity of 136–7
planning of 126–9
vocal ranges of 135–7
voice-types of 135–7, 193
York plays 5, 10, 19, 184–5
  revision of 135
  1 The Fall of the Angels (Barkers)
    245–6, 247, 331, 387
  7 Cain and Abel (Glovers) 46, 212
  8 The Building of the Ark
    (Shipwrights) 47
  9 The Flood (Fishers and Mariners) 46,
    194, 231, 241–3, 306
  10 Abraham and Isaac
    (Parchmentmakers and
    Bookbinders) 293
  11 Moses and Pharaoh (Hosiers) 45,
    47, 195, 237–8, 248–9
  12 The Annunciation and Visitation
    (Spicers) 24, 27, 185, 244–5, 322, 331
  13 Joseph's Trouble about Mary
    (Pewterers and Founders) 184
  14 The Nativity (Tilethatchers) 55, 77,
    236–7, 239, 257
  15 The Shepherds (Chandlers) 55, 88,
    331, 347–8, 352–3, 358
  16 Herod, the Magi (Masons,
    Goldsmiths) 44, 77
  17 The Purification (Hatmakers,
    Masons, Labourers) 48, 83, 259–61,
    263
  18 The Flight into Egypt (Marshals)
    185, 331
  19 The Slaughter of the Innocents
    (Girdlers and Nailers) 47, 323
  21 The Baptism (Barbers) 23, 47, 177,
    283–4, 331
  22 The Temptation (Smiths) 332
  23 The Transfiguration (Curriers) 47
  23A Jesus in the House of Simon the
    Leper (Ironmongers: not registered)
    273
  24 The Woman Taken in Adultery,
    Lazarus (Cappers) 47, 330
  25 The Entry into Jerusalem (Skinners)
    34, 55, 270, 308, 317, 330
  27 The Last Supper (Bakers) 274, 278
  29 Christ before Annas and Caiaphas
    (Bowers and Fletchers) 23, 47, 212
  30 Christ before Pilate 1 (Tapiters and
    Couchers) 34, 286–7, 325
  31 Christ before Herod (Litsters) 47,
    202, 212
  33 Christ before Pilate 2 (Tilemakers)
    44
  34 The Way to Calvary (Shearmen) 22,
    248
  35 The Crucifixion (Pinners) 32, 238–9,
    248, 369
  36 The Death of Christ (Butchers) 291
  37 The Harrowing of Hell (Saddlers)
    31, 208, 229, 280, 283
  38 The Resurrection (Carpenters) 189,
    248, 330, 332
  41 The Incredulity of Thomas
    (Scriveners) 19
  42 The Ascension (Tailors) 25, 330, 332
  43 Pentecost (Potters) 330
  44 The Death of the Virgin (Drapers)
    185, 330
  45 The Assumption of the Virgin
    (Weavers) 6, 12, 86, 121, 137, 191,
    193, 221, 230, 233, 246–8, 328–9, 330,
    340, 381
  46 The Coronation of the Virgin
    (Hostelers) 31, 239–41, 330, 372
  47 The Last Judgement (Mercers) 28,
    29, 30, 48, 55, 231, 330
'York Realist' 34, 35, 135, 189, 233, 369
York, Stonegate x